Hayner Public Library District-Alton
0 00 30 0322960 0

No Longer the Property of
Hayner Public Library District

P9-DCJ-557

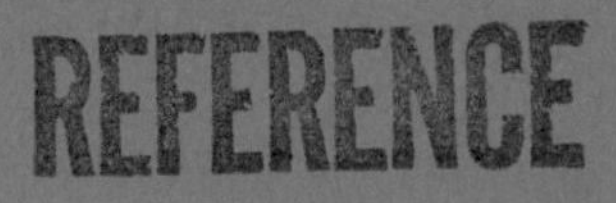
REFERENCE

ENCYCLOPEDIA OF AMERICAN HISTORY

Expansion and Reform
1813 to 1855

VOLUME IV

ENCYCLOPEDIA OF AMERICAN HISTORY

Volume I
THREE WORLDS MEET
Beginnings to 1607

Volume II
COLONIZATION AND SETTLEMENT
1608 to 1760

Volume III
REVOLUTION AND NEW NATION
1761 to 1812

Volume IV
EXPANSION AND REFORM
1813 to 1855

Volume V
CIVIL WAR AND RECONSTRUCTION
1856 to 1869

Volume VI
THE DEVELOPMENT OF THE INDUSTRIAL UNITED STATES
1870 to 1899

Volume VII
THE EMERGENCE OF MODERN AMERICA
1900 to 1928

Volume VIII
THE GREAT DEPRESSION AND WORLD WAR II
1929 to 1945

Volume IX
POSTWAR UNITED STATES
1946 to 1968

Volume X
CONTEMPORARY UNITED STATES
1969 to the Present

Volume XI
COMPREHENSIVE INDEX

ENCYCLOPEDIA OF AMERICAN HISTORY

Expansion and Reform 1813 to 1855

VOLUME IV

Malcolm J. Rohrbough, Editor
Gary B. Nash, General Editor

Facts On File, Inc.

Encyclopedia of American History:
Expansion and Reform (1813 to 1855)

Editorial Director: Laurie E. Likoff
Editor in Chief: Owen Lancer
Chief Copy Editor: Michael G. Laraque
Associate Editor: Dorothy Cummings
Production Director: Olivia McKean
Production Manager: Rachel L. Berlin
Production Associate: Theresa Montoya
Art Director: Cathy Rincon
Interior Designer: Joan M. Toro
Desktop Designers: Erika K. Arroyo and David C. Strelecky
Maps and Illustrations: Dale E. Williams and Jeremy Eagle

Facts On File, Inc.
132 West 31st Street
New York NY 10001

Library of Congress Cataloging-in-Publication Data

Encyclopedia of American history / Gary B. Nash, general editor.
p. cm.
Includes bibliographical references and indexes.
Contents: v. 1. Three worlds meet — v. 2. Colonization and settlement — v. 3. Revolution and new nation — v. 4. Expansion and reform — v. 5. Civil War and Reconstruction — v. 6. The development of the industrial United States — v. 7. The emergence of modern America — v. 8. The Great Depression and World War II — v. 9. Postwar United States — v. 10. Contemporary United States. — v. 11 Comprehensive index
ISBN 0-8160-4371-X (set) ISBN 0-8160-4364-7 (v. 4)
1. United States—History—Encyclopedias. I. Nash, Gary B.
E174 .E53 2002
973′.03—dc21 2001051278

Facts On File books are available at special discounts when purchased in bulk quantities for businesses, associations, institutions, or sales promotions. Please call our Special Sales Department in New York at (212) 967-8800 or (800) 322-8755.

You can find Facts On File on the World Wide Web at http://www.factsonfile.com

Printed in the United States of America

VB FOF 10 9 8 7 6 5 4 3 2 1

This book is printed on acid-free paper.

Contents

List of Entries

About the Editors

General Editor: Gary B. Nash received a Ph.D from Princeton University. He is currently director of the National Center for History in the Schools at the University of California, Los Angeles, where he teaches American history of the colonial and Revolutionary era. He is a published author of college and precollegiate history texts. Among his best-selling works is *The American People: Creating a Nation and Society* (Addison Wesley, Longman), now in its fifth edition.

Nash is an elected member of the Society of American Historians, American Academy of Arts and Sciences, and the American Philosophical Society. He has served as past president of the Organization of American Historians, 1994–95, and was a founding member of the National Council for History Education, 1990.

Volume Editor: Malcolm J. Rohrbough, University of Iowa, holds a Ph.D. from the University of Wisconsin. He is the author of several books, including *Days of Gold: The California Gold Rush and the American Nation* (University of California Press, 1996), and is coeditor of a 10-volume history of the trans-Appalachian frontier to be published by the University of Illinois Press.

Foreword

The Encyclopedia of American History series is designed as a handy reference to the most important individuals, events, and topics in U.S. history. In 10 volumes, the encyclopedia covers the period from the 15th century, when European explorers first made their way across the Atlantic Ocean to the Americas, to the present day. The encyclopedia is written for precollegiate as well as college students, for parents of young learners in the schools, and for the general public. The volume editors are distinguished historians of American history. In writing individual entries, each editor has drawn upon the expertise of scores of specialists. This ensures the scholarly quality of the entire series. Articles contributed by the various volume editors are uncredited.

This 10-volume encyclopedia of "American history" is broadly conceived to include the historical experience of the various peoples of North America. Thus, in the first volume, many essays treat the history of a great range of indigenous people before contact with Europeans. In the same vein, readers will find essays in the first several volumes that sketch Spanish, Dutch, and French explorers and colonizers who opened up territories for European settlement that later would become part of the United States. The venues and cast of characters in the American historical drama are thus widened beyond traditional encyclopedias.

In creating the eras of American history that define the chronological limits of each volume, and in addressing major topics in each era, the encyclopedia follows the architecture of *The National Standards for United States History, Revised Edition* (Los Angeles: National Center for History in the Schools, 1996). Mandated by the U.S. Congress, the national standards for U.S. history have been widely used by states and school districts in organizing curricular frameworks and have been followed by many other curriculum-building efforts.

Entries are cross-referenced, when appropriate, with *See also* citations at the end of articles. At the end of most entries, a listing of articles and books allows readers to turn to specialized sources and historical accounts. In each volume, an array of maps provide geographical context, while numerous illustrations help vivify the material covered in the text. A time line is included to provide students with a chronological reference to major events occurring in the given era. The selection of historical documents in the back of each volume gives students experience with the raw documents that historians use when researching history. A comprehensive index to each volume also facilitates the reader's access to particular information.

In each volume, long entries are provided for major categories of American historical experience. These categories may include: African Americans, agriculture, art and architecture, business, economy, education, family life, foreign policy, immigration, labor, Native Americans, politics, population, religion, urbanization, and women. By following these essays from volume to volume, the reader can access what might be called a mini-history of each broad topic, for example, family life, immigration, or religion.

—Gary B. Nash
University of California, Los Angeles

Introduction

In the 60 years from 1800 to the opening of the Civil War, the American nation expanded, matured, and divided. Expansion came first. It began in 1803 with Thomas Jefferson's purchase of the Louisiana Territory, and in 1819 the United States acquired the rest of Florida by treaty. Then, in the decade of the 1840s, with stunning suddenness amidst a burst of expansionist sentiment, the country extended its boundaries westward. The nation first annexed Texas (1845) as the 31st state, gained the Oregon Country by treaty (1846), and, after a war, seized the northern third of Mexico (1848), which would become the states of California, New Mexico, and Arizona. The Gadsden Purchase of 1854 would complete this expansion. At the conclusion of this growth, the United States had become a continental nation, stretching from the Atlantic to the Pacific.

At the same time that the United States expanded, and in part because of it, the civil contract of the nation and its political unity began to unravel. The issue of African slavery became the dominant theme of American political life. Opposition to the "peculiar institution" grew as the country expanded to the West. And the abolitionist movement, as it would be called, was only one of many reform movements that engaged the energies of men and women. Among the more important of these were women's rights and the temperance movement. These issues would continue to engage the nation through the Civil War and well into the 20th century.

—Malcolm J. Rohrbough

ENTRIES A TO Z

A

abolition movement

Opposition to SLAVERY in America dates to the early years of European settlement, when small numbers of Quakers criticized the practice. Antislavery sentiment increased during the revolutionary period, when American protests against the "slavery" enforced by the English king made some question the morality of enslaving Africans in the colonies. After the American Revolution, antislavery sentiment grew, as the rhetoric of liberty influenced the way some Americans thought about owning other people. In the northern states, where slaves were fewer in number and less essential to the ECONOMY, abolitionist societies began to form in the 1780s. These societies successfully lobbied for abolition in the state legislatures of the North. By 1800, most northern states had abolished slavery—either immediately or through gradual manumission (e.g., upon reaching a certain age, a slave would be freed). In the Northwest Ordinance of 1787, Congress prohibited slavery in the Northwest Territory. In 1808, Congress outlawed the foreign slave trade. To antislavery activists, both of these measures seemed to point to the eventual dissolution of the slave economy.

Thus, with the successes of antislavery advocates in the North, many Americans thought that the slavery system was becoming untenable in the new land of liberty and would soon die out. But with the invention of the cotton gin and new opportunities for expansion into the Southwest, slave-centered AGRICULTURE flourished after 1800. Also, because the U.S. Constitution did not grant the federal government the power to regulate slavery, southern states maintained enormous power to defeat any antislavery measures proposed in their state legislatures. Antislavery groups had effected change in the northern states where most of their members lived, but these groups had little influence in the South. Without an obvious way to combat slavery in the South, abolition societies became less powerful and lost momentum.

But the conflict over slavery did not disappear. Indeed, as white Americans moved west, became property owners, and gained more political rights, the rhetoric of American liberty became ever more tied to ideas of white supremacy. Just as Indians were being removed from land to make way for white settlers, some also worried that the presence of free blacks was a danger to white liberty. The number of free blacks had increased since the Revolution, but they were ill-treated and denied the rights of citizens. The presence of free blacks was, therefore, a problem for a society that was supposed to provide equal opportunity. With this growing skepticism about whether blacks could ever be accepted as free American citizens, societies such as the AMERICAN COLONIZATION SOCIETY began to emerge in the 1810s. These groups advocated removing free blacks from American society and sending them back to Africa.

The motives of the colonizationists varied. Some whites supported colonization because they wanted to rid the nation of African people, whom they deemed unfit to live in a democracy. Some southern slave owners promoted the removal of free blacks, whom they considered a threat to their ability to control their slaves. Other whites were more sympathetic about the discrimination experienced by free blacks in the United States; they argued that blacks would be free from such racism if they returned to Africa. Other whites advocated colonization because they believed ex-slaves who returned to Africa could bring Christianity and European civilization to the continent. But all of these factions were doubtful about whether African Americans would ever be accepted by a white populace whose political identifications were increasingly racist. Fearing the social consequences of freeing a previously subject group, many argued that removal was the only way to abolish slavery while preserving order.

Some free blacks also doubted whether they could ever prosper in America and supported colonization because they believed they would never be treated fairly if

An engraving of an antislavery meeting on Boston Common showing free blacks among the crowd *(Library of Congress)*

they stayed in the United States. They also thought that southern slave owners might be more likely to free their slaves if the ex-slaves were safely removed from threatening former masters. But many free blacks disagreed with the concept of colonization, arguing that blacks should stay in the United States to fight for their rights as citizens and to demand the abolition of slavery. Implicitly they argued that American identity was not race-specific, that African Americans had the capacity to be good citizens and the right to demand inclusion in the promise of American liberty. This more positive view of the purposes of abolition would grow as the movement focused more on inherent human equality.

The colonization movement was only moderately successful. The American Colonization Society (ACS) established the West African colony of LIBERIA, and several thousand free blacks emigrated. But the removal plan was costly, impractical, and therefore affected very few African Americans. Also, the ACS was attacked by other reformers who saw colonization as a cynical strategy designed to appease slave owners and vilify blacks. Black leaders such as James Forten and David Walker accused the colonizationists of the same racism that made life so difficult for African Americans. In the 1820s new reform societies arose in opposition to colonization, thus laying the groundwork for the next phase of the abolition movement.

Anticolonizationists in the black communities of the North protested the influence of the ACS. They realized that in order to challenge the ACS, they needed to build a coalition with sympathetic whites. By the early 1830s a new radical kind of abolitionism was growing. These new abolitionists advocated an immediate end to slavery, based on the concept of universal human equality. "Immediatists" argued that slavery was such a great moral evil that it must be ended at once. The most prominent proponent of immediatism was William Lloyd Garrison, a white newspaper editor. Once a colonizationist, Garrison was greatly influenced by Forten, Walker, and other black leaders to become more radical in his approach. In 1831, he began publishing *The Liberator* in Boston. Most of his early subscribers were black, and many welcomed his commitment to the movement. It was politically expedient for the immediatists to put forth a white man as the leader of the movement, but Garrison was not alone. Many other black and white writers contributed to the magazine. Other sympathetic leaders emerged, such as the fiery lecturer THEODORE DWIGHT WELD and ARTHUR AND LEWIS TAPPAN, wealthy New York City merchants who were prominent in the evangelical movement. The charismatic influence of the immediatists converted many people who were previously attached to the colonization cause. In 1832 the New England Anti-Slavery Society was formed—the first such organization in the United States. The following year the AMERICAN ANTI-SLAVERY SOCIETY (AASS) was founded, a national group that combined efforts of the many local groups. By 1837 there were more than 500 local societies in northern states. Some of these societies were founded and operated by women—and were often interracial. Indeed, several women, such as ANGELINA AND SARAH GRIMKÉ, became outspoken leaders in the movement.

So what was the immediatist strategy? The mainstream movement could not advocate violent change and remain respectable. Nor could abolitionists campaign for federal action, since the Constitution gave the federal government no authority over state slavery laws. Thus, abolitionists hoped to change slave owners' minds through moral persuasion and indirect political pressure. As was the standard practice of many contemporary reform movements, the abolitionists got their message across by public speaking tours, disseminating tracts, and selling subscriptions to antislavery periodicals. They attacked slavery as, first and foremost, a sin. They dismissed economic arguments as a distraction from the true cause: uplifting American society by eradicating the corrupting presence of slavery. Some abolitionists seemed more concerned with the endangered souls of slave owners than with the circumstances of the slaves themselves. But others, especially free black abolitionists, were primarily concerned with the liberation of enslaved black people. Whatever the emphasis, the strategy that evolved in the 1830s centered around convincing southern slave owners that abolition was morally right. If slave owners came to believe that they were committing a sin, they would voluntarily free their slaves.

But by the end of the 1830s it became clear that slave owners were not changing their ways, no matter which tactic the abolitionists employed. Tensions arose within the movement as well. The more conservative leaders, such as the Tappan brothers, protested the involvement of women on committees. In 1840 the AASS split into two organizations because of this dispute. Conservative abolitionists worried that Garrison and the radicals were too unconventional and controversial and would damage the respectability of the movement. This schism was the first of many splits among abolitionists, as the debate over slavery became increasingly high-pitched and volatile.

While Garrison was unwilling to compromise on the principle of human equality, some black abolitionists began to question the effectiveness of his "moral suasion" strategy. They began to formulate their own separate strategies, again centered on the right of slaves to revolt and take their freedom. The specter of black violence frightened many white abolitionists, who insisted that the movement could only succeed by seeming morally above reproach (and by being led by elite whites). It was clear by 1850 that not only had the abolitionists failed to transform southern slave society, but the plight of slaves had actually worsened. Southern politicians misused the federal authority over the mail in order to keep abolition material out of the South. In addition, the passage of harsher FUGITIVE SLAVE LAWS signaled a northern complicity with southern slavery that seemed catastrophic to abolitionists. Some black leaders began to see the situation as hopeless and revived the emigration solution. Some promoted emigration to Liberia, while others argued for going to Canada or Haiti.

Political opposition to slavery developed along several lines. The "Free-Soil" advocates in the new Republican Party viewed the slave system of labor as a threat to the liberty of all Americans because it endangered the ability of ordinary farmers and laborers to prosper. This kind of antislavery thought was centered more on the problems slavery created for whites than on the problems of slaves themselves. Only a minority of northerners opposed slavery because it was a racist system; most were persuaded to oppose slavery for other reasons: economic resentment of the South, a belief that slavery corrupted the spirit of liberty, concern about whether new territories would be slave or free. These reasons for being antislavery were connected to Garrison's moral suasion argument, but they were more about self-interest and less about social welfare. Many of the people who subscribed to antislavery politics in the 1850s were extremely prejudiced against blacks and not especially concerned about integrating freed slaves into American society.

When tensions over slavery and territorial expansion erupted into civil war, abolitionists were still a minority presence among Abraham Lincoln's Republicans. They continued to push the administration to take a bolder stand on ending slavery. Many abolitionists enlisted in the Union army and encouraged the army to open its ranks to black soldiers. Others worked in army hospitals, and some traveled south, setting up services for freed slaves in Union-occupied areas (an endeavor that would continue with the

Freedmen's Bureaus and other educational efforts during Reconstruction).

Abolitionists felt a sense of triumph with the Union victory, and, most important, the passage of the Thirteenth Amendment, which abolished slavery. Judging that their work was done, some of the older abolition organizations like the AASS dissolved. Other abolitionists recognized the need to continue helping freed slaves by providing education and fighting for their legal rights. Indeed, the violent backlash against African Americans after Reconstruction troops withdrew pointed to the continuing relevance of the abolitionist cause. Some former abolitionists realized what freed blacks learned almost immediately—that achieving equality required more than simply changing the laws. Unfortunately, without abolition to mobilize around, reformers who were concerned about the plight of African Americans lost an easy rallying point after the Civil War.

The abolition cause was never embraced by the majority of Americans, nor did abolitionists possess the political power their southern opponents accused them of having. However, this small section of society did change the debate about slavery in 19th-century America. And in retrospect, they helped achieve the abolition of slavery in a relatively short period of time. As one of the first organized reform movements, the abolition cause has served as an example to 20th-century activists advocating civil rights.

Further reading: David Brion Davis, *The Problem of Slavery in the Age of Revolution, 1770–1823* (New York: Oxford University Press, 1975); Martin Duberman, ed., *The Anti-Slavery Vanguard: New Essays on the Abolitionists* (Princeton, N.J.: Princeton University Press, 1965); Eric Foner, *Free Soil, Free Labor, Free Men: The Ideology of the Republican Party Before the Civil War* (New York: Oxford University Press, 1970); Lawrence J. Friedman, *Gregarious Saints: Self and Community in American Abolitionism, 1830–1870* (New Rochelle, N.Y.: Cambridge University Press, 1982); Benjamin Quarles, *Black Abolitionists* (New York: Oxford University Press, 1969); Ronald Walters, *The Antislavery Appeal: American Abolitionism after 1830* (Baltimore, Md.: Johns Hopkins University Press, 1976).

—Eleanor H. McConnell

Adams, John Quincy (1767–1848)

Born in Braintree (now Quincy), Massachusetts on July 11, 1767, John Quincy Adams was the most gifted American diplomat during the early republic and later served as the sixth president of the United States. Adams was uniquely qualified for a life of public service. The son of the revolutionary leader John Adams and Abigail Adams, he was also a gifted and articulate supporter of the revolution.

John Quincy Adams received his earliest education from his parents. At the age of 10, the younger Adams accompanied his father on diplomatic missions to Europe. He became fluent in French and was educated in a private school in Paris and at the University of Leiden. In 1782–83 he served as secretary and interpreter for the American diplomat Francis Dana on a journey to the Russian court in St. Petersburg. They traveled by way of Holland, the German states, and Scandinavia. When Adams returned to the United States in 1785, age 18, he was extraordinarily well-traveled, an accomplished linguist, and well-read in the classics, history, and mathematics. He completed his education at Harvard College, graduating in 1787, then read law in Newburyport, Massachusetts under the supervision of Theophilus Parsons, a distinguished and conservative Massachusetts jurist. In 1790, he was admitted to the bar and settled down to practice law in Boston.

Like his father, Adams identified with the emerging Federalist Party. He came to the attention of President George Washington as the author of newspaper articles defending the administration's neutrality policies during the wars of the French Revolution (1789–1815). In consequence, Washington appointed the younger Adams as the American minister to the Netherlands (1794–97). After serving in the Hague, Adams represented the United States at the Prussian court from 1797 to 1801. While on diplomatic business in London, he met and courted Louisa Catherine Johnson, daughter of Joshua Johnson, an American diplomat in Britain; they were married on July 26, 1797.

President John Adams recalled his son from Berlin after he lost the bitterly contested election of 1800, and the younger Adams returned to Boston to pursue his legal career. Public life continued to exert a pull on him, and in 1803 he was elected to represent Massachusetts in the U.S. Senate. Although a Federalist, Adams was independent-minded, and to the dismay of his party, he voted in support of the Jeffersonian embargo in 1807. Because of his independent stance, he was not reelected to the Senate, so he returned to Boston to resume his legal career and serve as Boylston professor of oratory and rhetoric at Harvard.

Adams's return to Massachusetts would be brief, as President James Madison appointed him the first American ambassador to Russia, a post he held from 1809 to 1814. He left the Russian court to act as the chief of the American mission at Ghent during the negotiations to end the WAR OF 1812 (1812–15). When the TREATY OF GHENT (1814) was concluded, Adams served as the American ambassador to Britain, a post his father had held 30 years before. He represented the United States in Britain from 1815 to 1817. (Between 1794 and 1817 Adams had represented the United States in the Netherlands, Prussia, Russia, and Great Britain. During that period he was an astute observer and reporter of the French Revolution and the Napoleonic Wars.)

President JAMES MONROE recalled Adams from London to serve as his secretary of state, a post Adams held from 1817 until 1825. Schooled in European ways and experienced in European affairs, Adams believed strongly that the United States should remain isolated from Europe's conflicts, articulating this view as the chief architect of the MONROE DOCTRINE. As secretary of state, Adams was responsible for negotiating the ADAMS-ONÍS TREATY, by which the United States acquired East and West FLORIDA and recognized the border of the United States as extending from the Gulf of Mexico to the Rocky Mountains and thence along the 42nd parallel to the Pacific Ocean. He also asserted that the border between Oregon and British Canada should run along the 49th parallel.

John Quincy Adams enjoyed a varied and successful career as lawyer, scholar, and diplomat until he ran for president in 1824. A crowded field of five candidates divided the popular vote. ANDREW JACKSON won the popular vote, but as no candidate had a majority in the electoral college, the election was thrown into the House of Representatives, and HENRY CLAY supported Adams to make the New Englander president. His presidency, undermined from the beginning by the circumstances of his election, encountered much opposition. The Jacksonians attacked his presidency as an exercise in "bargain and corruption," the term used to describe the charge that Adams and Clay colluded to cheat Jackson out of the office. Adams's nationalist views and his reluctance to make use of patronage further hindered his four years in office. In 1828 he lost the election to Jackson.

Adams was 62 years old when he left the White House in 1829. Rather than retire to Quincy, he ran for Congress and represented Massachusetts in the House of Representatives from 1830 until his death in 1848. During this period, Adams emerged as an articulate and forceful opponent of slavery. He crusaded against the "gag rule" that forbade the House from considering antislavery petitions, and in 1844 the House repealed the rule. In 1841 Adams actively participated in the successful arguments before the Supreme Court over the legal status of a group of former African slaves who had revolted and seized the Spanish ship *Amistad*. He also vigorously opposed the annexation of Texas and the U.S. declaration of war against Mexico as attempts to expand the institution of slavery. He died at his desk in the House of Representatives on February 23, 1848.

Further reading: Samuel Flagg Bemis, *John Quincy Adams and the Foundations of American Foreign Policy* (New York: A. A. Knopf, 1949); Paul C. Nagel, *John Quincy Adams: A Public Life, A Private Life* (New York: Knopf, 1997); William Earl Weeks, *John Quincy Adams and American Global Empire* (Lexington.: University Press of Kentucky, 1992).

Adams-Onís Treaty (1819)

The Adams-Onís Treaty (or Transcontinental Treaty) of 1819 is significant in the expansion of the United States for adding the FLORIDA territory to the country at relatively little cost and for giving the United States its first internationally recognized claim to territory on the Pacific Ocean.

Spain had established its control of the territory of Florida, which included the entire Gulf of Mexico shore from the Mississippi River to the current state of Florida, in the early 16th century. In 1763 Spain was forced to cede control to England after being on the losing side in the Seven Years' War, but the Treaty of Paris ending the American Revolution restored Spanish authority in Florida. After making the Louisiana Purchase in 1803, however, the United States slowly began to seize pieces of Florida from Spain. Settlers occupied the area around Baton Rouge in 1810, prompting its annexation to the United States. The U.S. Army then occupied Mobile Bay and other parts of West Florida during the WAR OF 1812, ostensibly to keep those lands from falling into British hands. In 1818 General ANDREW JACKSON, on the pretext of fighting Seminole Indians who were raiding the southern United States from Florida, occupied much of the rest of the territory. Meanwhile, there was an ongoing dispute between the United States and Spain concerning the boundary of the Louisiana Purchase. The United States claimed that the Louisiana Purchase territory extended to the Rio Grande; the Spanish rejected this, asserting the Sabine River as the boundary.

Negotiated by Secretary of State JOHN QUINCY ADAMS with Luis de Onís, the Spanish ambassador in the United States, the Adams-Onís Treaty contained several provisions. First and foremost, the Spanish relinquished all claim to Florida. Additionally, the treaty settled the southwestern boundary of the Louisiana Purchase at the Sabine River. In exchange for the United States, accepting the Spanish interpretation of the Louisiana boundary, Spain relinquished its claims to the Oregon Territory in the Pacific Northwest, fixing the boundary between United States and Spanish territory on the Pacific coast at the 42nd parallel. Oregon remained disputed territory, however, as the United States and England had agreed to joint occupation in the Convention of 1818; the boundary between the United States and Canada in the Northwest would not be settled until the OREGON TREATY OF 1846. Finally, although the United States did not "buy" Florida from Spain, the Adams-Onís Treaty relieved the Spanish government of $5 million worth of monetary claims made by American citizens against it. No actual money changed hands between the two countries.

The U.S. Senate readily ratified the treaty in 1819, though some criticism of Adams emerged for surrendering Texas when Onís might have been induced to cede that land as well. The Spanish, however, delayed ratification,

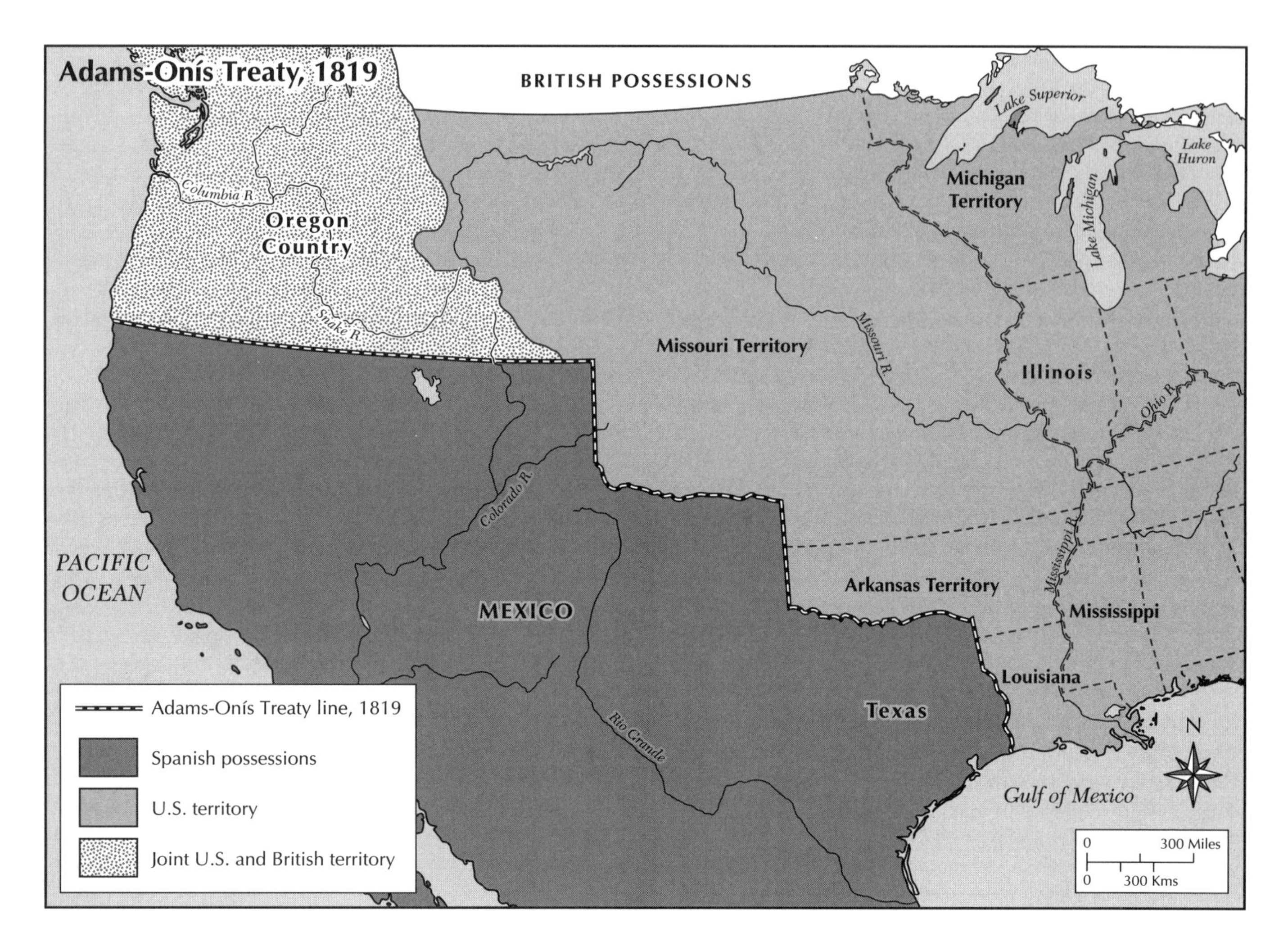

hoping to secure a promise from the United States not to aid revolutions in Spanish colonies in Latin America. The United States demurred, and two years later, after Spain accepted the original treaty, the Senate ratified the treaty again on Washington's birthday in 1821.

Further reading: Bradford Perkins, *The Creation of a Republican Empire,* vol. 1 of *The Cambridge History of American Foreign Relations, 1776–1865,* ed. Warren I. Cohen, general editor (New York: Cambridge University Press, 1993).

—Russell L. Johnson

African Americans

African-American men and women in the antebellum United States shared common experiences in their struggle for freedom. Despite disparate lives created by regional differences, labor patterns, religious beliefs, and legal sanctions, enslaved and free people alike fought an unending battle to define and possess their own liberty. Freedom was not simply the opposite of SLAVERY, nor did slavery mean the absolute absence of freedom. Liberty was experienced across a spectrum and won by deliberate and conscious action.

Most African Americans in the antebellum period were enslaved. After the abolition of the external slave trade in 1808, the majority of enslaved men and women were born in the country, rather than imported from Africa or other slaveholding nations in South America and the Caribbean. As slaves, men and women shared a common legal status. They were considered property, and as such could be willed, sold, and transported at the whim of their owners. For the purposes of the census and the legislative districting based on that count, slaves were considered three-fifths of a person. This guaranteed the South greater representation in Congress than if free people had been counted alone. Despite their importance to the business of legislative representation, however, enslaved men and women could not vote. They were rarely granted legal redress against physical or sexual abuse, and their marriages and families enjoyed no legal protection. Education, unsupervised religious meetings, large social gatherings, and the freedom to travel were all prohibited or restricted to some degree.

The experience of slavery did not simply depend on legal restrictions, however, but on the type of labor enslaved men and women were expected to perform. Most slaves worked in AGRICULTURE, raising cotton, rice, tobacco, indigo, and food crops on small farms. Each crop demanded a different labor cycle. Tobacco required constant attention but facilitated a steady pace of work. Rice cultivation was a relentless process requiring that the crop be dried, buried, stacked, threshed, winnowed, and pounded by hand to transform it into a marketable good. Accidents were common from the complexity of the work and the exhaustion felt by those involved in production, while water-borne diseases were a constant hazard. Cotton cultivation required physical strength and endurance, especially during picking season, when an average enslaved man or woman was expected to pick between 150 and 200 pounds of cotton a day. The rhythms of each production cycle dictated how much time slaves had to spend on their own concerns, such as raising and tending their own gardens, maintaining their homes, performing chores, and enjoying each other's company. Hard labor also affected the life expectancy of each slave.

Not all slaves lived in rural communities, however, and urban slaves generally enjoyed greater freedom of movement, the chance to earn money from their labor, and the opportunity to acquire and perfect a marketable skill. Many urban slave owners allowed enslaved men and women to hire themselves out for wages in return for a weekly fee. Enslaved men often worked in construction, in skilled trades such as carpentry, at railroad terminals, and on docks. Women were sometimes employed as midwives, although they were more usually hired for domestic work. Urban enslaved men generally enjoyed greater freedom than enslaved women as they were less likely to work in a home under the direct and constant supervision of an owner or employer and had a greater range of jobs open to them.

All of these factors, however, constituted a range of expectations placed upon enslaved men and women by those outside the slave community. Slaves themselves took conscious action to carve out different liberties from the system that held them. While labor patterns were largely dictated by the industry in which slaves worked, those demands could be alleviated to a degree. Slaves broke tools and engaged in slowdowns in order to ease the pressure of the workday. Some slaves took more dramatic action, committing arson or sabotage in order to slow the pace at which tasks were performed. Throughout the 19th century, slaves ran away in order to gain their freedom or reunite with loved ones. There were also outright rebellions in which slaves violently resisted the demands of white southerners and attempted to secure their personal liberty and that of others.

On a day-to-day level, enslaved men and women resisted the attempts of outsiders to establish meaningful relationships and family life for them. While their status as slaves prevented them from entering into legally recognized contracts such as marriage, they formed such relationships, regardless of their legality, and solemnized them through local customs. Men and women enjoyed long and short-term sexual relationships and bore children who were raised, where and whenever possible, within a family unit. Even when parents were separated from one another, family ties remained extremely important, as demonstrated by the tireless attempts of many newly freed men and women to reunite with loved ones during and after the Civil War. The concept of family was, in and of itself, something that slaves negotiated in their own way. While mothers, fathers, and children were central to the concept of family, kinship was experienced and perpetuated in a much more expanded fashion, drawing in cousins, aunts, uncles, grandparents and friends. Family structures drew from African traditions as well as American models, and obligations extended beyond individual households to the community and neighborhoods beyond.

Despite the best attempts of slaveholders to restrict their pastimes, some enslaved men and women did receive a rudimentary education from literate members of their community or sympathetic free whites and blacks. While large gatherings of slaves were often prohibited, owners could do little to prevent women from performing chores such as laundry and cooking together, and such labor gave participants the chance to spend time together away from the eyes of overseers or employers. Religious meetings also

This engraving shows a group of free blacks worshiping at an African-American church in Cincinnati, Ohio. *(Library of Congress)*

took place, with slaves creating their own interpretation of the Bible and often drawing on their African heritage to create their own expressions of spirituality.

Yet not all African Americans were enslaved, and the free black population of the United States grew throughout the 19th century. Prejudice, however, tempered what it meant to be free. Local and state laws often prohibited free African Americans from unrestricted freedom of movement, owning property, or voting. In the North, racial prejudice against African Americans resulted in segregated neighborhoods and the threat of violence. Competing with new immigrants for employment, few northern African-American men and women were able to significantly change their economic status over time. In the South, free African Americans faced less competition for the jobs they held, but white fears of cooperation between slaves and free blacks leading to rebellion meant that their lives outside the workplace were greatly circumscribed.

The political and social activism of free African Americans was nevertheless wide-ranging. Through churches, fraternal orders, and voluntary organizations, free African Americans often provided social services to their communities, aiding one another in times of economic or medical hardship. Such organizations were also key to the expansion of literacy within the African-American community.

Free African Americans were a central force of the 19th-century ABOLITION MOVEMENT. While individuals and religious groups such as the Quakers had opposed the operation of slavery in the United States, it was not until the 1830s that a formal abolition movement coalesced. In 1832, the New England Anti-Slavery Society was founded by William Lloyd Garrison, a white liberal, in Boston. In that same year, the first Female Anti-Slavery Society was established in Salem, Massachusetts, convened by a group of free African-American women. Since women of all colors were originally excluded from Garrison's society, the Boston Female Anti-Slavery society was also founded in 1832. The society welcomed white and black members, as did the Philadelphia Female Anti-Slavery Society, founded by LUCRETIA MOTT in 1833. Throughout the antebellum

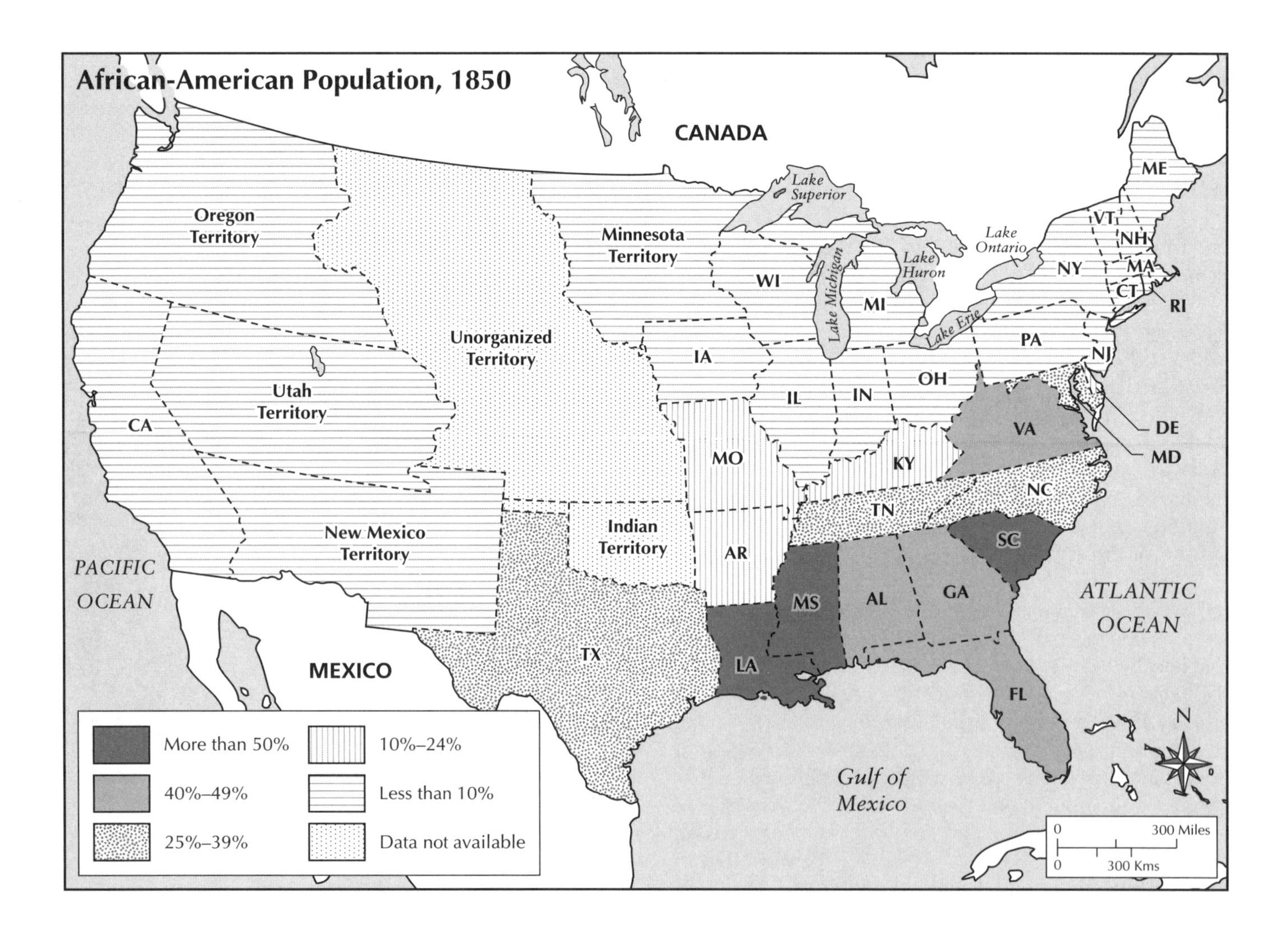

period, whites and free African-Americans, along with a growing number of fugitive slaves, worked to attain the abolition of slavery through speaking tours and the publication and dissemination of antislavery literature. Some of the most significant publications to spring from the movement were the autobiographies of escaped slaves, including *Narrative of the Life of Frederick Douglass, A Slave,* published in 1845.

The success of the Underground Railroad also depended on the activism of many free African Americans and escaped slaves. The Underground Railroad was neither underground nor a real railroad. Instead, it was a loose coalition of free men and women of all racial backgrounds, as well as a number of escaped slaves, who aided enslaved men and women in their quest to escape to the North. Many black abolitionists, including Frederick Douglass and Sojourner Truth helped shelter or guide fugitive slaves on their journeys. Perhaps the most famous participant in the work of the Underground Railroad, however, was Harriet Tubman. Born into slavery in 1821, Harriet was married to John Tubman, a free black, in 1848. Her marriage did not secure her freedom, however, and her husband opposed any talk of escape. Rather than be sent to Georgia after the death of her original master and the failure of an escape attempt (her husband's opinion notwithstanding), Harriet escaped again and made it to Philadelphia. She then went back into the slaveholding territories to assist her sister and her children to escape, and continued to travel into the South to do the same for others. It is estimated that she aided over 300 enslaved men and women in her lifetime, acting as their guide and directing them to homes where they would be sheltered before the next leg of their journey. Numerous other African Americans made similar journeys or offered their homes as "stations" along the railroad.

While the contentious issue of whether they were considered the property of another human divided free and enslaved African-Americans in the 19th century, many other considerations joined the communities together. All African Americans battled against racial prejudice and its effect on their legal and economic status. All experienced, to a greater or lesser degree, the presumption that whiteness was an inherent part of citizenship in the United States. Despite the definitions and expectations of mainstream America, African-American men and women refused to ever acquiesce completely to the demands of those outside their communities. Whether free or enslaved, African Americans faced the challenges of legal, social, and political prejudice with creativity and established patterns of association and activism that would support them far into the post–Civil War period.

Further reading: Frederick Douglass, *The Life and Times of Frederick Douglass, An American Slave, Written by Himself* (1845; reprint, Boston: Bedford Books, 1993); James Oliver Horton, *Free People of Color: Inside the African American Community* (Washington, D.C.: Smithsonian Institution Press, 1993); Harriet Tubman and Sarah Hopkins Bradford, *Scenes in the Life of Harriet Tubman* (1869, reprint, Freeport, N.Y.: Books for Libraries Press, 1971).

—Catherine J. Denial

agriculture

In the first half of the 19th century, agriculture defined the U.S. way of life economically and socially. It was the primary means of sustaining the ECONOMY, through the production of raw products such as cotton, which between 1815 and 1845 generated between one-third and more than one-half of the value of all U.S. exports. On the more than 2 million farms that existed by 1860, most farmers were able to juggle a mix of commercial and subsistence farming and to see profit. What accounted for these advancements in agriculture during the antebellum years? In large part, it depended on geographic expansion and technological innovation. Both changed the face of U.S. agriculture before the Civil War.

Throughout the 19th century, various regions developed crops that reflected their particular geographic riches. Tobacco was grown across Virginia and the entire Upper South. Rice was harvested along the tidal rivers of Georgia and South Carolina. Hemp was produced in Kentucky, sugar in Louisiana. Across the South and West, cotton was grown. In the North, Ohio was known for pork, Ohio and Illinois for cattle. New York and Ohio were centers for cheese.

Also during this period, migration patterns, which moved largely westward, reflected the search for new fertile land. The rapid settlement of rich agricultural lands west of the Appalachians led to the founding of several states during the antebellum period: Indiana (admitted to the Union in 1816), Mississippi (1817), Illinois (1818), Alabama (1819), Michigan (1837), Texas (annexed in 1845), and Iowa (1846).

The first major changes in farming came about through new technologies. As the 19th century began, a farmer's main agricultural tools were the axe and plow. Led by the cotton gin in 1793, a number of labor-saving devices were invented, reducing the hours of labor involved in nearly all aspects of farming. Among the labor-saving items that came into common use during the first half of the 19th century were the thresher, reaper, iron and steel plows, grain drills, corn and cotton planters, seed drills, and iron harrows and cultivators. Distinguishing many of these implements was the fact that they were designed to employ animal rather than human power, which reduced the farmer's workload.

For settlers and farmers, clearing land was a central task, and most northern and southern farmers in the early 19th century did so with a Carey plow. Using its wooden moldboard and wrought-iron share, farmers plowed up to one acre per day. For much of the antebellum period, prairie farmers employed the breaking plow or prairie breaker, which could crack fibrous soil. A major drawback was that it required multiple oxen and men. Much more efficient were steel plows, which were devised by various inventors beginning in the 1830s and refined by blacksmith JOHN DEERE. As refining processes reduced the price of steel during the 1840s and 1850s, the steel moldboard plow, known as the "singing plow," became popular on the prairie. By 1835, iron and steel plows also entered common use in the North; but in parts of the South, a one-horse wood-and-wrought-iron shovel plow was used. The cast-iron Eagle plow, with a long, curved moldboard, was popular in the North and South.

Other mechanical advances included the hand corn planter and the horse-drawn corn planter, which was developed in the 1850s. These planters greatly increased the amount of seed a farmer could plant with a hoe. Developed in the 1820s, the horse-hoe used horse-drawn power to cultivate crops more efficiently. For harvesting crops, farmers finally found a labor-saving alternative to the scythe when the horse-drawn reaper was developed. Created in 1831 and patented in 1834 by CYRUS HALL MCCORMICK, it cut down 10–12 acres of wheat per day. By 1860, the reaper was used in 70 percent of U.S. farms. Shortly before the end of the antebellum period, in 1854, an automatic raking mechanism was developed to gather cut grain for harvest. It later gained common use.

The thresher, which separated the grain from the stalks, was developed in the 1820s. It was refined in 1837 with a device that separated the chaff from the straw. By the 1850s they were in common use. The grain combine, which joins the reaper, thresher, and winnower, was developed in 1835, but its weight and multiple-horse requirement made it unappealing to small to medium-sized farmers. This implement was refined later in the century. Other advances of the period include the steam planter and steam-powered cotton gin.

The movement toward agricultural mechanization also involved the building of factories for food production. Beginning in the 1820s meatpacking facilities handled pork and cattle at Cincinnati, Chicago, and other sites. By the 1850s factories in the North and West produced cheese in standardized form. This form of industrialization rid homes of the chore of producing cheese for commercial use while also providing farmers a ready outlet for excess dairy products.

In the South the lifetime labor of slaves was central to the region's agricultural expansion and success. Male slaves, controlled by the white overseer and African-American driver, were expected to pick about 200 pounds of cotton per day, plow fields, and plant, among other tasks. Female slaves picked about 150 pounds of cotton per day and wove linen and wool, in addition to other domestic jobs. The increased production of bonded workers encouraged plantation farming and especially enriched owners. Given the South's large population of 11 million people and the region's dependence on a single, slave-driven crop, there was also a large market for corn and beef from northern states.

In all regions, farm women planted and harvested crops in addition to supervising the household, cooking, and caring for the gardens and household livestock. Women of slave-owning families also supervised slaves' domestic activities. As one farm woman wrote, it was "boiling and baking, turning the spinning wheel and rocking the cradle." They also engaged in a variety of home manufactures for trade. In the North, dairy products were popular home manufactures, and until factory-made clothing became available, women spun flax and wool as well as made linen cloth for trade. The rise of manufactured goods increased the ability of a woman to leave the farm but decreased her ability to contribute directly through farm manufactures to the family economy.

In general, life for the farm family was one of work, isolation, and limited social contact. The church provided social connections, with its rhythms of baptisms, marriages, and funerals. Similarly, communal labor-related activities such as barn-raisings and threshings contributed to the frontier society. To fuel increasing demand and in response to the changing soil, farmers developed new varieties of crops and refined animal breeds for specific agricultural uses. In Virginia during the 1850s, farmers created a new variety of tobacco called bright yellow, which, when specially cured, was used to wrap chewing tobacco. In the North, farmers bred and fed their cattle to produce dairy products with revenue-producing higher butterfat content. Western farmers also pioneered the importation of cattle such as the Shorthorn variety to improve livestock quality. Dairy farmers imported the Jersey cow in 1817, the Guernsey in 1830. Farmers also adjusted their crops to fill specialized markets. For example, when western farmers cornered their market by delivering low-cost grain, corn, and livestock, eastern farmers responded by adapting their crops and focusing on perishables such as dairy products and produce for ongoing delivery to cities.

Driven by increased demand for and production of foodstuffs, antebellum inventors developed various improvements to transport crops. Refined in 1807 by Robert Fulton, the steamboat, which could navigate a river or ocean, came into use from the 1810s to transport foodstuffs from west to east and along coastlines. By 1850, just under 750 steamboats were transporting raw materials and food along the Delaware, Hudson, and Mississippi Rivers, and along the coastlines. To link various strategic bodies of water, more than 1,000 miles of canals were dug following the success of the ERIE CANAL. Built between 1817 and 1825, the Erie Canal connected the agriculture-rich Ohio Valley at Lake Erie to the Hudson River and the commercial hub of New York City.

Finally, while steam-powered water and wheel-based land transportation dominated much of early 19th-century transport, RAILROADS come into use for agricultural transport by the 1840s and within decades became the dominant form of transportation for humans and foodstuffs alike. Some 30,000 miles of track were in use by 1860.

Financed in part through state and federal funds, transportation routes also increased and became more efficient during this period. The barriers to transatlantic trade during the WAR OF 1812 gave rise to trade along the Atlantic coast, with important northern ports in Boston and New York and southern ports in Mobile and New Orleans. Inland transport of foodstuffs, particularly from the western states of Ohio and Pennsylvania, was improved by the NATIONAL ROAD, which linked the Ohio Valley and the mid-Atlantic states, and the many side roads constructed during the period. In addition to streamlining food transport, these improvements spurred productivity and shifted areas of agricultural specialization. For example, the West became a major supplier of food and grain to the Northeast once farmers in the Ohio Valley region could ship wheat and corn along the Erie Canal and Ohio and Mississippi Rivers.

Conservation practices among most U.S. farmers of the age centered on labor conservation through the widespread use of implements such as the cotton gin (1793). Time conservation was also practiced through transportation advances such as the steamboat. But as of the mid-19th century, there was relatively little soil conservation. Given the amount of fertile land in the United States and the crudeness of fertilizers, farmers who had exhausted their land migrated to new soil. This practice was evident in the migration south and west to plant cotton once the soil in the Upper South had been exhausted in the early 1800s. One observer of the time said of the South, "The new country seemed to be a reservoir . . . and every road leading to it a vagrant stream of enterprise and adventure."

Despite these anticonservation tendencies, some farmers and agricultural reformers formulated soil and other conservation practices. The U.S. government helped the cause, to an extent. Beginning in 1839, the U.S. Patent Office offered reports on farming advances and technology, including a lengthy annual report distributed to farmers free of charge. The work of the Patent Office, along with the advocacy of the U.S. Agricultural Society, laid the groundwork for the development of the U.S. Department of Agriculture.

Of all farmers, northeasterners were generally the most well-versed in the common preservation practices of crop rotation and letting land lie fallow. These practices were not applicable for farmers of a single crop in great demand, such as cotton. However, one group of farmers along the coasts of Georgia and South Carolina did practice a form of crop rotation, turning to rice after the soil had been depleted by cotton or when rice might yield a higher return than cotton, as it did in the 1830s. Still, given generally declining prices for rice over the antebellum years, only large-volume, slave-labor plantations could still make money from the crop. In any event, cotton eclipsed rice, moving rice cultivation westward after the Civil War.

As the antebellum years came to a close in 1860, agricultural products remained central to the U.S. economy, accounting for 82 percent of U.S. exports. Producing 838 million bushels of corn, 172 million bushels of wheat, and over 2 billion pounds of cotton, the United States was its own primary supplier to domestic food processors and manufacturers. These products from across the nation's 2 million farms included food-related crops such as corn, wheat, other grains, fruits, and vegetables as well as livestock; and raw materials such as cotton and tobacco. Together, they revealed the wealth of the U.S. agricultural landscape and the efficiency of new cultivation methods and technological refinements. By the last quarter of the 19th century, these advances, coupled with the large number of working U.S. farmers, would provide the means by which the United States (along with the rest of North America and Australia) would overtake Europe as the world's leading producer of food.

Apart from the measurable advantages of improving farming practices and increasing productivity, the country's success with commercial agriculture brought lasting changes to the ways U.S. citizens lived. Farmers who once produced all the items they needed for daily life now purchased manufactured goods. This practice pointed to another overall shift, toward regional interdependence. As one region like the Ohio Valley specialized in grain, it depended on another specialized region, such as the Northeast, for textiles. Although for the most part the South produced its own foodstuffs, it depended on the North for many manufactured goods, for storing some of its cotton before export, and for providing credit to establish planting sites. In all, these practices promoted a national sense of self-sufficiency.

As the century moved on, agriculture continued to dominate the economy, but challenges to its position were in process. Increasingly, people were moving to urban areas and engaging in nonagricultural vocations. In 1860 more than 75 percent of southerners made their living through agriculture, but this percentage would erode greatly during the next several decades.

Still, whether small-time farmer or plantation owner, farmers of the 19th century believed in the importance of owning land. To this end, the U.S. government offered several bills which, to varying extents, served settlers' needs. After the PANIC OF 1819, many farmers were unable to pay for the lands they had purchased from the government on credit. In response, the government ended its credit practices and opened land at $1.25 per acre, to be paid by farmers in full. Still unable to pay for the land, the squatters who had settled their land were granted another chance through the Preemption Act of 1830. This law allowed them to buy surveyed land from the federal government and granted a year to pay costs. Given that this provision was used in large part by speculators, the law was superseded by the Preemption Act of 1841, which required claimants on surveyed land to live on and settle the public-owned land. Unclaimed or western lands came to be subject to the Gradation Act of 1854, which reduced the price of land not sold over the course of 10–30 years. Politically, this developed into a battle between established southern landowners who wished to retain power, the westerners who wished to settle large quantities of land, and a government undecided on whether selling land or providing it for quick settlement would best serve the economy. These questions would be debated on a national level for years to come.

Further reading: Paul Wallace Gates, *The Farmer's Age: Agriculture, 1815–1860* (New York: Holt, Rinehart & Winston, 1952); R. Douglas Hurt, *American Agriculture: A Brief History* (Ames: Iowa State University Press, 1994); John Mayfield, *The New Nation 1800–1845,* rev. ed. (New York: Hill and Wang, 1982); Peter D. McClelland, *Sowing Modernity: America's First Agricultural Revolution* (Ithaca, N.Y.: Cornell University Press, 1997).

—Melinda Corey

The Alamo

The Alamo, a mission fortress located in San Antonio, TEXAS, is the site of one of the most famous battles in American history, although it was located outside of the United States at the time of the siege that made it famous in 1836. The original building was a Spanish mission that Franciscan priests established in 1718. The Spanish government converted it into a fort and army barracks in the late 18th century.

In the early 19th century the Spanish, seeking to revitalize parts of their American empire, encouraged white citizens of the United States to settle the desolate province of Texas. Not many did at first. In the meantime the new republic of Mexico gained its independence from Spain in 1821, and its government urged its own citizens to settle in Texas. In part as a reaction to the economic distress caused by the PANIC OF 1819, land-hungry Americans from the South were pushing toward the lands beyond the boundaries of the United States in the 1820s. "Gone to Texas" was the cry of emigrants from Kentucky, Tennessee, and other states. Initially, the new Mexican government considered this immigration to be illegal, but, realizing they could not stop it, they finally welcomed the Americans to Texas, as long as the immigrants agreed to live by the laws of Mexico. Texas then became a state in the new republic of Mexico.

American *empresarios,* adventurers who were given land in return for bringing in new settlers and families to Texas and converting to Catholicism, tended to be aggressive, ignoring Mexican laws and customs, and thought of themselves as Americans, not Mexicans. They also remained Protestant. Some of the settlers brought their slaves into the rich cotton fields of east Texas, even after Mexico had outlawed slavery. Alarmed by these developments, Mexico passed a law in 1830 banning further immigration into Texas, but it was widely ignored. By 1835 Texas was home to 27,000 Americans, some of whom were small slaveholders; 3,000 of their slaves; and only 4,000 Mexicans, most of whom lived in the towns of Goliad and San Antonio.

The government of the United States tried to buy Texas from Mexico in the middle of the 1830s but was rebuffed. This interest in Texas was encouraged by the idea of MANIFEST DESTINY, which held that the United States was destined by God and nature to rule all of North America; there was even some talk that the nation would eventually encompass all of the Western Hemisphere. Concerned that it might eventually lose Texas to the United States, Mexico tried to exert its authority over the region and enforce the ban on slavery. In response, the Texans split into two camps. A "peace party" under STEPHEN AUSTIN's leadership favored working with the Mexican government for more local autonomy and recognized the ultimate sovereignty of the national government in Mexico City. But another group of Texans, the "war party," wanted no negotiations and immediate independence from Mexico. Austin did got some concessions from the Mexican government, but then General ANTONIO LÓPEZ DE SANTA ANNA became president and then dictator. Uninterested in negotiating with the Anglo-Texans, he appointed a military commander for Texas who answered directly to Mexico City, and he ordered Mexican troops into Texas as a show of strength. The American settlers rebelled and forced out the small contingent of Mexican soldiers. Santa Anna, angered by this defiance, personally led a large army into Texas to subdue the rebellion, reaching San Antonio in February 1836. Texans in the meantime had declared their independence from Mexico and adopted a constitution.

Santa Anna's army of 5,000 advanced on the Alamo in San Antonio, which was defended by about 180 men. Most prominent among them was DAVY CROCKETT, the legendary frontiersman and former Whig congressmen from Tennessee; and JIM BOWIE, the well-known adventurer and popularizer of the "Bowie Knife." The small garrison's commander was WILLIAM B. TRAVIS, another southerner and a slave owner. Travis was only 26 and was originally supposed to share the command with Bowie, but the latter fell seriously ill and had to be confined to bed. Although most of the garrison were Anglo-Americans, half from Kentucky, Tennessee and Alabama, their number also included native Mexicans who opposed Santa Anna and his dictatorship.

Santa Anna ordered the immediate surrender of the Alamo by its defenders. One of the many legends that have shaped popular understanding of the siege at the Alamo holds that Travis gave permission to his men to leave if they wished, but supposedly only one took the chance to leave the fort. Travis also sent appeals throughout Texas asking for volunteers to defend the Alamo. Only a few dozen men found their way to the besieged fort. Having refused to surrender, the defenders of the Alamo faced hopeless odds as Santa Anna's huge army prepared to attack. In the early morning of March 6, 1836, the Mexicans launched their assault on the Alamo, and suffered heavy initial losses. Eventually some of the attackers were able to scale the walls of the fort, however, and they engaged in ferocious hand-to-hand combat with the Texans in the courtyard and interior of the Alamo. By the time the fighting had ended, all of the Alamo's defenders had been killed, along with about 1,500 soldiers in Santa Anna's army. Travis's slave, Joe, was among the handful of noncombatants who survived the slaughter.

The Mexicans quickly moved on to the settlement of Goliad, hoping to deliver the Texas rebellion a second crushing blow. There a small and overwhelmed army of 371 Texans surrendered with the expectation that they would be treated as prisoners of war. Instead, Santa Anna declared them pirates and ordered them executed, after which he believed the rebellion to be over, with more than 500 Texas insurgents now dead. However, the fallen defenders of the Alamo became instant heroes and legends in the United States, immortalized in penny newspapers from New Orleans to New York. Santa Anna and his men were portrayed as henchman of the pope and a threat to American liberty. There were demonstrations in U.S. cities against Mexico, and Santa Anna was burned in effigy. Buoyed by the spirit of revenge, adventurers and soldiers from all over the United States rushed to Texas and joined an army led by SAM HOUSTON. At this point, Santa Anna made the mistake of dividing his army, which allowed Houston and his Texans to defeat his forces decisively at San Jacinto in April of 1836. Texas had won its independence, and the cry of "Remember the Alamo" had entered American lore.

Further reading: Virgil E. Baugh, *Rendezvous at the Alamo* (Lincoln: University of Nebraska Press, 1985); William C. Davis, *Three Roads to the Alamo* (New York: HarperCollins, 1998); Jeff Long, *Duel of Eagles: The Mexican and U.S. Fight for the Alamo* (New York: Morrow, 1990).

—Jason K. Duncan

American Anti-Slavery Society

Founded in Philadelphia on December 4, 1833, the American Anti-Slavery Society (AASS) advocated the immediate and complete abolition of slavery throughout the United States and its territories.

Although abolitionism became a nationwide movement in the 1830s, its roots go back to the American colonies. Prior to the Revolutionary War, Quakers and other religious groups opposed slavery as anti-Christian. Free blacks, many of whom had escaped slavery, spoke out vociferously against the "peculiar institution" and helped publicize many of its horrors.

At the founding convention of the AASS, three key figures shaped the fledgling organization: William Lloyd Garrison and two brothers, ARTHUR and LEWIS TAPPAN. Arthur Tappan became the group's first president. Impetus for forming the AASS had come from the first Black National Convention, which had taken place in Philadelphia two years earlier. Organizers had invited several white men to the meeting, where delegates determined that an immediatist, biracial organization was needed. According to a contemporary account by John G. Whittier describing the 1833 meeting, most of the 60 attendees were white, with only "two or three colored members." Those black men—Robert Purvis, James G. Barbadoes, and James C. McCrummell—were all prominent abolitionists. Also attending the 1833 convention were four white women, all Quakers.

Garrison drafted the new society's constitution, which pledged its members to work for emancipation through nonviolent means, such as "moral suasion," and "the overthrow of prejudice by the power of love." Membership in the organization grew rapidly; by 1835 there were more than 400 chapters, and by 1838 the number had grown to 1,350, with more than 250,000 members. Many of the offshoot groups included African Americans and women, although black and women's auxiliaries were also common. The local chapters of the AASS sponsored meetings, adopted resolutions, signed antislavery petitions to be sent to Congress, published journals, and sponsored lecturers to carry the antislavery message to northern audiences.

THE

AMERICAN

ANTI-SLAVERY

ALMANAC,

FOR

1839,

EMANCIPATION, RUIN—SLAVERY, SALVATION!!

A West India paper, in 1838, says: "Institutions undreamt of in the days of slavery, have been founded for agricultural, literary and scientific purposes. New villages and towns are rising in various parts of the island; new streets and houses are daily being erected in the old; and new churches and chapels are rearing their heads in almost every district of the colony. A heathen is now as rarely to be met with, as was a Christian ten years since. Hundreds of children are brought weekly to the baptismal font; thousands are daily receiving the rudiments of education. The vices peculiar to slavery are gradually wearing away; nightly orgies and licentious practices are fast falling into disuse; concubinage is receding before matrimony, and the long night of superstition rapidly evanishing before the sun of Christianity."—"*The West Indian,*" *Spanish Town, Jamaica.*

NEW YORK & BOSTON:

NEW YORK: S. W. BENEDICT.—BOSTON: ISAAC KNAPP.

Shown here is *The Anti-Slavery Almanac,* published yearly by the American Anti-Slavery Society. *(Library of Congress)*

Antislavery petitions were sent to Congress at such a high rate that a number of southern members of the House, with the support of a significant portion of northern representatives, succeeded in passing the Gag Rule in 1836. This regulation prevented any petition regarding slavery from being read aloud; instead, antislavery petitions would be tabled indefinitely. By 1844 the Gag Rule, which had come under fire from JOHN QUINCY ADAMS, was repealed.

Garrison, one of the best-known abolitionists of the mid-19th century, is considered by many historians to have been more of a lightning rod than a true leader. Although he served as president of the AASS from 1843 through 1865, his was largely a symbolic role, as he was not known as an effective organizer. His outspoken editorials in *The Liberator,* a newspaper he published between 1831 and 1865, called for an immediate end to slavery without reparations to slaveholders. Most of the general public of the North considered this an extreme position; even those who felt morally opposed to slavery preferred a more gradual phasing out of a complex political economic system that was protected by the Constitution. But Garrison, who drew a clear moral distinction regarding the ownership of human beings, was not one to consider compromise an option. Advocating secession from the Union by northern states on the grounds that the Constitution permitted slavery, he even burned a copy of the Constitution in protest on July 4, 1854.

During a meeting of the Boston Female Anti-Slavery Society in 1835, Garrison was attacked by a mob of seemingly peaceful attendees. This event gained him considerable sympathy and inspired WENDELL PHILLIPS, a Boston lawyer, to devote himself full-time to the cause of eradicating slavery. Phillips contributed frequently to *The Liberator.* He became known for his impassioned and eloquent speeches against slavery, most notably his 1837 address delivered after the assassination of fellow abolitionist ELIJAH LOVEJOY. Along with Garrison, Phillips supported women's rights.

THEODORE DWIGHT WELD, a minister and skillful political organizer, is considered by many historians to have been more influential than Garrison. In 1834, while a teacher at Lane Theological Seminary in Cincinnati, Weld organized a series of infamous student debates. These debates spurred a rash of student abolitionist organizing, which led to Weld's dismissal from the faculty. Weld married ANGELINA GRIMKÉ, a fellow abolitionist and women's rights activist, in 1838. A skilled writer, he edited AASS's paper *The Emancipator* from 1836 to 1840. Weld published many writings pseudonymously, including the highly influential *American Slavery as It Is* in 1839, which served in part as a basis for Harriet Beecher Stowe's *Uncle Tom's Cabin.*

The AASS published a number of books and periodicals, including *The Emancipator, Human Rights, Slave's Friend, Quarterly Anti-Slavery Magazine,* and the *Anti-Slavery Record,* with highly regarded writers of the period contributing their talents. The *Slave's Friend* was aimed at children and included poems, songs, and drawings. In addition to supporting the formation of juvenile antislavery societies, the *Slave's Friend* also encouraged children to collect money for the cause.

In addition to its prolific publications, the AASS sponsored lectures by its own members as well as former slaves like Frederick Douglass, publisher of *The North Star,* an abolitionist newspaper; and William Wells Brown, a novelist.

The AASS provided fertile ground for debates over many of the period's most controversial issues. The organization opposed the movement to send free blacks to Africa under the auspices of AMERICAN COLONIZATION SOCIETY, arguing that removing free blacks was a means of strengthening slavery. Garrison railed against colonization time and time again in *The Emancipator*, many issues of which were devoted exclusively to anticolonization arguments.

Perhaps the most divisive issue faced by the AASS was that of the place of women in the antislavery movement as well as in society at large. By the mid-1830s more than 100 female antislavery societies had been created, and female abolitionists were circulating petitions, editing abolitionist tracts, and organizing antislavery conventions. This issue reached the boiling point in 1840 at the annual meeting of the AASS in New York, leading the Tappan brothers, who opposed the full inclusion of women out of fear of alienating the churches, to form a new organization, the American and Foreign Anti-Slavery Society.

The American Anti-Slavery Society elected ABIGAIL KELLEY FOSTER to its business committee and named three women delegates (Foster, LUCRETIA MOTT, and Elizabeth Cady Stanton) as delegates to the World Anti-Slavery Convention in London. These women were then relegated to seats in a balcony on the grounds that their participation would offend British public opinion. The exclusion of women from the floor led Garrison and three other male abolitionists to boycott the convention and sit with the women in the balcony.

The American Anti-Slavery Society disbanded in 1870, after the Fifteenth Amendment to the U.S. Constitution granted black men the right to vote.

Further reading: American Anti-Slavery Society, "Constitution" [1833], in *American Abolitionists,* ed. Stanley Harold (London: Longman, 2001); Henry H. Simms, *Emotion at High Tide: Abolition as a Controversial Factor, 1830–1845* (Richmond, Va.: William Byrd Press, 1960).

—Eva Pendleton

American Colonization Society

The American Colonization Society (ACS) was formed in 1816 to send free African Americans to African shores. Created by a coalition of white philanthropists who wanted to provide incentives for ending SLAVERY and slaveholders who wanted to deport free blacks (whom they deemed to be subversive to plantation discipline), the colonization society grew steadily during the 1820s and 1830s. In fact, it became one of the largest reform organizations of the early antebellum era, with more local chapters than even abolitionists had in such northern states as Pennsylvania. In addition, the colonization society attracted the support of some of the nation's leading political figures, such as ex-president James Madison, presidential hopeful Henry Clay of Kentucky and Massachusetts governor and renowned orator Edward Everett. The colonization society sponsored the expatriate colony of Liberia and generated intense debate among black as well as white reformers over the society's goals and motivations. The group existed through the Civil War before formally ending operations in 1865.

The American Colonization Society operated through national and branch organizations. It held an annual convention and published its proceedings every year. In addition, it printed a newspaper promulgating the society's activities, *The African Repository*. Perhaps the group's most famous single undertaking was the establishment of Liberia, a colony of former slaves located on the western coast of Africa. Founded in 1823, Liberia achieved independence in 1847, becoming a destination for a number of free black activists, including former anticolonizationist John Russwurm, a coeditor of the first black newspaper, *Freedom's Journal,* published in New York City between 1827 and 1829; Martin Delany; and Thomas Morris Chester. The American Colonization Society garnered donations totaling nearly $2.5 million for the colony of Liberia. Roughly 12,000 free blacks and former slaves eventually traveled there. The ACS initially headed most of the colony's main posts: White appointees from the American Colonization Society controlled Liberia until 1841, although black settlers held a variety of powerful administrative positions, including secretary to the colonial agent, acting governor, and superintendent of education.

Beyond Liberia, the American Colonization Society spurred two important and interrelated events after its founding in 1816. The first involved colonization's impact on black activism; the second, colonization's impact on the broader cause of abolition. Although some African-American leaders, such as James Forten of Philadelphia, listened to early colonizationist plans with an open mind, most black Americans vehemently opposed the group. Arguing that the American nation was a black homeland too, and that Americans must end slavery immediately rather than export black activists, they organized against colonization in cities and towns ranging from Boston to Baltimore. The largest black anticolonization demonstration occurred in Philadelphia at Richard Allen's African Methodist Episcopal Church. Several hundred protesters forced the city's black leaders to publicly condemn colonization. Black leaders in other communities did likewise between 1817 and the early 1830s.

This groundswell of black activism was the only public movement against colonization before the 1830s, when a new generation of radical abolitionists emerged in American culture. The nation's leading antislavery societies during the early 1800s disavowed colonization as a strategy for ending slavery but also refrained from publicly attacking the American Colonization Society or its leaders. Early abolitionists, led by the Pennsylvania Abolition Society and the New York Manumission Society, sought to curry favor with the nation's leading politicians, jurists, and philanthropists. In this manner, early reformers hoped to slowly but surely build political support for gradual abolition plans. Early abolitionist groups did not accept black members, either, although they did work with local black leaders in community schools and in courts of law.

African Americans hoped to prevail upon early white abolitionists to support their anticolonizationist struggle. They petitioned white reformers and met with them privately on several occasions. For over a decade, however, the Pennsylvania Abolition Society and American Convention of Abolition Societies refused to unleash public condemnations of colonization. African-American reformers filled this void. During the 1820s Boston's David Walker issued perhaps the most famous black pamphlet of the antebellum era, "An Appeal to the Colored Citizens of the World." Walker called on African Americans to organize anew against slavery and racial injustice. In particular he focused on the evil of colonization, arguing that the plan merely sought to rid the country of free blacks as a means of strengthening slavery. According to Walker, African Americans had to raise national voices of protest in response.

In this way, colonization became a springboard for a new and more radical brand of abolitionism. William Lloyd Garrison, the famed editor of *The Liberator,* was influenced by black anticolonization protest during the late 1820s. After meeting such black activists as James Forten and Baltimore's William Watkins, both of whom provided Garrison with black protest documents, the young white printer shifted his beliefs. No longer a quasicolonizationist or gradual abolitionist, he vowed to become the most ardent opponent of slavery and colonization in the country. Garrison began publishing his own newspaper in Boston in 1831, and he consistently debated colonization speakers throughout the mid-Atlantic and New England. In 1832 Garrison also published a pamphlet opposing colonization, "Thoughts on African colonization," which prominently featured black protest documents.

Further reading: P. J. Staudenraus, *The African Colonization Movement, 1816–1865* (New York: Octagon Books, 1980).

—Richard Newman

American Fur Company

A fur-trading company started in New York by JOHN JACOB ASTOR in 1808, the American Fur Company eventually came to monopolize the American fur trade. Originally the only stockholder, Astor began the company in an effort to compete with two Canadian fur companies that were encroaching into American territory to do business, mainly in beaver hides. To challenge the North West Company and the Michilimackinac Company, Astor first tried to gain trading rights to the Great Lakes region. In 1811 he made an agreement with the two Canadian companies to form a partnership called the Southwest Fur Company, which would restrict its business to south of the Canadian border.

Also in 1811, his employees established ASTORIA, a trading post in Oregon located where the COLUMBIA RIVER meets the Pacific Ocean. These efforts to control the Pacific Northwest through another subsidiary, the Pacific Fur Company, were thwarted when Astoria was captured by rival trading companies and then fell into British hands during the WAR OF 1812. When Astoria was restored to the United States by the TREATY OF GHENT in 1814, the Astor interests had already been sold to the North West Company. But while some of the company's trading activities were temporarily sidelined during the war, Astor's enterprises recovered soon after and continued to grow. By 1817, he had bought out the two Canadian companies and established his own northern department of the American Fur Company as the main trading company in the Great Lakes area, centered at the Mackinac trading post. From this time on, he was no longer the only stockholder but added partners as he bought out or negotiated with competitors.

After securing his stake in the North, Astor began establishing his presence in the rapidly developing western fur trade, which was then centered in St. Louis. Upon negotiating terms with existing St. Louis companies such as the St. Louis MISSOURI FUR COMPANY (see also CHOUTEAU FAMILY), Astor was able to open a western department of his firm by 1822, concentrating on the Missouri River fur trade. Still intent on monopolizing the American fur trade as much as possible, Astor continued to plan ways to undermine his competitors. He still faced formidable competition from Kenneth McKenzie's Columbia Fur Company and from federally supported Indian factories. Started in 1795, the Indian factory system was intended to protect Indians from exploitation by private traders and promote peaceful relations between the United States and Indian nations by establishing trading posts at which Indians could trade pelts for goods, priced at cost. Astor and other independent traders opposed the factory system as a corrupt operation that hindered profitable trade. Along with powerful political allies such as THOMAS HART BENTON and LEWIS CASS, Astor pushed the federal government to end the factory system, which it did in 1822.

This was neither the first nor the last time that Astor would use financial dominance and political connections to aggressively push the interests of his company in order to eliminate competition. The American Fur Company prompted the federal government to pass laws that excluded foreigners from trade and established official trading locations—both of which favored Astor's interests over those of other companies and individuals. After merging with its main remaining rival, the Columbia Fur Company, in 1827, the American Fur Company finally acquired, if not a monopoly, then at least a formidable financial edge in the fur trade of the United States.

From 1828 to 1834 the company became more systematized and began to look more like a modern bureaucratic business. At their headquarters in New York City, Astor and his son oversaw general operations and supervised the head agents for each division of the company. Ramsay Crooks acted as the company's general manager. Pierre Chouteau, Jr., ran the western department out of St. Louis. Robert Stuart managed the Great Lakes region. Kenneth McKenzie (the former head of the Columbia Fur Company) acted as the main agent in the West, managing the Fort Union post at the convergence of the Missouri and Yellowstone Rivers.

Partly through McKenzie's influence, the company's trappers infiltrated the fur-rich lands of the Blackfeet Indians in 1829. By 1830 they had built a new post, Fort McKenzie, on the Marias River. While these actions secured Astor's hold on the upper Missouri, he still faced challenges in the Rocky Mountains. From 1830 to 1834 the American Fur Company fought another trading war with St. Louis entrepreneurs (WILLIAM HENRY ASHLEY, WILLIAM SUBLETTE, and THOMAS CAMPBELL) who were attempting to take over the Rockies trade. With Astor's financial resources and political clout, his interests eventually won out, and yet another group of rivals were absorbed into his company.

While profits from the American fur trade continued to grow, Astor realized that his business was built on a resource with inherent limitations. The fur trade depended on the accessibility of pelts and the continued demand for fur products. Past experience had shown him that the availability of beaver, bison, muskrat, bear, and other fur was readily affected by environmental factors human agents could not always control. Also, the rise of the textile industry meant that demand for fur to make hats and coats might decline over time. As a businessman interested in maximizing profit, Astor decided to sell out while the trade was still prosperous. He therefore sold his interests in the company to his partners in 1834. The western department, including the upper Missouri outfit, was bought by Pratte, Chouteau and Company. The northern department was purchased by a group led by Ramsay Crooks.

Crooks' group now took the name American Fur Company and continued to do business until 1842. Up to its 1842 failure, the company continued to operate in the region between Detroit, the Ohio River, and the Red River, diversifying from fur trading into shipbuilding and fisheries. The company continued a trading relationship with the West through Pratte, Chouteau and Company (later Pierre Chouteau, Jr., and Company), and attempted to compete with new rivals. The American Fur Company was reconfigured once more in 1846 as a commission house, but it was no longer a viable concern after 1847. Portions of the old company continued to exist until the 1860s, but the fur trade that thrived after the Civil War—most notably the trade in bison hides—was not transacted through the American Fur Company.

The American Fur Company and its subsidiaries were a powerful national (and international) presence for half a century. At the height of its power, the company controlled three-fourths of the American fur trade. As one of the nation's first monopolistic corporations, the American Fur Company set an early example for later American capitalists. Astor's method—using his formidable assets and political influence to intimidate and absorb rivals—became a standard strategy for American industrialists later in the 19th century.

Astor's imperious behavior and questionable ethics also set the standard for his capitalistic successors. His company has often been accused of using alcohol in trade to exploit the Indians. The American Fur Company was certainly not the only firm to use alcohol as leverage, however, and some scholars have pointed out that the trading relationship between Astor's agents and the Indians was not a completely one-sided story of exploitation through addictive commodities such as liquor. Indians were skillful bargainers who knew they had resources and knowledge traders would be willing to pay for. However, this leverage diminished over the first half of the 19th century, partly due to the abolition of the factory system and the forced cession of valuable lands to the United States. Indeed traders like Astor helped instigate a new relationship between Indians and whites that was much more one-sided: As Indians lost their economic clout and homelands through the efforts of interested parties like the American Fur Company, they became vulnerable and thus more easily exploitable.

Further reading: Hiram Martin Chittenden, *The American Fur Trade of the Far West: A History of the Pioneer Trading Posts and Early Fur Companies of the Missouri Valley and Rocky Mountains, and of the Overland Commerce with Santa Fe* (Stanford, Calif.: Academic Reprints, 1954); John D. Haeger, *John Jacob Astor: Business and Finance in the Early Republic* (Detroit: Wayne State University Press, 1991); David S. Lavender, *The Fist in the Wilderness* (Lincoln: University of Nebraska Press, 1998); David J. Wishart, *The Fur Trade of the American West, 1807–1840: A Geographical Synthesis* (Lincoln: University of Nebraska Press, 1979).

—Eleanor H. McConnell

American System

The American System was a philosophy of political economy in the 19th century which held that the federal government had a legitimate role to play in spurring economic development and growth. This program of economic nationalism was most closely associated with HENRY CLAY of Kentucky, first a representative and then for many years a senator. Clay borrowed some of his ideas from Alexander Hamilton, the first secretary of the Treasury and a Federalist. Hamilton was the most forceful and prominent spokesman in the early republic for the idea that the national government should take an active role in developing an integrated, commercial economy based in part on manufactures.

Early in his congressional career, Henry Clay had been one of the nationalist WAR HAWKS who pushed for war with England in 1812. He had also been among the majority who opposed the rechartering of the first Bank of the United States in 1811, believing it to be unconstitutional and unnecessary. However, the experiences of the WAR OF 1812, in which the United States struggled to fund its military effort, changed the minds of Clay and many other Republicans, who by the 1820s had formed the National Republican Party. This faction was crucial in the chartering of the SECOND BANK OF THE UNITED STATES in 1816. The war had also highlighted the inadequacy of existing transportation networks, which led to calls for improved transportation after the war.

It was during the administration of President JAMES MONROE that Henry Clay first articulated a program that became known as "The American System." It was in part a response to the changes, economic and otherwise, that the United States underwent after the War of 1812. Manufacturing was increasing, people were moving to cities for work, and there was a growing number of Americans migrating into the Ohio and Mississippi valleys in search of farmland. In 1819 during the crisis over the admission of Missouri as a state, the United States had a serious debate on the question of slavery, which caused some to fear for national unity. The PANIC OF 1819 also convinced some Republicans that the United States needed to provide safeguards against further panics or depressions. Clay and others believed that a series of policies was needed to make the ties between sections stronger and help to forge a more united country. With Clay now a committed economic nationalist as well, the core elements of his American System were (1) a high protective tariff to protect U.S. manufactured goods and secure the domestic market against foreign competition; (2) a federal bank to regulate domestic currency and the economy; (3) funding of internal improvements by the federal government, especially transportation networks to better enable the American people to distribute their goods and crops; and (4) the maintenance of a high price for lands that the federal government would sell to companies and individuals. The revenue from these sales would be sent to states to use on their own "internal improvements," as they were called.

Clay genuinely believed that the American System would encourage a harmony of interests from which all classes and regions would benefit. Much as Hamilton had before him, Clay argued that if the United States failed to develop its own manufacturing capability, it was destined to remain an economic colony of European powers. The lack of a strong manufacturing base to the national economy would place the nation's ability to defend itself in wartime in jeopardy. Such a situation was unacceptable to Americans who thought of their nation as destined for greatness. Clay believed that his system would benefit American cities, allowing them to become manufacturing and commercial centers and provide a balance in a nation that was still overwhelmingly rural and agricultural. Urban workers would see a raise in wages and jobs less prone to panics. Farmers would benefit as well, as by trading their produce to city dwellers for manufactured goods, their own standard of living, as well as their agricultural outputs, would rise. The improvements in transportation that the American System promised would help goods to move faster and more freely around the country. The Bank of the United States was needed to oversee and guide all of this financial activity and bring needed stability to an increasingly complex economy.

Henry Clay wanted to be president, and he was convinced that his advocacy for the American System would enable him to build a political base in all sections of the country and send him to the White House. Clay's ambitious plan, however, met with spirited opposition. From the founding of the republic, there had been a great many Americans, both northerners and southerners, who were resolutely opposed to enlarging the powers of government beyond those explicitly given to it in the Constitution. Originally this party, the Republicans, was led by Thomas Jefferson. Although James Madison had signed into law the chartering of the Second Bank of the United States, before he left office in 1817 he had also vetoed funds to help New York build a canal, asserting that the power to do so was not in the Constitution. His successor, JAMES MONROE, also believed that the federal government did not possess such authority under the Constitution. Therefore, Monroe vetoed a plan that would have allowed Washington to administer toll gates on the Cumberland Road. The dominant Republican Party subsequently divided in the 1820s, in part over the proper role of the federal government in making internal improvements.

Despite this formidable tradition in American politics, Clay did have some success in getting Congress to enact into law some parts of the American System. Proponents of the protective tariff passed several measures raising duties on imported goods, including one in 1824 and another in

1828. The latter was described as the "Tariff of Abominations" by its critics and nearly caused disunion, as South Carolina protested bitterly and claimed to have the right to nullify federal laws it believed not in its interest. Clay helped to craft a compromise tariff in 1833 that lowered duties and helped to mollify the South while maintaining the integrity of the Union. By that time, another distinct party, led by ANDREW JACKSON and MARTIN VAN BUREN, had emerged by 1830; they referred to themselves as Democrats. During his successful bid for the presidency in 1828, although Jackson had given the impression in the West that he was not opposed to the American System, over the course of his time as president he came to be a pronounced enemy of its principles. In 1830 Jackson vetoed the Maysville Road bill, which allowed federal monies to buy stock in a private company that was building a road that happened to run through Henry Clay's state of Kentucky. Jackson based his decision both on constitutional grounds and on the more pragmatic grounds that it benefited only one state. As former president JOHN QUINCY ADAMS described it, the veto was a blow to "the system of internal improvements by national energies.

Jacksonian Democrats believed that the American System was unjust because it put the federal government on the side of the wealthy and property-owning classes, and what was worse, it called for the government to exercise powers on behalf of the affluent that it did not possess under the Constitution. Some critics of the American System feared that it favored urban growth at the expense of farming interests and denied poorer Americans the opportunity to own land in the West because it promised to keep federal land prices too high. Southerners, led by JOHN C. CALHOUN of South Carolina, were wary of any plan that would bolster the powers of the federal government, which might then turn its increased authority toward the question of slavery. Slave owners also objected to the prospect of paying artificially high prices for manufactured goods, since their own agricultural products would suffer as trade between the United States and Europe declined as a result of the American System. Virtually all opponents of the American System feared that it was bent on creating a new aristocracy, this one economic, and that the creation of a small privileged class would gravely harm the republican ideals of equality before the law and a rough social egalitarianism.

Clay vigorously defended his system as in keeping with the Constitution. Indeed, he saw his plan as embodying the spirit of that document, which was to encourage a more perfect union. He also argued that the "necessary and proper" clause of the Constitution gave the federal government the power to build roads; after all, the same Constitution had created a national post office, the object of which was to deliver mail. This mission, Clay maintained, implied the building of roads and their maintenance, if necessary, by the federal government. Despite this, the American System suffered another serious defeat in 1832 when its opponents succeeded in abolishing the Bank of the United States. With the bank a key issue, Jackson easily won reelection in 1832 over his National Republican opponent, Henry Clay.

In 1834 the WHIG PARTY formed and became the proponent of the American System. But because the Democrats held the White House for most of the remainder of the antebellum period, the Whigs were unable to revive the Bank of United States or keep the price of federal lands high enough to suit them. The nation's economic growth and expansion continued in the 1830s and 1840s, however, even if the federal role in this process was not quite what Clay and the others had hoped for. Not until after the secession of southern states in the 1860s and then in the decades after the Civil War did Henry Clay's vision of an economically integrated United States come to pass, as the nation, with federal assistance, moved into an era of great industrial growth and improvements in transportation.

Further reading: Robert Remini, *Henry Clay: Statesman for the Union* (New York: W. W. Norton, 1991); Charles Sellers, *The Market Revolution: Jacksonian America, 1815–1846* (New York: Oxford University Press, 1991).

—Jason Duncan

Amistad incident

The *Amistad* controversy centered around a slave mutiny off the coast of CUBA in July 1839. The African captives who mutinied on board the Spanish ship *Amistad* had originally been transported to Cuba in a Portuguese slave ship sailing from Lombokor, an island off the West African coast. This transport violated the 1817 treaty between England and Spain which banned the trans-Atlantic slave trade. Thus, the contraband Africans were smuggled into Havana after dark. Two Spaniards, José Ruiz and Pedro Montes, purchased 53 of the Africans and sailed with them toward Puerto Príncipe aboard *La Amistad.*

The captives revolted soon after the ship set out from the northern coast of Cuba. Sengbe Pieh (also known as Joseph Cinqué) led the revolt. The captives freed themselves and then strangled the captain and stabbed some of the crew. Ruiz and Montes were spared, on the condition that they guide the ship back to Africa. Instead of returning them, the Spaniards deceived the mutineers by steering east by day, then west by night, slowly directing the vessel northward. By August the tattered ship had reached U.S. waters off the coast of Long Island near Montauk, New York, where the desperately hungry passengers went ashore to find food. The USS *Washington* discovered them,

This engraving depicts Joseph Cinqué and about 50 other enslaved Africans rising up against the captain and crew of the *Amistad*. *(Library of Congress)*

and the mutineers surrendered after some resistance. The Africans were sent to a New Haven jail, where they would remain for the next two years. News of the *Amistad* case spread quickly, and legal arguments over the fate of the Africans began in the Connecticut courts. Central to these legal proceedings was a conflict between the human right to rebel when held by force and the rights of property owners to recover their property. The same could be said for all legal arguments over slavery, but adding to this controversy was the problem of international laws and treaties. Thus, the fate of the Amistad rebels was shaped not only by state courts, but by federal and international concerns over U.S. relations to Spain.

Abolitionists in the United States reacted strongly to the incident, as did southern slave owners. Each side viewed the fate of the mutineers as a statement about the morality of the slave system. Ruiz and Montes maintained that the mutineers had been slaves in Cuba prior to the voyage, and thus as the legal property of the Spaniards, they were subject to punishment for their actions aboard the *Amistad*. Prominent abolitionist LEWIS TAPPAN and others created the Amistad Committee to help defend Cinqué and the other rebels. Tappan argued that the "Mendians" (as they became known because many were from Mende) were illegal captives who had the human right to defend their freedom through revolt.

The committee began to publicize the plight of the captives in an effort to raise money for their defense and promote awareness of the evils of slavery. Along with receiving substantial newspaper coverage, the Mendians were also sketched, and the sketches circulated at abolitionist speaking engagements. With the help of two African-born sailors, supporters were able to communicate with the prisoners, especially with the leader Cinqué. While imprisoned awaiting trial, sympathetic activists taught the Mendians some English and introduced them to Christianity. Tappan secured the services of attorney Roger Baldwin for the upcoming legal battle.

In September 1839 the *Amistad* case was brought before the U.S. Circuit Court in Hartford, Connecticut. This court denied the prisoners' pleas for release, remanding the case to the higher U.S. District Court. In January 1840 District Judge Andrew T. Judson ruled that the Africans had been illegally kidnapped and sold, in violation of the 1817 treaty. Judson also ruled that, as legally free people, Cinqué and his followers had the right to revolt against their captors in order to regain their freedom. Judson ordered that the mutineers be returned to Africa.

However, the federal government and President MARTIN VAN BUREN had expected a verdict that would have required the mutineers to be returned to Spain in accordance with Pinckney's Treaty of 1795 between the United States and Spain. Worried that Judson's verdict would provoke further diplomatic tension with Spain as well as southern hostility toward his administration, Van Buren appealed the District Court decision. The Court of Appeals upheld the verdict in May 1840, so the government continued the appeal at the highest level, the U.S. Supreme Court. The attorneys for the *Amistad* mutineers convinced former president JOHN QUINCY ADAMS to address the Court on their behalf. Baldwin's arguments and Adams's stirring address persuaded the Court. Although the majority of the justices (including Chief Justice Roger Taney) were southerners and slave owners, they affirmed the original District Court decision in March 1841 by a margin of 8-1: The mutineers had been kidnapped, which entitled them to use force to free themselves. The sanctity of property did not apply in this case, because the property was taken illegally through fraud and deceit. The rebels were free to return to Africa. Tappan and the Amistad Committee began to raise funds in order to return Cinqué and his comrades to Africa. Only 35 of the original captives remained, the others having died in the New Haven jail.

In November 1841 the remaining Africans, their translator, and five white missionaries set sail for Sierra Leone. Cinqué maintained some contact with Tappan after his return, but for the most part historians know little about the fate of the mutineers after 1841. Whether the Africans were able to return to their homelands and families is not known. Cinqué supposedly lived until 1879, coming to the surviving Tappan mission in Freetown to die. Still claiming material damages, Spain continued to ask for reparations from the United States for its lost "cargo." These demands for recompense were drowned out by the sectional controversies in Congress that eventually led to the Civil War.

The *Amistad* controversy itself helped kindle the flames of sectional dispute, pitting human-rights arguments against property-rights arguments in ways that influenced the domestic battle over slavery. The incident did not set a legal precedent that contributed to slavery's demise; indeed, the Taney Court that affirmed the mutineers' rights would go on to rule against the human rights of American blacks in the 1857 *Dred Scott* decision. Nevertheless, the arguments presented by Tappan, Baldwin, and Adams resonated within the antislavery community, and the publicity surrounding the captives helped illuminate the horrors of the slave trade and strengthen the argument for the human rights of African-American slaves.

Further reading: Mary Cable, *Black Odyssey: The Case of the Slave Ship Amistad* (New York: Viking Press, 1971); Howard Jones, *Mutiny on the Amistad: The Saga of a Slave Revolt and its Impact on American Abolition, Law, and Diplomacy* (New York: Oxford University Press, 1987).

—Eleanor H. McConnell

anti-Catholic riots

Beginning in the 1820s, the SECOND GREAT AWAKENING, which occurred among mainly evangelical Protestants, included an element of hostility against Catholicism. Some Protestants published novels and tracts which purported to expose the true, and menacing, face of Catholicism to the American public. This burst of religious enthusiasm occurred as the immigration of Catholics into the United States, mainly from Ireland and Germany, began to increase. These two factors contributed to a revival of traditional American anti-Catholicism, which was an inheritance of European religious rivalries. Between 1830 and 1860 there were numerous acts of group violence directed against Catholics and Catholic institutions.

One of the first such outbreaks occurred in Charlestown, Massachusetts, just outside of Boston, in 1834. A group of Ursuline sisters had established a convent there in 1818, and built a large school for girls on a hill overlooking the town. The size and extravagant design of the school drew much attention. There was also concern that the school enrolled wealthy Protestant girls, who, it was alleged, were held there against their will and were the victims of sexual abuse by Catholic clergy. These rumors contributed to raising the ire of local townspeople who were not Catholic. Adding to the tension was well known Protestant preacher Lyman Beecher, who began a series of sermons in Boston in August of 1834, the theme of which was the alleged threat of the Catholic Church to American republicanism. A group of local workingmen began to plot an assault on the convent and school, and shouting "no popery" and "down with the cross," burned down the school and an adjacent building belonging to the Ursuline sisters. This successful attack on the Charlestown school was followed by similar episodes in other cities, including New York and Detroit.

In the 1840s tensions between Catholics and Protestants flared up again when Catholics protested against the use of the King James Bible, which was essentially Protestant in character, in public schools. In response, Catholics requested public funds to set up their own private, religious schools. Many Protestants reacted strongly to this, accusing Catholics of using public money for their own purposes and for opposing the use of Bibles in the schools. As the immigration of Catholics from Europe continued into the 1840s, this contributed to fears on the part of some Protestants that the U.S. was in danger of being transformed by the large influx of Catholics, and anti-Catholic literature continued to flourish. In the summer of 1844 Philadelphia became the site of a serious anti-Catholic disturbance. "Native Americans" were encouraged to join a party of that name and fight the alleged threat to American institutions and liberties from the Catholic newcomers. Many of the Catholic immigrants were from Ireland, and they organized as well to prepare for what they believed were impending attacks on their churches and neighborhoods. A large crowd, proclaiming themselves "American Republicans," marched through an Irish section of Kensington, which was directly north of Philadelphia. They were met there with violence, with one of their number shot to death, possibly by an Irish Catholic sniper. Seeking revenge, nativist crowds reassembled a few days later, and once again marched through Kensington. They were encouraged by street corner speakers exhorting them to retaliate. Three days of rioting followed, in which nativist crowds burned to the ground three Catholic Churches, many of the homes in the Irish neighborhood, and an Irish fire company house. The fear among Catholics was so great that the bishop of Philadelphia, Francis Kendrick, ordered all Catholic churches in the area to be closed on the following Sunday.

CONSTITUTION OF THE UNITED STATES

"DANGER IN THE DARK"
IS DESTINED TO BE READ BY EVERY AMERICAN.

SHALL IT COME TO THIS?
ROMISH INTOLERANCE MUST NOT TRIUMPH!

THE AIM OF POPE PIUS IX.

"BEWARE! THERE IS DANGER IN THE DARK!"

WANTED IMMEDIATELY, Agents in every county in the United States, to aid in opening the eyes of the blind, by spreading throughout the length and breadth of our Glorious Republic, a new and important Book (which should be in the hands of every true American and Patriot), entitled

"DANGER IN THE DARK."

BY THE REV. ISAAC KELSO.

This distinguished Book, which has been published but a few weeks, has already reached its 31st edition, and there is an edition now in press of 10,000 copies. From

practised in our midst by the orders of the Jesuits—*A Brotherhood of Pious Assassins*, the vilest and most despicable of our race, who seek to stifle liberty and subvert the free institutions of our Glorious Republic, while they owe allegiance to a foreign despot, and BOW TO A MASTER AT ROME! Upon the guilty heads of those sworn enemies to Civil and Religious Liberty, the author hurls with giant force the fearful thunderbolts of a just condemnation, and especially repels with burning indignation their audacious assaults upon the COMMON SCHOOLS OF OUR COUNTRY!

To the cultivated mind, this book furnishes a rare intellectual treat; and happily combining, as it does, amusement with instruction, its pages cannot fail to delight

This cartoon of Pope Pius IX crumbling the U.S. Constitution captured the fears of American Protestants at the height of Irish immigration in the mid-19th century. *(Library of Congress)*

The hysteria soon spread to New York City, which by that point also had several Catholic churches as well and a growing population of immigrant Catholics. Nativists there blamed Catholics in Philadelphia for the disturbances in that city, and urged Protestant New Yorkers to gird themselves for similar trouble. To John Hughes, an Irish immigrant and Catholic bishop of New York City, this seemed to be a pretext for assaults on Catholics and Catholic property. Bishop Hughes issued the statement for which he is best known, warning that "if a single Catholic Church were burned in New York, the city would become a second Moscow," a reference to the burning of the Russian city in 1812. Acting with his encouragement, more than a thousand Catholics armed themselves and stood guard in front of the city's Catholic churches. This show of determination appeared to have its desired effect, as nativists, alarmed by Hughes's threat and the aggressive response of Catholics, called off plans for a mass meeting and the tension eventually dissipated. Disturbed by the violence, bloodshed and destruction of private property in Philadelphia and elsewhere, most Protestant Americans came to see the nativists as dangerous extremists. The immediate physical danger to Catholics ebbed after 1844, but anti-Catholicism remained a part of American political culture, as the rise of the Know-Nothings in the 1850s demonstrated. When an archbishop of the Vatican, Gaetano Bedini, toured the United States in the 1850s, angry nativist crowds burned his effigy in Boston, Cincinnati, New York, and Baltimore, and shots were fired into his hotel room in the latter city. Horrific clashes between Catholics and nativists in Louisville, Kentucky, in 1855 on what is known as "Bloody Monday" in that city's history, left at least 20 people dead. Along with fears of the slave power and Mormonism, fear of Catholicism was a defining feature of American life in the decades before the Civil War.

Further reading: Ray Allen Billington, *The Protestant Crusade: A Study of the Origins of American Nativism, 1800–1860* (Chicago: Quadrangle Books, 1938); Charles R. Morris, *American Catholics: The Saints and Sinners Who Built America's Most Powerful Church* (New York: Times Books, 1997).

—Jason K. Duncan

anti-Chinese agitation, rise of

It was the CALIFORNIA GOLD RUSH that first attracted large numbers of Chinese people to the United States, and more particularly to the American West. Chinese emigration from Guangdong Province to "Gold Mountain," as California was called, had begun in 1851 and reached substantial numbers in 1852, when perhaps as many as 25,000 Chinese came through San Francisco. The majority came as contract laborers, and from the beginning they were the most distinctive of the several groups that came from all over the world in response to the discovery of gold in California in 1848. Most of these sojourners—for they intended to return to their families and villages as soon as possible—arrived under a system of debt bondage that bound them to Chinese merchants for the price of their passage. They worked to pay this extended credit under such conditions and such terms that the indentured immigrants were slaves to well-to-do Chinese merchants.

Initially the new arrivals worked claims that were considered exhausted. That they would work for less and needed minimal subsistence gave them an advantage in the gold fields that soon generated hostility toward them. Since they worked for lower wages than Euro-Americans, and given the increasing competition in the California goldfields in the 1850s, the Chinese miners were targets for physical intimidation that could escalate into violence quickly. In addition to being mining competition, the Chinese were set apart from other foreign groups; they lived and worked together, they did not associate with other mining groups, they did not learn English, they made no attempts to assimilate, and they were non-Christian. Although they had come on a temporary basis, their financial bondage assured that their stay would be long. The California census of 1860 recorded almost 35,000 Chinese among the state's population of some 380,000. Of the Chinese enumerated (and the number is probably an undercount because of the difficulty of listing Chinese names), three-fourths were found in the mining counties. The rest were in San Francisco, where they found work in laundries and restaurants or as servants. Indeed, as the rich claims played out, the numbers of Chinese miners probably grew in proportion to the whole, and this only increased the hostility toward them.

Beginning in the mid-1860s, as the mining opportunities diminished, the Chinese took jobs as contract laborers on the railroads under construction across the West. Anti-Chinese feelings then transferred from the mining districts to the cities, especially San Francisco, where they became the targets of xenophobic political campaigns that sought scapegoats for unemployment, low wages, and hard times. Politicians vied with one another to make the most anti-Chinese statements in the course of their campaigns. That San Francisco was a growing city with a seasonal surplus of laborers (especially in winter, when there was an influx of miners into the city) added weight to the charge that Chinese laborers were taking jobs from Americans.

Further reading: Gunther Barth, *Bitter Strength: A History of the Chinese in America, 1850–1870* (Cambridge, Mass.: Harvard University Press, 1964).

anti-Masonry

The political and social movement that became known as anti-Masonry burst suddenly on the American scene in the 1820s. Anti-Masonry was a reaction to the Freemasons, who made up fraternal lodges of men active in fields such as commerce, politics, and law, primarily in the northern United States. Masonic groups, or lodges, had existed in the United States since the colonial period but had become more influential in the decades after the American Revolution. Many important leaders of the United States in the early republic were Masons, including George Washington. Masons, who were all men, engaged in a series of somewhat mysterious rituals, including secret handshakes and passwords. They believed that they should do good works for the new nation and inspire a sense of moral virtue and learning among its citizens. At ceremonial events such as groundbreakings and dedication of buildings, Masons were usually very much in evidence, as they laid cornerstones and inscribed them with their insignias. In 1793 for example, President George Washington laid the cornerstone of the U.S. Capitol in the District of Columbia wearing a Masonic apron.

Although Masons considered themselves pillars of republican society, others began to suspect them of having aristocratic and antirepublican tendencies, due in great part to the secretive aspects of their fraternal activities. Masonry was at its peak of influence and membership between approximately 1790 and 1825, when suddenly it became quite controversial. In 1826 William Morgan was a member of a Masonic lodge and a wandering stonemason who moved from city to city in search of work. He became embroiled in a dispute with a lodge in Batavia, New York, and threatened to publish a book that would reveal all the secrets of Masonry. Local Masons, angered by Morgan's threat, had him arrested and thrown in jail on charges of debt. After being released from jail, Morgan was immediately kidnapped by a group of Masons and was never seen alive again. It was generally believed that he was drowned in the Niagara River as punishment for his actions against Masonry.

Many people in western New York were not only shocked by Morgan's disappearance and apparent murder but outraged that local authorities, who were Masons, did not seem particularly eager to investigate and prosecute the case. An appeal by local residents to the state legislature went unheeded, and soon a growing number of residents in western New York became convinced that a conspiracy of silence was at work to protect Masonic wrongdoing. Anti-Masonry as a political movement was born when a growing number of citizens announced that they would support no candidates for office who would not renounce Masonry.

Anti-Masonry appealed to many different types of Americans. There were a number who believed that the Morgan case was conclusive proof that Masons considered themselves above the law. Masons were becoming an aristocracy of sorts, one that was incompatible with republicanism. Evangelical Christians, swept up in the SECOND GREAT AWAKENING that took hold in western New York and other parts of the North, found Masons to be a threat to Christianity. Anti-Masons decried the practice of meeting in secret, away from families, in places where alcohol was thought to be served. These practices offended those who were active in the various benevolent and reform movements, such as temperance (antialcohol) and sabbatarianism (those who wanted to keep Sunday free of commercial activity) that stemmed from the Second Great Awakening.

Anti-Masonry grew so rapidly in popularity in New York State that it began to be seen by some as a vehicle for opposing the Albany regency, the political faction of MARTIN VAN BUREN and the Democrats. The movement also spread into Ohio and Pennsylvania, as well as parts of New England. By the 1830s there were more than 100 anti-Masonic newspapers throughout the North. The anti-Masons by that time had become a genuine political party, winning state legislative seats in New York, and in the 1830s they elected governors in Vermont and Pennsylvania. There was little anti-Masonic activity in the South, however, nor in western states such as Illinois and Missouri. Even so, ambitious anti-Masons set their sights on national power. In 1831 they held what is generally regarded as the nation's first modern political convention, meeting in Baltimore to nominate William Wirt, a former attorney general, for president. Although not entirely committed to anti-Masonry, Wirt accepted the nomination as much out of ambition as principle. He won only Vermont's seven electoral votes in the 1832 presidential election, and about 8 percent of the popular vote nationwide. Much of his support appears to have come from voters who disliked the Jacksonian Democrats but saw National Republican candidate HENRY CLAY as morally compromised.

Anti-Masonry fell quickly from its peak of popularity and influence in the early 1830s. When the WHIG PARTY formed in 1834 in opposition to the Jacksonian Democrats, most anti-Masons joined it. Although that signaled the end of anti-Masonry as a formal political movement, their crusade was successful in that many Masonic lodges across the North closed in the 1830s as a result of the public pressure that anti-Masons brought to bear on them.

Further reading: Steven C. Bullock, *Revolutionary Brotherhood: Freemasonry and the Transformation of the American Social Order* (Chapel Hill: University of North Carolina Press, 1996); William Preston Vaughan, *The Anti-Masonic Party in the United States, 1826–1843* (Lexington: University Press of Kentucky, 1983).

—Jason Duncan

Aroostook War

The Aroostook War was an undeclared 1838–39 conflict between Maine and New Brunswick over contested territory in the Aroostook Valley (now Maine). It was resolved peacefully, with no violence or bloodshed.

The 1783 Treaty of Paris, which ended the American Revolution and established the United States as an independent nation, was vague on a number of boundary questions. One of these disputed regions was the Aroostook area north of the St. Croix River, a 12,000-square-mile piece of sparsely settled but timber-rich land, larger than the entire state of Massachusetts. The region was claimed by both the U.S. state of Maine and the Canadian province of New Brunswick. Neither of the central governments of Britain or the United States was much concerned about the inexactitude of the area's official borderline—after all, it took more than half a century for the matter to come to any sort of a head. But to local residents, especially after Maine achieved statehood in 1820, the boundary question was one of national importance and a matter of state honor. In an era when states' rights had come to the fore, this question demanded important consideration. In fact, it was Mainers' indignation over the national government's failure to resolve the Aroostook dispute that very nearly drove them to violence.

The new state of Maine had begun to grant parcels to settlers in the Aroostook Valley after 1820, despite New Brunswick's claim to the land. When Canadian lumberjacks began logging the area in the winter of 1838–39, the dispute finally boiled over. A Maine land agent, Rufus McIntire, attempted to send the Canadians home, and the loggers seized him in February 1839. That was enough for Maine to raise a 10,000-man militia and send it marching north. New Brunswick called up its own militia. The U.S. Congress authorized $10 million in spending for a 50,000-man contingent, and dispatched General WINFIELD SCOTT to Maine.

Scott quickly managed to negotiate a truce, and by March 1839—before any U.S. troops had had a chance to arrive, much less engage in battle—the "Bloodless Aroostook War" was over. But it was not until the WEBSTER-ASHBURTON TREATY (1842) that the border question was settled. In the end, more than half of the disputed territory was awarded to Maine, and both the United States and New Brunswick were given navigation rights on the St. John River. New Brunswick retained the northern part of the territory, thus preserving communication routes among the eastern Canadian provinces. Britain agreed to pay $150,000 to Maine and to Massachusetts for their lost land, and the U.S. federal government was to reimburse those states for the funds they had spent on the region's defense.

Further reading: Clarence A. Day, *Aroostook: The First Sixty Years* (Caribou: Northern Maine Regional Planning Commission, 1989).

—Mary Kay Linge

art and architecture

In the United States, the decades between 1810 and 1860 were a time of energy, invention, creativity, and accomplishment. It was also an exciting and inventive period for the arts, which reflected or reacted against remarkable changes happening in the nation.

Art

If American culture was still rooted in a European heritage, there was nevertheless a unique quality about the land. Unlike Europe, the United States seemed to have unlimited land available to all citizens, regardless of class. A romance grew out of the land, out of Americans' relationship to it, and out of their accomplishments on it.

In the East, Americans became nostalgic for a wilderness they knew they had lost to progress, as forests were cleared, factories rose, trestle bridges crossed rivers, and trains cut through the landscape. The doctrine of Manifest Destiny dictated that progress must take place across the land if America's future were to be fulfilled, and in the 19th century, few who went west doubted the rightfulness of their mission.

From about 1825 Americans wanted images of the land itself: its mountains, forests, prairies; the lives and customs of the Native Americans who dwelt in it; the adventurous men and women who moved into and settled it. To some the landscape became a metaphor for moral, religious, and poetic sentiments, and so it must be preserved. To others it represented the American Dream because of the opportunities it offered, and so it must be utilized. Some saw interminable forests as a biblical Eden, awaiting a new Adam and Eve in the form of the American pioneers, who had a chance to regain grace in a land uncorrupted by the Industrial Revolution.

The patrons of these artists were often prosperous merchants, bankers, or factory owners, desiring scenes of natural splendor as an antidote to the harsh world of business; or rural scenes reminiscent of the days spent on the farm, when life was slower and easier—somehow better. Armchair travelers enjoyed paintings of the exotic West, which they might never see for themselves. To satisfy this demand, a large and talented corps of landscape artists emerged to paint essentially naturalistic visions altered by romantic sentiment. Landscape painting before 1825 had been sporadic, often quite good, but generally lacking a strong thematic focus. After 1825, it enjoyed a great flowering.

Kindred Spirits, painting by Asher B. Durand, 1849 *(Library of Congress)*

The first American school of landscape painting was the Hudson River School. Many of these artists painted in and around the Hudson River Valley and the nearby Catskill and Adirondack Mountains. Beginning with the works of Thomas Cole (1801–48) and Asher B. Durand (1796–1886), the Hudson River painters helped to shape the mythos of the American landscape. At the time America was a nation yearning for artistic identity. The Hudson River style provided what Americans craved; dramatic and uniquely American landscapes. Artists, along with poets, novelists, and essayists, delighted in describing and depicting native scenery. Influenced by 17th-century European landscapes, the work of the Hudson River School is characterized by panoramic views rendered with precise detail. These serene and awe-inspiring vistas, in which a small figure often communes with nature, were intended to evoke elevated thoughts and feelings. With roots in European Romanticism, the Hudson River painters, nonetheless, heeded RALPH WALDO EMERSON's call "to ignore the courtly Muses of Europe" and define a distinct vision for American art. The artists who came to maturity in the years of egalitarian Jacksonian democracy and expansion translated these ideals into an aesthetic that was sweeping and spontaneous. Sharing the philosophy of the American Transcendentalists, the Hudson River painters created visual embodiments of the ideals set out in the writings of Emerson, HENRY DAVID THOREAU, William Cullen Bryant, and Walt Whitman. Concurring with Emerson, who had written in his 1841 essay, *Thoughts on Art,* that painting should become a vehicle through which the universal mind could reach the mind of mankind, the Hudson River painters believed art to be an agent of moral and spiritual transformation. A painting that has become a virtual emblem of the Hudson River School is the dramatic canvas by Asher B. Durand entitled *Kindred Spirits* (1849). In it Durand depicts himself, together with Thomas Cole, on a rocky promontory in serene contemplation of the scene before them, the gorge with its running stream, the Catskill mists framed by foliage. Tiny as the human beings are in this composition, they are nevertheless elevated by the grandeur of the landscape in which they are in harmony.

But America's fascination with landscapes was not solely confined to the eastern part of the nation. As America expanded beyond the Allegheny Mountains into the Great Plains, the arts soon followed. The frontier had its own chronicler in George Caleb Bingham (1811–79), who took his inspiration from the spirited life along the Missouri and the Mississippi Rivers. Bingham's work comes into historical focus with *Fur Traders Descending the Missouri* (ca. 1845). In the golden haze of a misty dawn, a French trader and his half-breed son move along the mirror-placid waters of the great river in a dugout canoe. They wear the typical colorful costumes of their culture, and have a wild-animal pet tied to the bow. Bingham saw something exciting and exotic in the men who lived in the solitary wilderness of the upper Missouri, running their traps or trading with Native Americans, and he captured the romance surrounding them. Pictures like this depicted a new type of folk hero, created by the land itself. Europe had no counterpart, and so here was a subject that was uniquely American.

There was another strain of American art that emerged in the first part of the 19th century, one associated with scenes of common men and women at work and at play. The most important artist of this genre was John Lewis Krimmel, a native of Germany who immigrated to the United States in 1809 and settled in Philadelphia. Krimmel first worked for his brother, a merchant, but he soon left business to pursue a career as an artist. In the course of his significant but brief artistic life (he accidentally drowned in Germantown, Pennsylvania, in 1821), he painted scenes from daily life, and he was probably the first American artist to do so. Among the paintings that he exhibited at the Pennsylvania Academy in 1813 were *Quilting Frolic* (a very American subject) and *The Blind Fiddler* (adapted from Sir David Wilkie's English painting of the same name, but given an American identity). Krimmel was the first painter of American scenes (he never became an American citizen) whose reputation rested on his adaptation of contemporary American life as an appropriate subject for an American artist.

As some American artists pursued American subjects, African-American artists found themselves severely restricted in artistic life, as they were in all aspects of civil and professional life in the United States. While their chances of pursuing careers as artists were severely circumscribed, they did find opportunities for artistic expression in painting signs, firebuckets, and helmets.

Architecture

The period 1825–70 produced an architecture that can only be described as romantic and eclectic. Architects adapted Greek, Roman, Gothic, Oriental, and Egyptian styles to suit American ambition, ideology, or institutions, as well as nationalistic, religious, or moral sentiments. The range reached from austere classicism to picturesque Victorian "gingerbread." New technologies and materials, such as cast iron, were forced into old forms, as in the classical dome of the enlarged U.S. Capitol.

The Greek Revival in America spanned the years 1820 to 1845. From the design of chairs to the style of women's dresses, the Greek mode was enormously popular. Americans identified strongly with the Greek cause when in the 1820s Greece fought to free itself from the Ottoman Empire and Turkish despotism. The Greek War for Independence was associated with America's own valiant struggle of a few decades earlier. Americans also recognized in Greece the cradle of democracy and the fountainhead of learning, culture, and the arts. To design a chair or a building in the Greek mode was to pay allegiance to the democratic spirit and to the timelessness of Western culture. For much of the mid-19th century, the Greek Revival style dominated residential and public architecture. Many European-trained architects designed in the popular Grecian style, and the fashion spread via carpenter's guides and pattern books. It was so popular it became known as the National Style. William Strickland (1788–1854) contributed greatly to the rise of the Greek Revival style in America. Strickland was the designer of the SECOND BANK OF THE UNITED STATES building in Philadelphia, which is a classic example of the American Greek Revival style. Strickland's influence extended from his designs to his instruction of a new generation of young architects. Among those who studied with him was Thomas Ustick Walter (1804–1887). Born in Philadelphia, Walter made the transition to architect about 1830, after several years as an apprentice in the building trades and of study with Strickland. Among his most important buildings were Girard College (1833–47) and the extension of the U.S. Capitol (1851–59). The work over his long career eventually included some 400 designs, most of them classical residences and churches.

The model for Greek Revival architecture was the ancient Greek temple, in which a series of columns support a horizontal superstructure called an entablature and a triangular pediment. (The pediment of a temple is the narrow end of a gable roof forming a triangle, often filled with a decorative relief.) In the United States, the style was based on the Greek orders: sets of building elements determined by the type of columns that were used. The columns ranged from the simple Doric, with a fluted shaft; the Ionic, with a capital shaped like an inverted double scroll; and the Corinthian, with a capital shaped in an elaborate leaflike form. The shape of the building was rectangular, with columns placed in various ways. They could be at the front of the building, full height, down the side, or all around it, and frequently they were indicated by pilasters at the corners or elsewhere on the building.

Brick and stone were the favored materials, though wood was often used and covered with a thin coat of plaster, then scored to resemble stone. The doorway was usually impressive. Paired columns with a pediment over the door, transom lights, side lights, and pilasters against the wall were all used to embellish the entry. Windows were often floor-length, double- or triple-hung. There were also often small horizontal windows set in a row under the cornice and sometimes covered by a decorative wooden or iron grille. In the early to mid-1800s Greek temples appeared everywhere from Maine to Mississippi. Colonnaded Greek Revival mansions—sometimes called Southern Colonial houses—sprang up throughout the American South. With its classic clapboard exterior and bold, simple lines, Greek Revival architecture became the predominant housing style in the United States.

The most enduring legacy of the Greek Revival style is the gable-front 19th-century farmhouse, often ornamented by only a flat pilaster doorway or corners. Usually called the New England Farmhouse, this became a popular form for detached urban houses in cities of the Northeast until well into the 20th century. In rural areas, the form of Greek Revival known as gable-front and wing (called, similarly, New England Farm) remained a popular form for farmhouses until the 1930s.

During the second half of the 19th century, Gothic Revival and Italianate styles captured the American imagination, and Grecian ideas faded from popularity. Most American Gothic Revival houses were built between 1840 and 1870. The Gothic Revival began in England and became the dominant style for country houses there. After it became accepted for English church building, it was promoted as the popular style for all English buildings from 1840 to 1870. Americans also liked this form, but only as one of several romantic styles to be modeled to Victorian American tastes.

The most important architect associated with the Gothic Revival style was Richard Upjohn. Born in England in 1802, in 1829 he immigrated to the United States, where he first worked in the building trades and, beginning in 1833, advertised himself as an architect. Among his first commissions were requests from the city of Boston to design street lamps and cast-iron fences and gates for the Boston Common. Upjohn's first important work was Trinity Church in New York City, which was a landmark Gothic Revival style and established Upjohn as one of the leading architects in the nation. Over the next 20 years, Upjohn designed a score of major churches and numerous minor ones, and in addition, he extended the Gothic style to domestic buildings. In 1852 he published *Upjohn's Rural Architecture*, in which he laid out a wide range of plans from cottages to churches for individuals and congregations unable to afford his personal services. Upjohn's eldest son, Richard Mitchell Upjohn, joined the firm in 1846, and in the 1860s the elder Upjohn gradually retired in favor of his son.

As a result of the economic opportunities of the Industrial Revolution, the growing middle class had more money to spend on housing and wanted to build attractive homes outside the cities in healthy surroundings. Horse-drawn railcars brought the man of the house to and from work, gas lights and indoor plumbing were becoming available, and all sorts of new devices and household machines (including iron cook stoves) were being invented. With these developments, the Gothic Revival bloomed.

Alexander Jackson Davis (1803–92) was the first American architect to champion Gothic domestic buildings. Works by him include the New York Customs House (1832), now the Subtreasury; the state capitols of Indiana (1832–35), North Carolina (1831), Illinois (1837), and Ohio (1839); and a number of villas along the Hudson River, including Lyndhurst (1838–42).

But it was Davis's friend Andrew Jackson Downing (1815–52) who expanded the Gothic Revival movement with pattern books and tireless public speaking about the virtues of the style. Previous publications had shown details, parts, pieces and occasional elevations of houses, but Downing's book *Cottage Residences* (1842), was the first to show three-dimensional views complete with floor plans. The Gothic Style fed public fascination with the romance of the medieval past. Downing's books—including *Architecture for Country Houses* (1850)—offered not only designs for houses but also site and landscape plans to ensure a "happy union." Downing is considered the founder of landscape gardening in this country. While Frederick Law Olmstead (1822–1903) dealt with the grander landscapes on a larger scale, Downing dealt more with American middle-class homes and emphasized gardening and plants, as he was also a nurseryman. Like those of Olmstead, his landscapes were influenced by the English style and were natural in appearance, as he described in his book *The Theory and Practice of Landscape Gardening* (1841).

Further reading: Calder Loth, *The Only Proper Style: Gothic Architecture in America* (Boston: New York Graphic Society, 1975); Judith K. Major, *To Live in the New World: A. J. Downing and American Landscape Gardening* (Cambridge, Mass., and London: The MIT Press, 1997); David Schuyler, *Apostle of Taste: Andrew Jackson Downing, 1815–1852* (Baltimore: Johns Hopkins University Press, 1996); Robert Kent Sutton, *Americans Interpret the Parthenon: The Progression of Greek Revival Architecture from the East Coast to Oregon, 1800–1860* (Niwot, Colo.: University Press of Colorado, 1992).

Ashley, William Henry (1778–1838)

Born in Chesterfield County, Virginia, in 1778, William Henry Ashley moved to Missouri in 1803, soon after the Louisiana Purchase had taken place. Over the next generation, he was a fur trader, land speculator, and politician. As a fur trade entrepreneur, Ashley outfitted expeditions that covered much of the Rocky Mountains and plateaus of the West. Ashley also organized the brigade system of trapping, including the annual RENDEZVOUS that would become associated with the emergence of free trappers and MOUNTAIN MEN as features of the American fur trade.

After Ashley settled in Missouri in 1803, he manufactured gunpowder and lead, items that became enormously profitable during the WAR OF 1812. As a result, when the war ended, he was a wealthy man. Ashley was also a prominent figure in the territorial (and later state) militia, where he was elected lieutenant colonel during the war and later rose to the rank of brigadier general. He would later use this title to enhance his political career, and when Missouri entered the Union in 1821, he was elected lieutenant governor.

Like many others, Ashley's economic circumstances suffered in the PANIC OF 1819, and he sought opportunities to recoup his losses. Even as he served his state in its second highest office, he remained active in fur-trade ventures. In 1822 Ashley and Andrew Henry advertised in the Missouri Gazette for "enterprising young men" to undertake an expedition into the upper Missouri. When eventually formed, the expedition was financed by Ashley and led by JEDEDIAH STRONG SMITH. Although the party of veteran fur traders penetrated as far as the Missouri's junction with the Yellowstone River, where they established Fort Henry, the opposition of the Arikara Indians was too strong. A second expedition the following year was ambushed by the Arikara, with the loss of a dozen trappers.

Concluding that the Missouri was too dangerous, Ashley sought other routes to the fur sources of the Rocky Mountains. His solution was to dispatch parties on horse-

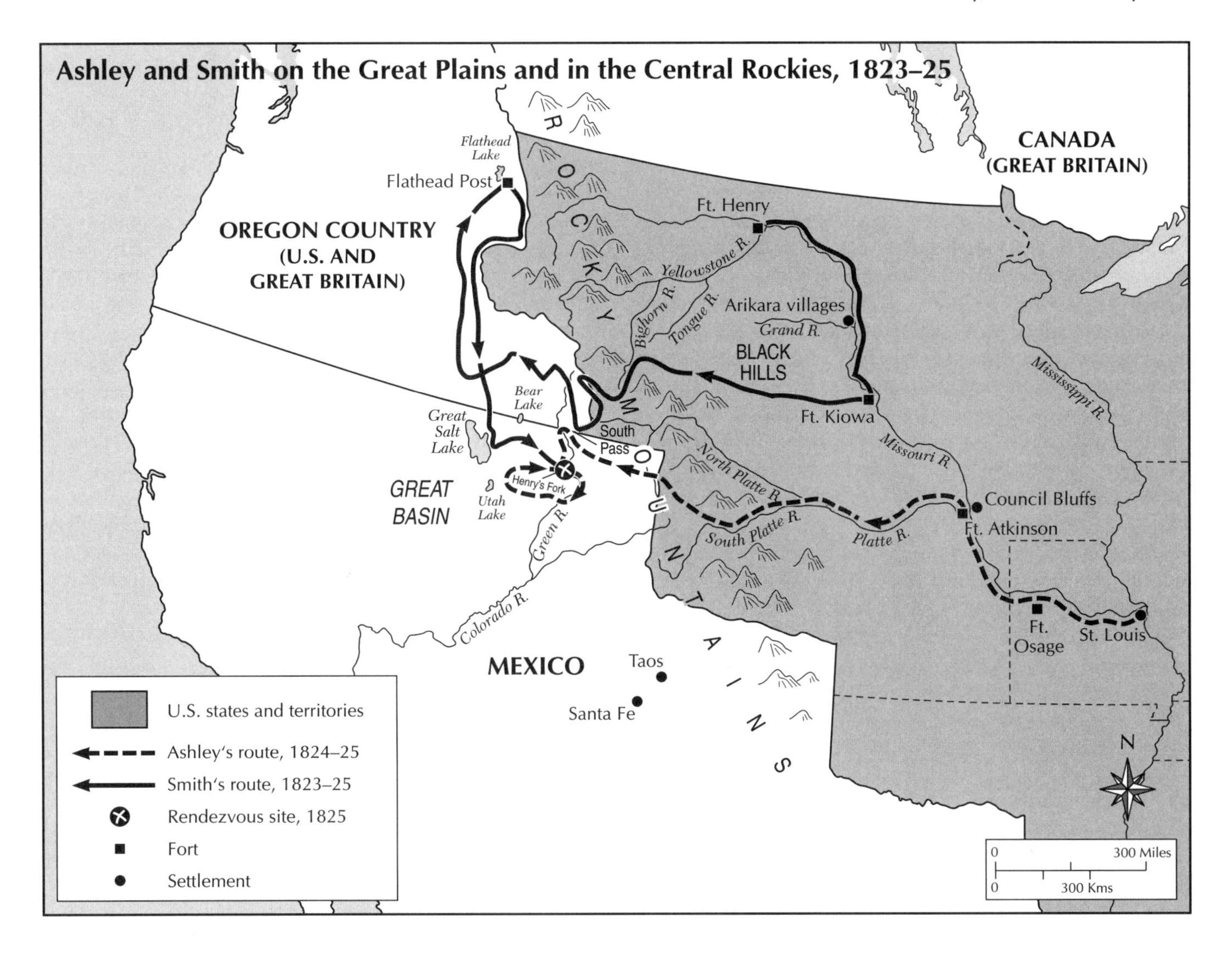

back overland to the Rockies; these groups of trappers were called "brigades." One of the first overland parties, under Henry, traveled across Nebraska to reach Fort Henry on the Yellowstone. Another, under Jedediah Smith, went by way of the Black Hills to the Wind River Mountains. In early 1824 Smith's party discovered South Pass (previously discovered by Robert Stuart in 1812), which was to become a key route through the Rockies on the overland trail to California and Oregon. Ashley soon followed Smith to the rich, fur-bearing streams of the Green River Valley. He subsequently redirected the fur trade away from Canada and his main rival, the Hudson's Bay Company, and into the southern areas of the Louisiana Territory.

In autumn 1824 Ashley started out from St. Louis with supplies for the trappers who were to remain in the mountains for the winter. His pack trains succeeded in making their way through the winter snows. In April 1825 his trappers dispersed to travel and trap in small groups, agreeing to meet on the Green River in the summer of 1825 (at the close of the trapping season). The first celebrated rendezvous was held near Henry's Fort on the Green River. It was to be followed by a series of annual rendezvous, in which trappers would convene at an agreed site to drink, gamble, fight, and generally make merry, and to trade their furs for Ashley's supplies. Ashley then brought the furs out of the mountains by pack train. The annual rendezvous continued in the Rockies until 1840. Ashley was present at the first two but after the second, in 1826, he sold his business for $16,000 to Jedediah Smith, David E. Jackson, and the William L. Sublette Company. This company was, in turn, succeeded in 1830 by the ROCKY MOUNTAIN FUR COMPANY. Although he had left the business and no longer participated in the annual rendezvous, Ashley remained active in the fur trade by handling financial matters for various St. Louis companies.

Ashley's strategies changed the direction of the fur trade. Previously, trappers had been forced to sign on for service in large companies, for only such an arrangement could provide supplies on credit and physical safety in numbers during the trapping season. In return, the trappers agreed to sell their furs to the company at a specified price. Amidst this large-scale organization, so-called free trappers or free traders were rare. Ashley revived the free trappers by giving them a support and safety system in the form of brigades and supplies provided in the field. Aside from the high degree of business acumen he displayed, Ashley also understood the demands of the trappers from personal experience. His presence on the expeditions and at the first two rendezvous made him not only a planner but also a participant. Furthermore, in addition to his use of free trappers in brigades and horses as transportation, his system supported St. Louis in its continuing connection to the fur trade, bounded on one side by the Hudson's Bay Company and on the other by the financial colossus of JOHN JACOB ASTOR'S AMERICAN FUR COMPANY. Ashley's personal bravery and ingenious business strategies for putting men in the field and supplying them made St. Louis an important city in the fur trade. Ashley himself was one of the first St. Louis-based businessmen (as opposed to Astor in New York) to make a fortune in furs.

Upon his retirement from the fur trade, the wealthy Ashley settled in St. Louis, where he pursued other trading and banking interests as well as politics. In his revived political career, he had the misfortune to be a dedicated member of the WHIG PARTY at a time when the Jacksonian Democrats had a large majority following in the state of Missouri. As a man of strong principles, Ashley refused to change his political allegiance, and he continued to campaign as a Whig throughout the next decade. As a result he failed in his campaigns for governor and senator, although he was elected to Congress for three terms, serving from 1831 to 1837. In the House of Representatives, he devoted himself to what he regarded as western interests, especially western expansion and the fur trade. Ashley also ran unsuccessfully for governor twice. He intended to run for Congress again when he was suddenly taken ill and died in 1838.

Although he was slight of stature, Ashley was acknowledged by those in the fur trade as brave and daring. He was also a natural leader in the field, perhaps reflecting his service in the militia. His business methods were enormously creative in an enterprise that had become increasingly the monopoly of two large groups, the Hudson's Bay Company and Astor's American Fur Company. Through such innovations as the trapping brigade and rendezvous, Ashley made St. Louis an important city in the fur trade. Furthermore, the geographic discoveries of those trappers in his employ would be significant in subsequent expansion across the continent.

Further reading: Richard M. Clokey, *William H. Ashley* (Norman: University of Oklahoma Press, 1968); Dale L. Morgan, *The West of William H. Ashley* (Denver, Colo.: Old West Publishing Company, 1964).

Astor, John Jacob (1763–1848)

The son of a poor butcher in Waldorf, Germany, John Jacob Astor was born on July 17, 1763. He would become America's most notable fur trade entrepreneur, and at his death, its wealthiest citizen. Astor's early life paralleled noteworthy changes in the continent of North America that would directly influence his career. Born at the close of the French and Indian War, in 1780 he immigrated to Great Britain, where he joined his brother George. He worked for his brother for three years, during which he learned English and saved his money for emigration to the United States.

Astor crossed the Atlantic in 1783, the same year that the Treaty of Paris confirmed America's independence. Because his vessel remained icebound in Chesapeake Bay for two months, it was not until March 1784 that Astor reached New York City, where he joined his brother Henry. Although he brought with him a modest capital in flutes, Astor's future was not in musical instruments but in the fur trade. He soon found a position in a fur store in New York City, where for two years he learned how to purchase furs in upper New York State and ship them through New York City to London. It was a lucrative business, and within two years, Astor had set up his own business.

After Jay's Treaty (1794) forced the British evacuation of the frontier posts in the Northwest Territory and reduced tensions and trade restrictions between the United States and Canada, Astor began to trade with the North West Company in Montreal. His business prospered, profiting from his astute negotiations with suppliers and his knowledge of the fur business in New York City. By 1800 he had amassed a fortune of $250,000, making him the leading fur entrepreneur in America. It was about this time that Astor began to ship furs to China; the first trading voyage to Canton netted him $50,000. He also made his first large purchase of New York real estate when in 1803 he bought 70 acres at the northern edge of the city, a tract that would become the heart of one of his several fortunes.

After President Thomas Jefferson acquired the Louisiana Territory from France in 1803, he dispatched Meriwether Lewis and William Clark to explore the region. Astor immediately recognized the significance of both the purchase and the expedition for the fur trade. Lewis and Clark crossed the continent to the Pacific Coast (1804–06) through some of the richest fur-bearing landscape on the continent, and Astor fully intended to exploit their discoveries. In 1808 he founded the AMERICAN FUR COMPANY as a corporation chartered by the state of New York for $2 million; Astor owned all the stock. At this time, the fur companies of St. Louis (the largest in the West) were each capitalized at less than $25,000.

Astor's strategy, as it developed over years, was to establish a post at the mouth of the COLUMBIA RIVER, from which his employees would trade with Indian peoples throughout the reach of the Columbia and its tributaries. Astor's ship would then carry the furs gathered at the mouth of the Columbia to Canton, where they would be sold to Chinese merchants. The goods acquired there would be traded in Europe, and eventually the profits would accrue to Astor in New York City. Astor calculated that on an annual basis, a single supply vessel would be sufficient to support the operation in the Pacific Northwest. In 1810 he organized the Pacific Fur Company—a direct competitor of the North West Company (Montreal) and the Hudson's Bay Company (London)—and recruited and dispatched two expeditions to the Pacific Coast. His employees founded ASTORIA at the mouth of the Columbia River in the spring of 1811, acquiring a key location in the fur trade for transshipping furs to Canton, and providing testimony to the capital that Astor was willing to invest. His triumph was brief. News of the declaration of war with Great Britain reached Astoria in January 1813. In autumn of that year, Duncan McDougall, head of Astor's operations, sold the fort and the surrounding tract of land to representatives of the North West Company for $58,000. This sum represented only a fraction of Astor's investment. Within little more than a month, a British warship arrived at the mouth of the Columbia, and on December 12, 1813, its captain took possession of the region and renamed the post Fort George, to honor the British monarch.

John Jacob Astor *(Hulton/Archive)*

Although Astoria was a severe financial loss, in other respects Astor found the war very profitable. His Manhattan real estate holdings rose in value throughout the conflict. He also profited enormously from a large loan to the federal government. By 1814 the American government was in a desperate financial situation. The WAR OF 1812 had been fought on credit, and in the face of military reverses, finances had become tight. Along with two Philadelphia bankers, Astor bought a large block of loan bonds from the government at 80 cents on the dollar. He then paid for the bonds with notes worth approximately half their face value. The war ended in less than a year, and Astor made a fortune from the government bonds. Although he always thought of himself as a patriotic citizen, he considered the war another of a series of business transactions, and he saw no reason not to take advantage of generous terms.

At the close of the war, Astor turned once again to the fur trade. The TREATY OF GHENT, signed in 1814, specified that territory seized during the war should be returned. As a result, Astor sued for the return of Astoria, but the British government argued that Astoria had been sold, not seized. In a technical sense, this was true, but Astor was able to show that the purchase price represented only a fraction of his investment. His case won, Astoria was once again in his hands.

When Astor had lost the outpost in the Pacific Northwest, he had also lost a considerable investment with it. No other entrepreneur associated with the fur trade could have absorbed such losses and remained in business. Whatever the size of Astor's operations—and they were huge—his company was an American concern at a time when the major competitors were British or Canadian. Thus, American officials at many levels applauded his aggressive plans as something that served the national interest. In 1816, at his urging, Congress passed a law that excluded foreigners from engaging in fur trading on American soil except as employees.

Astor also used his immense political power to force the U.S. government out of the fur-trade business. Under legislation passed in 1795, Congress had created a factory system through which the federal government established factories, or trading posts, to serve as a model of honest and ethical practices with Indian peoples. These government posts would offer high-quality goods at reasonable prices but without alcohol. However idealistic the concept, Indians continued to trade at the private posts, preferring traders as friends to doing business with government employees. Astor resented the federal competition, however mild. In 1822 Congress succumbed to the powerful political influence of the private American fur-trading companies and Senator Thomas Hart Benton of Missouri, the representative of fur interests in the Senate. Consequently, the private companies, reduced in number by fusion (including the melding of the North West Company and Hudson's Bay Company by Act of Parliament in 1821) but strong in influence, had the field to themselves.

After the War of 1812, Astor extended his trading operations to control the fur trade from the Great Lakes to the Ohio River. He established a key post at Mackinac, through which he expanding his trading operations into the upper reaches of the Mississippi and Missouri Rivers. To pursue this end, in 1822 he established the western department of the American Fur Company, In so doing, he gained a virtual monopoly of the fur trade in the upper Missouri country, and his operations bankrupted many small traders.

For years, Astor was hated and feared by the St. Louis fur-trade interests, which were much smaller operations. Although one of Astor's great skills as an entrepreneur was reaching an accommodation with the competition, he was never able to do so with the traders in St. Louis. Astoria and his plans for the Pacific Northwest bypassed these competitors, but his expanded operations in the 1820s brought him increasingly into direct competition with the St. Louis companies. He mounted a direct challenge to the ROCKY MOUNTAIN FUR COMPANY that was characterized by his usual daring and resourceful campaign, but his efforts failed. The returns were lower than expected, and conflicts with the Indians (especially the Blackfeet) resulted in serious losses. The Rocky Mountain Fur Company was composed of some of the best trappers and traders in the history of the fur trade—the Sublette brothers, Thomas Fitzpatrick, and Jim Bridger—but these were men at home in the mountains and around the lodge fires, not in the counting house. Although they managed to hold Astor at bay, their triumph was a short one. Fashion was changing, and the fur business was in decline. In June 1834 Astor sold his fur business. It marked the close of an era in the American West.

Astor spent his remaining years in New York City. His astute investments in real estate—financed by profits from the fur trade—had made him the wealthiest man in America. More than any other individual, including WILLIAM HENRY ASHLEY, Astor turned the fur trade into a profitable business. In order to survive against the rival North West Company and the Hudson's Bay Company, he created a series of large companies. That he succeeded was testimony to his remarkable acumen in corporate organization and in shrewdly assessing the rise and decline of the fur business. He died at his home in New York City in 1848, leaving an estate in excess of $40 million.

Further reading: John Denis Haeger, *John Jacob Astor: Business and Finance in the Early Republic* (Detroit: Wayne State University Press, 1992); David Lavender, *The Fist in the Wilderness* (Garden City, N.Y.: Doubleday, 1964).

Astoria

JOHN JACOB ASTOR had a vision of the fur trade as a worldwide business. With furs gathered in the northern reaches of North America's streams and mountains, ships would carry the harvest around the world. In 1800 China was an especially lucrative market. Astor's first step was the organization of the AMERICAN FUR COMPANY in 1808, but he needed a separate company to open the trade to the Pacific. To this end, in 1810 he organized the Pacific Fur Company. At a time when the fur trade also represented national interests, Astor's companies represented the United States, and they were arrayed against powerful rivals: the Canadian-based North West Company and the British-owned Hudson's Bay Company. Thus as relations with England became tenser in the decade after the Louisiana Purchase (leading to the WAR OF 1812), Astor and his fur-trading companies might be seen as representing American strategic interests. Nowhere was this confrontation more evident than in the Pacific Northwest. It was there that Astor hoped to build a post, thwart the North West Company and the Hudson's Bay Company, and establish trade with China.

The foundation of Astor's plan was information derived from the expedition of Meriwether Lewis and William Clark (1804–06). Lewis and Clark had traveled across some of the richest fur-bearing lands on the continent. Their experiences demonstrated that furs could be gathered and transported to the Pacific Coast and from there shipped to China. This could be done with less expense than shipping from the East Coast, as his rivals and he were currently doing. Astor gained additional knowledge from some Canadian friends in the North West Company who were also in competition with the Hudson's Bay Company.

To establish his post and put it into operation, Astor organized two separate parties, the first to travel to Oregon overland and the second by sea. To staff the companies, he hired the very best fur traders and explorers, most of them from the North West Company. The most important of these was Alexander McKay, who had been a member of Alexander Mackenzie's expedition to the Pacific

Coast in 1793. Astor offered shares in his enterprise to McKay and other recruits from the North West Company and also signed on several veteran French-Canadian and American independent trappers. In 1810 the seagoing expedition left with 33 men on the brig *Tonquin* from New York City to sail around Cape Horn to the Oregon coast. These Astorians suffered from a tyrannical captain, who had little experience or sympathy for his cargo of fur trappers. After the vessel reached the mouth of the COLUMBIA RIVER in March 1811, the company immediately laid out the site of the future post and began construction. Within a few weeks, Captain Jonathan Thorn provoked the surrounding Indian peoples into an attack that destroyed the *Tonquin* and its crew.

The "overland Astorians" were slower but, in the end, more successful. Wilson Price Hunt's party of 64 left St. Louis in April 1811 to cross the continent. It was a hard passage, with desertions, hostile Indians, and missed trails. The party eventually splintered into smaller groups, Hunt and his group reached the site of Astoria in February 1812, and they soon constructed the fort. Astor's dream seemed on the verge of success; at this point, his investment was more than $200,000.

Astor's expensive gamble seemed to have succeeded, but then fate intervened in the form of war between the United States and Great Britain. Most of Astor's employees were Canadian, and they did not support the United States in the conflict. In October 1813 Astor's representative, Duncan McDougall, sold Astoria to the North West Company for $58,000, a price that represented only a fraction of Astor's investment in the enterprise. Within a month a British warship appeared at the mouth of the Columbia, and on December 12, 1813, its captain took possession of the fort and renamed it Fort George, in honor of the British monarch.

In October 1814 the TREATY OF GHENT ended the war between the United States and Great Britain. The terms of the treaty specified that property should be restored to a condition that had existed before the declaration of war. The trading post of Astoria had been sold, not seized, but Astor sued to recover the post on the grounds that the sale had been forced and made for only a fraction of his original investment. The international tribunal agreed.

Astor again had his post on the Pacific, but the fur trade was changing. Twenty-five years of war had impoverished much of Europe, especially the rich merchants and nobility who were the buyers for American furs. Astoria as the center of the fur trade in the Pacific Northwest had already been replaced by FORT VANCOUVER, the headquarters of the Hudson's Bay Company operations. In 1821 Astoria was absorbed into the Hudson's Bay Company.

In its brief history, Astoria was an important strategic location for the fur trade and a symbol of the American presence in the region. At a time when the young American nation could mount only a single expedition of exploration, an American entrepreneur, John Jacob Astor, built a trading post that flew the American flag and proclaimed America's presence. The significance was the greater because Astoria was located at the mouth of the Columbia River, already seen as the great inland waterway of the West Coast.

Further reading: John Denis Haeger, *John Jacob Astor, Business and Finance in the Early Republic* (Detroit: Wayne State University Press, 1991).

Atkinson, Henry (1782–1842)

Henry Atkinson was a professional soldier who spent much of his career on the frontier of the trans-Mississippi West. Born in North Carolina in 1782, he entered the army as a captain of the Third Infantry Regiment in 1808 and was promoted to colonel of the Sixth Infantry Regiment in May 1815. With the close of the WAR OF 1812, the American government determined to make its influence felt among the Indian nations of the trans-Mississippi West, some of whom were heretofore allied with the British. To this end, Secretary of War JOHN C. CALHOUN organized an expedition to the mouth of the Yellowstone River. Calhoun named Atkinson to command the expedition, which would include an army of 1,000 men. The main force never traveled past Council Bluffs, but in summer 1820 Atkinson dispatched parties of exploration under Major Stephen H. Long and Captain Matthew M. Magee to the foothills of the Rocky Mountains (Pike's Peak) and to the mouth of the Minnesota River. That same summer, Atkinson was promoted to brigadier general and transferred to St. Louis, where he assumed command of the western department.

In 1824 Atkinson was given command of a second expedition to the Yellowstone River, and with 476 soldiers he left Council Bluffs on the voyage north on May 16, 1825. The group successfully reached its objective, and Atkinson opened negotiations with several Indian groups along the way. These treaties inaugurated relations between the U.S. government and several of the most important tribal groups in the interior of the continent. While on the headwaters of the Missouri River, Atkinson met WILLIAM HENRY ASHLEY returning to St. Louis with furs and escorted him downriver. In autumn 1825 Atkinson returned to St. Louis and chose the site of Jefferson Barracks nearby. Two years later, he authorized the expedition of Colonel Henry Leavenworth that established FORT LEAVENWORTH in what would become eastern Kansas.

When the BLACK HAWK WAR broke out in 1832, Atkinson was in command of the U.S. force. He supervised the pursuit of the Black Hawk and his band, culminating in the Battle at Bad Axe in August 1832, when the Sauk peoples were virtually destroyed. In 1840 Atkinson directed the removal of the Winnebago people from Wisconsin to Iowa. Fort Atkinson, established that year, was a tribute to his long service on the frontier.

Atkinson died June 14, 1842, at Jefferson Barracks with the rank of brigadier general.

Further reading: Roger L. Nichols, *General Henry Atkinson: A Western Military Career* (Norman: University of Oklahoma Press, 1965).

Audubon, John James (1785–1851)

One of America's best-known naturalists, John James Audubon is remembered principally for his bird paintings. He was born in Santo Domingo (Haiti) in 1785, the illegitimate son of Jean Audubon, a French ship captain, and Jeanne Rabin, a French domestic servant who died soon after his birth. Audubon grew up in France, where he was adopted by his biological father and his wife, Anne Moynet Audubon. As the son of a wealthy member of the bourgeoisie, Audubon studied serious academic subjects as well as music and fencing. For the most part, however, he was an indifferent student. The one subject that interested him was art—especially the depiction of natural subjects in the scientific spirit of Théodore Rousseau, George-Louis Leclerc de Buffon, and Jean-Baptiste Lamarck. He also claimed to have studied with the famous painter Jacques-Louis David, but the authenticity of this assertion is open to question. From an early age, he was interested in painting and cataloging wildlife. By the age of 15 he had created a considerable collection of drawings of French birds.

Audubon served as a naval cadet at Rochefort-sur-Mer from 1796 to 1800. After his time in the French military, he immigrated to the United States in 1803 to manage Mill Grove, an estate in Norristown, Pennsylvania, owned by his father. There he lived as a well-to-do planter, hunting and exploring his natural surroundings. Intrigued by the behavior of the local birds, he became the first person in America to conduct a "banding" experiment, tying threads to the legs of young peewees and observing their return the following year to a spot near their birthplace.

In 1808 he married Lucy Bakewell, the daughter of a neighbor. The couple subsequently moved to Louisville, Kentucky, where Audubon had established a general store with his business partner, Ferdinand Rozier. He was drawn to Louisville because of the frontier town's commercial potential and its closeness to the wildlife he wished to paint. As a recently settled part of the young nation, Kentucky was much closer to wilderness than Pennsylvania, providing Audubon with fresh ideas and numerous new birds to paint. While in Louisville, he met the Scottish ornithologist Alexander Wilson, who had come to the area to paint birds. Realizing that his own artistic efforts were superior to Wilson's, Audubon began to consider developing his hobby into a career.

In the meantime, he and Rozier continued to seek financial gain by relocating farther down the Ohio River to Henderson, Kentucky, in 1810. Their first years in Henderson were prosperous, and Audubon continued to paint new bird species he encountered on his business travels. By 1818, however, he was in debt after several businesses failed. He was forced to sell his family's belongings, and the Audubons moved back to Louisville, where he was jailed for a short time for failure to pay debts. He was finally bankrupted by the PANIC OF 1819. During this low period, two of the Audubons' children died in infancy. The family then moved across the Ohio River to Cincinnati, where he found work as a taxidermist at the new Western Museum. He also painted portraits and gave lessons in painting.

By 1820 Audubon had determined to end his business career and set out to publish his bird paintings. He and his assistant, Joseph Mason, embarked on an expedition to catalog and depict the birds of North America. The two men traveled down the Ohio and Mississippi Rivers, through Louisiana, and around the Great Lakes region, attempting to document all the birds in the United States east of the Mississippi River. Audubon created paintings of all the birds they found; in the background, Mason illustrated the plants and landscapes in which the birds lived. Audubon planned to publish his paintings in a comprehensive collection.

Audubon attempted to publish his work in the United States, but encountered scorn and opposition from the influential ornithologist Wilson. He subsequently joined his wife and children in Louisiana, where Lucy Audubon was working as a governess and teacher to support the family. After several years of helping his wife by teaching drawing and music to her students, he used the family savings to travel to Great Britain in 1826, where he hoped to generate interest for his project. Unlike the cold response he received in New York and Philadelphia, Audubon and his ideas were greeted with great enthusiasm in Liverpool and Edinburgh, where he was elected to the Royal Society. He began to sell subscriptions to raise money for his publication, upon which he traveled to London, where he eventually secured the support of a crucial subscriber: the king. With this support, he was able to publish *The Birds of America* incrementally over the next 11 years (1827–38). The massive collection contained 435 hand-colored aquatint engravings depicting 1,065 different birds, all in life size. To pay for this extravagant book, Audubon continued to sell subscriptions to wealthy patrons for about $1,000 each. He also returned to America to find more birds and generate more subscriptions. Later he wrote the five-volume *The Ornithological Biography* (1831–39) to complement the color plates; and a catalog of the birds, *Synopsis of Birds of North America* (1839).

John James Audubon *(Hulton/Archive)*

His reputation established, Audubon returned to the United States in 1839. He purchased an estate on the Hudson River, which he named Minnie's Land. He also began working on *The Viviparous Quadrupeds of North America,* in which he planned to document mammals in the same manner that he did birds. Various sections of his work were published incrementally between 1842 and 1854 and included 150 hand-colored lithographs. By the late 1840s, Audubon was becoming senile. Thus, his son, John Woodhouse Audubon, painted or completed roughly half of the illustrations in *Viviparous Quadrupeds.*

John James Audubon envisioned his subjects romantically, showing the beauty and grace he saw in the natural world. He created anthropomorphic compositions that showed birds and animals as heroic Americans. Despite this tendency to idealize his subjects (and to place them in anatomically unrealistic poses), his paintings are closely observed and remain scientifically and historically significant. His works also provide important documentation of the American landscape that was altering quickly during his lifetime. Audubon died on January 27, 1851, at his Hudson River home.

Further reading: Shirley Streshinsky, *Audubon: Life and Art in the American Wilderness* (New York: Villard Books, 1993); Alexander D. Wainwright, ed. *John James Audubon*. (Princeton, N.J.: Princeton University Press, 1960).

Austin, Moses (1761–1821)

An important figure in the early American lead industry and later a pioneer American entrepreneur in the settlement of TEXAS, Moses Austin was born in Durham, Connecticut. Orphaned at 15, he worked in the family dry goods business in Middletown, Connecticut, and later in Philadelphia, Pennsylvania. Eventually, he moved his general merchandising business to Richmond, Virginia, where he became interested in lead mining and processing. In 1789 he gained control of Virginia's richest lead deposits, and three years later he imported experienced lead miners and smelter workers from England. In so doing, he established the American lead industry, but his expanded ambition led him to look west.

In 1797 Austin moved to Missouri, then in Spanish upper Louisiana, where he acquired the rights to a rich lead deposit. There, near present-day Potosi, he established what was perhaps the first Anglo-American settlement west of the Mississippi River in what was to become Missouri. Near Potosi, he opened LEAD MINES and soon built smelting furnaces. Austin brought with him the advanced techniques that he had put into place in Virginia, and his Missouri lead enterprise soon prospered. With the most efficient smelting furnaces, he soon outdistanced his competitors, gradually taking control of the lead mining and smelting in the region. His techniques were to become standard in the lead industry for the next two generations, changing only after the Civil War. He also established a town at Herculaneum as a point from which to ship his lead product downriver.

Although Austin made a substantial fortune, his economic prospects, like so many others at the time, fell victim to the changing international situation. After Thomas Jefferson's purchase of the Louisiana Territory in 1803, Missouri was a part of the new, enlarged United States, and Austin was once more a citizen of the republic. As Jefferson and his successor, James Madison, attempted to deal with worsening relations with Great Britain, they tried a variety of strategies, including an embargo and on-intercourse acts forbidding trade with European belligerents. None of these would work, and finally Madison sent a declaration of war to Congress in spring 1812. The prolonged controversy of the previous decade had severely disrupted those portions of the American economy concerned with trade and exports. Austin's lead-mining enterprises suffered, and his substantial fortune disappeared. His economic prospects continued to decline with the depression that followed the end of the war. In 1816 Austin left Potosi and his lead mines to the management of his son, STEPHEN F. AUSTIN. By this time, he had become a prominent citizen of the territory. To bring relief to his economic difficulties and the hardships of others, he helped to establish a bank in St. Louis. The enlarged money supply would have assisted all debtors. Unfortunately, the bank fell victim to the economic crunch associated with the PANIC OF 1819. Austin was now on the edge of bankruptcy.

It was at this point, in 1819, that he developed a plan to settle an American colony in what was then Spanish Texas. He was spurred in this direction by the economic crisis of 1819, whose baneful results had created a substantial pool of willing immigrants; and also by the recent ADAMS-ONÍS TREATY, which laid out the boundaries of the Louisiana Purchase. In 1820, Austin traveled to San Antonio de Bexar to make the case for his colony to Spanish officials. His argument was that he was a former subject of the Spanish king (in Spanish Louisiana before 1803), that he proposed to swear loyalty again to the monarch, and that in exchange for a substantial grant of land he would provide a large number of settler families who would also become Spanish subjects.

The Spanish governor refused his request, but Austin was persistent. Working through influential friends, he eventually convinced the governor to accept the plan. In March 1821 officials notified Austin that he had received a land grant of some 200,000 acres, which he could settle with 300 families in accordance with the conditions that he had proposed. Austin would choose the families and serve as the intermediary between his colony and government officials. In exchange for a generous grant of land, the immigrants would swear allegiance to the Spanish Crown and become Catholic. Austin returned to St. Louis and was preparing to carry out the provisions of his grant when he became ill from the effects of his trip and died. He left the responsibilities of the colonization scheme to his son, Stephen Austin.

Further reading: David B. Gracy, *Moses Austin: His Life* (San Antonio, Tex.: Trinity University Press, 1987).

Austin, Stephen F. (1793–1836)

The most important figure in the American colonization of Spanish and later Mexican Texas, Stephen Fuller Austin was the son of MOSES AUSTIN. Born in Virginia, Austin attended Yale College and Transylvania University. His formal schooling ended, he moved to Missouri, assisting his father in lead mining and in the mercantile business in Potosi. The younger Austin was a public figure of some importance in the early history of the territory, serving as a militia officer and a member of the Missouri Territorial Legislature from 1814 to 1820. With the decline of the family fortunes in Missouri, Stephen Austin moved to Arkansas Territory in 1820, where he accepted an appointment as judge in the first circuit court. He left before assuming the judgeship, however, traveling downriver to New Orleans, where he read law and worked on a newspaper. In 1821, when Austin was 27 years old, his father died. He returned to Missouri and prepared to carry out the TEXAS colonization project that Moses Austin had begun. Although he was originally skeptical of his father's plans to colonize Texas, Stephen Austin eventually became a wholehearted convert and entered into the arrangement with enthusiasm and great intelligence.

In implementing his father's plans, Austin was to exhibit extraordinary qualities of tact and patience in the face of continually changing circumstances. He visited Texas in 1821, confirmed the arrangement to settle 300 families, and selected the Brazos and Colorado River valleys as the site of his colony. His colonists arrived at the site in late 1821, but in the meantime Mexico had established its independence from Spain. As the holder of a Spanish land grant, Austin became the object of suspicion for his loyalty to the Spanish colonial government. In the face of these mounting difficulties, he journeyed to the capital, Mexico City, to make his case to the government of the new, independent Mexican nation. Austin had to wait a year for his colonization plan to be confirmed, but he was a patient man who used the time wisely in the study of language and history of his new country. He also made numerous influential friends in the new government.

Austin returned to his colony in Texas with great authority. In an attempt to establish order in its distant north, the Mexican government had made him chief executive, judge, and military commander. Perhaps most significant, he had absolute authority in granting land to settlers. By 1825 Austin had met the terms of his original grant, settling some 300 families on his huge tract. The passage of a general colonization law spelled out the terms under which Austin had acted. This system, reflecting the original Austin colony, named agents of the government, known as *empresarios,* to contract for the introduction of families into Texas. The empresarios were responsible for selecting the families, granting lands, and maintaining order. Settler families chosen were entitled to as much as a league of land (4,428 acres) under generous terms. In exchange for these responsibilities, empresarios received large land grants from the government and great authority over the immigrants. Several individuals contracted with the Mexican government under this system, but Austin was the most prominent in both influence and numbers. Under the law, Austin contracted in 1825, 1827, and 1828 to bring in 900 families; he succeeded in settling more than 750. The scale of his work was astonishing, and his influence was in like proportion. As land grantee and governor, Austin distributed—and settled innumerable disputes over—land titles. Increasingly, he also mediated relations between Mexican officials in Texas and the Anglo-American settlers. The terms of the land grants specified that the settler families should become Roman Catholic and citizens of Mexico. In reality, the American settlers paid little attention to such provisions.

During the first decade of the colonization of Texas, Austin labored tirelessly on behalf of the Mexican government, to whom he gave complete and unqualified allegiance, and on behalf of his colony and its settler families. Among the many items to which he gave his attention were the land system, mapping the state of Texas, pacification of the Indians, and the growing commercial functions of the American colony. He supervised the construction and operation of cotton gins and saw mills and also promoted the construction of public schools. Throughout his work on all these projects, he maintained great influence with the government in Mexico City. Indeed, he persuaded the government to permit the continued introduction of slaves into the Texas colony at a time when the government of Mexico was committed to the abolition of slavery in the nation at large.

The very success of the colonization system generally and Austin's colony in particular aroused growing concerns on the part of both the colonists and the Mexican officials. By 1830 the newly arrived American colonists in Texas had become increasingly numerous. These Americans were predominantly Protestant and indifferent or even hostile to the government of Mexico and its officials. When a new Mexican law in 1830 forbade the immigration of Americans into Texas, Austin worked for its repeal. At the same time, his role as arbiter between the growing tide of American settlers and the Mexican officials in the state of Coahuila-Texas and Mexico City was becoming increasingly more difficult. The Americans were impatient with Mexican authorities and their insistence on observance of local and national laws. Mexican officials thought of American Texans as disrespectful of Mexican authority and indifferent to the conditions under which they had been granted their lands. In the midst of these divergent views, Austin advised patience and tolerance in permitting Mexican officials to work out relations with the Texas colonists. Austin's neutrality extended to Mexico itself, where, in spite of his influence, he never entered into the many national political contests. Instead, he continued to argue that the interests of Texas and Texans were best served in the long run by their continuing loyalty as citizens of Mexico.

However, events in Mexico City that Austin could not control made his counsel moot. In 1832 General ANTONIO LÓPEZ DE SANTA ANNA seized power in Mexico, and his authority was soon absolute. Declaring that democracy was not appropriate for the nation of Mexico, Santa Anna abolished the federal constitution of 1824. Texans began to organize in defense of what they saw as their rights. A convention called in 1833 petitioned the federal government of Mexico for a separation of the states of Coahuila and Texas and the establishment of a separate state government in Texas. It also urged a series of judicial reforms to make the legal system more responsible to the needs of Texas settlers. As the most influential Texan and a known Mexican loyalist, the convention chose Austin to carry the petitions to Mexico City and plead for their acceptance. Austin himself thought the reforms appropriate, that the separation of Texas was the only way to prevent a separatist movement. But he suspected that the conventions and the petitions would be seen in Mexico City as little short of treason. He was soon proved right. Many officials in Mexico had long viewed the establishment of a separate state of Texas as a prelude to a revolution for independence on the part of Texans. In the political confusion of Mexico City, Austin and his arguments were seen as the essence of disloyalty. Mexican officials charged Austin with organizing a rebellion in Texas and imprisoned him. He was incarcerated for a year and then under house arrest for another six months. As Santa Anna moved to consolidate his power and bring Mexico under his authority, Austin—the one figure who might have found a compromise—was under arrest in Mexico City. Never brought to trial, he was finally released in July 1835 under a general amnesty law.

Austin returned to find Texas in revolt. Santa Anna's attempts to unite all of Mexico (including Texas) under his authority by force had generated grave apprehension. In spite of his imprisonment, Austin remained opposed to Texas independence. He thought Texans were not strong enough to establish independence, and he thought the interests of Texas were best served by a political alliance with Santa Anna's opponents in Mexico City. But before Austin could organize a convention to draft a response to the crisis, he was overtaken by a series of events beyond his control. Armed clashes between Texan military groups and elements of the Mexican army made his efforts at compromise no longer credible. As Texans struggled to organize a military resistance to what they regarded as an invasion of their homeland, military leaders such as SAM HOUSTON came to prominence as civil leaders like Austin faded in influence.

In the aftermath of military disasters at THE ALAMO, Austin was briefly head of the new revolutionary government of Texas and commander of its armed forces. Acceding to the argument that he was the Texan best known to the American people, he undertook a diplomatic mission to the United States. He served in this capacity from 1835 to 1836, while Houston became commander of the Texas army. Although Austin was warmly received by the American people, the government of ANDREW JACKSON attempted to maintain a neutral stance regarding the conflict in Texas. Accordingly, Jackson was cool to the idea of annexation.

After Houston's decisive victory at San Jacinto assured Texan independence, Austin returned to Texas. Although he had been the most influential and significant Texan over the previous 15 years, he lost decisively in September 1836 to Houston in the contest for president of the Republic of Texas. Houston's decisive triumph confirmed the preference of citizens for the military in the aftermath of a successful revolution. Austin accepted Houston's offer to serve in the new government, and he was appointed secretary of state for the new republic. He died in December 1836 at the age of 43. He never married and was survived by his sister and her children.

Austin was slight of stature and never robust. His health was seriously damaged by his 18 months (six in solitary confinement) in a jail in Mexico City. It is one of the ironies of that period in Texas and Mexican history that he had gone to Mexico City in search of a compromise that would keep Texas a part of the Republic of Mexico. His physical condition continued to deteriorate under the stresses of trying to influence a society on the edge of a revolution for independence, and later, as a diplomat dispatched to the United States.

Although Austin did not prove successful in taking control of a revolution that demanded military leaders, he was ideally suited to the role of colonizer that he practiced so successfully for 15 years. He was an excellent manager, whether in his father's store in Potosi or in planning the settlement of the hundreds of families who would settle on his grants. His early sojourn in Mexico City gave him an understanding of language and culture that no other Texans could match. Having accepted the land and trust of the Republic of Mexico, he was intensely loyal to that country, and he worked tirelessly in search of compromises that would keep Texas a part of the republic. Austin's very success proved, in the end, his undoing. His Texan colonies (in addition to the hundreds of families brought in by other empresarios) created a presence that looked north to the United States rather than south to Mexico City. Few leaders on the American frontier made such an impact; and it is for this reason that Stephen F. Austin is considered the Father of Texas, at least the independent Republic of Texas and, later, the state of Texas, after its annexation by a U.S. joint resolution in 1845.

Further reading: Eugene C. Barker, *The Life of Stephen F. Austin, Founder of Texas, 1793–1836* (Austin: University of Texas Press, 1929); Gregg Cantrell, *Stephen F. Austin, Empresario of Texas,* (New Haven, Conn.: Yale University Press, 1999).

B

Baltimore, Battle of (September 12–14, 1814)

As a result of this battle in the WAR OF 1812 (1812–15), the British were driven back during their offensive in the Chesapeake Bay region. After they had burned Washington, D.C., the British turned their attention to the northern Chesapeake Bay and the seaport of Baltimore. This city had commissioned many privateers that wreaked havoc on British commerce. Baltimore was also the seedbed of strong Anglophobia and thus domestic support for the war. On the morning of September 12, British general Robert Ross landed 4,500 troops at North Point, about 14 miles from the city. As they proceeded to Baltimore, they were met by 3,200 American militia led by General John Stricker. Although they forced the Americans to retreat, the British suffered heavy casualties, and an American sharpshooter killed Ross. The next day, demoralized by the loss of their commanding officer and confronted by even more American troops dug in just outside of Baltimore, the British decided to halt their assault by land.

At the same time, Admiral Sir Alexander Cochrane conducted an unsuccessful naval approach up the Patapsco River. Cochrane had hoped to capture Fort McHenry, defended by 1,000 Americans, and thus support the British land attack. Cochrane used bomb-and-rocket ships to fire more than 1,500 rounds at the fort on September 13 and 14. This spectacular bombardment did little serious damage, killing only four and wounding 24 Americans. An attempt to send 1,200 men in barges to force their way up the river to Baltimore was driven back by American fire from the shore. The British withdrew and left the Chesapeake area. As they did so, they liberated more than 2,000 runaway slaves, most of whom subsequently settled in British Maritime Canada.

The inability to capture Baltimore, after their great success in sacking the nation's capital, reflected the difficulty the British had in invading any population center. Despite their superior training and firepower and their ability to capture territory, the 10,000–15,000 American militia in Baltimore provided too strong a defense.

The Battle of Baltimore is also noteworthy as the inspiration for FRANCIS SCOTT KEY's "Star Spangled Banner." Key had boarded a British ship to negotiate the release of a prisoner of war. Although he was successful in this effort, the British did not allow him to return to the American lines until after the bombardment of Fort McHenry. Key thus watched the "rockets' red glare" and the "bombs bursting in air" throughout the night of September 13 and 14. In the morning, despite the tremendous uproar and incredible fireworks, and with the American flag somewhat tattered, Fort McHenry remained in American hands. Inspired by this sight, Key penned the words, which he put to the MUSIC of an 18th-century drinking tune. The song became popular instantly, and Congress made it the national anthem in 1931.

Further reading: Donald R. Hickey, *The War of 1812: A Forgotten Conflict* (Urbana: University of Illinois Press, 1989).

Baltimore & Ohio Railroad

Chartered by Maryland in 1827, the Baltimore & Ohio Railroad (B&O) was the first railway projected westward over the Allegheny Mountains to the Ohio Valley. The businessmen of Baltimore were worried about the increased western trade that New York City was gaining from the ERIE CANAL. They feared that the NATIONAL ROAD could not successfully compete with either the Erie or a proposed canal system planned by Pennsylvania. The Baltimore leaders soon decided that a railroad to the West was the answer to the commercial competition from the North. Of the $3 million of capital stock issued by the company under the charter, the state of Maryland took $1 million and the city of Baltimore $500,000, while the remainder was made available to individuals and corporations. The company was organized in April 1827, and a merchant banker from Baltimore, Philip E. Thomas, was elected president. Surveying parties were sent out to seek a route to the Potomac, and the first stone for the new railroad was laid on July 4, 1828.

The first track was laid in the English standard gauge of 4 feet, 8 1/2 inches in October 1829; in May 1830 daily passenger service was started from Baltimore to Ellicotts Mills, 13 miles west of Baltimore. Horses pulled the first trains on the B&O even though some experts thought steam locomotion was practical. A small experimental steam engine, the Tom Thumb, built by Peter Cooper, convinced the B&O directors that steam power was possible; in 1831 they ordered steam locomotives for their road. B&O officials soon learned that such locomotives could pull moderate loads up a 2-percent inclined plane, an important ability considering the mountainous terrain of western Maryland and Virginia. In fact, the multitude of engineering problems faced and solved by B&O officials was so great that D. Kimball Minor, the editor of *American Railroad Journal,* described the Baltimore & Ohio as the Railroad University of the United States.

The B&O reached Frederick, 61 miles west of Baltimore, late in 1831 and Harpers Ferry in 1837. A 32-mile branch to Washington, D.C., was opened in 1835. By 1836, the revenue on the 84-mile Main Stem to Harpers Ferry was $281,000, more than 40 percent of which came from passenger service.

Under the presidency of Louis McLane (1836–48) much of the original line of the B&O was upgraded, and the line was pushed westward to Cumberland. Late in 1842, the line to Cumberland, the eastern terminal of the National Road 128 miles west of Baltimore, was opened to service. Important coal mines were located in the Cumberland area, and by 1848 coal moving to Baltimore made up 40 percent of eastbound tonnage. Thomas Swann, who succeeded McLane as president from 1848 to 1853, financed the building of the B&O over the mountains of Western Virginia to Wheeling by obtaining new stock subscriptions and selling bonds in England. The last rails of the new line to Wheeling were laid on December 24, 1852. Between 1851 and 1857, a second route to the Ohio River (the B&O-controlled Northwestern Virginia Railroad) was built. The 104-mile road ran from Grafton, 100 miles west of Cumberland, to Parkersburg, 90 miles downstream from Wheeling. By 1860 B&O revenue on the 379-mile main stem from Baltimore to Wheeling amounted to $4 million. The economic importance of the growing B&O was reflected in the population of the city of Baltimore, which climbed from 80,000 in 1830 to 212,000 in 1860.

John W. Garrett, a Baltimore commission merchant and banker, became the B&O president in 1858, a position he would hold until his death in 1884. He was a champion of the individual shareholder and successfully pushed for more frequent dividends on the common stock. He also ran the company during the crisis of the Civil War, which came early to the Baltimore & Ohio when John Brown stopped a B&O passenger train during his raid on the U.S. arsenal at Harpers Ferry in October 1859. Because of its location in a border state, the B&O was destined to experience far more than its share of the violence and destruction in the Civil War. Early in the conflict Garrett spoke of the line as a "southern" railroad, but the increasing destruction of B&O property by Colonel Thomas J. (Stonewall) Jackson led him to speak of Confederates as "rebels." Because of the destruction, portions of the B&O in the mountains of Virginia could not be fully restored for weeks and months at a time. In early autumn 1863 Garrett played a major role in helping to direct the rail movement of 25,000 Union troops from Washington, D.C., via the B&O and other lines in Ohio, Indiana, Kentucky, and Tennessee, to the aid of General Rosencrans near Chattanooga. Throughout the war, the Baltimore & Ohio line to Washington, D.C., was the only rail connection to the nation's capital. Despite the destruction it suffered, the B&O prospered during the war years. By 1865 annual revenue on the main stem was up to $10 million.

In the years after Civil War, John Garrett greatly expanded his railroad. In the late 1860s he started to build two giant wrought-iron bridges across the Ohio River. Between 1868 and 1873 he built the metropolitan branch northwest of Washington and linked it with the main stem near Point of Rocks. In the early 1880s Garrett began to build a line into Philadelphia.

The B&O, which was operating only 520 miles of line in 1865, had grown to a rail network of 1,700 miles by 1884. Most of the expansion had been paid for with borrowed money rather than new share capital. During the postwar years, Garrett's railroad had engaged in several rate wars with the Pennsylvania, the New York Central, and the Erie, with the final result being a general lowering of freight rates. During the late 1880s and early 1890s, operating expenses on the B&O climbed faster than the total revenue. On March 1, 1896, the Baltimore & Ohio was placed in the hands of receivers.

Further reading: Edward Hungerford, *The Story of the Baltimore & Ohio Railroad: 1827–1927* (New York: Putnam's, 1928); John Stover, *History of the Baltimore & Ohio Railroad* (West Lafayette, Ind.: Purdue University Press, 1987).

banking and currency

As institutions that safeguard, lend, invest, and exchange money, banks have been vital to economic growth since the earliest days of the United States. With the economy expanding vigorously in the early 19th century, issues related to the country's banking and currency, or the medium of exchange, were hotly debated. For 50 years from 1791 to 1841, the focus of the debate was the Bank of the United States, a federally created central bank that housed the federal government's revenues and acted as its fiscal agent. The Bank of the United States was established twice, the first time in 1791, over opposition from Thomas Jefferson, who claimed that the Constitution did not grant Congress the authority to create a bank. Shortly afterward, in 1792, a national currency was established, using the decimal system of coinage, with the dollar as the national monetary unit. A mint to produce currency was established in 1794.

With eight branches in major cities, the first Bank of the United States issued banknotes exchangeable for gold as legal tender and operated a commercial business, making loans to state-chartered banks (known as state banks) and to the public at large. State banks issued their own paper money, but the central bank exerted a conservative influence by refusing to accept state banknotes not redeemable in specie, or gold and silver actually possessed in their vaults.

State banks varied considerably in their structure throughout the antebellum period. Some were state monopolies, with the state as principal stockholder and all other banks prohibited. In other states, competing, privately owned banks were permitted, while in still others, no banks were allowed.

In any case, the Bank of the United States was opposed by state bankers, who chafed at the restrictions on their activity, and by those who followed Jefferson in favoring agrarian interests over mercantile interests. Because of the heavy political opposition, the bank's 20-year charter went unrenewed in 1811, and the first Bank of the United States went out of existence.

Events soon prompted Congress to reconsider. During the WAR OF 1812, the lack of a central bank made it difficult for the federal government to finance the war. Financial chaos spread as 120 new banks were chartered in the wake of the first bank's demise, often with little regulation and a

In this cartoon, President Andrew Jackson refuses to renew the charter of the Bank of the United States. Pandemonium ensues amid "The Downfall of Mother Bank." *(Hulton/Archive)*

tendency to extend credit out of proportion with their reserves. Many of these banks failed. In 1816 Congress granted a 20-year charter for a SECOND BANK OF THE UNITED STATES, this one even larger, with $35 million in capital stock and, eventually, 25 branches. Its constitutionality was affirmed in *MCCULLOCH V. MARYLAND* (1819), in which the Supreme Court decided that the federal government was permitted to operate a national bank exempt from state regulation.

The Second Bank of the United States had a rocky start. Its first president, William Jones, encouraged overspeculation by state banks and nearly ruined the institution. The second president, Langdon Cheves, appointed in 1819, rescued the bank by calling in loans and foreclosing mortgages, but many state banks were too overextended to pay their debts, and hundreds of businesses closed down, ruining investors. The result was the PANIC OF 1819, a depression that sent prices tumbling and unemployment soaring, and left widespread enmity against the bank as a ruthless institution answerable to no one.

In 1823 Nicholas Biddle became president of the second bank. Under his management, the bank prospered and the nation's currency was stabilized, counteracting the inflationary tendencies of the era and earning a degree of public approval. To get around congressional restrictions on the bank's printing of small-denomination notes, Biddle created branch drafts, bank-issued checks payable to the bearer that served as a uniform, stable form of money.

While many Americans supported the second bank, others opposed it, especially state bankers, thwarted credit-seekers, and small farmers who argued that it served the exclusive interests of wealthy businessmen in the East. The champion of the antibank movement was ANDREW JACKSON, a self-made backwoodsman and war hero who claimed to defend the small farmers of the South and West against the eastern moneyed elite. The first candidate of the emerging Democratic Party, Jackson narrowly lost the election of 1824 but won in 1828, setting the stage for a struggle with Congress over the Second Bank of the United States.

With the encouragement of Senator HENRY CLAY, Biddle applied to renew the bank's charter four years early, in 1832, and both houses of Congress passed a bill to do so. But in July 1832 President Jackson vetoed the bill, arguing that some of the bank's powers and privileges were "unauthorized by the Constitution, subversive of the rights of the States, and dangerous to the liberties of the people." He even charged that the bank had interfered in the electoral process by using bank funds to try to defeat him in the 1828 election. Jackson's veto set off what became known as the Bank War.

Reelected in 1832, Jackson took his electoral victory as a mandate to destroy the bank, which he called "this hydra of corruption." In 1833 he and the bank's supporters waged war against each other with all the legal means at their disposal. Jackson ordered Secretary of the Treasury William Duane to withdraw federal funds from the bank. When Duane refused, Jackson fired him and replaced him with Roger B. Taney, who removed the funds as ordered and distributed them among selected state banks known as "pet banks." In 1834 the Senate fought back by adopting two resolutions to censure Jackson and rejecting Taney's permanent appointment to the Cabinet. Jackson formally protested the censures, which were removed from the Senate record in 1837. Bank president Biddle restricted credit and called in state bank loans. With public opinion supporting Jackson, Biddle was pressured into restoring the credit and loans.

In 1836 the second bank's charter was not renewed, but Biddle obtained a state charter from Pennsylvania, and the bank became known as the Bank of the United States of Pennsylvania. The reconstructed institution didn't last long. With the bank's finances rocked by the PANIC OF 1837, Biddle resigned as its president in 1839, and the bank's doors closed in 1841.

The Panic of 1837 was a worldwide depression, but its particular force in the United States could be traced to the Bank War and to Jackson's policy of transferring federal funds to the pet banks. Thanks to income from tariffs and the sale of western public lands, Jackson succeeded in paying off the national debt, but this economic good news was short-lived. The surplus of government funds was deposited in the pet banks, which, unhampered by federal oversight, used the monies for risky speculation. In an era of economic expansion, there was no shortage of ventures craving capital, including land deals, industrial projects, and canal and railroad construction. The pet banks overextended credit to these ventures by issuing banknotes that greatly exceeded their specie reserves. Following their example, wildcat banks, so called for their financial recklessness, did the same, particularly in the West. State banks freely printed paper money, until there were hundreds of different kinds of notes in circulation. The ratio of paper notes to gold or silver reached 12 to 1.

Under these conditions, inflation mushroomed, as prices climbed to keep up with the perceived low value of the money in circulation. Interest rates rose, as the Bank of England, suspicious of the stability of the U.S. boom, raised the interest rates it charged to American borrowers. Since the U.S. government accepted paper money for sales of western land, speculators eagerly bought up vast tracts, leaving the government with banknotes of questionable value while the speculators made exorbitant profits by reselling the land to settlers.

In 1836, alarmed at the growing chaos, Jackson issued the Specie Circular, which decreed that henceforth only gold and silver coin would be accepted for the purchase of public lands. The presidential order brought a halt to the speculation, but it also led to the collapse of the pet banks. Taking the Specie Circular as a vote of nonconfidence in paper money, investors rushed in panic to their banks to demand that their banknotes be exchanged for gold and silver. The banks lacked enough specie reserve to pay all the debts, so they called in loans that borrowers could not repay. Banks closed, businesses failed, investors were ruined, production ground to a halt, and many people were thrown out of work. The ensuing depression lasted for seven years.

In the midst of the economic calamity, newly elected president MARTIN VAN BUREN, handpicked by Jackson as his successor, tried to prevent a recurrence of the damage done by Jackson's policy of placing federal funds in pet banks. In 1837 he proposed that federal funds be placed in an independent treasury, or subtreasury, separate from all banks. The proposal met with much congressional opposition and failed to pass in three successive sessions. Congress finally enacted it in 1840, founding the Independent Treasury System. By that time, Van Buren's political support was so low that he was easily defeated in the 1840 election by WILLIAM HENRY HARRISON, the candidate of the WHIG PARTY that had formed in the 1830s to oppose Jackson.

In 1841, before the Independent Treasury act could be completely carried out, congressional Whigs repealed it, hoping to establish a new central bank with Harrison's support. But Harrison died only one month after taking office, and his successor, JOHN TYLER, a former Jacksonian Democrat, alienated the Whigs by vetoing the bills that would have restored the Bank of the United States. In 1844, the Democrats won back the presidency, and in 1846 the Independent Treasury System was resurrected. Public revenues were to be stored in the Treasury building and in subtreasuries across the country. All payments to and by the federal government were to be in specie, and the Treasury would be completely independent of the country's banking system. In practice, however, the Treasury continued to exert influence on the banking system, because specie payments to and by the government affected the amount of gold and silver in circulation.

The Independent Treasury System was not ideal. It did restrain overspeculation, but it also kept gold and silver out of the market and tightened credit more than was necessary. The effect was to dampen legitimate economic expansion in good times and delay economic recovery in bad times.

Meanwhile, the banking and currency system underwent its own changes. Free-banking laws, enacted in New York in 1838 and adopted by about half the states by 1860, widened the banking system by permitting anyone to open a bank who complied with stated statutory conditions. The number of banks swelled, each issuing its own banknotes. States imposed regulations on the banks, including reserve requirements and mandatory reports to public officials. Yet counterfeiting, speculation, and other abuses were commonplace. By 1852 nine of the 31 states, convinced that banks were incorrigible, prohibited banking altogether. Some have called the period from the demise of the Second Bank of the United States to the early 1860s the dark decades of American banking.

The situation did not improve substantially until the Civil War, when military necessity led Congress to revisit the Independent Treasury System and reform the banking system. The National Currency Act (1863) and the National Bank Act (1864) created a national banking system and national currency alongside the state banking system. The national currency took hold as a uniform medium of exchange after a tax on nonnational banknotes in 1865 made them unprofitable for their issuers. The Civil War–era legislation also established exceptions to the bans against placing government funds in private banks and paying the government with paper. Nevertheless, the subtreasuries continued in existence until 1921.

Also in flux throughout the early 19th century was the preferred metal for coining. At this time America's monetary system was on a bimetallic standard, in which both gold and silver could be coined without limit and were legally acceptable for payments. The ratio of value between gold and silver was fixed by legislation; for example, the Coinage Act of 1792 made 15 ounces of silver equivalent to one ounce of gold, a mint ratio of 15:1. In practice the commercial value of the metals was always changing, so that one metal was usually worth more on the open market than the mint ratio indicated. That metal was usually hoarded by members of the public, who tended to pay their debts with the commercially cheaper metal. In the early 19th century the commercial value of one ounce of gold was higher than 15 ounces of silver, so gold was hoarded as a metal while silver was coined and used as money. However, relatively few coins were minted each year, and paper money and foreign coins were widely used. In the Coinage Acts of 1834 and 1837, Congress changed the mint ratio to 16:1, and silver became undervalued at the mint. After 1849, with the commercial value of gold falling because of gold strikes in California, silver became the metal to hoard while gold was increasingly minted and used as money. In 1873, the United States shifted to a gold standard, abandoning bimetallism altogether.

Further reading: Howard Bodenhorn, *A History of Banking in Antebellum America: Financial Markets and Economic Development in an Era of Nation-Building* (Cambridge, U.K.: Cambridge University Press, 2000); Seymour E. Harris, ed., *American Economic History* (New

York: McGraw-Hill, 1961); Robert V. Remini, *Andrew Jackson and the Bank War: A Study in the Growth of Presidential Power* (New York: Norton, 1967).

—George Ochoa

Bank of the United States, Second (1816–1836)

The Second Bank of the United States existed between 1816 and 1836 as a controversial institution of national finance and economic regulation. The bank came into being in 1816, following the national financial difficulties that became clear during the WAR OF 1812 (1812–15). The war had been fought without benefit of a national bank, owing to its rejection by a divided Congress in 1811. Since 1814 members of Congress and a few wealthy Jeffersonian (Democratic-Republican) merchants had been publicly attempting to bring back a national bank. In 1816 President James Madison proposed a new national bank to institute and maintain a stable national currency in the absence of a consistent currency from the state banks. To Madison and the bank's supporters, the war had exposed considerable problems stemming from the lack of a national institution to raise revenue and stabilize the money supply.

The second bank's 20-year charter passed both houses of Congress and was signed into law by Madison in 1816. It represented one component of the economic nationalism that had become popular in the postwar years. Other components of economic nationalism included protectionist legislation and national INTERNAL IMPROVEMENTS. The prevailing theory behind the idea was to develop a more economically independent nation that was based on domestic production rather than foreign commerce. Maintaining a stable source of capital for the federal government was key to this effort and the overriding reason for another national bank.

The bank was established at a difficult financial moment due to a growing currency crisis over too many different and unequal banknotes in circulation. Under the direction of bank president William Jones, the new bank soon implemented a strict policy to build up its own reserves of hard money (specie) as a way to develop its own credit and satisfy a new United States Treasury requirement that all payments to the federal government be in specie. However, the plan did not work, and the bank soon resorted to borrowing specie from abroad and severely curtailing its own lending. The bank's actions contributed to the financial chaos that ensued as notes issued by rural southern and western banks plummeted in value and the central bank had no ability to provide regulation or direction. A severe economic depression took place in part due to the national financial problems, which coalesced into the PANIC OF 1819.

The bank's early years were also marked by substantial political and legal controversy. Many Americans remained unconvinced of the bank's legitimacy, and a grassroots movement to get rid of the institution emerged between 1817 and 1819. This led to a number of state legislatures passing taxes on branches of the bank that were designed to drive it out of business in their states. In Maryland, the branch bank at Baltimore refused to pay its exorbitant tax and took the issue to court under the direction of its president, James McCulloch. The case ended up in the Supreme Court as *MCCULLOCH V. MARYLAND* (1819) and stirred up a considerable amount of controversy in the process. Chief Justice John Marshall issued a definitive judgement for the bank and against the state of Maryland. The court's decision is an important one, since it defined the Supreme Court of the era as nationalist. It also spurred considerable anger among bank opponents who felt that the court had affirmed an unconstitutional act of Congress, which violated the states' rights principle that only state governments could charter and control banks.

Following the Supreme Court's action and under new management, the bank functioned as a repository for government funds, government creditor, and lending agent for state banks, and also contributed to the regulation of national finance through 1831. At that time old political antipathies against the bank resurfaced under the leadership of President ANDREW JACKSON. The bank became a major political issue in 1831–32 after Jackson vetoed its recharter. The bank's president, Nicholas Biddle, had successfully waged an early congressional campaign for an early recharter, but in doing so he aroused the ire of Jackson, a longtime opponent of the bank. After vetoing the recharter, Jackson used the issue in the election of 1832 by portraying himself as the people's champion against the business and political elites symbolized by the national bank. In his second term Jackson ended the federal government's close association with the bank by removing government deposits from it and relying instead on state banks for capital and repositories of federal funds. In the wake of the new circumstances, the bank severely curtailed its own credit allocations. After losing its federal charter in 1836, the bank won a state charter from Pennsylvania as the United States Bank of Pennsylvania. It continued to operate until 1841, when it went out of business due to excessive loans made on stock security rather than actual capital, and economic conditions caused by the PANIC OF 1837.

See also BANKING AND CURRENCY.

Further reading: Bray Hammond, *Banks and Politics in America: From the Revolution to the Civil War* (Princeton, N.J.: Princeton University Press, 1957); Stuart Weems Bruchey, *Enterprise: The Dynamic Economy of a Free People* (Cambridge, Mass.: Harvard University Press, 1990);

Ralph Catterall, *The Second Bank of the United States* (Chicago: University of Chicago Press, 1960); Charles Gries Sellers, *The Market Revolution: Jacksonian America, 1815–1840* (New York: Oxford University Press, 1991).

—James R. Karmel

Bear Flag Revolt (1846)

The Bear Flag Revolt was a rebellion against Mexican rule by American settlers in CALIFORNIA, who adopted a flag featuring a black bear. During the 1840s, the number of American settlers drawn to the Pacific coast was small but steadily growing. Lured by rumors of free land, the settlers began to swarm into California. Only 30 arrived in 1841, but by 1845 that number had increased to 250. The Mexican government at the time prohibited these settlers from owning land or holding office, but it was so involved with affairs closer to home that its influence over California was beginning to slip away. Many Californios—the Mexican population of California—were becoming increasingly dissatisfied with Mexican rule. At that time, it was feared that Mexico might transfer California to Great Britain in an effort to keep the region out of American hands, given the possibility of war over increasing tensions regarding the U.S.–Mexico border in TEXAS. Concerned that some foreign power might take control of California, President JAMES K. POLK sent his "confidential agent," THOMAS OLIVER LARKIN, to make known to the Californios that they would be received as brethren should they decide to unite with the United States.

Early in 1846 U.S. Army captain JOHN C. FRÉMONT and a force of 60 men entered the Mexican province of Alta California, ostensibly to map the West Coast area. Although Frémont made contact with the Mexican authorities, his movement around the province was a point of consternation to Mexico's northern regional commander, General José Castro. Although Frémont at first defied the Mexican authorities by establishing a temporary base at Hawk's Peak near Salinas in the San Joaquin Valley, he withdrew northward to the region around Klamath Lake in the Oregon Country. There, in May 1846, he was contacted by an American agent, Lieutenant Archibald Gillespie of the U.S. Marine Corps, who instructed him to return to northern California and lend assistance if hostilities broke out between the United States and Mexico.

In the meantime, a group of American settlers heard about Frémont's presence in California, and this was enough to spur them into action. Leaders of this group, who called themselves the "Osos" (Spanish for bears), included Ezekiel Merritt and William B. Ide. At Sonoma, California, the settlers under Merritt and Ide organized an uprising against the Mexican government, fueled in part by a simmering personal vendetta against the Vallejo family, who wielded Mexican authority in the North. Added to this was the rivalry between General Castro and the civilian governor in Los Angeles, Pío Pico. Captain Frémont gladly accepted the 20 Osos and appointed Merritt as a lieutenant of the irregulars. On June 14, 1846, Merritt, Ide, and the American settlers rode into Sonoma and arrested Colonel Mariano Vallejo at his northern headquarters. With the acceptance of Colonel Vallejo's surrender, the Osos declared California a republic, independent of Mexican rule.

Finding that they could not count on the support of Frémont and the U.S. military, some of the Osos wanted to abandon the town and retreat. At this crucial moment, William Ide made a rousing speech declaring that he would rather die than retreat in disgrace. The party rallied around Ide, declaring him "president" of the new republic, and raised the famous Bear Flag.

On July 9, 1846, after learning that the United States had declared war on Mexico, the settlers lowered the Bear Flag and raised the American flag. California became a protectorate of the United States until it was made a state in 1850.

Further reading: Fred B. Rogers, *William B. Ide, Bear Flagger* (San Francisco: J. Howell, 1962).

Becknell, William (ca. 1790–1865)

A trader and explorer, William Becknell was probably born in Amherst County, Virginia, around 1790, but little is known of his early days. He apparently settled as a merchant in Franklin, Saline County, Missouri, just following the WAR OF 1812. In September 1821, to circumvent the effects of a nationwide depression, Becknell and four compatriots took a small convoy of pack animals from Missouri and into Colorado. They originally intended to trade with Indians along the southern Rocky Mountains, but while en route a group of Mexican soldiers informed them of Mexico's newly acquired independence from Spain. Prior to this, Spanish officials had scrupulously arrested any American traders found on their territory, so Becknell was eager to market his wares in Santa Fe. He did so at considerable profit and determined to return the following year.

In August 1822, Becknell organized a larger expedition, including the first wagons laden with goods to travel west. However, this time he cut across the Kansas plains and followed the Cimarron River to the south and into New Mexico. It was a move calculated to circumvent the treacherous Colorado mountain passes and allow wagons to be taken directly to Santa Fe for the first time. However, this new route also occasioned considerable hardship to men and draft animals alike owning to its arid climate and lack of water. Nevertheless, Becknell's expedition again proved successful and highly lucrative. Moreover, he had inaugurated a new trade route that came to be known as the SANTA FE TRAIL. This quickly developed into a major avenue of commerce with Mexico, and within a few years hundreds of traders and wagon trains were making the journey. Becknell's success constituted a major turning point in the development of trade between the two nations and lent greater impetus for migration and settlement into the southwestern plains region. The sheer volume of trade, coupled with the menace of hostile Indians, also impelled the government to assign the first sizable contingent of U.S. military forces on the southern plains.

In 1824 Becknell conducted an even larger expedition of 25 wagons and 81 men, again acquiring considerable profit. He is also known to have explored the region around the Green River Valley, Colorado, but this proved his final trading venture. By 1828 Becknell was operating a small ferry service on the Missouri River. That year he developed a taste for politics, and subsequently he was twice elected to the Missouri state legislature representing Saline County. In 1835 Becknell relocated to Texas, where he commanded a ranger company during the war for independence against Mexico. He eventually settled at Clarksville, Texas, dying there on April 30, 1865. His pioneering efforts established him as the "Father of the Santa Fe Trail."

Further reading: Larry Beachum, *William Becknell: Father of the Santa Fe Trail* (El Paso: Texas Western Press, 1982); David Dary, *The Santa Fe Trail: Its History, Legends, and Lore* (New York: A. A. Knopf, 2000); Stephen G. Hyslop, *Bound for Santa Fe: The Road to New Mexico and the American Conquest, 1806–1848.* (Norman: University of Oklahoma Press, 2002).

—John C. Fredriksen

Beckwourth, Jim (James) (ca. 1798–ca. 1866)

African-American mountain man, trapper, trader, miner, and pioneer, James Pierson Beckwourth was born in Virginia, the son of Sir Jennings Beckwith (from a family of Irish aristocrats) and a mulatto slave woman. In 1810, his father moved to Louisiana Territory and eventually settled in St. Louis. Beckwith apparently freed his slave son when the young man reached legal age in Missouri.

In 1822 Jim Beckwourth (he had changed the spelling of his last name) was part of the rush to the LEAD MINES in northern Illinois. The important change in the direction of his life occurred in 1824, when he joined the supply caravan of WILLIAM HENRY ASHLEY to outfit the fur trappers in the Rocky Mountains. Ashley's expedition became the first RENDEZVOUS at the Green River in the summer of 1825. Once in the mountains and exposed to the freedom associated with the lives of MOUNTAIN MEN, Beckwourth left

Jim Beckwourth *(Hulton/Archive)*

Ashley's employ and became a trapper, spending the winter of 1825–26 with the celebrated mountain man JEDEDIAH STRONG SMITH. Over the next few years, he followed the seasonal cycle of trapping during the winter and spring in the mountains, and enjoying the society of other mountain men at the annual rendezvous in the summer. He also took part in skirmishes against Indian parties. Although his main employer was the ROCKY MOUNTAIN FUR COMPANY, like all trappers his allegiance was flexible. Mountain men generally owed loyalty to each other rather than to an absentee employer in St. Louis, Montreal, or London.

In 1828 Beckwourth was adopted into the Crow nation. He lived with the Crow for extended periods over six years and was married at least three times, to women from the Blackfeet, Crow, and Shoshone nations. He became an honorary chief of the Crow and joined them in raiding parties against other Indian groups, earning him the nickname "Bloody Arm." After he left the Crow, he used his influence to promote the trade in furs between Indian peoples and his new employer, the AMERICAN FUR COMPANY. In 1837 Beckwourth left the company's employ and went to Florida, where he served as a mule wrangler for a volunteer Missouri company in the war against the Seminole Indians. After he returned to St. Louis, he worked for Andrew Sublette (the young brother of WILLIAM SUBLETTE) in the Santa Fe fur trade. He then found employment as a teamster at BENT'S FORT, after which he became a trader in Taos and, in 1842, a settler on the land near Pueblo, Colorado.

Two years later Beckwourth left Colorado for CALIFORNIA, where he engaged in political intrigue against Mexican officials and worked as a horse trader (some said horse thief). With the arrival of American military forces in California on the outbreak of war with Mexico, Beckwourth served as a guide for the U.S. Army. After the discovery of gold in California, he immediately left for the mining camps, where he operated a ranch, trading post, and hotel, all occupations associated with the CALIFORNIA GOLD RUSH. Most significantly, in 1850 he discovered a pass through the Sierra Nevada that made access to California easier for miners and pioneers. It was named Beckwourth Pass and is still used today.

In 1854 Thomas D. Bonner, a New Englander who was also a justice of the peace in the gold country, interviewed Beckwourth and published *The Life and Adventures of James P. Beckwourth, Mountaineer, Scout, Pioneer and Chief of the Crow Nation.* This account, which established Beckwourth's reputation as a pioneer a generation across the West, has gone through several editions and is still in print.

Beckwourth returned to St. Louis in 1858, but when he heard news of the discovery of gold in Colorado, he immediately headed west again to work at his old occupations of supplier, trader, and storekeeper. Later, as a guide and interpreter, he joined the Colorado troops that massacred the Cheyenne camp at Sand Creek in 1864. He died in 1866 or 1867, at a place still in dispute.

Further reading: Elinor Wilson, *Jim Beckwourth: Black Mountain Man and War Chief of the Crows* (Norman: University of Oklahoma Press, 1972).

Bent, Charles (1799–1847)

The oldest of four Bent brothers, Charles Bent was an important figure in the opening of the Southwest to Anglo-American settlement, a leader in the development of trade connections with Santa Fe, and one of the founders of the trading company that built BENT'S FORT. He was born in Charleston, Virginia (later West Virginia), the son of Silas and Martha (Kerr) Bent. His father was an educated man who constantly moved his growing family (ultimately seven sons and four daughters) to the West, eventually settling in St. Louis in 1806.

Charles Bent grew up in St. Louis, a frontier community energized by the Louisiana Purchase and the Lewis and Clark Expedition. He was always attracted to the fur trade. Before he went west, however, he attended Jefferson College in Canonsburg, Pennsylvania. He never received a diploma and what he studied is not known, but the years at Jefferson College showed that the Bent family valued education and a degree of formal learning rare on the frontier at the time. By 1822 Bent was a member of the MISSOURI FUR COMPANY; three years later, he became a partner in the company. The trade on the upper Missouri was both competitive and dangerous. The Indian groups, especially the Blackfeet, were often hostile. Both the Hudson's Bay Company and the AMERICAN FUR COMPANY offered continuous cutthroat competition. With the failure of the Missouri Fur Company, Bent turned his attention to the Southwest and the emerging trade with Santa Fe. He made his first visit to Santa Fe in 1829 as the head of a wagon train, experimenting with oxen as draft animals and organizing his train to defend against an attack by a large group of Kiowa Indians.

In 1830, with the pioneer merchant Ceran St. Vrain, Bent organized Bent and St. Vrain (later Bent, St. Vrain and Company), which would become the largest trading firm in the Southwest. Bent's brother WILLIAM BENT became an early partner, and their younger brothers George and Robert also joined the firm, which had trading stores in Taos and Santa Fe. In 1833, the company built BENT'S FORT on the upper reaches of the Arkansas to tap into the Indian trade. The fort became the center of an extraordinarily successful trading enterprise, with goods from Mexico and St. Louis exchanged for buffalo robes and beaver pelts. The fort also became the outfitting center for the last generation of Anglo-American MOUNTAIN MEN who trapped in the southern Rockies, and it possibly replaced the RENDEZVOUS, which disappeared after 1840. Certainly Bent's Fort performed the same kinds of function on a regular (not simply seasonal) basis: as a way to resupply, market furs, and provide recreation and sociability. Charles Bent pursued a policy of accommodation with the Indian peoples, and in 1842 his peace with the Comanche and Kiowa further expanded his trading range and options.

Increasingly interested in the economic development and politics of New Mexico (then part of the independent Republic of Mexico), Bent moved to Taos and married Maria Ignacia Jaramillo, a widow with a four-year-old daughter. The couple had five children of their own, two of whom died in infancy. As Bent's trading empire expanded, he became allied politically with Manuel Armijo, the Mexican governor of New Mexico, and used his influence with Armijo to extract several large land grants for favored friends. This favoritism made him powerful enemies. Yet despite his alliance with Armijo, when the MEXICAN-AMERICAN WAR began, Bent immediately supported the Americans. After the arrival of an American force under General STEPHEN WATTS KEARNY, Bent achieved great influence under the military occupation authorities, and Kearny made him governor of New Mexico. But the whole region of New Mexico was unsettled by the violence of war, which seemed to offer the opportunity to play out personal grudges. Bent had made many enemies. Various Indian groups resented his trade practices, while old Mexican (formerly Spanish) settlers were outraged by the large land grants with which he was associated. He had allied himself with one political faction, making enemies of the others. Although he had a Mexican wife and lived in a Mexican community, on the outbreak of war, he favored the United States and then became the political appointee of the conquering army. In January 1847 the Taos Indians rebelled against American occupation, and they assassinated Governor Charles Bent. Bent was 48 years old when he died, having lived a full and eventful life on the frontier of the Southwest.

Further reading: David Lavender, *Bent's Fort* (Garden City, N.Y.: Doubleday, 1954).

Bent, William (1809–1869)

One of several brothers who pioneered in the development of trade in the Southwest, William Bent was an important figure in relations between Americans and Indian peoples in the generations after 1840. He was born in St. Louis in 1809, the younger brother of CHARLES BENT and the second son of Silas Bent, a native of Virginia. The elder Bent had moved to St. Louis in 1806 and was a deputy surveyor for the Louisiana Territory and later a justice of the supreme court of the territory from 1813 to 1821.

William Bent followed his brothers into the fur trade, trapping on the upper Arkansas in 1824 and then becoming a partner in trade with his brother Charles and another merchant, Ceran St. Vrain. When the company made the decision to build a trading fort on the upper Arkansas River, Bent supervised the construction and was also its first manager. Indeed, the fort was sometimes called William's Fort because of his central role in its building and early operations.

Although he had trading ties to Mexico through Santa Fe, William Bent also favored the American side in the MEXICAN-AMERICAN WAR, which began in 1846. That same year, he guided General STEPHEN WATTS KEARNY's American army from Bent's Fort to Santa Fe. Upon the death of his brother Charles in 1847 and St. Vrain's retirement from the trade in 1849, William Bent became the sole owner of the firm and the fort. He subsequently offered to sell Bent's Fort to the U.S. government for what he thought was a reasonable price. The sale made sense, since the government already used the fort to outfit expeditions of exploration, and during the war against Mexico, it became a center of American military logistics. But the government refused, and, deeply affronted, William used powder stored there to blow up the fort, an act of destruction that he personally supervised. Three years later, he built another fort, generally known as New Bent's Fort, some 40 miles downstream.

Immediately on his entrance into the Southwest in the 1830s, Bent developed close relations with its Indian peoples. He liked the life of the MOUNTAIN MEN, and he liked trading with individual Indians and tribal groups. He had three marriages, each to an Indian woman. Of all the Bents, he was the one most associated with the open life of the frontier and the fur trade.

Even as Bent expanded his operations on the upper Arkansas with New Bent's Fort, the fur trade was in decline, and relations among Americans, Mexicans, and Indians were increasingly strained, in large part because of the war with Mexico. The COLORADO GOLD RUSH to the area of Pike's Peak in 1859 was a final act of closure. The large numbers of miners who crossed the plains that summer—something on the order of 50,000—forever fractured relations between Americans and Indians. The Great Plains had scant natural resources to maintain life throughout the year, and the march of thousands of settlers across the landscape endangered and depleted these natural resources. Physical confrontations were numerous and inevitable. Bent's trading empire, which had been based on forbearance and toleration in the interests of trade, was lost. Now the Americans, empowered by the doctrines of MANIFEST DESTINY, pursued gold, using whatever resources they needed, and they would thrust aside any individual or group that attempted to restrict them.

Bent worked as an Indian agent, attempting to bridge the gap between the two sides. The outbreak of the Civil War and the perceived Confederate threat to Colorado further inflamed relations. Periodic clashes degenerated into open warfare. The climax of this conflict was the attack of territorial volunteers led by Colonel John M. Chivington against a Cheyenne encampment at Sand Creek. The deaths of some 400 Indians might be said to mark the end of the world of William Bent, whose part-Indian son, Robert, participated in the battle.

Bent did leave one physical monument. A stockade that he built in 1857 at the mouth of the Purgatoire River became the site of an expanding community of settlers, the first American settlement within what would become the state of Colorado. The longest lived of the four Bent brothers, William Bent spent the remainder of his life in Westport, Kansas, near his longtime friend and fellow mountain man JAMES BRIDGER.

Further reading: David Lavender, *Bent's Fort* (Garden City, N.Y.: Doubleday, 1954).

Benton, Thomas Hart (1782–1858)

A leading Jacksonian Democrat, Thomas Hart Benton was a longtime, senator from Missouri. He was born during the American Revolution on March 14, 1782, in Hillsborough, North Carolina, to an affluent Loyalist family. His father died when the young Benton was only eight. As a youth of 16, Benton enrolled at the University of North Carolina at Chapel Hill. After a promising beginning, he was expelled for stealing money from his roommates. The memory of that shame and humiliation stayed with him for the rest of his life, driving him to prove himself worthy and to overcome his mistake. It also made him very touchy on questions of personal honor and perhaps kept him from running for president, lest his early scandal become general knowledge.

In 1799 the Benton family left North Carolina for Tennessee, where they owned land near Nashville. In 1809, at the age of 27, Thomas Hart Benton was elected to the Tennessee state senate as a Jeffersonian Republican. He served two years and was admitted to the bar in 1811. When the WAR OF 1812 broke out, Benton became a captain in the Tennessee Militia, which was commanded by Major General ANDREW JACKSON. Although Benton and Jackson initially got along well, trouble arose when a tavern brawl broke out involving, among others, Benton, his brother Jesse, and Jackson. In the confusion, one of the Benton brothers shot and wounded Jackson.

Sensing that his path to power might be blocked by Jackson in Tennessee, Benton removed to St. Louis, Missouri, where he became active in land speculation and banking and rose quickly in politics. He was, however, also involved in a duel in which he shot and killed his opponent, Charles Lucas, a U.S. attorney. Mortified by what he had done, Benton never dueled again. This scandal notwithstanding, Benton was elected one of the first two U.S. senators from the new state of Missouri in 1820. During the campaign, Benton, who himself owned several slaves, was adamant in his opposition to all attempts to limit slavery in Missouri. Soon after becoming senator, in March 1821, he married Elizabeth McDowell, who came from a well-known Virginia family.

In the Senate, Benton quickly became known as a champion of "hard money," working against the speculation of bankers, whom he blamed for the PANIC OF 1819. Early in his Senate career, he also became a strong advocate for the small farmer, and was especially interested in making western lands available to them at a cheap price and as quickly as possible. One idea he embraced, which anticipated the Homestead Act of the 1860s, was that settlers be granted 160 acres of land free if they improved the property over five years. He was an exuberant champion of American expansionism, declaring that the United States would eventually spread its institutions all the way to Asia. Marking himself as a firm democrat, Benton also urged, unsuccessfully, that the electoral college be abolished and that the president be elected directly by the people.

As Andrew Jackson became a serious candidate for president in the 1820s, he and Benton put aside their old feud and became political allies. Although he had supported HENRY CLAY in 1824, Benton was firmly in Jackson's camp for the latter's successful bid for the White House in 1828. He became President Jackson's leading spokesman in the Senate, especially during the Bank War of the early 1830s. He denounced the SECOND BANK OF THE UNITED STATES in flamboyant terms, saying that "All the flourishing cities of the West are mortgaged to this money power. . . . They are in the jaws of the monster! A lump of butter in the mouth of a dog! One gulp, one swallow, and all is gone!"

Benton so strongly favored "hard money," or gold and silver, over paper currency that he earned the nickname "Old Bullion." Benton also became staunchly opposed to southern proslavery champions such as JOHN C. CALHOUN of South Carolina, believing that their uncompromising views threatened the Union. As a firm supporter of western expansion, he also concluded that slavery hindered the movement of yeoman farmers into the West, and while he was by no means an abolitionist, he did think that the eventual demise of slavery was in the nation's best interests. This view put him at odds with many of his constituents and ultimately damaged his political fortunes. When MARTIN VAN BUREN ran for president in 1848 on a Free-Soil ticket that

Thomas Hart Benton *(Library of Congress)*

opposed the extension of slavery, Benton remained neutral, declining to support Democratic nominee LEWIS CASS. This, along with his opposition to the concessions granted to the South in the Compromise of 1850 (which was contrary to the wishes of the Missouri legislature), made him an increasingly isolated figure within the DEMOCRATIC PARTY.

Denied reelection in 1850, Benton made a political comeback when he was elected to the House of Representatives two years later. In Congress, he strenuously denounced the Kansas-Nebraska Act of 1854, which effectively repealed the MISSOURI COMPROMISE of 1820. However, his long political career came to a disappointing end when he was defeated for reelection in 1854 and then lost a bid for governor of Missouri in 1856. That same year, his son-in-law JOHN C. FRÉMONT, the husband of his daughter JESSIE BENTON FRÉMONT, ran for president as the first nominee of the Republican Party. Despite the family ties, Benton campaigned for Frémont's opponent, Democrat James Buchanan. A staunch unionist to the end, he feared that a Republican victory would mean the end of the Union.

In his retirement and facing death from cancer, Benton nevertheless managed to write one of the most valuable and important memoirs of American politics in the first half of the 19th century. Entitled *Thirty Years View,* the book was based on his recollections of the eventful years of 1820–50, in which he had played such an important role. He also published the *Abridgement of the Debates of Congress from 1789 to 1856,* finishing it less than a day before he died in Washington, D.C., on April 10, 1858.

Further reading: Elbert B. Smith, *Magnificent Missourian: The Life of Thomas Hart Benton* (Philadelphia: Lippincott, 1958); Robert Remini, *Andrew Jackson*, Vol. 3 (New York: Harper & Row, 1984).

—Jason Duncan

Bent's Fort

A trading post located in southeastern Colorado on the north bank of the Arkansas River near the mouth of the Purgatoire River, Bent's Fort was one of the most successful fur-trading posts on the Great Plains. In 1831 CHARLES BENT and Ceran St. Vrain established Bent, St. Vrain, and Company, which would become the largest venture of its kind in the Southwest. By 1833, the company had set up stores in Taos and Santa Fe. That same year, they constructed Bent's Fort to confirm its presence and dominate the trade of the region.

In considering the significance of the fort as a physical presence, it should be remembered that at the time of its construction, it was the most imposing structure of its kind in the 2,000 miles between the Mississippi River and the Pacific Ocean. As planned by WILLIAM BENT, Charles's brother and a partner in the firm, the fort was a large adobe structure, not quite rectangular, and built around an interior quadrangle. In its final form, Bent's Fort measured 137 feet by 178 feet. It was surrounded by walls 14 feet high and some 30 inches (three adobe bricks) thick. There was also an irregular second story in places, rows of apartments added as the numbers of permanent occupants of the fort grew in response to the growing trade. The structure was topped by a watchtower with a belfry that signaled the alarm and meals; atop the belfry was a flagstaff flying the Stars and Stripes. Some 150 Mexican laborers were brought from Taos to make the adobe bricks and lay them. These workers were probably paid $10 a month, most of the wage in trade goods. When completed, in addition to warehouses for trade goods and living quarters for the permanent residents and itinerant visitors, the fort contained a kitchen, a dining hall, and shops for blacksmithing and carpentering. There was also, within the main court, a reliable well for fresh water, a press for packing buffalo, and a brass cannon. In 1839, a reporter for a New Orleans newspaper estimated that the fort could garrison 200 men with twice that number of animals.

Bent's Fort was strategically located at the crossroads of a trading network that included the Cheyenne, Comanche, Arapaho, Ute, and Kiowa Indians. These dispersed peoples traded buffalo robes, animal hides, and beaver pelts with the Bent brothers and St. Vrain. The fort also did a substantial business with Mexican traders and white trappers, as well as with the army. The fort kept on hand a large number of horses and mules that were always in demand. Bent's Fort also outfitted U.S. Army exploratory expeditions into the Southwest. The Bent brothers had an anchor at the west end of the SANTA FE TRAIL, with connections to the army, to Mexican officials in Santa Fe, and to the most important white trappers of the period as well as leading Indian trading groups. Thus, Bent's Fort had powerful political influence, making it more than just a trading post. Unlike many similar enterprises in the American West, Bent's Fort was soundly financed, with established financial backers and lines of credit. Business was conducted with a high degree of integrity, as the Bents sought to maintain a balance among diverse groups of people. They soon established a principle that any conflicts among their clients should not be played out at the fort. As a result, Bent's Fort became an island of peace in a region of growing unrest.

The strategic location of the fort was, in a sense, its undoing. As the U.S. government became more interested in the Southwest, the military presence increased. Although the army was a good customer, it had the effect of inhibiting other trading groups, many of whom resented both its presence and its expeditions. The success of the TEXAS REVOLUTION and the establishment of the independent Republic of Texas contributed a national edge to the tensions of the region. The Republic of Mexico refused to recognize the independence of Texas and conducted an ongoing armed struggle over independence and boundary lines. Texas, for its part, embarked upon an expansionist policy that included claims to the upper reaches of the Rio Grande and, finally, a military expedition against Santa Fe. That this expedition was a fiasco did not lessen the sense of uneasiness over the lack of stability in the region. The outbreak of the MEXICAN-AMERICAN WAR in 1846 was a final blow to trading patterns that had depended on peace and forbearance among the many groups involved.

Charles Bent, appointed the first American governor of New Mexico, was assassinated in the Taos Indian rebellion of January 1847. The TREATY OF GUADALUPE HIDALGO ceded the landed area of northern Mexico to the United States, including California and the future states of Arizona and New Mexico, and ended the war. In 1849 William Bent offered to sell Bent's Fort to the U.S. government. The price seemed reasonable, but the government refused, apparently believing that the fort would eventually come into its possession for nothing. Angered by this snub, Bent blew up the fort with gunpowder. Four years later, he built a new fort 40 miles downstream, which he leased to the government in 1860.

Bent's Fort was a powerful presence in the Southwest for 16 years. Located at the intersection of streams of Mexican, Indian, and Anglo-American trade and exploration, the fort served as a peaceful gathering point for diverse elements of Indians, trappers, and soldiers. It was a large and impressive physical presence, which dominated the landscape even as it controlled the fur trade. As the largest trader's base in the region, Bent's Fort was also influential in directing the fur trade north and east toward St. Louis rather than south and west to Mexican settlements.

Further reading: David Lavender, *Bent's Fort* (Garden City, N.Y.: Doubleday, 1954).

Bidwell, John (1819–1900)

A California pioneer, politician, and rancher, John Bidwell was born in upper New York State in 1819 and later moved with his family to Pennsylvania. In 1839, he claimed a 160-acre tract near Weston, Missouri, that he subsequently lost to a claim jumper. He then made the decision to go to California, and in the winter of 1840–41, he organized the Western Emigration Society and signed up some 500 members to make the trip west. When the caravan left in the spring, he had 69 emigrants in his party. As Bidwell had no experience in traveling to the West, he signed on a group of MOUNTAIN MEN led by Thomas Fitzpatrick. At the Bear River in Idaho, the party divided; the Oregon emigrants headed west with the fur trappers, and the California group turned south. The California party suffered great hardships, got lost, and were hungry much of the time. Arriving in California on November 4, 1841, Bidwell's party was the first to make the journey over what would become the CALIFORNIA TRAIL.

Once in California, Bidwell found work at Fort Sutter. He eventually received a grant of land, and in 1846, on the outbreak of the BEAR FLAG REBELLION, he joined the American rebels and rose to the rank of major. At the close of the MEXICAN-AMERICAN WAR, he prospected in the CALIFORNIA GOLD RUSH without success, and in 1849 he received a grant of 22,000 acres in Northern California. This would become the Rancho Chico, which later gave its name to a nearby town. For the rest of his life, Bidwell worked to develop his ranch, and over half a century, he became a pioneer in California agriculture.

Bidwell was also politically active. He was elected to the California House of Representatives in 1864, and he ran for governor three times without success. In 1892 he was the presidential candidate of the National Prohibition Party. His lack of success never dimmed his interest in political life, although the ranch and its development remained his main interest. At the time of his death in 1900, he was probably the most celebrated agriculturalist in California. Bidwell's life spanned the continent from East to West and over the best part of the 19th century. At a time when much of California was mesmerized by mining, he saw its future in agriculture.

Further reading: John Bidwell, *A Journey to California* (1841; reprint, Berkeley, Calif.: Friends of the Bancroft Library, 1964).

Black Hawk War

The Black Hawk War of 1832 was the last attempt of the Sac (Sauk) nation to hold on to their traditional fishing, hunting, and planting grounds on the east side of the Mississippi River, in what is now Illinois and Wisconsin.

Black Hawk, or Makataimeshiekiakiak (1767–1838), was the war chief of the Sac at a time when pressure from white settlers had begun to mount. He fought with Shawnee chief TECUMSEH on the side of the British during the WAR OF 1812. Previously, Sac representatives had signed the first treaty of land cession in 1804, giving up their territory east of the Mississippi River. In 1816, at another treaty gathering at Fort Armstrong on Rock Island, Black Hawk and other Sac chiefs confirmed the original cession, although the Indians surely did not understand fully its final nature. Taken together, these treaties evicted the Sac and their allies, the Fox, from their fertile homelands on and near the Rock River in Illinois and Wisconsin.

As American settlers moved to the West in increasing numbers, the time for the Sac's evacuation approached. With the help of Indian agents, a substantial portion of the Sac under the leadership of Chief Keokuk moved across the Mississippi River into Iowa and established new villages. Black Hawk, however, refused to leave the old territory, remaining at the principal Sac village, Saukenuk (now Rock Island, Illinois). The local Indian agent continued to press for his departure, and white settlers began to occupy tracts of land around the village—even claiming the village graveyard and Black Hawk's own lodge. In autumn 1831, under threat from the Illinois militia, Black Hawk finally moved his people across the Mississippi.

Black Hawk had made the journey to Iowa, but he remained irate over the treaties of cession. Over the winter, he gathered around him others who were discontented over the land cession and some who objected to Keokuk's leadership. Black Hawk believed that in the event of an armed clash with the Americans, the British would send supplies from Canada as they had so many times in the past. He also believed that the Winnebago in Wisconsin would support his resistance. Driven by the desire to return to his village and confident of Winnebago assistance, he crossed the river into Illinois in April 1832.

Black Hawk *(Hulton/Archive)*

His party, numbering perhaps as many as 1,000, included a large number of warriors as well as women and children. They initially moved up the Rock River to a Winnebago village where, Black Hawk later stated, he had come to grow a crop of corn. When word of Black Hawk's return reached the frontier settlements, families began to flee their homes. A military force of volunteers and regulars, under the command of General HENRY ATKINSON, moved north to confront Black Hawk and force his return to Iowa. Black Hawk now recognized that his hopes of assistance from the Winnebago and the British were without foundation. He attempted to surrender in order to ensure the safe conduct of his band across the river, but overeager soldiers fired on his flag of truce, and one of his negotiators was killed. Black Hawk assumed that henceforth the only recourse for himself and his band of followers was war.

As Black Hawk and his party of warriors began to raid isolated settlements, the civil population and state political leaders demanded the active intervention of Illinois militia volunteers and the U.S. Army. The ranks of the volunteers were rapidly swelled by those anxious to battle against an ancient enemy of barbarous reputation, and editors and politicians led the cry for the use of overwhelming force in a campaign to be conducted without mercy.

In May Black Hawk won a series of bloody skirmishes, but the state and federal forces continued to gather strength. By midsummer, about 8,000 members of the Illinois state militia (including the future president Abraham Lincoln, elected captain of his company) and several companies of federal troops had arrived on the scene. Black Hawk led his Sac band in a retreat north toward Wisconsin, but their mobility was severely restricted by the presence of women and children. Throughout the march north, the Indians had to forage for food as they moved, increasingly harassed by pursuing soldiers. The troops followed them across northern Illinois and into Wisconsin. In July, at the Wisconsin River, the troops and militia defeated a portion of the Sac force, using a steamboat-mounted cannon.

Still led by Black Hawk, the remaining Sac continued to retreat. At the Bad Axe River, a small tributary of the Mississippi, they were trapped by the militia and 1,300 newly arrived federal troops. There, on August 3, as Black Hawk and his band attempted to cross the Mississippi, they were defeated in what came to be known as the Battle of Bad Axe. Troops firing from the shore and boats virtually annihilated the Indians exposed in open boats. Only a remnant of the original band reached the safety of Iowa.

The so-called Black Hawk War lasted about four months. It was characterized by few encounters, but these produced numerous casualties. Killed on each side were an estimated 70 soldiers and settlers and between 450 and 600

Indians. Most of the Indians were killed in the crossing of the Mississippi in August, although some were killed by the Sioux, ancient enemies of the Sac and Fox who attacked the survivors.

Black Hawk and a small number of his band survived the battle and fled to safety in a Winnebago village. They surrendered on August 27. The terms of the peace treaty were dictated by Governor John Reynolds of Illinois and General WINFIELD SCOTT representing the U.S. Army. As punishment for the war, the Sac were forced to cede the eastern half of their Iowa territory, a 50-mile wide tract of land running from the southern boundary of the neutral line to the Missouri border—some 9,000 square miles of land. Under the terms of the treaty, the Indians pledged never again to claim or attempt to plant, fish, or hunt in their old home in Illinois. In exchange for the large cession of land, the government of the United States assumed debts of the Sac band up to $40,000 and promised an annuity of $20,000 a year for 30 years, plus 40 barrels each of tobacco and salt.

After being imprisoned for a time in Virginia, Black Hawk was conducted on a tour of eastern cities, during which he met President ANDREW JACKSON. When he finally returned to Iowa, Black Hawk was allowed to settle on the Sac and Fox reservation lands governed by Keokuk. He died there in 1838, near Fort Des Moines, Iowa.

The Black Hawk War was a brief but intense confrontation between Indian peoples being forced from their lands and the advancing American settlers who intended to occupy them. It was a rare interlude of war in the generally peaceful period between the close of the War of 1812 and the outbreak of the wars against the Seminole. The Black Hawk War reflected divisions within the Sac nation, as Black Hawk led a dissident group that refused to accept Keokuk's leadership of accommodation. It recalled the support of the British and the confederation of several Indian nations (associated with Tecumseh) to block the further cession of Indian lands. It also spotlighted the continuing view of white Americans that Indians were basically treacherous and not to be trusted, that they waged war in the most barbaric manner, and that they could only be dealt with by the use of overwhelming force. And in a new state like Illinois, where the removal of Indians had become a powerful political issue, the cry of politicians for the use of the state militia and the summoning of units of the federal army meant that only a military solution was possible.

Further reading: Perry A. Armstrong, *Sauks and the Black Hawk War* (New York: AMS Press, 1977); Bruce E. Johansen and Donald A. Grinde, Jr., *The Encyclopedia of Native American Biography.* (New York: Henry Holt & Co., 1977).

—Mary Kay Linge

Bleeding Kansas See Volume V

Bloomer, Amelia (1818–1894)

Although her name has become synonymous with a particular type of dress reform, Amelia Bloomer's greater claim to fame is as a publisher, editor, lobbyist, women's rights activist, and member of the TEMPERANCE MOVEMENT. Born Amelia Jenks in Homer, New York, on May 27, 1818, Bloomer attended a local school and spent a great deal of time in personal study. As a young adult, she worked as both a teacher and governess. In 1840 she married a Quaker named Dexter Chamberlain Bloomer in a service where she omitted the promise to "obey." The couple established a home in SENECA FALLS, New York, where her husband was a newspaper editor. There Amelia Bloomer became increasingly interested in matters of social justice and formed a lifelong commitment to the issue of temperance. She also took up a position as the deputy postmistress of Seneca Falls.

In July 1848 the first women's rights convention convened in Seneca Falls. Bloomer attended the two-day event but had strong reservations about the ideas that she heard there. Four years later, Elizabeth Cady Stanton, one of the organizers of the event and a leader of the women's rights movement in the United States, would recall in a letter to Susan B. Anthony that Bloomer "stood aloof, and laughed at us." Nevertheless, Amelia Bloomer would go on to become a fierce champion of women's rights. The first step in that process was the January 1849 publication of *The Lily,* a monthly publication that initially focused on temperance issues and cost 50 cents for a year's subscription. Bloomer was the newspaper's owner, publisher, and editor. While other women had owned newspapers in the United States, she was arguably the first woman editor of such a publication. Over time *The Lily* grew in circulation and scope. Approximately 300 subscribers bought the newspaper in its first year; in four years that number had swollen to 6,000. Thanks to contributions from women such as Elizabeth Cady Stanton, the paper grew to tackle questions of suffrage, legal marital rights, and public policy. It also became a vehicle for the advocacy of dress reform.

Fashion and culture dictated that free women in mid-19th century America should wear a very specific style of clothing. Small waists were imperative, so women wore tight corsets lined with steel or whalebone and laced at the back in order to achieve this end. Corsets were uncomfortable, could displace internal organs, and made it difficult for women to breathe or move about easily. Large skirts, supported by layers of petticoats and hoops, also emphasized a woman's small waist. The effect often required 20 petticoats at a time, and the entire costume could weight between 15 and 30 pounds.

Amelia Bloomer wearing the "trousers" she designed, which were called "bloomers" *(Hulton/Archive)*

Dress reform was not a frivolous issue. A woman's freedom of movement and therefore her liberty of person were intrinsically tied to what she wore. Numerous women's rights advocates such as Elizabeth Cady Stanton, Susan B. Anthony, LUCRETIA MOTT, and ANGELINA AND SARAH GRIMKÉ therefore adopted a style of dress that eliminated the corset, shortened a woman's skirt, and added a pair of loose trousers to the outfit, gathered at the ankles. The costume was most likely introduced to the group by Elizabeth Smith Miller, yet since Bloomer not only wore the outfit but promoted and defended it in *The Lily,* she became most famously associated with it.

The Bloomer costume was ridiculed in the press. Opponents believed that it was immodest, that it compromised a woman's femininity, and that it was an example of the gross disorder that would result from allowing women to tamper with American culture and law. While the publicity and debate surrounding the costume was helpful to women's rights advocates for a time, they ultimately feared that it would undermine their efforts to effect other kinds of change. One by one, the advocates went back to their old styles of dress.

Bloomer continued to work on temperance and women's rights issues throughout the 1850s, and she began giving public lectures on such subjects after 1852. In the mid-1850s, Bloomer moved to Mt. Vernon, Ohio, with her husband, and later to Council Bluffs, Iowa, where she adopted and raised two children. *The Lily* was sold to Mary Birdsall in 1856, but this did not mark the end of Bloomer's activism. She continued to write, became involved in local groups such as the Good Templar lodges, and worked in the Soldiers Aid Society during the Civil War. After the war, Bloomer went on to petition Congress for the political rights she felt were owed her for her payment of taxes, as well as to lobby for woman suffrage both in Iowa and across the United States. She died in Council Bluffs on December 30, 1894, 26 years before American women finally gained the right to vote.

See also WOMEN'S STATUS AND RIGHTS.

Further reading: Dexter C. Bloomer, *Life and Writings of Amelia Bloomer* (Boston: Arena Publishing Company, 1896; reprint, New York: Schocken Books, 1975); Anne C. Coon, ed., *Hear Me Patiently: The Reform Speeches of Amelia Jenks Bloomer* (Westport, Conn.: Greenwood Press, 1994).

—Catherine J. Denial

Bodmer, Karl (1809–1893)

Considered one of the premier frontier artists of his day, Karl Bodmer was born near Riesbach (Zurich), Switzerland, on February 11, 1809, the son of a cotton merchant. He was apprenticed to his uncle, noted draftsman Johann Jakob Meier, for the purpose of learning art, and was tutored in sketching, engraving, and water colors. He subsequently received advanced artistic training in Paris while studying under Sebastian Cornu. By 1828, Bodmer had settled in Germany, where he enjoyed considerable success as a landscape illustrator. Even at this early stage, his art was well received and frequently utilized for book and magazine engravings. In 1832, while traveling in the Moselle region, Bodmer met Prince Alexander Philipp Maximilian von Wied, a naturalist and explorer of some repute. This aristocrat had previously undertaken an extensive exploration of the Brazilian coastal forests in 1815–17, which was subsequently published. The prince at this time was contemplating an extended journey in the American West for the purpose of studying Native American tribes, flora, and fauna. He naturally required an artist to chronicle the sights, and Bodmer readily agreed to accompany him. In July 1832, both men arrived at Boston, Massachusetts, and they spent several months wintering in Bethlehem, Pennsylvania, and New Harmony, Indiana, in preparation for their outing.

In March 1833 Bodmer's party arrived at St. Louis, Missouri, and contracted with the AMERICAN FUR COMPANY for transportation up the Missouri River. Their sojourn commenced by steamboat up to Fort McKenzie (present-day Great Falls, Montana), which largely retraced the steps of Lewis and Clark three decades earlier. While at Fort McKenzie, Bodmer became intimately acquainted with the Blackfeet men residing there. The Indians he encountered proved amicable and cooperative, although periodic wars among them made travel somewhat hazardous. While soliciting portraits, he witnessed a surprise attack on the Blackfeet by Assiniboine and Cree Indians, an event he later rendered as a painting. Bodmer and the prince then traveled south to winter at Fort Clark (modern Bismark, North Dakota), where they wintered among the Mandan and Hidatsa Indians. It was here that Bodmer produced some of his most impressive and significant works, capturing on canvas numerous and long-forgotten tribal ceremonies, costumes, and scenes from everyday life. He plied his craft by producing around 400 watercolors, including landscapes and Native American portraiture. Bodmer had thus become the first European artist to venture west of the Mississippi River and, as events proved, among the most talented and prolific.

Though never previously known for portraiture, Bodmer's work established him as one of the premier frontier artists of his day. In fact, he is celebrated for his uncanny ability to render highly lifelike, detailed renditions of his subjects. His use of color, lighting, attire, composition, and facial expression render his techniques superior to his closest American contemporary, the celebrated GEORGE CATLIN. Collectively, his work constitutes a valuable historical source of ethnographical information, and it is seldom matched as artwork.

Within a year, Bodmer and Maximilian departed the West for New York, and they arrived back in Europe by July 1834. Ironically, within a few years of their departure, the Mandan Indians with whom they had become so well-acquainted were nearly wiped out by smallpox, a disease introduced by white men. Bodmer's paintings are an important historic record of their way of life.

Once home, Maximilian published a detailed account of his experiences, *Travels in the Interior of America,* in 1838. The book featured 81 engraved aquatints based on Bodmer's watercolors, and the artist ventured to Paris in 1836 to supervise preparation of the plates for publication. The book was well received and ultimately published in German, French, and English editions, but, being a limited edition and highly expensive, it failed to produce the windfall expected. Nevertheless, the book is generally regarded as one of the greatest examples of Native American iconography published in the first half of the 19th century.

This publication concluded Bodmer's collaboration with Maximilian, and he subsequently settled among the artistic community of Paris. But for many years thereafter, his American works were continually engraved and reproduced for various publications, being copied, recopied, and embellished by innumerable European and American artists. It is likely that few, if any, of these individuals had ever beheld a live Native American.

The remainder of Bodmer's artistic career proved productive, but critically unremarkable. Around 1850, he became part of the flourishing Barbizon art community south of Paris and struck up useful relationships with such early impressionists as Théodore Rousseau and Jean-François Millet. He initially sustained his previous reputation as an illustrator and engraver of popular magazine illustrations. As late as the 1860s, his watercolors remained standard fare throughout the numerous Paris art salons, and in recognition of his work, he received the prestigious Legion of Honor from the French government. By the 1880s, however, his artistic style was soon increasingly passé, and a period of financial distress ensued. Bodmer died at Paris in poverty and relative obscurity on October 30, 1893.

The majority of the paintings produced by Bodmer during his North American sojourn remained with the family of Prince Maximilian. These were largely forgotten until after World War II, when they were successively purchased by a New York art gallery, the Northern Natural Gas Company, and the Josyln Art Museum, the latter two both of Omaha, Nebraska. Bodmer's works thus remain on permanent display not far from the region which inspired their creation and are still highly regarded depictions of the early upper Missouri region. Ironically, Bodmer himself came to regard his American interlude with regret, feeling that the experience had actually retarded his growth as an artist.

Further reading: William H. Goetzmann, ed., *Karl Bodmer's America* (Lincoln: Josyln Art Museum and the University of Nebraska Press, 1984); Robert J. Moore, *American Indians: The Arts and Travels of Charles Bird King, George Catlin, and Karl Bodmer* (New York: Stewart, Tabori, and Chang, 1997); Prinz Maximilian von Wied, *Travels in the Interior of North America During the Years 1832–1834* (New York: Taschen, 2001); Raymond W. Wood, *Karl Bodmer's Studio Art* (Urbana: University of Illinois Press, 2002).

—John C. Fredriksen

Bonus Bill (December 23, 1816; vetoed March 3, 1817)

The Bonus Bill promised to provide federal funding for roads and canals, but President James Madison vetoed it in 1817 because he believed the U.S. Constitution did not grant the power to provide money for INTERNAL IMPROVEMENTS.

With the increase in population and territory, the expanding market ECONOMY, and the introduction of steam-powered ships, the United States needed a new infrastructure of roads and canals. The WAR OF 1812 (1812–15) convinced even many Democratic-Republicans that the federal government had to provide assistance in its development. The eloquent South Carolinian congressman JOHN C. CALHOUN passionately advocated programs to enhance the wealth and power of the American nation. The main problem was the funding of such expensive programs. Most Americans rejected the idea of federal taxes. In the face of this opposition, Calhoun proposed a bold plan, the so-called Bonus Bill to raise funds for the construction and maintenance of roads and canals.

On December 16, 1816, Calhoun recommended that the House of Representatives appoint a committee to investigate the possibilities of creating funds for internal improvements by tapping into the profits of the SECOND BANK OF THE UNITED STATES. Calhoun, the chairman of this committee, introduced a bill on December 23, 1816, to appropriate a $1.5 million bonus payable to the federal government for chartering the bank and the future profits of the bank stock owned by the government. The plan would have provided for a series of canals and roads across the Appalachians, improvement of river transportation on the Ohio and Mississippi Rivers, and a NATIONAL ROAD to the Deep South through the interior to New Orleans. With the support of HENRY CLAY, the Bonus Bill passed both houses.

To the surprise of Calhoun and many congressmen, President James Madison vetoed the bill on March 3, 1817, two days before he left office. Although Madison supported federally funded internal improvements, he objected to the bill on the grounds that the constitutional power to provide for the "common defense and general welfare" did not authorize the national government to subsidize internal improvements. Madison recalled that the power to build federal canals had been explicitly rejected in the Constitutional Convention of 1787. Thus, he objected to the doctrine of implied powers in the "general welfare" clause of the Constitution. However, he suggested an amendment to the Constitution to allow for the appropriation of funds for federal projects.

After attempts to pass an amendment or override the presidential veto failed, New York State began building the ERIE CANAL without federal support in 1817. The issue of federal funding and planning for internal improvements was raised again in 1822 when Congress sought to collect tolls on the Cumberland Road; it was finally settled by Jackson's Maysville Road Veto in 1830.

Further reading: Drew R. McCoy, *The Last of the Fathers: James Madison and the Republican Legacy* (Cambridge and New York: Cambridge University Press, 1989).

—Dirk Voss

Bowie, Jim (1796–1836)

One of the legendary figures of the early TEXAS frontier, James (Jim) Bowie is best known for his death at THE ALAMO in 1836 and for the hunting knife he helped to make famous. Although the details of his birth are sketchy, Bowie was most likely born in Logan County, Kentucky, in 1796 to Rezin and Elvy Jones Bowie. The Bowie family was of Scottish ancestry and had been in America since the early 18th century. When he was a boy, young Jim moved with his family to Rapides Parish, Louisiana, shortly before the United States bought that land from France as part of the Louisiana Purchase.

In early 1815, Jim Bowie and his older brother Rezin enlisted in the Louisiana Militia and started out for New Orleans to join General ANDREW JACKSON'S army. However, the BATTLE OF NEW ORLEANS concluded before their arrival. After the war, Bowie joined a group of adventurers, including his brother, who went to Texas in the hope of separating that land from Spain. The Bowie brothers became involved with the pirate JEAN LAFITTE in a scheme to smuggle slaves into Louisiana, by then one of the United States, through Texas. It was at that point that Bowie first began to acquire a reputation as an especially tough character who was more than willing to defend his interests and honor with his fists and any other available weapon. It was in one of his many fights that Bowie supposedly first used the knife that was later named for him. However, it is quite possible that his brother Rezin actually designed the knife, which many on the southwestern frontier used.

Bowie went back to Texas and was baptized into the Catholic Church, which Mexican authorities required for all those who desired to settle there and own land. He also married Ursula María de Veramendi, whose father was a vice governor of one of the Mexican states. This union with the daughter of a wealthy man boosted Bowie's financial fortunes considerably. Although his search for a lost mine in Texas yielded no riches, his reputation as a tough frontiersman grew when he led a group of adventurers in fighting off a party of raiding Caddo Indians; he barely escaped with his life. Bowie experienced personal tragedy when a cholera outbreak claimed his wife Ursala in 1833. Still seeking wealth, he turned to a more profitable venture: land speculation. He acquired the title to considerable acreage in Texas by persuading Mexicans to apply for land grants and then buying the land from them for a reduced price.

In the 1830s, tensions developed between those who favored more autonomy for Texas and those who wanted a closer connection to the central Mexican government in Mexico City. Bowie sided with other expatriates from the United States who were increasingly skeptical of Mexican authority and were beginning to agitate for resistance. He fought with Texans in the Battle of Nacogdoches in 1832, one of the early confrontations in what became the TEXAS REVOLUTION. When that movement grew more serious two years later, Bowie became one of its leaders as a member of the first committee of safety. He later became a colonel in the fledgling Texas army, fighting to expel Mexican troops from Texas in 1835. When Mexican president ANTONIO LÓPEZ DE SANTA ANNA returned with a large army of several thousand in early 1836 to punish the Texans, Bowie was among a force of about 180 men who took up defensive positions at the Alamo, an abandoned Spanish mission in San Antonio.

Bowie became the commander of an informal volunteer militia that converged at the Alamo along with the regular Texas army. He apparently did not take well initially to the idea of being subordinate to the army's leader, Colonel WILLIAM BARRET TRAVIS, who was much younger than Bowie. The two managed to work out a plan for joint command, but they disagreed about whether to seek a negotiated end to the conflict before the shooting started in earnest. Bowie favored doing so and sent a message to Santa Anna to that effect through a messenger. When the Mexican leader refused to consider any compromise, Travis and those in the Alamo, including Bowie, rejected any surrender. In the meantime, Bowie had become seriously ill, most likely with typhoid, and was in his sickbed when the Mexicans began their siege of the Alamo. His worsening condition left Travis to lead the beleaguered Texans. With no help coming from other Texas armies and with the Alamo now completely surrounded, the situation quickly became hopeless. The Mexicans, after a sustained artillery barrage, began to scale the walls of the mission on March 6, 1836. Bowie by this time was far too sick to join in the defense and was killed by Mexican troops in his bed as the Alamo fell. Along with Travis and DAVY CROCKETT of Tennessee, Bowie became among the most celebrated of the defenders of the Alamo, all of whom were elevated to the rank of American legends.

Further reading: William C. Davis, *Three Roads to the Alamo: The Lives and Fortunes of David Crockett, James Bowie and William Barrett Travis* (New York: HarperCollins, 1998); Jean Flynn, *Jim Bowie: A Texas Legend* (Burnet, Tex.: Eakin Press, 1980).

—Jason K. Duncan

Bridger, James (1804–1881)

James Bridger was one of the most famous of the celebrated MOUNTAIN MEN and a guide whose knowledge of the geography of the West made him a legend in his lifetime. He was born in Richmond, Virginia, but his family soon moved to St. Louis, Missouri. When his parents died, the 13-year-old Bridger was apprenticed to a blacksmith, but he left the trade in 1822 to accompany WILLIAM HENRY ASHLEY on his first expedition to the Rocky Mountains. The next year, he and Thomas Fitzpatrick made the trip west overland with Major Andrew Henry. Another man on the journey was Hugh Glass, who had been severely mauled by a grizzly bear near Grand River, South Dakota. Although Henry had instructed them to care for and comfort Glass, Bridger and Fitzpatrick abandoned him in the belief he was about to die. Glass survived, and the story followed Bridger the rest of his life.

In late 1824 or early 1825 Bridger discovered the Great Salt Lake; he was probably the first American to see it. After Ashley's retirement, Bridger went to work for the company ran by JEDEDIAH STRONG SMITH and WILLIAM SUBLETTE. He was later employed by the ROCKY MOUNTAIN FUR COMPANY as a partner from 1830 until the dissolution of the company in 1834. In 1838, he signed on with the AMERICAN FUR COMPANY.

By 1843 Bridger had retired from the fur trade. With Louis Vasquez he built Fort Bridger at the Black Fork of the Green River in present-day western Wyoming. Here he offered an outfitting station for transcontinental emigrants headed to Oregon and California, with goods at high prices, fresh draft animals, and useful advice on schedules and routes. He sold his share in the fort to the CHURCH OF JESUS CHRIST OF LATTER-DAY SAINTS 10 years later. Throughout these years, he continued to be in great demand as a guide. He found and named Bridger's Pass and Cheyenne Pass in the Wasatch and the Rockies. On the outbreak of the MORMON WAR in 1856, Bridger guided

Colonel Albert Sidney Johnston's federal troops to the Great Salt Lake. Two years later, he accompanied Captain William Raynolds's expedition to the Yellowstone River. Bridger also guided exploring parties over the Powder River route (1865–66) and surveyed the Bozeman Trail for the federal government. He subsequently worked with Colonel Grenville M. Dodge on a survey for the Union Pacific Railroad.

During his years in the West, Bridger married three Indian women: a Flathead, a Ute, and a Shoshone. He sent the children of these marriages to Missouri for education. In 1868, his eyesight having declined, Bridger left the employ of the Union Pacific and bought a house at Westport, Missouri, near his friends WILLIAM BENT and Louis Vasquez.

Bridger's knowledge of the western landscape was unsurpassed, and his knowledge of the Indian peoples who had lived there was almost as great. He was one of those rare western pioneer figures who lived long enough to be celebrated as an icon of the American frontier. He appeared in the reports of the many prominent military officers, explorers, and writers whom he had guided. E. C. Judson, who wrote under the pen name Ned Buntline, wrote popular adventure stories about Bridger's career in the West. When he died in 1881, Bridger had joined that select group of western heroes who seemed to exemplify the human responses to the challenges of the frontier: uneducated but savvy, a man who could respond to every challenge from Indians to snowstorms, and who emerged with a story to tell.

Further reading: Dale L. Morgan, *Jedediah Smith and the Opening of the West* (Indianapolis, Ind.: Bobbs-Merrill Company, 1953); Stanley Vestal, *Jim Bridger, Mountain Man* (New York: Morrow, 1946).

Brook Farm

Former Unitarian minister George Ripley and his followers founded this experimental farm, also known as the Brook Farm Institute of Agriculture and Education, on 200 acres of land in West Roxbury, Massachusetts, in April 1841. The farming operations were designed around the ideals of cooperative living, in which members combined manual labor and intellectual activities in an effort to regain a sense of higher calling that they felt was being destroyed by industrialization and the increasing division of labor.

At the beginning, prospective members financed the farm through a joint-stock company, with stocks selling for $500 per share. Individual Brook farmers were supposed to devote part of each day to the manual labor necessary for agriculture and another part of the day to developing their minds and improving their souls. Artistic and social pursuits were highly valued, and the members enthusiastically participated in plays, musical performances, cardplaying, picnics, and other amusements. Several important social thinkers and artists joined this experimental farm, including Nathaniel Hawthorne, Isaac Hecker, and Charles A. Dana. The farm also attracted many prominent visitors such as MARGARET FULLER, RALPH WALDO EMERSON, William Ellery Channing, and Horace Greeley. These influential visitors spread the word about Brook Farm and its philosophy in their writings. As such, Brook Farm was an embodiment of the TRANSCENDENTAL MOVEMENT, and was also influenced by George Ripley's experiences with Unitarianism.

The farmers produced crops for subsistence and for sale, but their agricultural efforts were hampered by poor soil and inexperience. More economically successful was the Brook Farm school, which implemented the farmers' progressive ideas about learning by doing. This combination of thought and action was part of Ripley's desire to reconnect the social classes by requiring each person to engage in both manual and intellectual tasks. By requiring members to participate in all aspects of farm living, the founders hoped to reach greater social harmony and personal development in society.

Influenced by the writings of French philosopher CHARLES FOURIER, the members of Brook Farm decided to convert to his phalanx model in 1844. Fourier's ideas fitted well with the original aims of Brook Farm, since he advocated the reorganization of civilization into agricultural groupings (phalanxes). These phalanxes would develop social harmony through an economic system in which people worked on the tasks for which they were most suited, shedding the confines of industrial society and cultivating their whole selves. Each phalanx would live in a community dwelling called a phalanstery. The Brook Farm phalanstery burned down in 1846, while still under construction. The fire was a major financial setback for the farm and led to its dissolution in 1847. Even though Brook Farm existed only briefly, the ideas it tried to embody continued to be influential among Transcendentalists and other social utopians. Other more successful phalanxes were founded in the United States, and Ripley's experimental farm continued on in the memories and writings of the people who participated in it.

Further reading: Richard Francis, *Transcendental Utopias: Individual and Community at Brook Farm, Fruitlands, and Walden* (Ithaca, N.Y.: Cornell University Press, 1997); Lindsay Swift, *Brook Farm: Its Members, Scholars, and Visitors* (Secaucus, N.J.: Citadel Press, 1961).

—Eleanor H. McConnell

Brown, John See Volume V

Burns, Anthony (1829–1862)
A fugitive slave whose capture and return to his owners generated controversy among northern abolitionists, Anthony Burns was born in Stafford County, Virginia, on May 31, 1829. Though denied a formal education, he learned the alphabet from playing with white children and taught himself to read and write. He subsequently converted to the Baptist faith and found fulfillment serving as a "slave preacher" to his fellow African Americans. Having injured his right hand and being no longer capable of sustained labor, Burns became convinced that deportation to the Deep South and even harsher treatment was imminent. He thereupon decided to escape and, while working as a stevedore and with the assistance of an obliging white sailor, he fled to Boston in March 1854. There, on May 24, 1854, Burns was arrested at the behest of his former master under the controversial FUGITIVE SLAVE LAW of 1850. This legislation reaffirmed the status of slaves as property and mandated returning them to their rightful owners. Failure to comply was a federal offense.

Word of Burns's arrest and impending extradition back to Virginia caused considerable unrest among Boston's abolitionist community. A mass protest was staged by WENDELL PHILLIPS outside of Faneuil Hall, and when violence broke out in an attempt to free Burns from the municipal court house, a deputy sheriff was killed. During court proceedings, Burns was represented by noted attorney RICHARD HENRY DANA, who argued strenuously but futilely for his release. The following day, the militia was called out to escort the prisoner from the court to the dock, where he was placed on a boat and shipped back to Virginia. The entire episode cost the U.S. government an estimated $15,000 for the return of one fugitive slave.

THE
BOSTON SLAVE RIOT,
AND
TRIAL
OF
Anthony Burns,
CONTAINING THE
REPORT OF THE FANEUIL HALL MEETING; THE MURDER OF BACHELDER; THEODORE PARKER'S LESSON FOR THE DAY; SPEECHES OF COUNSEL ON BOTH SIDES, CORRECTED BY THEMSELVES; VERBATIM REPORT OF JUDGE LORING'S DECISION; AND, A DETAILED ACCOUNT OF THE EMBARKATION.
BOSTON:
FETRIDGE AND COMPANY.
1854.
Press of J. S. Potter & Co., 2 Spring Lane and 130 Washington Street.

Cover of *The Boston Slave Riot and Trial of Anthony Burns* *(Hulton/Archive)*

Once back in Virginia, Burns was imprisoned for five months as punishment. During this time, he was sold by his original owner to David McDaniel, a speculator. McDaniel had been contacted by a group of Bostonians who procured $1,500 to purchase Burns's freedom. Accordingly, in March 1855 he returned north a free man and was publicly hailed as the "Lion of Boston." Further donations allowed Burns to attend the Preparatory Department of Oberlin College, Ohio, where he formally studied theology and became a Baptist minister. He preached briefly in Indianapolis before an atmosphere of racial intolerance induced him to relocate to St. Catherines, Ontario, as pastor of the fugitive slave community. He died there in that capacity on July 27, 1862. Burns's notoriety had been brief but decisive; in the wake of his ordeal, no other fugitive slave was forcibly returned. Moreover, the entire episode added greater moral and political impetus to the rising cause of abolitionism. Eight northern states subsequently passed "personal liberty laws" to further infringe on compliance with the Fugitive Slave Law.

Further reading: Kevin L. Gilbert, "The Ordeal of Edward Greeley Loring: Fugitive Slavery, Judicial Reform, and the Politics of Law in 1850s Massachusetts." (unpublished Ph.D. dis., University of Massachusetts, Amherst, 1997); Albert J. Von Frank, *The Trials of Anthony Burns: Freedom and Slavery in Emerson's Boston* (Cambridge, Mass.: Harvard University Press, 1997).

—John C. Fredriksen

C

Cabet, Étienne (1788–1856)

A socialist community founder, Étienne Cabet was born into a working class family in Dijon, France, in 1788. He grew up in an atmosphere suffused with the sights and sounds of the great revolution of 1789. Educated at the local lycée (school), he became a medical student, but law was his real interest. After pursuing legal studies, he was admitted to the bar and then took a doctoral degree in law. When the courts in Dijon became hostile toward his legal defense of political radicals, he moved to Paris, where he identified himself with radical causes, culminating in his support of the July Revolution of 1830. The new monarch, Louis-Philippe, appointed him procureur-general for Corsica, but his extreme views led to his recall. He then sought political office and was elected to the Chamber of Deputies, where he allied with the radical faction. In 1833, Cabet established his own newspaper, *Le Populaire,* which became a voice for the workers. The following year, he published articles that incited readers to overthrow the government. He was indicted, and in order to avoid prison, he went into exile in London for five years.

In London, Cabet wrote a utopian novel, *Voyage et Aventures de Lord William Carisdell en Icarie.* When he returned to France in 1839, he republished the volume with the title *Voyage en Icarie.* The book was an immediate sensation. Into the economic and political ferment of the 1840s, Cabet and his book spoke to a vision of a just and equitable society. In May 1847, he wrote an article that described a utopian community in the United States.

Cabet correctly sensed that the PUBLIC LAND POLICY of the United States offered opportunities for land acquisition not available elsewhere. Unfortunately, instead of dealing with the federal land system, he negotiated with a Texas land company for 1 million acres on the Red River in Texas. When the advance party of some 70 Icariens arrived at the site, they found the holdings widely scattered and not especially fertile. Cabet gathered the main body of 500 adherents in New Orleans for a new start. In 1849, he leased the land and buildings of the former Mormon community at NAUVOO, Illinois. The community of Icariens settled into the new site under Cabet's leadership, and New Icaria began a six-year period of prosperity and growth.

In the midst of this success, Cabet found himself besieged by the courts in France and by a dissident faction in Nauvoo. Some of the French Icariens, irate at the failure of the Texas colony, brought suit for fraud against Cabet in French courts. The French courts supported the plaintiffs and sentenced Cabet in absentia to prison and a fine. In 1852, Cabet returned to Paris to defend himself against the judgment. Even as he achieved a degree of vindication in the French courts, the dissident faction in Nauvoo grew. In 1856, this group elected a majority to the board of directors governing the colony. Cabet challenged the legitimacy of the election, but civil authorities in the state of Illinois upheld the results of the election. Cabet then moved with 180 followers to the outskirts of St. Louis, where he suffered a stroke and died in 1856. The Icarien colonies survived him, including communities at Cheltenham, Missouri; Corning, Iowa; and Cloverdale, California.

Although French in origin and French in his views of society, the economy, and politics, Cabet's great social experiments were in the United States. As a part of his commitment to the nation that offered a refuge to himself and his followers, he became a citizen of the United States in 1854. Ridiculed in much of the French press, Cabet's communities nevertheless continued to attract adherents on a regular basis throughout the 19th century well after his death.

Further reading: Christopher H. Johnson, *Utopian Communities in France: Cabet and the Icarians, 1839–1851* (Ithaca, N.Y.: Cornell University Press, 1974).

Calhoun, John C. (1782–1850)

One of the leading senators of the first half of the 19th century as well as the most prominent ideological and political defenders of southern rights and slavery, John Caldwell Calhoun was born on March 18, 1782, in what is now Abbeville, South Carolina. The Calhouns were a prominent slave-owning family of Scotch-Irish ancestry. John Calhoun was named for his uncle, John Caldwell, his mother's brother, who was killed by Tories during the intense civil struggle that marked the American Revolution in the Carolinas. His father, Patrick Calhoun, rose to political prominence, and as a member of the South Carolina legislature he opposed the federal Constitution during the 1780s.

Young John Calhoun attended school in Georgia, where he studied history and philosophy, including the works of the English political thinker John Locke. After graduating from Yale College with a strong academic record, he enrolled at the well-known law school in Litchfield, Connecticut, run by Tapping Reeve. In both New England schools, Calhoun was a rare Republican, and, unlike his classmates, he exhibited little interest in formal religion. After completing his legal education, Calhoun returned to South Carolina, where he opened a law office in Abbeville and quickly gained a reputation for sharp thinking and honesty. He soon turned to politics, making his inaugural speech a defense of American national honor as he lambasted Britain for its navy's attack on the U.S. ship *Chesapeake* in 1807.

Shortly after his political debut, Calhoun won election to the South Carolina legislature in 1808 at the age of 26. While serving there, the legislature devised a plan to share power between the lowland section of the state, ruled by large slave-owning planters and merchants, and upcountry, which was home to yeoman farmers. Each section of the state was effectively given control over one house of the legislature when it reapportioned its seats. This was Calhoun's first experience with the idea of the "concurrent majorities," by which two competing interests would each be equally represented within one government.

John C. Calhoun's service in the South Carolina legislature was brief. Following his first term, he was elected to the U.S. Congress as a Republican. Around the time of his election, Calhoun married his distant cousin Floride Bonneau Calhoun, who was 11 years younger than he and a member of a prominent Charleston family of French Huguenot, or Protestant, ancestry. The couple had 10 children, seven of whom survived until adulthood. The marriage served to advance Calhoun's political status in South Carolina.

Upon his arrival in Washington, Calhoun and the rest of Congress were faced with a growing crisis with Britain and the likelihood of a second war with that country. Calhoun and a group of young congressmen, mainly from the South and West, emerged as fierce advocates of defending national pride and were named the WAR HAWKS for their exuberance. Although a newcomer to Washington and to Congress, Calhoun was named chairman of the House Foreign Relations Committee, and it was his committee that passed a key resolution calling for war with Britain. Once the WAR OF 1812 had commenced, Calhoun was active in organizing and sustaining logistical and financial support for the war. The pace and scope of his actions were such that one observer of wartime Washington described him as "the young Hercules who carried the war on his shoulders."

Once the war had ended, Calhoun resumed his fervent and strengthened nationalism in Congress; he was instrumental, for example, in chartering the SECOND BANK OF THE UNITED STATES in 1816. He also advocated federal support for internal improvements and for a high tariff to protect American goods from foreign competition. Calhoun also spoke for the need for a standing federal army, even in peacetime, as well as for strengthening the navy. He dismissed objections to nationalist measures that were based on sectional interests and on what he called "refined arguments on the constitution."

Calhoun's nationalism, which was forged in the War of 1812, would not ultimately govern the rest of his career. He did, however, resign his seat in Congress to join the cabinet of President JAMES MONROE as secretary of war. He served with distinction in that office, although his mind had more of a philosophical bent than an administrative one.

In 1824 Calhoun briefly entered the presidential contest to succeed the retiring Monroe. Unable to garner enough support for the presidency, he accepted the Republican nomination for vice president and assumed that office when JOHN QUINCY ADAMS became president. Although part of the Adams administration, Calhoun soon forged a political alliance with ANDREW JACKSON and New Yorker MARTIN VAN BUREN. They and others began building support for Jackson's 1828 White House bid almost immediately after Adams took office. This tactical decision by Calhoun did not mean that he had abandoned his own presidential ambitions. His hope was to succeed Jackson after the aging general served one term in the White House.

It was during his years as vice president that Calhoun started to modify his unqualified nationalism. Southerners came to despise the high tariffs designed to protect New England manufacturing interests, which they believed artificially raised their agricultural costs. South Carolina took the lead in opposing what its political leaders in the 1820s referred to as the "Tariff of Abominations." In his trips back home to his native state, Calhoun could not but notice how the deep feeling of resentment toward the North was based not only on the tariff but on a more general and wide-ranging critique of the nation's federal system. Calhoun for his

John C. Calhoun *(Library of Congress)*

part agreed to write a political treatise in which he insisted that South Carolina had the right to nullify any national law it determined was contrary to its own interests. He further argued that the federal union was made by the states, and they remained the sovereign body within it. The Constitution itself was fundamentally an agreement, or compact between the states, and the federal government was their instrument. Hence, Calhoun took a crucial step away from his nationalism and began to embrace fully the doctrine of states' rights. His newfound sectionalism helped to end any hopes that he had of succeeding Jackson. Calhoun resigned the vice presidency in 1832 and was subsequently elected to the U.S. Senate from South Carolina.

The dispute between South Carolina and the federal government over the tariff issue came to a head in 1833. At one point, President Jackson threatened to lead an army into South Carolina and hang John Calhoun. Hoping to avoid a crisis, Calhoun helped to forge a compromise on the tariff. But in the wake of Nat Turner's rebellion in Virginia and as abolitionism burgeoned in the North, Calhoun emerged as the leading spokesman for the cause of southern rights. A slaveholder and confirmed believer in white superiority, Calhoun began a vigorous defense of SLAVERY, which covered the final two decades of his life, on a range of political, economic, philosophical and moral grounds. He asserted that the rights of slaveholding states must should be protected within a nation that was increasingly dominated by the North and its manufacturing- and wage-based economy. One way to do so, Calhoun argued, was by a concurrent majority, a concept he had originally encountered in the South Carolina legislature.

Calhoun's antiabolitionist activity included supporting the "Gag Rule" by which Congress refused to even consider antislavery petitions; he also strongly favored the right of southern postmasters to remove abolitionist literature from the mail. Calhoun served briefly as secretary of state under President JOHN TYLER, and in that post he enthusiastically supported the U.S. annexation of TEXAS and argued for adding more slave states to the Union. Upon his return to the Senate in 1845, however, he came to oppose the MEXICAN-AMERICAN WAR, in the belief that the incorporation of so much new territory into the United States would push the question of slavery once again to the forefront and threaten the Union. Unfortunately, Calhoun was right in that fear; Congress soon found itself debating a proposal to ban slavery in all lands that the United States would gain in the war with Mexico. Calhoun stepped forward once more to defend the interests of the South, arguing that the addition of the free states of Oregon and CALIFORNIA would tip the balance of power against the South and cripple its ability to protect slavery from abolitionists.

The culmination of Calhoun's thinking on this subject came in his two essays, "The Disquisition on Government" and "Discourse on the Constitution." In them, he once again spelled out the need for southern interests, unique as they were, to be guaranteed with special safeguards or else the continuation of the Union would not be possible. He repeated his view that the American political system was uniquely federal, not national, with ultimate sovereignty residing not with the federal government but rather with the people of the states. He went so far as to propose that the North and South would each elect its own president, and the consent of both would be needed to enact legislation into law.

In his final year of life, Calhoun remained opposed to compromise over the question of the territory acquired from Mexico. Sick and rapidly failing, he sat by in the Senate while a colleague read his final speech on March 4, 1850, in which he traced the change of the United States from a federal republic to a "consolidated democracy" increasingly dominated by the North. The South, meaning its slaveholders, would have no way to protect their rights and interests in such a transformed polity. Having offered little hope for saving the Union, he died on March 31, 1850, and was buried in Charleston, South Carolina. The COMPROMISE OF 1850 staved off civil war for another decade, but John C. Calhoun had already laid the intellectual foundation for the doctrine of states' rights and of secession itself.

Further reading: Irving H. Bartlett, *John C. Calhoun: A Biography* (New York: W. W. Norton, 1993); Richard N. Current, *John C. Calhoun* (New York: Washington Square Press, 1963).

—Jason Duncan

California

The original human inhabitants of what was to become California were Indians who had crossed the bridge from Asia to northern North America some 15,000 years ago. As Indian peoples spread across the continent, south and then east, they extended human habitation across the range of South and North America. Amidst this movement over generations and centuries, large numbers remained clustered in what would become California. The pleasant climate and the varieties of accessible foods—fish, game, and seeds especially—made the place attractive for permanent settlement. As the natural resources were so extensive, California Indians had little reason to make a transition to agriculture, and they remained hunters, fishers, and gatherers. They were also diverse in their cultures, with the northern Modoc and Shasta connected culturally to the nations of the Pacific Northwest, the Miwok in the central valleys, the several nations of the south, and the Mojave and Yuma in the eastern deserts. These varied groups were sedentary and generally peaceful. The plentiful natural resources and mild climate had reduced the friction associated with expansion in search of food sources.

The ships of several European nations had passed up and down the California coastline for 200 years before European settlement began. Spanish explorers landed and spied out Alta California (the name given to Upper California by the Spanish) as early as the 1540s. In spite of its physical appeal, California did not fit easily into the Spanish empire. There was no readily exploitable source of wealth, and the ocean currents and winds made it difficult to sail up the coast from Mexico.

Among those in the first expedition who established a permanent Spanish settlement in San Diego in 1769 was Father Junípero Serra, who would found many of Alta California's missions. Spain's resources for expansion were declining, and given the great distances in Upper California, it was the missions that became the centers of Spanish settlement. Ultimately, there were 21 missions established on important sites. The missions established effective agricultural enterprise aided by the attractive weather and fertile soil, but they were far less successful in bringing together large numbers of Indians on a voluntary basis. Instead, missionaries frequently enslaved the Indians to establish an agricultural labor system and keep it in place. Partly because of this failure and partly because of the pleasant life they enjoyed, the padres made no effort to secularize the missions and deliver them into Indian hands after a period of years. It should also be noted that the important sites and lands in Alta California were in the hands of the church rather than secular entrepreneurs, and the missionaries hoped to isolate the Indians on the missions from what they regarded as dangerous temptations of the secular world.

In 1821 Mexico revolted against Spanish imperial rule and established its independence, upon which Alta California became a state in the Republic of Mexico. As the new Mexican republic worked to establish its authority over an enormous area with a diverse population, the state of California came to exercise a high degree of independence. The appointed governors resident in Monterey were a long way from Mexico City, and the authority of the republic was weak at such a distance.

The new republic felt strongly about one aspect of life in California. In the aftermath of the revolution of 1821, the federal government of the Mexican republic turned its attention to the missions of California, which it thought exploited the native peoples. After extended deliberations, the missions were secularized. Unhappily, the Indians themselves did not benefit from the secularization process; instead, the fertile mission lands were appropriated by large ranchos that were to spread across much of southern and central California following independence from Spain.

After 1821 the new government of Mexico also set up plans to develop the nation's northern provinces. The new settlements would protect the distant reaches of the new, independent nation from the incursions of the Russians from the North or the Anglo-Americans from the East. Spain had used the missions to establish its nominal control; Mexico turned to independent ranchos in the hands of individual families. It was a solution to the problem appropriate to the new nation: secularization mixed with private land ownership. The spread of the rancho system was also natural because the experiences of the missions over two generations had demonstrated that California was an ideal climate and landscape for the pastoral industry.

The federal government in Mexico City now made a number of large grants to individuals. In 1820, there were perhaps 20 sizable private land holdings in Upper California; in 1840, there were 600 such tracts. Most of these new land grants were very large, up to several thousand acres. Ranchos became distinct and separate independent political, economic, and social units. They were run by families as private fiefs with total control over every aspect of life. Much of the work was done by former mission Indians, now laboring under conditions of debt peonage, or an economic situation close to permanent slavery. This semifeudal system did not owe allegiance to any central government, and other than making further land grants, the government in Mexico City exercised little influence or sovereignty in California, where the dominant influence had become that of the local ranchos.

As the pastoral industry of livestock grazing took hold on a large scale and soon prospered, the ranchos became, inevitably, involved in trade with the outside world. The traders turned out to be New England sea captains and their ships, which began to make regular stops at sites along the California coast to pick up cargoes of cattle hides and tallow. The classic description of this trade is depicted in RICHARD HENRY DANA's *Two Years Before the Mast.* Over a period of 20 years after independence, the strongest influence in Alta California was not the federal government in Mexico City but the resident trade representatives established by New England merchant companies in the port towns of California. By the 1840s, there were many such agents, of whom the most significant was THOMAS OLIVER LARKIN. Seagoing commerce made the California ranchos wealthy, and the dependence of the ranchos on trade made the agents of trading companies enormously influential. This relationship was the beginning of a widening American influence in California affairs.

The numbers of Euro-American peoples involved remained small. In 1845, after a quarter-century of Mexican independence and on the eve of war between Mexico and the United States, the non-Indian population of California was probably on the order of 7,000. American immigration overland had begun on what would become the CALIFORNIA TRAIL, a branch of the OREGON TRAIL. Perhaps as many as several hundred people a year were arriving in California after a transcontinental journey.

In 1846, as relations between the United States and Mexico worsened, a group of itinerant hunters and trappers organized a rebellion against Mexican rule in California with a view to its annexation to the United States. Known as the BEAR FLAG REVOLT, this miscellaneous force was led by JOHN C. FRÉMONT. However, their ineffectual but sometimes violent actions were overtaken by larger events.

The outbreak of the MEXICAN-AMERICAN WAR in May 1846 changed the direction of California's history. The harbor at San Francisco Bay was considered the most important naval anchorage on the West Coast, and California had always played a central role in American expansionist plans. As part of military operations, General STEPHEN WATTS KEARNY's army reached California in December 1846. Kearny and Commodore ROBERT FIELD STOCKTON, in command of American naval forces, defeated the Mexican army at Los Angeles on January 8, 1847, and on March 1, Kearny established an American civil government in California. At the TREATY OF GUADALUPE HIDALGO, signed on February 2, 1848, Mexico ceded to the United States one-third of her northern national territory, including California.

Even before the signatures had been affixed to the treaty, the U.S. plans for California were overtaken by an unforeseen event. On January 24, 1848, at the site of JOHN SUTTER's mill in Coloma on the American River, a carpenter named James W. Marshall discovered gold. The ensuing immigration from around the world, known as the CALIFORNIA GOLD RUSH, would change the face of California and shape its development for the next half-century. By 1850, the census of California showed nearly 100,000 people, almost all of them arrived in the previous year. This influx of humanity would submerge the Mexican population of California, call into question many of the land grants made by the Mexican government, and quickly make California an American area. The constitution drafted at Monterey in the autumn of 1850 prohibited slavery, in large part because of the fear on the part of miners that slaves would become competition for free miners. Congress conferred statehood in 1850, as part of a settlement of territorial acquisitions from the Mexican-American War known as the COMPROMISE OF 1850.

California grew rapidly in the 1850s as mining expanded and prospered; AGRICULTURE developed on the fertile soil, tended by a burgeoning population; and San Francisco became the leading metropolitan center on the West Coast, with a population that became the most cosmopolitan in the nation. To the waves of Americans who came across the continent in 1849 and 1850—and in subsequent years by sea—were added large numbers of Mexicans, Chileans, Peruvians, and Hawaiians; from Europe, Germans, English, and French; and finally Australians and Chinese. All were subject to a growing unhappiness with the influx of foreigners, and in response to such sentiments, the legislature passed a heavy tax of $30 a month against foreign miners in 1850. After extensive protests, the tax was reduced in 1851 to $4 a month.

Of these groups, the Chinese would become the most visible feature of life in California. Arriving in large numbers for the first time in 1852, they had come in response to the lure of "Gold Mountain," the opportunity associated with the gold rush for poor men without name or education to make a fortune. The Chinese came, for the most part, as contract laborers, and of all the immigrant groups, they were the most distinctive. As the economic opportunities associated with the gold rush waned, they became the universal victims of the rising discontent against newcomers.

Indians were also targets of violence. Isolated raids against itinerant miners in the mountains were met with massive reprisals. The state government promulgated an official policy under which Indians were to be hunted down as dangerous to civil order. The Indian population in

California was decimated within a decade of the opening of the gold rush.

By 1860, on the eve of the Civil War, California had completed a decade of extraordinary growth. Agriculture had begun to take hold in the central valleys. The towns of Sacramento and Stockton were growing as commercial centers. Yet it was also a time of uneasiness and civil disorder. In response to a rising level of crime and violence, "committees of vigilance" took power in San Francisco in 1851 and 1856, enforcing justice through extra-legal means. In the latter year, a private army controlled the city for three months, and several notorious characters were hung. Nevertheless, despite its uneasiness and violence, San Francisco emerged as a financial center of the West Coast as well as a cosmopolitan center of theater, literature, and journalism. In 1859, for example, San Francisco had 12 daily newspapers. They all paid tribute to the fastest-growing city in the rapidly growing Golden State.

Further reading: Walton Bean, *California: An Interpretative History* (New York: McGraw-Hill, 1973); Andrew F. Rolle, *California: A History* (New York: Crowell, 1969).

California gold rush

The California gold rush was the mass movement of men and women to California in response to the discovery of gold by James W. Marshall, a carpenter, who found nuggets at JOHN SUTTER's mill on January 24, 1848. Although Marshall and his employer Sutter tried to keep the news quiet, rumors spread quickly. First arrivals came from along the West Coast, from Sonora and Oregon, and from the HAWAIIAN ISLANDS. The news then spread to the eastern states, from Maine to Mississippi, Wisconsin to Florida, and finally around the world. In response to the news of gold that was available to everyone, Americans initially set forth by sea as early as the winter of 1848–49, some on voyages of 8–10 months around Cape Horn; others took a shorter route to Panama, where they crossed the isthmus and then sought a ship to take them up the coast to San Francisco. Overland emigration began in the spring of 1849 from Independence and St. Joseph, by way of the CALIFORNIA TRAIL. The appeal of gold in California turned out to be universal. Those who would become known as the FORTY-NINERS came from farms, small towns, and large cities, with representatives of every class, from the wealthy to those in average circumstances and from every state and territory, including slaves brought by their owners to the goldfields.

The prospect of the wealth opened by news of the dazzling discoveries at Sutter's mill offered young people escape from what they thought of as the limited horizons of the village, the farm, or the shop, and the daily demand of labor associated with these places. It was not the young alone, however, who were spurred into action. Men of all ages and conditions made plans to go to California, and a surprising number of women wished to join them.

The response to the California gold discoveries was the greatest westward migration in the history of the nation. Some 80,000 went to California in 1849 and probably 300,000 by 1854. It was an immigration that was made by land across half a continent and by sea over thousands of miles of ocean to new and heretofore unimagined adventure and wealth. In the end, the California gold rush drew people from all over the world, including peasants from China and lawyers from Paris, miners from Wales and merchants from Chile. California would become in a few short years the most cosmopolitan place in the world, and San Francisco the most cosmopolitan city.

Astonishing as it might seem (and did to the Americans at the time) in a world of rumor and exaggeration, the stories of riches in California were true. The Golden State—it would join in Union in 1850—produced a seemingly endless flood of gold. While agricultural laborers in the East earned a dollar a day for 12 hours of work in the fields, and artisans and craftsmen received perhaps a dollar and a half for the same hours, men who were recently farmers and mechanics made $16 and even $20 a day washing gravel in the streambeds of California's foothills. In the six years from 1849 to 1855, the argonauts (as they were sometimes called) harvested some $300 million in gold from California.

The other astonishing feature of the California gold rush was that gold was available to everyone. This greatest bonanza in the history of the young republic and newly crowned continental nation was open to all, regardless of wealth, social standing, education, or family name. No experience was necessary, mining skills could be learned in 15 minutes, and the only tools necessary were a pick, pan, and a shovel, at least in the early years.

Those who went to California overland in 1849 and subsequent years often did so with their friends and neighbors, joining together in what they called a company. This was a group of people who shared the duties of work on the trail and looked after one another—in other words, a support network. As the young and inexperienced argonauts confronted an unknown adventure involving great distances and a strange and alien landscape, such a network was both welcome and necessary.

The first companies went by ship or by wagon overland from St. Joseph or Independence, Missouri, to Placerville (or Hangtown, as the argonauts affectionately referred to it). By 1852, the newest victims of gold mania—and it seemed to produce annual outbreaks in different parts of the nation—were traveling by railroad to steamships and then by sea to the golden shores of California in a fraction of the time taken by their predecessors in the first great overland emigration only three years earlier.

Gold mining in California *(Hulton/Archive)*

Once arrived in California, whether by land or by sea, the Forty-niners reassembled once more in groups for living and working. They called these groups mining companies or messes, after the domestic duties that were as much a part of their lives as the work in the rushing streams of the mountains. It was one of the unexpected characteristics of the California gold rush that mining, viewed as a lonely and selfish enterprise, was in reality an intensely cooperative experience.

With his new companions, the average Forty-niner established a new set of economic and social bonds. As early as the summer and fall of 1848, the first observers in the goldfields commented on the advantage of working in groups of at least three or four. These divisions for mining, with its unending hard physical labor, long hours, and collective work, also helped to develop the new living arrangements. For the argonauts, it was cheaper and more practical to live in groups. As few as three men, but often from six to eight, would occupy a large tent or cabin, where they would take turns cooking, cleaning, and making trips to town for food and mail.

The mining company as a unit of work and living offered support in case of sickness and even death. The Forty-niner's companions would sit up with an ill miner, fetch the doctor, and arrange the burial. They would settle the estate, and they would write to the dead man's family and carry out his last wishes.

The work of mining was arduous, repetitive, and took place under difficult physical conditions. Gold mining in California at mid-century—called placer mining—was among the most onerous work performed by free labor anywhere. Working a claim was a continuous round of digging, shoveling, carrying, and washing that continued unabated and with little variation throughout the day from sunrise to sunset. For many members of the company or mess, the work was carried out in swift, ice-cold, moving water up to their knees. Overhead was the burning summer California sun that shone into the canyons and watercourses. The summer months were crucial for digging and washing, for the dry season meant a drop in the water level, exposing the bars and riffles with the richest dirt. So hot were the days that even during the best mining season, the company often rested during the heat of the day. Placer mining was repetitive and exhausting.

When the miners had finished a day's work, they returned to the cabin and a round of chores. The domestic duties associated with the goldfields were as necessary and repetitive as the search for gold itself. They included cooking, serving, and fetching firewood and water, all rotated on

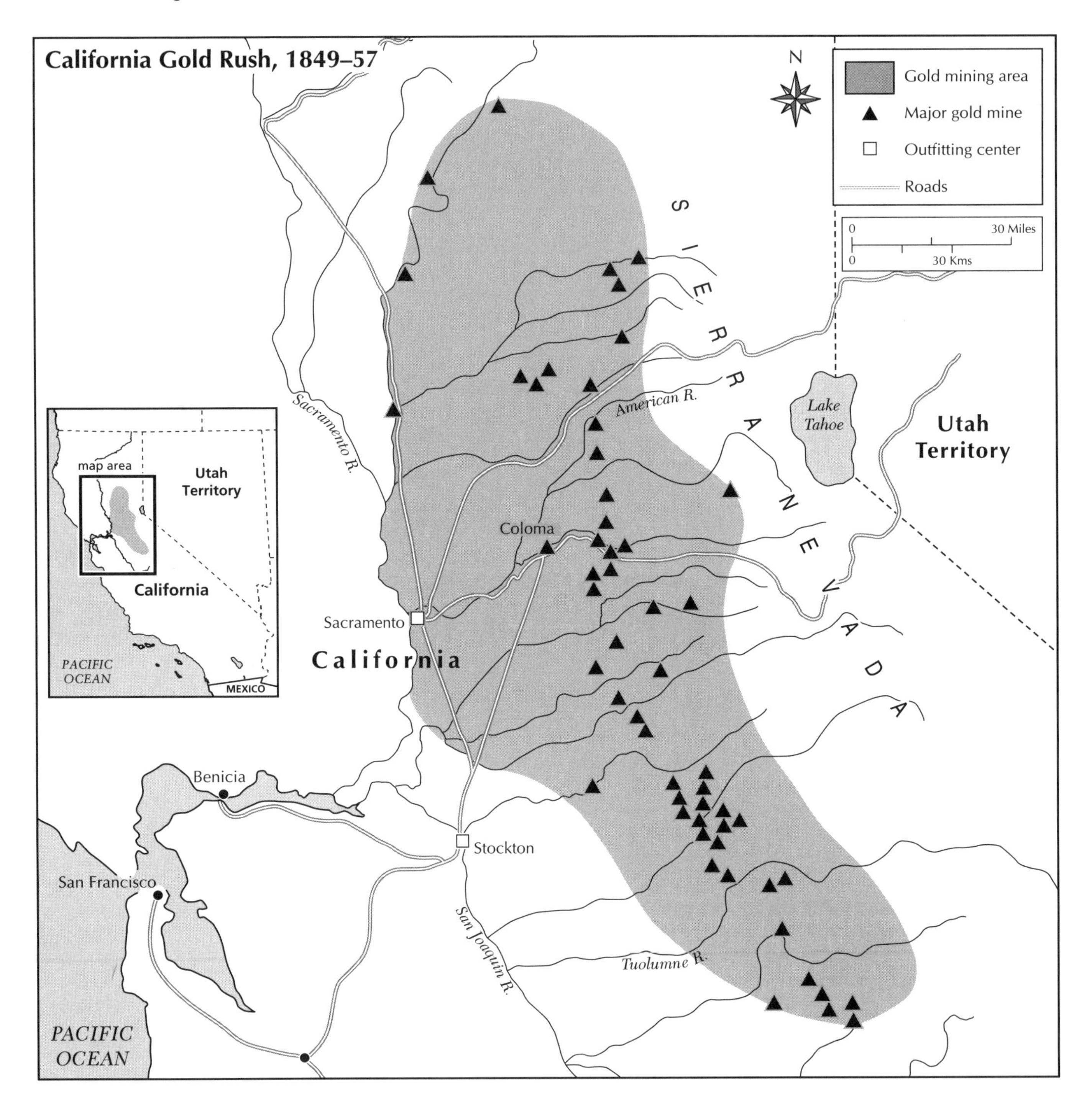

a weekly basis. For those who preferred to live alone, there were boardinghouses, complete with meals. Miners also washed and mended their clothes. Although cleanliness does not seem to have been a high priority, mending had a certain practical aspect, saving the cost of expensive new clothing.

The domestic dimension of the gold rush reflected the powerful influence of women, who dominated aspects of life in California by their absence rather than their presence. With the mining counties 97% male, the gold rush was also a continuing search for a scarce and valuable commodity—women, who turned out to be, for some years, even rarer than gold. The Forty-niners came from a world in which they had taken the presence of women for granted, but in California the argonauts confronted for the first time the prospect of a society without women, and they struggled to make the adjustment.

The growth of numbers in the goldfields was explosive. At the end of 1848, observers estimated there were 5,000 miners in California; 50,000 at the end of 1849; 100,000 at the close of 1850 and 125,000 miners in subsequent years. These numbers produced great returns, although unevenly spread across the range of mining and miners. Such astonishing numbers of miners generated new markets for goods and services. Every crossroads and mining camp of any size had a store, and towns had three or four or more. Miners took Sunday as a day off and went into town, so the entertainment business flourished, especially gambling. San Francisco became a thriving port of entry for people and goods, and the volume of commerce demanded a growing transportation network of wagons, animals, and facilities to care for them. Saloons, eateries, and boardinghouses sprang up everywhere in the goldfields, and they flourished.

The annual immigrations of new argonauts continued throughout the 1850s. As new Forty-niners arrived, others went home. The patterns of movement to and from the goldfields were continuous. Mining gradually changed, becoming less and less the work of individuals or even mining companies. First, large groups of miners joined together to build a dam to divert the flow of a stream, with a view to mining the streambed. This technique, known as river mining, demanded large numbers of miners and a substantial capital investment for a major construction project. River mining was soon followed by quartz mining, digging shafts into the sides of hills to follow seams of gold; and then hydraulic mining, in which a powerful stream of water would be used to wash away a hillside and produce gravels that could be processed for gold. All these techniques needed capital investment, and mining entrepreneurs soon began to sell stock in such ventures to the public.

From the first primitive venture, mining changed the landscape, and with larger numbers and larger-scale techniques, the changes created devastation. Beyond the physical reconfiguration of the streams and rivers of central California were the endless signs of indifferent human habitation. Old camps and mining sites marked the passage of tens of thousands and eventually hundreds of thousands through the California landscape. The common quality that bound all these individuals over a generation was that they had come to get rich, and since they intended to stay the briefest possible time, they were not interested in the devastation wreaked on the countryside. Most miners were not purposefully destructive; they were simply intent on wealth.

The California gold rush also had a catastrophic impact on the Indian peoples of California. Driven from the meadows and streams that had provided their places of habitation for centuries, they retreated to the isolation of the high mountains. But no matter how remote the location, prospecting parties of miners would invade their habitats. As their economic condition worsened, the Indians raided mining camps in search of food. Their incursions were met with organized violence by large numbers. Miners and others reacted with a rage born of uneasiness and racial superiority. They organized expeditions into the distant Indian sanctuaries, especially in the winter when miners were idle. These expedition were often undertaken as official acts of the state government. The violence, in conjunction with a legalized form of indentured service, reduced the Indian population from 250,000 to 15,000 between 1850 and 1900. This was among the most calamitous outcomes of any Indian group from first contact with Euro-Americans.

By the end of the 1850s, gold production in California had stabilized at about $40 million annually. Agriculture had become increasingly significant for the Golden State, especially the development of wheat and grazing in the Central Valley, while San Francisco had made the transition from mining town to a cosmopolitan city. Yet the influences of the California gold rush were everywhere. The discovery of gold had affected the history of California and its peoples (including Mexican and Indian peoples) in dramatic and sometimes final ways.

Further reading: Rodman W. Paul, *California Gold: The Beginning of Mining in the Far West* (Cambridge, Mass.: Harvard University Press, 1965); Malcolm J. Rohrbough, *Days of Gold: The California Gold Rush and the American Nation* (Berkeley: University of California Press, 1997).

California missions

California missions were established by Spain as a way of extending its imperial authority. By the middle of the 18th century, Spain's resources had become strained, and the far northern boundaries of the empire needed to be extended and safeguarded against incursion by European rivals. Committed missionaries became the means to this end. That the mission enterprises saved the souls of heathen Indian peoples also fitted in with Spain's goals for New Spain in the Western Hemisphere.

The extension of missions into CALIFORNIA began in 1769 with an expedition to Alta (Upper) California, led by Gaspar de Portolá and Father Junípero Serra, that established a Spanish outpost and mission at San Diego. Over the next 20 years, Father Serra and other missionaries established a total of 21 missions—Father Serra personally founded nine—within Upper California, stretching from San Diego to Sonoma, including sites at Santa Barbara, Santa Clara, San Carlos (Carmel), San Jose, San Francisco, and San Luis Obispo. Missions were established at strategic points, especially those on the ocean, and they were about 30 miles apart (a day's ride on horseback).

The mission in California was a self-contained economic, social, and religious unit. The padres would gather Indian peoples into the mission and give them religious instruction and have them labor to establish a self-sufficient agricultural enterprise. The religious instruction would lead to conversion and the saving of souls; the work would provide systematic discipline that would lead the Indian peoples toward European values; the success of the mission as agricultural enterprise would attract other Indian peoples; the mission system would serve the Spanish imperial policies at little or no cost to the Crown.

That the missions generally succeeded and even flourished owed much to the attractive landscape and gentle climate of California, but the presence of Indians was increasingly involuntary. The missionaries thought physical compulsion to remain was necessary to save souls and to ensure the continuing success of the enterprise. Many Indians sought the missions as places of safety from the raids of other native peoples, but when they wished to leave, they were restrained. Those who did leave the missions were pursued, returned to the mission, and punished. Although individual missions had devoted native resident families, the system was characterized by intimidation and force, policies that kept the Indian presence in the missions at a fixed number. The missions continued to prosper economically, but the relationship of native peoples to the missionary system often remained an uneasy one, and as a result, the padres' work of religious and cultural conversion was not very successful.

As the missions became established and prospered economically, the entire system became embroiled in larger church and national issues. According to the directive conveyed from New Spain, the missionaries were to establish the missions, give the native peoples religious instruction, train them in the management of agricultural or grazing enterprises, and then hand the mission over to them, depart, and establish another mission elsewhere. However, the padres did not make plans for the secularization of the missions, arguing instead that the Indians were not ready to take over the economic initiatives. The issue resonated in Spain itself, where clergy and state clashed over greater freedom of popular expression. Furthermore, wars of liberation and independence had begun in the Spanish colonies in the early years of the century, uprisings that gathered momentum with Napoleon's invasion of Spain. In this period of confusion, the church appeared as a conservative bulwark against change. The missions were a symbol of the traditional values of church and Crown.

The missions were a symbol of the traditional values of church and crown. Although the mission was an important instrument of imperial expansion for the Spanish, expanding the area of their control without colonization, in many respects, the missions were a failure. They systematically destroyed autonomous Indian cultures, and the effects of disease and malnutrition may be seen in the dramatic decline of California's Indian peoples, from about 150,000 in 1500 to some 98,000 in 1832.

With the independence of Mexico in 1821, the new Republic of Mexico assumed sovereignty over California and its missions. The Mexican government pressed forward the issue of secularization of the missions. The reasons for promoting secularization were the long apprenticeship of the Indians and their readiness for such a step as well as the knowledge that the Catholic Church was generally a conservative influence against the revolution and the independence of Mexico. A law providing for the secularization of the missions was enacted in 1834, but its impact was mixed. The government in Mexico City was far from California and only able to enforce its will sporadically. Furthermore, the padres were reluctant to leave and the growing rancho system in California seized the mission lands as soon as secularization took place. In the end, the Indian peoples of the missions were driven into the hills or enrolled as laborers under a form of debt peonage.

Further reading: Albert N. Hurtado, *Indian Survival on the California Frontier* (New Haven: Yale University Press, 1988); David J. Weber, *The Spanish Frontier in America.* (New Haven: Yale University Press, 1994).

California Trail

The trail that carried immigrants from Independence, Missouri, and St. Joseph, Missouri, to CALIFORNIA, was heavily used between 1849 and 1860 by FORTY-NINERS on their way to the California goldfields. The early section of the California Trail was the original OREGON TRAIL. It ran from the Missouri outfitting towns of Independence and St. Joseph north to the Platte River, west along the Platte, and then across SOUTH PASS. From this point, the trail moved along the Snake River until it struck out across the Blue Mountains to the Columbia River Valley.

The difficulty with travel to California lay in the landscape imposed by the wide and sterile intermontane plateaus, leading to the abrupt barrier of the Sierra Nevada, with its high passes and 14,000-foot peaks. Because of these obstacles, access to California in the 1830s was mainly by sea. Here, on the western coast, the trading ships of New England maintained a lively seagoing trade in hides and tallow, as depicted by RICHARD HENRY DANA in *Two Years Before the Mast.* Fur traders were the first Americans to make overland expeditions to Mexican California, and JEDEDIAH STRONG SMITH led a party of trappers across the Sierra Nevada in 1827. Although there were other groups that crossed in the next decade, no reliable route for immigrants could be found across the mountains.

In 1841 an immigrant party led by JOHN BIDWELL left the Oregon Trail in Idaho and followed the Humboldt River across the Carson Sink to the Walker River, which they followed across the sierra to the headwaters of the Stanislaus in California. They were the first to travel a large part of what would become known as the California Trail. Bidwell's party was composed almost entirely of young men (there was one woman and child), but it was the first group of overland immigrants (as opposed to trappers and traders) to make the journey. In 1844 the first overland party with wagons made the crossing. The necessary variation was the route of the Truckee River, which was to become the route of access by trail, and later by railroad and highway. The next season of immigration, 1845, was noteworthy for the increase in numbers to a half dozen parties with perhaps 250 immigrants, among whom was JOHN C. FRÉMONT. Remembering the surge of American immigrants to TEXAS that led to the TEXAS REVOLUTION, officials in Mexican California were suspicious of the rising number of American immigrants. Nevertheless, JOHN SUTTER offered a warm welcome at his large estate in the valley of the Sacramento River. For the immigrants on the trail, Sutter's New Helvetia was the end of their long journey.

The outbreak of the MEXICAN-AMERICAN WAR in spring 1846 changed the dynamics of immigration to California. By summer of that year, American troops and naval contingents had taken possession of much of strategic California—the main towns and the coastal harbors—and immigrants were coming to what was assumed would shortly become an American possession. Perhaps as many as 1,500 men, women, and children followed the California Trail that year, of which the most famous would be the DONNER PARTY (who left in 1846; survivors reached California in 1847).

The discovery of gold in California in January 1848 led to a dramatic rise in numbers using the California Trail. In 1849, the first big season of overland immigration, perhaps 80,000 Forty-niners crowded the trail from May to the end of September. The demands of the overland trail itself were basic and uncompromising. Over the 2,000 miles from Independence or St. Joseph in Missouri to Placerville, California, the immigrant gold-seeker moved into a landscape that was progressively drier and higher. The first landmark was FORT LARAMIE in Wyoming, some 800 miles out. Here, the Forty-niner companies would resupply, repack, trade tired mules or oxen for fresh draft animals, send mail, trade stories, and sign the register. Most of them did not tarry long. The overlanders of 1849 and subsequent years thought of the search for gold as an intensely competitive business. The advantage would go to those who arrived first and worked hardest. So they soon departed Fort Laramie, repacked and reenergized, following the Sweetwater River to South Pass. From this almost level crossing of the Continental Divide, they moved to Fort Hall on the Snake River, a second major stop for rest and supplies.

Leaving Fort Hall, the California Trail offered two options. The first ran through Salt Lake City, where the companies of argonauts entered Utah and BRIGHAM YOUNG's Mormon Church empire. Alternatively, the immigrant train might head overland to the source of the Humboldt, follow this watercourse to its disappearance, and then cross the desert of Nevada to the Truckee. Throughout, the second half of the trail was drier and harsher than the first, and it offered fewer places where the overland parties could find supplies or assistance. The immigrant groups who used the California Trail went heavily armed against possible attack by the Indians of the plains and the intermontane plateaus. In truth, however, the real dangers of the trail turned out to be accidents with firearms and the hazards of dangerous river crossings.

The California Trail was heavily used, beginning with the 1849 overland immigration of the Forty-niners. The more than 400 surviving diaries of immigrants using the trail in that year alone celebrated its landmark status as part of America's pioneering experience. Between 1849 and 1860, something on the order of 200,000 immigrants journeyed over it to California. The crossing was less expensive than the sea route—at least in the early years—and it used wagons, draft animals, and supplies widely available to Americans at the time. It also required skills shared almost universally by families from the farms that were characteristic of the nation at the time. As ship services expanded and the cost declined, many newer argonauts went to California by sea. The development of the transcontinental railroad, completed in 1869, ended the use of the California Trail.

Further reading: John Unrah. *The Plains Across; The Overland Emigrants and the Trans-Mississippi West, 1840–1860* (Urbana: University of Illinois Press, 1979).

Campbell, Thomas (1763–1854)

Thomas Campbell was a Protestant minister and, with his father, Thomas, cofounder of the Christian Church (Disciples of Christ). Thomas Campbell was born in County Down, Ireland, on February 1, 1763. Though raised an Anglican, he joined the Seceder branch of the Presbyterian church, was educated at the University of Glasgow, and was especially trained for preaching in the Antiburgher faction of the church. Adept at classical Greek and Latin, Campbell also adopted the Common Sense theories of the Scottish philosopher Thomas Reid. He began preaching in 1798 and assumed the pulpit of the Ahorey Church but grew disillusioned by the rampant factionalism he encountered. In 1805 he made a concerted attempt to unite the Burgher and Antiburgher cliques of the Seceder Church during their annual synod, but failed. Discouraged, by 1807 he had begun questioning Presbyterian practices, and he subsequently relocated to the wilds of western Pennsylvania to hone his theological concepts. In 1808, Campbell was assigned to the presbytery of Chartiers, Pennsylvania, where he expressed doubts as to the legitimacy of creeds, confessions, fast days, and other facets he ascribed to human authority. This apostasy resulted in Campbell's dismissal from the Presbyterian Church in September 1808, but he continued on as an itinerant preacher.

In August 1809 Campbell founded the Christian Association of Washington (Pennsylvania), which served as a pulpit for his Restorationist program. Here he formally denounced creeds and confessions as divisive and espoused a primitive form of Christianity based solely on New Testament precepts. "Where the Scripture speak, we will Speak," the church dictum rang, "Where the Scriptures are silent, we are silent." Campbell further enunciated his principles by publishing *A Declaration and an Address* (1809), which held that understanding the Bible, being the word of God, is within the grasp of any rational person. Furthermore, any church practices not mentioned in Scripture are human and not divine in origin, hence irrelevant. To Campbell, the New Testament alone formed the sole basis for uniting all Christians.

By 1812 Campbell was joined by his son, Alexander Campbell, and together they preached and established small academies throughout the Old Northwest. Reaction was mixed: Although the laity responded favorably to calls for unity, the Presbyterian community looked askance at the notion of Restorationism. In 1812 Campbell enjoyed a brief union with the Redstone Baptist Association, but he became a pariah for attacking Baptist emotionalism at the expense of rationalism and was expelled.

Eventually the Campbellites merged with Barton W. Stone's followers, thus giving rise to a new church, the Disciples of Christ. Thomas Campbell continued working closely with his son and successor until his death in Bethany, (West) Virginia on January 4, 1854. His advocacy of unity and rationality amongst Christians renders him an important theological figure, whose tenets found their greatest expression in the forthcoming Fundamentalist Movement.

Further reading: Lester G. McAllister, *Thomas Campbell: A Man of the Book.* (St. Louis: Bethany Press, 1954); Thomas A. Steed, "Alexander and Thomas Campbell's View of the Nature of Reality and Church: A Phenomenological, Rhetorical, and Metaphoric Analysis of the Restoration Movement." (unpublished Ph.D. dis., Southern Illinois University, 2000).

—John C. Fredriksen

canal era

From the beginning of the 19th century until the rise of the railroads, canals were extremely important to the internal transportation and trade of the United States. Best described as artificially constructed waterways or existing rivers modified, canals straightened and regularized water passages to make them more accessible to boat traffic. River transportation into the West had been limited because of the Appalachian Mountains and the fall line (the line of waterfalls on major American rivers that marked a significant drop in the land level). Through a sophisticated system of locks and levels, canals provided a dependable, controllable route over the uneven terrain that separated the East Coast from the developing frontier.

Canal building fed on the dream of connecting all of the major American waterways into a continuous, low-cost transportation network. The construction of a series of canals made the mass transport of goods and people to the inland frontier easier, and triggered wild speculation along the developing canal routes. The enthusiasm for canals during the first half of the 19th century exemplified the energetic optimism of American entrepreneurs looking to maximize opportunities in the developing West.

The earliest canals operated in limited areas near the eastern coast, but some of these engineering projects did succeed in bypassing the fall line. The first American canals to circumvent the line were the Patowmack Company's canal at Great Falls, Maryland (built between 1786 and 1808), and the Western Inland Lock Navigation Company's canal on the Mohawk River near Little Falls, New York (1795). Other canals connected important rivers and commercial centers, such as the Santee and Cooper Canal in South Carolina (1792–1800); and the Middlesex Canal, which connected Boston to the Merrimac River and thus to the interior of New England (1793). These early canals often had engineering flaws due to the builders' lack of knowledge about their proper construction. Gradually, experienced engineers—mostly from England—were recruited to correct these problems.

The true test of canal engineering skill would be the ERIE CANAL, for many years the most important and successful of all the canal projects. Built from 1817 to 1826, the Erie Canal connected the Atlantic Ocean to Lake Erie, and thus the entire Great Lakes region, creating a commercial artery able to transport goods easily to and from the developing Northwest. The Erie was so profitable that tolls collected from it financed a system of auxiliary lateral canals in New York State. This canal also provided a valu-

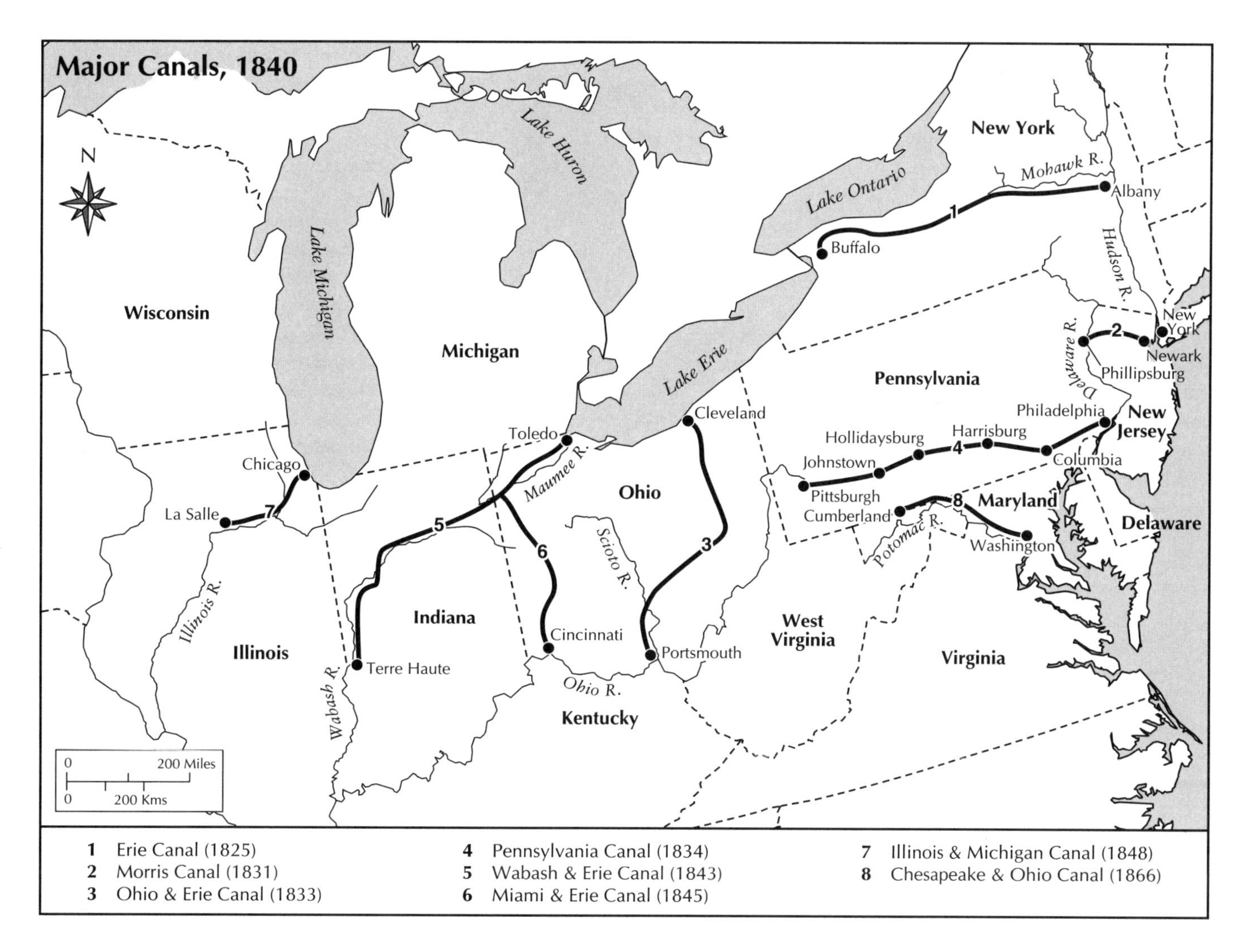

able basis for future canal engineering. Led by Benjamin Wright, the "Erie School" of engineers would go on to build canals across the expanding United States.

The Erie Canal transformed the economy of New York City and brought about the rapid development of the inland towns located near the canal in upstate New York. Successfully completed through state and private—but no federal—funding, the Erie example inspired other engineers and entrepreneurs to propose canal projects in other states. No canal project would approach the success of the Erie Canal, but builders tried. Some of the other canals built during the height of the canal era include the Pennsylvania Main Line Canal (1826–34), the Chesapeake and Ohio Canal (1828–50), the Lehigh Canal (1827–29), the Whitewater Canal (1836–43), and the Union Canal (1821–27).

Financing canal projects was a risky, complicated proposition. Usually canals were funded either by states or by private companies. States bore the brunt of costs in cases where canals were planned in newly developing areas without established industries. When canals were proposed along existing trade routes or centered on the transport of a single resource, private companies usually financed them. State-funded projects received land subsidies and other advantages but were the least successful ventures due to poor management or unsound construction. Privately funded canals were more profitable, since they were constructed to meet business needs, not to accommodate political objectives. Besides land subsidies, the other financing methods common in promoting canals included issuing stock, conducting lotteries, toll collecting on existing canals, local grants, and direct cash funding.

The success of the Erie Canal encouraged speculators and investors to believe that every canal project would be equally profitable. With the opening up of the Northwest to settlement, entrepreneurs and state boosters considered canal building the best way to capitalize on the abundant natural resources in new states like Ohio, Indiana, and Illinois. "Wildcat" bankers gambled on far-fetched projects, and gullible foreign investors were encouraged by the federal government to buy state bond issues in order to finance canal construction. These states were not as fiscally strong as the national government, and they were often unable to repay the enormous debts they took on to build canals. During the 1840s, four states defaulted on their canal debts: Indiana, Maryland, Pennsylvania, and Illinois. None of these projects combined the ingredients that made the Erie Canal prosper.

The construction and operation of canals required enormous manpower. Construction crews—many of them recent immigrants from Ireland and Germany—carved out the canals with only horsepower and blasting powder. Once constructed, canals required numerous specialized personnel, including lock tenders, maintenance people, ratters (to control the vermin population), level walkers, carpenters, and section bosses. Personnel on the canal boats usually consisted of a captain, mule or horse driver, and sometimes a night crew for around-the-clock operation.

People and goods traveled on canals in two different kinds of canal boats. Packet boats carried passengers and were drawn by horses. Before the railroad, packet travel was the fastest form of inland transportation available. Freight was transported by two different kinds of vessels: company boats and private boats. Company boats were more uniform in size and design and carried greater weight. Operated by the established industries along the canal route, these boats comprised a line distinguished by specific markings. Private boats were, as the name would indicate, individually owned and varied in size, capacity, and design. Freight boats were drawn by mules and thus slower than packets. Packet travel declined rapidly with the advent of railroads, but freight boats continued to operate profitably for considerably longer. Rail transportation eclipsed canals by the 1870s, offering a quicker, more versatile way to move people and commodities. The American canal system did not die out completely—in many coastal regions and along major rivers, canals still provide the most efficient method for shipping goods. While canals failed to become the national transportation network, the mania for canal building presaged many of the patterns visible in later efforts to build transportation infrastructure through railways and roads.

Further reading: Carter Goodrich, ed., *Canals and American Economic Development* (New York: Columbia University Press, 1961).

—Eleanor H. McConnell

The *Caroline* affair

On the night of December 29, 1837, Canadian militia operating under British command burned the U.S.-flagged steamer ship *Caroline*, which was moored in U.S. waters at the settlement of Fort Schlosser, New York, at Niagara Falls. The incursion briefly threatened to throw the United States and the British Empire into war.

In 1837 anticolonial uprisings had broken out in Lower Canada (now Quebec and vicinity), Upper Canada (now Ontario and vicinity), and the western British territories. The rebel "Patriots" (or *"Patriotes"* in the francophone sections) called for the establishment of independent republics and eventual annexation to the United States.

Seeking to nip the brewing revolution in the bud, the British had preemptively arrested the rebel leaders, forcing the Patriot volunteers into battle before they had organized as a militia. Consequently, the disorganized and poorly led Patriot army in Upper Canada had been routed almost from the moment the new republic was declared. The rebel leader, William Lyon MacKenzie, made a daring flight to safety in the United States, where sympathizers were already forming support organizations, called "Hunter's Lodges" along the Upper Canada border and *"Freres Chasseurs"* along Lower Canada, to help launch a guerrilla campaign. Arriving in Buffalo, New York, on December 11, 1837, MacKenzie was given a hero's welcome by the citizenry, many of whom immediately volunteered for his cause.

Having procured the use of the USS *Caroline* and a considerable arsenal from local law-enforcement and militia groups, MacKenzie established himself on Navy Island, lying between the Canadian and American shores just above Niagara Falls, and began to ferry arms, ammunition, and supplies to the republican guerrillas across the river. Two weeks later, loyalist units assaulted the island and burned the *Caroline* as it lay off the opposite shore. An American was killed in the assault, and when one of the loyalists, Alexander McLeod, was later arrested on the New York side of the river, he was criminally charged with murder and arson.

Great Britain, already enraged by the widespread participation of American citizens in the guerrilla attacks, threatened full-scale war. The British threat to widen and formalize the hostilities grew out of their belief that Canada was ultimately indefensible in the face of a sustained onslaught from the populous new American nation. The threat was intended to remind American officials that the British navy could still inflict vast damage on the already troubled American economy in retribution if Canada was lost.

For their part, President MARTIN VAN BUREN and his advisers were well aware that only last-minute American victories had turned humiliating defeat to honorable peace in the WAR OF 1812. Already struggling with the unprecedented economic crisis of the PANIC OF 1837, they had no desire for a costly rematch with their nemesis. Van Buren's administration applied increasing pressure on the local authorities along the northern border to disarm the Patriot armies and halt the smuggling of supplies. MacKenzie and other Patriot leaders were arrested and jailed for violation of the Neutrality Act. By the end of 1838, the Canadian revolution had been brutally crushed through the execution and deportation to Australia of rebels, including U.S. citizens.

The 1837–38 revolution prompted sweeping reforms in Canada, but their experience in the United States embittered MacKenzie and other Patriot leaders towards the republic they had previously idealized. A general pardon allowed them to return to Canada in 1849. Relations between the United States and Great Britain remained tense, however, and raw anger along the border fed the so-called AROOSTOCK WAR of 1838–39.

Further reading: Mary Beacock Fryer, *Volunteers and Redcoats, Rebels and Raiders: A Military History of the Rebellion in Upper Canada* (Toronto, Canada: University of Toronto Press, 1987); William Kilbourne, *Firebrand: William Lyon MacKenzie and the Rebellion in Upper Canada* (Toronto, Canada: General Publishing, 1977); Major L. Wilson, *The Presidency of Martin Van Buren* (Lawrence: University Press of Kansas, 1984).

—Dorothy Cummings

Carson, Kit (1809–1868)

Kit Carson was a frontier scout and Indian agent whose contributions to westward expansion made him a folk hero. Christopher (Kit) Carson was born in Madison, Kentucky, on December 24, 1809, and shortly thereafter moved with his family to Howard County, Missouri. He was almost bereft of education and functionally illiterate throughout his life. In 1824, while he was in his teens, Carson's father died, and the young Kit became apprenticed to a saddle maker. Finding the work distasteful, he ran away by joining a wagon train on the SANTA FE TRAIL in 1826. For three years, he worked as a teamster, interpreter, and cook, but in 1829 Carson accompanied Ewing Young on a fur-trapping expedition into the Southwest. The experience impressed him indelibly, and over the next 10 years Carson hunted, trapped, and roamed throughout the western interior. He took readily to such an arduous, adventurous lifestyle and eventually became renowned as a skilled, honest, yet soft-spoken frontiersmen. Also well known among the various Plains Indians, he successively took Arapaho and Cheyenne women as wives. Carson met his third and final wife, Maria Josepha Jaramilla, at Taos, New Mexico, where he was also baptized into the Roman Catholic Church. The dusty frontier community of Taos then became the beloved home to which he inevitably returned.

The defining moment in Carson's life occurred in 1842, when he had a chance encounter with Army explorer Lieutenant JOHN C. FRÉMONT, then headed west on an expedition to SOUTH PASS. The two men formed an abiding friendship, and Carson became employed as a scout. In 1843, he again assisted Frémont on a second expedition to the Rocky Mountains, and accompanied a third to CALIFORNIA in 1846. There Carson became caught up in the BEAR FLAG REVOLT against Mexico at Frémont's behest and also participated in the capture of Los Angeles and San Diego. In 1847, he was entrusted with carrying important dispatches back to Washington, D.C., but en route he ran into Brigadier General STEPHEN WATTS KEARNY. In need of an experienced guide, Kearney ordered Carson to accompany his column back to California, and he complied. He subsequently played a conspicuous role in the ill-fated, December 1847 Battle of San Pascual against mounted Californians, and he further distinguished himself by riding singlehandedly back to San Diego for reinforcements. Given this exemplary performance, President JAMES K. POLK proffered him a lieutenant's commission in the elite Mounted Rifles Regiment. However, the Senate obstructed his confirmation in an attempt to further embarrass Frémont, who was then being court-martialed over a dispute with Kearny.

Christopher "Kit" Carson *(Hulton/Archive)*

After the Mexican-American War, Carson returned to Taos and served as an Indian agent among the Ute, Pueblo, and Apache tribes. He functioned quietly and capably in this capacity and distinguished himself from many contemporaries by calling for better and fairer treatment of NATIVE AMERICANS. Shortly after the Civil War commenced in April 1861, Carson was commissioned colonel of the First New Mexico Volunteer Infantry. He skirmished with an invading Confederate column advancing from Texas and won plaudits for his handling of the Navajo crisis of 1863. When this large nation refused to move peacefully onto reservations, Carson was dispatched by General James H. Carlton to subdue them by force. This he accomplished by waging a scorched-earth policy that destroyed dwellings, crops, and livestock. Such harassment eventually drove the weary and half-frozen warriors onto the Bosque Redondo Reservation. However, when war erupted in the Texas panhandle, Carson further enhanced his reputation as a peerless Indian fighter by battling several thousand mounted warriors to a standstill at the Battle of Adobe Walls, November 1864. In light of such sterling service, Carson's final wartime rank was brevet brigadier general of volunteers.

After the war, Carson resigned his commission, resumed his Indian agent activity at Taos, and gained appointment as superintendent of Indian affairs for Colorado Territory. However, he had no sooner assumed that office than he died at Fort Lyon, Colorado, on May 23, 1868. Carson's remains were subsequently interred near his home at Taos. By this time, he was a legendary frontier figure, renowned for his honesty, humility, and sagacity. Carson's activities were also celebrated nationally, thanks to the various publications of Frémont, and he had proved supremely important to the exploration, conquest, and settlement of the far West. Short and physically nondescript, Carson was certainly among the most skilled frontiersmen of his generation, an icon whose reputation only increased with his passing. A river, a mountain pass, and the capital of Nevada perpetuate his memory.

Further reading: Thomas W. Dunlay, *Kit Carson and the Indians* (Lincoln: University of Nebraska Press, 2000); R. C. Gordon-McCutchan, ed., *Kit Carson: Indian Fighter or Killer* (Niwot: University Press of Colorado, 1996); Daniel Roberts, *A Newer World: Kit Carson, John C. Frémont, and the Claiming of the American West* (New York: Simon and Schuster, 2001).

—John C. Fredriksen

Cass, Lewis (1782–1866)

Lewis Cass's 54 years of public service spanned the tumultuous early to mid-19th century. Born in Exeter, New Hampshire, Cass emigrated to the Northwest Territory in 1801, where he studied law privately and was admitted to the bar in 1802. In 1806 he was elected to the Ohio legislature, where his staunch opposition to Aaron Burr's endeavors and strong support of President Thomas Jefferson resulted in his appointment by Jefferson as United States Marshal for the District of Ohio in 1807.

At the outbreak of the WAR OF 1812, Cass resigned his position as marshal to enlist in the army where he served as a colonel of the Third Infantry under the command of General WILLIAM HULL, a former Revolutionary War hero who was in command of Fort Detroit and who surrendered the fort to a much smaller British force without firing a shot. Cass was present at the surrender, wrote a report scathingly critical of Hull's performance, and testified against Hull at the court-martial proceedings. Hull was found guilty of treason and was sentenced to death by firing squad. Only his Revolutionary War service record allowed him to avoid execution.

Promoted to brigadier general in March 1813, Cass went on to be instrumental in the American victory at the BATTLE OF THE THAMES the following year. Cass's distinguished military service, as well as his Jeffersonian political views, resulted in his appointment as military and civil governor of Michigan Territory, a post he would hold until 1831. During his tenure, Cass secured the territory around the Great Lakes, improved the territory's infrastructure, and negotiated treaties with the Chippewa and other Native American nations.

Cass's experience in dealing with the NATIVE AMERICANS of the Northwest Territory and his ideas about the "Indian Question" were instrumental in his appointment by President ANDREW JACKSON as secretary of war in 1831. Cass was at the forefront of formulating government policy regarding Native Americans, and he was a central figure in promoting their removal as a general policy during his tenures as governor and as secretary of war.

In 1836 Cass resigned from the cabinet when Jackson appointed him to a diplomatic post, envoy extraordinary and minister plenipotentiary to France. He served in this capacity until 1842. While Cass was successful in many of his diplomatic endeavors regarding American and French relations, he was often at odds with the Jackson administration because of his outspoken anti-British views. Such negative public rhetoric led to a serious disagreement with Secretary of State DANIEL WEBSTER and prompted Cass's resignation in 1842.

Returning to Detroit, Michigan, Cass decided to reenter public service. He was easily elected to the U.S. Senate in 1845, but resigned his seat when he received the presidential nomination of the DEMOCRATIC PARTY in 1848. The nominating conventions and presidential election of 1848 reflected the divisiveness of the nation over the issue of the expansion of SLAVERY. Cass favored letting the residents of territories decide for themselves whether they wanted slavery—a concept that he termed POPULAR SOVEREIGNTY. That did not sit well with southern Democrats, who wanted the areas acquired as a result of the MEXICAN-AMERICAN WAR to allow slavery. The WHIGS nominated Mexican War hero ZACHARY TAYLOR. His long military record would appeal to northerners; his ownership of slaves would lure southern votes. Taylor would not commit himself on the issue of Congress's power over slavery in the territories.

A third party, the FREE-SOIL PARTY, made its debut in 1848. Formed by New York Democrats who unequivocally opposed the extension of slavery into the new territories, the Free-Soilers nominated former president MARTIN VAN BUREN. The Free-Soil platform appealed to antislavery Whigs and northern Democrats, and Van Buren won more than 10 percent of the national vote. In New York, he won more than 120,000 votes—votes that otherwise would have been cast, largely, for Cass. This effectively gave Taylor New York's electoral votes.

After his unsuccessful bid for the presidency, Cass returned to the U.S. Senate, serving there until 1857, when President James Buchanan named him secretary of state. As a senator, Lewis Cass was a strong advocate of compromise, and worked diligently for passage of the COMPROMISE OF 1850. However, after joining the Buchanan cabinet as secretary of state, Cass became convinced that stronger measures were necessary. When President Buchanan refused to fortify Fort Sumter and other federal garrisons as the South began to threaten disunion, Cass resigned from the cabinet. He retired to his home in Detroit, where he spent his last years writing and where he died on June 17, 1866.

Further reading: Willard C. Klunder, *Lewis Cass and the Politics of Moderation* (Kent, Ohio: Kent State University Press, 1996); Frank B. Woodford, *Lewis Cass: The Last Jeffersonian* (New Brunswick, N.J.: Rutgers University Press, 1950; New York: Octagon Books, 1973).

—Richard L. Friedline

Catlin, George (1796–1872)

Best known for his paintings of NATIVE AMERICANS and Western scenes—the first American artist to focus on these subjects—George Catlin was born in Wilkes-Barre, Pennsylvania, in 1796. His interest in Native American cultures can be partially traced to his family experiences. Catlin's mother, Polly Sutton Catlin, was captured by Indians as a child. He learned about Indian ways from her and from the visitors to the Catlin home during his childhood: trappers, traders, and soldiers who had dealings with the Indian of the trans-Appalachian region. Although Catlin received little formal education, he learned hunting, fishing, and other skills necessary for life in rural Pennsylvania. He was always interested in exploring nature and collected Indians artifacts on his outings.

In 1817 Catlin went to Litchfield, Connecticut, to study law in the offices of the well-known jurist Tapping Reeve. While in Litchfield, he began to make a name for himself as an amateur artist, painting mostly portraits of political figures. After finishing his studies in 1818, he practiced law in Luzerne, Pennsylvania, until 1823. He then moved to Philadelphia, determined to paint professionally. He studied painting at the Pennsylvania Academy of Fine Arts and at the National Academy of Design in New York. For the next few years, he earned his living by painting portraits, many of prominent figures such as New York governor DeWitt Clinton and former First Lady Dolly Madison. From 1824 to 1829 he spent most of his time in Washington, D.C., painting political figures. In 1828 he married Clara B. Gregory in Albany, New York. She was supportive of his career and joined him on many of his later journeys to the West.

During his time in Philadelphia, Catlin encountered Indian chieftains who visited Charles Willson Peale's famous American Museum. The young artist was enthralled with these Native Americans and the cultural artifacts they brought with them. Believing that the Indians and their ways of life were declining, he decided to use his artistic abilities to document their vanishing culture for posterity. He began by painting Indians on reservations in western New York, and then traveled to the Ohio River and Mississippi River regions. Catlin's premonition that he was documenting an endangered culture was perceptive. As European-American settlement moved further west, demand for Indian lands increased, and thus the trans-Appalachian Indians were forced further west onto reservations. The decline of the fur trade and the spread of disease also threatened their cultural stability. Catlin's paintings depict a conflicted, chaotic time for these displaced nations as they struggled to maintain their cultural practices and economic viability.

From 1830 to 1836 he spent his summers following various Indian nations; in winter, he would return to the East to paint what he had seen and to raise money so he could return to the West. One of his most important early works was his moving portrait of the aging Shawnee Prophet, Tenskwatawa (brother of Tecumseh), painted in 1830. Also that year, Catlin met explorer William Clark, then the superintendent of Indian affairs at St. Louis. He accompanied Clark on a trip to solidify Indian treaties. During the journey, he painted Iowa, Missouria, Otoe, Omaha, Sauk and Fox, and Sioux Indians. In 1832 he traveled up the Missouri on the *Yellow Stone*. Owned by the *American Fur Company*, this steamboat was the first to reach Fort Union at the mouth of the Yellowstone River. By traveling to this remote territory, Catlin was able to depict nations not previously familiar to Americans in the East and Europeans, such as the Blackfeet, Crow, Plains Cree, Mandan, and Yankton Sioux. He continued to travel further west, journeying to Pawnee and Comanche country in 1834 and becoming the first non-Indian to see the red stone quarry in southwestern Minnesota. The distinctive red stone, used by many tribes to make pipes, was later named Catlinite in his honor.

During the 1830s Catlin painted over 500 portraits of Indian men and women in native dress. He also painted scenes of Indian villages, religious ceremonies, games, and legends. From 1837 to 1852 he lectured and exhibited his paintings in the United States and Europe. Called "Catlin's Indian Gallery," this exhibition was a success in other countries but not particularly well received in America. In an attempt to ease his financial woes, he offered to sell his collection of Indian paintings to Congress in 1852 but was refused. Instead, he borrowed money from Joseph Harrison of Philadelphia, who took the collection as collateral. Catlin was never able to recover the paintings, but Joseph Harrison's family eventually donated the collection to the United States National Museum.

After 1852, Catlin continued to paint and write about his experiences with Indians. His most important early writings were published in a series of accounts, "Notes of Eight Years Travel Amongst the North American Indians," in the New York *Daily Commercial Advertizer* from 1830 to 1839. Other works include: *Letters and Notes on the Manners, Customs, and Condition of the North American Indians* (1841); *Catlin's North American Indian Portfolio: Hunting, Rocky Mountains and Prairies of America* (1845); *Catlin's Notes of Eight Years' Travels and Residence in Europe* (1848); and *Life Among the Indians* (1867). In later years, he traveled among and depicted the Indians of South America as well, writing *Last Rambles Amongst the Indians of the Rocky Mountains and the Andes* (1868).

Catlin's paintings of Indian life are important because he captured a disappearing way of life, depicting Indians specifically and candidly. He respected his Indian subjects and worked tirelessly to educate whites about their culture. His works provide valuable records of nations that did not survive contact with Europeans. His documentation of the Mandan of the upper Missouri was particularly important, since they were practically wiped out by smallpox in 1837. Most respected for his descriptive powers, he was less concerned with technical accuracy in perspective. Thus, his paintings evoke historically significant figures and themes, not classical aesthetic concerns. Most of his works are now owned by the Smithsonian Institution in Washington, D.C.; the Joslyn Art Museum in Omaha; and the American Museum of Natural History in New York.

George Catlin died in Jersey City, New Jersey, in 1872. Although he was financially unsuccessful and received only little recognition during his lifetime, he is now considered one of the most important and original American artists of the 19th century. As he had intended, Catlin's works have visually preserved the vital Indian cultures that were forever transformed by the American expansion to the West.

Further reading: George Catlin, *The George Catlin Book of American Indians* (New York: Watson-Guptill, 1977); William H. Truettner, *The Natural Man Observed: A Study of Catlin's Indian Gallery* (Washington, D.C.: Smithsonian Institution Press, 1979).

—Eleanor H. McConnell

Chouteau family

The Chouteaus were successful businessmen on the American frontier, facilitating the lucrative FUR TRADE between Indians (particularly the Osage), white Americans, and Europeans for nearly a century. They were also influential in the development of St. Louis and the surrounding region, acting as bankers, land speculators, public officials, and governmental advisers for the frontier settlement. Originally from New Orleans, René Auguste Chouteau (1749–1829) began his life as a trader at age 14, working for his stepfather, fur trader Pierre Laclede. In 1764 he helped establish a fur-trading post and fort near the confluence of the Mississippi and Missouri Rivers, the area now known as St. Louis. He became Laclede's partner in 1768 and acquired principal ownership after his stepfather's death in 1778. In the late 18th century the Chouteau company monopolized trade with the Osage and would continue to be closely connected to their interests for the next half-century. René Auguste also acted as a diplomat to the Osage from the Spanish government during the years they controlled the Louisiana area. In 1809, he became the chairman of the board of trustees in the newly incorporated town of St. Louis. He also represented the United States in various treaty negotiations with Indians in the Louisiana Territory.

Jean Pierre Chouteau (1758–1849) joined his brother René Auguste's enterprise and established a trading post at Salina, Oklahoma, in 1802. He was appointed as U.S. Indian agent for the upper Louisiana region by President Thomas Jefferson in 1804. In this role, he mediated relations between whites and Indians, helping to keep the peace by negotiating trade between these groups. Because trade was encouraged as the way to maintain peace, some accused Jean Pierre of taking advantage of his position as both a trader and a government agent to advance his own commercial interests. Whatever his motive, Jean Pierre's diplomatic efforts among the Osage helped secure that nation's loyalty during the WAR OF 1812 and saved St. Louis from direct attack. Asked to leave his position as agent in 1818, he returned to the family's trading business in Salina, occasionally advising the U.S. government about Indian affairs.

Jean Pierre's eldest son, Auguste Pierre Chouteau (1786–1838) was born in St. Louis. He attended the U.S. Military Academy at West Point (he was nominated by Meriwether Lewis), after which he joined the family business. He was also instrumental in founding the St. Louis-based MISSOURI FUR COMPANY, along with his father Jean Pierre, William Clark, Manuel Lisa, and others. He served in the War of 1812 as a captain of the territorial militia. After the conflict, Auguste Pierre continued to expand his family's trading empire by extending trade relations to the southern Arapaho and to fur traders in the Rocky Mountains. He also acted as a government representative, helping to mediate treaties between the United States and the Kiowa and Comanche from 1834 to 1838.

Jean Pierre's younger son, Pierre Chouteau, Jr. (1789–1865), was also born in St. Louis, and entered the family business in 1805. He later became an agent for JOHN JACOB ASTOR's AMERICAN FUR COMPANY and eventually bought the Missouri River interests of the company from Astor in 1834. In 1838 he started the highly successful Pierre Chouteau, Jr., and Company, which traded over the vast region between the Mississippi River and the Rocky Mountains until about 1865. He became the most powerful financier in the West in the years immediately preceding the Civil War. He spent his final years in New York as a wealthy fur trader and as an investor in newer western endeavors such as mining and railroads.

As clever and cosmopolitan entrepreneurs, the Chouteaus played a major part in shaping the development of the trans-Mississippi West before 1865. While their private business ventures thrived in this new market, they also acted as public leaders, mediating relations among France, Spain, Great Britain, the United States, and Native Americans in this contested region.

Further reading: William E. Foley and C. David Rice, *The First Chouteaus: River Barons of Early St. Louis* (Urbana: University of Illinois Press, 2000).

—Eleanor H. McConnell

Church of Jesus Christ of Latter-day Saints

The Church of Jesus Christ of Latter-day Saints (more commonly known as the Mormon Church) was organized by JOSEPH SMITH, JR., in 1830 in Fayette, New York. In 1820, according to his own account, Smith received a direct revelation in the form of God the Father and his son, Jesus Christ, who anointed Smith a prophet, through whom the new church of Christ would be restored on earth. In later revelations, an angel named Moroni gave Smith the location of Golden Plates and the means to translate them. Smith completed the translation of the Book of Mormon from the plates in 1829. With its publication in 1830, Smith incorporated his church under New York law and began to preach his gospel to all who would listen to him.

The history of the church under its founder and first prophet, Joseph Smith, falls into three divisions. In the first, the church was located in Kirtland, Ohio, south and east of Cleveland, where Smith moved his headquarters after one of his disciples converted a congregation there. The Kirtland community of Saints grew rapidly, and Smith laid plans to erect the first church temple. Completed in 1836, the temple became the center of new religious ceremonies received by Smith in divine revelations. The church and its leaders were part of the prosperity associated with the time and place, and to take further advantage, Smith sought to establish a bank. His application denied, the bank went into operation anyway. When the PANIC OF 1837 brought chaos to the state banking system, the Kirtland Anti-Banking Society Bank collapsed, along with most of the other local banks. This failure intensified divisions within the church, based in part on the rumors that Smith had sanctioned POLYGAMY (plural wives) as a part of church doctrine. Some members of the church left, and Smith and his loyal followers left Kirtland and moved to Mormon settlements in Missouri.

The Mormon community in Missouri dated from a missionary enterprise of the early 1830s, which had gone west to convert Indians. The centers of Mormon settlements were originally in Jackson County, north of Kansas City, and later farther north in Ray County. The sudden growth of the Mormon community by the influx from Kirtland began a period of expansion. Tensions with the surrounding population eventually developed, centering around the Mormons' growth and prosperity, their strong sense of group loyalty, their sympathy toward slaves, and their belligerence in defending what they thought of as their rights. As their neighbors began armed raids against outlying Mormon settlements, church leaders responded by organizing a paramilitary group known as the Sons of Dan, or the Danites. The attacks on the Mormons grew to include armed raids, arson, and murder. The Mormons responded in kind to what they saw as unprovoked aggression and the failure of the civil legal system to protect them.

The governor of Missouri, Lillburn W. Boggs, called out the militia. Believing that the Mormons were an undisciplined mob of religious fanatics, Boggs ordered them to leave Missouri or face extermination. Smith realized that his followers, however loyal and disciplined, stood no chance in conflict with a militia that had unlimited numbers and artillery, and he ordered the surrender of the church. He and other church leaders were imprisoned for several months without formal charges, while the members of the church were driven from the state. After six months in prison, Smith and the church leaders were permitted to leave the state of Missouri.

The third site of the Mormon community was a town on the Mississippi River north of Quincy, Illinois. Church leaders purchased the site in 1839, and Smith changed the name of the town from Commerce to NAUVOO, which he said derived from the Hebrew word for "beautiful." The new Mormon settlements came to embody the church's continuing growth and Smith's search for security in what seemed a perpetually hostile world.

As the Mormon settlements grew, enlarged by natural increase and the arrival of Mormon converts from England, the population swelled from 1,000 in 1839 to more than 10,000 in 1844. By 1845, Nauvoo was one of the largest cities in Illinois. In addition to economic prosperity, these numbers gave Smith a degree of political power. With the Whigs and Democrats evenly balanced within the state, he used the voting bloc of the Mormons to bargain for the security of the church community. The state legislature voted the Mormon community a special charter, the so-called Nauvoo Charter, which seemed to give the community, its city, and its leaders special privileges and rights. These rights included a university, founded in 1844 although never actually organized. Smith was elected mayor of Nauvoo in 1842, and the governor of Illinois appointed him a lieutenant general in the state militia. With state arms, Smith enrolled and trained the Nauvoo Legion, a carefully selected body of men whose training, discipline, and zeal was reassuring to members of the church community and threatening to outsiders. This series of events culminated in spring 1844, when Smith announced himself a candidate for president of the United States.

As the community grew in numbers and political and military power, Smith's revelations brought new theological directions for the church. Among these were the baptism of the dead, so that all might have the benefit of a church baptism. In conjunction with these revelations, Smith ordered the construction of a temple. Amidst distinctive religious rituals that became part of the church doctrine, rumors again circulated that church leaders sanctioned and, indeed, practiced polygamy. These rumors generated a strong degree of dissent within the church itself.

In spring 1844, a group of estranged members of the church published a single issue of a newspaper that exposed polygamy and other practices by church leaders. Smith called a special meeting of the town council, declared the newspaper and its press a public nuisance, and ordered the press destroyed. The dissident leaders sought refuge outside the Mormon settlements and charged Smith with arson. After his safety was guaranteed by the governor, Smith surrendered and was imprisoned with other church leaders at Carthage, where he was to stand trial. On June 27, 1844, a mob broke into the jail and shot Smith and his brother Hyrum. The death of the church's founder and prophet closed the first crucial period in the church's history.

Among the leaders who sought to follow Joseph Smith as the church's leader, BRIGHAM YOUNG was the logical choice. He took charge of a community in mourning over the death of their founder and prophet, divided internally over the issue of polygamy, and under physical assault from the outside. As soon as he received the sanction of the Quorum of the Twelve Apostles (a committee of senior Mormon leaders), Young displayed the remarkable qualities of leadership that he would bring to the church over the next 30 years. He first sought a truce to stave off further mob violence and attempted to negotiate an orderly departure of the church from Nauvoo, but he was only partially successful. Even as he and other church leaders prepared for an emigration to the West, the Mormon settlements in Nauvoo were under attack from the surrounding countryside. Invading mobs burned homes and pillaged what they did not burn. In winter 1846, the Mormons fled across the river and headed west to a new and as yet undisclosed location.

After crossing the state of Iowa, the Mormon migration paused for a year in Winter Quarters (near Omaha, Nebraska). Here, Young and other leaders prepared the organization of a large encampment of church members near Omaha and began to lay plans for an emigration of the church into the distant Inter-Mountain West.

The first wagon company, led by Young himself, departed Winter Quarters in the spring of 1847 and reached the Valley of the Great Salt Lake in July 1847. Here, Young declared that the valley was to become the site of the future City of Zion. What followed was the systematic immigration of the church from Winter Quarters to the Valley of the Great Salt Lake, a process that lasted two years. Even then, later emigrations across the plains (some in the form of "hand cart brigades") took place for another decade.

Within what was to become the state of Utah (although Young initially called it the STATE OF DESERET), Young systematically organized the Saints into a theocracy that controlled land, water, and other natural resources. When the federal government organized Utah Territory in 1850, Young was appointed governor. However, the federal judges appointed to the territorial court were non-Mormons, and they feared the theocracy that surrounded them. The hostility against the Mormons received fresh impetus in 1852 with the announcement that polygamy, practiced in secret by certain church leaders, was indeed a fundamental belief and practice within the church.

The open avowal of polygamy began a half-century of conflict and hostility between the church and the rest of the nation. Mormons saw the practice as a normal custom and their right as a chosen people headed by a farsighted prophet, seer, and revelator. To non-Mormons, the practice of plural wives was a violation of every tenet held by 19th-century America.

The sense of the Mormons as living in violation of the laws of the nation reached its climax in 1857, when President James Buchanan dispatched units of the U.S. Army to Utah to suppress what he regarded as a rebellion. At the same time, he removed Young as governor of the territory. Aware of the impending arrival of federal troops, the Mormon community began defensive preparations for an armed conflict. In this tense climate, Mormons and Indians attacked a wagon train at Mountain Meadows in southwest Utah. Some 120 men, women, and children died in what came to be called "The Mountain Meadows Massacre." Young, who had originally ordered the wagon trains to pass in safety, did little to bring the perpetrators to justice, preferring loyalty to the church to a public exposure of the church members involved in the attack. Twenty years later, the federal government tried and executed John D. Lee, a Mormon leader and Indian agent, for the crime.

The federal army occupied parts of Utah, in what historians call the Utah War. Young decided not to oppose the invading expedition by force. Instead, he burned forts and towns and destroyed crops in hopes of delaying the army's advance. Eventually, the two sides reached a degree of mutual accommodation. In 1858, the federal government pardoned Young for offenses, and the army gradually retired, with the last of the forces leaving Utah on the outbreak of the Civil War.

The rest of the nation now turned its attention to the great war that divided it, and Young and the Mormon community turned their attention to growth and consolidation. Missionary efforts, an integral part of the church since its founding, revived and expanded. Converts from the East and from Europe (especially Great Britain) poured into Utah, whose church settlement had expanded across hundreds of miles, as far distant as Arizona and Nevada. When Brigham Young died in 1877, Utah's population was 145,000, almost all members of the church community. In this prolonged period of independence, the institution of polygamy developed without internal or external opposition to become an accepted part of the church.

Mormon economic affairs also prospered. The agricultural enterprises associated with arable land irrigation grew and expanded, viewed throughout as arms of the church. Economic activity at all levels revolved around the church and church leaders. The joining of the Union Pacific and Central Pacific Railroads at Promontory Point, Utah, in 1869, ended Utah's isolation from the rest of the nation. Thereafter, groups in Congress and the federal government were to launch a growing campaign of restrictive legislation against the church. These acts and court decisions against polygamy and the Mormon economic domination of the territory led to a series of compromises and Utah's eventual admission to the Union in 1896.

Further reading: Leonard J. Arrington, *Great Basin Kingdom: An Economic History of the Latter-Day Saints, 1830–1900* (Cambridge, Mass.: Harvard University Press, 1958); Jan L. Shipps, *Mormonism: The Story of a New Religious Tradition* (Urbana: University of Illinois Press, 1985).

cities and urban life

During the first half of the 19th century, American cities differed substantially from their European counterparts. The process had begun long before, when the cities were planned without the protective walls, highly structured street systems, or charters that characterized European cities. Instead, 19th-century American cities developed as independent entities. The differences intensified as U.S. cities transformed themselves from trade and commerce centers with limited populations to ever-expanding arenas of public services, economic growth, and fluid populations that reflected the influx of foreign and rural immigrants.

For the first years of the 19th century, the urban population of the United States remained relatively stable. Cities such as Boston, New York, Philadelphia, and Baltimore were, as they had been since colonial days, East Coast port cities situated on major waterways with populations of under 100,000. They generated their commerce by shipping raw materials to European countries and receiving their manufactured goods in return.

But beginning in the 1820s, U.S. cities experienced unbroken growth that would last for a century. In large part, the source of this increase was large-scale immigration. By the mid-19th century, 5 million Irish, German, English, and other Europeans entered the United States. Between 1820 and 1850 alone, the combined population of Baltimore, Boston, New York, and Philadelphia climbed to 1.2 million people. Moreover, western cities such as Pittsburgh marked an inland urban expansion and the population of urban areas overall increased as towns with populations of 8,000 or more grew by 36 percent. Between 1830 and 1840, the total urban population grew from 0.9 million to 1.5 million people, and by 1850, close to 15 percent of all Americans lived in urban areas.

An early fixture of 19th-century U.S. urban life was industrialization, seen initially in the adaptation of steam power for mechanical use. By mid-century, the power used to drive steamboats 30 years earlier was running factory machines. This development freed business owners from situating factories along abundant water supplies. Instead, industries could follow the population and be established near popular transportation hubs.

Technological advances helped to transform city transportation and extend the city's geographic reach. They opened the city beyond the bounds of those who could walk within it to include anyone served by a public transport system. To move the growing numbers of residents living far away from work and entertainment, inventions such as the horse-drawn omnibus and trolley became popular. Introduced in the 1830s, the omnibus was a horse-drawn roofed wagon that carried over two dozen riders. More successful as public transportation was the horse-drawn trolley, a conveyance holding dozens of riders that ran along railroad tracks installed flush with the street. So well-fitted to city life were trolleys that they remained in service into the mid-20th century.

From the late 1820s, railroads served an increasingly important role in providing inter- and extraurban transportation. They linked cities and towns across the United States, and as the century progressed, cities devoted considerable funds to their creation. In many cities, railroad construction was underwritten by transportation bonds. Other forms of transportation were less well advanced. Plank walkways were only occasionally available for pedestrians; roads were unpaved.

Advanced technology and necessity were combined to develop urban commercial and residential housing. To accommodate increasing urban industry in limited city space, architects and city planners tried to find ways to build upward. In the late 1840s, inventor James Bogardus developed a cast-iron support process for buildings; by the 1850s, this form of columnar support allowed for the construction of multistory buildings. Elevators would also lead to the increased construction of multistory buildings. Once inventor Elisha Otis had improved their design to incorporate safety features, elevators became particularly useful to construction in the 1850s and afterward.

Such advanced housing was unavailable for most mid-19th century urban dwellers. Instead, one- and two-story buildings, divided into small apartments, provided much of the housing. Inadequate in size and number for the many thousands of new city dwellers, these low-rise apartment houses resulted in severe overcrowding. Several dozen people might share a room meant for a few, and all parts of a building were used for shelter. In New York City in 1850, over 28,000 people lived in cellars. In response to the public-health risk posed by apartment overcrowding, some cities passed reform legislation. An early New York law was passed in 1860, mandating that apartment buildings have fire escapes.

Information exchange became increasingly important to maintaining order within a city, and it was achieved in large part through the large-circulation penny paper. While at the beginning of the 19th century, newspapers were primarily six-cent periodicals underwritten by a political party and sold by annual subscription, the penny paper was sold on the streets by newsboys and was supported by commercial advertising. Unlike its predecessors, the penny paper often declined to promote political ideologies and attempted objectivity and up-to-date reporting of events. The combination of news and objectivity proved highly popular among immigrants, laborers, and the middle class, resulting in an increase in the number of daily and weekly penny papers from 715 to 1,279 between 1830 and 1840 alone. Notable penny papers included the *New York Herald, New York Sun,* and *Baltimore Sun.*

For profit, prestige, and civic-mindedness, cities supported various types of entertainment, including libraries, theaters, concert halls, and outdoor entertainment palaces, which were very popular. Impresarios such as P. T. Barnum imported European artists, such as operatic singer Jenny (the "Swedish Nightingale") Lind for U.S. tours. Such displays of high artistic enjoyment increased the overall perception of the United States as an increasingly sophisticated nation.

While 19th-century cities improved their stature by attending to their arts and industries, they also faced wide-ranging and daunting problems of public health. For example, the average New York street was overrun with swine and manure; a former New York mayor called the city a "pigsty." Disease was also a major problem. With tens of thousands of people sharing the same water supply and refuse system, and ships from across the world arriving daily at port cities, contagious diseases spread quickly. A cholera epidemic occurred in New York City and Newark (New Jersey), Cleveland, Chicago, and other cities in 1832; in 1849, another cholera epidemic occurred when the disease spread from New Orleans to St. Louis and through the middle and eastern United States. Other epidemics during the period included smallpox and cerebral meningitis.

Establishing public services to alleviate these problems became a major concern for 19th-century cities. Eighteenth-century cities had distributed funds for basic uses such as street and public building maintenance and as alms to the poor, but the more diverse and populous 19th-century city required a broader range of services. Among them were schools, public works, transportation, public health services, and government administration.

For example, creating a waterworks for a city was a primary, extensive endeavor. The New York tunnel system, which extended 50 miles to the upstate Croton reservoir, took several years to build, from 1835 to 1842. Dozens of citywide water systems were built by the end of the 1850s. Funding them, as well as other public works projects, sometimes involved federal, state, and city government

Broadway in New York City, 1855 *(Hulton/Archive)*

funds. In one successful partnership, the U.S. Army and city governments cofunded various harbor and river projects, such as the Chesapeake and Ohio Canal in the mid-Atlantic region.

Similarly, crime-control units began to be expanded and developed during the mid-19th century. They were transformed from plainclothes night-watch groups into uniformed police departments. In addition, they were now designed to take a more active role than they had in the 18th century. Instead of simply responding to crimes, the 19th-century police force was expected to uncover and prevent crime. New York City became the first to have a department of regularly uniformed policemen in 1856. Similarly, government-controlled fire-fighting departments were being developed, if not yet implemented, during the mid-19th century. Created in part to replace the various groups of volunteers and private subscription companies, some of whom belonged to warring ethnic groups and gangs, the forces were also established to provide fire coverage to property owners and businesses.

Providing citywide public education was another concern for mid-19th century cities. Because cities such as New York had a large percentage of foreign-born students, educators and public policy planners viewed public education as vital to developing an able workforce and patriotic citizenry. As common school reformers like HORACE MANN and Catharine Beecher viewed it, schooling was both practical and idealistic. It would prepare U.S. citizens for an increasingly industrialized society and would decrease social unrest.

City planners and members of government viewed the need for such public works—for water, transportation, housing, crime control, EDUCATION—as crucial. Their thinking led to the transformation of city government into an active force. While at the beginning of the 19th century, city government depended on regulations to be devised as problems arose, the mid- to late-century city was marked by active government involvement, including civic promotion, health campaigns, and financial incentives. In the years after the Civil War, city governments would become more responsive, even as they fell under the control of corrupt political bosses.

To finance the increasingly expensive city, legislators in the 19th century granted cities the power to levy taxes. Property taxes became a major source of city funds; other sources included fees, fines, and property sales. Western cities also financed themselves by issuing bonds to established European countries or eastern U.S. cities, while some new cities and villages were formed through a process of general incorporation. A popular entrepreneurial effort, incorporation of a city, allowed founders to seek private investments and government loans.

As the 19th century reached its midpoint, some changes in cities were evident. New York City, with its favorable coastal position, large harbor, and proximity to the Hudson River was the commercial and information center of the East Coast, surpassing larger, 18th-century rival Philadelphia. In the Midwest, the dominant city of 1840 was St. Louis, with its central frontier location and population of 16,469. During the 1860s, it would be challenged and eventually overtaken by the port-and-market center city of Chicago, whose population would increase 60-fold between 1840 and 1870. Although southern cities did experience some effects of industrialization and increased immigrant population, they grew at slower rates. Important 19th-century southern cities included Birmingham, Memphis, and New Orleans.

In 1853 the nation's largest city hosted its largest promotional event, the New York Crystal Palace Exhibition. Modeled on London's 1851 Crystal Palace Exhibition, it was meant to mark New York's status as a cosmopolitan center on a par with London and promote the nation's industrial accomplishments and public entertainments. Although it lasted for more than two months, attracted a million visitors, and collected over $330,000, it was considered a failure by its promoters, lacking the international representation and prestige of London's Crystal Palace exhibition of 1851.

The fair may have been considered a disaster, but its size, examples of industry, and mass of people reflected the complexities of the contemporary U.S. city. Throughout the 19th century, U.S. cities would grow in size and population, become repositories and generators of American inventions such as the elevator and telegraph, and become home to industries such as steelmaking and textiles. Public entertainments would develop, and U.S. cities would continue to showcase themselves at even more elaborate expositions like the Centennial Exposition of 1876 and the World's Fair of 1904. Although in 1860, 80 percent of Americans still lived in farms or villages, the move toward widespread urban life was well underway.

Further reading: Christopher Collier and James Lincoln Collier, *The Rise of the Cities: 1820–1920* (New York: Benchmark Books, 2001); David Freeman Hawke, *Nuts and Bolts of the Past: A History of American Technology 1776–1860* (New York: Harper & Row, 1988); Eric H. Monkkonen, *America Becomes Urban: The Development of U.S. Cities & Towns 1780–1980* (Berkeley: University of California Press, 1988).

—Melinda Corey

Claiborne, William C. C. (1775–1817)

A territorial official and the first governor of the state of Louisiana, William Charles Coles Claiborne helped to bring the Louisiana Territory into the Union. Descended from an old Virginia family, Claiborne was born in Sussex, Virginia, in 1775. Through his family connections, he was appointed at the age of 15 as a clerk to Congress and soon thereafter began to study law. He later moved to Sullivan County, Tennessee, where he established a legal practice. Like many lawyers on the frontier, Claiborne gravitated to politics, and when Tennessee (territory southwest of the Ohio) sought admission to the Union, he was a member of the constitutional convention. After Tennessee became a state in 1796, he was appointed to the state supreme court. While serving on this court, he was elected to the U.S. House of Representatives to fill out ANDREW JACKSON's term. Although Claiborne was not yet 25 years old and thus ineligible to serve in the House of Representatives, he nonetheless took his seat. In 1798 his constituents reelected him to the House.

In Congress, Claiborne headed the committee to investigate charges made against Governor Winthrop Sargent of Mississippi Territory. Residents of the territory had petitioned that the territory be advanced to the second stage, which would permit them to elect a legislature and send a nonvoting delegate to Congress. Claiborne's committee's report supported the petitioners. When the presidential election of 1800 ended in a tie between Thomas Jefferson and Aaron Burr, the decision was thrown into the House of Representatives. Claiborne voted for Jefferson, and his reward was an appointment as governor of the Mississippi Territory, succeeding Winthrop Sargent.

During his two years as governor, Claiborne demonstrated his political skills. He supervised the first elections in the territory and was remarkably successful in reducing the bitter political partisanship that was characteristic of Mississippi and other territories. The achievement was all the more remarkable since Claiborne had arrived as an outsider. When Jefferson bought Louisiana in 1803, Congress soon established the Territory of Orleans, and the president made Claiborne governor of the new territory. It was an important appointment, for he was representative of the national governor to a political and social community that was generally not happy about coming under U.S. sovereignty.

Claiborne's early years in New Orleans were difficult, given that he was the representative of an alien government and he spoke no French. The president and Congress had chosen to give Louisianians a minimal share of self-government out of concern for the loyalty of the new region, and their actions made Claiborne's position even more difficult. The new government also imposed English as an official language and the English common law on the court system. Furthermore, the rigid enforcement of the customs duties after years of lax Spanish administration further angered the New Orleans trading community. However, Claiborne gradually won the trust of the citizens of New Orleans and the Territory of Orleans. He also married into a Louisiana family and learned French. When Congress admitted the Territory of Orleans to the Union as the new state of Louisiana in 1812, Claiborne was elected its first governor.

Claiborne was a political leader of consummate personal skills. Even as an outsider in the territories of Mississippi and Orleans, he laid the foundation of trust and compromise. Yet the turmoil of the frontier at the opening of the 19th century demanded more aggressive solutions on certain occasions. Claiborne's first encounter with such new challenges was the behavior of General James Wilkinson and former vice president Aaron Burr in the series of events that would become known as Burr's Conspiracy. Claiborne's responses were slow and indecisive. The same difficulties reemerged a decade later during the threatened siege of New Orleans by the British in late 1814 during the WAR OF 1812. Claiborne's slow response to a British invasion force infuriated General ANDREW JACKSON and other American military leaders. Throughout these mishaps, Claiborne retained the loyalty and support of Louisianans. In 1817, at the close of his term as governor, the legislature of the state of Louisiana elected him to the U.S. Senate, but he died that year before he could take office.

Further reading: Clarence E. Carter, ed., *Territorial Papers of the United States,* Vol. 10, *Territory of Orleans* (Washington, D.C.: Government Printing Office, 1934–59).

claim clubs

In the early decades of the 19th century, settlers who arrived in western lands (what is now the Middle West) ahead of government land offices established claim clubs, makeshift associations also known as claim associations or squatter courts, to protect themselves and provide order on the frontier. Each club usually assumed authority over an area the size of a township, settling disputes over land rights and, when no officers were present, enforcing general matters of law and order.

Although these clubs were not, strictly speaking, legal entities, they proceeded as though they were sanctioned. By meeting, electing officers, and often forming constitutions, the clubs tried to reproduce political structures from settled regions of the United States. They grew out of the settlers' desire to protect their claims from the intrusions of other unofficial settlers and, especially, from wealthy speculators. Before the Preemption Act of 1841, anyone squatting on land prior to its public sale could be ejected by speculators. After the law was passed, squatting on surveyed lands was legal, and the squatter had the right to preempt his claim before public sale, thus circumventing the bidding power of the speculators. This law did not solve squatters' problems with speculators completely, since many would-be claimants who wanted to preempt their claims lacked the funds to pay for the land up front. Thus, claim clubs mediated disputes between competing claimants and speculators as well.

Joining a claim club was a simple process. For one dollar, members of a claim club could register a claim with the association. Elected secretaries or registrars kept records of each claim. If more than one settler claimed a given piece of land, the club arbitrated the dispute through a five-member jury. Disputants could also appeal any jury verdict by consulting the entire membership. This procedure was designed to deal both with the powerful speculators and with another common problem in these newly settled areas: claim jumpers. Without the official federal presence necessary to decide who owned what, jumpers often attempted to claim land that had already been registered with the claim association by another party. In these cases, the association's elected marshal issued a verbal warning to the jumper. If this effort failed, the marshal and other members of the association would issue a "physical warning"—destroying a jumper's personal property and improvements or even physically harming the jumper. Sometimes these attempts to oust the claim jumper led to deaths. Even when clubs were unsuccessful in their attempts to expel a supposed claim jumper, they ostracized these outlaws from the community, refusing to do business with them.

Most common in territories such as Iowa, Nebraska, and Kansas, claim clubs often operated under different criteria than those authorized by federal land law. Against official policy, clubs allowed minors to make claims and allowed claimants to register more than the standard 160 acres. Clubs established a kind of order on the frontier designed to withstand the influence of more powerful outsiders. When public land auctions finally occurred, members of claim associations would mobilize to protect their gains from any rivals. Though only quasi-legal themselves, the organized claim clubs were able to persuade many speculators to leave them alone. At land auctions, squatters would gather around a designated bidder, who was supposed to bid the minimum government price for each claim. If any outsider or speculator tried to bid higher on the property, claim associates would intimidate him, sometimes physically. Any speculator who resisted this coercion could expect to be treated the same way claimants treated jumpers.

Claim associations provided a means through which squatters could register, transfer, and mortgage claims without the presence of the federal land office. The clubs promoted self-sufficiency and often developed into powerful speculative organizations in their own right. They also proved that in the absence of federal authority, settlers could govern themselves efficiently. The spirited philosophy of self-defense and self-government found among the claim clubbers influenced the way laws were formed in these developing regions. State and territorial legislatures often validated the doctrines of the claim clubs, upholding the claims of settlers who came first and improved their land. While speculators wielded considerable power on the frontier, claim club ideals—mobilizing individuals to protect against outsiders—also exerted significant influence in the Middle West.

The establishment of claim clubs in frontier areas continued as standard practice until about 1870. Usually these clubs lasted only a few years, until federal officials took control. Although short-lived, the clubs were crucial to the formation of local communities and shaped the beliefs and attitudes of settlers determined to stake a permanent claim on the American frontier.

Further reading: Roy M. Robbins, *Our Landed Heritage: The Public Domain, 1776–1970* (Lincoln: University of Nebraska Press, 1976); Malcolm J. Rohrbough, *The Land Office Business: The Settlement and Administration of American Public Lands, 1789–1837* (Belmont, Calif.: Wadsworth Publishing, 1990).

—Eleanor H. McConnell

Clay, Henry (1777–1852)

Henry Clay was an American statesman, secretary of state under JOHN QUINCY ADAMS, an unsuccessful candidate for the presidency in 1824, 1832, and 1844, and in 1850, the architect of an important compromise to preserve the Union. A representative for the border state Kentucky and spokesman for the middle-of-the-road Whig party, Clay sought to reconcile differences between the North and South on slavery. Clay also represented the nationalist outlook of the young, expanding Middle West. In support of the region's territorial interests, he boldly urged war with Britain in 1812. His AMERICAN SYSTEM political platform called for protective tariffs for eastern manufacturers, federal financing for internal improvements in the West, and a national bank as he sought to link the industrial East with the agrarian West.

Henry Clay was born on April 12, 1777, in Hanover County, Virginia, to a middle-class family. At the age of 20, after studying for the bar with the eminent George Wythe, Clay moved to Lexington, Kentucky, where he developed a thriving practice. He was blessed with a quick mind, a flair for oratory, and an ability to charm both sexes with his easy, attractive manner. That he loved to drink and gamble was no drawback in an age that admired both vices. Ambitious for worldly success, Clay married into a wealthy and socially prominent family and soon gained entry into Kentucky's most influential circles. While still in his 20s, he was elected to the state legislature, in which he served for six years, until 1809.

In 1810 Clay was elected to the U.S. House of Representatives, and from 1811 he served as Speaker of the House. As a spokesman of western expansionist interests and leader of the WAR HAWKS, he stirred up enthusiasm for war with Great Britain and helped bring on the WAR OF 1812. After a brief absence in 1814 to aid in the peace negotiations leading to the TREATY OF GHENT, Clay returned to Congress and began to formulate his "American System," a national program that ultimately included federal aid for internal improvements and tariff protection of American industries.

While Henry Clay was not the author of the MISSOURI COMPROMISE, he was instrumental in facilitating its final form and passage through Congress. In 1818 the Territory of Missouri, which was part of the Louisiana Purchase, applied for admission to the Union. SLAVERY was legal in the Territory of Missouri, and about 10,000 slaves lived there. Most people expected Missouri to become a slave state. When the bill to admit Missouri to the Union was introduced, there were an equal number of free and slave states. The admission of Missouri threatened to destroy this balance. But during the next session of Congress, Maine applied for admission to the Union. Missouri and Maine could then be accepted without upsetting the balance between free and slave states, and the Missouri Compromise became possible.

The compromise admitted Maine as a free state and authorized Missouri to form a state constitution. The compromise also banned slavery from the Louisiana Purchase north of the southern boundary of Missouri, the line of 36 degrees 30 minutes north latitude, except in the state of Missouri. This compromise was not immediately acceptable to all parties, especially those in Missouri Territory. Working hand-in-hand with Senator John Holmes of Maine, Clay ironed out the wrinkles, and in 1821 he pushed the amended Missouri Compromise through Congress.

In 1828 Clay again supported Adams for president, but Jackson won the White House. Three years later, Clay was elected to the U.S. Senate and led the National Republicans, who were beginning to call themselves the WHIG PARTY. Hoping to embarrass Jackson, Clay led the Senate opposition to the president's policies, but when the election came, Jackson was overwhelmingly reelected.

Around this time, a crisis developed over tariffs. South Carolina's nullification of the tariffs of 1828 and 1832 as well as Jackson's threats of an armed invasion of that state allowed Clay to gain political ground. Working, even at the cost of his own protectionist views, toward a compromise with the faction led by JOHN C. CALHOUN, he helped to promote the Compromise Tariff of 1833.

As a candidate for the presidency in 1824, Clay had the fourth-largest number of electoral votes. With no candidate having a majority, the election was decided in the House of Representatives. Clay released his electoral votes to John Quincy Adams in return for Adams naming Clay secretary of state. Adams won the election by a one-vote margin. The deal struck between Adams and Clay became referred to as the "corrupt bargain," and many thought Jackson had been "robbed" of the presidency. The public outcry was strong, and the stigma of the "corrupt bargain" would haunt Adams's presidency and be instrumental in his serving only a single term. It would also be an impediment to Clay's future political fortunes.

In December 1831 the National Republicans once again nominated Henry Clay for the presidency. Clay returned to the national spotlight feeling pessimistic about his chances of defeating Jackson. He therefore made his primary goal to bring a measure to Congress that would put the administration in an embarrassing position. Clay proposed a modification of the tariff. This would have reduced revenues and put off Jackson's intended repayment of the national debt by nearly a year. If Jackson vetoed it, he would alienate northern states, like Pennsylvania, whose votes he needed. If he signed it, it would alienate Jackson's southern supporters. In the end Clay's strategy failed when Congress passed a bill moderate enough to enable Jackson to sign it without alienating either faction.

Clay opposed the Jackson regime at every turn, particularly on the issue of a national bank. When, in 1833, Jackson had the deposits removed from the SECOND BANK OF THE UNITED STATES to various other banks, Clay secured a Senate resolution censuring the president.

In 1840 Clay lost the Whig nomination to WILLIAM HENRY HARRISON, but Clay supported him. When Harrison was elected, Clay was offered the post of secretary of state, but he chose to stay in the Senate, where he planned to reestablish the Bank of the United States. However, the unexpected accession of JOHN TYLER to the presidency upon the death of Harrison less than a month after taking office, and Tyler's vetoes of Clay's bills, caused Clay to resign his Senate seat in 1842.

Henry Clay *(Library of Congress)*

In 1844 Clay ran for president against JAMES K. POLK, an avowed expansionist. Earlier Clay had publicly opposed the annexation of TEXAS. During the campaign, however, he modified his position, agreeing to annexation if it could be accomplished with the common consent of the Union and without war. This shift probably lost him New York State, with which he could have won the election. His failure was crushing for him and for the Whig Party. In 1848, his party refused him its nomination, feeling that he had no chance, and his presidential aspirations were never fulfilled.

Slavery had been given limits by the Missouri Compromise of 1820 and for some time there was no opportunity to overstep those limits. However, the new territories made renewed expansion of slavery a real likelihood. After the MEXICAN-AMERICAN WAR, Texas, which already permitted slavery, naturally entered the Union as a slave state. But CALIFORNIA, New Mexico, and Utah did not have slavery, and when the United States prepared to take over these areas in 1846, there was great sectional conflict on what to do with them.

Southern opinion held that all the territories had the right to sanction slavery. The North asserted that no territories had that right. In 1848, nearly 300,000 men voted for

FREE-SOIL PARTY candidates who declared that the best policy was to contain and discourage slavery. The Midwestern and border-state regions (Maryland, Kentucky, Missouri) were even more divided, however, with many favoring popular sovereignty as a compromise.

After being reelected to the Senate in 1849, Henry Clay denounced the extremists in both North and South, asserted the superior claims of the Union, and was chiefly instrumental in shaping the COMPROMISE OF 1850. It was the third time that he had stepped forward to avert a breakup of the Union in a crisis, and thus he has been called the Great Pacificator and the Great Compromiser.

The key provisions of the compromise were: California was to be admitted as a Free-Soil state; that the remainder of the new annexation be divided into the two territories of New Mexico and Utah and organized without mention of slavery; that the claims of Texas to a portion of New Mexico should be satisfied by a payment of $10 million; that more effective machinery be established for catching runaway slaves and returning them to their masters; and that the buying and selling of slaves (but not slavery itself) be abolished in the District of Columbia. For the last time, Henry Clay had been instrumental in pacifying the growing sectional unrest. The country breathed a collective, albeit temporary, sigh of relief.

Clay was not to live much longer after the passage of the compromise. He spent the summer of 1851 at Ashland, where he made his will, providing for the disposition of his estate and the freeing of his slaves. Though dying of tuberculosis, he returned to Washington that fall and answered the first Senate roll call. Thereafter he was closely confined to his room in the National Hotel, where he died on the morning of June 29, 1852.

Further reading: Maurice G. Baxter, *Henry Clay and the American System* (Lexington: University Press of Kentucky, 1995); Robert Vincent Remini, *Henry Clay: Statesman for the Union* (New York: W. W. Norton, 1991).

—Richard L. Friedline

Clayton-Bulwer Treaty (1850)

The Clayton-Bulwer Treaty was an agreement between the United States and England to cooperate in the construction of any canal through Central America to link the Atlantic and Pacific Oceans. The end result of the treaty may have been to delay construction of an isthmian canal for more than 50 years. Nevertheless, in 1850 it represented an important diplomatic triumph for the United States since it forestalled British expansion in Central America and recognized the United States as equal to the more powerful British in the region. At the same time, however, it meant that American settlers in CALIFORNIA and Oregon had to wait many years for improved transportation links with the East.

During the period of American conflict with Mexico, both the United States and Britain made significant moves to enhance their position in Central America. In the 1840s, the most favored route for a potential isthmian canal went through Nicaragua. From their colony in British Honduras (Belize), the British asserted a protectorate over the Mosquito Coast (the Atlantic coast of Nicaragua), the most likely Atlantic starting point for a canal. Later, in 1849, they also temporarily occupied Tigre Island near the most likely Pacific terminus for a canal through Nicaragua. The United States had not been idle in Central America, either. Democratic president JAMES K. POLK's administration negotiated and signed two treaties with Latin American countries which would affect any canal-building effort. The first, the Bidlack Treaty (1846) with Colombia, gave the United States exclusive rights to build a canal via what was then the second most desirable route, the Colombian province of Panama. In exchange, the United States guaranteed Colombian control over the province and the canal's neutrality in times of war. The second treaty, this one with Nicaragua, offered the United States exclusive control over a Nicaraguan canal in exchange for guarantees of Nicaraguan sovereignty.

The OREGON TREATY OF 1846, the MEXICAN-AMERICAN WAR, the CALIFORNIA GOLD RUSH, and the consequent flow of settlers to Oregon and, especially, California increased both American and British interest in Central America and a possible isthmian canal. In the United States, a canal was increasingly popular with shipping magnates such as CORNELIUS VANDERBILT who sought to control trade with the West Coast. Central America was also attracting the attention of southern politicians who saw the region as potential slave territory to offset the free-state advantage gained in California and (later) ratified in the COMPROMISE OF 1850. Meanwhile, the British sought to maintain their dominant position in the Caribbean, a position that would be threatened by American control over an isthmian canal. The British also wanted to participate in the trade of the Pacific coast of the United States.

Thus, both the United States and Great Britain had interests in Central America and had reasons to be concerned about the other's moves in the region. Accordingly, conditions were favorable for a resolution of potential conflicts. During the Whig presidency of ZACHARY TAYLOR, Secretary of State John Clayton sat down with the new British ambassador to the United States, Sir Henry Lytton Bulwer, to resolve the disputes over Central America. The resulting treaty guaranteed both countries a role in any canal by denying either exclusive rights to any canal route. It also committed both to the neutrality of any canal and to policies of founding no new colonies and building no new fortifications in Central America. The treaty was ratified by the U.S. Senate on May 22, 1850.

Apart from the provisions relating to a possible isthmian canal, other provisions of the Clayton-Bulwer Treaty were violated almost immediately. Britain refused to surrender its protectorate over the Mosquito Coast, which the United States believed fell under the provisions of the treaty. More egregiously from the American perspective, in 1852 the British fashioned the Colony of the Bay Islands out of islands in the Bay of Honduras. For their part, the British were angered in 1856 when Democratic president Franklin Pierce recognized the government in Nicaragua established by American adventurer William Walker; though he disavowed any aim to join the United States, Walker seemed to be aiming for annexation. In the long run, these treaty violations came to little. The British gave up the Mosquito Coast and the Bay Islands in 1859 and 1860, and Walker's government was destroyed in 1857.

Finally, although the requirement of American and British cooperation in the construction of any canal seems to have made it more difficult to build a canal, an isthmian canal project was probably beyond the capabilities of mid-19th-century technology and science—as the French tragically discovered in Panama in the late 19th century when disease decimated their work crews. Nevertheless, the Clayton-Bulwer Treaty remains an important landmark in U.S. diplomatic history, with important consequences for westward expansion.

Further reading: Walter LaFeber, *The American Age: U.S. Foreign Policy at Home and Abroad Since 1750,* 2d ed. (New York: W. W. Norton and Company, 1994); ———, *Inevitable Revolutions: The United States in Central America,* 2d ed. (New York: W. W. Norton and Company, 1993); Bradford Perkins, *The Creation of a Republican Empire, 1776–1865,* vol. 1 of *The Cambridge History of American Foreign Relations,* ed. Warren I. Cohen, (New York: Cambridge University Press, 1993).

—Russell L. Johnson

Colorado gold rush

The name generally given to the surge of people across the Great Plains to Colorado in the summer of 1858 was the Colorado gold rush, whose predecessor was the CALIFORNIA GOLD RUSH a decade earlier. The response to the discovery of gold in Colorado was just as intense as that in CALIFORNIA, but the location and the circumstances made for a varied outcome.

In the aftermath of the discovery of gold in California in January 1848, the search spread across the breadth of the American West. Surely the riches of the Golden State lay in other locations just awaiting the enterprising prospector, or so ran the argument. In July 1858 a party of prospectors, led by William Green Russell, camped near the mouth of Cherry Creek and the headwaters of the South Platte River, where they found placer gold in modest quantities. Russell's report of the find exaggerated the richness and range of the discoveries, but America had long awaited another California bonanza, and news of their discoveries precipitated a flood of immigrants across the plains to the new diggings. The imagined Colorado goldfields were only 700 miles from Independence, Missouri, so the Colorado gold rush drew most of its participants from the eastern United States.

The so-called Pike's Peak rush in 1859 generated an enthusiasm and a movement of people not seen since 1849. Perhaps as many as 50,000 crossed the plains that summer, and some have estimated a higher number. The immigration created a mining culture in the town of Denver and in the camps farther into the Rockies, with boisterous and optimistic crowds intent on the prospect of wealth. The rush to Colorado had an early impact on the landscape of the plains and the lives of the Plains Indians. Heretofore, various groups of Indian peoples had largely escaped the impact of Euro-Americans on the West by accidents of geography and landforms. The tens of thousands who rushed to California had following the well-worn CALIFORNIA TRAIL along the Platte River Valley, and they pressed rapidly across the plains, intent on reaching the crest of the Sierra Nevada before the early snowfalls. The rush to Colorado in 1859 followed the Platte River and several alternative routes, arriving in the staging area around present-day Denver. The large numbers and the variety of routes meant extensive contact with Indians. On the dry plains, the Colorado argonauts found themselves in competition for the same natural resources as Indians, especially water, grass, and shelter. This competition for scarce resources produced inevitable conflicts.

Something in the order of 50,000 men (and a few women) reached the site of the new bonanzas in the spring and summer of 1859. In the traditional proportions that had emerged in California, about the half of the arrivals headed for the gold diggings; the other half turned their attention to the many ways of profiting from the miners. These included supplies, transportation of men and supplies to the gold camps, entertainment in all its various forms, and the many professional opportunities available to doctors, lawyers, and others.

The mining enterprise itself followed a cycle much like that in California, but accelerated in time. During the first season, miners wielded the pick, pan, and shovel in washing gravels, work routines familiar to their predecessors in California. Soon, however, prospectors found rich leads of gold ore that demanded more systematic and complex mining techniques. The Colorado gold rush soon passed from individual mining to larger operations requiring large capital investment and the latest in metallurgy techniques. Entrepreneurs soon built smelters in Denver to process the ores from the richest of the quartz leads. And, as in California and the more recent COMSTOCK LODE, mines began to burrow underground, following the gold leads as they sank farther and farther from the surface.

The immigration experience in the Colorado gold rush was markedly different from that of California. Because of the abbreviated distances, the prospective 59ers (as they were soon called) could return to the East. Many of them did; this was in the nature of mining enterprise. But the ease of return meant that miners could move back and forth almost seasonally. This continuous movement across the plains over the half-dozen years after 1858 further disrupted the lives of NATIVE AMERICANS. The Colorado gold rush began a period of continuous conflict on the plains, with the reinforcement of racial stereotypes that had long characterized contact between the two groups. In November 1864, in a campaign that reflected continuing racial hostility set in a context of the American Civil War, Colonel John M. Chivington led a force of 1,000 territorial volunteers in an attack on a Cheyenne camp at Sand Creek. The massacre of some 400 Indian people, who had been confident of the government's benevolent protection, was the climax to a continuing conflict begun by the great immigration to Colorado in the summer of 1859.

In these early years, the center of Colorado's mining enterprise was William Green Russell's original settlement on Cherry Creek. In 1860, the little mining town merged with Auraria, its main rival. The following year, the consolidated town was incorporated with the name of Denver. This collection of log houses, false storefronts, and a modest tent city would become the commercial center of the Colorado gold rush and most important city in the West between Kansas City and San Francisco. Its success was owed to effective promotion, continuing mineral production in Colorado, and, beginning in 1859, the presence of a newspaper, the *Rocky Mountain News.* Denver was initially a supply center, later the site of industrial processes associated with mining, and finally a financial base. The important mining towns, farther in the mountains, were Central City, Black Hawk, Georgetown, Silver Plume, and Idaho Springs. Most of the significant early mining was in Gilpin County.

Early Colorado mining camps drew their institutional form from California camps. With the organization of the territory some years away and the conflicts and tensions created by large numbers rubbing elbows and jockeying for a claim in shallow narrow streams, the miners soon formed districts and established rules to preserve order and to provide for the adjudication of disputes. Without formal structure for order, the miners established their own miners' courts and enforced a high degree of order. As in other camps, foreigners and non-English speakers were at a disadvantage, but unlike the California Gold Rush, the Colorado gold rush was not a world event; it attracted immigrants from the East Coast but few foreigners.

The Colorado gold rush provided the nucleus of a Euro-American population that offered the basis for organizing a territory. Town founders and promoters (who were generally the organizers) called the territory Jefferson Territory. Congress did not concur. Still, the initiative may have helped. In 1861, Kansas became a state, and soon thereafter, Congress created Colorado Territory, with the same boundaries as the present state.

Colorado's gold-rush country had every institution and facility that a prosperous El Dorado could provide—except the regular consistent production of gold. Gold leaders in quartz strata soon supplemented the placer mining of the first summer. But the gold harvest from placer mining was low—some would even have said disappointing—and the development of an effective deep quartz-mining enterprise was handicapped by the difficulties of extracting from Colorado's quartz with the technology then available. Colorado minerals presented difficulties beyond the mining techniques of the day. The quartz camps hung on while the new generation of mining engineers—appearing on the scene for the first time—searched for solutions that would transform Colorado's mining into another California.

The final resolution of the issue was largely the work of Nathaniel Hill, a professor of chemistry at Brown University in Rhode Island. Hill began his work in Colorado in 1864—even as most of the placer mining in Colorado was ending—and he sent a quantity of Colorado ore to Wales, where it was examined in the most modern mining laboratory of the day. Based on the findings, Hill organized a smelting company in 1867 and then began construction on a new kind of smelter in Black Hawk. Hill's smelter, which went into operation within a year, helped to revive Colorado's declining mining economy. Ten years later, a larger smelter was built in Denver, which became the center of Colorado's smelting industry. Denver's dominance was notably assisted by the development of a railroad network that connected the distant isolated mining camps to the Mile High City.

Further reading: Rodman W. Paul, *Mining Frontiers of the Far West, 1848–1880* (Albuquerque: University of New Mexico Press, 1963); Elliott West, *The Contest Plains: Indians, Goldseekers, and the Rush to Colorado* (Lawrence: University Press of Kansas, 1997).

Colt, Samuel (1814–1862)

Samuel Colt was a U.S. inventor most famous for his handgun, the Colt .45, and considered one of the first to use mass production techniques in America. He was born in Hartford, Connecticut, on July 19, 1814, the son of a successful fabric manufacturer. His mother died when he was seven, and Colt lived with various relatives during his early years, acquiring an imperfect education. However, even as a child he displayed great interest in and an aptitude for firearms and explosives. He was attending a prep school in Amherst, Massachusetts, in 1829 when, at the age of 13, he put on an impressive display of pyrotechnics on Ware Pond. However, his father decided he needed discipline, so in 1830 Colt accompanied the ship *Corvo* on a yearlong voyage to India. En route, while observing the mechanics of the ship's wheel and steering system, it occurred to him that the same principles could be applied to handguns. Thereafter, he spent many hours whittling a wooden model of what became his trademark legacy: the revolving pistol. The concept was not entirely new or original; multibarreled weapons (or "pepperboxes") had been in existence since 1813. However, Colt saw much greater practicality in employing a single barrel with a revolving cylinder. Such a mechanism promised much greater rates of fire than traditional, muzzle-loading handguns.

When Colt returned home in 1831, he dedicated his energies to having a working model of his device developed by local gunsmiths. To help raise money for the effort, he toured the country giving demonstrations of "laughing gas" (nitrous oxide), and in 1835 he applied for a U.S. patent on his pistol. That year he also traveled to England and France to promote his ideas, but with little success. It was not until the outbreak of the SEMINOLE WAR in 1836 that the military displayed any interest in his weapon. By this time, Colt had established the Patent Arms Manufacturing Company in Paterson, New Jersey, and he received a government contract for 100 weapons. Though crude, these functioned well in the swamps of Florida, and orders were received from the Texas Rangers, then engaged in a war of independence against Mexico. It was here that the high rate of fire and accuracy of Colt's revolvers became immediately apparent. Part of Colt's success was his system of manufacture, which was based entirely upon factory production, assembly-line procedures, and interchangeable parts, all of which facilitated both production and quality control. Despite this success, unfortunately, no future government contracts were forthcoming, and Colt liquidated his assets in 1842.

For the next four years, Colt applied his talents to creating a submarine battery (underwater mine) for the U.S. Navy, as well as a submergible battery system. The latter was instrumental in assisting SAMUEL F. B. MORSE to perfect his own telegraph cable. Fortunately, on the eve of war with Mexico, General ZACHARY TAYLOR dispatched Captain Samuel Walker to confer with Colt about producing more weapons. The result was a heavier, more refined

Samuel Colt *(Hulton/Archive)*

weapon, the "Walker Colt," which fired a .44 caliber ball and functioned as a standard sidearm throughout the conflict in 1846–48. However, lacking a factory of his own, Colt forged a partnership with Eli Whitney, Jr., to manufacture the new weapons at Whitneyville, Connecticut. His most significant weapon here was the Improved Holster Model, which was lighter and more manageable in the saddle. Over the next 20 years, an estimated 200,000 of this pistol were sold to military and civilian customers alike. In time, the fame of Colt weaponry spilled over into the civilian sector, where they became the most popular weapon during the conquest of the western frontier. Mass production brought down the price of individual weapons, thereby ensuring their availability to Americans of the middle and lower classes, who formed the bulk of settlers.

Buoyed by success, in 1856 Colt established a large manufacturing center at Hartford, Connecticut, where he turned out continually improved versions of pistols and rifles in ever-increasing numbers. His endeavors made him a millionaire, while his factory employed some of the best-paid and most highly skilled workers in the nation. In 1860, when civil war seemed imminent, Colt introduced a new model handgun, the New Model Army Pistol, of which 200,000 were purchased. Colt, however, proved somewhat over-businesslike in his dealings as he unhesitatingly shipped several hundred of the guns to southern sympathizers in Richmond, Virginia, prior to the outbreak of hostilities. Thereafter, he was firmly in the Union camp.

Colt died of heart disease on January 10, 1862; although only 47, he had a net worth estimated at $15 million at his death. Having become one of the most important arms manufacturers in American history, he had also wielded an indelible impact on the field of early mass production.

Further reading: Ellsworth S. Grant, *The Colt Armory: A History of Colt Manufacturing Company, Inc.* (Lincoln, R.I.: Mowbray Publishing, 1995); William N. Hosley, *Colt: The Making of an American Legend* (Amherst: University of Massachusetts Press, 1996); K. D. Kirkland, *America's Premier Gunmakers* (New York: Mallard Press, 1990).

—John C. Fredriksen

Colt revolver

The Colt revolver takes its name from both its inventor, SAMUEL COLT, as well as its firing method. Featuring a revolving cylinder, which contained a separate chamber for each bullet, the revolver was one of the first handguns capable of firing multiple rounds without reloading.

Colt patented his first model in 1836. By all accounts, his early revolver was flawed in many aspects: difficult to load, prone to accidental discharge, and in danger of exploding if dropped. Regardless of his pistol's imperfections, Colt was a master salesman; he conducted a relentless marketing and public-relations campaign aimed at the military, government officials, the press, and potential investors.

Initially based in Paterson, New Jersey, Colt's first factory manufactured approximately 3,000 pistols and 1,500 other guns during its six years in operation. But high manufacturing costs and an inherently flawed design led to the failure of Colt's early venture. In 1849, however, his fortunes began to turn. After being granted a renewal of his patent, he developed a much-improved .31-caliber revolver. Until the legendary Colt .45 came along in 1872, the 1849 revolver sold 325,000 and stood as the best-selling handgun of its time.

While this gun marked a definite improvement over the initial revolver, its success was not due to quality alone. Gun culture exploded during the 1840s and 1850s. MANIFEST DESTINY—the ideology that posited Americans as a kind of chosen people with an inalienable right of conquest—proved the best marketing tool possible. The CALIFORNIA GOLD RUSH, the MEXICAN-AMERICAN WAR, and other westward-expansion movements played a significant role in the Colt explosion. But Colt's greatest advocates, the men who would embody the spirit of the American West, were the Texas Rangers.

Captain Samuel H. Walker, a commander during an 1844 clash between 15 Texas Rangers and nearly 80 Comanches known as Hays's Big Fight, recounted the battle in a letter to Samuel Colt and credited his revolver with the Texan victory. Walker and Colt began working together, resulting in design improvements and government contracts that proved highly lucrative for Colt.

What distinguished the revolver was, of course, its rapid-fire capacity. In earlier skirmishes, the Rangers were armed with single-shot guns. Riding on horseback, they found the guns easy to shoot but awkward to reload. Comanche and Apache warriors developed a fighting strategy based on the limitations of the Rangers' weaponry. They would mount an initial assault, using just a few fighters, during which the Rangers would discharge their weapons. Then, as the Rangers dismounted in order to reload, the Indians would converge in much greater numbers and overwhelm the Rangers before they were able to fire again.

Walker credited the Colt revolver with intimidating the Indians enough to halt their attacks on TEXAS settlements and negotiate a treaty. He also brought the revolver into widespread military use during the Mexican-American War, giving the Colt revolver its reputation for being the "Gun that Won the West." SAM HOUSTON, the first U.S. senator from Texas, lobbied President JAMES K. POLK and his secretary of war to arm every soldier on the American frontier with Colt's pistols.

Colt harnessed the power of the Texas publicity, incorporating engravings of scenes from Hays's Big Fight and other Texan tableaux into the design of his pistols. He used his success in Texas as a springboard from which to generate military sales both within the United States and abroad. By the time of the Civil War, Colt had become the weapon of choice for the U.S. military.

Further reading: Jervis Anderson, *Guns in American Life* (New York: Random House, 1984); William N. Hosley, *Colt: The Making of an American Legend* (Amherst: University of Massachusetts Press, 1996).

—Eva Pendleton

Columbia River

Because of its location, the Columbia River played a vital role in the United States's expansion into the Pacific Northwest. Rising in southeast British Columbia, this river of southwestern Canada and the northwestern United States flows approximately 1,200 miles before emptying into the Pacific Ocean west of Portland, Oregon. After 465 miles, it enters the state of Washington, and thereafter forms the boundary between Washington and Oregon.

The Columbia pours the largest volume of water into the Pacific Ocean of any river in North America, and long before the Europeans arrived, the Native Americans fished it for salmon. The earliest archaeological evidence of human habitation in the Columbia River basin dates to 10,000 years ago. The earliest groups lived by fishing, hunting large mammals, and gathering plants for food. Cultures in the protohistoric and historic periods varied greatly along the river. On the lower Columbia, groups lived in large multifamily longhouses, while on the middle- and upper-river sections, people moved seasonally and lived in smaller groups. Native fishers took salmon at Willamette Falls on the Willamette River and at Kettle Falls on the upper Columbia. Celilo Falls on the middle river was the most important native fishery. Thousands gathered there during the spring and summer fish runs to harvest chinook salmon and trade. In the early 19th century, Pacific Fur Company trader Alexander Ross called Celilo "the great emporium or mart of the Columbia."

The Columbia River first appeared on European maps in the early 17th century as "River of the West," when the Spanish maritime explorer Martin de Aguilar located a major river near the 42nd parallel. Cartographers often labeled the "River of the West" as an estuary to the mythical Straits of Anian, or the Northwest Passage, and located it anywhere from the 42nd to the 50th parallel. In 1765, British major Robert Rogers called the river "Ouragon"—later spelled "Oregon" by Jonathan Carver in 1778—as a derivative name referring to the "ouisconsink" river in present-day Wisconsin. The first confirmation of its location came in 1775, when Bruno de Hezeta described a river estuary at the Columbia's correct latitude. In May 1792, American trader Captain Robert Gray sailed across the bar in the first documented visit to the river and named it after his ship, the *Columbia.* In October that same year, British explorer George Vancouver sent Lt. William Broughton up the river more than 100 miles, and Broughton produced the first detailed map of the lower river. Meriwether Lewis and William Clark explored the river in 1805–06 for the United States. Northwest Company fur trader David Thompson made the first map of the full river in 1811–12. After the War of 1812, England and the United States jointly occupied the Columbia River Basin territory.

In 1811 JOHN JACOB ASTOR established the first fur trading post, known as Fort ASTORIA, on the mouth of the Columbia River. Britain's Hudson's Bay Company (HBC) established a fur-trading hegemony in the region and built a headquarters post at FORT VANCOUVER in 1825. HBC trappers and traders spread throughout the Columbia River basin and beyond, bringing furs back to Fort Vancouver for shipment to England. Americans returned to the region as settlers during the 1840s, when overland migrants came to the Columbia and Willamette River valleys on the OREGON TRAIL. In 1846, the Oregon Country south of the 49th parallel became U.S. territory by treaty with Great Britain. Oregon achieved statehood in 1859, Washington and Montana in 1889, and Idaho in 1890.

Further reading: William Dietrich, *Northwest Passage: The Great Columbia River* (New York: Simon & Schuster, 1995).

Compromise of 1850

The Compromise of 1850 was a group of measures agreed to by northern and southern interests in Congress that imposed limits on the expansion of SLAVERY, but protected it where it already existed. After the MEXICAN-AMERICAN WAR and the TREATY OF GUADALUPE HIDALGO, the United States gained the territory north of the Rio Grande and south of the 49th parallel. The acquisition of new land rekindled the flames of animosity between northerners and southerners over the extension of slavery into the West. This controversy was really a continuation of the problems first addressed by the MISSOURI COMPROMISE in 1820, which had temporarily settled the issue of which states within the Louisiana Purchase would be free and which slave. This new territory, however, was not part of Louisiana and thus did not fall under the 1820 agreement. Tensions over slavery had worsened since the Missouri controversy, as abolitionists launched their impassioned antislavery campaigns and new FUGITIVE SLAVE LAWS were passed that angered northerners.

In 1842 the U.S. Supreme Court had ruled that officials in free states were not required to enforce fugitive slave laws—enforcement of a law that involves more than one state should be a federal responsibility. With this ruling in mind, southerners pushed for the creation of a national fugitive slave law. Usually the southern slaveholder position relied on the rhetoric of states' rights, but in this instance their economic interest in seeing runaway slaves returned outweighed their devotion to state sovereignty. At the same time, abolitionists were campaigning to end the slave trade in Washington, D.C., seeing this practice as especially offensive when committed in the capital of a democratic nation. Tensions were also rising on the border between TEXAS and New Mexico. Texas claimed almost half of what is now the state of New Mexico. The terms of Texas's annexation to the United States permitted the territory to be divided into as many as five new states. Because Texas was a slave state, the acquisition of the new territory in New Mexico could mean the creation of yet another slave state. Concern over balancing the number of free and slave states made the problems between Texas and New Mexico a troubling development.

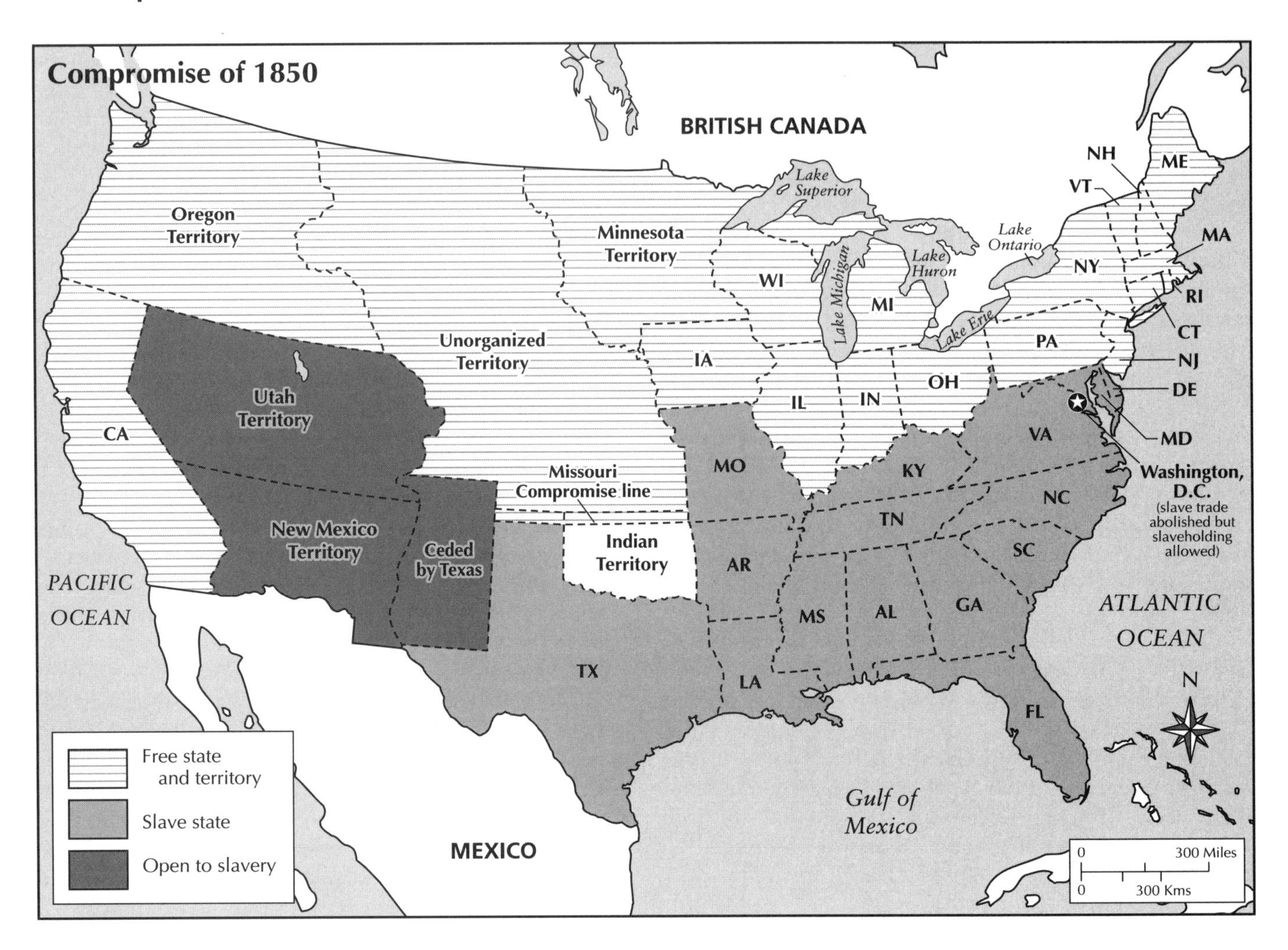

These three controversies—all connected to slavery and its future—angered southerners and northerners more than any problem since the Missouri controversy. Some southern states began to decry northern aggression and call for secession. Animosity was so great in Congress that representatives could not agree on a new Speaker of the House, and debates became shrill to the point of violence. Senator HENRY CLAY of Kentucky, the promoter of compromise in 1820, once again proposed a solution to save the Union, introducing eight proposals in the Senate in January 1850. The first six proposals were grouped in pairs, one favorable to the north, one to the south. In the first pair of proposals, California would be admitted as a free state while allowing the Mexico cession to be established without any restrictions on slavery. In the second, the border conflict between Texas and New Mexico would be resolved in New Mexico's favor, while Texas would be compensated for its loss by helping the state pay off bonds it had issued when it was a republic (a plan that benefited the mostly southern bondholders). In the third set of proposals, the slave trade would be abolished in the nation's capital, but slavery would remain legal there unless neighbor states Maryland and Virginia approved its abolition. The final two proposals eventually proved to be the most thorny and contradictory: Congress would have no jurisdiction over the interstate slave trade, while the last element of the proposal supported the creation of a national fugitive slave law.

Debate over Clay's compromise was prolonged and fierce. Senate leaders JOHN C. CALHOUN, DANIEL WEBSTER, and William H. Seward gave powerful speeches on the proposals. At the heart of their remarks was the basic conflict between states' rights and the preservation of the Union. Calhoun argued that the Constitution protected slavery and that states' rights were sacrosanct. Webster called for compromise, appealing to the idea of an American identity larger than any single state interest. In his desire to compromise, Webster accepted the national fugitive slave law. Seward rejected this compromise position. For him, slavery and compromise were both wrong. He appealed to the concept of a higher moral law, one that valued the liberty of all over the privileges of a few.

In the end, after exhaustive arguments, the compromise package that passed in the Senate resembled Clay's initial proposals closely. He had decided to group all the proposals in one bill, hoping the whole compromise would pass because senators and congressmen would vote for the parts of which they approved. The opposite happened: legislators mostly voted against the package because they opposed certain proposals within it. After months of hard work fashioning a solution, Clay was discouraged. Retreating to Newport for his health, he charged Senator Stephen A. Douglas with the task of defending the compromise. Douglas decided to shift tactics, separating the elements of the compromise into different bills and building coalitions to support each one. In July 1850 President ZACHARY TAYLOR died suddenly. Taylor had opposed the compromise, but the new president, MILLARD FILLMORE, approved of it. Fillmore's support, combined with Douglas's division of the proposals, led to the successive passage of the compromise measures in August and September of 1850.

Most legislators were pleased and relieved by the result, hoping the Compromise of 1850 would at last heal the divisions between North and South, but diehard partisans on both sides viewed the compromise as a betrayal. The results of the compromise were different than predicted: California and the western territories voted in favor of the South throughout the 1850s, and slavery would actually be legalized in New Mexico and Utah. But by far the most incendiary feature of the compromise was the passage of a national fugitive slave law, which allowed federal commissioners to issue warrants for fugitive slaves. Once runaways were captured, slaveholders came before the commissioner to prove ownership. The standards of proof were minimal, and fugitives were barred from testifying. These slave-catching endeavors were paid for with federal money, and federal marshals were required to assist in the retrieval of runaways. Northerners who harbored fugitives or refused to help find them could be heavily fined or even imprisoned.

Abolitionists condemned the law for violating civil liberties and accused southern slaveholders of immorality and hypocrisy. After decades of promoting states' rights, southerners were relying on the power of the federal government to return their property. This self-serving shift, and the blatant abuses of the slave-catchers, angered some northerners who had never before considered themselves abolitionists. Most did not consider blacks as equals, but they were shocked by the violation of liberties they witnessed as the fugitive slave law was enforced. Some northern states passed personal-liberty laws in the mid-1850s and refused to help southerners recapture their slaves. Thus, the divisions between North and South actually increased as a result of the Compromise of 1850. The violent incidents and political hostility steadily increased over the next 10 years, leading eventually to southern secession and the outbreak of the Civil War in 1861.

Further reading: Holman Hamilton, *Prologue to Conflict: The Crisis and Compromise of 1850* (Lexington: University of Kentucky Press, 1964); Edwin Charles Rozwenc, *The Compromise of 1850* (Boston: Heath, 1957); Mark J. Stegmaier, *Texas, New Mexico, and the Compromise of 1850: Boundary Dispute and Sectional Crisis* (Kent, Ohio: Kent State University Press, 1996).

—Eleanor H. McConnell

Comstock Lode

The Comstock Lode lies in the Carson Valley in northwestern Nevada, on the side of Mount Davidson, where the towns of Virginia City and Gold Hill would mark its presence. Beginning in 1859, the mines and mining operations associated with the deposits of the Comstock Lode were to be among the most significant in the history of mining. Between 1860 and 1880 alone, Comstock mines produced more than $300 million in gold and silver—the richest in the West at the time. Along with profits, the Comstock led to a series of innovations in mining technology that influenced mining across the length and breadth of the West.

The Comstock Lode had its origins in the enthusiasm for the CALIFORNIA GOLD RUSH, whose riches produced a widespread search for similar gold deposits across the American West. In the summer of 1859, Peter O'Riley and Patrick McLaughlin found the site of what would become the Orphir mine. The rush to the new El Dorado began with the discovery that the "blasted blue stuff" that interfered with placer mining for gold turned out to be very rich silver ore. In the rush to the region that following, prospectors and investors of varying degrees of skill would eventually register more than 17,000 claims, most of which were worthless. One-half of the Comstock's ore production and almost four-fifths of the mining dividends came from pairs of adjacent mines: the Belcher and Crown Point and the California and Consolidated Virginia. Such odds of success, however, were much like those of other mining districts in the West.

The Comstock Lode was to be the West's first great silver bonanza. Unlike the early CALIFORNIA experience, mining in the Comstock demanded large investments of capital, so the best claims soon passed into the hands of California entrepreneurs with capital to develop the sites. Because the ore lay deep underground in several major concentrations, experienced mining men and preparatory investment were required to bring it to the surface for processing. In this respect, the Comstock would become the first large mining enterprise in the West to resemble an industrial city. Furthermore, with investment demands that could be met only in San Francisco and other cities, the best mines in the Comstock were the property of absentee owners and developers almost from the beginning. The absentee nature of the exercise created all the benefits and disadvantages of such enterprise, and professionals on the site worked with shadowy and shady financial figures in San Francisco.

From the first ore discoveries in 1859, technology was crucial to opening the Comstock. With huge stamp mills soon in operation, vast underground mining works, and complex operations to treat the crushed ore, the Comstock was a complex operation far removed from individual miners. The first major difficulty was how to prevent cave-ins in the deepening shaft. The solution was the "square-set" timbering process that permitted deep mining in unstable rock formations. The invention of Philip Deidesheimer, a German-born engineer, the technique quickly spread to underground mines everywhere in the West. Very early in mining operations in the Comstock, large quantities of water had to be pumped out of the works by the Cornish pump. Soon the pan-amalgamation process evolved to allow the separation of gold and silver ores quickly and cheaply.

With the large capital investments and the rumors of the great profits to be made, the mines of the Comstock Lode soon made their appearance on the San Francisco Stock Exchange. Stocks in Comstock mines fluctuated wildly, producing some fortunes for the favored insiders, but whatever the results, the dramatic rises in the value of a few stocks kept the market in a state of continuous turmoil. The experience of the Comstock Lode first demonstrated that more money might be made in buying and selling shares of mining stocks than in actual mining operations. In this respect, the Comstock style of stock and stock manipulation would become a model for railroads and speculation in railroad stocks in the next generation.

Technical innovations contributed to the first boom period from 1860 to 1863, but then Comstock profits languished. However rich the silver ores—and they were very rich indeed—mining for them posed continuing difficulties: deep shafts, rising water, impossible heat, and poor ventilation. With the decline in production and the falling stock prices, officers in the Bank of California bought up large numbers of shares at low prices. With new discoveries in the early 1870s, the bankers were in a position to reap great profits, and they did.

Other mining entrepreneurs soon took control of the Comstock. The so-called "Silver Kings" combined practical mining experience with stock manipulation to gain control of the "Big Bonanza" mines that produced the next generation of great profits. From 1873 to 1882, these mines produced $105 million in silver bullion. The new discoveries were at astonishing depths, up to 3,000 feet underground. The technical difficulties of mining at such levels were notably eased by Adolph Sutro's four-mile tunnel under Mt. Davidson. The tunnel offered ventilation, drainage, and easy access to ores. Various mine owners had opposed Sutro's tunnel for a decade, fearful of the power that it would confer on him. Finally, with foreign capital, he completed the tunnel in 1878 and sold out the following year. Sutro's exit with his fortune to San Francisco marked the beginning of the decline of the Comstock Lode. By 1880, the output and the profits were falling. Although exploration continued for years, the Comstock never recaptured its former leadership in silver mining.

The Comstock Lode had an impact on mining in the West that went beyond even its great profits. The technical knowledge acquired from mining at such deep levels and in processing the ores brought to the surface was transferred to mines all over the West. In this sense, the Comstock was a mining laboratory of exceptional significance, and the mining engineers who labored there would later open the great silver mines in Leadville and Aspen (Colorado), the next generation of silver bonanzas. Finally, the profits of the Comstock produced a group of mining entrepreneurs who would take their money and skills not only throughout the West but also around the world. The most important of these was George Hearst, who would go on to become the owner of the Homestake Mine in Lead, South Dakota, and an important figure in California politics.

The Comstock was also significant in the development of a mining city. Virginia City was the first great mining city: the political, financial, and social center of mining enterprise in Nevada. Indeed, it was Nevada's most important site and mining its most important industry for a half century. Local editors and civic boosters declared that the population reached 30,000 in the bonanza years; the official census number from 1870 was 10,917. Not until the rise of legal gambling in the 20th century and the emergence of Reno and Las Vegas has any city been as influential in Nevada as Virginia City. By 1880, as the mines shut down, Virginia City had also declined.

Further reading: Dan DeQuille, *The Big Bonanza* (1876; New York: Knopf, 1947); Ronald M. James, *The Roar and the Silence: A History of Virginia City and the Comstock Lode* (Reno: University of Nevada Press, 1998); Rodman W. Paul, *Mining Frontiers of the Far West, 1848–1880* (Albuquerque: University of New Mexico Press, 1963).

cotton culture

During the first half of the 19th century, cotton defined the South as no other crop did before or since. Its growing range and yield were enormous, encompassing at least a dozen states from North Carolina to TEXAS and producing at rates that doubled every decade between 1820 and 1860. Already by 1820, cotton accounted for nearly 50 percent of the value of U.S. exports. It also brought great growth to the region, as the population, despite the relocation of thousands of NATIVE AMERICANS, increased fivefold. During the 1840s and 1850s, the population grew from 7 million to 11 million. Among them were as many as 3.5 million slaves, whose labor was central to the success of medium-sized farmers and large planters alike.

Accounting for more than 65 percent of the world's cotton by the 1850s, the south was a major contributor to the U.S. national ECONOMY. In 1855, David King published *Cotton Is King,* in which he noted that cotton was royalty, in constant international demand for textiles and other uses. The erosion of the practices that built an effective single-crop economy—on economic, political, and moral grounds—marked the later antebellum years and laid the foundation for the coming civil war.

Before the early 18th century, tobacco and rice were the primary commercial crops in the South, and both depended on slave labor. Although the southern states of Virginia and Maryland had successfully raised tobacco in the late 18th and early 19th centuries, with production levels climbing to what they had been before the Revolutionary War, by the 1810s and 1820s they had become transformed by cotton. Tobacco, which had yielded 15 percent of the value of U.S. exports in 1820 brought only 6 percent of that amount in 1845. Rice had also been an important export crop, but beginning at the end of the 18th century, exports stagnated and remained low until the 1850s. In the early 19th century, sugar developed into an important commercial crop, first in the Upper South and later in the Gulf region, and would be another slave-based crop that provided no economic reason for the South to free slaves, as would occur in the North during the late 18th and early 19th centuries.

At the same time, a new crop was being grown: cotton. It arose to serve an increasing export market for textile

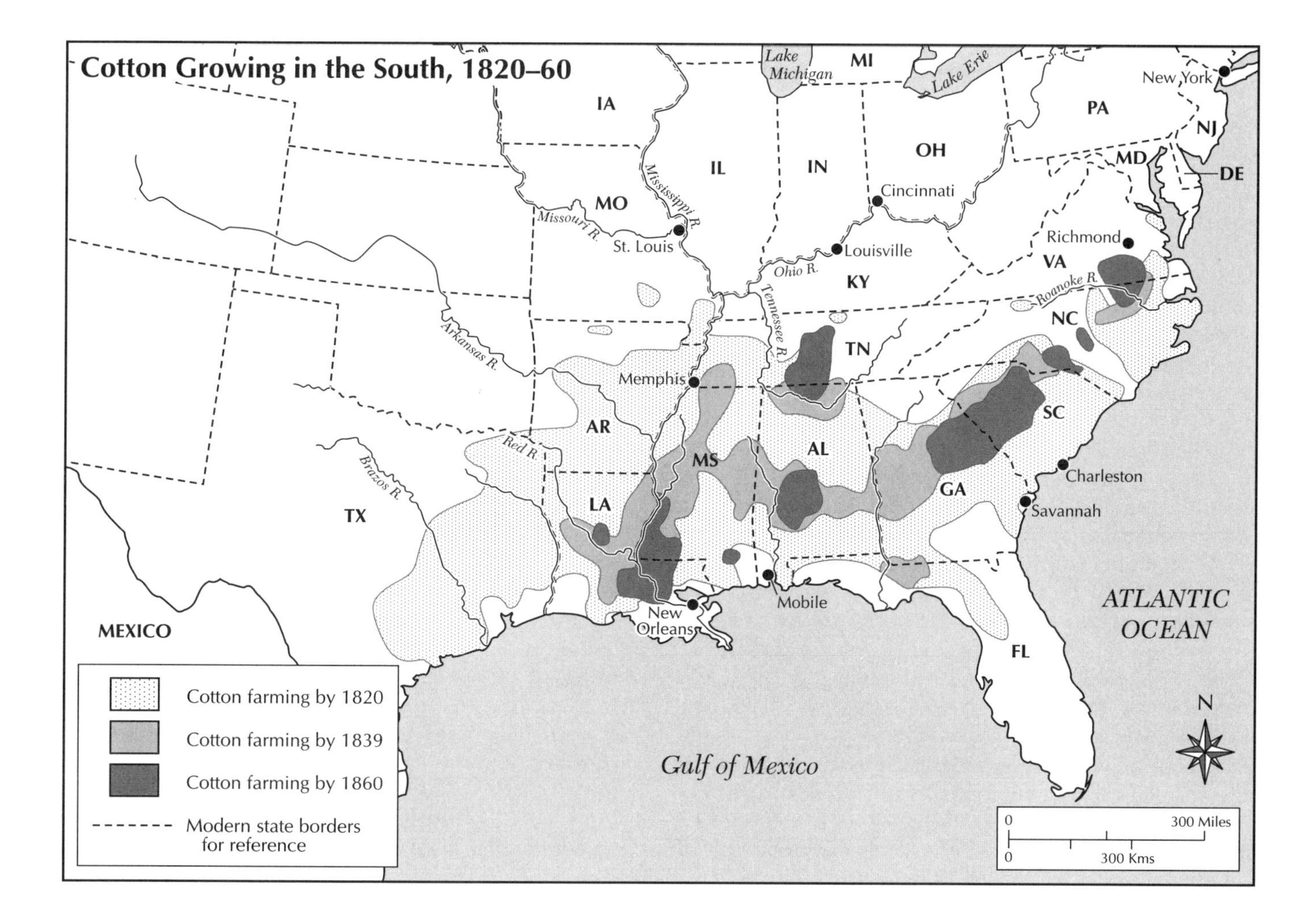

businesses in the newly industrialized Britain. But the type of cotton being grown, long-staple cotton, could be raised successfully only in the sea-island areas of Georgia and North and South Carolina. Another variety, short-staple cotton, was more geographically adaptable but had gummy seeds that were too labor-intensive to remove by hand and keep the crop profitable. The success in 1793 of Eli Whitney's invention of the cotton gin, which removed seeds from cotton, transformed short-staple cotton harvesting and began its titanic expansion across the South and West. In 1815, southern cotton production stood at 150,000 bales (one bale equals 500 pounds); by 1826, it was 600,000 bales per year; by 1851, it had reached 2.4 million bales per year.

Since their initial migration south and west to Alabama and the western parts of the Carolinas, Florida, and Arkansas, white planters fought with several Native American nations including the Creek, Cherokee, and Choctaw for control of the region. Agreements such as the 1814 Treaty of Fort Jackson ceded former Native American lands to the U.S. In the 1830s, nations in the Southeast including the Choctaw, Cherokee, and Chickasaw were relocated west of the Mississippi River, some traveling along the TRAIL OF TEARS to Oklahoma. Even nations that adopted settlers' ways, such as the Cherokee, were forced to remove themselves from the South during the 1830s.

At the same time (and continuing through 1860), up to a million slaves were brought to the South, particularly to the millions of acres of the soil-rich Lower South. To farmers and planters, slaves provided a secure, self-perpetuating source of labor that increased at the rate of 30 percent each decade between 1820 and 1860. Slaves were considered even more valuable to agricultural success than they had been two or three decades earlier, before the rise of cotton. As a result, the South considered any move away from SLAVERY to be a threat to self-preservation. Accordingly, southern support for the emancipation of slaves nearly vanished. While in the 1820s southern antislavery societies outnumbered those in the North, they were virtually nonexistent in the South by the late 1830s. In addition, the number of slave states in the region more than doubled, from six to 15.

Yet only a minority of the population was slaveholders, a number that decreased due to increased slave costs over the course of the 19th century. In 1830, 36 percent of southerners owned slaves; by 1850, it was 31 percent. In 1850, 347,825 of 6 million white residents of the South owned slaves. Further, as fewer planters owned slaves, cotton production, property, and wealth became concentrated in those families holding the largest number of slaves. Of the 10,000 families holding 50 or more slaves, the wealthiest among them were the 3,000 families owning more than 100 slaves each. About 90,000 farmers owned between 10 and 99 slaves; about 255,000 other farmers owned fewer than 10 slaves. Two percent of slaveowners owned half of all U.S. slaves.

There was great variety among slave-owning cotton farms in the South. While the 3,000–4,000 large slave-owning plantations had a greater role in cotton production by mid-century, much of 19th-century cotton was grown on small to medium-sized farms with limited slave labor. For example, a middle-class planter might have 10–50 slaves on his farm, which, if managed correctly, could yield substantial profit; a workingman's farm would have less than 10 slaves. Generally, such small farms were characterized by their overall poverty, with owner and slave working side by side in the field on cotton that yielded only $125 per year. As Mark Twain described it in *The Adventures of Huckleberry Finn,* this was "one of those little one-horse cotton plantations" with a "rail fence around a two-acre yard . . . [and] some sickly grass-patches in the big yard."

Life on large plantations was vastly different. The family home on the site would have been fashioned in what architect Frederick Law Olmstead called "a Grecian style," with wooden slave housing situated far from the house. Slave labor was monitored by the overseer, whom the plantation owner hired to discipline slaves and maintain profits. An intelligent and able slave was given the job of driver; he was the overseer's closest subordinate and was responsible for managing the slaves. One common factor for all slaves was the long workday, which ran for 12–15 hours per day, and longer if the moon allowed.

The demands and rewards of the "King Cotton" economy resulted in a fivefold population increase during the first six decades of the 19th century, but it kept the South an unsophisticated agricultural economy. Because it produced few other goods, it needed to import goods from northern manufacturing states; and because prices for cotton fluctuated greatly, the South had little capital to invest in manufacturing and therefore had to purchase goods and rent storage space for cotton from northern suppliers on credit. In the 19th century, such practices left the South in a chronic state of financial instability.

Some southern spokesmen attempted to counter encroaching northern dominance by rallying the next generation to embrace industrialism. In 1849, according to an editorial in the *Sumpter Banner* of South Carolina, the current generation should feel compelled to cast aside the timeworn call to preserve gentility and prepare "the rising generation for mechanical business." But it was too late to catch up to the urbanized, industrialized North. In the northeast, one-third of residents lived in cities and towns; less than 13 percent of residents of the Southeast were similarly urbanized. The distinction between industry and agriculture was similar: As late as 1860, 60 percent of northern workers were employed in nonagricultural jobs, while only 16 percent of southerners were employed in nonagricultural work. That meant there were 1.3 million industrialized workers in the North but only 110,000 in the South.

Meanwhile, the South encountered an immediate, chronic threat to cotton planting: overplanted, exhausted crop land. In 1826, the Upper, or old, South, accounted for more than half of cotton produced. But the cultivation of a single crop depleted the soil and reduced yields dramatically—in some areas, up to 50 percent. In response, planters entered what would become a common situation: being compelled to move westward for fresh soil. In the 1840s and 1850s, planters and slaves from the formerly fertile cotton states of Maryland, Virginia, and South Carolina moved to the rich Gulf and Mississippi River states of Louisiana, Alabama, Arkansas, Mississippi, and Texas. Over the next several decades, they moved even farther west, to Arizona and California.

While cotton production in the Lower South soon doubled or tripled the production of the old South, it resulted in wealth for only the few large plantations and farms, which were able to replenish their ranks of slaves from within. In response, smaller farms unable to find or afford slaves called for the resumption of African slave trade, which had been outlawed for several decades. This position, which stood in opposition to national law and Northern sensibilities, became one of the many factors that hastened the Civil War and brought an end to the "peculiar institution" of slavery and the cotton culture it supported.

Further reading: American Social History Project, *Who Built America: Working People and the Nation's Economy, Politics, Culture, and Society,* Vol. 1 (New York: Pantheon Books, 1989–92); David L. Cohn, *The Life and Times of King Cotton* (New York: Oxford University Press, 1956); John Mayfield, *The New Nation: 1800–1845,* rev. ed. (New York: Hill and Wang, 1982).

—Melinda Corey

Crockett, Davy (1786–1836)

Politician, soldier, and Texas patriot, Davy Crockett became most famous for his frontier exploits. Born in Greene County, Tennessee, in 1786, the young David Crockett had minimal schooling. By the time he was 12, he was at work, first as a cattle drover, then as a freight hauler, and, in slack times, as a farm laborer. He married Polly Finley, and on a rented tract of land he built a cabin and began to farm. Crockett was an excellent hunter and adept in the woods, but he had little interest in the regular labor associated with farming. In 1811, with his wife and two children, he moved from what was then eastern Tennessee to middle Tennessee, settling in Lincoln County near the Alabama line. The countryside was then in turmoil over Indian raids and news of a battle at Fort Mims. ANDREW JACKSON had begun to recruit volunteers, and Crockett immediately joined the local militia. He participated in the campaigns that followed the outbreak of the WAR OF 1812, but he was not present in 1814 at Jackson's great victory over the Creek Confederation at the BATTLE OF HORSESHOE BEND. In another twist of fate, Crockett joined a mounted Tennessee battalion that went to confront Indians in southern Alabama and northern Florida, as a result of which he missed Jackson's even greater triumph at New Orleans.

With the war over, Crockett returned to middle Tennessee. In 1816, upon the death of his wife Polly, he married a widow, Elizabeth Patton. Sometime during these years, he contracted malaria and only gradually recovered his strength. Meanwhile he tried, seemingly without success, to find some way to profit from the great internal migrations that characterized the years immediately after the war. In 1817, he moved to west Tennessee, and when Giles County was established, Crockett became a justice of the peace and was also elected a colonel in the militia. In 1821, he was elected to the Tennessee Legislature, where

David "Davy" Crockett *(Library of Congress)*

he supported the claims of squatters and small landholders. Reelected after a spirited campaign, he now represented a larger constituency, as west Tennessee had begun to grow. During this term, Crockett incurred the wrath of Jackson and his party by failing to support their candidate for the U.S. Senate.

Over the next decade, Crockett shifted his attention to the national political scene. In 1825, he was defeated in an election for the U.S. House of Representatives. He was subsequently elected in 1827, reelected in 1829, defeated in 1831, reelected in 1833, and finally defeated again in 1835. His mixed political success in contests for the House of Representatives reflected the close balance between the DEMOCRATIC PARTY and the WHIG PARTY. It also reflected a political fact of life about this 10-year period—namely, that Andrew Jackson (elected president in 1828) and his party were the dominant political force in Crockett's native Tennessee. Crockett was a Whig in a Democratic world. Jackson was the state's favored son, the first western president, and the pride of the state. Throughout his terms in Congress, Crockett generally voted against Jackson's measures. That he was elected to the House three times in this 10 years reflected his great personal popularity, an appeal that in the final analysis could not counter the power of the Democratic Party and the leadership of "Old Hickory."

With the end of his political career in the 1835 election, Crockett left his family and went to TEXAS in search of new opportunities. In February 1836, he and his companions arrived in San Antonio, where they joined the Texan force that was holding THE ALAMO. On March 6, the army of General ANTONIO LÓPEZ DE SANTA ANNA launched a frontal assault, and all the defenders of the Alamo mission died, including Crockett.

Crockett was one of the first politicians on the national scene to make a virtue of rural origins with minimal education. Throughout his career—whether as justice of the peace, colonel in the militia, or representative in Congress—he prided himself on his wide experience in the world and his good common sense. He delighted in debunking proper spelling and grammar. His autobiography, *A Narrative of the Life of David Crockett . . . Written by Himself* (1834) confirmed these eccentricities of style. Even in life, Crockett had been the subject of much legend and myth. His death at the Alamo further enhanced his qualities as the natural frontier figure, representing freedom of movement and action, good judgment, and common sense. His death also confirmed him as a man of principle, willing to die for the cause in which he believed.

Further reading: Davy Crockett, *Davy Crockett, His Own Story: A Narrative of the Life of David Crockett . . . Written by Himself* (1834; reprint, Bedford, Mass.: Applewood Books, 1993).

Cuba

The island nation of Cuba found itself the object of American advocates of MANIFEST DESTINY and proslavery expansionists in the antebellum period, as the United States sought to extend its influence and continue to wrestle with the issue of SLAVERY.

The sugar industry exploded after 1791, when French planters fled a slave revolt in Haiti and settled in Cuba. Sugarcane rapidly blanketed the island, and as a result 700,000 Africans were imported to work the plantations over the next 40 years; they eventually outnumbered whites on the island. Cuba was the world's largest sugar producer, and the newly independent United States was its biggest market. Meanwhile, the criollo bourgeoisie (born in Cuba of Spanish descent) was becoming wealthier and impatient with Spanish rule. By 1825, there were only two Spanish colonies left in the Americas: Cuba and Puerto Rico. The United States twice attempted to buy Cuba from Spain, in 1848 and 1854, but the colonial power refused to sell. In the 1850s, nationalist pressure for self-rule began to build and soon became unstoppable.

Having acquired EAST AND WEST FLORIDA from Spain in 1819, the United States had expanded to within 90 miles of Cuba. In a letter to Minister to Spain Hugh Nelson, Secretary of State JOHN QUINCY ADAMS described the likelihood of U.S. "annexation of Cuba" within half a century despite obstacles: "But there are laws of political as well as of physical gravitation; and if an apple severed by the tempest from its native tree cannot choose but fall to the ground, Cuba, forcibly disjoined from its own unnatural connection with Spain, and incapable of self support, can gravitate only towards the North American Union, which by the same law of nature cannot cast her off from its bosom." Cubans called this policy *la fruta madura* (ripe fruit); Washington would wait until the fruit was considered ripe for the picking.

By the end of the 18th century the United States had begun to play an increasingly prominent role in Cuba. With Spain involved in the European wars of the late 18th and early 19th centuries, the U.S. government was in a good position to take advantage of the situation. It was geographically well-positioned, since Cuba was only 90 miles away; the United States was growing in population; and the U.S. economy was expanding.

By 1850 the United States, Great Britain, and Spain accounted for 80 percent of Cuba's total foreign trade, with the Americans capturing 39 percent of the market, the British 34 percent, and the Spanish percent. Spain's importance to Cuba had diminished relative to that of the United States, and Spain could guarantee neither adequate markets for Cuban goods nor sufficient supplies. Yet while Spain's importance was declining, the government refused to relinquish its hands-on approach to Cuban affairs and continued to regulate Cuban trade by levying customs duties on imports and taxes on exports, thereby lowering profits for Cuban producers and increasing prices for the island's consumers.

In 1825 Mexico and Venezuela planned an expedition to Cuba in order to help the struggle for independence. But the United States, fearing an independent Cuba would lead to the end of slavery with repercussions in the southern states, let it be known that it would block any move to liberate Cuba from Spain.

Throughout the 1840s there had been several invasion attempts by southern expansionists, in the hopes that the slave-owning elite would declare independence from Spain. Once Cuba was independent, it would be invited to join the Union as a slave state. In October 1849, the first filibustering expedition by Narciso López, with the intention of invading Cuba, ended in abject failure. López led a second expedition in May 1850 and, after that failed, another expedition in August 1851. On this third attempt, López was captured by the Spanish army and publicly executed in Havana.

In 1853 President Franklin Pierce covertly supported a new Cuban expedition led by John A. Quitman, an associate of Narciso López and former governor of Missouri. While Quitman was building his forces, Pierce offered Spain $130 million for Cuba, which was refused. In Havana, Spanish police boarded an American merchant ship, the *Black Warrior,* and imprisoned her crew under the charge of "violating customs regulations." The Pierce administration tried to take advantage of the situation by threatening to declare war on Spain, but northern Democrats would not support Pierce's attempt to take Cuba by force, so the ploy failed.

Under instructions from Secretary of State William Marcy to put pressure on Pierce to seize the island, the American minister to Spain, as well as the ambassadors to France and Great Britain, sent an inflammatory message to Pierce that became known as the Ostend Manifesto. Invoking the rhetoric of manifest destiny, the three American diplomats declared that the United States was justified in seizing Cuba. Quickly leaked to the press by antiexpansionists, the Ostend Manifesto triggered a new wave of northern resentment against the South and forced Pierce to halt his efforts to acquire Cuba.

Further reading: Louis A. Perez, Jr., *Cuba and the United States: Ties of Singular Intimacy* (Athens: University of Georgia Press, 1990).

—Richard Friedline

D

Dana, Richard Henry (1815–1882)

Author and lawyer Richard Henry Dana was among a small group of Eastern literary figures (including Francis Parkman) who wrote about the West. Born in Massachusetts in 1815, Dana entered Harvard College in 1831 at the age of 16. Dogged by health problems, especially failing eyesight as a result of an earlier bout with measles, he withdrew from college. His family then sent him on a long sea voyage to recover his health. In 1834, he sailed as a common seaman on the brig *Pilgrim,* bound from Boston to CALIFORNIA by way of Cape Horn. Arriving in California in 1835, Dana witnessed the trade in hides and tallow characteristic of the California economy at the time. He returned to Boston in excellent health in 1836, reenrolled in Harvard College, graduated in 1837, and then read law and was admitted to the bar in 1840. That same year, he published *Two Years Before the Mast,* an account of his two-year voyage and sojourn in California.

Dana's book gave him something of a national literary reputation and became known for its descriptions of the brutal treatment of common sailors on ship. In additional to the physical hardships of poor food, little sanitation, and crowded living conditions, sailors were subjected to arbitrary and brutal punishment by officers, especially flogging, for a variety of transgressions. The book was also an invaluable account of life in Mexican California, if not the most important detailed description of the Californios's existence before their lands and culture were submerged by the great influx of Americans after the CALIFORNIA GOLD RUSH of 1849 and on. Dana's depictions of the California ranchos and the elaborate pastoral economic and social life built on trade in hides and tallow have become a necessary historical document for understanding life in California before 1848. The book was later reprinted in English and French editions.

Dana practiced law with great success, specializing in admiralty cases. He also pursued an interest in politics, becoming an important figure in the FREE-SOIL PARTY. In 1851 he acted as attorney for the defense for Shadrach Minkins, who was rescued by abolitionists, in Boston and also defended fugitive slave ANTHONY BURNS in 1854. Dana's interest in politics had a patrician slant to it. He believed strongly in the principles associated with political parties and their platforms (hence his support of the antislavery doctrines of the Free-Soil Party), but he had no taste for campaigning, and he intensely disliked the corruption and favoritism popularly associated with successful political campaigns.

Dana continued his successful law practice for the next 30 years. In 1866 he lost a contest for a seat in the U.S. Senate to Benjamin Butler. A decade later, President Ulysses S. Grant nominated Dana as ambassador to England, but the Senate refused to confirm him because Grant had acted without consulting party leaders. In 1882 Dana died in Rome, Italy, while on a tour of the continent.

Further reading: Robert L. Gale, *Richard Henry Dana* (New York: Twayne Publishers, 1968).

Dartmoor Prison

Located in southwest England near Plymouth, Dartmoor Prison was the compound used by the British in the WAR OF 1812 (1812–15) to hold as many as 6,000 captured American sailors and privateersmen. American prisoners of war hated its desolate location on a barren moor. While many suffered illness and malnourishment, others set up trades and stores within its walls to service their fellow prisoners. In a world unto itself, the prisoners even established schools to teach navigation, dancing, and boxing.

The most famous section of the compound was Prison Number 4. In 1814 the British placed all of the African-American prisoners in this prison, along with whites who were considered undesirable by other prisoners. The black prisoners were led by Richard Craftus, a huge African American also called King Dick, and they were known for holding religious services and theatrical performances in their prison house. The American prisoners were often unruly and challenged the authority of the British guards. Conditions became even more explosive after the peace agreement of the TREATY OF GHENT (December 24, 1814). Without an easy means of accommodating the prisoners and returning them to the United States, and preoccupied by the return of Napoleon to France in the spring of 1815, the British did not release their prisoners of war. The Americans rioted on April 4, 1815, when the British commissary attempted to serve them hard biscuits instead of the usual soft bread. The Americans won that confrontation, and the British found the appropriate bread for them.

On April 6, 1815, an incident along the wall of the prison, where some prisoners were thought to be trying to escape, led to a general alarm. Amid the confusion, and as the prisoners began to rush the gate, the British guards opened fire on the Americans, killing six and wounding many more. This event was called the Dartmoor Massacre and remained a searing testimony of British perfidy for the American maritime community. A joint American and British diplomatic commission, however, determined that no one was at fault, thus defusing a potentially divisive diplomatic incident immediately after the War of 1812.

Dartmouth College case (*Trustees of Dartmouth College v. Woodward,* 1819)

In 1816 the New Hampshire state legislature altered the charter of Dartmouth College (granted by the colonial New Hampshire legislature in 1769) to assert state control over the institution. The private board of trustees of the college opposed this action, but the New Hampshire supreme court decided in favor of the state. In 1819, the case was brought before the U.S. Supreme Court, with Chief Justice John Marshall presiding. DANIEL WEBSTER, a Dartmouth graduate, represented the college. He argued that the New Hampshire legislature's action was an abrogation of contract, since it altered the act of incorporation that created Dartmouth College. As such, the change was a violation of the contract clause of the U.S. Constitution and was therefore unconstitutional. In a 3–1 vote, Marshall and the Supreme Court were convinced by Webster.

Although the decision was rendered in a case involving the incorporation of a private institution of higher learning, it had a larger application to the world of business in that it helped to secure the sanctity of the corporation, a legal entity that was in this period just taking on much of its modern form. Because of the Dartmouth decision, private companies with acts of incorporation believed they were protected from state legislative interference. To get around this problem, many state legislatures started inserting a reserve clause into acts of incorporation creating private companies. The sanctity of the corporation was also subsequently weakened by the Charles River Bridge Case of 1837.

Further reading: G. Edward White, *The Marshall Court and Cultural Change, 1815–1835* (New York: Macmillan, 1988).

Decatur, Stephen (1779–1820)

Stephen Decatur was a swashbuckling officer of the American navy in the early 19th century. Born in Maryland on January 5, 1779, Decatur grew up in Philadelphia in a seafaring family. He became a midshipman in the U.S. Navy in 1798 and fought in the Quasi War (1798–1800) with France. But he first gained fame in action off the coast of Tripoli in the war against the Barbary pirates, by which time he had been promoted to lieutenant. In 1804, the American frigate *Philadelphia* had run aground off Tripoli harbor and been captured. On the night of February 16, 1804, Decatur led a raid into the harbor to deny the vessel to the Tripolitans. He and his men entered the harbor on a captured schooner named the *Intrepid,* seized and burned the *Philadelphia,* and made a safe getaway. Decatur was promoted to captain on the basis of this expedition. He also was involved in several other engagements at Tripoli, including hand-to-hand combat, that captured the imagination of the American public.

At the beginning of the WAR OF 1812 (1812–15), Decatur was captain of the frigate *United States.* On October 15, 1812, he outmaneuvered a slightly less powerful foe, the *HMS Macedonian,* pummeling her with over 70 broadsides, killing or wounding a third of her crew, and forcing the British captain to strike her colors. This action was one of a series of spectacular single-ship victories at the beginning of the war, but the British blockade kept Decatur trapped in American harbors for over two years. On January 15, 1815, unaware of the TREATY OF GHENT of December 24, 1814, Decatur took advantage of weather conditions to slip out of New York harbor in the frigate *President,* but he struck a sandbar off Sandy Hook, damaging the ship. Winds prevented his reentry to New York harbor, so he continued his efforts to run the blockade. Several British frigates pursued him. He was able to defeat the fastest of these, but, almost crippled from the battle and running aground while dealing with a storm at sea, he was compelled to surrender to the other two.

Later that year, Decatur took command of the American squadron sent to destroy the Algerian ships that had attacked and exacted tribute from American vessels. In a short and brilliant campaign, he defeated the naval forces of Algiers, forced Tunis and Tripoli officials to sign peace treaties and pay indemnities, and helped bring to an end the power of the Barbary Coast pirates who had been the scourge of the western Mediterranean.

When James Barron, who had been court-martialed after the *Chesapeake-Leopard Affair* in 1807, issued a challenge because of statements Decatur made concerning Barron's reinstatement in the navy the two agreed to meet in a duel. Decatur wounded Barron, but the shot he received was fatal. Decatur died on March 20, 1820. He is best remembered today for the toast he gave at a dinner: "Our country . . . may she always be in the right; but our country, right or wrong."

Further reading: William M. Fowler, Jr., *Jack Tars and Commodores: The American Navy, 1783–1815* (Boston: Houghton Mifflin, 1984).

Deere, John (1804–1886)

John Deere was an innovative inventor and manufacturer of the plows and farming equipment that helped make American AGRICULTURE more productive. Deere was born in Rutland, Vermont, on February 7, 1804, the son of a tailor. His parents were both formerly British subjects who had sided with Great Britain during the American Revolution and later settled in New England. Deere received scant formal education and was apprenticed to a blacksmith at 17. He proved himself an excellent worker and established a reputation for high-quality metalwork. For 12 years he worked at or owned several blacksmith shops around Vermont with considerable success, until fires and the depression of 1837 forced him into bankruptcy. To escape his debts, Deere relocated to Grand Detour, Illinois, at the behest of a friend, Leonard Andrus, through whom he established another shop. As before, Deere cemented his reputation for high-quality smithing. He also encountered farming conditions radically different from those of New England, especially difficulties associated with plowing on the prairie. He set about resolving them between bouts of the usual blacksmith work.

The soil of the Midwest was rich and fertile, but particularly heavy and sticky. Under these conditions, a farmer tilling land with a conventional iron plow was forced to stop and periodically clean the moldboards (which did the actual plowing), as sod accumulated in clumps. Deere immediately saw the need for a better-designed device that would clean itself while in operation. His first efforts were unsuccessful but displayed an innovative streak that characterized his later life. Deere's first plow was actually a broken blade saw made of steel, which he bent over a log, hammered into place, and fashioned into a curved plow blade. During trials it cut through the prairie clay better than any iron device extant. Thereafter, using only polished steel in place of iron, he perfected a series of new, wedge-shaped plows capable of tilling through heavy prairie soil without the necessity of constant cleaning. The result was greater acreage covered and far less effort expended. However, sales were slow. In 1837 Deere sold only three plows. Two years later, he sold 10 and in 1840 a mere 40, forcing him to concentrate upon his routine blacksmith activities for income. But by 1848 Deere had relocated to Moline, Illinois, by the Mississippi River; acquired a business partner; and expanded his sideline into a full-fledged business. This move afforded the company closer proximity to water power and river-borne transport, and hence easier access to raw materials and new markets.

Intent on producing the finest plows available, Deere had to import steel from Sheffield, England, and also took on several business associates. After the introduction of harder steel from the Bessemer-Kelly process, he was able to acquire high-quality steel from Pittsburgh. Significantly, the nation's first supply of agricultural steel was made at the behest of the John Deere Company in 1846.

Deere spent considerable effort perfecting his plows, especially developing the optimum curvature for steel moldboards. By 1857 the John Deere Company was firmly established and selling 13,000 plows a year, making him the largest farm-tool manufacturer in the Midwest. Moreover, his constant flow of inventions greatly enhanced the agricultural resources of his region, with tremendous profits to farmers and their attendant markets.

Outside the realm of improved farm technology, Deere was a pioneer in aggressive marketing techniques. Rather than wait for orders, he continually built up a backlog of inventory while dispatching company agents throughout the countryside and Canada to demonstrate his wares. Deere products were a common sight at state fairs nationwide, and he was among the earliest manufacturers to take out regular advertisements in publications such as the *Prairie Farmer.* He also established one of the earliest national networks of wholesalers and retailers. The result was a constant influx of capital, which Deere inevitably reinvested in upgrading and improving his line of products. At one point he was able to offer prospective customers five sizes of walking plows and three sizes of breaking plows. During the 1850s his company pioneered work in developing seed-drills and plows for large, steam-propelled tractors. By the mid-1860s he was making metal plows with interchangeable parts.

After weathering several national depressions, Deere became an important supplier of wagons, carriages, harnesses, and other useful articles for the Union army during the Civil War. His steady stream of effective plows also insured that the North enjoyed great abundance of food throughout this conflict. By 1868 the business was incorporated as Deere & Company, and actual leadership was passed on to his son Charles. Freed from administrative demands, Deere focused his energy and talents on continued development of agricultural equipment. His company also continued to be a leader with respect to sales, distribution, and service organizations nationwide.

Deere died in Moline on April 16, 1873, having significantly contributed to the expansion and profitability of American agriculture, along with modern promotional and servicing strategies. As such he was directly responsible for helping the first wave of farmers to populate the Midwest. Deere was not the first designer to use steel in designing a plow but, rather, the first to successfully market one. His was the plow, literally, that broke the plains.

Further reading: Wayne G. Broehl, *John Deere's Company: A History of Deere & Company and Its Times* (New York: Doubleday, 1984); John Gerstner, *Genuine Value: The John Deere Journey* (Moline, Ill.: Deere & Company, 2000); R. Douglas Hurt, "The Tractor: Iron Horse for the Farmer," *Journal of the West* 30, no. 2 (1991): 9–29; Yngve P. Magnuson, "John Deere: A Study of an Industrialist on the Illinois Frontier, 1837–1857" (unpublished master's thesis, St. Cloud State College, 1956).

—John C. Fredriksen

Delany, Martin See Volume V

Democratic Party

The Democratic Party of the 19th century traced its roots to the Democratic-Republicans in the early republic. This party emerged in the 1790s out of a dispute over the proper role of the federal government within the framework of the new Constitution. A group in Congress coalesced around the leadership of Representative James Madison of Virginia. In the first administration, the spokesman for the opposition was Secretary of State Thomas Jefferson, also of Virginia. This Democratic-Republican "interest" believed that the administration of President George Washington and Secretary of the Treasury Alexander Hamilton (the latter of whom was a Federalist) assumed powers for the national government that were not explicitly delegated to it in the Constitution. The Republicans, as they called themselves (the longer name Democratic-Republicans was sometimes used in the early 19th century), charged that Federalists also secretly desired to impose a monarchy on the young republic and harbored far too much sympathy for the English model of government and economy. They pointed to the Jay Treaty of 1795, negotiated by the Washington administration with Great Britain to resolve outstanding issues from the American Revolution, as further proof of this tendency on the part of the Federalists.

The party of Jefferson and Madison saw itself as representing ordinary people, including farmers and urban laborers in the North and plantation and slave owners in the South against the pretensions of would-be aristocrats in the Federalist ranks. In turn, Federalists derided Republicans as too enthusiastic for the excesses of the French Revolution and for being irreligious. The Republicans did attract the support of deists and free thinkers, as well as Catholics and others drawn to Jefferson's advocacy of religious tolerance and Republican championing of political equality for white men.

Republicans and Federalists both believed that the other posed a genuine threat to liberty and to the republic that must be resisted whenever possible. In one of the most important elections in the political history of the United States, Thomas Jefferson of Virginia and Aaron Burr of New York defeated Federalist incumbent John Adams in 1800. Although Jefferson was generally acknowledged to be the leader of the party, neither he nor Burr received a majority of the votes in the electoral college, thus leaving the election to be decided by the House of Representatives. Jefferson was finally elected president, and he and his party assumed power. Although outgoing Federalist president John Adams did not remain in Washington to see his successor inaugurated, the ascendancy of Jefferson to the presidency by a peaceful transition of power was the first in the history of the young nation, thus setting a precedent.

Once in office, the Republicans pursued policies of reduced government spending, an enhanced respect for states' rights, minimal federal authority, and a belief that the federal government should not serve the interests of economic elites. Under Jefferson's leadership, taxes were cut, the national debt was paid off, and the Alien and Sedition Acts—laws passed by the Federalists to squelch political dissent—were revoked or allowed to lapse. Republicans, especially those from the slaveholding states of the South, did not want the federal government strong enough to threaten the institution of SLAVERY. They also generally supported the aspirations of poorer white men to gain access to the ballot between 1800 and 1830, and most of these new voters supported Republican candidates when they gained the right of suffrage. Many workers in the cities and towns supported Republicans as well.

The Democratic-Republicans won every presidential election from 1800 through 1820 and took the country through the trauma of the WAR OF 1812, which the nation barely survived. After the war, the Federalists, due in part to their opposition to it, began a rapid decline into their final oblivion. During the 1820s—the so-called ERA OF GOOD FEELINGS—it seemed for a while that parties might fade from the American scene. When, for example, JAMES MONROE was reelected in 1820, he won every electoral vote but one. But in 1824, in a controversial election, JOHN QUINCY

ADAMS was elected as a National Republican over ANDREW JACKSON, most famously known for defeating the British in the BATTLE OF NEW ORLEANS at the end of the War of 1812.

MARTIN VAN BUREN of New York played a crucial role in revitalizing the old Jeffersonian party in the 1820s. Forging alliances with southerners such as Richmond, Virginia, newspaper editor Thomas Ritchie, Van Buren thought that political parties were crucial to the health of the nation in that they blunted sectional tensions and resulted in honest and healthy political competition. He saw the Democratic Party, as it was becoming known, as an alliance between "plain republicans of the North and planters of the South." Meanwhile, Jackson and his devoted supporters continued to campaign over the ensuing four years of John Quincy Adams's presidency, winning a convincing victory in the campaign of 1828.

The Democratic Party under the leadership of Jackson and Van Buren in the 1830s was committed to a strict interpretation of the Constitution and a limited role for the federal government in the life of the nation. Supporters of the party included farmers in the North and slave owners in the South, as well as mechanics and immigrants in the cities of the North. Jackson vetoed bills to promote internal improvements and the bill to recharter the SECOND BANK OF THE UNITED STATES, as the Democrats decried privilege and economic monopolies and saw itself as the party of the small producers, i.e., farmers and working men.

The "Bank War" of 1832 was crucial in shaping the second party system. In vetoing the rechartering of the Second Bank of the United States, Jackson saw himself as acting on behalf of the common people by striking at an economic power that had grown so powerful it threatened the integrity of the republic. Supporters of the bank saw Jackson as a demagogue playing on popular fears and overstepping his authority under the Constitution in issuing the veto. Opponents of the president, who was reelected in 1832 following the bank veto, began to call him "King Andrew."

The Democrats also defended the rights of slaveholders and supported the removal of American Indians to

This cartoon depicts Martin Van Buren, the presidential candidate for the Free-Soil Party, stretching over the Salt River (the slang term for political defeat) in his attempts to unite his party's Democratic and Whig factions against slavery. *(Hulton/Archive)*

lands west of the Mississippi. The party systematically rewarded its supporters with jobs and offices, as part of the so-called spoils system. Democrats also favored low tariffs, as they believed that a high tariff (or tax) on imported goods would enrich manufacturers and merchants at the expense of ordinary workers and farmers. Their support of such political rights did not, however, extend to women.

The Democrats between 1830 and 1860 opposed moral reforms such as the TEMPERANCE MOVEMENT, Sabbatarianism, and most important, abolitionism. They became the defenders of the desire of their constituents, including immigrants, to resist the reforming crusades that swept through the United States in the antebellum era. Democrats believed that the federal government should not coerce people on moral issues, just as it should not grant special privileges to economic elites. In this sense, the party's program was essentially negative.

Andrew Jackson's use of the presidential veto power encouraged the formation of an opposition party that called themselves Whigs. Using popular political techniques borrowed in part from the Democrats, the WHIG PARTY nominated the aging general WILLIAM HENRY HARRISON, who subsequently denied Van Buren, Jackson's successor, a second term in 1840.

Democrats in the antebellum period were not of one mind, however, especially on issues of the ECONOMY. In many states, especially in the North, Democrats were divided between those who favored extensive banking, paper money, and economic expansion and those who feared that changes in the economy, such as the growth of wage labor, were potentially harmful to ordinary people. In New York, the latter group were known as Locofocos, a name that to Whigs and probusiness Democrats became synonymous with economic radicalism.

Where Democrats were more united was on the question of political democracy. This included defending the rights of immigrants in the face of nativism and the KNOW-NOTHING PARTY. Although the Democrats had support from native-born Protestants in all regions, they came to rely on the votes of immigrants in the larger cities of the Northeast. It was these voters who helped to elect Democrat JAMES K. POLK of Tennessee over HENRY CLAY in 1844.

In the 1840s the Democratic Party was the party of expansion, encouraging the annexation of TEXAS and settlement of the Pacific Northwest. They also supported the rights of white planters to take their slaves with them into new territories. This expansionist impulse led to the MEXICAN-AMERICAN WAR (1846–48), a conflict begun and prosecuted by President Polk.

In the war's aftermath, growing sectional tensions over slavery caused severe conflicts within the Democratic Party. Northern Democrats were increasingly troubled by the expansion of SLAVERY, and one of them, Congressman David Wilmot of Pennsylvania, introduced a measure to ban slavery from all territory gained in the Mexican-American War. Martin Van Buren himself left the Democratic Party in 1848 to run as the nominee of the FREE-SOIL PARTY, which proposed that slavery be confined to those states where it already existed.

Despite the COMPROMISE OF 1850, the controversy over slavery continued to threaten the unity and stability of the nation and its political system. Although two northern Democrats were elected president in the 1850s—Franklin Pierce of New Hampshire and James Buchanan of Pennsylvania—neither was able to defuse the growing crisis. Tensions over slavery led to the collapse of the Whig Party in the 1850s. The Democrats desperately wanted to keep the entire question of slavery out of politics in order to keep the Union intact and to perpetuate their political alliances. But events overtook that strategy. The ill-advised Kansas-Nebraska Act, shepherded through Congress by Senator Stephen Douglas of Illinois, revoked the ban on slavery north of a line established by the MISSOURI COMPROMISE of 1820. Under the act's provisions, slavery was permitted north of this line if the settlers of a territory voted to accept it. Northern Democrats who found themselves in profound disagreement with Douglas's doctrine of POPULAR SOVEREIGNTY began to desert the party. Some of them joined the new REPUBLICAN PARTY that was emerging in the northern section of the country. President James Buchanan, acting in what he believed was the spirit of the decision handed down by the U.S. Supreme Court that forbade territories from outlawing slavery, supported the admission of Kansas to the Union as a slave state. This series of events outraged many Democrats in the North, who now saw the slaveholding power expanding its influence over the nation's political institutions and soon, they feared, over the land of the United States itself.

Meeting in convention at Charleston, South Carolina, in 1860, the Democrats could not agree on a candidate for president. Reconvening a few weeks later in Baltimore, they selected Stephen Douglas. Several southern delegations walked out, fearing that the national Democratic Party was no longer fully committed to protecting slavery and states' rights. Southern Democrats nominated John Breckinridge of Kentucky. Douglas lost every northern state except New Jersey to Republican nominee Abraham Lincoln and the South to Breckinridge. Seeing Lincoln's victory as tantamount to the abolition of slavery, 11 southern states seceded from the United States, thus triggering the Civil War (1861–65). The Democratic Party, which traced its roots to Thomas Jefferson and which had held national power almost continuously from 1800 to 1860, lay in shambles, discredited and seen by most northerners as the party of slavery and, after 1861, of treason. The party ultimately survived these calamities, but only in the defeated South of the old Confederacy would it regularly hold power in the decades following the Civil War.

Further reading: John Ashworth, *"Agrarians" and "Aristocrats": Party Political Ideology in the United States, 1837–1846* (New Jersey: Humanities Press, 1983); Robert A. Rutland, *The Democrats from Jefferson to Clinton* (Columbia: University of Missouri Press, 1995); Harry Watson, *Liberty and Power: The Politics of Jacksonian America* (New York: Hill and Wang, 1990).

—Jason Duncan

Deseret, State of

The State of Deseret was a Mormon political community in what is now Utah. Though its period of official existence was short, from 1849 to 1850, "Deseret" more broadly refers to the Mormon community in Utah in its early decades, after its migration there in 1847 and before the admission of Utah into the Union as a state in 1896.

Officially known as the CHURCH OF JESUS CHRIST OF LATTER-DAY SAINTS, the Mormon church was founded in 1830 in Fayette, New York, by JOSEPH SMITH, JR., who that year published the Book of Mormon, which he claimed to have translated from gold plates bestowed by an angel. (The name "Deseret" is said to mean "honey bee" in this book.) Based on the Book of Mormon and private revelations, Smith preached what he considered to be a restored version of Christianity, with a distinctive, highly centralized church structure and a strong emphasis on missionary activity and dedication to the community. The church grew rapidly, attracting converts from England as well as the United States. But the Mormons, or Saints as they called themselves, were repeatedly forced to move because of persecution from neighbors who objected to their unorthodox beliefs, communal economic practices, and bloc voting in public elections, among other sources of contention. The church's advocacy of POLYGAMY, by which men could have more than one wife, also attracted condemnation, although it did not become an official doctrine until 1852.

In the 1830s the church moved from New York to Ohio to Missouri to NAUVOO, Illinois. In 1844 Smith and his brother Hyrum were assassinated by a mob while being held in prison in Carthage, Illinois, on charges of treason. A schism developed over who should succeed Smith as leader of the church, but the largest group rallied behind BRIGHAM YOUNG, head of the policy-making body called the Quorum of the Twelve Apostles.

Young sought a safe haven for his church, a Mormon homeland far from "Gentiles" (as his people called non-Mormons). He identified it more than a thousand miles west in the Great Basin, an area of the Rocky Mountains then claimed by Mexico, though inhabited at the time only by Native Americans and a few American fur trappers and traders called MOUNTAIN MEN. Bordered by the Wasatch Range in the east and the Sierra Nevada and Cascade Range in the west, it was called the Great Basin because waterways drained into it as into an inland sink; it had no outlet to the sea. Full of strange and forbidding scenery, the region was protected from intruders by arid wastelands such as the Mojave Desert, and it contained several saline lakes, including the Great Salt Lake in what is now Utah. Young selected the Great Salt Lake Valley as the Mormons' destination. This would be the site of the "Gathering," the spiritually significant bringing together of all the Saints.

In 1846 Young led the first group of Mormon pioneers on the first leg of the journey, from Illinois to Winter Quarters (now Omaha, Nebraska). The following year, on July 24, 1847 (remembered in Utah as Pioneer Day), the epic migration, known as the Mormon trek, was completed when an advance party of about 150 Mormons arrived in Great Salt Lake Valley. Trees were scarce, but the soil was fertile. William Clayton, one of the Mormon pioneers, called it "one of the most beautiful valleys and pleasant places for a home for the Saints which could be found."

Wasting no time, the pioneers dammed a stream to provide water and planted corn, potatoes, winter wheat, and other crops. Land was parceled out to individual families. A city was planned in plots of 10 acres (four hectares) around Temple Square, a central plot of 40 acres (16 hectares) that would be reserved for a temple. That city received the name Great Salt Lake City, later (in 1868) abbreviated to Salt Lake City. In autumn 1847, Young was elected president and prophet of the Mormon church, officially becoming Smith's successor.

While the Mormon trek was underway, the United States fought Mexico in the MEXICAN-AMERICAN WAR (1846–48). About 500 Saints, known as the Mormon Battalion, served on the U.S. side, affirming Mormon loyalty to the United States (often questioned by the church's critics) and laying the ground for a claim to remain in the territory they had occupied. In the TREATY OF GUADALUPE HIDALGO, which ended the war in 1848, the Great Basin passed from Mexican to American sovereignty.

In 1849, expecting that the Mormon homeland would eventually become a state of the Union, Young called a convention to draft a constitution. The constitution that resulted that year formally created the State of Deseret, with Great Salt Lake City as its capital. The constitution provided for a bicameral legislature and supreme court, but in practice the state was a theocracy run by the church hierarchy headed by Young, who, running unopposed, was elected governor of Deseret on March 12, 1849. It was funded by tithing, the Saints' contribution of 10 percent of their incomes to the church. Among the state's official acts were the incorporation of the Church of Jesus Christ of

Latter-day Saints, a charter for Great Salt Lake City, the establishment of what is now the University of Utah, and the founding of a Perpetual Emigrating Fund to lend money for migration expenses to poor Saints who wanted to come to Deseret.

As conceived by Young, Deseret included not only the Great Salt Lake Valley but almost a half-million square miles of territory, including an outlet to the Pacific Ocean in southern CALIFORNIA. It encompassed all of present-day Utah, nearly all of Nevada, most of Arizona, and parts of California, Oregon, New Mexico, Colorado, and Wyoming. To stake the Mormon claim, Young founded settlements at key points throughout this vast region, selecting by name the Saints who would colonize them. The chosen colonists usually complied willingly, though not always gladly. One Mormon girl cried when she learned that her father had been selected, but told a friend, "I should not own him as a father if he would not go when he is called." In this manner, about 350 settlements were established, including Moab, Utah; Carson Valley and Las Vegas, Nevada; San Bernardino, California; Fort Supply and Fort Bridger, Wyoming; and Lemhi, Idaho.

Deseret petitioned the United States for territorial status, but Congress refused to consider the petition. Anti-Mormon sentiment was still high: President ZACHARY TAYLOR called the Mormons "a pack of outlaws" who "had been driven out of two states and were not fit for self-government." Territorial status did come soon, but on U.S. terms. In September 1850 Congress created the Territory of Utah, rejecting the name Deseret for one derived from the region's Ute Indians. The territory's scale, limited principally to Utah and Nevada and later reduced to Utah alone, was much smaller than that proposed for Deseret. However, President MILLARD FILLMORE, who had succeeded Taylor after the latter's death from cholera that year, allowed Young to continue holding power as territorial governor, and the territorial legislature continued to be dominated by Mormons. Although Deseret officially ceased to exist, the Mormon Church hierarchy was still the most potent authority in Utah. From at least 1862 to 1870 the State of Deseret was clandestinely revived, with a "ghost" government of Deseret, composed of the same Mormons as those in Utah's territorial government, meeting in secret as a sign of their commitment to Deseret as originally conceived.

In the meantime, the number of Mormons in Utah continued to grow, to about 40,000 by 1859. They included thousands of converts from England and Scandinavia and, from 1856 to 1860, thousands who came hauling handcarts because they were too poor to afford ox-drawn wagons. By 1869, when the opening of the transcontinental railroad made it easier to come to Utah, the territory's population had reached 80,000.

The early years were hard. In 1848 crickets devoured much of the harvest, with complete disaster averted only by the intervention of cricket-eating seagulls, an event the Mormons took to be a divine miracle. Young's efforts to establish industries, such as pottery, cloth, lead, and iron, were largely unsuccessful, though the CALIFORNIA GOLD RUSH provided a bonanza in 1849–50 as the Saints traded and did business with prospective gold diggers passing through Utah. There were some clashes with NATIVE AMERICANS, including the Walker War of 1853, though relations were relatively good, since the Mormons regarded Native Americans as descendants of Israel. The Ute learned to distinguish between "Mormonee" and "Mericats," or other Americans.

The Mormons' biggest problem was continuing animosity from white non-Mormons. The Saints had fled to Utah to escape conflict with Gentiles, but now that Utah was a U.S. territory, that conflict was renewed. Polygamy, which the Mormons began to preach openly in 1852, was considered immoral and barbarous by most Americans. The Mormon tendencies to band together economically and vote in unison were regarded as harmful to free enterprise and free elections. A new Mormon alphabet of 38 letters, which was meant to reform and replace the English alphabet, was viewed by outsiders as a nefarious secret code, while the Mormons' close relationship with Native Americans raised suspicions of treason.

Amid increasing reports of disloyalty and disregard for American law, President James Buchanan replaced Young with a non-Mormon governor, Alfred Cumming, and sent him along with federal troops to Utah in 1857 to put down what he saw as "substantial rebellion" and restore "the supremacy of the Constitution." In what was known as the Utah War (1857–58), the Mormons called in their distant colonists and missionaries and massed in their heartland, ready to defend themselves against what they saw as invaders. Mormon raiders destroyed federal property, but no lives were lost in combat. The affair was settled peacefully, with Cumming becoming governor, while Young remained as powerful as before in his capacity as head of the church. The most serious loss of life, the Mountain Meadows massacre of 1857, involved noncombatants: About 140 non-Mormon migrants bound for California were massacred by Native Americans and Mormon settlers.

Throughout the remainder of the 19th century, the relationship between the United States and the Mormons in Utah remained one of tension. Utah applications for statehood were refused, largely because of the polygamy issue. Congress passed laws against polygamy that were targeted directly at the Mormons, most notably the Edmunds-Tucker Act, or Anti-Polygamy Act, of 1887, which dissolved the corporation of the church, forbade Mormon participation in government, abolished woman suffrage (which the

Utah territorial legislature had granted in 1870, 50 years before women nationwide would receive the vote), and otherwise attempted to end the temporal power of the Mormon Church. The standoff did not end until 1890, when the church formally renounced polygamy. Statehood followed in 1896.

The beehive, a symbol of industriousness and a reminder of the meaning of Deseret, is featured in the State Seal of Utah. The *Deseret News,* a newspaper founded in 1850, is still in publication.

Further reading: Claudia Lauper Bushman and Richard Lyman Bushman, *Mormons in America* (New York: Oxford University Press, 1999); Michael S. Durham, *Desert Between the Mountains: Mormons, Miners, Padres, Mountain Men, and the Opening of the Great Basin, 1772–1869* (New York: Henry Holt and Company, 1997); Wallace Stegner, *Mormon Country* (New York: Duell, Sloan & Pearce, 1942); Jean Kinney Williams, *The Mormons* (New York: Franklin Watts, 1996).

—George Ochoa

diseases and epidemics

As American cities grew in the early 19th century, so did the risk to public health. The urban poor were increasingly crowded in filthy conditions ripe for the spread of infectious disease. The germ theory of disease—understanding the role of microorganisms in causing illness—would not be developed until the second half of the century, but improved trade and transportation were already enabling the swifter spread of germs around the globe. With no clear understanding of disease or how to combat it, it was not surprising that deadly epidemics frequently wracked antebellum America.

Perhaps the most devastating illness of this period was cholera. Also called Asiatic cholera, it is now known to be caused by the bacterium *Vibrio comma,* which spreads when water and food supplies are contaminated with stools from infected people. Cholera causes severe diarrhea, vomiting, and cramps, and, if left untreated, swiftly brings about death through dehydration in more than 50 percent of patients. In 19th-century epidemics, the mortality rate among cholera patients could run as high as 90 percent. Though still endemic in poorer nations, cholera has mostly been eradicated from developed countries by proper sanitation, especially safeguards to keep sewage out of drinking water. But in the early 19th century, when it first became pandemic, or epidemic over a wide region, its speed and brutality made it inexplicable to many except as the scourge of an angry God.

The first major cholera pandemic began in 1817 in India. It spread to most of Asia and East Africa, reaching China in 1820 and Russia in 1823. This first pandemic did not reach western Europe or America, but from 1826 to 1837, a new pandemic did. This one too began in India, reached Russia by 1831, and struck France and the British Isles by 1831–32. Irish immigrants carried it to North America in 1832, where it raged until 1834. It reached New York City in June 1832 and spread south and west across the country, killing thousands of Americans and sending people fleeing in terror from infected places. Wrote one diarist, "To see individuals well in the morning & buried before night . . . is something which is appalling to the boldest heart."

Many Americans considered cholera a disease of the sinful, visited selectively by God on immoral, dissolute, low-class people with filthy habits. "The cholera is not *caused* by intemperance and filth, in themselves, but it is a *scourge,* a *rod* in the hand of God," wrote one clergyman. Doctors of the time did what they could to save patients, which was very little. Common but futile remedies to treat the disease included bleeding, calomel (a mercury compound), and laudanum (an opium solution). Most physicians believed incorrectly that the disease had a miasmatic or atmospheric origin, arising from filth and foul fumes and spread through the air. One genuine health benefit of this view was the spread of public sanitation measures such as cleaning streets, installing sewers, and collecting garbage. Health reformers such as Sylvester Graham and William Alcott helped spread the view that cleanliness meant health. In many places, quarantines were instituted, though public opinion was divided as to whether cholera was contagious. In any case, the increasing efficiency of trade and transportation in the early 19th century ensured that cholera continued to spread.

In 1840 a new worldwide cholera pandemic began, this one killing millions of people into the 1850s. Reaching the United States in late 1848, it had struck every part of the country east of the Rocky Mountains by 1849. In that year of the CALIFORNIA GOLD RUSH, ships from Panama carried the disease to San Francisco, where it advanced throughout California. Meanwhile, in Great Britain, research was beginning to show a way of fighting cholera. In 1854, British physician John Snow demonstrated that cholera was spread through water contaminated by sewage. In one striking case, he brought an end to a local cholera epidemic by removing the handle from a pump that drew water from a sewage-laden area of the Thames River.

Yellow fever was another disease that regularly took epidemic form in antebellum America. Yellow fever is now known to be caused by a virus transmitted through the bites of infected mosquitoes. Symptoms include fever; headache; chills; and jaundice, the yellowing of the skin that gives the disease its name. In the worst cases, the disease ends in death through internal hemorrhage. Endemic

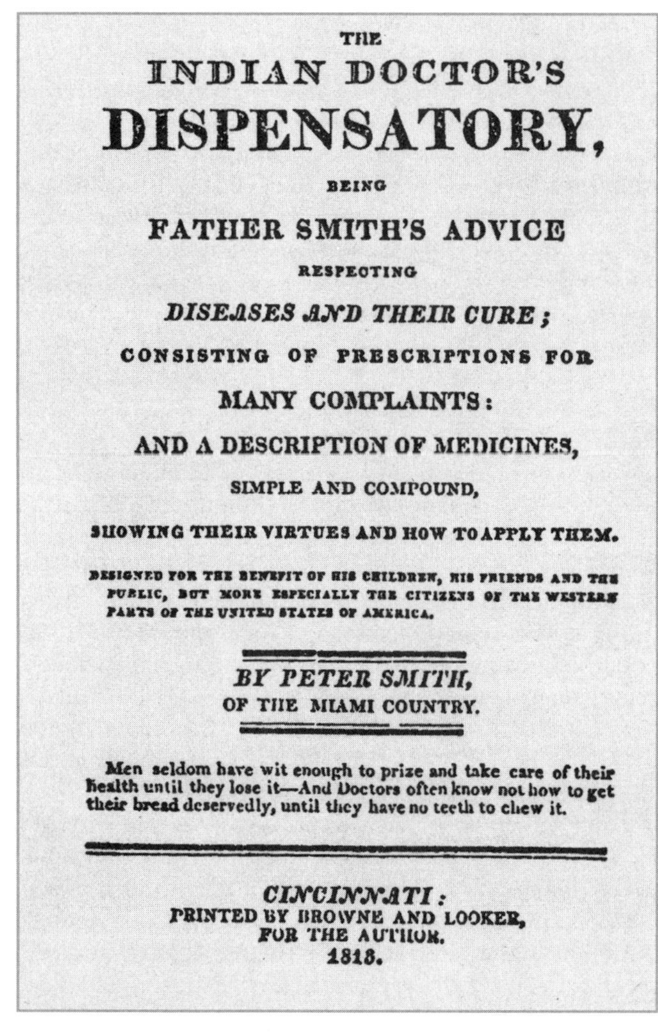

THE

INDIAN DOCTOR'S

DISPENSATORY,

BEING

FATHER SMITH'S ADVICE

RESPECTING

DISEASES AND THEIR CURE;

CONSISTING OF PRESCRIPTIONS FOR

MANY COMPLAINTS:

AND A DESCRIPTION OF MEDICINES,

SIMPLE AND COMPOUND,

SHOWING THEIR VIRTUES AND HOW TO APPLY THEM.

DESIGNED FOR THE BENEFIT OF HIS CHILDREN, HIS FRIENDS AND THE PUBLIC, BUT MORE ESPECIALLY THE CITIZENS OF THE WESTERN PARTS OF THE UNITED STATES OF AMERICA.

BY PETER SMITH,

OF THE MIAMI COUNTRY.

Men seldom have wit enough to prize and take care of their health until they lose it—And Doctors often know not how to get their bread deservedly, until they have no teeth to chew it.

CINCINNATI:

PRINTED BY BROWNE AND LOOKER,

FOR THE AUTHOR.

1818.

The title page of a medical guide published for the Native American population, which was devastated by diseases such as measles and smallpox *(Hulton/Archive)*

in the tropics, yellow fever can spread into cooler regions during warm seasons, as it did repeatedly in the United States in the early 19th century. During epidemics, the death rate could run as high as 85 percent.

In 1819 yellow-fever epidemics struck Baltimore and Philadelphia and reached as far north as Boston. In 1820, one-third of the population of Savannah, Georgia, came down with yellow fever. In 1822, New York suffered an epidemic. After that, areas north of Virginia remained free of yellow fever, but it remained a killer in the South. In 1843, yellow fever swept the Mississippi Valley, killing 13,000. An 1855 outbreak in Norfolk, Virginia, raged so uncontrollably that, according to contemporary accounts, "All Commerce stopped. The only industry became that of fighting yellow fever." The editor of the *Daily Southern Argus* had to suspend publication because only one employee was left in the plant. The editor wrote, "How doth the city sit solitary that was full of people!"

Dengue fever sometimes swept southern areas as well. Like yellow fever, it is a viral disease carried by mosquitoes, and has similar symptoms—fever, headache, chills, prostration—though it is rarely fatal. The two ailments are so similar that doctors sometimes had trouble distinguishing them, and sometimes epidemics of both occurred simultaneously. In the United States, the first pandemic of dengue fever struck in 1827–28, afflicting Charleston, New Orleans, Pensacola, and Savannah. Another pandemic in 1850–51 caused illness from Georgia to Louisiana.

Other deadly diseases of the period included typhus, which took epidemic form in Philadelphia in 1837; and influenza, which took pandemic form in 1847–48 and 1850–51. Spotted fever was another killer. Known today as meningococcal or cerebrospinal meningitis, this disease is caused by the bacterium meningococcus. It received the name spotted fever because it can cause spotting of the skin, along with fever, headache, projectile vomiting, delirium, and convulsions. An inflammation of the membranes of the brain or spinal cord, meningococcal meningitis can be fatal or can leave devastating aftereffects, such as paralysis or deafness. It was a new disease to the doctors who first encountered it in 1805 in Geneva, Switzerland; a year later, it appeared in the United States for the first time, in an outbreak in Medfield, Massachusetts, in which nine people died. Epidemics occurred periodically, notably in 1856–57 in North Carolina and New York State.

Though epidemic disease hit crowded cities especially hard, rural and frontier areas were not free of ailment. Settlers carried disease wherever they went, including Illinois, Indiana, Michigan, and other areas of what is now the Midwest. According to historian of disease Howard N. Simpson, "The most lethal dangers the pioneers had to face were neither savages nor wild animals. They were typhoid, malaria, dysentery, malignant scarlet fever, pneumonia, erysipelas in epidemic form, spotted fever, or what would now be called meningococcal meningitis, and diphtheria."

Certain situations made people particularly liable to disease. Soldiers camped in close quarters in unfamiliar places had reason to fear disease more than bullets. In the MEXICAN-AMERICAN WAR (1846–48), approximately 13,000 Americans died, but only 1,733 were killed in battle. Most of the remaining 87 percent died from disease. Slaves were more prone than their owners to most kinds of disease. Overwork, malnutrition, and poor living conditions increased the susceptibility of slaves to such killers as pneumonia and tuberculosis. However, slaves were more resistant than their masters to yellow fever and malaria, diseases to which the slaves' ancestors had become resistant in Africa.

NATIVE AMERICANS were particularly liable to disease when first coming into contact with white people. Low resistance to previously unencountered germs often resulted in fatal epidemics among Indians, as it had since the time of Columbus. From 1830 to 1833, influenza and other diseases swept through Native American communities in CALIFORNIA, Oregon, and British Columbia. In 1837, a smallpox epidemic ravaged the Mandan, Hidatsa, and Arikara peoples of the upper Missouri River.

Some diseases were specific to certain segments of the population. Women frequently suffered from puerperal fever, or childbed fever, an often fatal illness now known to be a bacterial infection that occurs in women after childbirth because of aseptic, or unclean, procedures during delivery. In 1843 Boston physician Oliver Wendell Holmes, father of the Supreme Court justice of the same name, used case studies to demonstrate that puerperal fever was contagious, spread by physicians who attended childbirths after being in contact with the living or dead bodies of puerperal fever patients. He urged physicians to wash their hands and wear clean clothes to prevent the spread of this disease. His findings were supported four years later by the studies of Hungarian physician Ignaz P. Semmelweis.

Other steps were taken in antebellum America toward improved cure and prevention of disease. One was the establishment in 1820 by New York physician Lyman Spalding of the *U.S. Pharmacopoeia*, a government-approved list of medical drugs that set standards for their formulation and purity. Another was the founding of the American Medical Association, inaugurated in 1847 to promote medical knowledge and maintain standards for medical education and ethics.

Further reading: W. H. McNeill, *Plagues and Peoples* (New York: Doubleday, 1976); Geoffrey Marks and William K. Beatty, *Epidemics* (New York: Charles Scribner's Sons, 1976); Charles E. Rosenberg, *The Cholera Years: The United States in 1832, 1849, and 1866* (Chicago: University of Chicago Press, 1962).

—George Ochoa

Dix, Dorothea (1802–1887)

Almost single-handedly responsible for changes in the way that mentally ill individuals were treated in 19th-century America, Dorothea Dix was one of the most effective activists and reformers of the era. Born on April 4, 1802, Dorothea was the eldest child of Mary Bigelow Dix and Joseph Dix, a traveling preacher. Her childhood—spent in Hampden, Maine, and Worcester Massachusetts—was dominated by her mother's ill health, her father's alcoholism, and the responsibility of caring for her two younger siblings. At the age of 12, Dix was sent to live with her wealthy grandmother in Boston, but she found adjustment to her new social status extremely difficult. By the age of 14, she was back in Worcester, living with her great-aunt. During the next year Dix began her career as a teacher, founding a dame school for young girls in the area. After breaking off an engagement in 1821, she returned to her grandmother's house in Boston and continued to teach there until the mid-1830s. Dix also published a number of books, including *Conversations on Common Things* in 1824, *Hymns for Children: Selected and Altered* in 1825, and *Meditations for Private Hours* in 1828.

Dix suffered from poor health through most of her life, and by the mid-1830s she was extremely sick with what many scholars now believe to be tuberculosis. She traveled to England to recuperate, staying at the home of the Rathbone family. There she met a number of intellectuals and activists, including Dr. Samuel Tuke, whose family was involved in mental health-care reform in England. During her convalescence, Dix learned that her mother and grandmother had died and that she had inherited enough money to give up teaching on her return to the United States. Influenced by the religious beliefs of her Methodist upbringing and her Unitarian sympathies, Dix took the

Dorothea Dix *(Hulton/Archive)*

opportunity to look for ways in which she could make the best use of this financial freedom.

In March 1841 Dix was invited to establish a Sunday school class in the East Cambridge House of Correction, Massachusetts. The conditions she witnessed inside the jail appalled her. Mentally ill individuals had been thrown into cells with criminals of every degree, left unclothed, without heat, and lacking anything but the most basic sanitary provisions. Many inmates were found chained to walls and had been flogged in an attempt to control their behavior. Determined to change the situation, Dix set out to tour prisons throughout Massachusetts. Her experience in East Cambridge was repeated over and over again, and Dix carefully cataloged the conditions she observed. In 1843 she submitted a report on her work to the Massachusetts legislature and lobbied fiercely for the overhaul of the penitentiary system. Thanks to her efforts, a law was passed to facilitate the expansion of the Worcester State Hospital in order to provide better care for the mentally ill.

Dix's career as a reformer had barely begun. Over the next 11 years, she toured prisons across the eastern United States and lobbied other state legislatures for changes in the treatment of the mentally ill. In 1845 she published *Remarks on Prisons and Prison Discipline in the United States.* As a direct result of her efforts, 15 states passed reform legislation, and 32 hospitals for the mentally ill were built.

In Dix's opinion, wholesale reform in mental health care could only be achieved with the assistance of the federal government. Dix repeatedly lobbied Congress to sell parcels of public land and channel the proceeds into the treatment of the mentally ill. Congress voted on the issue twice, rejecting the idea in 1848 and passing it in 1854. Vetoed by President Franklin Pierce, however, the legislation was never put into effect. Drained by the demands of her reform work, Dix left the United States that same year, hoping to be able to rest.

Once in Europe, however, Dix continued to work on issues of mental health reform, visiting jails across the continent over the next two years. At each stop, she advocated the building of new hospitals and better training for prison and hospital staff. In Italy, Dix personally persuaded Pope Pius IX to become involved in her cause and to witness the conditions in local jails.

Dix returned to the United States in 1856, where she continued her reform work despite lasting difficulties with her health. She would go on to become chief superintendent of nurses for the Union army during the Civil War, a job for which she was not well suited. After peace was declared, Dix continued to work as a reformer until her health deteriorated to the point at which she needed hospital care. In 1881 Dix admitted herself into the state hospital at Trenton, New Jersey, a hospital she had founded. It was there she died on July 17, 1887.

Further reading: Thomas J. Brown, *Dorothea Dix; New England Reformer* (Cambridge, Mass.: Harvard University Press, 1998); David Gollaher, *Voice for the Mad: The Life of Dorothea Dix* (New York: Free Press, 1995).

—Catherine J. Denial

Donner party (1846–1847)

This disastrous emigrant expedition to CALIFORNIA, which began in spring 1846, was planned by two prosperous brothers, Jacob and George Donner. The Donners were among the earliest and most successful settlers to begin farming in Sangamon County, Illinois, near Springfield. Along with hundreds of others at this time, the brothers were drawn by the lure of California and decided to uproot their families and head further west, searching for even fairer prospects. They were inspired to make the journey by reading the *Emigrant's Guide to Oregon and California,* an enthusiastic promotion of western settlement written by Lansford W. Hastings.

Hastings had encouraged his readers to follow a new and quicker route over the mountains, which he dubbed the "Hastings Cutoff." Instead of following the established CALIFORNIA TRAIL, Hastings suggested emigrants leave it at Fort Bridger and head towards the Great Salt Lake. The Donners decided to follow his advice. Their group, which now included the James Reed family and numbered 31 people in nine wagons, left from Springfield in April 1846. After reaching Independence, Missouri, they joined a wagon train captained by Colonel William H. Russell. The larger party traveled along the Platte River for a month, reaching FORT LARAMIE, Wyoming, where they discussed the Hastings Cutoff with a mountain man, James Clyman. Clyman had just traveled the route with Hastings himself and warned them not to take the cutoff, but they learned from another traveler that Hastings had promised to meet emigrant groups at Fort Bridger and lead them through his cutoff personally.

Now known as the Boggs company, the group continued on and, in mid-July, a large number decided to follow Hastings's shortcut and elected George Donner as their captain. Now known as the Donner party, they reached Fort Bridger a week later but found that Hastings had already gone, leading a different party across his trail. After resting for a few days, they continued on, hoping to catch up with him. Soon after, a few members of the party, led by James Reed, traveled ahead to find Hastings and get his advice. With the addition of other emigrants, the Donner party now numbered 87 people and 23 wagons. Reed's group soon returned with more specific directions.

The party crossed the Great Salt Lake Desert at the end of August, a trek that took six days, not the two that Hastings predicted. After this arduous leg of the journey, almost all the cattle were dead or lost, and food supplies were getting low. Donner sent two men ahead to Fort Sutter to obtain more supplies. At the end of September, they reached the California Trail, which they followed along the Humboldt River for two weeks. Tensions among the emigrants began to flare. In early October, James Reed killed another man in the party during a dispute. The party banished Reed from the wagon train, and he traveled ahead to find supplies. Troubles continued to multiply as they encountered hostile Paiute raiders, who killed at least one straggler unable to keep up with the wagon train.

The Donner party reached the Truckee River in mid-October and began their grueling journey across the Sierra Nevada. But they had lost precious time following a route that proved much longer and more difficult than Hastings had promised. Before they reached the pass through the mountains, snow stopped their travels. Some emigrants constructed makeshift cabins near the Truckee Lake, while others camped near Alder Creek. They waited, hoping this early snow was a fluke occurrence and would soon melt. But the snowfall persisted, and their attempts to cross the mountains failed. Although some supplies had been brought back from Fort Sutter, provisions remained meager, and they had slaughtered all their remaining livestock by the end of November. By mid-December, a small group known as "Forlorn Hope" set out on snowshoes to find help. Soon the Truckee Lake group learned that several people at the Alder Creek camp, including Jacob Donner, were dead. In late December, the Forlorn Hope expedition was caught in a blizzard, and many of their number died. The remaining people, out of food, were forced to eat their remains.

Seven members of the Forlorn Hope group survived, arriving at Johnson's Ranch in mid-January 1847. Word spread about the disasters that had befallen the Donner party, and in San Francisco, settlers began to plan rescue missions and raise money. Back at Truckee Lake, members of the Donner party began to die in large numbers. The first rescuers arrived at the lake in mid-February and found that 11 people had died; the rest were traumatized and weak. When the relief party began the journey west, they took 23 refugees with them. The second relief mission, led by James Reed, arrived at the lake on March 1 and learned that the remaining migrants had, like the Forlorn Hope group, resorted to cannibalism. The rescuers left with 17 people, but this party was trapped by a blizzard. A third rescue party reached them at "Starved Camp," then continued on to the lake and creek camps, where they found few migrants still alive. Most were too weak to travel. By the time the fourth rescue party arrived, only one man was still alive, surrounded by the horrifying evidence of cannibalism. Of the 89 original members of the Donner party, only 45 survived. All the rest, including George Donner, perished. Their journey became famous as the most horrible tragedy to befall emigrants heading for California.

Further reading: Kristin Johnson, ed., *"Unfortunate Emigrants": Narratives of the Donner Party* (Logan: Utah State University Press, 1996); Dale L. Morgan, ed., *Overland in 1846: Diaries and Letters of the California-Oregon Trail* (Lincoln: University of Nebraska Press, 1993).

—Eleanor H. McConnell

Douglass, Frederick

See Volume V

Dow, Lorenzo (1777–1834)

One of the most influential preachers of the early republic, known for his animated, fervent speaking style, Lorenzo Dow traveled across the United States and Great Britain, spreading his impassioned evangelism through camp meetings and other revivals. He was born in Coventry, Connecticut, in 1777, the fifth child of Humphrey and Tabitha (Parker) Dow. According to his own writings, he was drawn to spiritual matters from an early age.

In 1794 Dow began traveling and preaching. Two years later, he became associated with the Methodists, who assigned him to a circuit in New York State. This connection with an established church was short-lived because of Dow's unconventional exhortations. He continued to live as an impoverished itinerant preacher, often covering more than 100 miles in a week on horseback. The Methodist Conference readmitted him in 1798, but he almost immediately created new controversy when he went to Ireland in an unappreciated attempt to convert Roman Catholics. After this controversy, his formal association with the Methodists ended, but not his own adherence to Methodist doctrine as he saw it.

Returning to the United States after 18 months in Ireland, Dow sailed to Georgia to preach, went briefly to New York, and then returned to the South in 1802 for an extended evangelizing tour. His hellfire-and-damnation style of preaching won many converts in the newly settling inland South. He evangelized among both Indians and pioneering whites, preaching the first Protestant sermon in the Tensaw and Tombigbee settlements in Alabama in 1803. Dow also toured Tennessee, Virginia, and the Carolinas, offending some and inspiring others.

He returned to New York in 1804 to marry Peggy Holcomb, who agreed to allow his nomadic ministry to take highest priority; he returned to the South to preach on the day after their wedding. He continued to shuttle back and forth between New York and the southern states, and then embarked for England with Peggy, who gave birth to a daughter while they were abroad; the baby died soon after. In England, Dow popularized the camp-meeting revival and inspired the formation of the Primitive Methodists. Returning to the United States in 1807, the Dows resumed their revival tours across the country. Lorenzo Dow's reputation as a charismatic preacher grew, and he often referred to himself as "Cosmopolite," a wealthy and dashing prophet. As he railed against vice, Dow dazzled audiences with his dramatic long hair and convulsive movements. His wit, charm, and fierceness were especially compelling to backcountry settlers living under harsh conditions.

Peggy Dow continued to support his enterprises until her death in 1820. Soon after, he remarried and began to settle into a more sedentary, but still vigorous, lifestyle. He wrote journals and kept publishing numerous pamphlets, as had been his practice for several years. These religious tracts were as much self-promotion as they were spiritual instruction. Dow published several volumes, including sermons and accounts of the controversies he inspired. Notable among these publications were *Polemical Works* (1814) and *History of a Cosmopolite, or, the Writings of the Rev. Lorenzo Dow, Containing his Experience and Travels in Europe and America* (1848). He remained a persistent antagonist towards his opponents—namely Whigs, Catholics, and established Methodists. Lorenzo Dow died in Washington, D.C., in 1834. While always a maverick in American Protestantism, he greatly influenced mainstream spiritual beliefs and practices during the early decades of the 19th century.

Further reading: Lorenzo Dow, *The Dealings of God, Man, and the Devil: As Exemplified in the Life, Experience, and Travels of Lorenzo Dow* (Cincinnati, Ohio: Applegate, 1860); Charles Coleman Sellers, *Lorenzo Dow, the Bearer of the Word* (New York: Minton, Balch, 1928).

—Eleanor H. McConnell

***Dred Scott* decision** See Volume V

E

economy

The American economy, the nation's system for producing and distributing wealth, grew dramatically in the period 1813–55. Growth was fed by an expanding land base, a burgeoning and productive population, industrialization, an improved transportation system, and technological advances. It was facilitated by a stable government that encouraged private enterprise and investment, and it was fueled by the ambition, energy, and creativity of Americans. However, the generally bright economic picture contained dark areas. The economy was periodically rocked by panics, or financial alarms leading to depressions. The BANKING AND CURRENCY systems were unstable. The gap between rich and poor was growing, with NATIVE AMERICANS and enslaved AFRICAN AMERICANS left out of the nation's growing prosperity. Furthermore, a serious divide was developing between the economies of North and South, the former increasingly based on manufacturing and the latter on cotton farming by slaves.

By any measure, the antebellum economy was surging. Per-capita real gross domestic product increased by 60 percent from 1800 to 1840. Real reproducible wealth per capita, a measure of how much wealth each American possessed, grew from $166 in 1805 to $441 in 1850 (in 1929 dollars). In the late 1830s, the United States began to export more goods than it imported.

Territorial expansion was crucial to American economic growth in this period. In the TREATY OF GHENT (1814), which ended the WAR OF 1812, Britain acknowledged undisputed American possession of the Northwest Territory, or the Old Northwest, an expanse of 266,000 square miles that comprises what are now Indiana, Illinois, Ohio, Michigan, Wisconsin, and eastern Minnesota. Farther west, the Louisiana Purchase of 1803 added an additional 800,000 square miles of territory, while the acquisition of Florida (1821), the annexation of TEXAS (1845), the OREGON TREATY (1846), the Mexican cession (1848, comprising California and the Southwest), and the GADSDEN PURCHASE (1853) brought the United States to its present continental borders. From 1800 to 1860, the territory of the United States more than tripled.

Population growth more than matched territorial expansion. Thanks to natural increase and surging immigration from Ireland, Germany, and elsewhere, the U.S. population rose from fewer than 4 million to more than 31 million from 1790 to 1860. Much of the new territory was in the public domain, and the government made it available to settlers at low prices. In 1832, for example, a family could buy 40 acres of public land in the West for $50. As a result, pioneers to settle and create wealth in the new territory were easy to find. The percentage of Americans remaining in the East fell every decade from 1810 to 1860, so that by the latter date only 50 percent of Americans lived east of the Appalachians.

In the North, the Old Northwest attracted so many settlers that the region soon produced more agricultural goods than the Northeast, supplying sufficient food to allow the latter region to specialize in industrial production. In the South, farmers moved west to Alabama and Mississippi, in pursuit of new land for growing cotton, while the United States forced Native Americans in those areas to give up their lands and relocate farther west.

Another key to the nation's growth was an efficient transportation system. Frontier farmland was a worthless investment if crops could not be gotten to market. With federal and state aid, turnpikes proliferated throughout the antebellum period, including the NATIONAL ROAD, which linked Washington, D.C., with the Ohio Valley in 1818 and reached Vandalia, Illinois, by mid-century. By 1840 so many major arteries had been built east of the Mississippi that few others were added until the 20th century.

Waterways were even more attractive than roads for transporting goods, since a heavier load could be carried more cheaply on a barge than on a wagon. Steam power contributed to the growth in water traffic, by allowing goods and people to be shipped cheaply against a river's

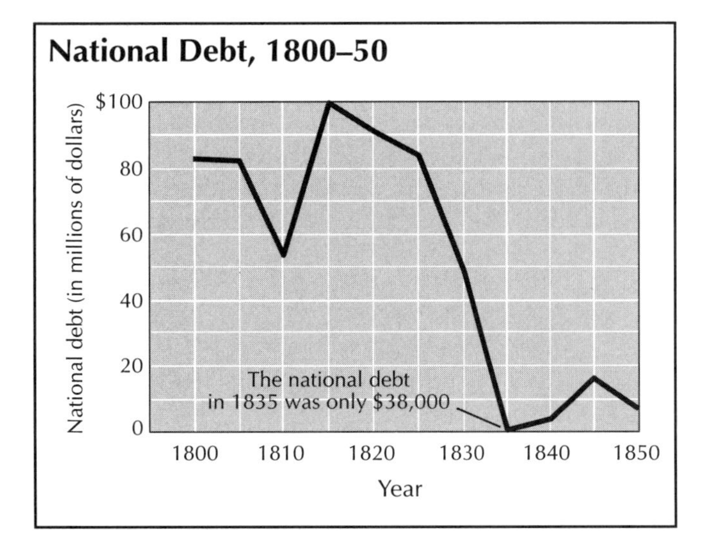

current or in the absence of favorable winds. Steamboats first became commercially viable in 1807, with American engineer Robert Fulton's launch of the *Clermont.* Where rivers and lakes did not connect with each other, canals were dug. By 1840, the nation had more than 3,000 miles of canals, including the ERIE CANAL, completed in 1825 and 13 times longer than any previously attempted. It spanned 365 miles from Albany to Buffalo, linking the Hudson River and the Great Lakes.

Railroads provided yet another transportation solution, one that soon eclipsed that of canals. The first railways, opening in the 1820s, were horse-drawn, but the steam locomotive was vastly more powerful, as Peter Cooper demonstrated in 1830 with the *Tom Thumb,* the first U.S.-built locomotive. By 1860, the country was crisscrossed by about 30,000 miles of railroad track laid down by many railroad companies, including the BALTIMORE & OHIO RAILROAD (B&O), the Pennsylvania Railroad, Pacific Railroad, and New York Central Railroad.

The growing web of transportation served an economy that was still largely agricultural. As late as 1860, agricultural products accounted for 82 percent of U.S. exports. Leading American agricultural products included corn, wheat, rice, livestock, cotton, and tobacco. Most farmers practiced both subsistence and commercial AGRICULTURE, meeting their own country's food needs while also producing goods for export. The South was particularly agricultural in character; as late as 1860, more than 75 percent of southern workers were farmers, with most of the rest involved in processing or otherwise handling agricultural products.

Yet the national economy as a whole was beginning to be industrialized, moving away from an agricultural basis toward one based on large-scale, mechanized factory production. The South's most profitable crop, cotton, was shipped to northern factories and transformed into textiles. The proportion of American workers engaged in agriculture declined from 71.8 percent in 1820 to 58.9 percent in 1860. By 1849, manufacturing was the economy's most rapidly growing segment.

Industrialization in America began with New England's textile industry, which flourished throughout the antebellum period. Entrepreneurs such as Samuel Slater and Francis Cabot Lowell adapted British textile machinery for use in American factories, including those in Lowell, Massachusetts, incorporated as a city in 1836. By 1840, about 2.25 million spindles were at work producing cotton cloth in 1,200 factories, most of them in New England. Woolen manufacturing also advanced during this period, as did other industries, everything from guns in Connecticut to straight pins in New York. From 1810 to 1850, the annual output of pig iron grew from 50,000 to 600,000 gross tons. Manufacturers such as Peter Cooper, SAMUEL COLT, Eleuthère Irénée Du Pont, William Colgate, and William Procter and James Gamble began to make fortunes that rivaled those of contemporaries such as CORNELIUS VANDERBILT, who made his money with shipping, and JOHN JACOB ASTOR, who made it with fur and real estate.

Technological innovation brought growth in both the agricultural and industrial sectors, including CYRUS HALL MCCORMICK's mechanical, horse-drawn reaper (1831); Charles Goodyear's process for vulcanizing rubber, rendering it elastic in all weather (1839); and SAMUEL F. B. MORSE's telegraph, a form of long-distance communication by wire (demonstrated in 1844). Federal and state government support also helped, including tariffs that protected domestic industries, tax exemptions, monopoly privileges, and laws that made it easy to organize corporations and obtain financing.

For economic growth to occur, capital (accumulated wealth) was needed to finance land purchases and new business enterprises. Most entrepreneurs in the young nation had relatively little capital, but they found financing from a variety of sources, including direct or indirect aid from federal and state governments, loans from banks, sales of stock to investors, and capital from overseas, mainly Britain. Up to 1839, Britain had invested more than $170 million in American businesses. Capitalization in general was growing rapidly. From 1820 to 1840, capital funds invested in the nation's factories grew fivefold, from $50 million to $250 million.

Banks played an important role by pooling capital, in the form of deposits, and lending it out at interest to those who could put it to use. Most banks were state-chartered institutions, known as state banks, each with a reserve of gold and silver, known as specie, and its own paper money, issued in the form of banknotes. (Both gold and silver could be coined freely at the time, a monetary system called bimetallism, though by mid-century gold was increasingly displacing silver as the preferred coin.) In the absence of a uniform national currency, the spread of banknotes as a fluid medium of exchange was itself a spur to economic development, especially in frontier areas, where farmers otherwise had to rely on awkward media such as animal pelts or old foreign coins to complete transactions. The banks' loans—for construction, manufacturing, commerce, agriculture, and other enterprises—further stimulated growth. One study found that commercial banks supplied about 90 percent of the short-term credit needs of eight prominent textile mills in Massachusetts.

Although state banks were important in fueling economic expansion, they were also a source of economic instability when they printed too many banknotes or extended credit out of proportion with their reserves. They thereby contributed to panics, financial collapses that resulted when frightened depositors, no longer confident in the banks, tried to withdraw their deposits en masse, and banks responded by calling in loans from borrowers who could not pay. Panics struck in 1819, 1837, and 1857, each time with devastating consequences for those thrown out of work or left with worthless banknotes or foreclosed property.

Proponents of a federal central bank twice established a Bank of the United States to exert a stabilizing influence by refusing to accept banknotes from state banks not redeemable in specie actually possessed in their vaults. The first Bank of the United States lasted from 1791 to 1811, the second from 1816 to 1836. Political opposition brought about the demise of both. In the second case, President ANDREW JACKSON led the opposition, arguing that the SECOND BANK OF THE UNITED STATES was antidemocratic and served the exclusive interests of wealthy eastern businessmen against farmers and western frontiersmen. Jackson waged a successful "Bank War" in Congress to ensure that the bank's charter was not renewed in 1836. Even before then, he drained the bank's assets, shifting them to state banks called "pet banks."

With income from tariffs and the sale of western public lands, Jackson succeeded in paying off the national debt in 1835. But his economic victories were short-lived. The risky speculation of the pet banks and of even more reckless institutions called wildcat banks led to higher interest rates and rampant inflation. In response to the growing financial chaos, Jackson in 1836 issued the Specie Circular, which declared that only gold and silver coin would henceforth be acceptable for purchase of public lands. Taking the Specie Circular as a sign that paper money had lost its value, investors rushed to their banks to demand that their banknotes be exchanged for specie. The result was the PANIC OF 1837. The ensuing slump, part of a worldwide depression, lasted seven years and left a trail of closed banks and failed businesses.

In 1846 Congress tried again to add a stabilizing force to the economy with the Independent Treasury System. Federal funds were placed in an independent treasury, or subtreasury, system separate from all banks, with all payments to and by the federal government in specie. The Independent Treasury System restrained overspeculation, but it also kept specie out of the market and tightened credit excessively. Meanwhile, banking abuses, such as overspeculation, remained commonplace, and currency remained confusing, with each bank issuing its own notes. The National Currency Act (1863) and the National Bank Act (1864) helped by creating a national banking system and national currency alongside the state banking system.

As the economy grew, society changed and new social tensions emerged. The lure of factory jobs drew immigrants and rural residents to towns and cities, increasing such urban problems as poor sanitation and epidemic disease. During the 1840s, towns and cities of 8,000 or more people grew by 90 percent, a rate much greater than that of the U.S. population as a whole (36 percent). Economic inequality grew as wealth became concentrated in fewer hands. A growing class of factory wage laborers took the place of a shrinking class of independent artisans and craft workers. From 1774 to 1860 the share of wealth owned by the top 1 percent of Americans grew from 13 to 29 percent. While industrialization improved standards of living by lowering prices for manufactured goods, in many cases it also made for bad working conditions. In the 1830s, labor unions began to grow as workers protested wage cuts and demanded that workdays be reduced from 13½ to 10 hours.

The most serious national tension in this period was that between North and South, which worsened as a result of economic change. North and South were increasingly becoming two nations, the former progressing through industrialization, the latter stagnating as a result of its commitment to a single crop, cotton, and an economically inefficient system of mobilizing labor, SLAVERY. That system was increasingly viewed by northerners as morally intolerable and defended by southerners as indispensable. The two societies, with their radically different economies, ultimately clashed in the cataclysm of the Civil War (1861–65).

Further reading: Stuart Bruchey, *The Wealth of the Nation: An Economic History of the United States* (New York: Harper & Row, 1988); Alex Groner, et al., *The American Heritage History of American Business & Industry* (New York: American Heritage Publishing Co., 1972); Seymour E. Harris, ed., *American Economic History* (New York: McGraw-Hill, 1961); Gary M. Walton and Ross M. Robertson, *History of the American Economy*, 5th ed. (San Diego, Calif.: Harcourt Brace Jovanovich, 1983).

—George Ochoa

education

American education in the first half of the 19th century was marked by idealistic reform and economic necessity. Its development was closely tied to the needs of a growing and geographically expanding populace as well as to the desires of a country determined to distinguish itself from Europe, in part by developing public and private roles for educating the country.

In 1797 the American Philosophical Society sponsored a contest requesting essays on a "system of liberal education and literary instruction, adapted to the genius of the government of the United States." Generally, the essayists called for an educational system that would create a literate citizenry who could support and defend the new country. Two decades earlier, in 1779, Thomas Jefferson envisioned a more expansive plan for a national school system that spanned free grammar schools to universities and encompassed training in the classical and modern arts and sciences. Further, he posited that those who excelled at school, whatever their social rank, should be called on to be the nation's leaders. This, he believed, would bring fresh ideas to the nation. Yet despite agreement on the importance of education among early American thinkers and philosophers, it took much of the first half of the 19th century to transform the government and its people into supporters of regulated public education.

In the early 19th century, movement toward public education began slowly. Most elementary schooling at the time occurred in the district school. Funded through taxation of district households, it was open to all children of the community, usually from ages three to 17. In the average school, students of all ages shared the same single classroom.

Beginning in the 1820s, Whig-affiliated educational reformers introduced one of the most successful movements of the century, the public-school program called the common school movement. Headed by leading thinkers such as Henry Barnard and HORACE MANN, the movement pushed for the public education of all elementary-age white children in local schools supervised by the state and regularized under the guidance of state boards of education.

Mann, in particular, was instrumental in promoting the common school and public education. A lawyer and Massachusetts state legislator, he became the first secretary of the Massachusetts Board of Education in 1837, in answer to a desire to engage in good works following his wife's death. He served in this role until 1848, working to raise statewide support for public education. He spoke throughout the state on how public education promoted an efficient workforce and a culturally and personally enriched citizenry. Through his *Common School Journal,* teachers gained pedagogical skills; through his annual reports,

This engraving shows a white teacher barring African-American children from entering a school. *(Library of Congress)*

circulated nationwide, the country became interested in public education. Also through his efforts, public schoolteachers' salaries were increased substantially.

Over the course of two decades, school construction increased, and by the mid-19th century, there were many varieties of educational facilities in the United States, reaching increasing numbers and types of students. In 1830, combined attendance for white students between five and 19 years of age was 35 percent; by 1850, it had increased to 50.4 percent. Public common-school attendance in 1850 totaled about 4 million, or over 55 percent of the common school-age population. The greatest number of public schools were located in New England, followed by the Midwest, while public schooling in the southern states would become commonplace within the next half-century.

Other changes accompanied this rise in school attendance. One was the development of mass teaching materials, particularly schoolbooks. While 18th- and early 19th-century children had been trained on Noah Webster's *American Spelling Book* and the Bible, many mid-19th century public schoolchildren learned from professor and Presbyterian minister WILLIAM HOLMES MCGUFFEY's *Eclectic First Reader* and its later editions. First published in 1836, the books were graded readers that presented a wide variety of material reinforcing Western morality and ethics as well as a common culture. By 1857, six McGuffey editions had been published, with 7 million copies sold.

Another change begun in the antebellum years was an increase in the number of female schoolteachers. Formerly a male preserve, the growing number of schools created a need for morally upright, low-wage sources of labor in large quantity. The feminization of education was championed by educator and reformer Catharine Beecher. Founder of academies for women, she wrote works including *An Essay on the Education of Female Teachers* (1835), which proclaimed that the expertise of women in developing moral sensibility would make them superior teachers. She also understood that teaching was one of the few professions open to women. Together, Beecher's moral and practical arguments served their purpose and turned the teaching profession into a women's bastion by the post–Civil War years.

Higher education was represented in great numbers of schools but educated relatively few students. According to estimates in the *American Journal of Education,* 6,000 academies existed in the United States in 1856, serving approximately 250,000 students. Given that the prewar secondary school–age white population of 15 to 24 totaled about 4.1 million, this meant that between 10 and 15 percent of students were receiving higher education. While overall involvement in higher education was lower than it was for primary grades, the increasing number of academies represented a commitment to U.S. secondary education.

This commitment extended to colleges, with several dozens founded between the American Revolution and the American Civil War. According to the *American Almanac,* 46 colleges were established by 1831; less than two decades later, the 1850 census listed 119 colleges. Many of these antebellum schools have been long-lived: Sixty-six of the 173 colleges lasting into the 20th century were founded in the 1850s. Notably, these colleges were established across the United States, not concentrated in one region. This development also attested to a national interest in developing educational outlets.

As the number of U.S. colleges grew, so did the percentage of college-educated students. According to historical estimates, in 1830, 17 out of 10,000 students had received some form of American college education. In 1850, the number had risen to 1.25 percent of the U.S. college-age population.

Despite this overall increase in college attendance, more sites for higher education were built than the populace could use. One reason for this overdevelopment in the first half of the 19th century was the financial worth of an academy or college to a new community. The promise of such an institution brought more settlers and more money to a community than did an elementary school.

Most of these antebellum schools were affiliated with religious denominations. In large part, these affiliations to various Christian denominations reflected the religion of the community and those leaders who would support the institution. In this early part of the 19th century, the affiliations were less concerned with the particulars of the religion than in providing a source of financial support. To convey their own religious tenets, many of these civic-minded school supporters would build their own religiously grounded colleges.

Befitting the many changes to education during the period, higher education was also being transformed, particularly at elite schools. After centuries of a standard classical curriculum, the educational programs at colleges such as Harvard or Yale were about to change. Up until the 1820s, students followed a course of study that included learning Latin and Greek languages and history in order to prepare them for entry into the professions. Specialized study of subjects was seen as secondary.

As late as the 1820s, this support of the classical standard was upheld by public statements such as the Yale Report of 1828, but several factors would change this approach. Among these factors were the pervasive effects of atheistic Enlightenment thinking; inadequate college teaching of the classical languages, which diluted their power; and the move toward granting specialized degrees in subject area and level of schooling. By the 1850s, religiously affiliated colleges were undergoing a period of transition that culminated in higher educational reform in the post–Civil War years.

Along with the founding of colleges was the flourishing of learning through noninstitutional means such as newspapers, agricultural fairs, and particularly the adult-education program known as the lyceum. Begun in 1826 in Massachusetts, lyceums soon expanded nationally, and within a decade, several thousand such institutions were operating. Culture in variety was the lyceum's hallmark, with major lyceums such as the Cooper Union in New York City presenting speeches and demonstrations by writers, artists, and statesmen. The lyceum was influential in promoting a national culture and ideas of social progress.

Throughout the first half of the 19th century, hundreds of thousands of AFRICAN AMERICANS faced increasingly stringent codes that forbade slave education. Although this undercut the 18th-century move toward building African free schools in the cities, educational training still continued, privately, among African Americans and with whites, though the literacy rate among slaves stood at about 5 percent. Just before the Civil War, in 1855, Boston became the first city to integrate its public schools.

By the mid-1850s, school enrollment on all levels was rising, mirroring growing government support and an increasing population, much of it foreign-born. With 50 percent of the population of New York City born outside the United States and other cities also containing high immigrant populations, public education was being viewed as vital public policy. Such thinking stemmed from reformers like Horace Mann and Catharine Beecher, who believed that schooling was both practical and idealistic. It would prepare U.S. citizens for an increasingly industrialized society and would decrease such potential social problems as, according to one reformer, "intemperance, avarice, war, slavery, [and] bigotry." By raising literacy and mathematical skills, American education would provide a surer social footing to immigrants and reduce their need to return to the country they once called home. After all, few countries—not France, Germany, Ireland, Italy, or Scotland—could match the 90-percent literacy rate among whites that the United States would enjoy in 1860.

Further reading: Robert L. Church, *Education in the United States: An Interpretive History* (New York: The Free Press, 1976). H. G. Good, *A History of American Education,* rev. ed. (New York: The Macmillan Company, 1962); Paul Monroe, *Founding of the American Public School System: A History of Education in the United States* (New York: Hafner Publishing Company, 1971).

—Melinda Corey

election of 1828

The election of 1828 is widely considered a watershed in the history of the American state, primarily because it brought ANDREW JACKSON to power, inaugurating a westward shift in the nation's center of political gravity and a dramatic increase in the power of the presidency. It is also significant for the emergence of the first true political party machine, created by MARTIN VAN BUREN to deliver the White House to Jackson.

Both Van Buren's machine and Jackson's election were direct consequences of the disastrous electoral deadlock of 1824. That year, the Democratic-Republican Party (or DEMOCRATIC PARTY) of Thomas Jefferson and James Madison, which had been without rival since the disintegration of the Federalist Party during the WAR OF 1812, had fractured. Unable to agree on a successor to the almost universally beloved JAMES MONROE, party leaders had broken into regional factions, with southern agrarian interests generally favoring Secretary of the Treasury William H. Crawford, northern traders and manufacturers halfheartedly backing Secretary of State JOHN QUINCY ADAMS, and Speaker of the House HENRY CLAY seeking to represent the settlers of the newer western territories. Unfortunately for Clay, the West chose a different champion: Andrew Jackson. Elected a U.S. senator of Tennessee, Jackson had skillfully positioned himself as the champion of the poor and the scourge of wealth and privilege, to the horror of his initial patrons.

Jackson won a plurality of both the popular and the electoral vote, but fell well short of the absolute electoral majority necessary. For the second time in the life of the young republic, the election was thrown into the House of Representatives. Jackson's partisans argued that his twin pluralities were a mandate to the House for his election; Henry Clay, having been eliminated by virtue of his fourth-place finish, disagreed and lobbied his colleagues assiduously for the election of Adams, who eventually emerged victorious in the House by a single vote. When Adams then appointed Clay secretary of state, a position he had long sought, furious Jacksonians denounced it as evidence of a "corrupt bargain" which had blocked the ascension of the "legitimate" victor, Jackson.

Whether an explicit deal had in fact been made and whether leading Jacksonians believed it had remain subjects of historical debate. What is clear is that the "bargain" led to an irreparable breach within the Democratic-Republican Party, with the supporters of the victorious Adams styling themselves as the National Republican Party (1825–1833) and the adherents of Jackson retaining the older name.

The Jacksonian movement is often seen as the product of a western clique. In truth, however, no man did more than New Yorker Martin Van Buren to ensure Jackson's ascent. It was Van Buren who led the four-year siege that was the John Quincy Adams administration. Van Buren fashioned a disciplined, nationwide network that relentlessly promoted the central myth of the Jacksonian cause: that Old Hickory, the simple honest man of the frontier, was chosen by the people but swindled of his and their destiny by the corrupt aristocracy of the wealthy and well connected. Van Buren oversaw the systematic placement of pro-Jackson editors atop newspapers across the country, most notably Duff Green, who as editor of the Washington-based *Telegraph* tirelessly questioned Adams's honesty and patriotism.

In this campaign of character assassination, the Jacksonians were ably assisted by Adams himself. Urbane, educated, and cosmopolitan, Adams was likely the finest mind on the North American continent. Unfortunately, his stubborn high-mindedness, aloof manner, and contentious nature were off-putting to many, who viewed him as snobbish and egotistical. His father's role as founder of the Federalist Party and an alleged monarchist likewise did not promote the image of Adams as "a man of the people." Even more serious, in his patrician disdain for factionalism of all kinds, Adams refused to reward friends and punish enemies. Seeking always to assemble the ablest men in the public's service, he did not discharge even those who openly joined his opposition or called for his defeat.

Adams's ambitious vision of strong federal leadership also hindered his cause. His calls for federal control of public lands to ensure more rational settlement and for federal protection of Native American lands to uphold treaty rights were anathema to Jackson's supporters in the West. His various proposals for a national university, an education system, scientific and artistic institutions, comprehensive public works, and infrastructure programs all generated fear among the southern elites, who increasingly viewed strong states' rights as a necessity in the maintenance of slavery. His support for the BANK OF THE

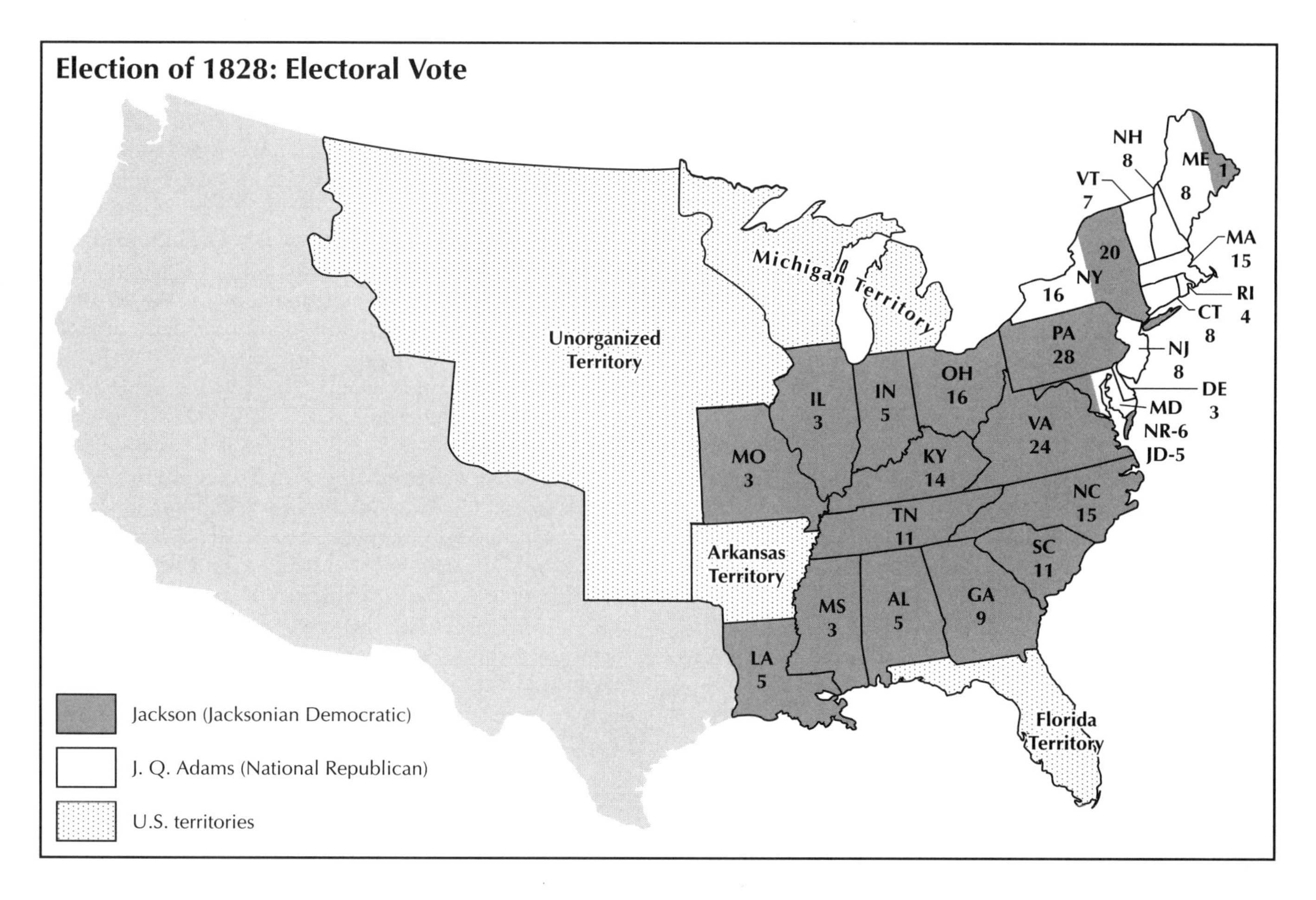

Election of 1828: Electoral Vote

UNITED STATES alienated a broad array of its debtors and competitors. Most damaging was his support for a strong tariff to aid the development of American manufacturing and development. The southern planters, who faced stiff retaliation on their agricultural exports by the European nations, denounced the 1828 tariff as the "Tariff of Abominations."

Led by Van Buren, the Jacksonians promoted their hero as everything they said Adams was not: self-made, gruff, plainspoken, passionate, agrarian, democratic, manly, anti-intellectual, a strict states'-rights constructionist, and, most of all, opposed to economic privilege. Jackson's image of inarticulate morality proved quite useful in his party's strategy. To be as many things to as many men as possible, Jackson avoided detailing his views on the complicated economic and legal issues of the day, instead campaigning on his personal biography and charisma.

Running on values and biography had its risks, however. Adams and his supporters did not appreciate being called "corrupt," "aristocratic," and "undemocratic," or being constantly portrayed as closet monarchists and stooges of the rich. They fought back hard, labeling Jackson as "vicious," "barbaric," and "bloodthirsty." They accused him of conducting atrocities against Indians and army deserters, and they described him as having ungovernable passions manifested by fits of fury and "intemperate behavior." (This last charge had the virtue of being true.) Most disgraceful of all were the aspersions spread by the Adams forces on the character of Jackson's wife, Rachel, for the unknowing bigamy of her first years of marriage to Jackson; so distressing were the slanders that Rachel died of a heart attack shortly after the election. In return, Jackson's followers accused Adams of misappropriating federal funds, spending public monies lavishly on extreme personal luxury, and of acting as a pimp.

The Jacksonians also made attractive campaign promises, perhaps the most significant of which was "rotation in office," more commonly known as the spoils system. Arguing the democratically flattering view that any decent man of basic education could perform most of the jobs in government, the Jacksonians promised to sweep out the hated appointees of Adams and, incidentally, replace them with Jackson loyalists. As Jackson adherent William Macy famously said, "To the victor belong the spoils!" How, in fact, this was different from the arrangement Adams allegedly made with Clay was tactfully left unexplained.

In the end, Jackson defeated Adams by a healthy margin, 56 percent to 44 percent in the popular vote and 178 to 83 in the electoral count. Van Buren went so far as to resign from the Senate and run for governor of New York to ensure that its electors would be in Jackson's camp.

Despite the outrageous mudslinging and the debates about the tariff, the rights of the states, and the power of the Bank of the United States, in the end there was really only one issue in 1828: the election of 1824. Jackson had not won in 1824, but in the scramble to build an enduring majority that followed, his party had built both a myth and a machine that would carry the day in 1828, and in five of the seven presidential elections thereafter.

Further reading: Arthur M. Schlesinger, Jr., *The Age of Jackson* (Boston: Little, Brown & Co., 1988); Harry L. Watson, *Liberty and Power: The Politics of Jacksonian America* (New York: Hill & Wang, 1990); Florence Weston, *The Presidential Election of 1828* (Philadelphia: Porcupine Press, 1974).

—Dorothy Cummings

election of 1840

The election of 1840 saw two milestones in American history. The victory of the WHIG PARTY opposition marked the end of the ad-hoc factionalism that had characterized the earlier era and firmly established the two-party system of American politics. At the same time, the innovative Whig campaign pioneered the modes and patterns of voter persuasion that have dominated campaigns ever since.

The nation approached the 1840 election preoccupied by four great issues: the extent of states' rights, the power of the executive, the structure of the financial system, and the expansion of the union. The contours of federalism continued to divide the nation into sections. On one hand, the NULLIFICATION CONTROVERSY of seven years earlier remained an open wound, estranging hard-line states' rights advocates like JOHN C. CALHOUN from the dominant DEMOCRATIC PARTY. On the other hand, nationalists such as HENRY CLAY and DANIEL WEBSTER had never reconciled themselves to the Democrats' states'-rights stance and became the organizing force of the new Whig coalition.

An individual's preference as to the relative power of the federal government and the states was not necessarily an indicator of his views on the balance of power between Congress and the presidency, however. Clay and Webster, for instance, both supported a strong central government but a weak executive within it; Calhoun opposed measures that strengthened either the national government or its president; while ANDREW JACKSON and MARTIN VAN BUREN supported states' rights and a powerful executive.

Disagreements over the proper model of federalism were enmeshed in the economic interests of the various factions and sections. These issues had come to a head in the struggle over the SECOND BANK OF THE UNITED STATES. After his reelection in 1832, President Jackson had refused to recharter the Bank of the United States, whose policies favored his political opponents. The efforts of bank president Nicholas Biddle to compel charter renewal by constricting the nation's credit supply had led to an alarming deflation. An unregulated increase in the issuing of state banknotes following the bank's closure in 1836 further aggravated the situation, leading to the PANIC OF 1837 and crashing the national economy just weeks after Van Buren's inauguration. President Van Buren correctly diagnosed the underlying cause of the nation's economic ills to be overspeculation and, true to his party's stated principles, called for an independent treasury to remove the federal government from the banking system altogether. Further hewing to laissez-faire economics, Van Buren declined to provide general relief to failing businesses. This stand provoked sustained public criticism from the Whigs, who insisted that the federal government was responsible for safeguarding the economic well-being of its citizens when prosperity failed; this novel view became an enduring theme of American politics.

Adding to the nation's sense of frustration were a long and inconclusive war with the Seminole nation of Florida and southern Georgia and Van Buren's deliberate foot-dragging on the annexation of Texas. The recent Texas revolution, led by close Jackson ally and Democrat Sam Houston, had successfully defeated the Mexican army, and sentiment in favor of the "inevitable" admission of Texas to the union was strong in the South and West. Van Buren was cautious, however. Mexico still claimed sovereignty and threatened war, and the admission of another slave state could upset the delicate balance on the smoldering issue of SLAVERY.

It was against this background of economic depression and expansionist frustration that the new Whig Party made its most important decision: to unite behind a single candidate. In 1836, the loose anti-Jacksonian coalition had nominated several sectional candidates for the presidency in an attempt to deadlock the electoral college and throw the selection of a president into the House of Representatives; that plan had proved disastrous in the face of the truly national party the Democrats had become. The Whig Party's single-candidate decision in 1840 sealed the future of American politics as a continuing clash between two broad, ideologically vague coalitions.

The Whigs would prove no less trailblazing in their decision as to who that single man would be. Henry Clay, the primary architect of the new coalition, wanted the job and was the expected choice. But the other leaders of the new party had learned much observing the hated Jackson and Van Buren. In 1840, they resolved to out-Jackson the Democrats in their choice of candidate and out-Van Buren them in their electioneering antics. Rather than initiating the "great debate" always sought by Clay, Webster, and Calhoun, the Whigs ran a cheerfully irrelevant campaign of images, slogans, and symbolism.

The nominee chosen for this new project was William Henry Harrison, who had run as one of the sectional candidates four years before. Tall and lean—like Jackson—Harrison was a former general and Indian fighter from the West—like Jackson. In truth, that was where the similarities ended. While Jackson had risen from humble beginnings on merit and compiled a glittering war record, Harrison was the scion of a wealthy old Virginia family who owed his military appointments and political career to social connections. His education was elite but undistinguished and his military record respectable but unimpressive in achievement.

By the time the Whig "Log Cabin and Cider" campaign was finished, all such distinctions between the hardscrabble Jackson and the aristocratic Harrison had been erased. Deliberately echoing Jackson's nickname of "Old Hickory," Harrison was christened "Old Tippecanoe" after his most notable military action, a minor Indian skirmish recast as a great and heroic American victory. In a campaign that marked the emergence of banners, placards, buttons, bunting, and grandiloquent nonsense as the trappings of American politics, the reserved Harrison was misrepresented to the public as a cider-drinking, two-fisted frontiersman who lived in a log cabin.

The Democrats rallied behind Van Buren—who was known variously as "The Little Magician," "The Red Fox of Kinderhook" and, in a bow to Jackson, "Old Kinderhook"—and fought back. Supporters organized themselves into "O.K. Clubs" (for "Old Kinderhook"), a phenomenon that introduced the idiom "OK" into the American vernacular. Van Buren"s partisans attacked Harrison's alleged lack of intellectual ability, citing no less an authority than Harrison campaign manager Henry Clay, who had referred to his party's standard-bearer as a "bumpkin." But their assaults proved no more effective than their opponents' similar charges had against Jackson. Indeed, Whig leaders managed to reprise many of the anti-intellectual and class aspersions Democrats had cast on JOHN QUINCY ADAMS.

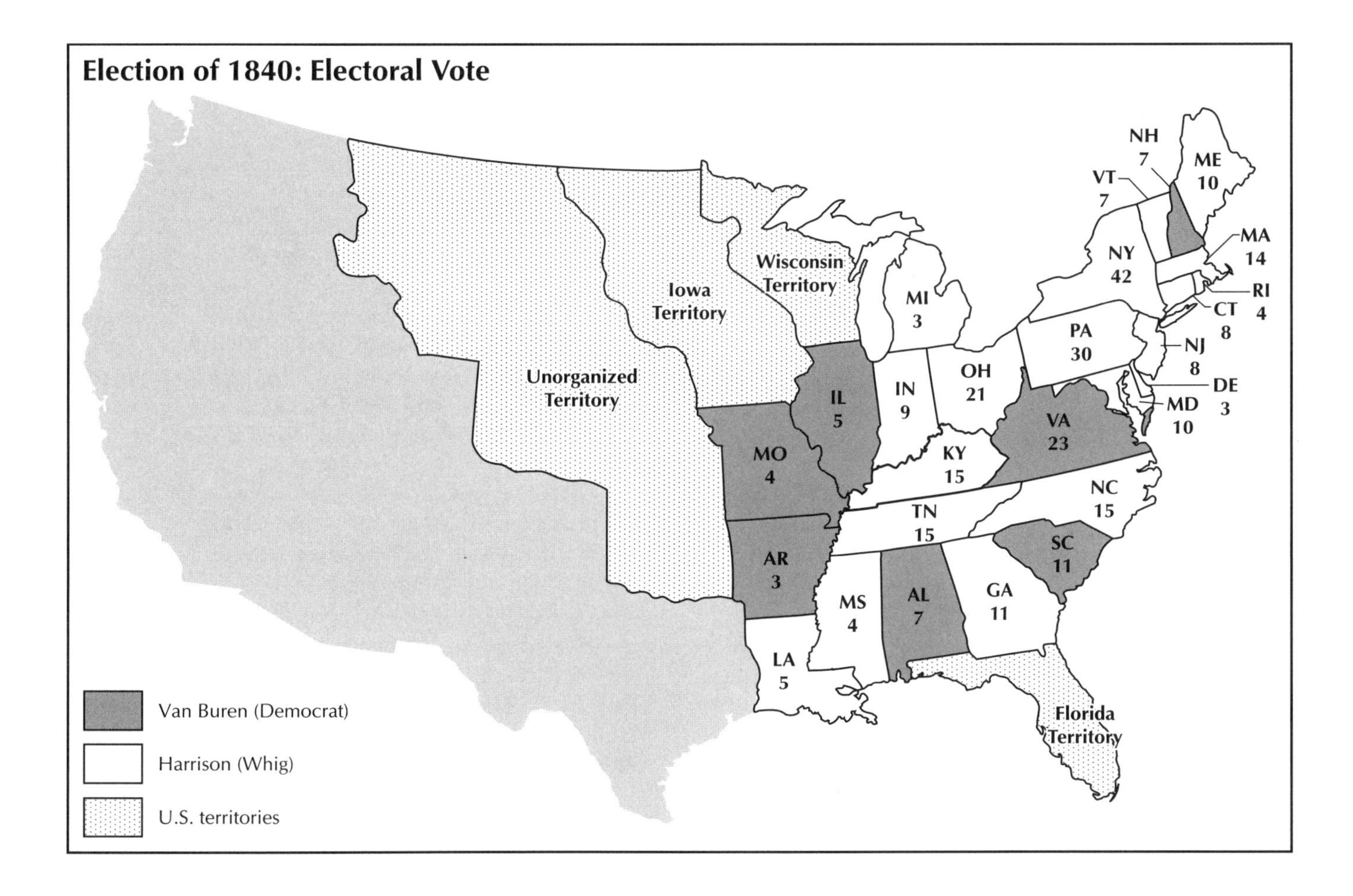

The result was another innovation that would become commonplace in American politics: an inversion in which Martin Van Buren, the self-made tavern keeper's son and dogged battler of entrenched privilege, was portrayed as an elitist, while William Henry Harrison, the aristocratic mediocrity, was presented as the common man's soul mate.

It is impossible in retrospect to determine which was more decisive in the race's result—Harrison's dynamic persona or the continuing economic malaise. What is clear is that the Whig refrain of "Tippecanoe and Tyler too!" (referring also to vice presidential candidate JOHN TYLER) carried the day. Harrison swamped Van Buren in the electoral college 234 to 60, though the popular vote was much closer at 53 percent to 47 percent.

Harrison, trying to live up to his freshly minted myth, went coatless on inauguration day and died of pneumonia a month later. The Whigs would survive only until 1858. But in their landmark campaign of 1840, they firmly imprinted both the underlying structure and the surface decoration on the American party system.

Further reading: Robert Gray Gunderson, *The Log-Cabin Campaign* (Westport, Conn.: Greenwood Publishing Group, 1977); Arthur M. Schlesinger, Jr., *The Age of Jackson* (Boston: Little, Brown & Co., 1972); Major L. Wilson, *The Presidency of Martin Van Buren* (Lawrence: University Press of Kansas, 1984); Harry L. Watson, *Liberty and Power* (New York: Farrar, Straus & Giroux, 1990).

—Dorothy Cummings

Emerson, Ralph Waldo (1803–1882)

Philosopher, lecturer, poet, essayist, and the father of transcendentalism, Ralph Waldo Emerson was also a passionate abolitionist whose writings condemned both southern slaveholders and those northerners who were not fully committed to freedom for AFRICAN AMERICANS. Initially unenthusiastic about Abraham Lincoln, Emerson became a supporter during the Civil War and delivered a widely reprinted eulogy upon the death of the president.

Born on May 25, 1803, Emerson was the son of a Unitarian pastor named William Emerson, who died in 1811, and Ruth Haskins Emerson. He was educated at the Boston Latin School, then at the Harvard Divinity School, and in 1829 he was ordained. After obtaining a position as second pastor at the Second Church of Boston, he married Ellen Tucker, who died only 18 months later. Because of his doubts about Unitarian doctrine, Emerson left the church and traveled to Europe, seeking knowledge and exposure to a wider range of thought.

In Britain, Emerson met Thomas Carlyle and other thinkers, whose ideas prompted a reexamination of his spirituality when he returned to Massachusetts in 1833. That same year, Emerson married for a second time, to Lydia Jackson. He began to lecture widely on spiritual issues, developing a philosophy that is known today as transcendentalism. In 1836, he published *Nature,* his first book, which outlined transcendentalism broadly. In 1837, at Harvard, Emerson delivered an address entitled "The American Scholar," which called for America to establish its own intellectual traditions apart from Europe. From 1840 until 1844, he and Margaret Fuller edited a literary journal dedicated to the TRANSCENDENTAL MOVEMENT called *The Dial.* Emerson would publish essays and poems throughout his life, always emphasizing individuality and the importance of the self.

Emerson succeeded Margaret Fuller as editor of *The Dial,* and during its continuance, until April 1844, he published more than 40 of his own pieces, prose and verse, in its columns. The poems included such famous ones as "The Problem," "Woodnotes," "The Sphinx," and "Fate." While the periodical contained much delicate and valuable writing, it failed due to lack of financial support. As chief intellectual leader of the idealists, Emerson took a close interest in the semisocialistic experiment at BROOK FARM (1840–47), with which some of the cleverest New England men and women of that day were connected, but he did not join the community. Nathaniel Hawthorne, who was actually a member and lost money in the undertaking, has been criticized for having viewed it independently; but Emerson, outside, held a similar neutral attitude, and wrote an account of the affair, in which, touching it humorously at points, he called it *"a French Revolution in small, an Age of Reason in a patty pan."*

In addition to its focus on individuality, transcendentalism also embraced change. Perhaps this reflected, in part, Emerson's conviction that the society in which he lived was flawed by SLAVERY. A committed abolitionist, Emerson traveled widely before the Civil War, arguing everywhere that slavery should be destroyed. Occasionally these beliefs spurred a violent reaction, as when he was mobbed in 1861. During the war, he wrote widely on the progress of the conflict and on its aims.

Early in the Civil War, Emerson's reaction to Abraham Lincoln was guarded. Lincoln's folksy manner and lack of interest in the trappings of refinement were distasteful to the philosopher. In addition, Emerson was disappointed by Lincoln's avowed preference for a war to save the Union rather than a war to abolish slavery. Over time, however, Emerson came to believe in Lincoln's leadership. The two men met in 1862, very close to the publication of Emerson's essay "American Civilization," which argued that northerners could not plead innocence with regard to slavery. Because northern citizens were not fully committed to abolition, he suggested, they bore a portion of the blame for slavery. In 1863, Emerson expressed his support of Lin-

Ralph Waldo Emerson *(Library of Congress)*

coln's Emancipation Proclamation in a poem entitled "Boston Hymn." After the president's assassination, he spoke at a memorial in Concord, Massachusetts, calling Lincoln "the father of his country."

Although Emerson continued to write and speak for the rest of his life, his work after the Civil War was focused mainly on his philosophy of life rather than on politics. On April 27, 1882, he died of pneumonia.

Further reading: Ralph Waldo Emerson, *The Essential Writings of Ralph Waldo Emerson,* ed. Brooks Atkinson (Princeton, N.J.: Princeton Review, 2000); Oscar W. Firkins, *Ralph Waldo Emerson* (New York: Dover Publications, 2000); Robert D. Richardson, Jr., *Emerson: The Mind on Fire* (Berkeley: University of California Press, 1995).

—Gina Ladinsky

Era of Good Feelings

The Era of Good Feelings (or Feeling) is usually placed between the TREATY OF GHENT (1814) and the election of JOHN QUINCY ADAMS in 1824. It was marked by three characteristics: nationalism, prosperity, and party unity. Although the WAR OF 1812 (1812–15) ended in a stalemate, Americans came to believe that it was a great triumph. In part, this sense of pride stemmed from the war's last battle, the BATTLE OF NEW ORLEANS (January 8, 1815), which was a tremendous victory for American arms. In part, too, just the idea of having fought the greatest power on earth to a standstill represented a victory for the republic. With the war behind them, Americans could concentrate on their own continent, acquiring FLORIDA in 1819 and coveting much of the rest of the continent. Everything seemed possible, and this optimism spread to the ECONOMY as a wild economic boom swept the nation. Land speculation was rampant, fed by the expansion of banking within the states and in the creation of the SECOND BANK OF THE UNITED STATES. Cotton prices, too, increased dramatically leading to greater production. Good feelings even seemed to enter politics. The first party system, pitting Federalists against Democratic-Republicans, disintegrated in the wake of the HARTFORD CONVENTION. The Federalists had been losing ground since 1800, and their opposition to the war destroyed them as a national force. JAMES MONROE won the 1816 election, 183-34, in the electoral college; by 1820, single-party government led to a 231-1 electoral college margin—and the single vote was for a member of Monroe's own cabinet.

Although the pride in American nationhood continued, neither the booming economy nor the party unity could last. The PANIC OF 1819 led to a recession that continued into the 1820s. Democratic-Republican politicians soon divided into warring camps and gave birth to a second-party system. By the time John Quincy Adams was elected president in 1824, growing conflicts over SLAVERY and other issues had brought the Era of Good Feelings to an end.

Further reading: George Dangerfield, *The Era of Good Feelings* (New York: Harcourt, Brace, 1952; Chicago: Ivan R. Dee, 1989).

Erie Canal

The most important and successful building project of the CANAL ERA was the construction of the Erie Canal. With the rapid increase of settlement in New York State after the American Revolution, businessmen and politicians began to discuss the possibility of constructing a waterway to facilitate trade and transportation between Lake Erie and the Hudson River, thereby connecting the port of New York City with the developing Northwest. As early as 1792, the Western Inland Lock Navigation Company began to build dams, locks, and canals, but never managed to construct more than a few miles of waterway. In the 1800s, new proposals for a canal system began to appear. In 1807, Jesse

Hawley wrote a series of essays arguing that an east-west route was indeed possible. He thought that the route of an "artificial river" had already been laid out by God and only needed to be finished by humans. The following year, the New York legislature passed a bill authorizing surveyors to search for possible routes. In 1810, a canal commission was created to begin searching for ways to finance this project. The commission asked for federal funding, but President James Madison eventually vetoed their proposal in 1817. That same year, DeWitt Clinton, one of the canal project's main promoters, was elected governor of New York. He decided to proceed with the proposed canal plan using state funding. He persuaded the legislature to authorize construction of the Erie Canal as well as the Champlain Canal, which would connect Albany to Lake Champlain in the northeastern corner of the state. On July 4, 1817, with much fanfare, Clinton and his supporters broke the ground for the beginning of canal construction.

Construction of the canal began in the middle section, 98 miles of which were completed by 1819. By 1820, the western and middle portions of the canal were already in use. In 1823 the canal finally reached the Hudson. Two years later, the enormous project was complete from Buffalo to Albany. This unprecedented engineering accomplishment was celebrated across the region, as farmers, merchants, and artisans looked forward to an expanded market for their goods. The Erie Canal was an instant financial and public relations success; tolls paid for its construction costs in only a short time. Almost immediately, the legislature authorized the creation of 17 lateral canals that would connect even more towns to the new trade artery. The Canal Board, which would manage the new waterway, was established in 1826. Only 10 years later, the Erie Canal Enlargement project began, to ease the traffic congestion which was by then a common feature of canal travel. This major expansion was not completed until 1862. Because of the Erie Canal's stunning success, the demand for canal construction intensified throughout the United States. Unlike the Erie, most of the later canals were federally or privately funded, not state-funded. But none of these projects proved as successful or culturally significant.

An engraving depicting the first barges en route from Buffalo to New York City via the newly opened Erie Canal. *(Hulton/Archive)*

The original canal was four feet deep, 40 feet wide, and 363 miles long. It cost $7 million to build and contained 83 locks and 18 aqueducts. Benjamin Wright and his associates (later referred to as the "Erie School" of engineers) oversaw the construction. In the process, Wright and his workers developed new machines to help remove roots and stumps and invented a new watertight mortar to line the canal bottom. They built aqueducts across valleys and rivers and locks to level out less-dramatic changes in elevation.

Canal-digging was backbreaking, dangerous work. Laborers were hired not by the state but by private contractors who placed bids for constructing certain sections of the canal. Many of the diggers were local farmers, hired by these contractors to work on the stretch of canal near their towns. Many other diggers were recent immigrants, mostly from Ireland. The presence of these immigrant wage-laborers concerned some of the canal's proponents. Often uneducated and without a permanent home, these men symbolized the kind of wage slavery that, according to popular ideology in the early republic, was not supposed to exist in the United States. The Erie Canal was supposed to embody the proposition that all men could become independent landowners, prospering through the democracy of property ownership and trade. The fact that this canal of progress was built by the seemingly un-American was unimportant. Once the canal was completed, some of these same workers became part of the huge workforce required to operate the canal and canal boats.

The new canal revolutionized travel and trade in the region as transporting goods became quicker and cheaper. Farmers who previously had no accessible market for their produce were now able make the transition from subsistence farming to commercial AGRICULTURE. Land near the canal rose in value, and new cities grew up seemingly overnight, ready to take advantage of the commerce the canal would create. The ease with which goods could be transported to New York City gave it an economic advantage over other American coastal cities. Always an important port, New York became *the* center of American and trans-Atlantic commerce—a preeminent position that would endure for more than a century.

The canal also promoted travel and tourism in the region. Sightseers reveled in the wild scenery and bustling towns. While canal travel could sometimes be uncomfortable, most people found it exciting at first. New kinds of travel boats were created, providing meals, foldout sleeping cots, and entertainment. Previously isolated from the outside world, families were able to visit commercial centers and keep in touch with relatives through the rapid transit of canal boats (and the increasingly speedy mail service). For the first time, big-city luxury goods could be easily shipped to the developing West, rapidly transforming the quality of life in the hinterland. Journeys that used to take weeks could now be completed in a few days.

But with the canal's triumphs came troubles. The canal cut across private property, and many landowners complained that they were never adequately reimbursed for losing their property. Farmers whose land had been bisected by the canal lobbied the Canal Board for the right to construct bridges over the canal. Without bridges, some landowners were unable to travel to the towns to sell their goods without trespassing on neighbors' property. In turn, shipping companies lobbied against these bridges, which created increased navigation obstacles and safety hazards.

The culture that developed among canal workers was troubling to merchants and civic leaders. These workers were mostly unmarried, often recent immigrants, and sometimes young boys. The mobile nature of boat life seemed to promote vice; saloons multiplied in port towns, and prostitutes became a visible presence along the route. The canal operated 24 hours a day, seven days a week, creating noisy nightlife and increased crime. In the 1830s, the Canal area became known as the "burned-over district" because of an explosion of evangelical fervor and reform campaigns. The reformers were especially concerned about the behavior of the canal workers and tried to force the Canal Board to close operations on Sundays, so that drivers and longshoremen could attend church. Others argued that, given idle time, vice among the workers would increase. Another serious problem was what to do with the canal workers during the winter months, when canal operations completely shut down. Port towns were forced to deal with groups of unemployed or marginally employed men for months at a time.

Of course, not all canal workers were dangerous and immoral; many boating operations were run by families, and not all single men were a threat to civilized life. However, troublemakers loomed large in the imaginations of local farmers, worried again that their vision of ordered, moral progress was being undermined by the seemingly alien values of canal culture.

The Erie Canal became too successful for its own good as swarms of boats crowded in, slowing down what was supposed to be the most rapid form of transit. The increased congestion and numerous locks in the eastern part of the canal proved so tedious that many shipping companies were forced to circumvent these sections in order to save time, transporting their goods by road during these sections of the journey.

Many observers worried that the progress created by the canal was made at too high a cost, morally and economically. The "canal mania" that accompanied its completion caused wild speculation among bankers and merchants that often resulted in ruin. Fortunes could be made and lost very quickly in this new environment, causing many to question whether the canal really was a financial boon. The structure that was supposed to stabilize and improve their lives was proving to be a volatile force beyond their control. Small farmers began to suspect that, while the state had originally built the canal to benefit everyone, the parties who ended up gaining the most were big corporations. More and more people in the canal region felt that the state government was more interested in protecting powerful companies than ordinary voters.

The Erie Canal permanently altered the landscape and economy of New York. It was one of the first INTERNAL IMPROVEMENTS designed to expand American mobility and trade during the early 19th century. Although it continued to prosper for many years, it was eventually eclipsed by railroads, which were much faster and could operate year round. The canal survived well into the 20th century as an important auxiliary method for transporting freight. It remains an important exemplar of American ambition, engineering, and resourcefulness. For historians, the Erie Canal provides a revealing case study about the complexities of labor, property, and ideas about progress in American culture.

See also CANAL ERA.

Further reading: Ronald E. Shaw, *Canals for a Nation: The Canal Era in the United States, 1790–1860* (Lexington: University Press of Kentucky, 1990); Carol Sheriff, *The Artificial River: The Erie Canal and the Paradox of Progress, 1817–1862* (New York: Hill and Wang, 1996).

—Eleanor H. McConnell

Essex, USS

The USS *Essex,* a 46-gun frigate, is most famous for its voyage to the Pacific in the WAR OF 1812 (1812–15), wreaking havoc on British shipping until it was captured by the frigate HMS *Phoebe* and another vessel. The *Essex* was built in Salem, Massachusetts, as part of the expansion of the U.S. Navy in the late 1790s. In 1799, along with the USS *Congress,* the *Essex* under Edward Preble was dispatched to the Far East to escort an American convoy of merchantmen back to the United States. The *Congress* was damaged in a storm soon after it left port, leaving the *Essex* to proceed on its own. The *Essex* was thus the first American naval vessel to cross the equator, venture into the Indian Ocean, and show its flag in the East Indies. She returned after almost a year at sea in 1800.

The *Essex* also participated in the campaign against Tripoli (1803–05), but only really became famous at the beginning of the War of 1812. In July 1812, the *Essex* under the command of Captain David Porter missed a British convoy in the Atlantic, but in two months she captured nine prizes, including the first British warship to surrender to an American vessel in the war. The total value of the prizes was over $300,000, an impressive sum at the time. In autumn 1812, the *Essex* was ordered to rendezvous with the *Constitution* and the *Hornet* in the South Atlantic. Those two ships, however, successfully fought with British counterparts and returned to the United States. Left on his own, and fearing that he was surrounded by British warships, Captain Porter headed for the Pacific. By early spring 1813, he was capturing British whalers and other vessels, accumulating a small fleet for himself. In September, he decided he needed to refit and set sail for the Marquesas. After spending seven weeks in the Pacific island paradise of Nukahiva, Porter left the island group with the *Essex* and a consort he had captured earlier and called the *Essex Junior.* Unfortunately, soon after they arrived in Valparaiso, Chile, then still a Spanish possession, two British ships appeared. Since they were in a neutral port, the British did not attack, but when Porter finally made an attempt to run past them, a gale came up and damaged some of the rigging of the *Essex.* Although Porter made it back to neutral waters, the two British ships pursued him and pounded him into surrender while remaining out of range of most of the *Essex*'s heavy guns.

Further reading: William M. Fowler, Jr., *Jack Tars and Commodores: The American Navy, 1783–1815* (Boston: Houghton Mifflin, 1984).

exploration

The U.S. purchase of the Louisiana Territory in 1803 opened up a vast area for American exploration, more than 800,000 square miles from the Mississippi River to the Rocky Mountains. After Meriwether Lewis and William Clark reconnoitered that region and, further west, the Oregon Territory, in their expedition of 1804–06, other explorers soon followed. In 1806–07, soldier ZEBULON PIKE ventured into what is now Colorado, where he sighted Pike's Peak, and into New Mexico, then held by Spain. John Colter and George Drouillard, veterans of the Lewis and Clark Expedition, explored what are now Montana and Wyoming in 1807. As the United States stretched its territory from coast to coast in the remaining antebellum years, many more explorers sent back reports about these and other little-known lands.

Not all expeditions were government-sponsored. Much exploration in the period 1813–55 was done by adventurous private citizens motivated by profit and working for themselves or on behalf of companies. They ventured not only into Louisiana but into the Spanish-owned, and later Mexican-owned, areas of CALIFORNIA and the present-day Southwest, as well as into the disputed Oregon Territory.

Among the most notable private explorers were MOUNTAIN MEN, professional fur trappers and traders such as JEDEDIAH STRONG SMITH, JAMES BRIDGER, Joseph Walker, and JIM BECKWOURTH. These men lived a rugged existence in the Rocky Mountain wilderness, trapping beavers and other animals. They learned survival techniques and cultural practices from the region's NATIVE AMERICANS and often married Indian women. The explorations of these frontiersmen were vital to charting the territories that became part of the United States.

The heyday of the mountain men began in the 1820s, when fur traders WILLIAM HENRY ASHLEY and Andrew Henry developed the brigade-RENDEZVOUS system for financing and supplying them. Brigades, or teams of trappers, lived and worked in the wilderness, supplied by pack or wagon trains from Missouri that would meet them every summer at a boisterous trading event called a rendezvous. A similar system developed in the Southwest, where the mountain men spent summers trading and carousing at town fairs, such as at Taos, New Mexico. The era of the mountain man faded in the 1840s, when overtrapping sent the beaver population into decline and changing tastes made beaver hats unfashionable. Mountain men also often served as scouts or guides for other people's expeditions, both before and after the decline of the FUR TRADE.

Probably the most renowned mountain man was Jedediah Strong Smith, who blazed several trails from 1822 until his death in 1831. In 1824 or 1825, he discovered an overland route to California through SOUTH PASS, which later became part of a well-traversed westward route known as the Overland Trail. (He actually rediscovered South Pass; it had first been discovered in 1812 by Robert Stuart of ASTORIA.) In 1826–27, Smith led his greatest expedition, becoming the first American to go overland to California through the Southwest. His route took him to the Great Salt Lake and across the Colorado Plateau, Mojave Desert, and Sierra Nevada to San Gabriel, California. On the return trip, he traveled northward through the San Joaquin Valley and through Ebbetts Pass across the Great Basin, where his party of three almost perished from thirst. They became the first non-Indians to cross the Sierras from the east and the first to traverse the Great Basin. Smith also explored the Black Hills of what is now South Dakota, survived a grizzly bear attack, and waged numerous battles with Native Americans. He was finally killed by the Comanche.

James Bridger worked with northeastern fur companies from 1822 to 1842. In 1824, Bridger became the first non-Indian to see the Great Salt Lake. He founded Fort Bridger, Wyoming, in 1843 and discovered Bridger's Pass in 1849. Joseph Reddeford Walker trapped and traded in the upper Missouri region from 1820 to 1840. His name was bequeathed to Walker Lake and Walker's Pass. He was a guide for several exploratory expeditions between 1832 and 1860.

James Pierson Beckwourth, an African American, had been born a slave but was raised free in Missouri. He took part in the Ashley-Henry fur-trading expeditions into the Rocky Mountains (1823–26) and lived with the Crow from 1826 to 1837. From 1837 to 1850, he was variously a guide, army scout, trapper, trader, and hunter. In 1850, he discovered the Beckwourth Pass in the Sierra Nevada, which opened a route to the Sacramento Valley of California.

Other mountain men included James Ohio Pattie and his father, Sylvester Pattie, who together in 1827 traveled from Santa Fe, New Mexico, to Southern California; and Ewing Young and William Wolfskill, who helped to blaze the Old Spanish Trail from Santa Fe to Los Angeles. KIT CARSON was a saddlemaker's apprentice who ran away to join an expedition to Santa Fe in the 1820s. He became a mountain man and served as guide for JOHN C. FRÉMONT's three government-sponsored expeditions.

Those who traded with mountain men also did their part in exploring the West. The SANTA FE TRAIL was established in 1821 by American merchant WILLIAM BECKNELL, who drew on knowledge of trails first used by Native Americans. The Santa Fe Trail ran about 780 miles from western Missouri to Santa Fe. Every summer from the 1820s to the 1840s, Becknell and other merchants brought wagon caravans laden with goods to trade with Mexicans, Indians, mountain men, and anyone else in New Mexico.

Another important trail that evolved during this period was the OREGON TRAIL. It developed from Native American trails, the explorations of Lewis and Clark, and the pioneering of mountain men such as Nathaniel Jarvis Wyeth, who founded Fort Hall, Idaho, in 1834. Stretching 2,000 miles from Independence, Missouri, to Oregon's Willamette Valley, the Oregon Trail passed through what are now Kansas, Nebraska, Wyoming, and Idaho. It was heavily used by westward-moving pioneers in the 1840s and 1850s.

As the era of the mountain men faded, government-sponsored expeditions became more important. In 1838, the Corps of Topographical Engineers was founded as a distinct army unit to explore, survey, and report on little-known lands. Their greatest officer was John C. Frémont, known as the Pathfinder, who in the 1840s surveyed areas along routes into Oregon and California. In 1841, he traced the headwaters of the Des Moines River. In 1842, guided by Kit Carson, he explored Rocky Mountain territory along the Oregon Trail. In 1843–44, Frémont and Carson explored the Nevada country, crossed the Sierra Nevada to California, visited Oregon, and returned home by a more southerly route. Frémont's reports roused interest back east about the western territories, especially California. In 1845–46 Frémont and Carson surveyed the central Rockies and the Great Salt Lake region.

The son-in-law of Senator THOMAS HART BENTON, Frémont was much admired back home, but he sometimes went too far, playing a central role, for instance, in the controversial BEAR FLAG REVOLT in 1846. He helped to capture California for the United States during the MEXICAN-AMERICAN WAR (1846–48), but was court-martialed for mutiny and insubordination when he fell out with a superior. His sentence was remitted, but he resigned from the army. In 1856, he became the Republican Party's first presidential candidate.

The 1840s brought many more Americans to the West, pioneers who aided in exploring and mapping territory even though they followed trails blazed by others. In 1846–47, in what was known as the Mormon trek, BRIGHAM YOUNG led a group of Mormons fleeing persecution from Illinois to Nebraska to the Great Salt Lake Valley in what is now Utah. They covered 1,300 miles, some of it over old Native-American trails and parts of the Ox-Bow, Oregon, and California trails. In the CALIFORNIA GOLD RUSH of 1849, the discovery of gold in California brought would-be prospectors into regions that had previously been little known. Missionaries, some of them foreign-born, also advanced the cause of exploration. Belgian-born Jesuit missionary Pierre Jean De Smet founded a chain of missions in the Pacific Northwest that ministered to Native Americans and added to knowledge of the region.

Once the TREATY OF GUADALUPE HIDALGO (1848) at the end of the Mexican-American War brought California and the Southwest into American possession, the era of exploration was gradually replaced by one of scientific mapping and pioneer settlement. By that time, Oregon had become a settled issue. Spain and Russia had abandoned their claims to the Oregon territory in, respectively, 1819 and 1824, leaving the United States and Britain to argue over it. In 1846, the OREGON TREATY set the border between U.S.-owned Oregon and Canada at the 49th parallel from the Rocky Mountains to the Pacific Ocean. Further south, the GADSEN PURCHASE (1853) expanded U.S. territory in the Southwest to its present boundaries. The Transcontinental Railroad Surveys of 1853–55, conducted

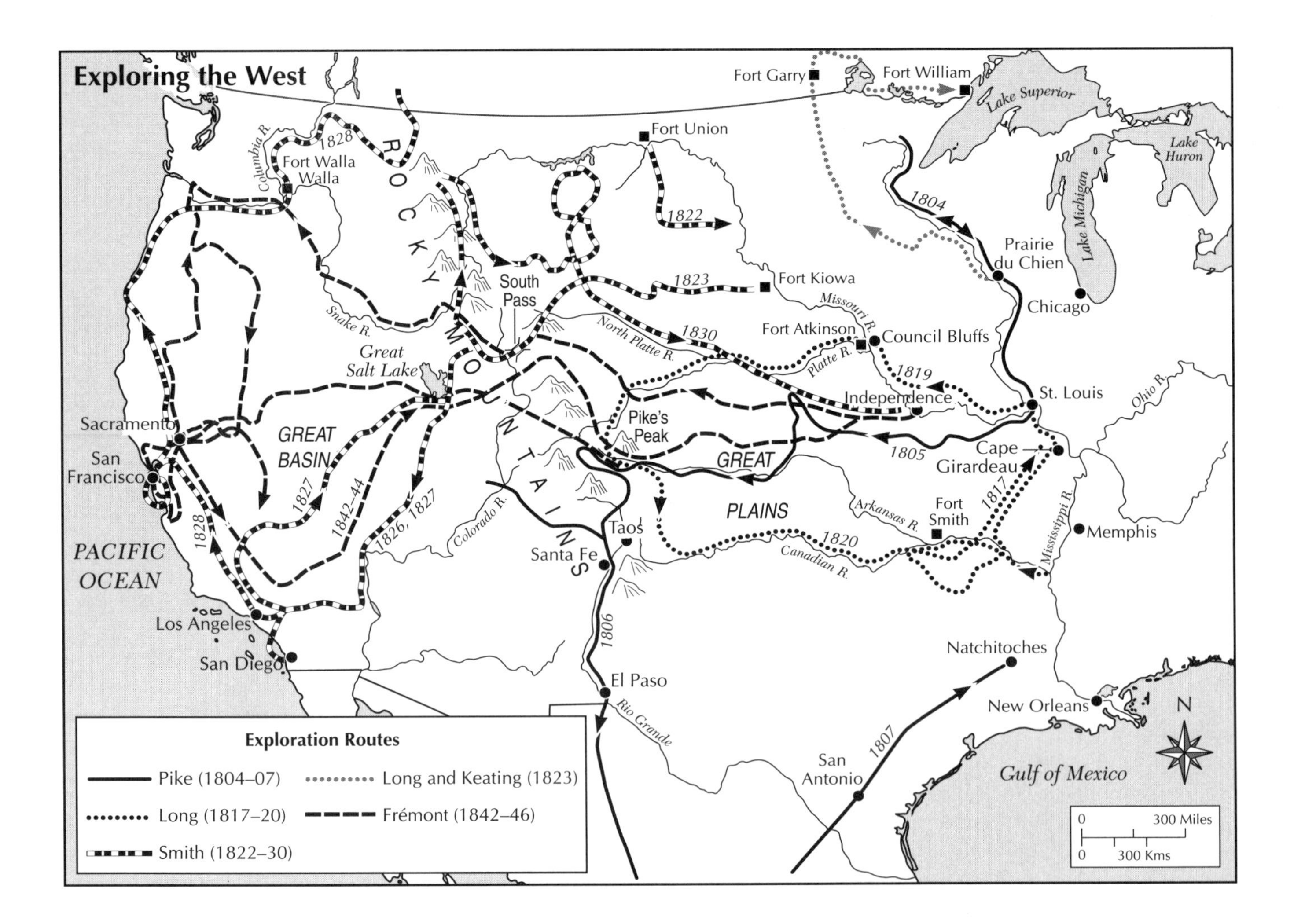

by the U.S. Army in search of a railroad route to the Pacific, added more knowledge of the West. By the end of the 1850s, the major features of the continent were well known, though more detailed mapping would be done after the Civil War.

With so much territory at home to explore, Americans had little time for more far-flung expeditions. Nevertheless, some intrepid Americans pushed beyond their country's shores. On a whaling voyage in 1820, American sea captain Nathaniel Brown Palmer reached the Antarctic Peninsula and the South Orkney Islands. In 1838–42, naval officer Charles Wilkes led the Wilkes expedition to Antarctica, Hawaii, the Pacific islands, and the Oregon coast. Wilkes is credited with naming Antarctica and discovering that it is a continent. Closer to home, in 1839, American traveler and author John Lloyd Stephens and English artist Frederick Catherwood conducted explorations in Central America, discovering Mayan ruins in Copán and elsewhere.

Further reading: John A. Hawgood, *America's Western Frontiers: The Exploration and Settlement of the Trans-Mississippi West* (New York: Alfred A. Knopf, 1967); Howard R. Lamar, ed., *The Reader's Encyclopedia of the American West* (New York: Thomas Y. Crowell Co., 1977); Clyde A. Milner II, et al., eds., *The Oxford History of the American West* (New York: Oxford University Press, 1994).

—George Ochoa

F

female antislavery societies

For as long as SLAVERY flourished in the United States, opposition to its existence was its dogged partner. Whether by individuals or by groups such as the Quakers, antislavery sentiment predated the Revolutionary War and continued through the early years of the new republic. It was not until the 1830s, however, that abolitionist opinion found formal expression through the formation of antislavery societies across the United States. The first such society is commonly considered to be the AMERICAN ANTI-SLAVERY SOCIETY, founded by William Lloyd Garrison in 1832. That group excluded women from its proceedings, causing Boston's female abolitionists to create their own organization, the Boston Female Anti-Slavery Society, in the same year. Independently of these bodies, a group of free black women formed the Female Anti-Slavery Society in Salem, Massachusetts, also in 1832. One year later, after being refused entry to the meetings of the Philadelphia Anti-Slavery Society, LUCRETIA MOTT founded the Philadelphia Female Anti-Slavery Society. At its inception, the society had 19 members, including two Quaker sisters from South Carolina, ANGELINA GRIMKÉ AND SARAH GRIMKÉ.

Female antislavery societies had much the same goal as their male counterparts: the end of the institution of slavery within the United States. Most abolitionists objected to slavery on moral grounds, believing that it was expressly wrong for one human to hold another in bondage, and, using the rhetoric of the new republic, calling for equality, justice, and liberty for all. Abolitionists convened public meetings to explain their position and used the power of the printing press to try to educate the general citizenry in their beliefs. Garrison and other prominent abolitionists such as Frederick Douglass published antislavery newspapers, while numerous activists wrote pamphlets and tracts for distribution across the North and South.

Female antislavery activists were central to these endeavors. Male abolitionists were generally comfortable with the idea of women raising funds for the movement, particularly as this mirrored the gender roles found in many churches of the period. Women also became adept at writing and circulating petitions, flooding the federal government with requests for the abolition of slavery through the 1830s and 1840s.

Although women, like men, often wrote and spoke publicly about their antislavery beliefs, they were frequently perceived to be stepping outside the acceptable boundaries of a woman's 'place' when they did so. To opponents of such female activism, it was especially disturbing that many female abolitionist writings appealed directly to other women, politicizing their roles as sisters, wives, and mothers. Angelina Grimké's 1836 pamphlet *An Appeal to the Christian Women of the South*, for example, pressed southern women to use their familial ties to men to exert influence over the business of the legislature and the ballot box. Sarah Grimké published a theological critique of slavery that same year, implicitly stepping into a sphere—ministry—that was generally, although not exclusively, the domain of men. When the sisters and other women, including Lucretia Mott, followed up their published works with lecture tours, outrage at their behavior reached fever pitch. Catharine Beecher publicly criticized the Grimkés for their "unfeminine" behavior, while the collective clergy of Massachusetts issued a pastoral letter condemning the sisters.

Regardless, female antislavery societies flourished in the North and by 1837 were of sufficient number to warrant the first National Female Anti-Slavery Society convention in New York. Eighty-one delegates from 12 states attended the convention, an event that was multiracial, as were the female antislavery societies themselves. Opposition to the political and abolitionist activism of women, however, continued, and after the second national convention was held in Philadelphia in 1838, the meeting hall in which it had taken place was burned to the ground.

By 1840 the American Anti-Slavery Society had, amid bitter acrimony, conceded women's right to join its ranks. It was as a delegate of that society that Lucretia Mott traveled to the World Anti-Slavery Convention in London in 1840. There she was refused admittance, male delegates arguing that the presence of women would trivialize the proceedings and undermine everything they hoped to achieve. Mott found a sympathetic supporter in Elizabeth Cady Stanton, the wife of another delegate to the convention. The two talked at length about the continued inequities experienced by women and resolved to hold a convention that expressly tackled the issue of women's rights. Helped by numerous other women's activists, that convention took place in SENECA FALLS, New York, in 1848.

Female antislavery societies were crucial to the success of the abolitionist movement and also acted as a catalyst to the formation of a women's rights movement later in the century. Using the tactics and political expertise they had gleaned from their abolitionist activism, women fought not only for the rights of the enslaved but for themselves. Their actions fueled the debate about gender equality for the rest of the century.

Further reading: Gerda Lerner, *The Grimké Sisters from South Carolina: Pioneers for Women's Rights and Abolition* (New York: Schocken, 1971); Jean Fagan Yellin and John C. Van Horne, ed., *The Abolitionist Sisterhood: Women's Political Culture in Antebellum America* (Ithaca, N.Y.: Cornell University Press, 1994).

—Catherine J. Denial

Figueroa, José (1792–1835)

José Figueroa was the Mexican governor of California responsible for establishing a central government. Born in Jonacatepec, Morelos, Figueroa made his appearance on the national scene in 1821 at the time of the movement for the independence of Mexico, when he served as the personal secretary of General Vincente Guerrero. After Mexico became an independent nation, Figueroa assumed several military and political positions. In 1824, he was commanding general of Sinaloa and Sonora, where he actively suppressed Indian revolts. He was appointed governor (commandante general and *jefe político*) of Upper (Alta) California in 1833. Among his duties were presiding over the education of the recently secularized mission neophytes, dividing up the Indian lands, and fostering the colonization of skilled workingmen and artisans into the province. He also had instructions to keep an eye on trade with the Russians and the American whaling ships.

Figueroa became embroiled in domestic political squabbles when he set about administering the law of the Mexican Congress to secularize the California missions. At issue were some of the most attractive lands in the province. Figueroa acted to thwart the schemes of José María Padres and José María Hijar (the latter already appointed as Figueroa's successor as governor) in their colonization plans for mission lands. When General ANTONIO LÓPEZ DE SANTA ANNA took office in 1834, he reappointed Figueroa to the office of governor of Alta California. Figueroa used the authority of his office to order the Padres-Hijar colonies off the mission lands and directed that they settle along the northern frontier of Sonoma, Solano, and Petaluma as a buffer against Russian expansion to the south. His quarrel with Padres and Hijar continued, and he eventually expelled them from California. He then wrote a political testament defending his actions, under the title *The Manifesto to the Mexican Republic.* Figueroa's last actions as governor were concerned with securing the northern border against Indian revolt and Russian penetration. In 1835, he died in Monterey and was buried in Santa Barbara.

Figueroa was an important figure in the establishment of the authority of the central government in California. During his administration, he worked on the issues that were important to the Republic of Mexico. These included the administration of the Secularization Law of 1833 and safeguarding mission lands, securing the northern frontier against penetration by the Russians, and monitoring the expansion of American companies into the trades in hides and tallow. Loyal to his superiors in Mexico City, he was a man who stood up against the corruption and cronyism associated with much of Mexican political life at the time.

Further reading: Jose Figueroa, *The Manifesto to the Mexican Republic* (reprint, Oakland, Calif.: Biobooks, 1952); C. Alan Hutchinson, *Frontier Settlement in Mexican California* (New Haven, Conn: Yale University Press, 1969).

filibustering See Volume V

Fillmore, Millard (1800–1874)

Born into poverty at the dawn of the 19th century, Millard Fillmore climbed to the highest office in the land—and inherited a nation breaking into fragments over the question of SLAVERY. Despite his best efforts, the lines of the future battles of the Civil War were drawn, and Fillmore found himself rejected by his own dying party and denied renomination.

The second of eight children, Millard Fillmore was born into an impoverished family on January 7, 1800. His family's small farm in upstate Cayuga County, New York, could not support them, and his father apprenticed him to a clothmaker, a brutal apprenticeship that stopped just short of slavery. Fillmore taught himself to read, stealing books on occasion, and finally managed to borrow $30 to pay his obligation to the clothmaker. Free, he walked 100 miles to get back home to his family.

Fillmore was obsessed with educating himself. He pored over every book he could get his hands on and attended school in a nearby town for six months. His teacher, Abigail Powers, encouraged and helped him and ultimately proved to be the most influential person in his life. She was only 19—not even two years older than her pupil. After Fillmore received a clerkship with a local judge, he began to court her, and the couple married in 1826.

As a young lawyer, Fillmore approached by a fledgling political party and asked to run for the New York State Assembly. In 1829, he began the first of three terms in the assembly, where he sponsored a substantial amount of legislation. In 1832, he was elected to the U.S. House of Representatives. At that time, ANDREW JACKSON was president. Jackson's repeated clashes with Congress and his ambitious attempts to expand presidential power united several parties against him. Fillmore's own Anti-Masonic Party merged with the Whigs, which represented the older, more entrenched power structure and opposed everything that Jackson and the Democrats represented. In 1843, at the end of four terms in Congress (interrupted by one defeat), Fillmore resigned from the legislature. The following year, he lobbied unsuccessfully for the vice-presidential nomination on the Whig ticket with HENRY CLAY and also lost an election for governor of New York. In 1847, he was elected New York State comptroller (or chief financial officer), winning by such a wide margin that he was immediately considered a prospect for national office.

The WHIG PARTY selected military hero General ZACHARY TAYLOR as their presidential nominee for the election of 1848, but the nomination of a slave owner who held property in Louisiana, Kentucky, and Mississippi infuriated abolitionist Whigs from the North. The party decided to balance the ticket by putting a northerner—Fillmore—in the vice-presidential slot. The Taylor-Fillmore ticket won a bitterly fought election over the Democratic ticket led by Michigan senator LEWIS CASS.

Taylor and Fillmore were an odd match—the products of very different backgrounds and educations, and far apart on the issues of the day. The two men did not meet until after the election and did not hit it off when they did. In a short time, Fillmore found himself excluded from the councils of power, relegated to his role as president of the Senate.

The critical issue facing President Taylor was slavery. Henry Clay had crafted a series of proposals into an omnibus bill that became known as the COMPROMISE OF 1850, a patchwork of legislation that forbade slavery in some states that had been formed from the new territory gained in the MEXICAN-AMERICAN WAR. The compromise also established a FUGITIVE SLAVE LAW guaranteeing that runaway slaves apprehended anywhere in the United States would be returned to their owners. Taylor refused to take a stand, and the compromise bill was stalled in endless debates in the Senate by mid-1850. But then the unthinkable happened: The president died, possibly of cholera.

As president, Fillmore strongly supported the Compromise of 1850. Allying himself with Democratic senator Stephen Douglas, the new president engineered its passage. By forcing these issues, Fillmore believed he had helped to safeguard the Union, but it soon became clear that the Compromise, rather than satisfying anyone, gave everyone something to hate. Under the strains of the failed agreement, the Whig Party began to come apart at the seams.

On the international stage, Fillmore dispatched MATTHEW CALBRAITH PERRY to "open" Japan to Western trade and worked to keep the Hawaiian Islands out of European hands. He refused to back an invasion of CUBA by a group of southern adventurers who wanted to expand the South into a slave-based Caribbean empire. This filibustering expedition failed, and Fillmore took the blame from southerners. At the same time, he offended northerners by enforcing the Fugitive Slave Law in their region. Weary and dispirited, he declined to run again but was prevailed upon to allow his name to be put forward—only to lose the nomination to General WINFIELD SCOTT. Shortly

Millard Fillmore *(Library of Congress)*

thereafter, his beloved Abigail died, followed by his 22-year-old daughter Mary.

In 1856, Fillmore ran for election as the presidential candidate of the Whig-American Party, a fusion of the remaining Whigs and the anti-immigrant American Party (nicknamed the KNOW-NOTHING PARTY). He won the electoral college votes of Maryland and 21 percent of the popular vote; but the newly organized REPUBLICAN PARTY, even in defeat, eclipsed Fillmore and the Whigs, winning 33 percent of the vote, and Fillmore's poor performance marked the end of his party.

While a Union supporter, Fillmore opposed Abraham Lincoln's policies during the Civil War and supported George McClellan for president in 1864. He also sympathized with Andrew Johnson's presidential struggles. Fillmore died of a stroke in New York State March 1874, 21 years after leaving the White House.

Further reading: Elbert B. Smith, *The Presidencies of Zachary Taylor and Millard Fillmore* (Lawrence: University Press of Kansas, 1988)

Finney, Charles Grandison (1792–1875)

One of the leading evangelical preachers of the 19th century, Charles Grandison Finney was a key figure in the series of revivals known as the SECOND GREAT AWAKENING that swept parts of the United States in the 1820s and 1830s. Widely considered to be one of the most important figures in the religious history of the United States, he saw himself as acting firmly in the tradition of Protestantism as articulated by John Calvin and the American Jonathan Edwards, among others.

Finney was born in western Connecticut, near Warren, on August 29, 1792, to Sylvester and Rebecca Rice Finney, Yankee farmers who traced their ancestry to the Pilgrims of Plymouth. The Finneys later moved to upstate New York, settling first in Oneida County before moving to Henderson, in Jefferson County, when Charles was eight. After receiving an education in New York and Connecticut, he taught school in New Jersey. While still a young man, he returned to Adams in northern New York to apprentice with a lawyer.

Over six feet in height and a natural leader, Finney seemed to be heading toward a successful career in law and perhaps politics. While a practicing attorney, he began to turn his attentions more to matters of religion, reading the Bible and leading the choir of the Presbyterian Church in Adams. As many around him began to be caught up in the excitement of religious revivals in the 1820s, Finney despaired at ever experiencing a dramatic conversion that would change his heart and lead him to Christ. He promised God that if he were ever to have such an epiphany, he would devote the remainder of his life to preaching the Gospel. On October 10, 1821, as he neared his 30th birthday, Finney had such a dramatic conversion during a community revival meeting near Adams. Recognizing his talent and potential, the local Presbyterian clergy shortly authorized him to begin preaching. Soon after, he married Lydia Andrews; the couple had six children, four of whom survived to adulthood.

Finney's style from the pulpit was simple, direct, and highly effective. He spoke without notes, urging his listeners to commit their lives to Christ at that moment or risk damnation. He spoke of hell in very vivid terms as a real place that awaited those who failed to believe. He was so persuasive that many in his audiences would convert on the spot, falling to the floor and weeping as they did. He preached throughout upstate New York, meeting with special success in towns along the Erie Canal, such as Utica and Rome, and, later, in Rochester. These were places that were on the forefront of economic change in the United States, and Finney's message of redemption found many willing listeners among the new middle class of managers, business owners, and professionals. He preached a somewhat more optimistic brand of Christianity than traditional Calvinism in arguing that the individual was not necessarily predestined to damnation and could overcome his or her sinfulness by a conversion of the heart and by establishing a personal relationship with Christ through prayer.

One of the other keys to the success of Finney's revivals was that he persuaded people they were more likely to experience God's saving grace if they came into the presence of others who had already undergone a conversion. The saved and the unsaved alike would pray together publicly at Finney's revivals. Another part of his method was to come into a community and create excitement by having his assistants, some of whom were women, go door to door, encouraging families and groups of friends and neighbors to attend the revivals together. Then he would hold all-night prayer meetings in which the conversions, often theatrical in appearance, would follow one after another. In one of his most successful revival campaigns, in Rochester during 1830–31, Finney first made use of "the anxious bench," calling forward members of his audience to give their heart over to Jesus at the bench placed near his pulpit, adding to the dramatic effect. As he described his manner for saving souls in his book *Lectures on Revivals of Religion* (1853), which was based on his work at Rochester and other places, appealing to the individual's precarious situation was crucial. He would directly ask the persons sitting in the rows before him: "Will you submit to God tonight—NOW?"

Finney ranged far and wide in the Northeast in his preaching, traveling to Delaware, Philadelphia, Boston (where he met with mixed results) and New York City. He eventually linked his religious message to social-reform causes such as temperance, which drew the support of many evangelical Protestants. In 1835, he accepted a position teaching theology at the new Oberlin Collegiate Institute in Ohio. His Christian mission led him to observe strict guidelines on personal behavior, as he avoided alcohol, tobacco, and caffeine. He also became a vigorous abolitionist, and Oberlin developed into an important station on the Underground Railroad. His work at Oberlin did not stop him from continuing to preach throughout the northern United States, even after he came the president of the college at Oberlin in 1851.

During middle age, Finney had a crisis of faith after the death of his wife Lydia, but he came out of it with a renewed belief in the redeeming power of Christianity. He remained active into his later years, even after retiring as college president and pastor in the 1860s. As a staunch opponent of SLAVERY, he did not support Abraham Lincoln in either 1860 or 1864 because he considered Lincoln too cautious on the questions of emancipation and racial equality. He successfully completed his *Memoirs*, which was published after his death on August 16, 1875, in Oberlin. He was survived by his wife Rebecca, whom he had married after his second wife, Elizabeth, died.

Charles Grandison Finney was a leading example of the evangelical and reform spirit which did much to shape the United States in the 19th century. A major figure of the Second Great Awakening and an innovator in terms of method, Finney considered himself a part of the great tradition of Anglo-American Protestantism and saw his duty as bringing the lone sinner to a new life in Christ.

Further reading: Charles E. Hambrick-Stowe, *Charles G. Finney and the Spirit of American Evangelicalism* (Grand Rapids, Mich.: W. B. Eerdmans Pub. Co., 1996); Keith J. Hardman, *Charles Grandison Finney, 1792–1875: Revivalist and Reformer* (Syracuse, N.Y.: Syracuse University Press, 1987).

—Jason K. Duncan

Florida, East and West

The area that is now the state of Florida was contested by the French, Spanish, British, and American governments for over a century before it became part of the United States in 1819. France and Spain fought a minor territorial war over the area in 1719. After fighting stopped, the two empires agreed that the border between French Louisiana and Spanish Florida would be the Perdido River (now the western border of the state). When France was defeated by Great Britain in the Seven Years' War in 1763, French Louisiana became the property of Spain, and Spanish Florida was given to the British. During this realignment, Britain claimed the strip of land running from the Perdido River west to the Mississippi River (what is now part of Alabama, Mississippi, and Louisiana), with the exception of the island of New Orleans, which remained Spanish. The British called this small, remote territory West Florida and administered it separately. They also extended West Florida eastward to the Apalachicola River and the town of Pensacola, which became the capital of the territory. The area east of the Apalachicola, including the entire peninsula, became known as East Florida.

In the Peace of Paris ending the American Revolution in 1783, Spain reacquired both Floridas from Great Britain, including the strip west of the Perdido River that had once belonged to France. The Floridas were under the Spanish colonial government of Louisiana until 1800, when Spain secretly ceded Louisiana once again to France. When the United States purchased Louisiana from France in 1803, the status of the Floridas was unclear. The Treaty of San Lorenzo in 1795 fixed the northern border between the United States and the Spanish Floridas at the 31st parallel, which seemed to imply that the Floridas were still separate from Louisiana. With the purchase of Louisiana, however, the United States argued that the acquisition included East and West Florida. Putting aside the misleading, confusing logic of this claim, the American government pressed its case for ownership of both Floridas. They based their claim on two different arguments. First, the American government argued that Napoleon had sold the Floridas when he sold Louisiana. Second, if Napoleon did not sell Florida and it was still Spanish territory, Spain should give it to the United States as compensation because the Spanish had not upheld the terms of the Treaty of San Lorenzo. The United States claimed that the Spanish had violated the treaty by failing to keep Indians from raiding American settlements and by protecting American slaves who escaped to Florida.

The dispute over which empire held the Floridas continued for the next 15 years. The United States slowly encroached on the territory, declaring West Florida a U.S. customs district in 1804 and then appropriating the territory up to the Pearl River in 1810. In 1812, most of West Florida was incorporated into the new state of Louisiana, while the section between the Perdido and Pearl Rivers became part of Mississippi Territory. In 1818, General ANDREW JACKSON invaded Pensacola, where he implemented violent frontier justice on those Spanish colonists who opposed him. The aggressive behavior of Jackson and President JAMES MONROE soon led to Spain's capitulation. In 1819, Spain agreed to the ADAMS-ONÍS TREATY, which ceded the Floridas to the United States.

Florida was a problematic territory not only because of contested ownership. It was ideally located to be a center for Caribbean trade, but the region's malarial climate and treacherous geography made permanent settlement difficult for the Spanish, British, and Americans. Indian resistance to white settlement was also more persistent in Florida than anywhere else in the eastern part of the country. Jackson established a skeletal civil government in Florida Territory, and a territorial legislature was created by 1826. Settlement and economic growth seemed to be progressing until the SEMINOLE WARS and the PANIC OF 1837 temporarily shut down speculation in Florida's future. Only after the second Seminole war concluded in 1842 did the stabilized territory begin pushing for statehood. Florida was admitted as a slave state in 1845.

In retrospect, the international feud over Florida may seem unimportant, but this struggle can be seen as one of the first acts of an imperial United States in an effort to gain more territory. Through the annexation of Florida, the nation began to develop strategies for becoming truly continental. These aggressive tactics for expansion eventually led to conflicts with the Republic of Texas and Mexico, as well as the eventual acquisition of the territory between the Rio Grande and the 49th parallel.

—Eleanor H. McConnell

foreign policy

National sovereignty, commercial freedom, and territorial expansion were the three primary objectives that shaped U.S. foreign policy over the course of the 19th century. Between 1800 and 1861, America emerged as a nation with great potential for global influence. The country expanded its borders from the Atlantic Ocean to the Pacific Ocean, while also establishing borders with Canada and Mexico. Before it plunged into the tragedy of the Civil War in 1861, the United States had begun cultivating what would become a seemingly insatiable hunger by the century's end for commercial, cultural, and military success beyond its own vast boundaries and onto the world stage.

At the dawn of the 19th century, the newly independent United States was grudgingly recognized by the great powers of Europe as a sovereign nation. Jay's Treaty with Britain (1794) and Pinckney's Treaty with Spain (1795) solidified U.S. territorial acquisition in the Northwest and Florida and secured American trade along the Mississippi River. Although these treaties represented a minor advance of U.S. legitimacy, the British and French continued their attempts to influence and manipulate the young and fragile nation.

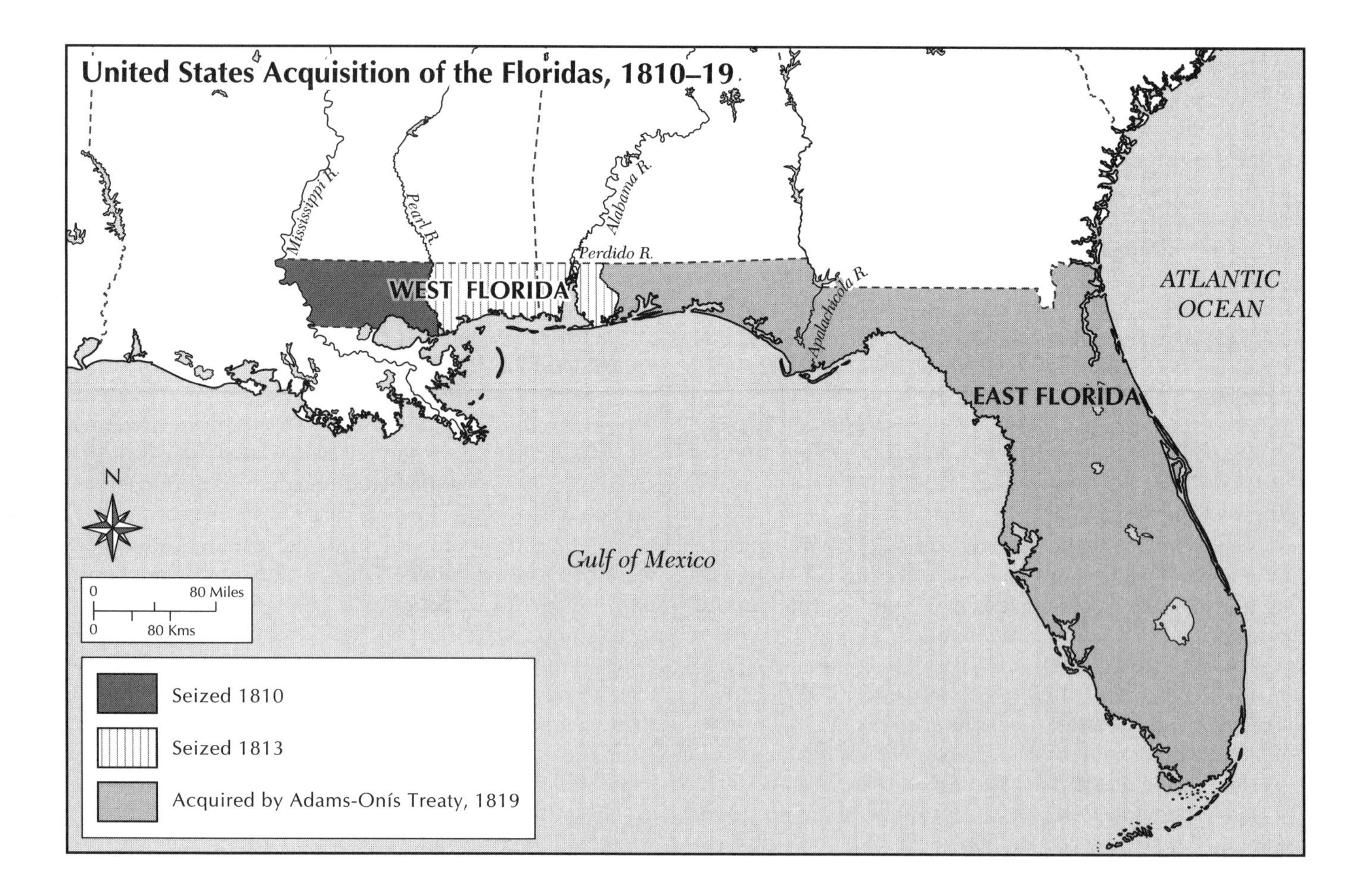

The wars between Britain and France that raged in Europe during the early part of the 19th century provided the United States and its people not only with significant challenges but also with great opportunities to achieve international integrity, commercial growth, and territorial acquisition. Despite its best efforts to remain neutral, the young nation was eventually swept up in conflict among several European powers. The United States and France nearly went to war over the so-called XYZ Affair in 1798, in which French officials demanded a bribe from American envoys in Paris as a prerequisite to begin negotiations over the growing differences between the two nations. Continuing disputes over U.S. neutrality in commercial shipping, over free navigation of the Mississippi, and over American use of the port of New Orleans heightened tensions.

Many of these problems were resolved in 1803, when the United States purchased Louisiana, including the port city of New Orleans, and vast, largely unexplored territories west of the Mississippi River from a financially strapped France. Although Napoleon Bonaparte had hoped to resurrect the French colonial empire in North America, his ambitions in Europe were more significant. Additionally, the inability of French forces to put down a slave rebellion on the Caribbean island of Hispaniola (now shared by Haiti and the Dominican Republic) led by the indomitable Toussaint Louverture severely limited the French emperor's designs on the Western Hemisphere. Although it meant abandoning direct influence across the Atlantic, the sale of the Louisiana territory provided Napoleon with sufficient funds to sustain his military campaigns in Europe and dreams of continental supremacy until his final defeat by Britain in 1815. The Louisiana Purchase was an unexpected windfall for the United States and President Thomas Jefferson, because he had instructed his emissaries to Paris only to acquire New Orleans and parts of Spanish Florida. With the Louisiana Purchase, the thrust of U.S. westward expansion took a great leap forward.

Although the United States avoided war with France, it would not do so with Great Britain. After 1803 and the resumption of fighting between Britain and France, the British resumed the seizure of American merchant ships suspected of carrying on trade with the French. The U.S. government demanded that the British respect American neutrality. Tension between the two nations mounted as the British navy ignored this demand and impressed over 10,000 American citizens into service. A frustrated President Jefferson and Congress knew that their navy was no match against the most powerful fleet in the world, so they first sought to boycott British imports. After this policy failed, the federal government imposed the 1807 Embargo Act, which was intended to harm Britain by denying it access to American raw materials. Like the boycott, the embargo also failed and, in fact, actually did more harm than good for American trade, as U.S. exports plummeted and desperate merchants continued to find ways to get their goods to Britain. Discouraged, Congress repealed the act in 1809 and passed subsequent acts to stop the harassment of U.S. vessels by both the British and the French, but witnessed little success.

The conflict between the United States and Britain was only made worse by the part the British played in the U.S. war with Indian nations in the Northwest Territory. Led by TECUMSEH, the charismatic and fiercely independent Shawnee leader, these NATIVE AMERICANS violently resisted American encroachment onto their lands. The British entered into various alliances with these Indian nations and encouraged their struggles against U.S. domination. Most Americans saw British support as yet another in a series of insults and outrages. The tension between the two countries finally resulted in open armed hostility in June 1812, when President James Madison sent a declaration of war to Great Britain.

With war declared by Washington, American forces invaded Canada to stop the British support of Indian nations. The invasion achieved little more than a stalemate at the U.S.-Canadian border. Additionally, it created regional conflict in the United States because the residents of New England states, who had British sympathies, ignored illegal trade across the Canadian border and refused to support the American cause with troops or supplies. Because the small U.S. Navy was no match for their own, the British easily blockaded the Atlantic seaboard. British troops attacked, sacked and burned many coastal cities, including Washington, D.C. Meanwhile, the Indian wars of resistance continued in the Northwest and the South. American forces under the command of ANDREW JACKSON won significant military victories in 1814 against Indian peoples in these territories. Native American resistance was suppressed, and some of their lands were ceded as part of the burgeoning American nation. Finally, fatigue brought on by the Napoleonic wars in Europe compelled the British to end their war in North America. The two nations signed the TREATY OF GHENT in December 1814, with the British ending their advocacy for a separate, independent state for neutral Indian peoples. Because of poor communication, Andrew Jackson's famous victory over the British in New Orleans in 1815 actually happened after the treaty was signed. Notwithstanding what appeared to be only minor U.S. gains, the war was significant because it marked the final British recognition of U.S. independence.

The conclusion of the WAR OF 1812 signaled the emergence of the United States as an independent and sovereign world nation, although a relatively underdeveloped one. Over the next half-century, U.S. foreign policy focused on further territorial acquisition. JOHN QUINCY ADAMS, President JAMES MONROE's secretary of state, proved an exceptionally skilled diplomat. He was a shrewd negotiator and one of the chief architects of early 19th century U.S. foreign policy. In 1817, he negotiated a fixed boundary between the United States and British Canada. More significant, however, was Adams's diplomacy in acquiring the Spanish territories of Florida for the United States. Adams's negotiating position was greatly enhanced when an overzealous General Andrew Jackson invaded Spanish Florida in "self-defense" against Florida's Seminole Indians. The Spanish protested what they considered to be an act of U.S. aggression. However, Adams countered by making the argument that Spain did not have an adequate military presence in its Florida territories to prevent Seminole incursion into the United States. Spain, recognizing that it did not have the capacity to control the Seminole or, for that matter, American invasion forces, ceded Florida to the United States with the ADAMS-ONÍS TREATY in 1819. Five years later, Adams also managed to obtain for the United States those parts of Oregon claimed by imperial Russia, thereby bringing the nation closer to continental unification.

Under Adams's guidance, in 1823 President Monroe articulated the famous MONROE DOCTRINE that would become one of the key pillars of U.S. foreign policy for the remainder of the century and well into the next. The doctrine called for the end of colonization in the Western Hemisphere and promised U.S. protection of newly independent Central and South American countries from European intervention. Monroe declared that any attempt by the European powers to violate the sovereignty of these new countries would be viewed "as the manifestation of an unfriendly disposition toward the United States." The nation would continue to take a special interest in the affairs of the Western Hemisphere throughout the 19th and 20th centuries, and Monroe's original doctrine would be rearticulated in various forms such as Theodore Roosevelt's Corollary at the turn of the century and the Good Neighbor policy of the 1930s.

Following Monroe's presidency, U.S. territorial acquisition and Atlantic-to-Pacific consolidation became chief cornerstones of both foreign policy and American cultural identity. In 1845, journalist John O'Sullivan gave the American expansionist urge a name: MANIFEST DESTINY. He declared that it was America's "manifest destiny to overspread the continent allotted by Providence for the free development of our yearly multiplying millions." Inspired by this mission statement, Americans continued to pursue expansion with both impressive zeal and ruthless violence. What this meant in terms of foreign policy was a near-war with Great Britain over the Oregon territory and a two-year war between the United States and Mexico. Until 1846, Great Britain and the United States accepted joint occupancy of Oregon. President JAMES K. POLK sought to claim all of Oregon below the 54th parallel as solely American. Peace was maintained through the OREGON TREATY OF 1846 that established the 49th parallel as the U.S.-Canada border. In exchange for this new boundary, the United States allowed the British to keep control of Vancouver Island.

Polk's claims for lands that belonged to or were claimed by Mexico led to the MEXICAN-AMERICAN WAR (1846–48). His justification for armed conflict was the American annexation of TEXAS, which the Mexican government disputed. The Mexican army's defeat by the forces of SAM HOUSTON in 1836 secured Texan independence from Mexico, and in 1845 the United States annexed Texas out of expansionist desires and concerns about foreign influence, namely that of the British. However, the Mexican government refused to recognize Texas's annexation. Polk had larger designs than adding Texas to the nation; he was determined to acquire, by force if necessary, large portions of northern Mexico, including the territory of California and what would become New Mexico. Using the dispute with Mexico over Texas and the Rio Grande border as a pretext, the United States invaded its southern neighbor in 1846. American troops pushed easily down to Mexico City and forced the Mexican government to surrender. According to the terms of TREATY OF GUADALUPE HIDALGO (1848), Mexico ceded to the United States two-fifths of its territory (including Texas, CALIFORNIA, and New Mexico) for $15 million. Whether they liked or not, the inhabitants of these lands were incorporated into the United States.

The war with and victory over Mexico only whetted the American appetite for territory and bolstered the federal government's confidence in international affairs. Polk offered Spain as much as $100 million for CUBA in 1848, but his offer was rejected. President Franklin Pierce made a similar offer and even threatened the use of force to compel the sale of Cuba. He withdrew this intimidating offer, however, because of negative domestic public reaction.

The expansionist lust of some Americans spurred them on to seek territory in the Caribbean and Central America as private endeavors. During the early 1850s, these adventuresome Americans, also called filibusters, attempted to invade and conquer Cuba, Nicaragua, and even parts of Mexico. Ardent proslavery southerners who professed the doctrine of Manifest Destiny, these filibusters hoped to increase the power and influence of the slave states through conquest, but none of their private expeditions was successful. Despite the filibusters' failure to seize new lands and that of U.S. presidents to buy them, Americans coveted much of what they saw south of Mexico for the remainder of the century.

U.S. expansionist desires did not stop in the Western Hemisphere. In an effort to establish a presence in the

Pacific, to promote commerce, to find coaling stations and to protect shipwrecked American sailors, President MILLARD FILLMORE sent U.S. Navy Commodore MATTHEW CALBRAITH PERRY to "open" Japan. In 1853, four U.S. warships, two of them intimidating steam-powered vessels that belched black smoke, dropped anchor off the coast of Japan. Perry's efforts and determination to fulfill his orders produced in 1854 a commercial trade treaty with Japan. The Tokugawa Shogunate rulers of Japan capitulated to Perry's demands because of superior U.S. military power. They also hoped to avoid the humiliating domination several European powers exercised over other Asian nations like India and China. The "opening" of Japan was only a beginning for the United States. The Americans would return to the Pacific later in the century in order to seize the HAWAIIAN ISLANDS and, during the Spanish-American War (1898), to secure a more permanent foothold and influence in Asia.

U.S. international concerns took secondary importance when civil war erupted at Fort Sumter off the coast of South Carolina in 1861. Following the defeat of the Confederacy in 1865, the United States would once again return to an expansionist foreign policy. For the next half-century and beyond, Manifest Destiny would encourage U.S. commercial and territorial desires well beyond national borders and into Central and South America as well as the far-flung Pacific. The lives of millions had been and would continue to be irrevocably changed as the American expansionist juggernaut pushed west and south. By 1899, the expansionism that drove U.S. foreign policy for over a century was ushering the country into the international arena and towards superpower ascendancy in the 20th century.

Further reading: Garry Clifford, Kenneth J. Haugan, and Thomas J. Patterson, eds., *American Foreign Policy: A History*, Vol. 1. (Lexington, Mass.: D.C. Heath, 1995); Michael H. Hogan, *Paths to Power: The Historiography of American Foreign Relations to 1941* (New York: Cambridge University Press, 2000).

—Charles Hawley

Fort Laramie

Built by 1834 by fur traders, Fort Laramie was a focal point of the FUR TRADE, the CALIFORNIA GOLD RUSH, and relations with NATIVE AMERICANS over a half-century, until its closing in 1890. WILLIAM SUBLETTE and Robert Campbell built Fort William (its original name) at the junction of the Laramie and North Platte Rivers as part of the expansion of the fur trade onto the northern Great Plains. Like BENT'S FORT farther to the south, it was designed to become a focal point of contact and exchange between the traders and the surrounding Indians. The stockade was soon called Fort Laramie, after a French trader who had been killed on the Laramie River. The appearance of these fixed posts reflected the declining significance of the RENDEZVOUS as an instrument of contact and trade. In 1835, Sublette and associates sold the fort to another fur-trading company headed by Thomas Fitzpatrick, and the next year, the AMERICAN FUR COMPANY absorbed Fitzpatrick's group. The fort attracted the trade of the Indians from the Rocky Mountains as well as several groups of Sioux, confirming the significance of its location. The fur business was steady, but trading on the Platte was never as important as that on the upper Missouri or that of the southern Great Plains (Bent's Fort).

As the fur trade stagnated, the fort assumed another significance. Beginning in 1841, a growing number of settler families began an annual overland trek to Oregon over what became known as the OREGON TRAIL. For the westward pioneers, Fort Laramie became the first significant stop after leaving Independence, Missouri. After 800 miles on the overland trail, settlers, guides, and draft animals all used the fort as a site to rest, refit, and organize for the mountain challenges ahead. As the numbers of overland immigrants grew, from 1,000 in 1843 to 5,000 in 1845, the significance of the fort as an oasis on the land trail grew even as the fur trade declined.

In 1849 the U.S. government bought the fort as a military post. The previous year, gold had been discovered in CALIFORNIA. The California gold rush stimulated the largest overland immigration in the history of the republic. In 1849, some 80,000 FORTY-NINERS took the overland trail to California, and Fort Laramie became the most important landmark on their way West. Every Forty-niner diary—and there are more than 400 preserved—remarked on the arrival at Fort Laramie and the significance of the place to travelers heading west. Among its other services, the fort (now under the command of an Army officer) kept a register of wagons and a roster of immigrants. National newspapers used these numbers as evidence of the large numbers rushing to California in search of gold.

The large overland immigrations of 1849 and subsequent years were the work of inexperienced argonauts intent on reaching California to find gold. They saw the CALIFORNIA TRAIL, as it came to be called, as an obstacle to their ambitions. Most of them carried too much, and the strain on their draft animals was obvious by the time they reached Fort Laramie. During the stop at the fort, the hurried and harried Forty-niners discarded weight and repacked their wagons. In the middle of the summer, observers commented on the piles of bacon and trunks outside the fort. Indians came not to trade but to pick up the bounty around the fort.

This painting shows a Native American encampment outside Fort Laramie in Wyoming. *(Hulton/Archive)*

As the focus and number of immigrants to California shifted from overland travel to seagoing transportation in the 1850s, Fort Laramie became a focal point of relations between the U.S. government and the Indian nations of the northern plains. The California gold rush, the annexation of new lands through the TREATY OF GUADALUPE HIDALGO, and the signing of the OREGON TREATY OF 1846 had intensified Euro-American traffic across the plains. The fur trade had begun to decline, and the Indians' bargaining power was reduced as increasing numbers of non-Indians moved over what they regarded as their hunting areas. In an attempt to settle Indian affairs on the northern plains and to fit Native Americans into new national policies, the federal government convened a large gathering of Indians. The year was 1851, and the site of the meeting was Fort Laramie. Perhaps as many as 10,000 Indians attended a series of meetings.

With the doctrine of the permanent Indian frontier now obsolete, the Treaty of Fort Laramie (1851) laid down federal policy toward the Indians of the plains. Even as nations east of the Mississippi River were moved to the vast area known as Indian Territory on the grounds that such landscape would never be attractive for American settlement, the movement of settlers farther onto the plains indicated that Indian policy must be recast. Under the terms of the Treaty of Fort Laramie, nations of the plains agreed to pursue peaceful relations among themselves and to permit the federal government to construct and maintain roads and other fixed posts within the Indian territories. The treaty also divided the northern plains into specific tracts for individual signatory nations. This division was part of the federal government's intention to assign specific boundaries to Indian groups, a legal nicety that was probably not clearly understood by the treaty signers. Even if the leaders had understood the various provisions, they lacked power to enforce their will on all members of their tribal groups, which were inherently decentralized. Among those who eventually affixed their marks to the treaty were representatives of the Sioux, Cheyenne, Arapaho, Crow, and Mandan nations. In return for these concessions, the federal government promised that the designated Indian lands would be theirs forever and that the government would protect the Indians from Euro-American trespassers. Finally, the representatives of the government agreed to pay annuities of supplies and provisions worth $50,000 for the next 50 years.

In an arbitrary decision that would become a pattern of relations with the Indians, the Senate reduced length of the annuity to 15 years and increased the amount of goods to $70,000. None of the Indian signatories agreed to these changes, and the peaceful respite was brief. The continuing movement of Euro-American settlers onto the plains, which accelerated after the Kansas-Nebraska Act (1854), produced the inevitable physical confrontations. The COLORADO GOLD RUSH and the immigration of 50,000 gold seekers across Kansas and Nebraska in the summer of 1859 brought the situation to a head. The large numbers of Colorado Fifty-niners were competitors for the scarce natural resources of the plains, making subsistence for the Plains Indians difficult if not impossible. Conflict between the two groups produced the inevitable number of depredations and reprisals, and within a decade of the great gathering and treaty-making exercise at Fort Laramie, the arrangements for peace had irrevocably broken down.

Fort Laramie remained an important post on the plains for another generation. The enlarged American presence in the form of settlers, the Pony Express, the telegraph, and, finally, the railroad led to escalating clashes. The American government was preoccupied by the Civil War, but with the end of this conflict, expansion onto the plains accelerated. The great Sioux War of 1876 was the most noteworthy example of U.S. and Indian clashes but far from the only one. Meanwhile, Fort Laramie continued to play a central role in affairs on the plains until its closure in 1890.

Further reading: Paul L. Hedren, *Fort Laramie in 1876: Chronicle of a Frontier Post at War* (Lincoln: University of Nebraska Press, 1988).

Fort Leavenworth

The U.S. Army established Fort Leavenworth in 1827 in what would become the territory and later state of Kansas, at the head of the SANTA FE TRAIL and OREGON TRAIL. It was named for Colonel Henry Leavenworth, one of the army officers most associated with the frontier. Built to protect western travelers and maintain a military presence against the Plains Indians, the fort was a significant anchor to American defense in the West.

Fort Leavenworth was the staging site for several important expeditions to the West, one commanded by Colonel Henry Dodge (1835) and two others led by Colonel (later General) STEPHEN WATTS KEARNY (1839 and 1845). On the outbreak of the MEXICAN-AMERICAN WAR in 1846, Kearny gathered a force of 1,600 at the fort, trained and outfitted his army, and began his trek to conquer New Mexico and California. During the Civil War, Fort Leavenworth served as an important supply depot and as the headquarters of the Department of the Missouri. In 1881, the army established a Command and Staff School at the fort, and this course of study became the required career step for all officers of staff rank. As such, the fort and its environs became one of the few (along with West Point) common factors in the experience of career officers. It continues to fill that same function up to the present day.

Further reading: Dwight L. Clarke, *Stephen Watts Kearny, Soldier of the West* (Norman: University of Oklahoma Press, 1961).

Fort Vancouver

The Hudson's Bay Company (HBC) built Fort Vancouver in 1824–25 to serve as the headquarters of its Columbia Department. The HBC was locked in a continuing competition with the AMERICAN FUR COMPANY of JOHN JACOB ASTOR for control of the rich FUR TRADE in the Pacific Northwest. Fort Vancouver—located on the north bank of the COLUMBIA RIVER about six miles from the mouth of the Willamette River (the gateway to the interior of the Oregon Country) and some 100 miles from the Columbia's mouth —was intended to perform the functions of physical presence and trading center, to rival Astor's ASTORIA.

For a quarter-century after its founding, Fort Vancouver dominated the trading and commercial life of the Pacific Northwest. That it did so was a tribute to its location, the influence of the Hudson's Bay Company, and above all, the leadership provided by Dr. JOHN MCLOUGHLIN, the chief factor of the company. McLoughlin commanded the respect of the Indians, and the fort and his presence were decisive influences in a generation of peaceful relations between Indians and Europeans and Americans in the Pacific Northwest. As the region's patriarch, McLoughlin welcomed growing numbers of European and American visitors, including MOUNTAIN MEN such as JEDEDIAH STRONG SMITH, who found safety at Fort Vancouver in 1828 after Indians had attacked his party at the Umpqua River. Of 18 men in the party, only Smith and three others escaped to reach Fort Vancouver, where McLoughlin assisted them and eventually negotiated to recover their lost furs. Later, Fort Vancouver and McLoughlin played host to the first group of American missionaries in the Oregon Territory, Jason Lee and, later, Marcus and Narcissa Whitman, to whom McLoughlin provided supplies, advice, and counsel.

As Oregon became the center of growing competition between Great Britain and the United States, Fort Vancouver became the symbol of both the British presence in the Northwest and the overwhelming local influence of the Hudson's Bay Company. As the HBC trapping brigades and the mountain men trapped out the streams of the Pacific Northwest, however, the fort became less and less important to the HBC. Responding to these changes and the rising international tensions over the Oregon Territory (enhanced by the election of JAMES K. POLK in 1844 on an expansionist platform), McLoughlin moved his base of operations from Fort Vancouver to Fort Victoria on Vancouver Island in 1845. The Oregon Treaty of 1846 established the international boundary line at 49 degrees and so left Fort Vancouver in American hands. After 1848, the U.S. Army used the fort as a military post.

For a quarter of a century, Fort Vancouver was the most important European presence in the Pacific Northwest. The location at the intersection of the Columbia and the Willamette Rivers offered a key to its significance, but more important were the authority of the Hudson's Bay Company and the continuing leadership and diplomacy of John McLoughlin.

Further reading: William R. Sampson, *John McLoughlin's Business Correspondence, 1847–1848.* (Seattle: University of Washington Press, 1973).

Forty-niners

The name usually given to the large numbers of men (and women) who went to California in 1849 in response to the discovery of gold was Forty-niners. In January 1848, James W. Marshall first identified gold in the race of the mill that he was constructing for John Sutter. News of the discoveries spread slowly, in part because Sutter wished to keep it secret and in part because it was disbelieved almost everywhere. However, after the presence of gold was confirmed in an address President James K. Polk gave to the Congress on December 5, 1848, enthusiasm reached a mania. Editors called it an epidemic of gold fever, an analogy that captured its capacity to infect families and entire communities.

This 1849 print, *The Way They Go to California,* lampoons the rush to California by gold seekers, many of whom went to outlandish lengths to get there and stake a claim before the next person. *(Library of Congress)*

The first great immigration from the East Coast to California was by sea and occurred during the winter of 1848–49. The Forty-niners left in companies composed of their friends and relatives. One or more companies would charter a ship, and individual members would share the cost. An important advantage for the seagoing Forty-niner was the opportunity to carry a substantial amount of cargo, including items for personal use or things to be sold in the magic market of San Francisco and the gold camps. Already newspapers were filled with stories of the high prices for basic goods (tools, food, and shelter) and services (medical, legal, and transportation). The disadvantage of the seagoing route to California was the long voyage around Cape Horn, perhaps as much as nine months in duration. When the vessel rounded the cape and emerged from the Straits of Magellan, it encountered strong headwinds up the coast, making the voyage up to California one of endless course adjustments. Alternatively, the company of Forty-niners might go to the port of Chagres in Panama, cross the isthmus by way of dugout and mule, and emerge on the Pacific shore to join hundreds and eventually thousands of other argonauts in the search for passage up the coast to San Francisco. Over the winter of 1848–49, some 25,000 Forty-niners (most of them men but not exclusively so) left the ports of Portland, Boston, Nantucket, New York, and Philadelphia on the East Coast; and, farther to the South, from Wilmington, Charleston, and New Orleans, bound for the goldfields of the new El Dorado in California.

With the coming of spring in 1849, a great body of Forty-niners assembled in the staging towns of Independence and St. Joseph in Missouri. There, they organized into companies, bought mules and broke them to the harness, acquired wagons, elected officers, and drew up constitutions. They also packed and repacked their supplies in order to conform to the general rule that with four men to a wagon, each could not exceed 250 pounds. The overland Forty-niners, using mules or oxen, would travel to California by traditional means, using the same wagons that had carried their grandparents to Ohio and Kentucky and parents to Wisconsin and Missouri and Mississippi. Overland Forty-niners expected to make the trip for a cost of about $250. The wagon trains would follow the Oregon Trail through South Pass, where they would turn west and then south for California. The distance of some 2,000 miles had to be covered by late September, when the snows would close the passes of the Sierra Nevada. Furthermore, the many wagon trains would become competitors for the same grass and water. Because grass would not appear on the prairies in sufficient growth to support draft animals until the end of May, all parties of overland Forty-niners had to leave at about the same time.

The overland Forty-niners left with strong feelings about the search for gold and the enterprise on which they were about to embark. They believed, first, that they were going to become rich, or so the stories from California indicated; the sober, hard-working miner must invariably make a fortune. Second, they were convinced that this wealth could be used for the benefit of the family as a whole. In this sense, the venture was not selfish but something for the advantage of many. Third, they supposed that they were doing both God's will and the national will. After all, part of the issue in the enterprise was to assist in the transformation of California (recently acquired through the TREATY OF GUADALUPE HIDALGO) from a Mexican to an American cultural identity. The Forty-niners saw themselves as embodying the ideas associated with MANIFEST DESTINY. Finally, the Forty-niners had a strong sense of history and the significance of their overland enterprise. They were part of a long line of heroic pioneers who opened the West for the benefit of the nation. Part of the evidence of this strong belief was the number of journal keepers on the overland voyage to California. Some 400 diaries and journals of Forty-niners survive for the summer of 1849 alone, and many others must have been lost. Their entries, taken in conjunction with the letters that the argonauts sent to their families, confirm their sense of a national destiny of which they were a part.

The Forty-niners had to cross 2,000 miles in five months. To assist them, they had companies of friends and relatives, constitutions that identified the responsibilities of every member, and elected officers. They were well equipped—although many had packed more weight than the livestock could carry over the journey—and they were heavily armed. Indeed, accidents with firearms would become one of the major sources of casualties. Another was the cholera epidemic of that summer, which reached the departure towns of St. Joseph and Independence and often went west with the Forty-niners. Dangers from Indians, of which all Forty-niners were conscious, turned out to be limited to occasional theft.

Once arrived in California, most Forty-niners ceased to keep a journal and dispersed to the mining camps to dig for gold or to the numerous and growing towns of California's gold-rush country, where they sought other ways to profit from the search for gold. Yet each one had been welcomed to that mystical club of Forty-niners that would become so significant in later life, in recounting the travels and deeds that made them a part of America's westward march of empire. The annual migrations to California continued for the next decade, increasingly by sea as steam connections joined the Atlantic Coast ports to Panama and the steamers on the West Coast side carried cargoes of later Forty-niners to California.

Within a few years, many Forty-niners returned to their homes. Their arrival was celebrated by their families if not always by their creditors. They resumed their lives in their communities, although some later moved elsewhere. Others remained in California to make their lives on the West Coast. Some simply disappeared from view, forever lost to their families in the vast landscape of the West. For those who returned or even those who remained in California, their years as a Forty-niner were almost certainly the most memorable of their otherwise routine lives. Forty-niners began to remember and celebrate those years as pioneers, individually and collectively. Some joined in family celebrations, perhaps on the date that the absent argonaut had returned. Others came together in groups, with annual dinners, speeches, and list of members.

The term Forty-niner came to have a general application to all those who went to California in search of gold over a decade, but the nation's true Forty-niners were forever enshrined in a special category. Not even the Civil War and its half-century of remembrance could diminish the permanent identification associated with the Forty-niner. Songs, speeches, poems, stories, and stage plays about Forty-niners served as a reminder of the time when America went west to California in search of gold.

Further reading: Rodman W. Paul, *California Gold: The Beginnings of Mining in the Far West* (Cambridge, Mass.: Harvard University Press, 1947); Malcolm J. Rohrbough, *Days of Gold: The California Gold Rush and the American Nation* (Berkeley: University of California Press, 1997).

Foster, Abigail Kelley (1811–1887)

Abigail Kelley Foster was a prominent abolitionist and advocate of WOMEN'S STATUS AND RIGHTS. Abby Kelley was born January 15, 1811, in Pelham in west-central Massachusetts. She was the fifth of Wing Kelley's seven children by his second wife, Diana Daniels. Abby spent her childhood in the rural districts of Worcester, Massachusetts, where her family moved in 1811. Reared in the Quaker faith, she early developed a spirit of independence and moral commitment, after completing her education, which according to her daughter included several years at the Providence Friends School. She then became a teacher in the Friends school at Lynn, Massachusetts. While there, she was converted to the ABOLITION MOVEMENT through reading William Lloyd Garrison's *Liberator.* As secretary of the Lynn Female Anti-Slavery Society, she circulated petitions, distributed literature, and raised funds. Also an officer of the Lynn Female Peach Society, she was among the first to accept Garrison's radical doctrine of nonresistance, and in 1838 she joined him in founding the New England Non-Resistant Society.

In 1837 Kelley attended the first national woman's antislavery convention in New York, where she met ANGELINA AND SARAH GRIMKÉ. When these abolitionist sisters lectured in Massachusetts that summer, the friendship deepened. Kelley shared with them the Quaker conviction that men and women were equally susceptible to the promptings of the "inner light,") and by December 1837 she was convinced that to "improve mankind" was "the only object worth living for."

Her deepening concern with both antislavery and the role of women in public life was demonstrated in May 1838, when she made her first public address before a "promiscuous," or mixed, audience, at the second women's antislavery convention. Held in Philadelphia at Pennsylvania Hall, the hall was burned to the ground by a proslavery mob after only one day. So effective was her speech that THEODORE DWIGHT WELD begged her to become an abolitionist lecturer, exclaiming, "Abby, if you don't, God will smite you!" Influenced by such appeals, she resigned her teaching post and returned to Millbury, Massachusetts, where her family had moved, for six months of soul-searching and studying in preparation for a reformer's vocation. Encouragement from the Grimkés, reformist and abolitionist Henry Wright, feminist and abolitionist LUCRETIA MOTT, and others helped counteract family efforts to dissuade her.

In May 1839 in Connecticut, Kelley began her long and tempestuous career as a lecturer and agitator. One village minister denounced her, taking as his text a Biblical reference to "that woman Jezebel, which calleth herself a prophetess." In Norfolk, where Kelley was forbidden to speak, a hotelkeeper explained that they believed her to be a bad woman, no better then the vilest of New York. Undaunted, she declared in the *Connecticut Observer:* "Whatever ways and men are right for men to adopt in reforming the world are right also for women to adopt in pursuing the same object." Notoriety also had its rewards, as the spectacle of a woman addressing the public attracted listeners otherwise cool to the antislavery message.

The abolition movement at this time was deeply troubled by dissension between moderate and radical factions over nonresistance, the role of women, political action, abusive language, and anticlericalism. These were all matters on which Abby Kelley had firm views, and she played a part in the open break, which came at the 1840 convention of the AMERICAN ANTI-SLAVERY SOCIETY. When a conservative attempt to block her appointment to the business committee was defeated by a vote of 560-450, a large block of delegates left the conference and organized a new antislavery group.

During the next 15 years Abby Kelley traveled great distances, carrying her message throughout New England and into New York, Pennsylvania, Ohio, Indiana, and Michigan. Preaching Garrison's doctrine of "No Union with Slaveholders" and his denunciation of the constitution as "a covenant with death," she also helped to advance the feminist cause by opening public platforms to women. In March 1841, she resigned from the Society of Friends because of its equivocal position on slavery. She then joined a small band of radicals who disclaimed allegiance to both church and state. One of these companions in the early 1840s was Stephen Symonds Foster, a New Hampshire radical who, after leaving Dartmouth with the intention of studying theology, had rejected all clerical institutions as proslavery and set out to topple them. He often interrupted religious services to denounce slavery. In 1843, he published the "Brotherhood of Thieves, or, A True Picture Of The American Clergy and Church."

In Foster, Abby Kelley found a man thoroughly in sympathy with her beliefs and practices. Their courtship extended for four years as their desire to wed conflicted with their devotion to abolition. Finally married on December 21, 1845, in Pennsylvania, they thereafter often traveled as a lecture team. A noteworthy example of their effectiveness together occurred early in 1846 when they visited Oberlin College during a religious revival. In a series of meetings that drew much interest, they attacked preachers, politicians, and the government. The faculty, including the evangelist CHARLES GRANDISON FINNEY, denounced them as infidels. Nevertheless, they returned in the fall, at which time Stephen conducted a brawling debate with Oberlin's president, Asa Mahan. At least one Oberlin student, Lucy Stone, was as deeply moved by the Fosters' visit as the faculty was dismayed.

An acrimonious break with Garrison, under whose strict regime the Fosters became increasingly restive during the 1850s, pushed Foster further to the margins of the movement. By 1856, the Fosters had become convinced that abolitionists must organize politically, or the growing Republican Party would win over their supporters with halfway measures. Their demand for an abolitionist third party was too extreme for Garrison, who saw some good in the rise of the Republicans. In 1859, at the annual meeting of the New England Anti-Slavery Society, Garrison publicly accused Foster of dishonesty in collecting funds. Although tempers cooled after the Civil War, the rift was never fully healed.

With the exception of a final fund-raising tour of New England in 1870, poor health and a failing voice generally limited Abby Kelley Foster, postwar activities to local affairs. She died on January 14, 1887.

Further reading: Dorothy Sterling, *Ahead of Her Time: Abby Kelley and the Politics of Anti-Slavery* (New York: W. W. Norton, 1991).

Fourier, Charles (1772–1837)

A French philosopher whose ideas influenced several American utopian movements, Charles Fourier was born at Besançon in 1772, the son of a businessman. Largely self-educated, he had hoped to join the military as an engineer but instead joined the family business, working as a tradesman in Marseilles. His lack of interest and skill in the business world, coupled with the family firm's financial difficulties, led him to abandon the trade in 1799 and take a job as a civil servant in Lyons. He wrote his first book, *The Social Destiny of Man: Or, Theory of the Four Movements,* in 1808. Little else is known about his life until 1816, when he inherited money from his mother and began spending all of his time writing. In 1823, he moved to Paris, where he would live and write until his death in 1837.

While Fourier's theories contained singular and peculiar interpretations of the cosmos, he also analyzed the burgeoning capitalist society around him. It is for these ideas about the social order that he is remembered today. Troubled by the chaos and volatile imbalances he saw in capitalist societies, Fourier proposed to reorganize them into balanced structures that would create social harmony. These new organizing units would be called phalanxes, agricultural groupings in which people worked on the tasks for which they were most suited, thus shedding the confines of industrial life and cultivating their whole selves. Each phalanx would live in a community dwelling called a phalanstery, where all residents could live in the apartments that best fit their budgets (Fourier even planned the dimensions of the rooms). Each phalanstery would operate efficiently and profitably by centralizing daily activities such as eating and cleaning and by assigning all other kinds of work to the people most interested in doing them. Fourier predicted that people would compete in a friendly way, thus producing good products without creating conflicts. All profits would be community property, divided among members of each phalanx along these lines: five-twelfths to labor, four-twelfths to capital, three-twelfths to ability.

Phalanxes would thus be cooperative organizations, where workers would ideally become part-owners as well. Once the entire world had been divided into phalanxes, human society would become more ordered and harmonious. Capitalist impulses would not be abandoned, but rather redirected. In Fourier's utopian vision, humankind would be able to cultivate the positive aspects of industrial capitalism (such as productivity and ingenuity) while eliminating the venality and despair that he saw in the industrial societies of his time.

Despite the bizarre aspects of Fourier's world view, his theories attracted numerous followers, most notably in France and the United States. His utopian notions about human perfectability corresponded well with some of the ideas being expressed by transcendentalists and religious reformers in America. The most famous American community to adopt Fourierist principles was BROOK FARM, which operated in Massachusetts from 1841 to 1847. Other Fourierist phalansteries were founded during these years, but none lasted long.

While Fourier's ideas seem impractical and naïve today, he and other utopian socialists are historically significant because they criticized a capitalist system that was creating enormous social change, anxiety, and financial insecurity, and proposed to reorganize society through rational planning and humane working conditions.

See also TRANSCENDENTAL MOVEMENT.

Further reading: Jonathan Beecher, *Charles Fourier: The Visionary and His World* (Berkeley: University of California Press, 1987); Robert L. Heilbroner, *The Worldly Philosophers: The Lives, Times, and Ideas of the Great Economic Thinkers,* 7th ed. (New York: Simon & Schuster, 1999).

—Eleanor H. McConnell

Franklin Institute

The Franklin Institute, organized as a memorial to Benjamin Franklin (1706–90), sought to study and promote mechanics and the applied sciences. Founded in Philadelphia in 1824, it is the oldest such institution in the United States. The institute publishes a peer-reviewed scientific journal on new theoretical developments and their practical applications, especially in engineering and mathematics; the *Journal of the Franklin Institute* has been issued continuously since 1826. The institute also bestows the annual Bower Award and Prize for advances in science and technology, as well the Cresson Medal, the Franklin Medal, and other awards and prizes. The list of its honorees includes Alexander Graham Bell, Marie and Pierre Curie, Thomas Edison, Albert Einstein, Max Planck, Niels Bohr, and a host of other leading scientists.

The institute was incorporated as the Franklin Institute of the State of Pennsylvania for the Promotion of the Mechanic Arts, and its first headquarters was in Independence Hall (then the Philadelphia County Court House). Intended as a lasting tribute to Franklin, the statesman, printer, and writer who was also well known for his scientific experiments and inventions, the institute's headquarters incorporates an impressive Franklin memorial and museum complex that was erected in 1933. Today, the Franklin Institute Science Museum includes exhibits on mechanics, aviation, meteorology, anatomy, electricity, transportation, astronomy, and the elements—some of the many subjects in which Franklin himself was most interested. A major part of its mission is providing educational programs for children, in the hope of inspiring new generations of scientists and inventors.

Further reading: The Franklin Institute Science Museum, "Legacy of the Franklin Institute." URL: www.fi.edu/tfi/legacy.html. Downloaded 2001.

—Mary Kay Linge

Free-Soil Party

The Free-Soilers were a small but influential political party that came into existence in 1847–48 and opposed the extension of slavery into the western territories. Democratic factionalism in a single state created the new Free-Soil Party. The New York Democratic Party represented a complex coalition particularly sensitive to shifts in national, state, and local developments. One of the most important of the northern state organizations, it achieved direct national importance with the 1836 election of MARTIN VAN BUREN, but his unwillingness to cooperate in the admission of TEXAS to the Union led to his abandonment by the party's southern wing in 1840 and its fierce hostility to him in 1844. On a statewide level, the party divided between "Hunkers" and "Barnburners," with whom Van Buren was identified. When the tenant-farmer and rural vote shifted against the Democrats, Barnburners blamed the Hunkers. Barnburners also opposed President JAMES K. POLK's use of patronage to secure southern control of the national party through Hunker cooperation.

The Wilmot Proviso was the cause of much debate. Introduced by David Wilmot—a Democrat from Pennsylvania—the proviso stated that the institution of slavery was forbidden in territories acquired from Mexico. The Democratic state convention at Syracuse on September 29, 1847, split over adopting the Wilmot Proviso, as the Barnburners walked out. The Hunkers met January 26, 1848, at Albany while the Barnburners held their own convention on February 16 at Utica. Both sent delegations to the May national convention at Baltimore. The conflict over which New York delegation should be seated split the party nationally. In the end, the Barnburners withdrew, calling another national convention for Utica, June 22. Delegations from Wisconsin, Ohio, Illinois, Massachusetts and Connecticut joined the Barnburners there to nominate Van Buren. The convention then called for another national convention to unite the country on a "free-soil" basis.

There were already several such moves underway. A similar convention had already been called by the People's Convention of Friends of Free Territory, which met in Columbus, Ohio, on June 20. The WHIG PARTY's nomination of ZACHARY TAYLOR at their convention on June 7 led to the departure of the "Conscience Whigs," which itself consisted of two factions, and the LIBERTY PARTY with its National Reform allies.

The Buffalo convention of August 9 was bedlam, more like a public mass meeting than a delegated convention. Managed by the Barnburners, a Committee of Conference transacted all the business while the majority sat in a big tent to hear speeches. The platform pledged to discourage slavery, abolish it where possible (e.g., in the District of Columbia), prohibit its extension, guarantee retrenchment, provide cheap postage, abolish unnecessary offices, create more elective offices, promote internal improvements, secure a homestead law, pay the public debt, and levy a tariff for revenue. Conscience Whigs generally concurred, although they had little confidence in the Barnburner Democrats who seemed to see the movement primarily as a means to put the Democrats back on the right track.

The party had momentous importance for the antislavery movement. Noted abolitionist William Lloyd Garrison thought the party was a good beginning toward a loftier goal, "a party for keeping Free-Soil and not for setting men free." Other political abolitionists and National Reformers around Gerrit Smith favored retaining the Liberty Party. Still, most abolitionists, including the prominent black spokesman Frederick Douglass, supported the party of "Free Soil, free speech, free labor, and free men."

The new party threatened components of both the existing parties. Whig statesman DANIEL WEBSTER called them "Free Spoilers" and the *National Intelligencer* denounced their hypocrisy and insincerity as a device for Van Buren's revenge. *The Democratic Washington Union* called the party simply a gathering of Whig Abolitionists. Free-Soilers in the "Old Northwest" demonstrated both the values and pitfalls of coalition politics. Michigan Free-Soilers rallied Whigs and others hostile to Democratic leader LEWIS CASS, while Ohio Free-Soilers worked with the Democrats who declared for free territory. In the 1848 election, Van Buren polled 291,616 votes, and the Free-Soil party elected 14 congressmen and two senators.

In Massachusetts, Henry Wilson and Charles Sumner engineered an understanding of sorts between the Free-Soilers and the Democrats who were desperate to overthrow the Whig dominance in the state. By 1850, the tentative coalition had won a majority in the legislature in which Free-Soilers agreed to leave the state offices to the Democrats in return for the Senate. As a result, Sumner joined the growing antislavery contingent in Washington.

In some ways, the party seemed to lose much in the East after the elections, as the New York Barnburners soon drifted back into the Democratic Party. However, the two major parties rallied to the COMPROMISE OF 1850 and its new fugitive-slave provision, repudiating some of its state and local professions of sympathy for Free-Soil.

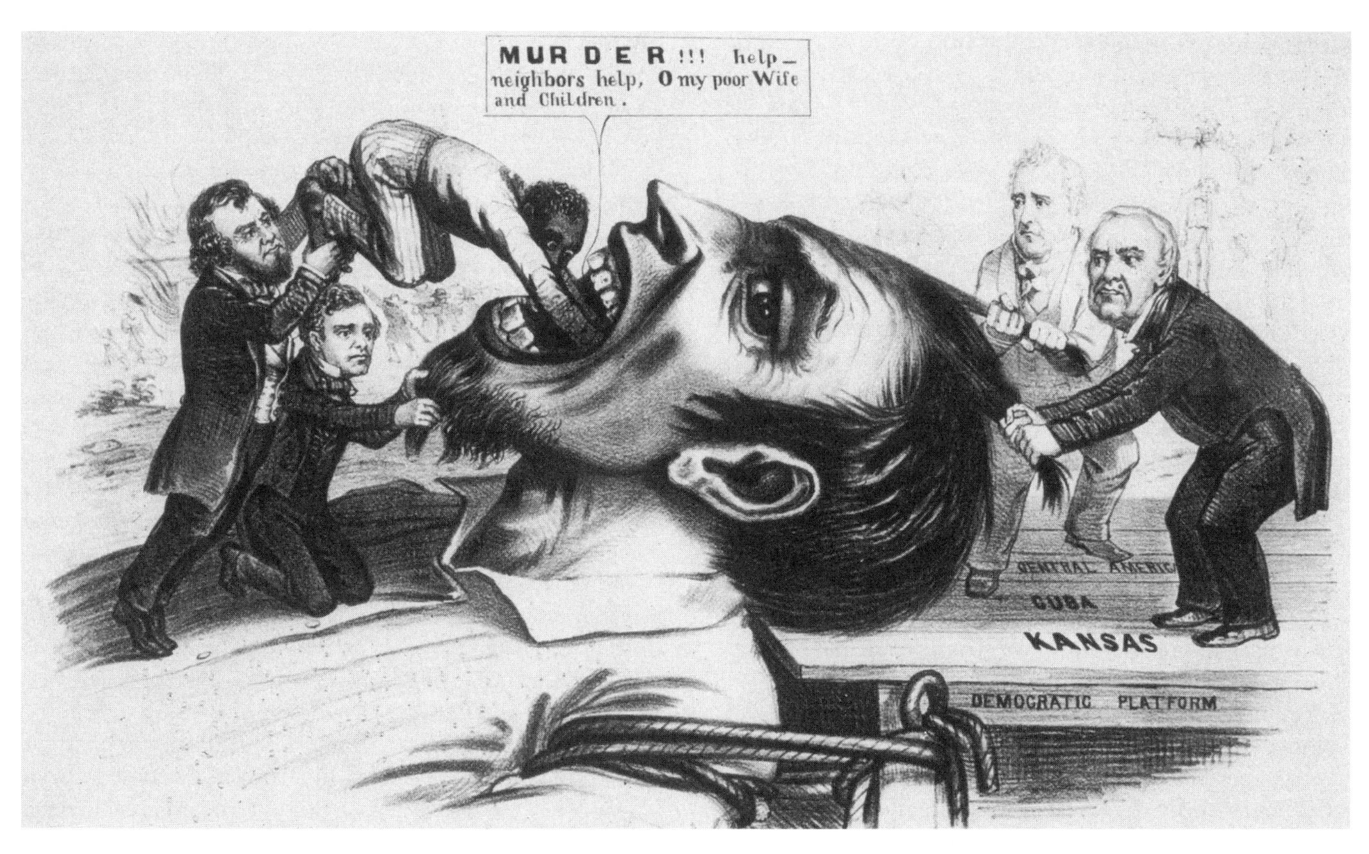

This cartoon depicting the Free-Soil controversy lays on the Democrats the major blame for violence perpetrated against antislavery settlers in Kansas. *(Hulton/Archive)*

While the process lost the party politicians, it radicalized its electoral base, particularly in the Old Northwest. The unrepentant Free-Soilers attacked these policies. Former Democrats like Preston King and David Wilmot and former Whigs like Giddings, Henry Wilson, and Charles F. Adams would not return to their old parties. An 1851 Cleveland, Ohio, meeting of the remaining leaders called a national Free-Soil Democratic Convention to meet August 11, 1852, at Pittsburgh. Under Giddings, this enthusiastic convention proclaimed themselves "Free-Soil Democrats," "Independent Democrats," or, most commonly "Free Democrats." It adopted a platform based on the 1848 Buffalo platform, but added planks condemning the Compromise of 1850 and the Fugitive Slave Bill, denouncing South Carolina's seamen laws, demanding recognition of Haiti, and stating that it was the duty of the U.S. government to protest against European monarchical intervention in countries trying to establish republican governments. The party nominated a presidential ticket of John P. Hale of New Hampshire and George W. Julian of Indiana as his running mate. In the 1852 election, the ticket polled only 156,297 votes, but these were far more radical than the earlier Free-Soil Party votes.

The party disappeared with the 1854 crisis over Kansas and the emergence of the new REPUBLICAN PARTY.

Further reading: Eric Foner, *Free Soil, Free Labor, Free Men: The Ideology of the Republican Party before the Civil War* (New York: Oxford University Press, 1970).

—Richard L. Friedline

Free Trade and Sailor's Rights

This political slogan became popular as the United States entered the WAR OF 1812 (1812–15). It represented in succinct form the two main maritime grievances that Americans had against Great Britain. "Free trade" referred to the various impositions that Great Britain had put on American neutral trading in the midst of the French Revolution and Napoleonic Wars (1793–1815), including the Essex Decision (1805) and the Orders in Council (1806–12). Americans claimed that as neutrals they had a right to trade with any country, whether that nation was at war with Great Britain or not. "Sailor's rights" referred to the right of a sailor to contract for himself on American merchantmen ships, and that once he did so, he should be protected from being seized and forced to serve in the British Navy.

Although it remains unclear when the slogan first appeared, it quickly gained widespread usage in the maritime community. Politicians like HENRY CLAY used the phrase in the halls of Congress, and it appeared in several publications. American privateers and warships sometimes flew a pennant from a mast with the slogan emblazoned on it. Captain David Porter raised such a banner from the masthead when he headed for the Pacific on the USS *ESSEX* in 1813, and Captain James Lawrence flew a similar banner when he left Boston aboard the *Chesapeake* to fight the HMS *Shannon* in May of the same year. American sailors made the slogan their own. When the captives held at DARTMOOR PRISON heard of the TREATY OF GHENT (1814), they were excited that they would soon be released. Confident that both impressment and limitations on American commerce had been ended by the treaty—officially it did not deal with either issue—they raised an American flag and a pennant proclaiming "Free Trade and Sailor's Rights" over the British compound. For many years thereafter, the slogan would appear occasionally as a statement not only of sailors' rights but of the rights of the poor. Day laborers in New York City struck for higher wages in 1816 and used a banner with the slogan on it. Whalers etched the phrase on whalebone for decades, and as late as 1840, banners appeared in election campaigns proclaiming "Free Trade and Sailor's Rights."

Frémont, Jessie Benton (1824–1902)

Born the daughter of leading Jacksonian Democrat THOMAS HART BENTON and his wife, Elizabeth, and later married to famous explorer and presidential nominee JOHN C. FRÉMONT, Jessie Benton Frémont was a strong presence and accomplished individual in her own right. She was born Jessie Ann Benton on May 31, 1824, on her grandfather's estate in the Blue Ridge Mountains of Virginia. As a young girl, she was known for her strong and energetic personality; the family often commented how she took after her father, a U.S. senator representing Missouri.

The Bentons had six children, but Jessie, the second-born, was usually the center of attention. The family spent part of each year in Washington, and Jessie as a young girl would accompany her father to the Capitol and also to the White House when he called on his friend and political ally, President ANDREW JACKSON. Jessie also spent considerable time at her grandparents' estate in Virginia as well as in St. Louis, where her parents had a home. She was educated in Washington, however, at Miss English's Female Seminary in Georgetown. It was in Washington that she met and fell in love with John Frémont, then a lieutenant in the Topographical Corps of the United States. Although her father was strongly opposed to the two getting married, in part due to his teenaged daughter's youth, Jessie Benton and John Frémont were married in Washington, D.C., on October 19, 1841.

Jessie Benton Frémont did not join her husband on his government-sponsored travels and explorations in the western part of the continental United States, but she was instrumental in popularizing accounts of his expeditions (which included the scout KIT CARSON). In addition to raising the couple's children, she and her husband collaborated on a series of reports, mainly written by Jessie, that proved to be very popular with the reading public. These reports included valuable and generally accurate scientific and topographical information, and also told of the natural beauty and adventures encountered on Frémont's expeditions. In 1849, she traveled west with her young daughter to meet her well-traveled husband and later published an account of her own journey, including observations on the environment in California, as *A Year of American Travel.*

During the 1850s, the Frémonts lived in both San Francisco and Washington, when John Frémont represented California briefly in the U.S. Senate and then ran for president in 1856 as the first nominee of the new REPUBLICAN PARTY. Although they made a strong initial showing, the Republicans went down to defeat. Jessie Benton Frémont, however, made a positive impression during the campaign and was the center of attention in a way that was truly remarkable for a woman in 19th-century America. Only 32 years old, she had charmed many of the leading politicians of the day, impressing them with both her vivacious personality and sharp intellect.

During the Civil War, the Frémonts entered in the national spotlight again when John C. Frémont was a general in the Union army. With Jessie at his side, he ran afoul of the Lincoln administration, in part because he had emancipated slaves in Missouri without prior approval from Washington. Relations between President Lincoln and the Frémonts deteriorated rapidly; at one point Lincoln denounced Jessie Frémont as "a female politician" and she in turn referring to him as "sly" and "slimy."

After the war, Jessie Frémont and her husband were much less prominent on the national stage, although she continued to write, publishing a number of stories for periodicals on her travels and history as well as some children's stories. John C. Frémont died in 1890, and Jessie lived for 12 more years, remaining active in women's clubs until her own death in Los Angeles in 1902. Given the norms of the society in which she lived, it would have been quite understandable if she had been entirely overshadowed by her dynamic and powerful father and husband, yet Jessie Benton Frémont succeeded admirably in making her own mark on the world.

Further reading: Pamela Herr, *Jessie Benton Fremont: A Biography* (New York: F. Watts, 1987).

—Jason K. Duncan

Frémont, John C. (1813–1890)

Previously well known as a western explorer and adventurer, John Charles Frémont, referred to as "The Pathfinder," was the first presidential candidate of the REPUBLICAN PARTY in 1856. He was born on January 21, 1813 in Savannah, Georgia, to Jean Fremon, a French immigrant, and Anne Beverly Whiting, who were not married. The young Fremon was five when his father died, and he grew up in Charleston, South Carolina, in circumstances that were less than prosperous.

Having added a t and an accent to his name, John C. Frémont as a young man was notable for being ambitious and proud as well as somewhat reckless and headstrong. After working in a Charleston law office, he entered the College of Charleston in 1829. Although considered very bright, especially in mathematics, he proved to be an indifferent student and was expelled for "incorrigible negligence" before he could graduate. He did, however, apply for and receive his degree five years later. Frémont later joined the navy as a math teacher, but resigned his commission to enlist in the U.S. Army as a second lieutenant in the late 1830s, joining a topographical study charged with surveying Cherokee lands in northwestern Georgia. This was Frémont's first real work as an explorer, and he took an instant liking to it, saying later in his memoirs that "through many of the years to come the occupation of my prime of life was to be among Indians and in waste places."

After the Georgia survey was finished, Frémont, who spoke French, was assigned by the U.S. government to assist Joseph Nicollet, a scientist and explorer from France who was surveying the land between the upper Mississippi and Missouri Rivers. Nicollet was among the best in his field, and he gave Frémont a solid grounding in natural sciences as they pertained to western exploration in the United States. Upon returning to Washington, the two men collaborated on a report of their travels and a map of the lands they had surveyed together. Senator THOMAS HART BENTON of Missouri, a vigorous champion of western expansion, invited them to his home to discuss their findings, and it was there that Frémont met Benton's teenaged daughter, Jessie. The two fell in love almost immediately, but Senator Benton thought his daughter too young to marry and arranged to have Frémont sent west to make an expedition in the Iowa Territory. Although Frémont went to Iowa and produced a generally reliable map, the journey did nothing to stem his romance with Jessie Benton, and the two (both Protestants) were married in secret by a Catholic priest in Washington in October 1841. Frémont thus gained not only a wife in JESSIE BENTON FRÉMONT but an influential patron in the powerful Senator Benton.

The following year, Frémont led his first major expedition along the OREGON TRAIL, and afterwards, with much assistance from his wife, he published *A Report of the Exploring Expedition to Oregon and California,* which captured the nation's imagination with its vivid descriptions of natural wonders and riches awaiting brave adventurers. It was on this trip that Frémont first met KIT CARSON, a scout who became famous in his own right from his travels with the Pathfinder. The two undertook another large expedition in 1843, traveling west from the Missouri River toward the Oregon territory, investigating the Great Salt Lake, going into Nevada and in the winter crossing over the Sierra Nevada and into CALIFORNIA, which then belonged to Mexico. The journey took the party nearly 6,500 miles, and the Frémonts subsequently published *A Report of the Exploring Expedition to Oregon and California.* The report was widely popular, as it included tales of adventure, scientific information, and a well-drawn map, along with information for anyone seeking to move west.

As relations between the United States and Mexico worsened, President JAMES K. POLK approved a third expedition for Frémont, and he generously supplied the Pathfinder with men and money. This journey lasted from 1845 to 1847, and when Frémont and his party moved once again into California, Mexican authorities ordered them to leave. Frémont defied the order by raising an American flag and later joined with other migrants from the United States in instigating what became known as the BEAR FLAG REVOLT.

When war between the United States and Mexico was formally declared, Frémont helped to capture the California city of Los Angeles. However, he became involved in a serious dispute between two high-ranking members of the American military, Commodore ROBERT FIELD STOCKTON and General STEPHEN WATTS KEARNY, both of whom claimed authority over California. Frémont backed Stockton's bid for leadership, and the naval officer appointed him governor of California. As Frémont was technically still an officer in the army, an incensed Kearny, upon learning from Washington that he was in fact the one entitled to appoint the governor, detained Frémont and then marched him eastward to FORT LEAVENWORTH, where he was arrested. Frémont was found guilty by a military court of mutiny and disobedience. President Polk, grateful for the services he had rendered and aware of his great popularity, overturned the verdict, but Frémont was humiliated by the entire affair and resigned his commission.

The Pathfinder subsequently set out on a fourth expedition, this one financed not by the federal government but by his father-in-law and some businessmen in St. Louis. Once again his party included Kit Carson, but this expedition met with tragedy during the winter as they got lost in the Rocky Mountains of Colorado while searching for a railroad route. Ten of the party's 30 members died as a result, and some of the survivors blamed Frémont for the disaster. He later ended up back in California, where in the late 1840s gold was discovered on land he owned. Armed with this new wealth, Frémont was elected as the first U.S. senator from California; a Democrat, he served for less than a year due to a prior agreement.

In 1856 the new REPUBLICAN PARTY nominated the still well-known and popular Frémont as its first presidential candidate. A born southerner, he had come out in favor of antislavery forces in Kansas earlier that year, and this, combined with his heroic persona and colorful past, convinced Republicans that he would be a natural vote-getter despite his limited political experience. The Republican rallying cry in 1856 was "Free men, free soil, free labor and Frémont!" At 43, Frémont was then the youngest man in the country's history to be nominated for president. During the campaign, the DEMOCRATIC PARTY spread the false rumors that he was a secret Catholic.

Frémont was essentially a sectional candidate, as the Republicans were only on the ballot in four southern states, all in the Upper South, and the party received virtually no votes in those states. There were thus two contests that year; Frémont vs. Democrat James Buchanan in the North and Buchanan vs. former President MILLARD FILLMORE, running on the American Party ticket, in the South. Frémont did very well in most parts of the North, winning 60 percent of the vote to Buchanan's 36 percent. He carried 11 states and won 114 electoral votes, but Buchanan won enough states in the lower North that, combined with his victory in the South, gave him a comfortable victory and the presidency.

During the Civil War, Frémont served unsuccessfully as a general, infuriating President Abraham Lincoln in 1861 by emancipating slaves in Missouri without authorization. In 1864 dissident Republicans dissatisfied with Lincoln's wartime leadership nominated him for the presidency, but Lincoln was able to persuade him to withdraw in return for a political favor. Although Frémont served as territorial governor of Arizona between 1878 and 1883, he depended on his wife's income from writing during his later years. He died in New York City in 1890.

Further reading: Allan Nevins, *Fremont: Pathmarker of the West* (Lincoln: University of Nebraska Press, 1992); David Roberts, *A Newer World: Kit Carson, John C. Frémont and the Claiming of the American West* (New York: Simon & Schuster, 2000).

—Jason K. Duncan

fugitive slave laws

Laws giving slaveholders the right to capture slaves who had escaped their bondage, as well as the enforcement of those laws, were at the center of much of the bitterness and growing divisions between North and South in the decade prior to the Civil War. The U.S. Constitution had given slave owners the legal right to capture runaway slaves and return them to servitude. Article IV, Section 2, stated that any "person held to service or labor in one state" who fled his or her bondage by going to another state "shall be delivered up on claim of the party to whom such service or labor shall be due." This original language proved to be somewhat vague, and in 1793 Congress passed a measure, which became law, that gave slaveholders the right to actually bring those persons they claimed were their slaves into any local or federal court to prove ownership.

During the court proceedings that eventually stemmed from this law, those accused of being runaway slaves were denied trial by jury or the right to testify on their own behalf. Such a situation did not sit well with an increasing number of people in the North, especially as the ABOLITION MOVEMENT gained strength after 1830. Northern states therefore responded by passing a series of PERSONAL LIBERTY LAWS. The measures included protecting the rights of runaway slaves by providing criminal punishments for kidnapping and allowing those brought to court as fugitives to testify on their own behalf, have a jury trial, and not be imprisoned without due process of the law. Some of these laws were challenged in the courts, and in 1842 the U.S. Supreme Court handed down an important decision when it ruled that the 1793 Fugitive Slave Law was constitutional. The Court also ruled, however, that state governments were not required to enforce the language in the Constitution pertaining to fugitive slaves, as that responsibility rested with the federal government. This ruling paved the way for another series of state personal liberty laws in the North between 1842 and 1850, which denied the use of state government facilities and prohibited state officers from assisting those involved in the capture and extradition of runaway slaves. Among the states passing such laws were Massachusetts, Vermont, and Ohio in 1843; Connecticut in 1844; Pennsylvania in 1847; and Rhode Island in 1848. These measures drew a torrent of criticism from the South, with slaveholders denouncing the North for aiding abolition and encouraging lawlessness and disrespect for property. Although the exact number of slaves who made their way to freedom in the North or to Canada remains in doubt, it is very possible that as many as several hundred enslaved people a year escaped their bondage along the route of the legendary Underground Railroad.

The question of fugitive slave laws remained a source of mutual hostility between North and South, and in 1850 Congress addressed the matter at the urging of southerners who wished to see the entire system of laws governing fugitive slaves strengthened to their advantage. The debate over the bill immediately broke down along sectional lines; predictably, southerners believed that the proposed measure did not do enough to protect their property, i.e., their slaves. Senators from the North complained that the proposed law did not give enough protection to free African Americans living in their states. The efforts of northern senators, mainly Whigs, to get amendments passed to the bill that would guarantee some rights to slaves were defeated. The Fugitive Slave Law was the only measure passed as part of the COMPROMISE OF 1850 that explicitly protected the rights of slaveholders. Consequently, it was the North that in general felt most aggrieved by it. Under the law's provisions, a person could bring an accused runaway slave before a federal commissioner and provide "satisfactory proof" of ownership, either by testimony of witnesses (whites only) or documentation from a court in a southern state. The law also included penalties for those, including federal officials, who aided or abetted runaway slaves or who refused to assist in their capture and extradition.

In practice, the enforcement of the 1850 law favored slaveholders at the expense of African Americans. During the decade after its passage, over 300 persons accused of being runaway slaves were forced to return to bondage, while only 11 were allowed to remain free. Tragically, some of those who were sent south against their will had been previously free. Abolitionists refused to accept the law as it was written, however. A crowd in Boston stormed a federal courthouse in 1851 and rescued a runaway slave named Shadrach Minkins, who was facing certain return to the South. Three years later, also in Boston, federal officials responded with force of their own when hundreds of deputies and soldiers escorted runaway slave ANTHONY BURNS to a ship waiting to return him to his owner.

Opponents of slavery challenged the law in the courts, but in 1859 the Supreme Court ruled that it was constitutional. Even so, opposition to the law helped to drive many Whigs and some Democrats who opposed slavery out of their parties and led them to create a new one, the REPUBLICAN PARTY. Southerners increasingly took the stance that strict enforcement of the Fugitive Slave Law was necessary for them to stay in the Union. As a result of some highly publicized cases in which runaway slaves were forcibly returned to the South under the provisions of the 1850 law, northern states from New England to the Middle West passed yet another series of personal liberty laws in the 1850s. Ultimately, it was the controversy over slavery in the Kansas and Nebraska Territories and the election of Republican Abraham Lincoln to the presidency in 1860 that led to the outbreak of the Civil War (1861–65). Even so, the intense disagreement over whether slaveholders had the right to capture runaway slaves and return them to the South from anywhere in the United States illustrated as much as anything that the slavery question was causing an unbridgeable gulf between North and South. During the Civil War, the Republican-dominated Congress revoked the Fugitive Slave Law of 1850.

Further reading: Stanley W. Campbell, *The Slave Catchers: Enforcement of the Fugitive Slave Law, 1850–1860* (Chapel Hill: University of North Carolina Press, 1970); Jane H. and William H. Pease, *The Fugitive Slave Law and Anthony Burns* (Philadelphia: Lippincott, 1975).

—Jason K. Duncan

Fuller, Margaret (1810–1850)

Born on May 23, 1810, in Cambridgeport, Massachusetts, Sarah Margaret Fuller went on to become one of the foremost American philosophers, feminists, and social critics of the 19th century. The eldest child of Margaret Crane Fuller and Timothy Fuller, Margaret received a classical education from an early age. Save for two years spent at the Misses Prescott's school in Groton, Connecticut, from 1824 to 1826, she was educated entirely by her father, a lawyer and U.S. congressman. By the age of seven, she was reading Ovid, Virgil, and Horace, and by adulthood she was proficient in French, German, Italian, Latin, and Greek. A formidable scholar, Fuller applied for and gained access to the libraries at Harvard University, a male-only institution.

In the mid-1830s, Fuller met RALPH WALDO EMERSON and became increasingly devoted to the philosophy of transcendentalism. She befriended many other New England intellectuals including Elizabeth Peabody, W. E. Channing, and Bronson Alcott, father of Louisa May. In December 1836, she became a teacher at Alcott's Temple School in Boston, before moving to Providence, Rhode Island, where she taught until 1839. That year she returned to Boston and founded a weekly group for women to discuss matters of art, philosophy, mythology, and women's rights. These 'conversations,' as the meetings were called, took place until 1844. Fuller concurrently deepened her commitment to the TRANSCENDENTAL MOVEMENT, helping to plan the utopian community of BROOK FARM in 1841 and cofounding *The Dial,* a quarterly journal, with Emerson and George Ripley in 1840. As editor of the journal from 1840 to 1842, and as contributor until its demise in 1844, Fuller was one of its most ardent supporters. In 1843, she published "The Great Lawsuit: Man *versus* Men. Woman *versus* Women," in *The Dial*'s pages, an essay that she would revise and expand to publish as *Woman in the Nineteenth Century* in 1845. Both works sharply criticized the inequality between men and women in 19th-century America, particularly in terms of education and legal rights. *Woman in the Nineteenth Century* is believed to have been a major influence on the organizers and participants at the women's rights convention of 1848 in SENECA FALLS.

In 1844 Fuller published *Summer on the Lakes,* a travel journal that contained her thoughts on America's westward expansion and included commentary on the education of women. Impressed by her literary skills, Horace Greeley hired Fuller as a critic for the *New York Tribune* in 1845. While she lived in New York for only a year, it was a year that compounded her commitment to social activism, particularly in support of abolitionism, prison reform, and women's rights. In 1846, she left New York to became the *Tribune*'s foreign correspondent, visiting England and France to meet with numerous writers and politicians. Eventually she settled in Rome, where she became an increasingly active participant in the revolutionary campaign to unify Italy. There she met Giovanni Angelo, Marchesse d'Ossoli, a fellow revolutionary with whom she conceived a son, born in 1848. Sometime in the next two years, Fuller and d'Ossoli were married, but not, to the chagrin of many of Fuller's compatriots, until after the birth of their son. In 1849 the revolution was defeated, and the d'Ossolis fled Rome. Hoping for a new beginning and, some suggest, in spite of a nagging feeling of impending disaster, the d'Ossolis boarded the ship *Elizabeth,* bound for New York in 1850. A mile from the shores of Fire Island, New York, the ship ran aground and sank. Only the body of Eugene, the d'Ossolis' son, was ever found.

Further reading: Elizabeth Ann Bartlett, *Liberty, Equality, Sorority: The Origins and Interpretation of American Feminist Thought: Frances Wright, Sarah Grimké and Margaret Fuller* (Brooklyn, N.Y.: Carlson Publishing, 1994); Jeffrey Steele, ed., *The Essential Margaret Fuller* (New Brunswick, N.J.: Rutgers University Press, 1992).

—Catherine J. Denial

fur trade

From the beginning of European contact with North America, the fur trade drew entrepreneurs who hoped to tap its lucrative potential. For three centuries, the fur business shaped the international economy, Indian-white relations, and the American landscape and settlement patterns. As European colonization in North America moved west from the Atlantic Ocean and east from the Pacific, trappers and traders traveled with explorers, continuously expanding into new territories possessing new sources of fur. Much of the diplomatic and economic relationship between Native Americans and Europeans depended initially on the trade in beaver pelts in the Northeast, deer in the Southeast, sea otters along the Northwest Pacific coast, and bear in the Rocky Mountains. These furs were in high demand in Europe for manufactures such as coats and felt hats.

Of the commodities Europeans found in North America, fur was the easiest to acquire and sell for immediate profit. Both officially government-sanctioned companies and private individuals competed for trading rights, which were contested among the European nations then involved in international trade and colonization: Spain, France, Great Britain, Russia, and Holland. Each of these countries developed trading agreements with different groups of NATIVE AMERICANS, often using existing animosities among Indian nations to strengthen their own trading alliances. Cooperation with Indians was absolutely necessary, since they understood the American terrain and how to hunt most effectively for beaver and other valuable fur producers. Initially, Indian men hunted, and Indian women prepared the pelts for trade. Then middlemen or certain tribes would trade these pelts for items produced in Europe such as tinware, tools, textiles, and liquor.

In the early years, non-Indian hunters stayed clear of activities that would compete with Indian hunting, preferring to act only as traders. This arrangement, however, did not last, and the trading networks that had been established between whites and Indians were disrupted by competition among different nations and their European allies. These changes led to the disastrous Iroquois wars of the 17th century, in which the Iroquois and their trading allies from England and Holland decimated the Huron, the major intermediaries in the inland fur trade and key allies of France.

After these conflicts, English and French trading interests continued to clash, especially in northern Canada and the Great Lakes region. By sending missionaries, traders, and explorers inland and establishing successful trading posts at Montreal and Detroit, the French successfully expanded their trading power. English influence also grew with the establishment of the Hudson's Bay Company in 1670. While the French strategy for capitalizing on North American trade was to mingle with Native Americans and promote political as well as economical allegiances between the royal France and its American subjects, the aims of the English trading companies were more driven by private profit and economic power. French and English animosities continued to grow, eventually leading to the French and Indian War, or Seven Years' War, which ended in 1763 with the fall of New France. Old French trading companies in Montreal continued to compete privately with the Hudson's Bay Company by forming the new North West Company. These two firms continued to contend for new trade among Indians from the Great Lakes all the way to the Pacific Ocean, finally merging their operations in 1821.

During the first half of the 19th century, the American fur trade was dominated by the AMERICAN FUR COMPANY and other powerful trading organizations such those run by the CHOUTEAU FAMILY and Manuel Lisa. Because exten-

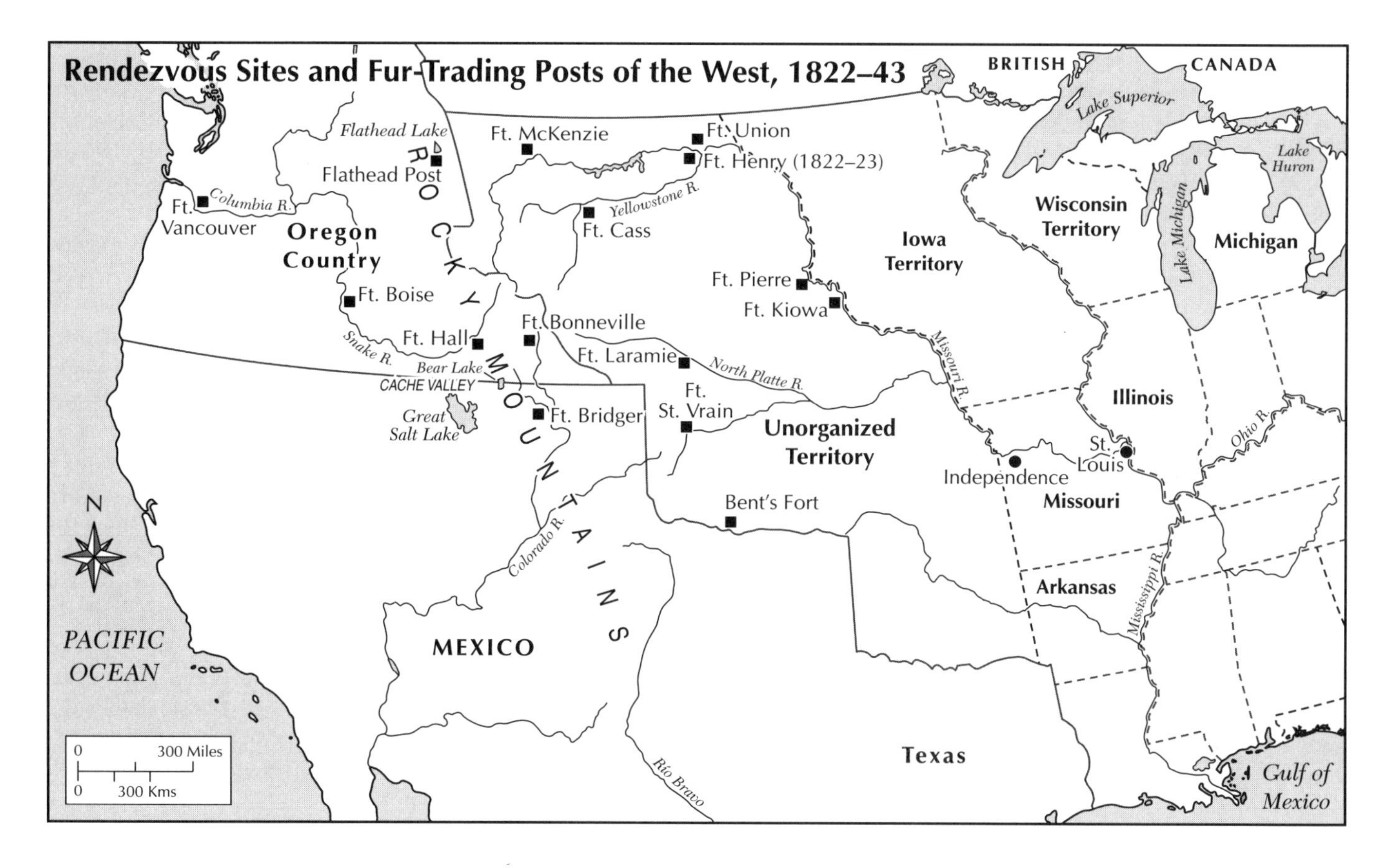

Rendezvous Sites and Fur-Trading Posts of the West, 1822–43

sive settlement in the eastern United States before and after the Revolutionary War had eradicated the fur-producing animals from that region, traders needed to expand to the interior and find new sources of fur. After the Lewis and Clark Expedition (1804–06) mapped potential trade routes through the trans-Mississippi West, this vast territory and its fur resources were easier for traders to exploit. In 1822, WILLIAM HENRY ASHLEY's expeditions explored and discovered routes for travel across the Rocky Mountains and the Continental Divide, which opened up this region to transcontinental trade. The various branches of JOHN JACOB ASTOR's American Fur Company dominated the American market from 1808 to the mid-1840s, establishing trading posts from St. Louis to Oregon. Beginning in 1810, St. Louis was the market center of the western fur trade for three decades.

By the beginning of the 19th century, it was clear that the fur trade and its subsequent industries had transformed Indian economies and ways of living, leading Native Americans to primarily supply pelts while relying on trade for goods they had once produced for themselves and for new goods they wanted, such as kettles, guns, and blankets. In a larger sense, the fur trade transformed Indian ideas about how to live with the world, giving monetary value to things that were previously not commercial in their cultures. Until the abolition of the Indian factory system in 1822, Native-American groups could compete with the fur companies and maintain some level of economic power in the production of fur goods. The Indian factory system consisted of U.S. government–owned and –operated fur trading posts, whose policies of fair prices and no alcohol were designed as a model of fur trading posts. After the factory system was eliminated by the federal government (at the strong urging of its competitor, Astor), Indians became more dependent for their trading livelihood on white traders and white companies. Native Americans had participated willingly in the fur trade, drawn to the prospect of materially improving their lives just as white Europeans were doing. But over time, Indian participation in the American market economy became less negotiated and more coerced. From the beginning, the fur trade introduced Native Americans to an international capitalist economy—one that would eventually contribute to the depletion of their resources and their eviction from valuable lands. As their lands were taken and the finite resources (such as fur) that they depended on for economic agency diminished, Indians were increasingly forced into debt with white traders in order to survive.

The fur trade altered Native-American cultures permanently. Social interactions and family relationships changed as the older customs gave way to new practices that disrupted old roles. The economic imperative to process more and more pelts meant that older limits imposed on hunting were discarded, which led to over-hunting and the destruction of the food chain in many areas. As beaver and other desirable fur-bearers declined in number, Indians and white traders relocated to fresh hunting grounds, and the process was repeated. Disease spread from European traders to Indians along trade routes. Because Native Americans had not developed immunity to European diseases such as smallpox and measles, the death toll could be devastatingly high, destroying whole villages and tribes. The ravages of disease and the destruction of North American ecosystems followed in the wake of traders and settlers as they penetrated further into the continent in search of furs and other commodities.

The fur trade eventually dwindled in importance due to the depletion of available pelts and changes in European fashions and market demands. In North America, the major fur companies were finished by the 1870s. But the lure of fur as a quick moneymaker continued. Despite the breakdown of trading companies and reciprocal trade relationships, the fur trade continued with the availability of a new product: bison. As the Plains Indians were cleared from their lands by settling Europeans after the Civil War, companies and individuals hunted the Plains bison nearly to extinction. Even without the powerful fur companies or Indian trading partners, American and foreign entrepreneurs were still drawn to harvest the abundant fur in America, and continued to threaten the future of the ecosystem.

Further reading: Hiram Martin Chittenden, *The American Fur Trade in the Far West: A History of the Pioneer Trading Posts and Early Fur Companies of the Missouri Valley and Rocky Mountains, and of the Overland Commerce with Santa Fe* (Stanford, Calif.: Academic Reprints, 1954); LeRoy R. Hafen, ed., *Mountain Men and Fur Traders of the Far West: Eighteen Biographical Sketches* (Lincoln: University of Nebraska Press, 1982); David S. Lavender, *The Fist in the Wilderness* (Lincoln: University of Nebraska Press, 1998); Richard White, *The Middle Ground: Indians, Empires, and Republics in the Great Lakes Region, 1650–1815* (Cambridge and New York: Cambridge University Press, 1991); David J. Wishart, *The Fur Trade of the American West, 1807–1840: A Geographical Synthesis* (Lincoln: University of Nebraska Press, 1979).

—Eleanor H. McConnell

G

Gadsden Purchase

The Gadsden Purchase was, in essence, a diplomatic follow-up to the MEXICAN-AMERICAN WAR, which was brought to a formal conclusion by the TREATY OF GUADALUPE HIDALGO in 1848. In the years immediately after the end of the war, Mexico accused the United States of not fulfilling some of its obligations under the treaty, including protecting Mexico from incursions of American Indians who lived in the United States. There was also a boundary dispute between the two nations over land south of the Gila River. This territory had not been sufficiently surveyed to reflect the boundaries agreed to in the treaty. These lands in Mexico also included important low mountain passes that American investors looking to build a southern railroad from New Orleans to the Pacific Ocean sought to acquire. In addition, two American speculators, P. A. Hargous of New York City and A. G. Sloo had purchased tracts of land in the disputed territory and demanded that the United States protect their property in Mexico.

In 1853 President Franklin A. Pierce, a Democrat and leader of a party favoring westward expansion, appointed James Gadsden, a native of South Carolina, as minister to Mexico. Secretary of War Jefferson Davis, a friend of Gadsden who also favored the building of a southern railroad, was instrumental in the appointment. The grandson of Christopher Gadsden, a leader of the American Revolution in South Carolina, James Gadsden was a railroad promoter who in 1840 was elected as president of the Louisville, Cincinnati and Charleston Railroad and later successfully managed the South Carolina Railroad, the most extensive railroad in the southern United States. Gadsden had been less successful in politics, having failed on several occasions to win election to Congress as delegate from the Florida Territory. He had earlier served as an officer under General ANDREW JACKSON in the First Seminole War in Florida.

At the time of his appointment as minister to Mexico, Gadsden had a financial interest in the disputed territory. Pierce instructed him to arrange a purchase of the land in question from Mexico. The original hope of the Pierce administration was to acquire lower CALIFORNIA as well, which belonged to Mexico. However, there were many in Congress, especially those from the northern states staunchly opposed to the expansion of SLAVERY, who were wary of Gadsden, suspecting him of seeking the land in order to create more slave states. This was a reasonable assumption, because as early as 1850 he favored not only the extension of slavery and the construction of a southern railroad, but, if need be, the South's secession from the United States to protect its rights.

After arriving in Mexico City, Gadsden offered Mexican president ANTONIO LÓPEZ DE SANTA ANNA $50 million for about 250,000 square miles in the northern part of the country. That square mileage represented nearly one-third of Mexico's entire territory. Since his country needed the money badly, Santa Anna agreed to a treaty with the United States by which he would sell 55,000 square miles for $15 million. Opposition to the treaty persisted in the Senate, and a contentious debate ensued that contributed to the growing sectional tension between North and South. Supporters of the proposed treaty were also hampered by the flagrant lobbying of speculators looking to enrich themselves, and there was opposition in the Senate to providing Santa Anna, a hated figure to many Americans dating back to the attack he led on THE ALAMO in 1836, with such a large sum of American money.

The Senate narrowly approved the treaty on April 25, 1854, but only after cutting 9,000 square miles and $5 million from the original agreement that Gadsden had reached with the Mexican government. Reflecting the fears over the expansion of slavery, it also reduced the territory that the United States stood to acquire to only that land deemed necessary for the railroad route. The Gadsden Purchase benefited the United States much more than it did Mexico. The year after the treaty was signed, Santa Anna was overthrown, the Gadsden treaty being a contributing factor in his demise. Railroad interests in the United States

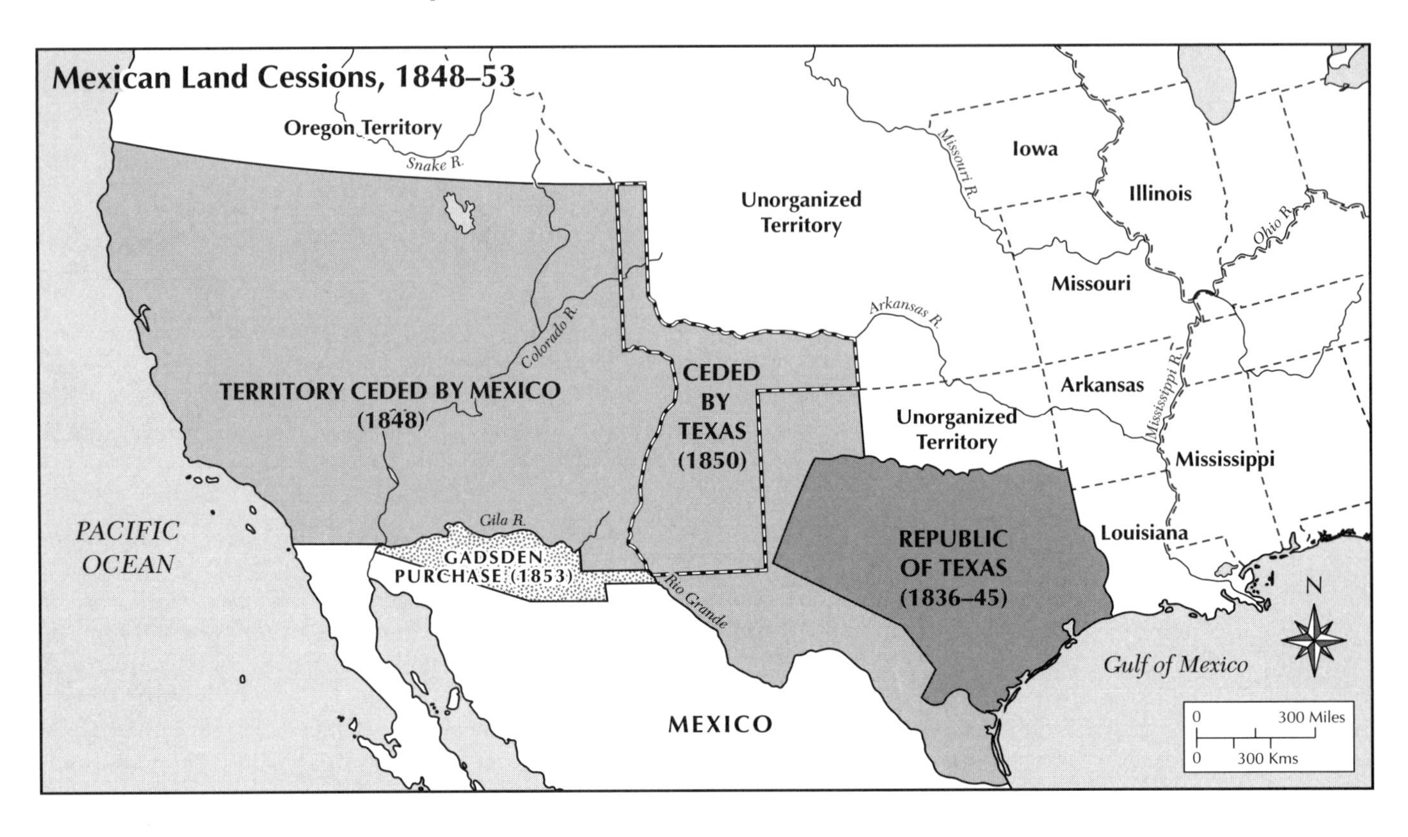

subsequently succeeded in building a line through the territory acquired from Mexico as part of the Southern Pacific Railroad in the 1870s and 1880s.

Further reading: Paul Neff Garber, *The Gadsden Treaty* (Philadelphia: Press of the University of Pennsylvania, 1923); John F. Stover, *Iron Road to the West: American Railroads in the 1850s* (New York: Columbia University Press, 1978).

—Jason K. Duncan

Genius of Universal Emancipation (1821–35)

This antislavery periodical was started in 1821 by Benjamin Lundy (1789–1839) in Mount Pleasant, Ohio. While not the first serial publication to advocate the abolition of SLAVERY, the *Genius of Universal Emancipation* was the first to be entirely devoted to the abolitionist cause. Previous newspapers such as the *Emancipator* and the *Philanthropist* considered other reform issues in addition to slavery, and were addressed primarily to the Quaker community. A Quaker himself, Lundy realized the limited usefulness of addressing only fellow Quakers. After witnessing the failure of abolitionists to influence policy during the Missouri controversy of 1820, he began to think that a more effective way to force changes in the slave system would be to use his newspaper to galvanize the general public about the evils of slavery.

Soon after the periodical's beginning, Lundy moved his operation to Jonesborough, Tennessee, publishing his antislavery views from within a slave state. For most of the 1820s, the *Genius* was the only newspaper in the United States focusing exclusively on the slavery question. Lundy's efforts attracted the anger of the opposition, and he was threatened with physical harm several times. The newspaper, however, continued to grow in circulation and influence. Tireless in his efforts, Lundy traveled widely, spreading the word about abolition and the *Genius*. He later moved its operations to Baltimore, while continuing in his attempt to build a nationwide antislavery movement with the political clout necessary to challenge proslavery interests. He organized antislavery societies in New England with the help of clergymen and abolitionist William Lloyd Garrison, whom he convinced to embrace slavery as the crucial reform issue. Garrison coedited the newspaper with Lundy after 1829.

With a combination of zeal and practicality, the *Genius of Universal Emancipation* advocated the end of slavery by various possible means. Lundy at first considered the efforts of the AMERICAN COLONIZATION SOCIETY to be legitimate but later repudiated the proslavery elements of the movement. Open to any ideas that would undermine the slave system, he also advocated gradual emancipation through political means and the inclusion of former slaves into American society. While based on many of the moral appeals that characterized the later ABOLITION MOVEMENT, Lundy was also interested in undermining slavery politically by creating a groundswell of voter opposition through the *Genius*. His newspaper continued to be published in various incarnations until his death in 1839.

Further reading: John W. Blassingame and Mae F. Henderson, eds., *Antislavery Newspapers and Periodicals* (Boston: G. K. Hall, 1980–84); Merton L. Dillon, *Benjamin Lundy and the Struggle for Negro Freedom* (Urbana: University of Illinois Press, 1966).

—Eleanor H. McConnell

Ghent, Treaty of (1814)

The Treaty of Ghent between the United States and Great Britain ended the WAR OF 1812 by restoring the status quo antebellum. On the one hand, that result disappointed many Americans who believed the country had important grievances against the British. On the other hand, since the war had been a near-disaster for the United States, a treaty that effectively declared the war a draw was a better result than might have been expected. Further, following the Treaty of Ghent, the British withdrew their support for the Native American nations in the U.S.-held Great Lakes territories. Removal of this support made the Great Lakes region—the Old Northwest—more open for non-Indian settlement.

War engulfed Europe in the early 19th century. On the fringes of this struggle, the United States tried to assert its neutrality and its right to trade with both sides in the European conflict. This failed as the European combatants, primarily the British and the French, each tried to block the other's trade with the United States. The British went further, however, boarding American ships on the high seas and impressing (removing) any sailors who either had been members of the British navy or were former British subjects; the latter category included many American citizens, since the nation had gained its independence from England as recently as 1783. In one incident, aboard the USS *Chesapeake*, American citizens were killed as alleged deserters from the British navy. The United States also accused the British of encouraging Native Americans to resist U.S. authority and to attack settlers in the Great Lakes region. Each of these grievances—interference with trading rights, impressment, the *Chesapeake* incident, and the problems with the Native Americans—was featured in President James Madison's war message to Congress in 1812.

Interestingly, although the United States had declared war on England, the nation did not become an ally of France but chose instead to enter and fight the war alone. It was almost a fatal mistake. The Americans wrongly believed that they could easily conquer Canada; indeed, they expected the Canadians to welcome incorporation into the American nation. Instead, the Canadians fought successfully against the American invasion, though American forces did burn the Canadian capital city. The most notable American military successes before the end of the war came in naval battles on the Great Lakes and WILLIAM HENRY HARRISON's defeat of the Native Americans led by Tecumseh at the BATTLE OF THE THAMES. By summer 1814, Napoleon's France had been defeated in Europe, and the British had turned their full attention to the war in North America. They tightened their blockade of the U.S. coast and invaded the Chesapeake area, capturing Washington, D.C., and burning the Capitol building and the president's residence. Both sides were ready for peace, however, and in December 1814, negotiators concluded the Treaty of Ghent. Two weeks later (because of poor communications), the last battle of the War of 1812 occurred at New Orleans, where ANDREW JACKSON repelled a British invasion force.

In fact, like the BATTLE OF NEW ORLEANS, the war itself was perhaps unnecessary. Shortly after the American declaration of war, the British repealed their Parliamentary acts that had interfered with American trade, a change brought about by a depression and a change of government. Meanwhile, the war was deeply unpopular in certain parts of the United States, especially in New England, where merchants continued to trade with the British, and at the HARTFORD CONVENTION, Connecticut hinted at the possible secession of New England from the Union. Under such circumstances, it is not surprising that negotiations to end the war started soon after it began; the two countries even maintained diplomatic relations throughout the war.

The war's ebb and flow directly affected the negotiations. Early on, the Americans demanded that a peace treaty redress all their grievances involving trade, neutral rights, and especially impressment. By 1814, American negotiators had dropped the impressment issue and sought a treaty which merely restored the status quo antebellum. By then, however, the British were demanding more: territorial concessions in Maine, northern New York State, and the northern part of the future state of Minnesota; and an independent Native-American state in the Great Lakes region as a buffer between the United States and Canada. War weariness and the still-volatile situation in Europe soon led the British to drop their most extreme demands and accept the American idea of status quo antebellum.

For the United States, the Treaty of Ghent had advantages. The end of war in Europe—temporary, as it turned out—had removed the causes for interference with neutral trading rights and impressment. The treaty also restored to the United States the territories the British had occupied during the war. Further, it demilitarized the Great Lakes and established a lasting peace between the United States and the British in North America and in the world, laying the groundwork for later Anglo-American friendship. Finally, British abandonment of their Indian allies in the treaty, combined with the death of Tecumseh in 1813 and the consequent collapse of his dreams for an Indian confederation in the Old Northwest, largely ended the Native-American threat to white settlement in the Great Lakes region.

Though the United States failed in its primary objective of adding Canada to the Union, the Treaty of Ghent confirmed certain gains made during the War of 1812. In particular, American nationalism had been enhanced. New England sectionalists failed to disrupt the Union, and important symbols of American patriotism emerged from the war, including the "Star Spangled Banner" (written as FRANCIS SCOTT KEY watched the British bombard but fail to invade Baltimore), "Uncle Sam" (a character based on a real person who helped get supplies to American troops), and the White House (painted to cover smoke damage from the fire that had burned it).

Further reading: Alexander De Conde, *Growth to World Power (1700–1914),* vol. 1. of *A History of American Foreign Policy,* 3d ed. (New York: Charles Scribner's Sons, 1978); Bradford Perkins, *The Creation of a Republican Empire, 1776–1865,* vol. 1. of *The Cambridge History of American Foreign Relations,* ed. Warren I. Cohen (New York: Cambridge University Press, 1993).

—Russell L. Johnson

gold, discovery and mining

The first important gold mining within the United States took place in the states of North Carolina and Georgia in the 1820s and 1830s. While they camped on the rushing streams of the Appalachian Mountains, this first generation of American miners panned and washed for gold (a process called placer mining). In the years 1828, 1829, and 1830, placer gold discoveries in Georgia drew a crowd of prospective miners. Gold production in Georgia reached $110,000 in 1828, a dramatic amount for the age, which would within a generation be dwarfed by events in CALIFORNIA.

The important gold discoveries were those connected with California at mid-century. On January 24, 1848, James W. Marshall, employed by the entrepreneur JOHN SUTTER to construct a sawmill on the American River, picked some mineral flakes out of the tailrace. He identified these specimens as gold, and later primitive tests confirmed his view. Marshall's gold discovery began a series of events that would change the history of California and the history of mining, by bringing the discovery and mining of gold to the center of events associated with the American West. These influences would last for the rest of the century.

From the first news of its discovery, gold production in California was large and it grew for the next few years, before stabilizing for the rest of the decade. In the first six years from 1849 to 1855, the argonauts (as they were sometimes called) harvested some $300 million in gold from California.

Gold mining was important to Americans everywhere at mid-century because of the nature of the enterprise. From the beginning of mining in California in spring 1848, the gold was available to everyone, regardless of wealth and technical skill, and it was an enterprise that rewarded hard work, without need for capital investment—or so it initially seemed. New arrivals in the goldfields could learn the rudiments of mining in 15 minutes. Anyone with a pick, pan, and shovel could become a gold miner, and in 1848, 1849, and even 1850, a miner could expected to make unheard-of sums. Indeed, ordinary miners expected to make from $15 to $20 a day, at a time when the normal wage for agricultural laborers was $1 a day. It is no wonder that so many FORTY-NINERS headed west to the Golden State to participate in this bonanza.

From the beginning, miners worked in groups called "mining companies." As early as the summer and fall of 1848, the first arrivals in the goldfields immediately understood the advantages of working in clusters of at least three or four; most companies settled on six to eight. By the mining season of 1849, the "mining company" was everywhere in the goldfields.

Whatever the organization, the basic unit of work in the CALIFORNIA GOLD RUSH—at least for the first half-dozen years—was the human body. The hard, repetitive labor of digging, carrying, and washing was often done in swift, ice-cold, moving water. Contrasting with the icy water of the snowmelt watercourses was the heat of the summer California sun, beating down on the bars and into the still canyons. The work was exhausting, and during the long workdays that stretched into a long mining season, Forty-niners drove themselves forward on a daily basis through a combination of restless energy, hope, self-interest, and group loyalty. The mining companies carried over to living arrangements. For the Forty-niners, it was cheaper and more efficient to live and work in groups. From five to eight men would occupy a large tent or cabin as close to the work site as possible, where they would take turns cooking, cleaning, and making trips to the larger camps for food and mail.

The act of mining in California in the middle of the 19th century was straightforward. Gold was found in the nooks and crannies of old streambeds and in the bottoms of existing watercourses, where it had been left during thousands of years by moving water carrying the mineral downstream until the flow was insufficient to support the weight. Thus, water was a crucial agent in early gold mining, as an instrument in transporting and dropping the mineral, and as a force for its separation from the dirt around it. The first American miners—often tutored by early-arriving Mexicans—quickly mastered the primitive techniques by which moving water flowing through a tin container would separate the gravel carried off by the force of the flow of water from the heavier gold particles, which would sink to the bottom of the pan, where they could be easily retrieved and stored in a small sack. The widespread presence of gold in the streams draining the western slope of the Sierra Nevada and in gold streambeds—where it might be uncovered by removing a layer of top soil—meant an accessibility that made the early gold rush an exercise open to everyone. All that was necessary to participate were the most elementary and easily available tools.

Furthermore, the search for gold was uninhibited by institutional influences. Access to the rivers, streams, and valleys was open, and no licenses were issued by any kind of central authority (although the state of California levied a tax on alien miners in 1850). The issue of land ownership was in abeyance, since the land was sparsely settled and largely unclaimed in a European sense (except for the tracts belonging to John Sutter). The California Indians were sufficiently weakened by two generations of the mission experience and the trauma associated with its destruction to offer little or no resistance, although this did not prevent American miners and politicians from waging an undeclared war against California's NATIVE AMERICANS.

As mining became more crowded—the number of miners in the goldfields grew from 50,000 in 1849 to 100,000 in 1850 to 125,000 in 1851—the Americans felt a rising hostility toward other national groups. The issue began as a struggle over attractive mining claims and the xenophobic argument that the mines were for Americans alone. The initial targets were the Mexicans, followed by the Chileans and the French. This animosity toward foreigners reached a climax with attacks on the Chinese—who came in large numbers after 1851—the group most different by appearance and culture. Anti-Chinese riots became a focus of politics in San Francisco over the last half of the 19th century.

Advances in technology quickly changed the nature of mining. The first new machine was the "rocker" or "cradle" earlier in use in the gold mines of Georgia and North Carolina. The cradle was a rectangular box six or eight feet long, open at the foot, with a coarse grate and sieve at its head and small cleats nailed across a rounded bottom. The principle was the same as before—namely, to let the water do the work of separating the gold from the gravel. The difference was the economy and efficiency provided by a machine that would allow men to pool their labor into larger units. The pan and the cradle—simple to purchase or easy to make from boards of lumber and both relying on the washing action of the water—provided the technology for the first two years of the California gold rush. Most companies operated one or more "cradles." The universality of both instruments, in spite of rising prices in accordance with supply and demand, ensured that every prospective argonaut could have access to the latest technology in the goldfields.

Mining was changing in other ways, too. By the close of 1849, some miners had banded together to construct dams to divert streambeds for washing. Mercury to separate the gold particles from gravels was rapidly introduced, and by the beginning of 1851, miners had begun what they called quartz mining: the retrieval of gold-bearing rock from deep shafts, the crushing of these gravels, and their processing to capture the gold. River damming, hydraulic mining, and quartz mining gradually transformed or at least severely restricted the opportunities of individuals in opposition to large-scale companies with substantial capital that soon sold shares to the public. Larger units of production with new techniques had replaced simple placer mining, and individuals had become parts of larger companies, with increased investment in season-long mining enterprises. The expanded opportunities for gold recovery were associated with the concentrations of capital and increasingly the sale of shares to the public. Capitalists (or even individuals of modest means) could invest in distant gold-mining enterprises or water companies (almost as profitable as gold) without leaving the comfort of their homes in San Francisco.

It is impossible to overestimate the significance of the California gold rush for mining in the American West. The 10 years of the rush would produce an explosive immigration to the goldfields; transform California into an American state; and establish the basic institutional forms for mining (that would later be codified in the Mining Law of 1872), especially the principle that mining was to proceed without interference from the federal government. It would also serve as a laboratory for the development of mining technology for the next half-century, especially as an introduction to the COMSTOCK LODE, where so many of these technical skills were perfected. Finally, the rush introduced the large-scale forms that would transform mining from an individual into a corporate enterprise, with a large labor force, sophisticated technology, and large capital investment, including absentee ownership and investment. California also proved that in the face of mining strikes, neither well-meaning individuals nor governments at any level could protect the rights of Native Americans from rapacious prospectors, and the California experience outlined a future in which foreign miners (especially non-

English speakers) would be subject to discrimination and harassment. California was also the site of the first struggles over mining and the environment.

The gold strikes in California in 1848 and over the next decade generated an ever-widening search for gold throughout the West. Among the most significant of the new discoveries was that associated with the Comstock Lode, which a decade later would become a great silver-producing complex in the future Nevada Territory.

The more immediate gold discoveries that followed the pattern of the rush to California took place in Colorado. The COLORADO GOLD RUSH began in 1857, with strikes along the Platte River close to the present site of Denver, and spread into the mountains in subsequent months. Soon news of the gold finds spread east and west, ushering in a great movement of gold seekers to Colorado in the summer of 1858. Most of these prospective miners came from the East, and they crossed the plains in companies (like their California counterparts a decade earlier) to the village of Denver, from where they moved into the mountains. The Colorado gold rush showed many of the same characteristics as the original rush to California, but in Colorado the actual discoveries were less rich and numerous. For the rest of the century, the California gold rush was the standard by which other gold strikes around the world would be judged.

Further reading: Paula Mitchell Marks, *Precious Dust: The American Gold Rush Era, 1848–1900* (New York: William Morrow, 1994); Rodman W. Paul, *Mining Frontiers of the Far West, 1848–1880* (Albuquerque: University of New Mexico Press, 1963).

Grimké, Angelina (1805–1879), and Grimké, Sarah (1792–1873)

The children of wealthy planters, Sarah and Angelina Grimké worked the greater part of their lives to abolish the institution of SLAVERY that surrounded them from birth. Born to Mary Smith Grimké and John Faucheraud Grimké—Sarah on November 26, 1792, and Angelina on February 20, 1805—the sisters were raised on a plantation in Charleston, South Carolina. There they received an education considered fitting for young southern women, consisting mostly of basic literacy and social arts. In addition, the sisters attended the law classes that their father, a legislator and judge, held for his sons. Perhaps the most lasting EDUCATION they received in the South, however, was on the cruelties of slavery. Both Grimké sisters grew to hate the institution that supported them.

In 1816, Sarah Grimké traveled with her father to Philadelphia, where the latter hoped to find treatment for his continued ill health. It was there that Sarah first came into contact with Quakers and became increasingly impressed by their simple lifestyle and opposition to holding slaves. When John Grimké died in 1821, Sarah moved to Philadelphia and joined the Society of Friends, immersing herself in Biblical studies. Angelina Grimké followed her sister to Philadelphia in 1829 and quickly joined the Philadelphia Female Anti-Slavery Society. Over the next six years, the sisters became regular attendees at antislavery meetings. In 1835, Angelina Grimké wrote a letter of support to William Lloyd Garrison, editor of the abolitionist newspaper *The Liberator*. When Garrison printed her letter, the Grimkés' public life had begun.

Joined in their commitment to abolitionism, the Grimké sisters nevertheless had their own particular strengths. Angelina began the sisters' public attacks on the institution of slavery with her 1836 pamphlet *An Appeal to the Christian Women of the South*. In it she urged southern women to embrace the political nature of their roles as mothers, wives, and daughters. While the formal avenues of power were closed to women—they could not vote and they could not run for elected office—they were ideally disposed, she argued, to influence the hearts and minds of the men who did. "[I]f you really suppose *you* can do nothing to overthrow slavery, you are greatly mistaken," she wrote. Her ideas caused outrage across the South, and pamphlets sent to her hometown were burned by the postmaster before they could be distributed. Sarah, meanwhile, used her biblical training to write *An Epistle to the Clergy of the Southern States*, published in the same year. In it she flatly denied that there was any scriptural defense for slavery. The sisters followed up their publications with lectures, first in private homes and then at public meetings, attended by men and women alike.

Opposition to the Grimké sisters' work was varied and strong. In the South, the sisters were reviled for their abolitionist opinions and warned never to return to South Carolina. In the North, however, their public speaking engagements were considered by many to be improper. It was rare for women to speak in public, and even more so for them to address mixed crowds. The collective clergy of Massachusetts were so disturbed by the Grimkés' public appearances that in 1837 they issued a pastoral letter condemning the sisters. Women, they argued, were weak and dependent, their "appropriate duties and influence . . . clearly stated in the New Testament. . . . But when a woman assumes the place and tone of man as a public reformer . . . her character becomes unnatural." The Grimké sisters, they suggested, were opening the way for general "degeneracy and ruin."

Rather than persuade the sisters to stop their public work, the letter rejuvenated their determination. In 1838, Sarah published *Letters on the Equality of the Sexes and the Condition of Women*. The book argued that women deserved nothing less than full equality with men in every area of life, including the right to speak in public, and that all women should work toward that end. In turn, Angelina wrote *Letters to Catharine Beecher* (1838), answering that prominent reformer's similar charge that their work stepped too far outside the boundaries of acceptable female behavior. The idea that equality and human dignity were off-limits to women was unacceptable to either sister. As such, their fortitude and eloquent defense of their beliefs became an inspiration to later advocates of women's rights.

On May 14, 1838, Angelina Grimké married Theodore Weld, a fellow abolitionist. The next day, she attended the Anti-Slavery Convention of American Women, one of her last public acts before retiring to private life. Both sisters withdrew from the limelight after Angelina's marriage. Angelina bore three children, whom Sarah helped to raise, and both sisters became teachers in New Jersey as the children grew. On December 23, 1873, Sarah Grimké died in Hyde Park, now part of present-day Boston. Angelina followed on October 26, 1879.

Further reading: Larry Ceplair, ed., *The Public Years of Sarah and Angelina Grimké: Selected Writings, 1835–1839* (New York: Columbia University Press, 1989); Gerda Lerner, *The Grimké Sisters from South Carolina: Pioneers for Woman's Rights and Abolition* (New York: Oxford University Press, 1998).

—Catherine J. Denial

Guadalupe Hidalgo, Treaty of (1848)

Named for the small town near Mexico City where it was negotiated, the Treaty of Guadalupe Hidalgo ended the MEXICAN-AMERICAN WAR by settling the TEXAS border with Mexico, confirming American control of CALIFORNIA, and granting the United States control of the territory of New Mexico, a vast area containing all or parts of six future states. Although the treaty achieved the territorial goals of President JAMES K. POLK and his administration going into the war, it satisfied few. Many northerners believed the Mexican War had been started under false pretenses simply to acquire more territory for slave states, and they opposed dismembering Mexico for such a purpose. For their part, southerners demanded the right to move their slaves into any territories acquired from Mexico. There was also a political faction throughout the country which believed that, since the United States had conquered all of Mexico, it should annex the whole country. In the end, the extremes cancelled each other, and the treaty was ratified. The controversy over the status of slavery in the new territory, however, helped provoke the Civil War in the 1860s.

Ostensibly worried about British and French designs in California, after taking office in 1845, Polk had tried to purchase California as well as New Mexico. The Mexicans' refusal to sell was one of the issues cited in Polk's declaration of war in 1846. Another issue was the yet-to-be-determined southern border of Texas, which the United States had annexed in 1845. The United States wanted to set the border at the Rio Grande, while Mexico insisted the Nueces River had been the boundary of Texas before 1836, when it was a Mexican province. The latter dispute most directly precipitated the Mexican-American War, when Polk directed General ZACHARY TAYLOR to occupy the disputed territory, and Mexico sent its army to dispute the occupation.

Once the war began, Polk sent an emissary, Nicholas P. Trist, to accompany General WINFIELD SCOTT's army, which landed on the Mexican coast at Veracruz and marched inland toward Mexico City. Trist, chief clerk at the State Department, was chosen as much for his loyalty as a Democrat and lack of political aspirations (in each case a contrast to Taylor and Scott) as for his acknowledged ability, record of success in Latin American diplomacy, and Spanish language skills. Polk instructed Trist to continue to offer to end the war in exchange for California, New Mexico, and the Rio Grande border for Texas; Trist could also offer up to $30 million in compensation. After joining Scott's army in May 1847, Trist accepted a British-mediated armistice in August to begin negotiations. The armistice soon broke down, but before it did, Trist indicated his willingness to accept less territory for Texas than Polk wanted. After the war resumed, Scott's army continued its march through Mexico, and by mid-September it had occupied Mexico City. Meanwhile, Polk had gotten wind of the armistice (which he opposed) and of Trist's willingness to make concessions on the Texas boundary. Displeased, the president recalled his emissary to Washington.

Events outpaced Polk's efforts to control them, however. His order for Trist to return to Washington did not reach the diplomat until mid-November, by which time the Mexican government of General ANTONIO LÓPEZ DE SANTA ANNA had fallen and been replaced by one more amenable to negotiations. General Scott and the British consulate in Mexico City urged Trist to ignore Polk's instructions and stay long enough to conclude a peace treaty. This Trist did, and in February 1848 he forwarded the proposed Treaty of Guadalupe Hidalgo to Washington. Perhaps justifiably angry at what he considered Trist's insubordination, Polk nevertheless decided the treaty was one he could accept. Most important, it met his minimum territorial requirements, including the Texas border he wanted at the Rio Grande. Further, Polk decided the treaty could prevent a political collision damaging to the nation. Early in the war, northern antislavery forces had introduced the Wilmot Proviso, trying to prevent the spread of slavery into territory acquired in the war but also angering the president's southern Democratic friends. At the end of the war, ardent expansionists, primarily northern and western Democrats, demanded that the United States annex all of Mexico as the only appropriate compensation for the loss of American lives in the war. Southerners were unhappy that slavery apparently would be excluded from California and had an uncertain status in New Mexico. Still, opponents of the treaty could muster just 14 votes against it in the Senate; 38 Senators voted to accept it.

As approved by the Senate in March 1848, the Treaty of Guadalupe Hidalgo acknowledged the American conquest of California, ceded control of the New Mexico Territory to the United States, and established the Rio Grande as the southern border of Texas. Adding Texas, which had become part of the United States in 1845, Mexico lost over one-half of its territory to the United States in the 1840s. For its part, the United States agreed to pay Mexico $15 million and to take responsibility for more than $3 million owed by Mexico to U.S. citizens. In sum, apart from the territory acquired from Mexico in the GADSDEN PURCHASE (1854), the Treaty of Guadalupe Hidalgo completed the United States' continental empire from the Atlantic to the Pacific.

Perhaps because the nation's continental empire was complete, the controversy over the status of slavery in the territories worsened after the Treaty of Guadalupe Hidalgo. Northern opponents of slavery periodically reintroduced the Wilmot Proviso in Congress, without any success in enacting it into law. An important part of the COMPROMISE OF 1850 allowed for slavery's status in New Mexico to be determined by POPULAR SOVEREIGNTY; this idea held that the actual inhabitants of a territory should decide whether or not they wanted slavery in that territory. Popular sovereignty ultimately satisfied neither pro- nor antislavery forces, and the issue of slavery in the territories, reopened by the acquisition of California and New Mexico, remained unresolved until the Civil War.

Further reading: Alexander De Conde, *Growth to World Power (1700–1914)*, vol. 1 of *A History of American Foreign Policy,* 3d ed. (New York: Charles Scribner's Sons, 1978); Bradford Perkins, *The Creation of a Republican Empire, 1776–1865,* vol. 1. of *The Cambridge History of American Foreign Relations,* ed. Warren I. Cohen, (New York: Cambridge University Press, 1993).

—Russell L. Johnson

H

Hale, Sarah Josepha (1788–1879)
One of the most influential women of letters in the 19th century, Sarah Josepha Hale was born in rural Newport, New Hampshire, the third child of Gordon Buell and Martha Whittlesey Buell. Her family encouraged her in her EDUCATION and intellectual development, an advantage not normally available to girls at this time. She studied literature and the classics at home, and her older brother, a student at Dartmouth, tutored her. When she was 18, she started a private school for boys and girls, where she taught for seven years.

In 1813 Sarah Buell stopped teaching to marry David Hale, a local attorney. While no longer instructing students, she continued her own education and began publishing her prose and poetry in local newspapers. The Hales had four children, and Sarah spent most of her time raising them. She became ill with tuberculosis in 1819, but ultimately survived this affliction. Then, in 1822, David Hale died suddenly of pneumonia, just a few weeks before the birth of their fifth child.

Sarah Hale was now the sole provider for her family, a responsibility she assumed with characteristic vigor and creativity. After a brief stint in her sister-in-law's millinery shop, she decided to earn her living by writing. Only a year later, she published a book of poetry, *The Genius of Oblivion* (1823). She also wrote articles for magazines such as the *Boston Spectator* and *Ladies' Album,* and published the influential novel *Northwood: A Tale of New England* (1827). Hale's successes attracted the admiration of Boston publisher John Lauris Blake. In 1828, he asked her to be the editor of his new venture, *Ladies' Magazine.* Thus the 39-year-old Hale began the editing and writing career that would bring her national influence and regard.

At a time when most American periodicals merely reprinted English articles, Hale published the work of American writers such as Lydia Sigourney and Lydia Maria Child. She also wrote a large portion of the magazine's text. Her articles were republished in two collections, *Sketches of American Character* (1829) and *Traits of American Life* (1835). In 1830, she published *Poems for our Children,* a collection that included her most famous verse, "Mary's Lamb" (more commonly known as "Mary Had a Little Lamb"). She continued to produce and edit works for children and briefly edited *Juvenile Miscellany,* a children's magazine. Many of her verses for children also appeared in the popular children's readers created by WILLIAM HOLMES MCGUFFEY.

In 1836, the *Ladies' Magazine* failed and was purchased by Philadelphian Louis Godey, successful publisher

Sarah Josepha Hale *(Hulton/Archive)*

of the *Lady's Book,* a fashion magazine. Godey offered Hale the highest position in the new joint publication, which she accepted. She ran the magazine from Boston until 1841, when she moved to Philadelphia. It was as editor of this publication, soon renamed *Godey's Lady's Book,* that Sarah Josepha Hale became a nationally influential figure. Uninterested in fashion, she nevertheless continued to print the innovative engravings of new women's fashions that set *Godey's Lady's Book* apart from other women's magazines. More interested in literary pursuits, Hale elevated the magazine's profile by commissioning the work of respected writers such as Emerson, Longfellow, and Hawthorne. She also wrote large portions of the text, examining numerous topics. She was best known for her articles on what she called "domestic science"—parenting, homemaking, health, and fitness.

Hale also promoted political reforms in her editorials, advocating women's education and the reform of women's property rights. Like her friend EMMA WILLARD, she believed in expanding women's educational and career opportunities but opposed woman suffrage as unfeminine. She advocated separate spheres for men and women and argued that women could best change public morality through private, domestic example. Yet she herself was a public figure who sought changes in the condition of American women.

While she transformed *Godey's Lady's Book* into a literary power, she continued to write books for women, including volumes on cooking and household management. She also compiled an ambitious 900-page reference, *Woman's Record; or, Sketches of All Distinguished Women from "the Beginning" till A.D. 1850,* first published in 1853. She persistently updated this reference, aiming to give her readers a more accurate picture of women's accomplishments throughout history. She kept up her support for philanthropic and civic causes, helping to found the Women's Medical College of Philadelphia and the Philadelphia School of Design for Women. During the years leading to the Civil War, she wrote books and editorials advocating the gradual abolition of slavery and the repatriation of former slaves to Africa. Her most famous civic endeavor was undoubtedly her effort to make Thanksgiving a national holiday. After years of campaigning on her part, Abraham Lincoln proclaimed this holiday in 1863.

By 1860 *Godey's Lady's Book* was the most widely read periodical in America, with a paid readership of 150,000. Sarah Josepha Hale continued to edit the magazine until 1877, when she retired at the age of 89; she died two years later. In her 50-year publishing career, Hale became a powerful force in American culture, promoting her belief in domesticity while gaining a kind of public stature and power rarely attained by women in the 19th century.

See also WOMEN'S STATUS AND RIGHTS.

Further reading: Norma R. Fryatt, *Sarah Josepha Hale and Godey's Lady's Book: The Life and Times of a Nineteenth-Century Career Woman* (New York: Hawthorne Books, 1975); Patricia Okker, *Our Sister Editors: Sarah J. Hale and the Tradition of Nineteenth-Century American Women Editors* (Athens: University of Georgia Press, 1995).

—Eleanor H. McConnell

Harpers Ferry See Volume V

Harrison, William Henry (1773–1840)

Soldier, statesman of the WHIG PARTY, and ninth president of the United States, William Henry Harrison was born in Charles City, Virginia, on February 22, 1773, the son of Benjamin Harrison, a signer of the Declaration of Independence. He was educated at Hampton-Sidney College and subsequently studied medicine at the College of Physicians and Surgeons in Philadelphia. However, he became attracted to military service and joined the U.S. Army as an ensign in August 1791. Reporting to the army of Major General Anthony Wayne in western Pennsylvania, he initially served as an aide-de-camp. On August 20, 1794, Harrison distinguished himself at the victory of Fallen Timbers, whereby the Shawnee coalition of Blue Jacket and Little Turtle met defeat. He consequently advanced to captain in May 1797 and assumed command of Fort Washington, Ohio, but then resigned his commission the following year to pursue politics.

In 1799 Harrison gained an appointment as secretary of the Northwest Territory under Governor Arthur St. Clair. The following year he was elected the territory's first congressional delegate. His most notable accomplishment was passage of the Land Act Bill of 1800, which encouraged settlement and granted borrowers up to five years to pay back loans. In May 1800, President John Adams made Harrison governor of the Indiana Territory, a large wilderness tract encompassing present-day Indiana, Illinois, Wisconsin, and western Michigan. Harrison held this post for 12 years, proving instrumental in establishing a legal system, managing land disputes, and supervising Indian affairs. His tenure was also marked by sincere attempts to maintain peace with indigenous Native American nations in the region and included efforts to suppress the sale of liquor and widespread inoculation to curtail smallpox.

Unfortunately, Harrison was also authorized to negotiate as much Indian land away from them as possible. His efforts climaxed in the 1803 Treaty of Fort Wayne, whereby the United States acquired 2.9 million acres of pristine wilderness in exchange for annual subsidies. However, within six years further negotiations were thwarted by two

Shawnee brothers, TECUMSEH and his one-eyed brother, Tenskwatawa ("The Prophet"). Tecumseh maintained that the chiefs who signed the Fort Wayne treaty did not represent all Indians present and therefore it was invalid. His brother, meanwhile, had originated a new religion that called for the expelling of Americans and their culture from the Indian world. Indian resistance to further white encroachment coalesced around these two figures. Harrison met with Tecumseh repeatedly at Vincennes, the capital of Indian Territory, to seek accommodation but failed to sway his mind. The course was now set for a confrontation between civilizations.

In autumn 1811 Tecumseh ventured south to recruit Creek Indians into his anti-white confederation. Harrison availed himself of this absence by advancing with 1,000 men toward the Indian village of Prophetstown on Tippecanoe Creek. This was a move calculated to intimidate the inhabitants, but on November 7, 1811, Tenskwatawa's warriors suddenly lashed out at the intruders. A stiff fight ensued with heavy losses to both sides, but Harrison ultimately prevailed. The victorious Americans then burned Prophetstown and retired back to Vincennes without ceremony. Harrison's "victory," a close call militarily, was portrayed in the newspapers as decisive, and he basked in the newly acquired glow of national fame. Tippecanoe, however, was simply the first salvo in a bloody and protracted frontier war. It also threw Tecumseh's people into an armed alliance with Great Britain just as the WAR OF 1812 was beginning.

When war with England recommenced in June 1812, Harrison was not a major contender for a regular army commission, so through the intercession of HENRY CLAY he became a major general of the Kentucky militia. By August, the war effort was in serious trouble, and he became a brigadier general in the regular army. His orders were to recapture Detroit, disgracefully surrendered that month by General WILLIAM HULL. However, he was unable to weather endemic manpower and supply shortages, and his campaign stalled. Worse, when the army of General James Winchester was destroyed at Frenchtown, Michigan, in January 1813, British forces under General Henry Procter went on the offensive. Harrison, now a major general, countered by constructing Fort Meigs at the headwaters of the Maumee River, Ohio, and awaited their approach. Procter besieged the Americans and defeated a determined sortie by Harrison on May 5, 1813, but he lacked the manpower to storm the fort. The British withdrew to Canada, while Harrison kept accumulating men and supplies. Once Procter returned and suffered a sharp repulse at Fort Stephenson in August 1813, he withdrew from American soil altogether. Harrison then waited for Commodore Oliver Hazard Perry to win the decisive BATTLE OF LAKE ERIE on September 10, which gave American forces

William Henry Harrison *(Library of Congress)*

command of the waterways. Detroit was finally recaptured, and Perry thereupon transported the bulk of Harrison's army across the lake and into Canada. Several days of hard marching ensued before Harrison cornered Procter and Tecumseh at the Thames River on October 5. The affair was settled quickly by a mounted cavalry charge under Colonel Richard M. Johnson that crushed all opposition. Procter managed to escape, but Tecumseh was slain and with him died the last hope of a viable Indian confederation. In 1815 a victorious Harrison presided over the Spring Wells Treaty, which sealed the fate of Indian lands in the Old Northwest. In light of his services, Harrison was feted as a national war hero, and he received a congressional gold medal.

After the war Harrison settled in Ohio, where he gained election to state office. He returned to the U.S. House of Representatives in 1816 and also served a term in the Senate from 1825. Harrison initially functioned as a close ally and confidant of Henry Clay, a longtime aspirant to the presidency, but the two ambitious men drifted apart. In 1828 President JOHN QUINCY ADAMS appointed Harrison ambassador to Colombia, where he remained until the election of ANDREW JACKSON to the presidency. His only notable accomplishment was to enter into a dispute with

General Simón Bolívar over the latter's alleged intention to establish a monarchy. Harrison then resumed a quiet life at his home in North Bend, Ohio. As a politician and diplomat, he had handled himself competently but without great distinction. Meanwhile, growing resistance to Jackson and the DEMOCRATIC PARTY culminated in the foundation of a new political party, the Whigs, in 1836. This prompted Harrison to reenter politics, and he campaigned to win the Whig nomination for president against Democrat MARTIN VAN BUREN. However, he failed for being a sectional candidate whose name appeared in only a few states. Fortunately for the Whigs, the PANIC OF 1837 ensued the following year, and public support for the Democrats dropped precipitously.

In 1840 Harrison again determined to run for the White House. Taking a leaf from Andrew Jackson, popularly known as "Old Hickory," Harrison sought broad-based, national voter appeal by packaging himself as "Old Tippecanoe," a reference to his War of 1812 endeavors. Moreover, the Whig party leadership was searching for a candidate that, in contrast to the assertive Jackson, would be more pliant towards congressional wishes. For this reason, Harrison edged out Clay as the party's nominee, despite the latter's attempt to portray him as something of a bumpkin. Thus was born the "Log Cabin and Hard Cider" campaign. Harrison was quick to adopt and exploit the imagery, contrasting his "homespun" persona against the solidly aristocratic credentials of Van Buren. His efforts were greatly abetted by a new political strategy that bore all the trappings of a modern presidential campaign: souvenirs, slick campaign publications, songs, and slogans all emerged in abundance for the first time. Harrison himself broke new ground by becoming the first American presidential candidate to stump for votes around the country. Buoyed by the famous slogan "Tippecanoe and Tyler, Too" (in reference to running mate JOHN TYLER of Virginia) Harrison easily defeated Van Buren in autumn 1840 to become the first Whig president.

Harrison did not live long enough to savor his victory. He caught a cold during his inauguration in March and died of pneumonia on April 4, 1841. Having become the first American executive to die in office, he was succeeded by Tyler, and his political legacy remains conjectural. Harrison is best remembered as a competent, if not brilliant, militia leader during the War of 1812, who did much to resurrect the reputation of American "citizen-soldiery." Regardless of his shortcomings as a politician, the memory of his earlier victories was sufficient to carry him into the White House.

Further reading: Sandy Antal, *A Wampum Denied: Procter's War of 1812* (East Lansing: Michigan State University Press, 1997); Freeman Cleaves, *Old Tippecanoe: William Henry Harrison and His Times* (New York: Scribner's, 1939); Reginald Horsman, "William Henry Harrison: Virginia Gentleman in the Old Northwest," *Indiana Magazine of History* vol. 96, no. 2(2000): 124–149; Gary W. Pond, "William Henry Harrison and United States Indian Policy in the Northwest and Indiana Territories, 1783–1813" (unpublished master's thesis, Central Missouri State University, 1996); Kenneth R. Stevens, *William Henry Harrison: A Bibliography* (Westport, Conn.: Greenwood Press, 1996).

—John C. Fredriksen

Hartford Convention

Beginning December 15, 1814, delegates from the five New England states, representing the Federalist Party, met at Hartford, Connecticut, to discuss the alleged encroachments of the national government. The convention was primarily a protest of the WAR OF 1812 (1812–15), and much has been made of the fact that the delegates discussed secession from the Union. Although such drastic steps were not taken, the Hartford Convention still made its mark by declaring the rights of states to deny the legitimacy of government acts that they believed were unconstitutional.

Some tension had begun prior to the start of the war, as New England Federalists had opposed the embargo of 1807 and other government measures against the British. Since their ECONOMY was closely linked to Britain, New Englanders were understandably alarmed by the declaration of war between the United States and Great Britain in June 1812. However, the increased wartime demand for provisions was quite a benefit, and many New Englanders ignored the embargo Congress had passed and sold supplies to British troops. On the other hand, the war was harmful to other foreign commerce and to the fishing industry. In spite of whatever profits there were to be gained from the conflict, Federalist leaders believed the interests of New England were being pushed aside for the interests of the southern states and the Democratic-Republican Party. Some New England states began to try to hinder the war effort, initially by refusing to supply militia to the federal government, and they did not support the federal loan of 1814. Finally, in 1814, several leaders in Massachusetts issued a call for a convention to address the regional grievances.

In December that year, 26 Federalists representing Connecticut, Rhode Island, and Massachusetts, sent by their state legislatures, and New Hampshire and Vermont, chosen by the Federalist Party, met in Hartford, Connecticut. George Cabot, a moderate Federalist from Massachusetts, presided, while Theodore Dwight served as secretary of the convention. The underlying aim of the convention was to protect the privileges of the individual states against apparent violations by the federal government. The meetings were held in absolute secrecy. Although the moderates prevailed at the convention, some extremists proposed secession from the Union and others suggested a separate peace between New England and Great Britain. The proposal to secede was ultimately rejected, but the delegates did produce a final report that was critical of James Madison and the war. The convention also recommended several changes to be enacted through constitutional amendments that would remedy the advantage New Englanders felt the South had gained. The convention urged that taxation and representation in each state should be proportionate to its free population, that no naturalized citizens should be allowed to hold office in the federal government, that the presidency should not exceed one term and the president should never be chosen twice successively from the same state, and that Congress should not interfere with foreign commerce or declare offensive war except by a two-thirds vote.

Unfortunately for the cause of the Federalists, their recommendations had little power, because the TREATY OF GHENT had been signed on December 24, 1814, while the convention was still in session. The futile Hartford Convention, which concluded on January 15, 1815, signaled the approaching end of the Federalist Party, which was already in decline because of its pro-British reputation.

Further reading: James M. Banner, Jr., *To the Hartford Convention: The Federalists and the Origins of Party Politics in Massachusetts, 1789–1815* (New York: Knopf, 1970).

—Crystal Williams

Hawaiian Islands

The "Hawaiian pear is now fully ripe, and this is the golden hour for the United States to pluck it," declared the U.S. minister to the Hawaiian Islands John L. Stevens in 1893. Five years later, Hawaii was "picked" by the United States and officially annexed by the government of President William McKinley. The archipelago was fully incorporated into the nation when it became the 50th state in 1959. The U.S. government had been eager to absorb the Hawaiian Islands into its plans for expansion into the Pacific and Asia at the end of the 19th century. However, it was private American citizens more than government officials who took the lead in wresting the islands away from the Hawaiian monarchy and securing them under U.S. sovereignty.

Hawaii is composed of eight main islands (including Kauai, Oahu, Maui and Hawaii, also called the "Big Island") and located nearly 2,500 miles from the U.S. mainland. Various Polynesian peoples, principally the Marquesans and Tahitians, originally settled the archipelago more than 1,000 years before English naval captain James Cook first reached it in 1778. Over the course of its early history, Hawaii existed in virtual isolation and remained unknown to the world beyond Polynesia.

The unification of the Hawaiian Islands under a single indigenous monarch, KAMEHAMEHA I (also known as "the Great") occurred almost simultaneously with the arrival of the first European explorers. As late as the 1780s Hawaii was divided into three kingdoms. By the end of the 1790s Kamehameha had conquered a significant portion of the archipelago, including the islands of Hawaii, Oahu, and Maui. In 1810 the islands of Kauai and Niihau submitted to his rule and signaled the unification of the entire island chain under the Kamehameha dynasty, which would last until the 1890s.

During Kamehameha's early struggle for domination over Hawaii, Captain James Cook and the crews of his ships the HMS *Resolution* and the HMS *Discovery* first sighted Oahu on January 18, 1778. Two days later, they made landfall on the island of Kauai, introducing the isolated archipelago to the western world. Cook stumbled across the islands as he was attempting to find the legendary pathway across the North American continent known as the Northwest Passage. The initial interaction between the British and the Hawaiians was generally very cordial; the British traded various metal trinkets, which completely fascinated the Hawaiians, for essential provisions.

Almost immediately, social and sexual fraternization began between Cook's crew and Hawaiian women. The local *kahunas* (Hawaiian shamans) encouraged this interaction as a way to test the divinity of the British in the belief that if these men were gods, they would not desire the women. Cook's men proved themselves to be quite mortal. Unfortunately, sexual exchange introduced various forms of venereal and other diseases to the Hawaiians. The native population, which was estimated to have been about 300,000 at the time of Cook's arrival, fell to under 150,000 by 1820.

Cook named the island chain the Sandwich Islands in honor of his patron, the British noble John Montagu, the Fourth Earl of Sandwich. The name would eventually be replaced as American influence overtook that of the British in subsequent decades. Despite this auspicious beginning, which included Cook's deification as a local god, hostility developed between the British and Hawaiians over the theft of one of Cook's boats. This antagonism turned into armed conflict on a return visit in 1779 during which Cook was killed.

Cook's death, however, did not signal the end of relations between Hawaii and the West. The islands became a significant provisioning port for American and European trading ships sailing to and from Asia. The Hawaiians felt the impact of the West, and not only in terms of trade and the unfortunate consequences of disease. Kamehameha made use of two captured sailors, John Young and Isaac

Davis, as well as a confiscated American vessel and cannons, in his efforts to consolidate power over the archipelago.

Whites, called *haoles* by the native population, began settling the islands in the early 19th century. Although most of the white settlers were sailors and entrepreneurs, Christian missionaries also came to Hawaii in search of new converts. They played a significant role in imposing western domination over the islands. Under their influence, the traditional Hawaiian cultural system, *kapu*, was terminated, the Hawaiian language was altered, and an extensive public school system was created. Not only were whites exercising social influence in the islands, but they came to dominate local politics and threaten the power of the Hawaiian monarchy throughout the 1800s. In 1840 Kamehameha III called for a change in rule from an autocracy to a constitutional monarchy with a bicameral legislature. Hawaiians also adopted their first constitution and bill of rights that same year. Missionaries were influential in these reform efforts.

Under the Great *Mahele*, carried out in 1848, royal lands were made public and commoners were granted the right to purchase their own property. Unfortunately for the majority of Hawaiians who hoped to benefit from this land distribution, foreigners were granted permission to buy lands in 1850. By the end of the century, rich white businessmen had purchased almost four times as much land as Hawaiians, reducing much of the local population to propertyless tenancy.

White settlement also had great economic impact on the islands. The early 19th century witnessed the massive expansion of whaling in the northern Pacific. As a consequence, Hawaii became the chief port for whaling vessels, particularly those owned and operated by Americans. Much of Hawaii's agriculture was directed towards provisioning whaling vessels. Yet by the 1850s, interest in whaling was declining and sugar production, introduced to the islands by the American George Wilfong in the late 1840s, was expanding. Sugar production in Hawaii exploded in the second half of the 19th century as an almost insatiable demand for refined sugar in the United States grew. The sugar industry would irrevocably change Hawaiian society.

Because sugarcane production is labor-intensive and the Hawaiian labor force was declining as a result of disease, planters began to import labor in massive numbers with the passage of the 1850 Masters and Servants Act. More than 200,000 laborers, mostly Japanese and Chinese, would be brought to the islands by the turn of the century. This demographic shift would make Hawaii a veritable rainbow of ethnic diversity. However, it would also push indigenous Hawaiian influence to the periphery of social and political life.

The final blow to Hawaiian rule came in the 1890s. American planters and merchants, led by Sanford B. Dole, instigated the overthrow of the Hawaiian government. The Americans saw their economic interests endangered by indigenous rule and sought closer ties to the United States. They carried out an outrageous, if bloodless, coup in January 1893. They were given armed assistance by Marines from the USS *Boston* and easily toppled the Hawaiian monarchy. Not wanting to see any of her people killed, Queen Liliuokalani reluctantly capitulated. Upon taking over the government, Americans sought the islands' annexation by the federal government, which happened in August 1898. In June 1900 Hawaii became a U.S. territory, and all those residing in Hawaii, whether they wanted to or not, became U.S. citizens.

Further reading: Edward Joesting, *Hawaii: An Uncommon History* (New York: W. W. Norton and Company, 1972).

—Charles Hawley

Hicks, Elias (1748–1830)

A Quaker reformer, Elias Hicks was born in Hempstead Township, Long Island, New York. His parents were formally Anglicans, but his father joined the Society of Friends (Quakers) shortly before his birth. As a youth, Hicks received little formal education and was apprenticed as a carpenter. In 1777 he inherited his family farm, which he managed until his death 53 years later. Throughout his early manhood, Hicks behaved like a typical Quaker of his class. Being well versed in the Bible, early Quaker literature, and basic Christian history, he was commonly present at annual gatherings of Friends in New York and Philadelphia. However, by the early 19th century, he began espousing a radically different interpretation of his sect's beliefs.

During childhood, Hicks had apparently experienced visitations of "divine grace." As he matured, he frequently lectured on the fundamental necessity of acknowledging the "Inner Light." This manifestation of God's will and love, he maintained, was self-evident and open to all. Furthermore, in placing great emphasis on personal revelation from God, he openly downplayed the significance of the Bible as a guide to salvation. He also reinterpreted the story of Jesus as an example of a perfect man aware of the presence of God within him. Hicks's teachings were a radical departure from the established tenets of Quakerism and the source of a contentious schism among the Friends. Henceforth, from 1828, the Quakers became divided between two distinct sects. The so-called Hicksites embraced their founder's notion of personal revelations for spiritual guidance, while the more traditional Orthodox reaffirmed their emphasis on the Bible and the teachings of Christ as the only source of salvation. Hicks's centrality of the importance of personal salvation also called into question the moral and religious authority of elders guiding the Quaker movement.

In a more practical sense, Hicks was at odds with modernity. He waxed highly critical of fellow Quakers who had grown wealthy and participated actively in the larger community about them. He demanded that they remain aloof from the world and not pursue money or other activities that ground "the faces of the poor." Moreover, Hicks was profoundly abolitionist in outlook and openly condemned Quakers who owned slaves. His beliefs mandated that AFRICAN AMERICANS should enjoy the same intrinsic right to liberty as all human beings, and he advocated the boycott of slave-produced goods such as rice and cotton.

Hicks died at his farm in Jericho, New York, on February 27, 1830. The schism he started, and the theological recriminations it engendered, endured among the Society of Friends long after his passing. For this reason, Hicks is regarded as a major religious reformer of the early to mid-19th century.

See also RELIGION.

Further reading: Paul Buckley, "'Thy Affectionate Friend': The Letters of Elias Hicks and William Poole" (unpublished master's thesis, Earlham School of Religion, 2001); Bruce Dorsey, "Friends Becoming Enemies: Philadelphia Benevolence and the Neglected Era of American Quaker History," *Journal of the Early Republic* 18, no. 3 (1998): 395–428; H. Larry Ingle, *Quakers in Conflict: The Hicksite Reformation* (Knoxville: University of Tennessee Press, 1986).

—John C. Fredriksen

Horseshoe Bend, Battle of (Tohopeka)
(March 27, 1814)

This battle between American forces and rebel Creek (Muskogee) Indians known as the "Red Sticks" effectively ended the Red Stick War of 1812–14. The Red Sticks resisted the Americanization (adoption of white cultural practices) of the Creek, which had been taking place within the nation for decades. There was increasing pressure on the Creek to abandon communal land ownership and adopt the white practice of private land ownership, which would allow them to sell much of their land to the United States. Many of the Creek, led by mixed-blood chiefs, were open to change. However, a considerable number rejected the changes taking place and erupted into open rebellion with the United States and the pro-American Creek in 1812, causing a civil war within the nation. These rebel Creek, or Red Sticks, wished to return to a more traditional way of living centered on a new prophetic movement designed to restore traditional values. This new religious movement also called for little or no contact with white people and an abandonment of most facets of white culture which the Creek had adopted.

Throughout 1812 and 1813 the Red Sticks skirmished with the pro-American Creek. In 1813, the United States and the Red Sticks began open warfare at the Battle of Burnt Corn. By March 1814 about 1,000 Red Stick warriors and 400 women and children had assembled along the Tallapoosa River in modern-day Alabama. Tohopeka, the town the Red Sticks built there, lay in a horseshoe-shaped bend in the river. Under the guidance of the war chief Menawa, they built fortifications on the land side of the town, enclosing it effectively against attack. Less than one-third of the Red Sticks had guns (although they did not reject the use of guns, they could not acquire any); most had clubs, knives, and bows and arrows. However, the Red Sticks did not fear the upcoming battle, for their religious leaders (or shamans) had assured them that they were protected by sacred forces and could not be harmed by their enemies' bullets.

As the Red Sticks prepared for war, about 1,500 Americans—commanded by ANDREW JACKSON and supported by 500 Cherokee and 100 pro-American Creek—marched to Tohopeka. On March 27, 1814, the Americans attacked. The Red Sticks withstood the siege for hours, despite the much larger force and superior arms of their attackers. However, the Americans charged the fortifications while their Cherokee allies crossed the river and assaulted the Red Sticks from the rear, which cut off their means of escape and broke their resistance.

Andrew Jackson promised that no quarter (mercy) would be given to the Red Sticks if they chose to fight. As a result, many of the rebel Creek were killed in the river while trying to escape. The Red Sticks suffered catastrophic losses, as 800 warriors died and 350 women and children were captured. Many of the surviving Red Sticks surrendered after the battle, while some fled to FLORIDA to join with the Seminole. Many of these rebel Creeks fought in the subsequent SEMINOLE WARS of 1818–19. However, the Battle of Horseshoe Bend effectively ended the Red Stick War and allowed for further American expansion into the southern United States.

Further reading: Joel W. Martin, *Sacred Revolt: The Muskogees' Struggle for a New World* (Boston: Beacon Press, 1991).

—Michael L. Cox

Houston, Sam (1793–1863)

Born in Virginia and later a congressman from Tennessee as well as a political protégé of ANDREW JACKSON, Sam Houston was most significant for his role in the early history of TEXAS. Immigrating to that territory in 1832, he became commander in chief of the army during the TEXAS

REVOLUTION and later first president of the Republic of Texas. After Texas was admitted to the Union as a state in 1845, he served as a U.S. senator and finally as governor.

Houston had minimal formal schooling in Virginia. His family moved to Tennessee when he was 13, and he grew up on the Tennessee frontier. During the WAR OF 1812, he served as a lieutenant in the army commanded by Major General Andrew Jackson, and he participated in Jackson's campaigns throughout the South. When the war ended, Houston returned to Tennessee, read law, and became a practicing attorney. It was a youth and adolescence similar to that of many ambitious young men on the early frontier of the trans-Appalachian West.

Like other energetic young men, Houston found himself drawn to politics. He was a friend and partisan of Andrew Jackson's at a time when Jackson was the most famous figure in the state. Houston was elected to the U.S. Congress in 1823, and four years later, he was elected governor of the state of Tennessee. In 1829 he married Eliza Allen. At this point, his successful personal and political career took another direction. For reasons that he never explained, but perhaps because his wife had left him, Houston resigned the governorship and took up residence in Indian Territory (now Oklahoma), where he became a member of the Cherokee nation, taking an Indian name, assuming the dress of that nation, and marrying a Cherokee woman. He lived among the Cherokee until 1832, when he and his Indian family moved to Texas.

Sam Houston *(Library of Congress)*

Texas was then a state called Coahuila-Texas in the Republic of Mexico. Nevertheless, its population was predominantly Anglo-American settlers recently arrived from the Mississippi Valley. These approximately 20,000 settlers had come to Texas under a system of contracted immigration, arranged by STEPHEN F. AUSTIN, another figure who would be indelibly associated with the formative years of the American occupation of Texas. Houston was a natural leader with important political connections with the government of the United States, and his arrival was widely noted. There were even suggestions that he had come as the personal representative of his friend, President Andrew Jackson, although this connection was never made directly.

Houston found Texas in a state of uneasy confusion. Many prominent Texans were agitating for a greater degree of autonomy—perhaps even independence preparatory to a future union with the United States. The officials of the Republic of Mexico in both Texas and Mexico City were aware of this interest and opposed to it. Austin, the most prominent figure in Texas, favored searching for a redress of grievance through official means, and he supported a continued connection with the Republic of Mexico. When the American settlements drafted a series of petitions to the government in Mexico City, Austin was the unanimous choice to make the case for the Anglo-Texans. Although he gained much of what the Texans sought, Austin was arrested and confined in Mexico City. During his two-year absence, others, including Houston, assumed positions of leadership in the Texas community.

Houston was among those who wanted greater independence for Texas, and this feeling was increasingly shared after the ascendancy to power of General ANTONIO LÓPEZ DE SANTA ANNA, who seemed to threaten the rights that Texans thought were guaranteed to them under the Mexican Constitution of 1824. As Santa Anna pursued a series of military campaigns to solidify his power, he eventually turned his attention to the north, where he saw Texas in what he considered a state of open rebellion. Divided Texan voices and poor military leadership led to military disasters at Goliad and at THE ALAMO, but these defeats only strengthened their resolve for independence. Houston was a delegate to the Convention of 1836, and he signed the Declaration of Independence drafted by that body. In March 1836 the delegates to the convention chose him as commander in chief of the Texas army. Given charge of a small and poorly trained body of men, he pursued an unpopular policy by retreating to the east and north toward the Louisiana border. Then, in a surprise move, he marshaled his forces to confront Santa Anna and the much larger Mexican army near the San Jacinto River, where Houston ordered a frontal assault. In 20 minutes the Texas army had won an overwhelming victory. The Mexican army lost 630 killed and an equal number taken prisoner; the Texan losses were a mere handful. Against all odds, Houston had saved Texas.

As the most popular figure in the republic, Houston easily defeated Austin for the presidency of the new Republic of Texas. The election showed that the immediacy of a military victory had easily overshadowed Austin's contributions in building Anglo-Texas over 15 years. As president of the republic, Houston pursued a cautious policy of engagement with the United States. The American government had backed away from immediate annexation, sensitive to diplomatic criticism of its conduct during the war. Texas's status had also become embroiled in the controversy over SLAVERY, since it was sure to make application to enter the Union as a slave state. In spite of these difficulties, Houston remained convinced that the destiny of Texas was inevitably bound to the United States.

Houston's policy of correct diplomatic engagement with the United States and European nations and even his attempts to come to terms with Mexico aroused political opposition within Texas itself. Furthermore, he was a strong personality who made no secret of his likes and dislikes. Mirabeau B. Lamar led the opposition, and he became Houston's political rival over the next decade. At the end of Houston's first term as president of the Republic of Texas (he could later serve a second, though nonconsecutive, term), Lamar was elected his successor. Lamar pursued a policy of expansion and confrontation with Mexico, with the Indian peoples of Texas, and eventually with the United States over Texan claims to the upper reaches of the Rio Grande. Most important, Lamar moved the capital from Houston to a frontier village soon renamed Austin; it was the most enduring of all his policies.

When Houston was elected governor again, he resumed his patient negotiations with the United States over annexation. With the election of JAMES K. POLK in November 1844, the American nation signaled its expansionist interest, and Texas was a logical object of it. Consequently, both houses of Congress approved a joint resolution for annexation in January 1845. Houston's policy of engagement with the United States had succeeded.

Upon the admission of Texas to the Union in 1845, Houston was elected a U.S. senator. Throughout the 1850s he walked a fine line in his allegiance, always the Texas patriot but often critical of rising southern nationalism. By the mid-1850s he had come to support the KNOW-NOTHING PARTY as an alternative to southern sectionalism. Increasingly, he showed a strong commitment to the preservation of the Union in the face of growing southern sentiment for secession.

Again elected governor of the state in 1859, Houston immediately expressed his opposition to the convention called in support of secession. When the convention met in early 1861, he refused to take an oath of loyalty to the newly formed Confederate States of America. The state legislature declined to impeach him, probably because of his many services to the republic and the state over 30 years. Instead, it simply declared the office of governor vacant, and his duties were assumed by the lieutenant governor. Houston retired to his home, where he declined to accept an offer of federal troops to support him and his stand. Houston firmly supported the Union, but he refused to engage in a policy that would pit Texan against Texan in a violent confrontation. Houston spent the rest of his life at his home, embittered by Texan secession and the loss of the governorship. He died in 1863.

Further reading: Llerena Friend, *Sam Houston: The Great Designer* (Austin: University of Texas Press, 1954); Marquis James, *The Raven: A Biography of Sam Houston* (New York: Blue Ribbon Books, 1929).

Hull, William (1759–1825)

Distinguished service marked the beginning of William Hull's military career, and a court-martial brought it to an end. Hull was born in Derby, Connecticut, on June 24, 1753. He attended Yale College, where he contemplated entering the ministry but later decided on a career in law. He practiced law in Litchfield, Connecticut, but even the legal profession did not hold Hull's attention. At the onset of the Revolutionary War (1775–83), he devoted himself to the military. Serving admirably in the Continental army, he was promoted to major in 1777 and lieutenant colonel in 1779. He also fought at the battles of Trenton (December 26, 1776) and Princeton (January 3, 1777). After the war, Hull practiced law in Massachusetts and married Sarah Fuller in 1781. In 1787 he assisted in putting down Shays's Rebellion (1786–87). Elected to the Massachusetts state senate in 1798, he openly sided with the Democratic-Republican Party. In 1805 President Thomas Jefferson appointed Hull governor of Michigan Territory, where he served for seven years. During his terms as governor, Hull successfully acquired land cessions from Indian nations in the territory, including the Chippewa, Ottawa, Potawatomi, Shawnee and Wyandot. Many Indian leaders, such as Tecumseh, disliked Hull for his dealings with NATIVE AMERICANS.

The WAR OF 1812 (1812–15) brought Hull back to the military when he reluctantly accepted a position as a general in the Old Northwest. President James Madison ordered him to invade upper Canada at the onset of the war, but the campaign foundered immediately. British general Sir Isaac Brock drove Hull's force of 2,000 soldiers back to Detroit, even though the American troops were larger in number. Meanwhile, the British and their Native

American allies (many of whom were injured by Hull's Indian policy as governor of Michigan Territory) cut off reinforcements. On August 16, 1812, fearing for the town's population, Hull surrendered Detroit to Brock and returned ignominiously to the United States to face a court-martial. The court found him guilty of cowardice, neglect of duty, and misconduct as an officer, and sentenced him to death for the Detroit debacle. However, President Madison pardoned Hull from the death penalty because of his service during the Revolutionary War and his advanced age. Hull's nephew, Commodore Isaac Hull, restored the family name with his naval performance during the War of 1812.

Hull spent the rest of his life acquitting himself. He wrote two books—*Defense of Brig. Gen. Wm. Hull* (1814) and *Memoirs of the Campaign of the Northwestern Army of the United States: A.D. 1812* (1824)—which sought to explain his actions at Detroit. He died in Newton, Massachusetts on November 29, 1825.

Further reading: Maria Campbell, *Revolutionary Service and Civil Life of General William Hull* (New York: D. Appleton; Philadelphia: G.S. Appleton, 1848); Donald R. Hickey, *The War of 1812: A Forgotten Conflict* (Urbana: University of Illinois Press, 1989).

—William J. Bauer, Jr.

I

immigration

In the first great wave of 19th-century immigration, about 5 million people entered the United States between 1820 and 1860. Nearly 1.6 million were natives of Ireland, and 1.5 million more were from Germany. During the 1820s, the Irish and Germans accounted for more than 40 percent of immigrants; in the 1830s, they accounted for approximately 60 percent; and in the 1840s and 1850s, they made up more than 70 percent of immigrants. English immigrants accounted for 15 percent or less of the total. Small numbers of Scandinavian and Canadian immigrants also entered the United States during the time. Approximately 80,000 Mexicans became U.S. residents during the mid-19th century, but not through immigration. Instead, they gained the rights of American citizens following the American absorption of TEXAS and much of the American Southwest (comprising modern-day CALIFORNIA, Nevada, Utah, and parts of New Mexico, Arizona, Wyoming, and Colorado) following the MEXICAN-AMERICAN WAR (1846–48). These lands were ceded in the 1848 TREATY OF GUADALUPE HIDALGO between the United States and Mexico. Also in the late 1840s, some 25,000 Chinese immigrants arrived during the CALIFORNIA GOLD RUSH and established residence.

Necessity and opportunity were the primary driving forces for immigration. From the 1830s, declining economic conditions led Irish farmers to emigrate to the United States. During the mid-1840s, the numbers of immigrants increased sharply after potato blights destroyed Ireland's primary source of food and commerce. Compounding the problem was the treatment of farmers by the landowners. Although dairy products and other foodstuffs were raised successfully in Ireland, they were used mainly for export to England. This left tenant farmers dependent on potatoes, and when those rotted from blight, many starved. One million of Ireland's 8 million inhabitants died of hunger and other related conditions during this time. One quarter of those remaining eventually immigrated to the United States, in what became known as the Great Migration.

For Germans, economic necessity and failed revolutionary movements in 1830 and 1848 led them to migrate to North America. So many thousands came to the U.S. after the failures of the 1848 European revolutions that they were known as Forty-Eighters. As they had been for decades, peasants and artisans were also solicited by U.S. labor agents, who offered work in a rapidly industrializing country. Agents further enticed potential immigrants with the chance to own inexpensive land in the West. For many European Jews, the United States also offered a chance to escape religious discrimination.

Other Europeans became immigrants for economic reasons. Certain factors were common to all these groups; industrialization and commercial agriculture played important roles. As the large-scale practices of commercial agriculture increased during the early 19th century, small farmers throughout Europe were unable to support themselves. Similarly, the low-cost, factory-made products that industrialization brought to the market ended the livelihood of many European craftsmen. A further stimulus to migrate to the United States was the low cost of steamboat transportation, which made the transoceanic trip possible.

One characteristic of migration was its growth as the 19th century progressed. During the 1820s, 152,000 immigrants entered the United States, which had a population in 1820 of 9.6 million. The 1830 population was 12.9 million, and in the decade that followed, 599,000 immigrants entered the country. The population in 1840 was 17 million; 1,713,000 immigrants entered during the next 10 years. By 1850, the population was 23.2 million; that decade saw the entry of 2,598,000 immigrants. In the 1820s, slightly more than one of every 1,000 U.S. residents was a new immigrant; in the 1850s, it was more than nine of every 1,000. Immigrant Irish brought New York City unprecedented increases in numbers, accounting for 343,000 of the city's 1850 population of 515,547. Overall,

This engraving shows Irish emigrants getting ready to leave famine-stricken Ireland for the United States. *(Library of Congress)*

the millions of immigrants and a fertile young populace combined to make the United States grow more quickly than any other nation during the 19th century, increasing from 5 million to about 31 million between 1800 and 1860.

The boat voyage that brought immigrants to North America was lengthy and hazardous, usually taking place aboard a steamer (known to Irish immigrants as a "coffin ship") that was overcrowded and invited disease. In 1832, Irish immigrants carried cholera aboard ship to Canada and through to New York, resulting in hundreds of deaths. Most of these and other Irish immigrants were young (under 35 years old) and without money, traveling in small groups or alone. Other family members came when the new immigrant was able to raise funds. In contrast, most German immigrants traveled as families, and, at least with the early groups, had more money. From 1849, most European immigrants entering New York passed through a receiving station called Castle Garden, in lower Manhattan.

Immigrants from all countries adopted various methods to adjust to an unfamiliar land. From friends and relatives, they learned about the country and of relatively hospitable regions. Although both Irish and German groups settled in northeastern coastal cities, including Boston, New York, Philadelphia, and Baltimore, some settlers moved into the nation's midsection to work on canals, railroads, and roads. Eventually, many German immigrants settled widely across the United States, establishing farms and homes in the Ohio Valley, along the Mississippi River to Missouri, within the Great Lakes region in Wisconsin and Minnesota, and in Texas. To some of these more sparsely populated regions of what is now the upper Midwest, Irish and German immigrants arrived in such great numbers during the 1850s that the region's population grew from 5,000 to just under 150,000. This was but a portion of the record number of more than 950,000 Germans who migrated to the United States during the 1850s. So great and varied was German settlement that its well-populated states formed a continuous line from New York to Minnesota known as the "German Belt." Only one in eight of all new immigrants entered the cotton-dominated South.

Once arrived, new immigrants turned to formal and informal ethnic networks that provided information and leads for housing and jobs. Although most colonial-era Irish and German immigrants were Protestants, those arriving during the 19th century were largely Roman Catholics who looked to the church for social support. Ethnic newspapers and social clubs, particularly those for German immigrants, also provided community support.

Types of work and working conditions varied among these immigrants. Although there were some skilled craftsmen, professionally trained people, and intellectuals in the immigrant mix who became artists, journalists, shopkeepers, and political leaders, most immigrants were former farmers and manual laborers. This was particularly true among Irish immigrants. Along the eastern coastal cities, laborers found work (much of it day labor) in construction sites, factories, canals, railroads, or textile mills. Given their need for labor, textile mills were favored sites of employment for Irish immigrant families, since they provided ready sources of work for entire families that needed money. Female Irish immigrants, however, were often subjected to faster work paces and lower pay rates than their native-born counterparts. Some Irish immigrant women were also employed at home doing piecework or as domestic servants. As one journalist wrote in 1860, "There are several sorts of power working at the fabric of this Republic: water-power, steam-power, horse-power, Irish-power. The last works hardest of all." German immigrants were more likely to work in light industry or crafts work, which utilized their earlier training as artisans. Other immigrants of the era from England, Canada, or elsewhere were less likely to take jobs as domestic servants or day laborers. Instead, they worked as farmers, in construction, or in higher-level machinery work.

Over time, immigrant groups also developed various social and cultural specialties that allowed them to enrich and be integrated into the American way of life. German immigrants became known for their ability to provide various types of entertainment, which spanned the popular venues of dance halls and beer gardens to choral and classical music. For example, in 1835 German immigrants founded the first U.S. vocal music society, the *Maennerchor* (Men's Choir); in later decades, they led in the formation of musical societies in other cities. German immigrants were also central to bringing classical music to the United States; in 1855, an early conductor of the New York Philharmonic Symphony Orchestra was German immigrant Carl Bergmann.

Many Irish immigrants developed a political expertise that won them local and statewide positions. (President ANDREW JACKSON was the son of Irish immigrants who arrived before the Great Migration.) They were able to establish voting blocs and infiltrate traditionally English and old-immigrant neighborhoods.

From the 1830s through the 1850s, the influx of 2.2 million immigrants, many of them destitute and Roman Catholic in an overwhelmingly Protestant nation, roused deep anti-immigrant sentiment in the United States. Most earlier Irish immigrants were Protestants from northern Ireland and thus easily accepted into American society. Newly arrived German Roman Catholic immigrants held beliefs that were more agreeable with prevailing northern thinking, such as participation in public schools. Pro-Union, in later years they were instrumental in the presidential victory of Abraham Lincoln. Additionally, when they arrived in the United States, German immigrants often had more money than their Irish counterparts and possessed greater training for skilled work.

These anti-immigrant attitudes, which represented the first large-scale nativist movement in U.S. history, were manifested in many ways. Newspaper postings for work and housing often included the catchphrase "Nina"—"No Irish Need Apply." Beginning in the 1830s, periodicals featured warnings of "popish" plots for the Catholic appropriation of the nation. One notable anti-Catholic spokesman was SAMUEL F. B. MORSE. Now best known for his invention of the telegraph, he was famous then for his 1834 series of letters, *A Foreign Conspiracy Against the Liberties of the United States.*

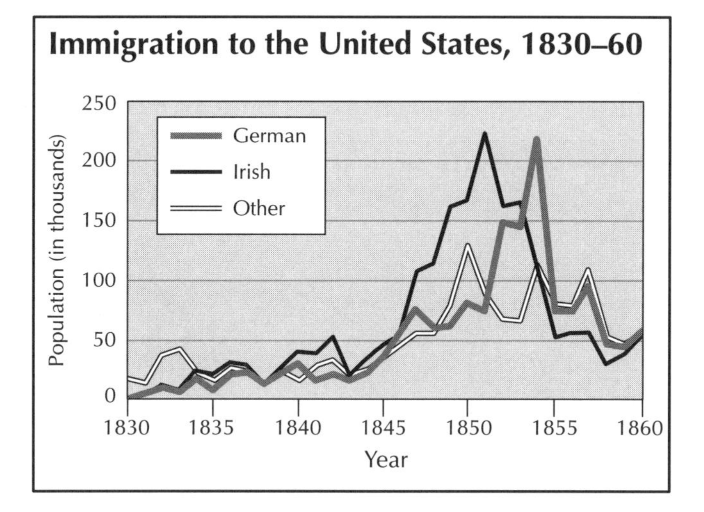

Violent demonstrations of anti-Catholic opinion occurred throughout the period of the Great Migration, usually in cities with large immigrant populations. One prolonged argument centered on the ongoing Irish objection to using the Protestant King James Bible in public schools and one school board's response to it. In 1844 the Philadelphia school system exempted Catholics from using Protestant-leaning textbooks and permitted the use of the Catholic Douay version of the Bible. In response, Protestant and Catholic rallies and demonstrations erupted and resulted in two riots, ending in 30 deaths, 150 injuries, and the destruction of two Catholic churches. It was the most violent religious confrontation in the United States to date. In the 1850s ANTI-CATHOLIC RIOTS occurred in Boston and elsewhere.

Anti-immigrant forces also attempted to control immigration and immigrants' rights through political means, forming various political parties to promote their goals. In 1837 the Native American Association was founded to counter nonnative groups, particularly Catholics; its formal political party, the Native America Party, was founded in 1845. Also organized to curtail immigrant rights was the American Republican Party, founded in 1843. Its goal was to prevent immigrants from holding elected office. Most influential nationally was the American Party, more commonly known as the KNOW-NOTHING PARTY. Founded in mid-century as memories of the bloody 1844 Philadelphia riots faded, the Know-Nothing Party aimed to bar immigrants and any Catholic from public office. Affiliated with this party was MILLARD FILLMORE, who became president following the death of ZACHARY TAYLOR in 1850.

In the West during the gold rush, Chinese immigrants faced what would in later decades become escalating discrimination. As prospectors, they were granted access only to gold claims already examined by white prospectors.

Nativist movements and focus on anti-immigration diminished at the end of the 1850s as conflicts escalated between the North and the South. Immigrants were needed to defend the Union; thousands did, serving in many Irish- and German-immigrant divisions. Their participation in the Union army during the Civil War was important to the Northern triumph. Among notable Irish commanders were General Philip Sheridan and immigrant General Thomas Francis Meagher, leader of a Union Irish brigade. German immigrant Civil War generals included Carl Schurz, who later worked for President Lincoln. Such soldiers helped to contribute to the assimilation of all 19th-century immigrants into the United States.

Despite adversity, immigrants who arrived between 1820 and 1860 would be the last group to have relative freedom from immigration laws. The second wave of immigrants, who would arrive between 1880 and 1920, would face more stringent legislation, beginning with an 1862 law prohibiting American ships from bringing Chinese immigrants to the United States. Such legal measures would increase in scope throughout the century. Still, the immigration surge that began in the early 19th century continued to grow until World War I, seeing its largest number of arrivals—20 million—during the highly regulated period of 1880 to 1920.

Further reading: Louis Adamic, *A Nation of Nations* (New York and London: Harper Brothers Publishers, 1945); American Social History Project, *Who Built America: Working People and the Nation's Economy, Politics, Culture, and Society*, Vol. 1 (New York: Pantheon Books, 1989–92); Stephen A. Flanders, *Atlas of American Migration* (New York: Facts On File, Inc., 1998).

—Melinda Corey

Indian Affairs, Bureau of

The Bureau of Indian Affairs (BIA) is the office of the federal government responsible for many aspects of NATIVE AMERICAN life. Among the several different activities within its jurisdiction in the 20th century are EDUCATION, employment, police, welfare, AGRICULTURE, and industrial development. Because of the BIA's enormous influence over Indian affairs, from the beginning it has been the source of great controversy among Native Americans and white Americans over its duties and their execution.

The BIA has a long history that is deeply enmeshed in the thorny relationship between the United States's majority population and its Indian minority. After the U.S. Constitution was written and ratified, the new government organized in 1789 gave the War Department responsibility for overseeing all relations with native peoples. This structure reflected the view that Indian peoples were a military issue, and so they were to be dealt with by the military arm of the government. Given the continuing confrontations between settlers and Native Americans in the 1780s and early 1790s, this position was understandable.

In 1806 a separate Office of Indian Trade was organized, again under the aegis of the War Department, to manage the factory system, an attempt to regulate trade with Indian peoples in a fairer and more honest manner than that pursued by private fur-trading companies. Although the factory system was a success in fostering better relations with Indian peoples, it was constantly under attack by fur-trading interests as unfair competition, and Congress abolished the system in 1822. Two years later, Secretary of War JOHN C. CALHOUN established a Bureau of Indian Affairs within the War Department, appointing Thomas L. McKenney its first chief. McKenney had been superintendent of Indian trade from 1816 to 1822. His duties, as defined by Congress, were to supervise the financial arrangements that arose out of "laws regulating intercourse with the Indian tribes." In his reports, McKenney called the agency the "Office of Indian Affairs." (The name remained in use until 1947, when "Bureau of Indian Affairs" again came into use.) In some ways, McKenney was more a financial officer than one concerned with policy. But as in so many cases having to do with the federal government, especially in the 19th century, financial issues became closely associated with issues of policy.

In 1830, when Congress passed and President ANDREW JACKSON signed the INDIAN REMOVAL ACT, it became clear that removal was to become the government's favored solution to the Indian presence east of the Mississippi River. Partly in response to this new direction, Jackson replaced McKenney, although the latter had strongly supported the Removal Act in 1832. Congress then established the bureau-level Office of Indian Affairs, headed by a commissioner appointed by the president and confirmed by Congress. The office was still an agency of the War Department, and the new commissioner reported to the secretary of war. The commissioner was charged with the "direction and management of all Indian affairs and all matters arising out of Indian relations." Two years later, another law provided for the reorganization of the Department of Indian Affairs, establishing several new agencies and superintendencies.

The Office of Indian Affairs was responsible for conducting removal negotiations as well as for oversight of existing treaties. In cooperation with the U.S. Army, the Office directed the removal of the remaining nations east of the Mississippi to new reservations in Indian Territory (later the state of Oklahoma). This process was accomplished through a series of treaties of questionable legality and legitimacy, and, where necessary, through the use of force. The most noteworthy example of enforced removal and its disastrous results was the roundup of the remaining Cherokee in Georgia in autumn 1838, and their enforced removal during the winter of 1838–39 on a march known as the TRAIL OF TEARS.

With the removal of Indians east of the Mississippi to the West, debate began anew over whether the management of Native American affairs properly lay within the War Department. In 1849, the Office of Indian Affairs was transferred to the newly created Department of the Interior. By this time, the bulk of its responsibilities had to do with the administration of the Indian Territory reservations as well as the other reservations scattered throughout the nation. The office has frequently been accused of fostering government dependency among native peoples during this period by arbitrarily depriving them of their traditional lifeways, social structures, and even their own names. Certainly, there have been many examples of unscrupulous government agents. Some agents were known to withhold food rations from recalcitrant individuals; others cheated nations out of funds that the government had held in trust. Such experiences spurred feelings of bitterness and distrust on the part of Native Americans toward the government.

The agency's name was changed to the Bureau of Indian Affairs in 1947, although its mission and its place within the Department of the Interior remained the same. Today, the BIA attempts to work in concert with tribal governments to establish health, education, and economic development programs to benefit native groups.

Further reading: National Archives and Records Administration, "Records of the Bureau of Indian Affairs." URL: http://www.nara.gov/guide/rg075.html. Downloaded 2001; Francis Paul Prucha, *The Great Father: The United States Government and the American Indians,* 2 vols. (Lincoln: University of Nebraska Press, 1984); James Wilson, *The Earth Shall Weep* (New York: Atlantic Monthly Press, 1999).

—Mary Kay Linge

Indian Removal Act

The Indian Removal Act was passed by Congress on May 28, 1830. Most commonly associated with the removal of the Choctaw, Chickasaw, Cherokee, Creek and Seminole nations from the American Southeast, the act authorized the president of the United States to facilitate the exchange of NATIVE AMERICAN lands anywhere in the East for lands west of the Mississippi River. Passed because of pressure from whites, the act marked the beginning of vigorous era of government-sponsored removal. For American Indian nations, the policy would exact a tremendous material, spiritual, and human cost.

Pressure for the government to institute a national removal policy came from several sectors of American society. Proponents of such a policy shared two main concerns. The first was that the United States had a compelling need to expand westward. The second was a fear of Indian attack as such expansion took place.

At the turn of the century, the United States had yet to significantly expand its territory. The fur trade provided the most important contact between white settlers and American Indians across the Midwest. The government had long hoped to open the Ohio Valley up to settlement, believing it would provide the means to settle war debts. The region was rich with timber, while its waterways offered the makings of a transportation network and source of mechanical power. In the Southeast, American Indian communities controlled a significant part of Georgia and most of present-day Florida, Mississippi, and Alabama. To white Americans, this region's fertile soil held the prospect of expanded cotton production, a lucrative enterprise thanks to improvements in spinning technology in industrial

Britain. This and the increase of the American population pressured the government to smooth the way for expansion into the West.

American designs on Indian lands were compounded by cultural prejudice. Few Americans believed that American Indians made productive or sensible use of their land. Many observers, journalists, and politicians argued that Native American groups relied on hunting, an enterprise that ought to give way to settled agriculture under the principles of natural law. Confusion over appropriate gender roles lay at the root of much of this belief. To white Americans, a society was best judged by the actions of men. Observers therefore viewed the business of hunting, diplomacy, warfare, or limited participation in AGRICULTURE as a male prerogative. In most American Indian communities, farming was a female activity, a fact that many observers argued showed the laziness of Indian men and the backwardness of Native American culture. In real-

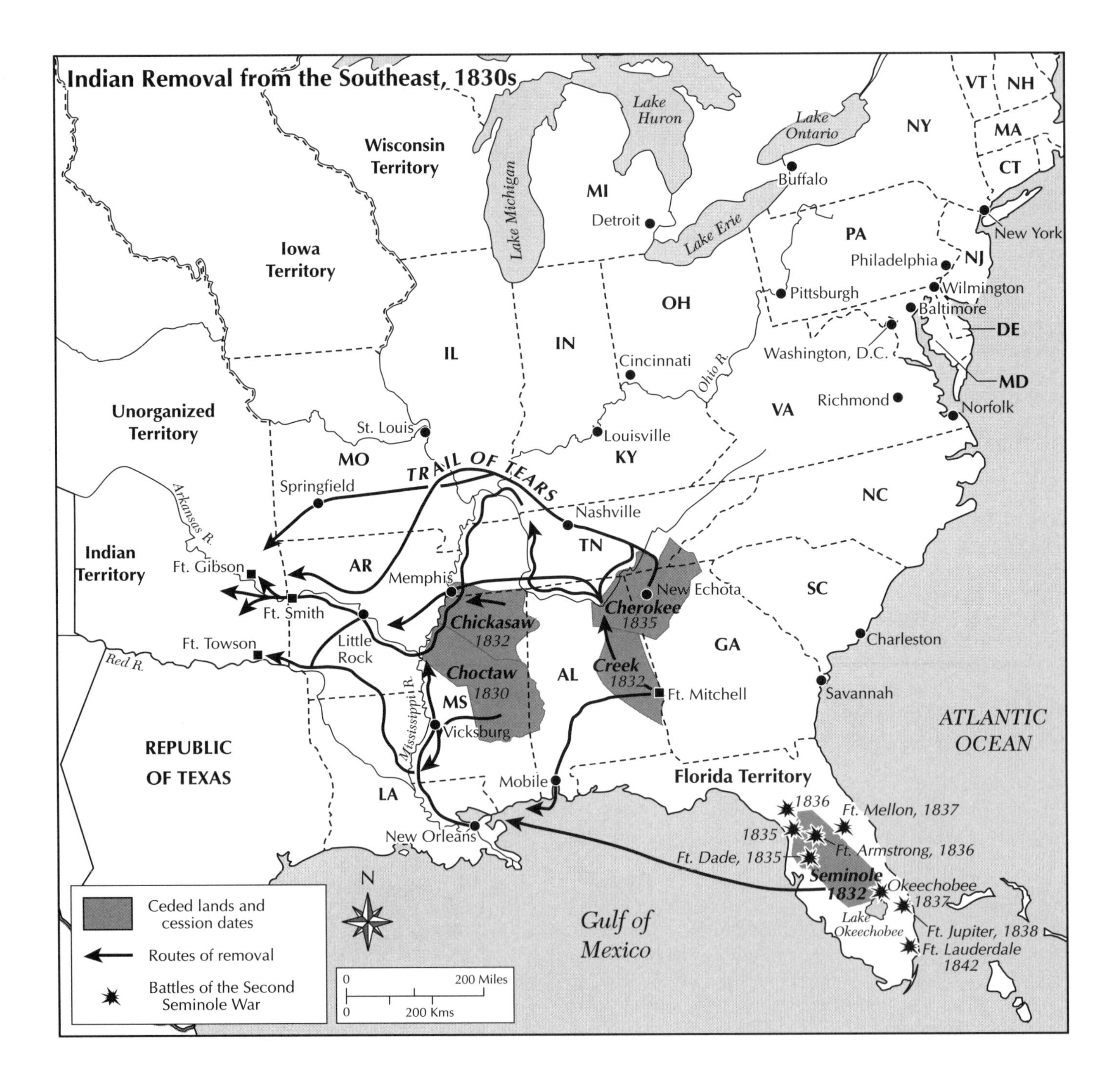

ity, many American Indian communities across the Southeast thrived on the intensive agriculture they practiced. Men and women had their own particular responsibilities which contributed to the health of the nation, and even those native groups who relied on hunting and gathering engaged in the careful and purposeful cultivation of wild food sources.

While most Americans shared the idea that Indian communities were a 'problem' for the expanding nation, not all agreed that removal was an appropriate response. A reform movement flourished in the first three decades of the 19th century, arguing that through education and religious instruction, Native American communities could be remade in the image of the U.S. ideal. Religious groups such as the Quakers, Moravians, and the American Board of Commissioners for Foreign Missions made heavy investments of time and money to this end.

Many Americans believed, however, that Native American groups were fundamentally hostile. In 1800, peace in the Ohio Valley was only five years old. After the Revolutionary War, a series of fraudulent treaties were imposed upon the Iroquois and their allies, who had battled to protect their lands. In the South, the Creek and Cherokee had engaged in similar conflicts. Skirmishes between American settlers and American Indian nations continued through the early 19th century, becoming particularly fierce during the WAR OF 1812. The result was that a generation of Americans, living at the boundaries of the existing United States, remembered war with Indian nations from personal experience. They demanded protection from the threat they perceived.

The fusion of these considerations resulted in pressure for Indian removal. ANDREW JACKSON was the president who put the policy into effect. A renowned Indian fighter who had personally negotiated treaties between the government and the nations of the American Southeast, Jackson was in favor of removal for economic and military reasons. A shrewd politician, Jackson used the rhetoric of reform to further justify his ideas during his presidential campaign. Native American communities must be moved out of the way of white settlement, he argued, in order to give them a real chance to adapt to western ways of life.

While Jackson supported removal, it was events in Georgia that forced him to act on his beliefs. Many of the southeastern nations had made cultural adaptations over the course of the early 19th century, in an effort to nullify criticism of their lifestyles and forestall attempts to remove them. While adaptations took place among each southeastern nation, it was the Cherokee who made the most widespread changes. Indigo, tobacco, and cotton were grown as cash crops, while prominent families built large, plantation-style homes and kept slaves. By 1817, the Cherokee had their own legislature, judicial system, and chief executive, and a written constitution was passed in 1827. Education was readily available at a number of schools, and in 1821 a Cherokee syllabary (vocabulary) was adopted. The Bible was at least partially available in Cherokee by 1824, and by 1828 the nation was publishing a bilingual newspaper, *The Cherokee Phoenix.*

Rather than assuage the concerns of white Americans in the region, however, these changes convinced them that the Cherokee would never give up their lands of their own free will. In order to force the issue, proponents of Cherokee removal pointed to splits in the nation between those who had made cultural adaptations to the world around them and those who had not. The latter suffered grave poverty and alcoholism, and Georgian citizens argued that it was imperative that all Cherokees be removed for their own survival.

The passing of the Cherokee constitution infuriated Georgia's legislators. Claiming that it was unconstitutional for a state to exist within a state, Georgia extended jurisdiction over the Cherokee nation on December 20, 1828. The state gave notice that it would refuse to recognize Cherokee laws or law enforcement and would make Cherokees citizens liable for taxation. These changes would go into effect on June 1, 1830. Newly elected as president of the United States, Andrew Jackson had until that date to resolve the conflict between the two groups.

Jackson's solution was to press forward with removal. In his first State of the Union address, the president committed himself to the policy of moving Indians to the West and urged Congress to act on the matter with haste. By February 24, 1830, the removal bill was out of committee and the subject of bitter debate in Congress. Despite eloquent arguments made in favor of leaving American Indian communities alone, the bill passed the Senate 28-19 on April 23, 1830, and passed the House 102-97 on May 24. Jackson signed the bill into law that same day.

The Removal Act was used to displace Native American communities across the United States, often by force. The experience of the southeastern tribes was particularly harrowing. Despite appealing their case to the Supreme Court and insisting that the government treat them fairly, the nations were ultimately divested of their lands. Forced to travel to present-day Oklahoma without adequate notice, clothing, food, or transportation, thousands of Indian men, women and children died. The removal process became known as the TRAIL OF TEARS.

Further reading: Theda Perdue and Michael D. Green, *The Cherokee Removal: A Brief History with Documents* (Boston: Bedford Books, 1995); Anthony F. C. Wallace, *The Long Bitter Trail: Andrew Jackson and the Indians* (New York: Hill and Wang, 1993).

—Catherine J. Denial

industrialization

Industrialization is the process by which an agricultural society is transformed into one based primarily on large-scale, mechanized factory production. It first occurred in Great Britain in the Industrial Revolution starting in the mid-18th century, and began to spread to the United States in the early 19th century, though a full-scale industrial revolution did not take place there until after the American Civil War (1861–65).

Industrialization in America first took root in New England. The WAR OF 1812 stimulated manufacturing in New England by encouraging reliance on domestic industries rather than those of the British enemy. But just as important was the ingenuity of enterprising textile manufacturers. Britain prohibited export of its profitable textile machinery, but British-born Samuel Slater memorized blueprints and brought them to America, where he and partner Moses Brown built the country's first mechanized cotton-spinning mill, or factory, in Rhode Island in 1790. Soon several mills owned by their firm, Almy, Brown, & Slater, were churning out mass quantities of cotton yarn. As is characteristic of industrial facilities, Slater's mills achieved efficient, inexpensive mass production of goods by using machines worked by large numbers of employees.

In 1814 Francis Cabot Lowell, a Boston merchant, developed the first American power loom, an improved version of English prototypes. With partners, he founded the Boston Manufacturing Company in 1813, the first mill or factory in America to handle all the operations involved in turning raw cotton into finished cloth. After his death in 1817, his partners gave his name to Lowell, Massachusetts, a textile manufacturing center incorporated as a city in 1836.

Through operations such as Slater's and Lowell's, the factory system for cotton spinning and weaving became established. It depended on raw cotton from the South, a product that had itself been affected by mechanization: The cotton gin, invented by Eli Whitney in 1793 to separate seeds from fibers, had greatly increased the profitability of cotton farming and made it the basis of the southern economy. By the presidency of JAMES MONROE (1817–25), manufacturing was overtaking shipping as the primary interest in New England and Pennsylvania. By 1840 about 2.25 million spindles were in use in 1,200 cotton cloth factories, two-thirds of them in New England. Woolen manufacturing also advanced during this period, though at a slower pace. By 1850 more than 1,500 wool factories at places like Lawrence, Massachusetts, were producing flannel and blankets.

In addition to textile plants, numerous other kinds of factories sprang up in antebellum America. Near New Haven, Connecticut, Eli Whitney developed a system of interchangeable, standardized parts to mass-produce guns for the U.S. government. The system worked well enough to be widely copied, and Whitney applied it to making clocks. In Delaware, Oliver Evans founded a grist mill that mechanized the entire process from grinding to packing. In North Salem, New York, in 1835, the Howe Company began mass-producing straight pins at the rate of 50 a minute. In Philadelphia, Stuart & Company manufactured hollow ironware while the Disston Company made saws. SAMUEL COLT perfected Whitney's techniques for mass-producing guns in his arms plant at Hartford, Connecticut, where, beginning in 1848, he turned out six-shooters (pistols with six revolving chambers). Other thriving industries in this period included gunpowder, associated with manufacturer Eleuthère Irénée Du Pont; soap and candles, linked with such entrepreneurs as William Colgate and the partnership of William Procter and James Gamble; and rubber, which flourished after Charles Goodyear discovered in 1839 how to vulcanize rubber to keep it elastic in all weathers.

As a result of all this activity, from 1819 to 1849 private production income from manufacturing grew from $64 million to $291 million. In 1850, more than $1 billion worth of manufactured goods were produced in America. In the late 1830s the United States began to export more goods than it imported, a characteristic shift in nations undergoing industrialization. However, manufactured goods remained a relatively small percentage of sales to other countries, accounting for only 12 percent of exports as late as 1860.

Manufacturing in America at this stage was mainly powered by water. The domestic coal industry, essential to steam power, was still developing, as were the iron and steel industries. By 1850 Americans were still importing almost twice as much iron and steel as they were manufacturing at home. But iron production had begun to move out of small blacksmith shops to industrial forges and mills. From 1810 to 1850 the annual output of pig iron increased from 50,000 to 600,000 gross tons. Peter Cooper was among the entrepreneurs who shaped the American iron industry in this period.

In many cases, industrialization was helped by government support. For example, at the urging of textile magnate Francis Cabot Lowell, the tariff law of 1816 imposed duties on imported cotton cloth, aiding the domestic textile industry. Local, state, and federal governments directly or indirectly financed many enterprises through such means as tax exemptions and special franchise and monopoly privileges. Increasingly liberal state laws made it easier for enterprises to obtain financing from banks and to be organized as corporations that could sell stocks and bonds to raise money.

From 1820 to 1840 capital funds invested in the nation's factories increased fivefold, from $50 million to $250 million. Much of the capital came from overseas: Up to 1839, the British had invested more than $170 million in American businesses. The relatively unrestricted flow of capital spurred industrial growth but also contributed to financial instability and devastating panics, or depressions, when confidence in the economy fell, notably the PANIC OF 1819 and PANIC OF 1837.

For industrialization to increase its pace, it was vital to have faster ways to get finished goods to far-flung markets and to get food, supplies, and raw materials to industrial centers. Steamboats, canals, and RAILROADS provided solutions. In 1807 American engineer Robert Fulton launched the first commercially viable steamboat, the *Clermont,* and this mode of transportation was improved and adapted throughout the antebellum years. In 1815 regular steamboat service began on the Mississippi River. However, rivers and lakes did not connect every market or production center, so a spate of canal-building began. From 1817 to 1825 the ERIE CANAL was constructed, spanning 365 miles from Albany to Buffalo, linking the Hudson River and the Great Lakes. By 1840 there were over 3,000 miles of canals in the United States. (See CANAL ERA.)

Horse-drawn railways went into operation, such as the Granite Railway in Massachusetts between Quincy and the Neponset River, opened in 1826. But these were only a precursor to the steam locomotive, which was soon everywhere. Industrialist Peter Cooper introduced the first U.S.-built locomotive, the *Tom Thumb,* in 1830, the same year that the BALTIMORE & OHIO RAILROAD (B&O), based in Baltimore, began using steam locomotives for rail service. Other railroads followed quickly, linking cities along the eastern seaboard to each other and the West. The Pennsylvania Railroad was chartered in 1846; the Pacific Railroad Company, the first railroad west of the Mississippi, was begun in 1849; and the New York Central Railroad was started in 1853. By 1850 there were more than 9,000 miles of railroad track; by 1860, about 30,000 miles. Railroad manufacturing itself became an important industry, as factories were established to build locomotives, car parts, and track. The telegraph, demonstrated by SAMUEL F. B. MORSE in 1844, became important in scheduling and dispatching trains, as well as in facilitating other kinds of business communications.

Improved transportation was useful not only for shipping goods, but for moving people. By steamboat or train, as well as by older modes of transport, rural residents and new immigrants migrated to urban centers to take up jobs in factories. During the 1840s alone, towns and cities of 8,000 or more people grew by 90 percent, a much faster rate than the U.S. population as a whole, 36 percent. Between 1820 and 1850 the combined population of Baltimore, Boston, Philadelphia, and New York more than tripled to 1.2 million. The state of transportation was such that daily commutes over long distances were still difficult

Showing the power looms of textile manufacture, this label was the early trademark of the Merrimack Manufacturing Company. *(Museum of American Textile History)*

to manage, so company towns, built to house workers, sprang up around mills.

Farm mechanization freed laborers for factory work while also ensuring enough food for the growing cities. In 1831 CYRUS HALL MCCORMICK invented a mechanical, horse-drawn reaper that dramatically improved the efficiency of harvesting. In 1838 JOHN DEERE began manufacturing steel plows, which was an improvement over iron plows and initiated a new industrial empire, that of Deere agricultural equipment.

As is usual with nations undergoing industrialization, the economy grew and per capita income rose, but it did not do so equally. It is estimated that the share of wealth owned by the top 1 percent of Americans grew from 13 percent in 1774 to 29 percent in 1860. In Boston from 1833 to 1848 alone, the share of wealth held by the top 10 percent grew from 75 percent to 82 percent, while the share owned by the bottom 80 percent fell from 14 percent to 4 percent.

Industrialization lowered prices for many goods, making them more available to the middle and lower classes and so improving their standard of living. Wages were relatively high at first, especially for skilled mechanics who understood or could learn how to repair and build machines. American factories attracted immigrants by paying wages that were a third to a half higher than were available in Europe. But as more workers became available, wages fell. Men in general earned more than women or children: Men in Massachusetts earned $5 a week, women $1.75–$2.50, and children $1–$2.

Working conditions were often hard. Factory workers typically toiled from dusk to dawn for 11–13½ hours a day. The Lowell Mills, under the influence of British socialist Robert Owen, offered a neat, educational, chaperoned environment for the young women who worked there as

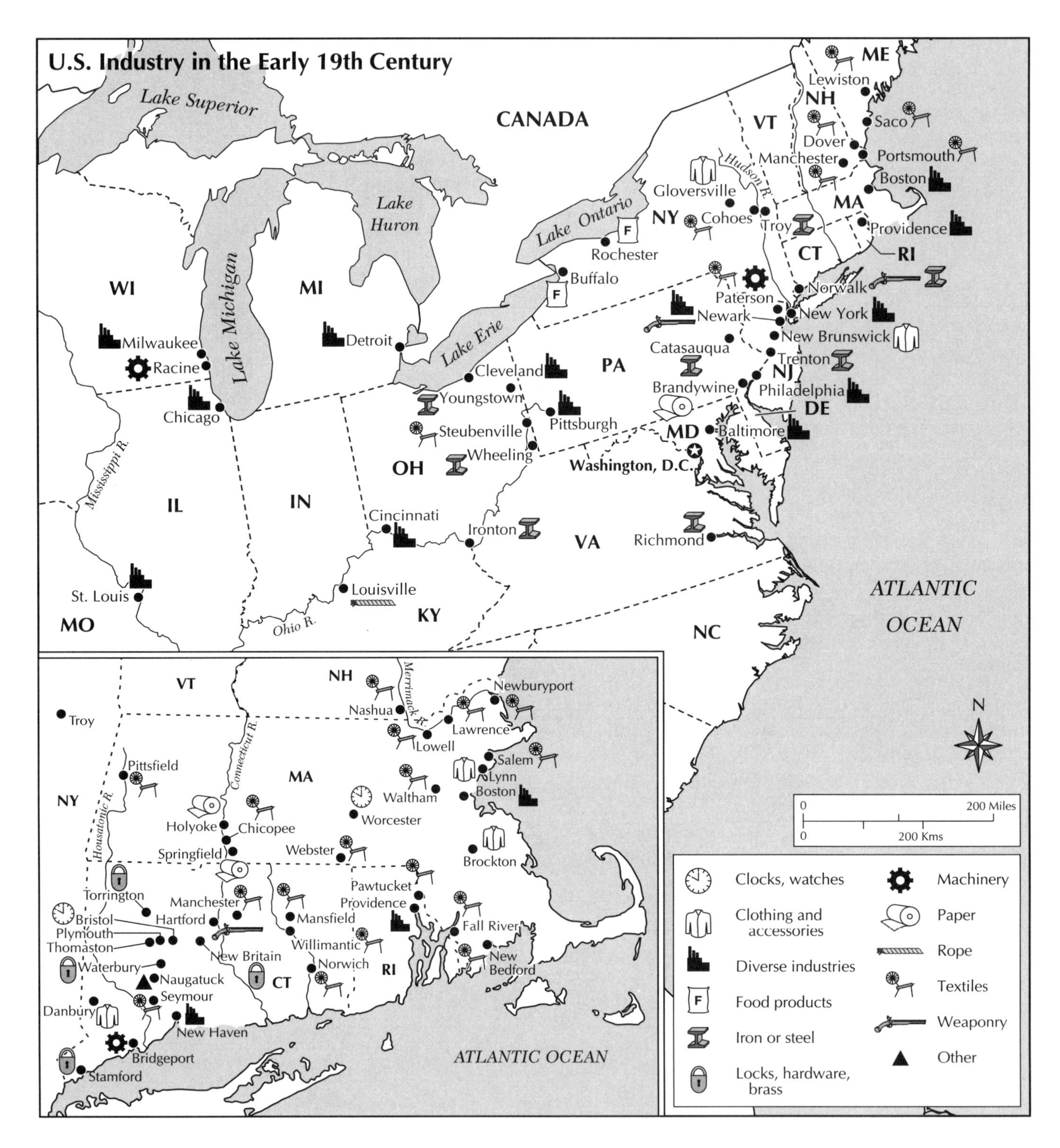

"factory girls." But working conditions in other factories were not so attractive. In the company towns of New York and Pennsylvania, workers had to buy what they needed at company-owned stores, frequently going into long-lasting debt to their employers.

The factory system was rapidly making domestic craft labor obsolete. Before industrialization, most manufactured products had come out of the homes and workshops of skilled artisans. Cloth manufacturing, for example, had been done at home, in domestic weaving operations where the worker owned her own tools. Increasingly, domestic enterprises were replaced: by 1840, more goods were manufactured in mills than in homes and workshops. However, in many businesses, such as boot- and shoe-making, skilled craftsmanship and domestic manufacturing remained the norm until after the Civil War.

Even as workers carried the burden of industrialization, capitalist entrepreneurs prospered. Whereas wealth before the 19th century had been primarily measured by land ownership, industrialists such as Lowell, Cooper, Du Pont, Colt, and Colgate made fortunes. By the 1840s, the phrases "millionaire" and "labor union" had both entered the American lexicon, an indication of the development of new social classes and of the growing struggle between them. In the 1830s, textile and craft workers organized to demand a 10-hour day. From 1834 to 1837, union membership grew from 26,000 to hundreds of thousands.

The benefits of manufacturing were distributed unequally by region as well as class. The North was far more heavily industrialized than the South, particularly in the Northeast, site of the first textile factories in New England; and in the Midwest, where Cincinnati, Chicago, and St. Louis became industrial centers by the 1850s, providing manufactured goods for settlers. In the South, however, the heavily agricultural economy was centered on cotton farming, with slaves picking cotton to be shipped north to be spun and woven into textiles.

By the end of the antebellum period, the majority of American workers were still on farms, but industrialization was clearly in the ascendancy. The proportion of American workers engaged in AGRICULTURE declined from 71.8 percent in 1820 to 68.6 percent in 1840 and to 58.9 percent in 1860. By 1849, private manufacturing income amounted to an eighth of total national income from private sources, with manufacturing the economy's most rapidly growing segment. The pace of industrialization quickened even more from 1860 to 1890. By the late 19th century, the United States was the world's largest industrial power.

Further reading: Thomas V. DiBacco, *Made in the U.S.A.: The History of American Business* (New York: Harper & Row, 1987); Alex Groner et al., *The American Heritage History of American Business & Industry* (New York: American Heritage Publishing Co., 1972); Robert Heilbroner and Aaron Singer, *The Economic Transformation of America: 1600 to the Present,* 3d ed. (Fort Worth, Tex.: Harcourt Brace College Publishers, 1994).

—George Ochoa

Interior, Department of

The Department of the Interior, a cabinet-level office of the federal government's executive branch, was established by an act of Congress on March 3, 1849. The department was originally organized to bring together many of the government's disparate procedural responsibilities. A number of independent offices and bureaus, as well as large departments such as the Department of State and the Department of War, had been in charge of such tasks as patent registration, census administration, supervision of federal buildings, oversight of Indian affairs, enforcement of land laws, and the administration of military pensions. All these areas were reorganized under the auspices of the new Department of the Interior.

Over time, the department's mandate has changed. Today it is responsible for the protection and use of the United States' natural resources, national parks, historic sites, and wildlife. While many of its original responsibilities have now been given over to other federal agencies, the BUREAU OF INDIAN AFFAIRS remains within the Department of the Interior, as it has since 1849.

Further reading: National Archives and Records Administration, "Records of the Office of the Secretary of the Interior," URL: http://www.nara.gov/guide/rg048.html. Downloaded 2001; John Upton Terrell, *The United States Department of the Interior; A Story of Rangeland, Wildlife, and Dams* (New York: Duell, 1963).

—Mary Kay Linge

internal improvements

By the beginning of the 19th century, Americans began to advocate for the construction of new transportation routes in order to facilitate western settlement and efficient trade. These "improvements" on the natural landscape—roads, canals, bridges, turnpikes, and, later, RAILROADS—would allow Americans to take advantage of the abundant resources in the West. Proponents also argued that, by connecting different regions, these improvements would create a more unified and prosperous nation. By the 1830s, enthusiasm for the transformative power of internal improvements was widespread, as various states and the federal government planned new transportation projects.

In newly settling western states, officials thought that they could encourage rapid development by building canals and roads, thereby providing access to huge tracts of federally owned land. Once transportation routes had been provided, settlers would be more likely to buy tracts in these unsettled areas. The sooner these areas were settled, the sooner the state could become solvent via a substantial tax base. With increased revenue, still more infrastructural improvements could be started.

Beginning in the first two decades of the 19th century, the first major improvement to receive federal support was a system of toll roads or turnpikes. By 1810, approximately

300 turnpike companies had been chartered in the Mid-Atlantic states and New England. By the 1820s, all major northern cities were connected by roads; in the South, efforts to improve transportation routes would proceed much more slowly. But how would roads be established in the new western territories? Thomas Jefferson's original grid plan for western settlement did not include space or provisions for roads. Congress began to rectify that oversight in 1802 and 1803. In the acts that admitted Ohio as a state, members of Congress placed stipulations requiring that 5 percent of the proceeds from the sale of public lands be used to build roads in the state. These funds financed construction of the Cumberland Road, also called the NATIONAL ROAD. This western road would begin in Cumberland, Maryland, then go to Wheeling, Virginia, then on to Columbus, Ohio, and then Indiana, terminating in Vandalia, Illinois. The plan for the National Road was approved in 1806, with the Army Corps of Engineers responsible for surveying and constructing it. Actual construction began in 1811, and the road reached Wheeling by 1818, Columbus by 1833, and Indianapolis by 1850. At this point, the federal government handed over funding and construction to the states through which the road would run. In thinly populated states like Wisconsin, Michigan, and Indiana, settlers asked the federal government to help build other roads. The government offered land grants to construct three roads in this region. Slowly, a system of smaller roads developed that connected larger areas to the main arteries. In the trans-Mississippi West, most roads were constructed by military forces as part of their efforts to impose white settlement and contain Native American populations. These efforts were assisted by the INDIAN REMOVAL ACT, which became official federal policy in 1830.

The evolving road system was heavily traveled, but maintaining it was difficult and expensive. Enthusiasm for completing the National Road project diminished as roads became more common, and less-cumbersome transportation methods, such as canals, emerged.

Thus, the second great improvement initiative centered around the construction of artificial waterways, or canals. Although costly and difficult to build, canals were supposed to be quicker and easier routes than the bumpy, muddy roads. The stunning success of the ERIE CANAL in New York encouraged other states to view canals as an essential element of development. State officials hoped these canals would promote rapid settlement in the Northwest and strengthen regional economies. While the Erie Canal was state-funded, most of the canal projects in the West relied more heavily on federal support and private funding, because the new states had few sources of capital. One of the few states to succeed on the New York model, Ohio began to construct a canal system the year before the Erie Canal was completed.

By 1833, 341 miles of canal had been built from Portsmouth (on the Ohio River) to Cleveland, and from Cincinnati to Dayton. As hoped, this canal system raised land values and increased settlement and commerce. Other projects meant to connect the Northwestern states to the Great Lakes through lateral canals were not completed until the 1830s, when the states were finally able to borrow the money they needed for construction. Still, many states defaulted on loans they had taken out to build canals. The PANIC OF 1837, along with risky and unsound planning, caused many improvement projects to fail. Nevertheless, traveling by canal or by Robert Fulton's new steamboats was the fastest, most efficient method of transportation until the 1840s, triggering rapid development in the trans-Appalachian West.

Railroads displaced canals as the favorite internal improvement by the 1850s. Faster and more versatile than canal or river travel, railroads became the major carriers of people and goods to and from the West. The first railroad companies, such as the Mohawk and Hudson Railroad (1826), connected coastal cities and seaports with the surrounding regions. The first American rail company to reach over the Appalachians, the BALTIMORE & OHIO RAILROAD (B&O) was chartered in 1828 and began running trains in 1830. Construction to Wheeling was completed by 1852. The Chicago and Rock Island Railroad reached the Mississippi River in 1854, connecting this crucial river system with the Great Lakes region for the first time. Other important early railroads include the New York Central Railroad; the Chicago, Burlington, and Quincy Railroad; the Chicago and Northwestern Railroad; and the Chicago, Milwaukee, and St. Paul Railroad. Just as the Erie Canal had transformed New York City into the most important American seaport, the railroad system made Chicago the center of the expanding western market. While the whole nation would not be connected from sea to sea until 1869, railroads were well on their way to transforming space, time, and production before the Civil War.

Throughout this period of infrastructural expansion, Americans contended with a key question: Who should fund these improvements—private parties, states, or the federal government? Officials debated whether the federal government should be financing such projects, since the Constitution did not specifically name internal improvements as a federal responsibility. HENRY CLAY and other Whig proponents of the AMERICAN SYSTEM argued that federal funding for improvements was necessary for the nation to grow economically strong. In order to reach a compromise with Democratic opponents (among them President ANDREW JACKSON), Clay proposed that the proceeds from land sales be distributed to the states, where they could then use this money to build improvements. A similar plan proposed by JOHN C. CALHOUN was eventually passed in 1836, making

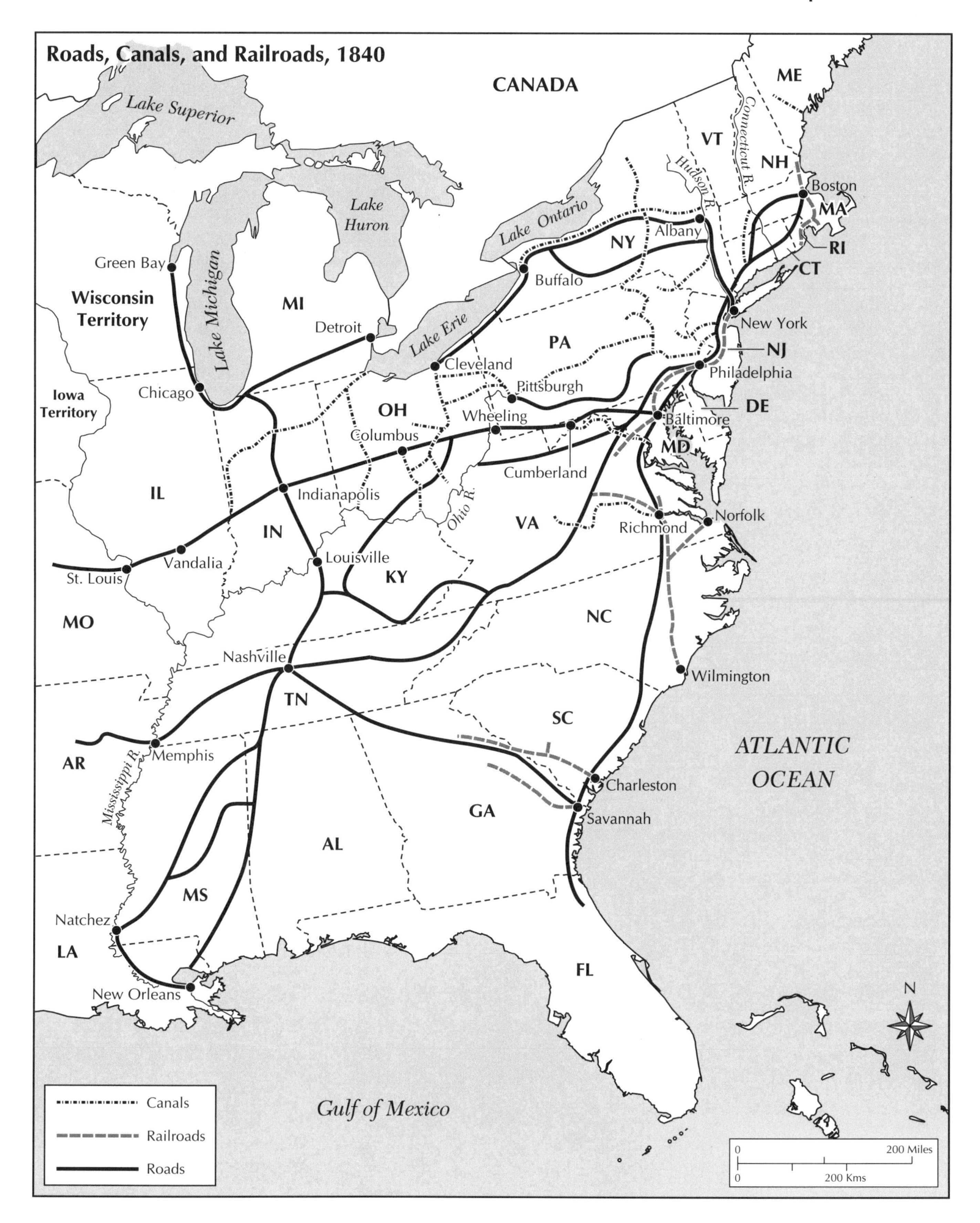
Roads, Canals, and Railroads, 1840
CANADA
Lake Superior
Lake Huron
Lake Michigan
Lake Ontario
Lake Erie
ME
VT
NH
MA
RI
CT
NY
PA
NJ
DE
MD
VA
NC
SC
GA
FL
AL
MS
TN
KY
OH
IN
IL
MI
MO
AR
LA
Wisconsin Territory
Iowa Territory
Boston
Albany
Buffalo
New York
Philadelphia
Baltimore
Pittsburgh
Cleveland
Wheeling
Cumberland
Columbus
Detroit
Green Bay
Chicago
Indianapolis
Vandalia
St. Louis
Louisville
Nashville
Memphis
Natchez
New Orleans
Richmond
Norfolk
Wilmington
Charleston
Savannah
Hudson R.
Connecticut R.
Ohio R.
Mississippi R.
ATLANTIC OCEAN
Gulf of Mexico
N
Canals
Railroads
Roads
0
200 Miles
0
200 Kms

$28 million available to states to build improvements. Before this point, some projects had been funded federally, others by the states or private parties.

In 1841 Congress tried to equalize the federal contributions to state road construction. Through the Distribution-Preemption Act, Congress granted half a million acres of public land to every state that had not yet received federal money for constructing internal improvements. Less-populous western states were angry about the distribution method, which granted funds based on population figures. But preemption rights, or giving settlers already on the land the right to purchase that land first, was a welcome change in the law. The distribution requirement was eliminated in 1842. Some states used the half-million acre grant to complete existing canal and road projects; others used the acreage to begin building that most revolutionary 19th-century improvement, railroads. In 1850 Congress began to grant lands specifically for railroad construction, usually by designating alternate sections along a proposed route.

In the first half of the 19th century, the craze for internal improvements exemplified high hopes about the nation's future growth and a commitment to rapid economic expansion in many segments of American society. The antebellum debate over how to accomplish internal improvements reveals concerns over the role of government in promoting the economy that still divide Americans today. The first improvements in road, canal, and rail construction provided the initial transportation web that enabled Americans to spread throughout the continent and begin connecting regions together in trade networks.

Further reading: Paul W. Gates, *History of Public Land Law Development* (Holmes Beach, Fla.: William W. Gaunt, 1987); Forest Garrett Hill, *Roads, Rails & Waterways: The Army Engineers and Early Transportation* (Norman: University of Oklahoma Press, 1957); George Rogers Taylor, *The Transportation Revolution, 1815–1860* (New York: Harper and Row, 1968).

—Eleanor H. McConnell

J

Jackson, Andrew (1767–1845)

Seventh president of the United States and the first president who did not reside in one of the original thirteen colonies, Andrew Jackson was a frontier general and Indian fighter. Elected president on a platform that anointed him as the candidate of democracy and the common man, he served two terms of office (1829–37) that were marked by bitter controversies over states' rights, the tariff, the spoils system, Indian removal, and banking policies. A man of volatile temperament and strong convictions, Jackson used his presidential power vigorously and left his mark on the era.

The period of Jackson's influence, approximately 1820–45, has been dubbed by many historians as "The Jackson Era," or "The Age of Jackson." This was a time of rampant economic, political, and social growth, as the market economy burgeoned with revolutions in transportation and manufacturing, and westward expansion took place at an amazingly fast pace. Regional diversification was the result of much of this expanding economy, but so was regional separation and enmity; the views of North and South moved toward diametrically opposed positions regarding matters of states' rights and the expansion of SLAVERY.

The child of poor Scotch-Irish immigrants, Jackson grew up in the backcountry of the South Carolina-North Carolina border, where he attended frontier schools. He was orphaned during the American Revolution when his widowed mother died of smallpox. Although still a boy, Jackson participated in the war as a messenger and orderly. Afterwards, he set himself up as a saddlemaker and sometime schoolteacher on the South Carolina frontier. He eventually moved to Charleston and then to North Carolina, where he read law and gained admission to the bar. In 1787 Jackson established a law practice and soon became a successful lawyer and land speculator. Shortly thereafter, he migrated to Nashville, Tennessee, where he became involved in politics.

In 1791 Jackson married Rachel Donelson Robards. This was Rachel's second marriage, which was risk enough to an aspiring politician during this period. However, when it was learned that no divorce from her first husband had ever been granted, it became a personal and political nightmare for the Jacksons. After Robards's divorce, they remarried in 1794, but the damage had already been done. Gossips and political opponents attempted to make a scandal out of Jackson's happy marriage. While Rachel suffered the slanders in silence, Andrew often preferred to use dueling pistols to avenge his wife's honor.

Jackson served as a delegate to the Tennessee constitutional convention in 1796 and as congressman from Tennessee (1796–97). His congressional career was undistinguished, marked primarily by his fierce opposition to the Washington administration's conciliatory stance toward Great Britain and the western Indian nations. He was elected U.S. senator in 1797, but financial problems forced his resignation and return to Tennessee in less than a year. After serving as a Tennessee superior court judge (1798–1804), he retired from the bench to devote all his energies to business ventures and to his plantation, the Hermitage, near Nashville. His political career seemed to be over, as his efforts to gain appointment as governor of Louisiana were rebuffed by President Thomas Jefferson.

The WAR OF 1812 changed his political fortunes. In March 1814, assisted by Native American allies, Jackson crushed Creek resistance at the BATTLE OF HORSESHOE BEND. As terms of surrender, he demanded and got enormous tracts of land ceded by Indians—friend and foe alike—in both Alabama and Georgia. This stunning victory impressed the federal government sufficiently to place him in command of the defense of New Orleans, which "Old Hickory," as Jackson was called by his admirers, swiftly organized. On January 8, 1815, his forces completely routed an invading British army, unaware that Britain and the United States had signed a peace treaty several weeks earlier.

Andrew Jackson *(National Archives)*

Jackson's victory at New Orleans, coming at the end of a war marked by military ineptness and humiliating defeats by the United States, was seized upon widely by an American public hungry for vindication of national honor. Not even the news that the war had been officially over could diminish the national fervor attached to its new hero. The BATTLE OF NEW ORLEANS had made Andrew Jackson a legend—a symbol of American virtue and power.

General Jackson continued to add to his legend during subsequent years. After pursuing the Seminole Indians into FLORIDA (a Spanish possession) in 1818, Jackson exceeded his authority when he deposed Spanish authorities and executed two British subjects. This brought about the U.S. acquisition of Florida in 1819. Not only did Jackson avoid censure and dismissal for his actions, he was appointed territorial governor of Florida in 1821.

A traditional westerner, pro-tariff and pro-internal improvement, Jackson became a presidential candidate in 1824. The demise of the Federalist Party, long out of presidential power and now discredited by its opposition to the War of 1812, had left the nation, for all practical purposes, with a one-party system in 1824. The Democratic-Republicans were unable, however, to agree on a common presidential candidate. Riddled with factions, the party put four major candidates on the ballot: William H. Crawford of Georgia, Henry Clay of Kentucky, Andrew Jackson of Tennessee, and John Quincy Adams of Massachusetts.

Jackson won the popular vote but not a majority of the electoral vote, forcing the election to be decided in the House of Representatives. Henry Clay released his electoral votes to Adams in return for Adams naming Clay secretary of state. Adams won the election by a one-vote margin. The deal struck between Adams and Clay became referred to as the "corrupt bargain," and many thought Jackson had been robbed of the presidency. The public outcry was strong, and the stigma would haunt Adams's presidency; it would be instrumental in allowing him only a single term.

Capitalizing on the public and political outrage over the Adams-Clay "corrupt bargain," MARTIN VAN BUREN, a staunch Jeffersonian Republican, put his formidable skills as an organizer to work and began to forge a national alliance between the Democratic-Republicans of the North and the planters of the South. Because of these changes, the Democratic-Republicans became known as the Democratic Party, which nominated Jackson as their candidate for president in 1828.

Critical of Adams's nationalist policies and lack of concern for states' rights, the Jackson organization represented Old Hickory as a champion of the common man. They attacked Adams and Clay for the "corrupt bargain" that, they alleged, revealed the aristocratic principles of both men and their contempt for democracy. Adams's supporters in turn attacked Jackson for the irregularity of the first years of his marriage and portrayed him as an ignorant and uncouth barbarian. Yet the Jacksonian Democracy was triumphant in 1828. In an election marked by mudslinging and character assassination on both sides, Jackson defeated Adams's bid for a second term.

Jackson's victory was marred when Rachel Jackson died of an apparent heart attack soon after the election. While the occasional local reference to the "bigamist" Rachel had occurred over the years, for the most part the Jacksons' marriage scandal blew over until the 1828 election, when Adams tried to raise the old slurs and gossip for his advantage. Jackson was convinced that his wife's death was the fault of Adams and his administration, and he never forgave them for it. As president, Jackson introduced the spoils system into national politics, which rewarded party loyalty and service with political offices. The system, with its official label of "rotation in office," was hailed by Jackson as a Democratic device for allowing the common man a voice in the government. In any event, he relied more heavily on his "Kitchen Cabinet" of personal advisers than he did on his official cabinet.

In 1830 Jackson signed the INDIAN REMOVAL ACT, which called for the general resettlement of Indians to lands west of the Mississippi River. The following year, the Supreme Court ruled in *Cherokee Nation v. Georgia* that the Cherokee were not a "foreign nation" within the meaning of the Constitution, but a "dependent nation." This essentially made the Indian Removal Act of 1830 unconstitutional. Undaunted, Jackson was reputed to have said, "[Chief Justice] John Marshall has made his decision. Now let him enforce it." The decision was ignored, and between 1831 and 1839 the Five Civilized Tribes of the Southeast (Choctaw, Chickasaw, Cherokee, Creek, and Seminole) were forcibly relocated to Indian Territory (Oklahoma). On the TRAIL OF TEARS, thousands of Native Americans perished in this removal. Henry Clay called Jackson's Native-American policy "a stain on the nation's honor." However, Jackson's antipathy toward Indians was typical of the frontier mindset, and because this policy opened more land to settlement, a majority of the public and Congress supported it with enthusiasm.

In December 1831 the National Republicans once again nominated Henry Clay for the presidency. Clay, senator from Kentucky, returned to the national spotlight feeling pessimistic about his chances against Jackson. His main goal was to bring a measure to Congress that would put the administration in an embarrassing position. He therefore proposed a modification of the tariff, lowering it but leaving the protective elements in. By lowering revenues, this would have put off Jackson's intended repayment of the national debt by nearly a year. If the president vetoed it, he would alienate northern states, like Pennsylvania, whose votes he needed. If he signed it, it would alienate his southern supporters. In the end, Clay's strategy failed when Congress passed a bill moderate enough that Jackson could sign it without alienating either faction.

The election of 1832 marked the first time that presidential candidates were chosen by party conventions. The chartering of the SECOND BANK OF THE UNITED STATES was the most important campaign issue. The National Republicans, with Henry Clay as their candidate, supported the bank, while Jackson and the Democrats were adamantly opposed to it. Jackson won a second term easily.

Before Jackson entered his second term, South Carolina threatened nullification of the tariff of 1832. Although Jackson was a champion of states' rights, he always stood firm behind the supreme powers of the federal government in any struggle that placed the interests of a state above those of the Union. He therefore made it clear that he considered a state's nullification of a federal law to be unconstitutional, inconsistent with the principles and spirit on which the union was founded, and destructive to its continued existence. Jackson also pushed through Congress a force bill that authorized the use of federal troops to collect the tariff.

The crisis was eased when Henry Clay promoted a compromise tariff in 1833 along with the force bill. As a last defiant gesture, South Carolina accepted the tariff but nullified the force bill. Jackson had preserved the Union, but NULLIFICATION remained a great question.

In spring 1833 Jackson embarked on a tour of the country, mostly in the Northeast, where pro-Union sentiment was especially strong. He was greeted by huge cheering crowds wherever he went and received an honorary doctorate of law from Harvard, to the disgust of John Quincy Adams. He finally had to cut the trip short because of "bleeding at the lungs," at least partly due to a bullet he had carried in his chest for more than 20 years (the result of a duel).

At this height of his popularity, Jackson set out to ensure the demise of the Second Bank of the United States. He spent the summer of 1833 looking for banks into which federal deposits could be made should they be withdrawn from the Bank of the United States. As the withdrawal of funds went forward, the bank began a severe tightening of funds, restricting loans, and calling in as many debts as it could. This caused a financial panic resulting an economic recession.

As the recession continued and deepened in 1834, the country became more polarized. It was during this period that the National Republicans became the WHIG PARTY. This name conjured the ghost of the antiroyal, pro-Parliament, English factions of the 17th and 18th centuries. In that spirit, Whigs labeled Jackson "King Andrew I" and drew political cartoons depicting him as a king, with a scepter labeled "Veto."

Before 1834 was over, many former friends of the Second Bank became disgusted at its conduct, and in the end, the Bank of the United States was stripped of the funds the government had placed in its keeping. It lost its friends, including Clay, and quietly lost its standing as a national bank. Rechartered as a state bank in Pennsylvania, it only lasted a few years more.

Jackson lived to the age of 78, despite chronic sickness and a bullet in his chest, and died peacefully at home on June 8, 1845. His era had radically changed the American party system and methods of electioneering. The firmness and arguably violent nature of his positions and actions gave birth to a strong new opposition, the Whigs. He left the presidency much stronger than it had been, and he strengthened the notion of the United States as a nation rather than a number of states with an agreement to act in concert.

Further reading: Robert Vincent Remini, *The Life of Andrew Jackson* (New York: Harper & Row, 1988); Harry

L. Watson, *Liberty and Power: The Politics of Jacksonian America,* Eric Foner, consulting editor (New York: Hill and Wang, 1990).

—Richard L. Friedline

journalism

During the first half of the 19th century, technological advances, the growing U.S. population, an emerging market economy, and a widespread egalitarian sensibility brought tremendous growth to the popular press. Between 1830 and 1840 alone, the urban U.S. population increased by over one-third to 1.5 million; the number of weekly newspapers swelled from 650 to 1,141, and daily newspapers increased from 65 to 138.

Nearly all of these papers were inexpensive journals called "penny papers" such as the *New York Journal,* which drew a large circulation of two to five times as much as an 18th-century paper. Antebellum magazine readership also grew markedly, with the *Godey's Lady's Book* reaching the highest circulation—150,000 by the end of the 1850s.

While traditional newspapers continued to be published, they were eclipsed in number and importance by penny papers. These self-proclaimed democratic publications gained popularity by serving all members of society and by offering a variety of up-to-date information that came to be known as "news."

Newspapers

From the 18th century into the 1820s, most newspapers were relatively expensive items that cost a few pennies—usually six cents—and were sold by subscription to a select portion of society, the mercantile class and political leaders. These papers depended on political parties, not commercial advertising, to support them. Popular newspapers of the era included the *Boston Daily Advertiser* and the *Baltimore Daily Advertiser.*

Reflecting their audience, subscription newspapers held definite views on what were considered proper topics for coverage and advertising. Among them were business-related segments such as stock listings, ship dockings, and foreign reports; political information consisted largely of editorials, which favored the party supporting the newspaper. Considered unfit for the paper were topics concerning everyday life, from local problems to crime. Also improper were advertisements for personal products and services as well as entertainment.

During the 1830s, the look and content of newspapers were transformed with the introduction of the commercially driven "penny paper." Unlike the six-cent paper, this newspaper was priced at a penny. Not underwritten by political parties, it accepted advertising to pay for itself. It was also not sold by yearly subscription to those who could afford it, but rather bought on the streets by all social classes. It was particularly favored by middle-class urban dwellers—shopkeepers and salesmen, for example—who bought the paper from roaming child vendors known as newsboys.

Within months of their introduction, the penny papers' circulation more than doubled subscription paper rates and became the cities' primary sources of information and idea exchange. In New York, 11 penny papers were available by 1835; among the most influential were New York's *New York Sun* (founded 1833), *Evening Transcript,* and *New York Herald* (both 1835). Other notable urban newspapers included Philadelphia's *Philadelphia Public Ledger* (1836), Boston's *Boston Daily Times* (1836), and Baltimore's *Baltimore Sun* (1837).

Who ran the penny papers and what did they contain? Many of the founding editors of the penny papers were entrepreneurial businessmen whose newspaper ownership reflected the increasingly heterogeneous society in which they lived. Among them were James Gordon Bennett, who controlled the *New York Herald* (1835), the most widely read penny paper in the United States and Europe. Bennett founded the paper in 1835 on $500 and simple goals: to concentrate on news reporting but aim it, in his words, "to interest the merchant and man of learning, as well as the mechanic and the man of labor." Politician and veteran newspaper editor Horace Greeley founded the *New York Tribune* in 1841 and distinguished it from competitors through its eclectic views, which included abolitionism, women's rights, and nationalism. Influential in shaping public opinion, the *Tribune* was also known for such writers as MARGARET FULLER and Karl Marx, who was a foreign correspondent.

Other notable editors included Benjamin Day, founder of the *New York Sun,* whose newspaper grew to a readership of 10,000 within months of its 1833 founding. Day was also known for his early use of newsboys to sell papers. Borrowing from the London practice of selling newspapers on the street, Day sold boys and girls copies of 100 papers wholesale (at 67 cents) or on credit (at 75 cents); the street sellers then sold papers at a profit to readers.

Amidst the general-interest newspapers were several important specialized papers arising during the period. Representing the African-American audience was the pioneering black-press–published *Freedom's Journal,* founded in 1828 by the Reverend Samuel E. Cornish and John B. Russwurm. Before ceasing publication in 1831 (under the name *Rights of All*), the newspaper championed the antislavery movement and contested black stereotyping in other newspapers. Abolitionist William Lloyd Garrison inaugurated his weekly newspaper *The Liberator* in 1831. Campaigning in print against SLAVERY and other social ills, it generated violent public response before it ended publication in 1865.

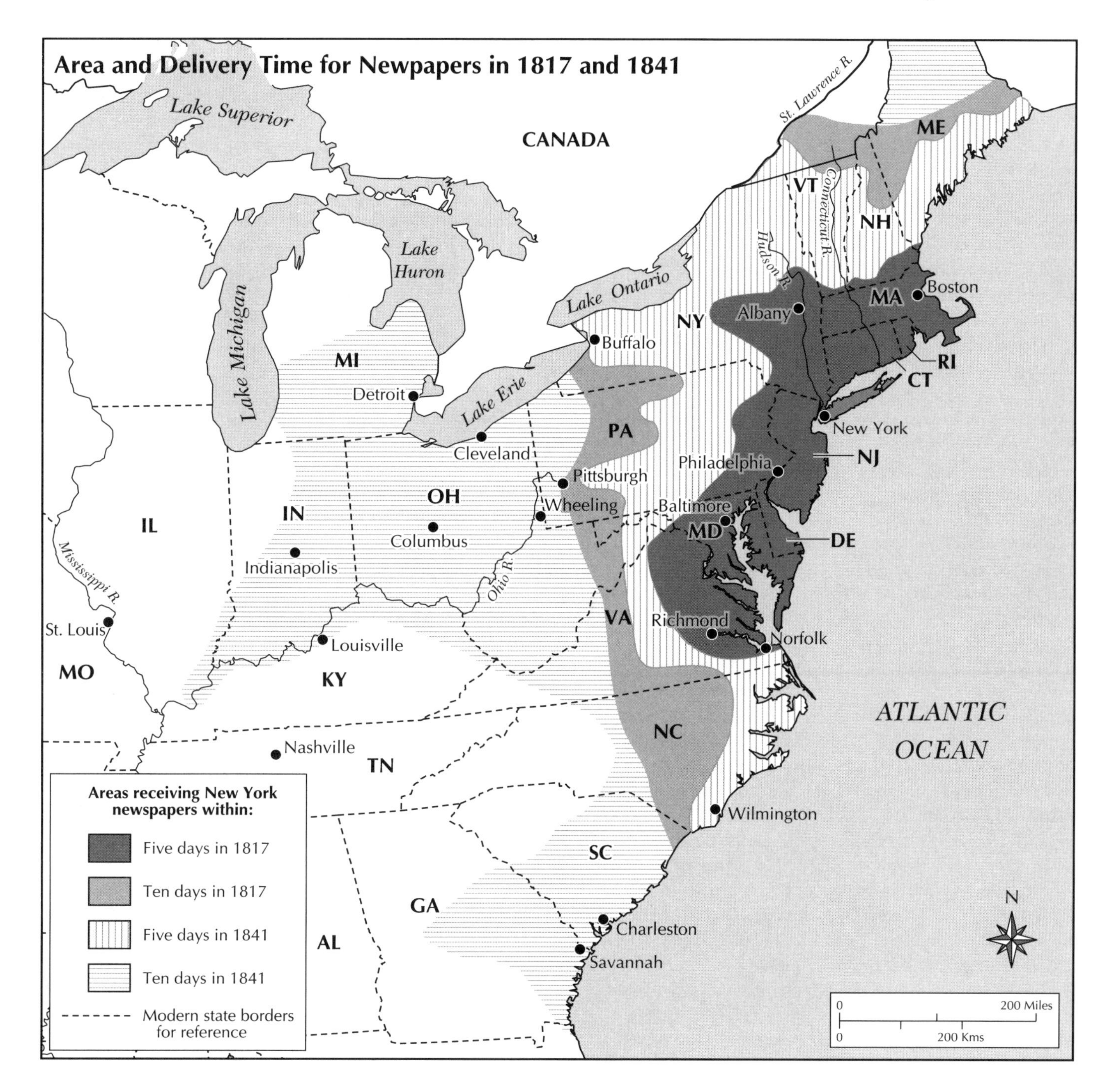

Influential as specialized newspapers were, they did not have the large audience of the general-interest penny-press newspapers. In part, this was due to the overriding aim of most penny papers: to appeal to the widest possible audience by following no set political views and being nonpartisan in reporting. While some papers, such as the *New York Transcript,* initially professed disinterest in political issues, most, like the *New York Tribune,* pledged itself to covering the broad world of politics and local events. This shared stance of the penny papers marked the beginning of modern-day news coverage: the timely, accurate, and adept presentation of events.

As reporting of news events increased in the penny papers, the importance of the editorial page of opinion declined. A central element of the six-cent paper, the editorial page had previously been written for a circumscribed audience. Such a set opinion would not represent the varied penny-press audience. Instead, accuracy and timeliness became the impartial standards by which a heterogeneous audience judged a newspaper.

The up-to-date information required for the penny paper sharpened the role of the news reporter. Rather than reprinting a political speech as was done in six-cent papers, penny-press newspapers unearthed news. They did so through the innovative practice of assigning reporters on regular assignments or beats, or postings at foreign locations. For example, by the mid-1830s New York papers established reporters on regular court, police, sports, and society duty; others were stationed domestically in Washington, D.C., in eastern cities, and in Europe.

In addition to offering reporting from specified beats, some penny papers offered analyses of important issues. Pioneered by the *New York Tribune,* these writings, notably what became known as the "money articles," provided original analysis and business speculations for readers who might otherwise have shunned the inexpensive paper. Through this coverage, penny papers came to represent varieties of everyday life, from marriages to habits of political and cultural leaders to analysis of economic trends.

Central to the proliferation of the popular press were the technological and transportation advances that improved the speed and efficiency of the printing and delivering of periodicals. Printing advances had been improving the speed and quality of printing since the early 19th century and entered domestic use in 1823, when the European-based steam-driven press was first used to print U.S. books. Simultaneously, printing for major newspapers and other periodicals was also being adapted to the cylinder press, which was first used in 1835 by the *New York Sun.* After being refined into a two-cylinder version, it was used to print a newspaper, the *Philadelphia Public Ledger,* in 1847, and gained widespread use shortly after the Civil War.

Making fast newspaper delivery possible was the growth of the railroad across several states during the antebellum years. Between 1830 and 1850, several thousand miles of train track were laid over several states, a vast increase from the several dozen miles of track laid in the 1820s.

Another technological development increased the speed of information delivery and raised questions about the content of reporting: the telegraph. Invented in the 1840s, the telegraph made it possible to transmit news by wire nationwide. In an early application, the telegraph was particularly useful to penny papers in delivering news during the MEXICAN-AMERICAN WAR (1846–48).

To provide the largest number of newspapers with this timely information, several New York-based newspapers formed the first wire service, the Associated Press, in 1848. To resolve the problem of how to present the information to varying newspapers, the Associated Press reported news without political slant or commentary. Other similarly objective wire news services followed, including United Press (later United Press International).

Another change in newspapers was its source of financial support. Unlike its subscription predecessors, the penny paper paid for itself through commercial advertising. No longer limiting its advertising sources, penny papers accepted ads from various commercial sources, including personal products and popular entertainments. Summarizing the common penny-press position, one paper wrote, "It is sufficient for our purpose that the advertisements are paid for, and that . . . we are impartial, and show no respect to persons, or to the various kinds of business that fill up this little world of ours."

Magazines

To a lesser extent during this period, magazines also gained wider readership and influence. The 19th century began with the dominance of literary and political journals such as *The Monthly Magazine and American Review* (1799) and *The American Register* (1807), both founded by Charles Brockden Brown; and the Federalist *Port Folio,* edited by Joseph Dennie (1801).

Founded in 1815, the intellectual journal the *North American Review* was an early champion of American letters and the most influential journal of its kind until the mid-19th century. Contributors included Henry Wadsworth Longfellow and historian Francis Parkman; editors included clergyman Edward Everett and historian John Palfrey. Other notable journals of the 1820s included *American Quarterly Review* (1828).

The introduction of penny-press newspapers and the technology that accompanied them gave rise to a new kind of periodical, the general circulation monthly magazine. Influential representatives of the era included *Graham's Magazine* (1826). Founded by Samuel C. Atkinson and Charles Alexander as the *Casket,* it gained dominance under the editorship of George Rex Graham, who changed the magazine's name and paid unprecedented fees for contributions by important writers, such as James Russell Lowell and RICHARD HENRY DANA. Also prominent during the era, particularly in New York, was the *Knickerbocker Magazine,* founded in 1833 and edited by Washington Irving.

Also gaining popularity was the diverse regional weekly, which was designed to offer a wide range of information for weekend readers. Prominent among these entries was the *Saturday Evening Post.* Founded in 1821 by Charles Alexander and Samuel Atkinson, it became hugely popular in the 1840s and 1850s after incorporating the magazine the *Saturday Bulletin* in 1832 and including popular serial fiction.

Notable antebellum literary quarterlies included the literary magazine the *Dial* (1840), which represented the thinking of the TRANSCENDENTAL MOVEMENT through its contributors and editors RALPH WALDO EMERSON and Margaret Fuller. Southern writing was represented in *The Southern Review* (1828) and the *Southern Quarterly Review* (1842).

Political magazines during the period were often distinguished by their regional views. Reflecting northern attitudes were the *Democratic Review* (1837), which featured noted writers of the day including Nathaniel Hawthorne; and *Niles' Weekly Register*, a newspaper digest. Southern views were presented in the *Southern Literary Messenger* (1834) and *DeBow's Review*, the former edited for two years by Edgar Allan Poe.

Female readers were considered an important, separate group that was represented largely by *Godey's Lady's Book* (1830). Reaching an audience of 40,000 readers, *Godey's Lady's Book* was the most influential women's magazine during the pre–Civil War years and beyond. Founded by Louis A. Godey, it was driven by SARAH JOSEPHA HALE, who became its editor in 1836. In addition to shaping opinion on fashion and matters of domestic life, it published works by leading writers including Edgar Allan Poe and Ralph Waldo Emerson. In later years, Hale and the magazine were central to establishing Thanksgiving as a national holiday. *Godey's* closest competition was *Peterson's Ladies' National Magazine* (1842).

Another magazine that proved influential after the Civil War was founded in 1855 by Frank Leslie. Combining the magazine *Frank Leslie's Ladies Gazette of Fashion and Fancy Needle Work* and the *New York Journal*, a newspaper, he founded *Frank Leslie's Illustrated Newspaper*, a hybrid of periodical and newspaper that would become known for its timeliness and colorful writing.

Aside from the observable changes of INDUSTRIALIZATION and the growth of the urban population, newspapers and periodicals during the 19th century grew in popularity for an intangible reason: The U.S public considered newspapers important on a personal basis. As a more democratic, commercial ECONOMY developed, newspapers and periodicals became significant items that an up-to-date household could acquire.

Along with this attraction to periodicals came a growing skepticism at the press's aims. Nearly two centuries before current critiques of the media, author and critic James Fenimore Cooper perceived the problem. In his 1838 nonfiction work *The American Democrat*, he wrote, "If newspapers are useful in overthrowing tyrants, it is only to establish a tyranny of their own. The press tyrannizes over publick [sic] men, letters, the arts, the stage, and even over private life."

At the same time, the American press was coming to view its own role as central to promoting democracy. Unlike subscription papers of the past, whose titles reflected their business or political ties, papers founded in the mid-19th century bore names such as the *Beacon* or *Herald* that looked outward to the wider world. As the *Baltimore Sun* promised, "Our object will be the common good, without regard to that of sects, factions, or parties; and for this object we shall labor without fear or partiality." The ideal of the honorable presentation of knowledge has clung to newspapers for two centuries.

Further reading: Robert Rutland, *Newsmongers: Journalism in the Life of the Nation* (New York: Dial Press, 1973); Michael Schudson, *Discovering the News: A Social History of American Newspapers* (New York: Basic Books, 1978); Carl Senna, *The Black Press and the Struggle for Civil Rights* (New York: Franklin Watts, 1993).

—Melinda Corey

K

Kamehameha I (ca. 1753–1819)

Historians are uncertain when and under what circumstances Hawaii's great warrior king and national unifier was born. The year ranges between 1753 and 1758. According to legend, Kamehameha's mother, Kekuiapoiwa, gave birth to the future king on the island of Hawaii (the "Big Island") in secret because *kahunas* (Hawaiian shamans) prophesied that he would grow up to slay his rival chiefs and rule the HAWAIIAN ISLANDS. To protect her son from the murderous plots of chiefs who saw the infant as a threat, Kekuiapoiwa entrusted Kamehameha to a faithful servant. Kamehameha was raised in relative isolation, and because of this he acquired the nickname "the Lonely One."

Kamehameha proved himself to be a ferocious, intelligent, and successful warrior. When the great chief of the Big Island and Kamehameha's uncle, Kalaniopuu, died, he passed his kingdom on to his son Kiwalao. However, he made Kamehameha the keeper of the family war god. The result of this was jealous rivalry between cousins. Kamehameha began a war against his cousins Kiwaloo and Keoua for dominance of the Big Island; it lasted almost nine years. The result of this warfare was a shaky truce between Kamehameha and Keoua; Kiwalao was killed in battle.

By the 1780s, the Hawaiian Islands were divided roughly into three kingdoms. The Big Island and a small portion of Oahu were under the rule of Kalaniopuu and his heirs. The chief Kahekili ruled the rest of Oahu as well as the islands of Kahoolawe, Lanai and Oahu. His brother Kaeo had control over Kauai. As Kalaniopuu's heirs were struggling for power on the Big Island, Kahekili conquered Kalaniopuu's portion of Oahu and gained influence over Kauai through family marriage. Power in the islands was at a deadlock, and only the arrival of westerners and their technology tipped the balance in Kamehameha's favor. The Lonely One made an immediate and lasting impression on British captain James Cook and other westerners he met. According to one of Cook's officers, Kamehameha had "as savage a looking face as I ever saw, it however by no means seemed an emblem of his disposition, which was good natur'd & humorous."

Following a fatal encounter between Hawaiians and an American vessel, which occurred shortly after Cook's death in 1779, Kamehameha took two sailors, Isaac Davis and John Young, prisoner. He also captured their vessel, the *Fair American*. The two sailors were soon won over by Kamehameha's humane treatment and, with the *Fair American*'s cannons, helped him vanquish his rivals and gain control over the entire archipelago. By 1796, Kamehameha was the undisputed ruler of all the major islands of Hawaii. The entire chain fell under his sovereignty in 1810 when Kauai, which was nominally independent, and Niihau submitted entirely to him.

Under Kamehameha's rule, which lasted from 1796 to his death in 1819, Hawaii flourished in peace and enjoyed its last period of traditional Polynesian culture and society. The political economy resembled European feudalism with the *ali'i* (warriors) and the *maka'ainana* (peasants) functioning as vassals and serfs respectively. The *kahunas* served in significant positions as advisers and doctors. The Lonely One also enacted laws that gave greater equality to commoners by restricting their exploitation at the hands of the nobility. Finally, under Kamehameha, Hawaiians lived according to the traditional *kapu* system that regulated daily life, family relations, divisions of labor, and gender dynamics. Kamehameha made Lahaina, on the island of Maui, the royal court. The monarchy he established would continue for another 100 years. However, as more westerners came to settle in the islands after 1819, particularly whalers and missionaries from the United States, the Hawaiian society Kamehameha created would gradually give way in almost every respect to American political, economic, and cultural dominance.

Further reading: Richard Tregaskis, *The Warrior King: Hawaii's Kamehameha the Great* (New York: Macmillan, 1973).

—Charles Hawley

Kansas-Nebraska Act See Volume V

Kearny, Stephen Watts (1794–1848)

An American general in the Mexican War, Stephen Watts Kearny's expeditions in the Southwest served to enlarge U.S. territorial holdings by more than a million square miles. Born in Newark, New Jersey, Kearny enrolled at Columbia College. On the outbreak of the WAR OF 1812, he served as an officer in the Thirteenth Infantry Regiment. A brave troop leader, he was wounded and captured by British forces. At the close of the war, he remained in the army, transferring to the Second Infantry Regiment. In 1819, he was transferred to the West, where he joined an expedition exploring a part of the Louisiana Purchase acquired by the United States in 1803. Meriwether Lewis and William Clark had first crossed this vast landscape between 1804 and 1806. Further exploration had been delayed by worsening relations with Great Britain and with the Indian nations of the region. After signing the TREATY OF GHENT in 1814, ending the war of 1812, the government renewed its interest in the huge domain west of the Mississippi River. Kearny was among the first army officers to make a professional career in the West.

As a means of exerting control over the many Indian peoples of the region, Kearny commanded a regiment of mounted dragoons that established the nation's military presence on the Great Plains. He was an excellent unit commander, a strict disciplinarian, and a fine representative of the strength of the American government. He made the dragoons into an elite unit, renowned for their discipline, mobility, and ability to intimidate. As a result, over the next 20 years, Kearny rose steadily in rank.

With the outbreak of the MEXICAN-AMERICAN WAR in 1846, the War Department ordered Kearny to organize an army to conduct a campaign across the West into New Mexico and California, two of the main objectives of American military operations. With 1,600 men in his command, Kearny and his "Army of the West" left FORT LEAVENWORTH for the Southwest. In August 1846, they entered Santa Fe, where the officials in New Mexico surrendered without a fight. Kearny declared New Mexico a part of the United States and appointed CHARLES BENT as governor.

It was in Santa Fe that Kearny received news of his promotion to brigadier general. He soon left New Mexico and headed west to CALIFORNIA by way of the Gila River. With a much-reduced army numbering no more than 120 men, he defeated a Mexican force at San Pasqual, California, and early in 1847 he and his army reached San Diego. There he joined Commodore ROBERT FIELD STOCKTON in a brisk and bloody campaign to subdue Mexican forces along the coast of Southern California. The combined force won a series of engagements and captured Los Angeles in January 1847.

Stephen Watts Kearny *(Library of Congress)*

Before Commodore Stockton retired, he appointed Captain JOHN C. FRÉMONT as governor of the conquered province of California. Kearny was outraged and challenged the appointment, arguing that Stockton had no authority to appoint the governor. On March 1, 1847, Kearny organized his own government with himself as governor, but Frémont refused to recognize this authority. Kearny charged Frémont with insubordination (failure to obey the orders of a superior officer) and mutiny. A court-martial found Frémont guilty, and he resigned from the army.

In summer 1848, Kearny was military governor at Vera Cruz and Mexico City. Promoted to the rank of major general, he returned to St. Louis to command the Sixth Military Department. In autumn that year, he died from yellow fever.

Further reading: Dwight L. Clarke, *Stephen Watts Kearny, Soldier of the West* (Norman: University of Oklahoma Press, 1961).

Key, Francis Scott (1779–1843)

Best known as the author of "The Star Spangled Banner," Francis Scott Key was a lawyer from Maryland. His moment of fame came near the end of the WAR OF 1812, when he was a spectator aboard a British ship during the attack on Fort McHenry in the BATTLE OF BALTIMORE (September 12–14, 1814). Key had traveled through the British lines to arrange the release of Dr. William Beanes, who had been taken captive in the British campaign against Washington, D.C. Although the British agreed to release Beanes, they detained the Americans during the night of September 12–13, as they launched a massive bombardment on Fort McHenry. After watching the attack from aboard a British warship, and seeing the American flag still flying in the morning, Key was inspired to write a poem—"The Star Spangled Banner." Although it is not known with certainty when he wrote the words, family and friends claim that he did so while in a British longboat taking him ashore on September 13. Nevertheless, he soon shared the lines with others, and within days of the great victory at Baltimore, the poem was published as a handbill. Soon it was being sung to the tune of the British drinking song, "To Anacreon in Heaven," in taverns throughout the nation.

Key wrote some other poetry, but little of real note. He focused most of his energies on his law career and served as the U.S. district attorney in Washington, D.C., from 1833 to 1841. Written at a time of rising American nationalism, his best-known work remained popular. In 1931, Congress adopted "The Star-Spangled Banner" as the U.S. national anthem.

Further reading: Sadyebeth Lowitz, *Francis Scott Key* (Minneapolis: Lerner Publishing Company, 1967); Sam Meyer, *Paradoxes of Fame: The Francis Scott Key Story* (Annapolis, Md.: Eastwind Publishing, 1995).

Know-Nothing Party

The Know-Nothings were members of a nativist political movement in the United States in the 1840s and 1850s that was organized to oppose the great wave of immigrants who entered the United States after 1846. Know-Nothings began as a secret fraternity called the "Order of the Star Spangled Banner" who enlisted over a million members across the country in 1854 and 1855. When asked any questions about it they replied "I know nothing." Thus, they were swiftly labeled the "Know-Nothings."

IMMIGRATION grew sharply in the 1830s and 1840s and became increasingly Roman Catholic with the arrival of large waves of Irish and Germans. Simultaneously, a Protestant revival flourished in a climate of economic change and insecurity. Evangelists demonized Catholics as "Papists" who followed authoritarian leaders, imported crime and disease, stole jobs, and practiced moral depravities. A barrage of such agitation led Protestant workingmen to burn the Ursuline Convent near Boston and to riot in several cities; 30 were killed and hundreds injured in Philadelphia in 1844. The Know-Nothings grew out of this increasingly nativist atmosphere. Their anti-immigrant doctrines became even more popular when Irish and German Catholic immigration swelled to unprecedented numbers after 1845.

The new immigrants appeared to assimilate too slowly, clinging tenaciously to their old ways. The Germans retained their language, and the Irish adhered closely to the Catholic Church. Both, moreover, depressed the labor market while the Irish, especially, showed considerable political zeal—and usually voted the Democratic ticket.

The Know-Nothings attracted working-class and middle-class voters angered by the job competition from immigrants, the increase in crime, public drunkenness, and pauperism that accompanied immigration; the supposed pollution of the body politic by ignorant immigrant voters; and an assertiveness by Catholic clergymen that supposedly threatened the nation's Protestant values and institutions. Such nativist sentiments had long existed among many Americans, but they had never before been expressed in such powerful form.

Among the chief legislative aims of the Know-Nothings were an extension in the period required for naturalization from five to 21 years, the exclusion of the foreign-born and Catholics from public office, the limitation (or prohibition) of alcohol sales, and the restriction of public-school teaching to Protestants.

As early as the 1840s, there were local nativist parties in several northern states that drew support away from the DEMOCRATIC PARTY and WHIG PARTY. The movement was temporarily eclipsed by the MEXICAN-AMERICAN WAR and the debates over SLAVERY. However, when the slavery issue was temporarily quieted by the COMPROMISE OF 1850, the nativist movement again came to the fore. By the early 1850s, there was a trend to organize nationally against the presumed immigrant threat. The old parties, the nativists said, had not confronted the danger. The Democrats, it was charged, were supported by the aliens; the party needed their votes and catered to their whims.

Growing rapidly, the Know-Nothings allied themselves with the group of Whigs who followed MILLARD FILLMORE. In the 1854 election, they almost captured New York State, swept the polls in Massachusetts and Delaware, and had local successes in other states. The disintegration

A pronativist cartoon that depicts an Irish and a German immigrant stealing a ballot box *(Library of Congress)*

of the Whig Party aided them in their strides toward national influence. Looking toward extension into the South, in 1855 they openly assumed the name American Party and cast aside much of their characteristic secrecy. By the mid-1850s the nativist American Party (a.k.a. "Know-Nothings") had won six governorships and controlled legislatures in Massachusetts, New Hampshire, Connecticut, Rhode Island, Pennsylvania, Delaware, Maryland, Kentucky, and California. They enacted numerous laws to harass and penalize immigrants (as well as newly annexed Mexicans), including the first literacy tests for voting, which were designed to disenfranchise the Irish in particular.

By 1855, 90 U.S. congressmen were linked to the party. They attracted many northern Whigs to their point of view, along with an important number of Democrats. Southern Whigs also joined because of growing sectional tensions caused by the reintroduction of the slavery issue into national politics in 1854. For a time it seemed as if the Know-Nothings would be the main opposition party in the United States.

By 1856, when the party had abandoned secrecy and campaigned publicly as the American Party, many people expected it to elect the next president. But at the national convention in February 1856, which nominated ex-Whig Millard Fillmore for president, Know-Nothings split along sectional lines over the slavery extension issue. The Know-Nothings of the South supported slavery, while northern members opposed it. At the 1856 convention, 42 northern delegates walked out when a motion to support the MISSOURI COMPROMISE was ignored. This time the slavery issue split the Know-Nothing movement as it had the Whigs. While the American Party presidential candidate, Fillmore, won more than 21 percent of the popular vote and eight electoral votes, the national strength of the Know-Nothing movement was broken.

That same year, the great majority of northern Know-Nothings joined the Republicans in supporting JOHN C. FRÉMONT for president, and between 1856 and 1860 almost all the rest of Fillmore's northern supporters became Republicans. Those converts helped Lincoln garner 500,000 more votes in 1860 than Frémont had won in 1856.

Know-Nothing parties remained strong in a number of northern states in the late 1850s, but the party was spent as a national force before the election of 1860.

Further reading: Tyler Gregory Anbinder, *Nativism and Slavery: The Northern Know Nothings and the Politics of the 1850s* (New York: Oxford University Press, 1992).

—Richard Friedline

L

labor movements

Given the divergent regional economies in the antebellum North and South, laborers' efforts to get fair treatment for their work varied widely. In the North, wage-earning workers fought and sometimes struck for direct improvements to work conditions and in the ability to organize as an affiliated group, such as a union. Although these efforts were often bloody, they marked what would become a standard employee-owner/employer state of coexistence. In the slave-labor South, slaves lacked the standing as employed workers to present such demands. Nonetheless, slaves entered into varieties of negotiations and work slowdowns with planters, overseers, and other members of the staple-crop (cotton, rice, sugar) hierarchy to acquire and maintain a modicum of independence.

The North

After the American Revolution, many people searched for ways to create a more just and perfect society. At the same time, an increasingly industrialized workplace was bringing various constraints to workers. The interaction of high-minded reform and the practical fight for humane work conditions helped to fuel early labor movements during the first half of the 19th century. Since the late 18th century, skilled urban workers had joined in local groups to protest wage cuts, but trade unions did not begin in earnest until the 1820s, with the formation of unions such as the Mechanics' Union of Trade Associations in Philadelphia in 1827. Over the next decades, several skilled trade unions formed, with some, such as the International Typographical Union (1852), representing several countries.

As industrial capitalism increased over the period, workers experienced growing financial and social distance between themselves and owners. In addition to work-related demands, this perceived inequality fostered another reason for labor reform: changes that would build a more socially equal society. Thus, in addition to fighting for higher wages, the labor movement also enacted reforms such as labor-related political parties and campaigns for equal rights. These two strands of the labor movement—one for improving job-related concerns, one for improving society—would dominate northern labor reform during the antebellum years.

For much of the antebellum period, journeyman workers (those less experienced and below master workers) linked their case for better working conditions to the ongoing universal aim of a just society, the ideal that Americans fought for during the American Revolution. For example, when the ECONOMY revived after the PANIC OF 1819, many unions called for improved conditions, such as the ongoing call for the 10-hour workday. Among them were New York workers in 1827, who contended that employers who sought to extend the workday to 11 hours were "aggressors upon the rights of their fellow citizens . . . [and] justly obnoxious to the indignation of every honest man." At mass demonstrations in eastern cities such as Philadelphia and New York, workers of various craft unions united in their goals for what the Philadelphia Mechanics' Union of Trade Associations called the need to fight "the desolating evils which must invariably arise from a depreciation of the intrinsic value of human labour . . ."

Workers also took direct action in the form of strikes to demonstrate displeasure with owner actions. Continuing a practice that began with artisans during the late 18th century, workers often staged a turnout, in which a group of workers remained unemployed until wages reached a given level. Generally, strikes in the early 19th centuries occurred in cities and involved skilled members of trade groups, such as shoemakers and tailors. Concerns involved improving the pay scale or reducing the length of the workday. As strikes increased during the 1820s and 1830s, small labor groups that discovered shared goals united to form larger and potentially more powerful associations. Although violence occurred during these strike protests, no strike-related deaths occurred until 1850, when two tailors were killed as police attempted to break up a striking crowd.

To increase the chances for labor reform, laborers and reformers during this time sought political representation and power by forming political parties. In the late 1820s, the Philadelphia Mechanics' Union, a pioneering multicraft union, formed the Workingmen's Party of Philadelphia. Other Workingmen's Parties arose in eastern cities, including Boston and New York, and at least one representative was elected to a position in local government. Some party leaders' positions undercut support among more moderate party members. New Yorker Thomas Skidmore, for instance, called for equal rights, an end to inherited land, and the redistribution of wealth. But some ideas, such as reducing special privilege among the financial elite, controlling monopolies, opening public lands for homesteading, and creating a large-scale public school system, gained widespread popularity between the 1820s and the 1840s. Further, many of the Workingmen's Party's ideas came to be expressed by more powerful political parties, notably Democrats and Whigs. As a result, most Workingmen's Parties dissolved during the 1830s.

However, the unity among trade unions that developed during the 1820s continued and resulted in several dozen new multitrade unions during the next two decades, such as the General Trades Union and the National Trades Union. These unions embodied an increasing understanding of the need for all workers to pool their efforts to counter increasingly sophisticated campaigns of commercial interests. Such efforts were epitomized in an opinion in the *Journal of Commerce,* which equated strikes with "war with the order of things which the Creator has established for the general good." Debate over which public policy was true to democratic ideals—building a society upon accepted views of equality and justice or allowing society to emerge amidst economic freedom—continued throughout the antebellum period (and beyond).

Shortly after strikes became regular practices after the close of the 18th century, employers sought defense through the courts. Successful prosecutions of striking workers were mounted before the 1820s on criminal conspiracy charges. By 1829 in New York, a law was passed to censure any collective action that is "injurious to public morals or to trade and commerce."

Despite such rulings, strikes for improved hours and pay continued through the 1830s, as did employer and other forms of community-based attacks. In 1836, New York journeymen tailors began a strike over violations of negotiated agreements on pay rates and hiring union labor. After an outdoor protest, a grand jury indicted several of the protesters, 20 of whom were convicted on conspiracy charges. A massive demonstration that included over 10 percent of all New York residents protested the decision.

Although popular support for the labor demands of male workers was increasing, women often gained little favor for their labor protests. Since the 1810s, females dominated the textile mills in Massachusetts and formed associations in the 1820s. Many male laborers disparaged female workers and considered the presence of women in the workforce a twofold attack. The female worker attacked domestic society, in which women were to restrict their sphere of influence to the home; and the workforce in general, where their menial jobs lowered the overall standard of a trade. Still, female workers continued to form other trade associations, such as the Tailoresses' Society, and protested wage cuts. At the Lowell, Massachusetts, textile mills in 1834 and 1836, women staged two widespread strikes over increases in room and board charges and reductions in pay, one involving over 15 percent of mill workers. At one point, more than 1,000 girls marched through Lowell streets, singing, "Oh, isn't it a pity, such a pretty girl as I / Should be sent to the factory to pine away and die?"

As mid-century approached, unions began to gain more rights under U.S. law. In 1842, the appeal ruling of Chief Justice Lemuel Shaw in *Commonwealth v. Hunt* granted unions the right to organize. The case involved an 1840 conviction of seven labor leaders for criminal conspiracy in calling a strike by the Boston Journeymen Bootmakers' Society against the hiring of nonunion employees. Justice Shaw's ruling allowed the right of a union to make its presence and requests known by a strike. Nonetheless, strikes did not resume in earnest until the early 1850s, when hundreds of strikes were launched.

Well into the 1830s, trade unions represented only skilled workers such as tailors and printers. But the issue of unskilled labor and unionization came into discussion as tens of thousands of European, primarily Irish, immigrants entered the United States during the 1820s and 1830s to toil as unskilled laborers. Working at ship construction, railroad building, and as dock workers, these workers often formed secret groups to stage protests and targeted acts of violence. In 1835, skilled and unskilled workers united for a general strike in Philadelphia. This joint experience led the large General Trades Union to open membership to unskilled workers and pointed to the workers' understanding that all workers share common goals. As striking tradesmen on the street yelled, "We are all day laborers!"

Throughout the antebellum decades, economic conditions directly affected union growth. Particularly destructive were economic declines. The depression of 1819 caused businesses to close, dismiss workers, or drastically reduce wages. In turn, workers viewed unions as tangential to creating work, and many of them ended their existence. Businesses welcomed the erosion of unions; the *Journal of Commerce* called it a welcome step toward eliminating morally diseased unions "thoroughly." The PANIC OF 1837 and a depression that lasted from 1839 to 1843 generated prolonged unemployment that similarly diminished union power.

By the early 1850s unions and union membership had increased, with ethnic groups such as the Irish and Germans now actively mobilizing and joining forces. While craft hierarchy and ethnic tensions continued, labor leaders sought to unite workers. As one leader said of business in 1855, "They wish to separate the American mechanics from the German, and the German from the Irish; they want to keep you in a divided condition so that you cannot concentrate your action for the benefit of yourselves and fellow workingmen." This solidarity aided workers in the panic of 1854–55 and for decades to come, as voiced by a German worker: "We all belong to one great family—the Workingmen's family!"

The South

Although large-scale plantation owners viewed themselves, in the words of one planter, as "kind masters" and the slaves' lot as protected, the millions of slaves who worked the farms viewed their lives differently: as paths of modification and resistance. The negotiations that slaves devised in working under their owners and overseers mark the primary form of labor action in the South during the antebellum period and the slaves' main method for achieving some scraps of independence.

Slaves on large plantations, which held between 20 and 100 of them, had the greatest chance for family stability; their work was needed, and for that reason families might be kept together. How they would be treated by their masters was less predictable. All masters wanted productivity from their slaves, but some used physical punishment to achieve it, while others employed various types of personal inducements. Among them might be the right to hunt, fish, and plant one's own garden and market its crops. Such activities allowed slaves to have some portion of life that belonged to them, not to the plantation.

In coastal cities, transient day laborers (who were often white but without land) working the plantations and farms displayed different methods for gaining acceptable treatment. They argued with workers and owners, were unruly and unpredictable, and maintained a sense of social superiority. Through these actions, they demonstrated that they were above slaves and had no connection to the plantation (where slaves worked).

Acts of slave resistance were common, as they consisted of any action not requested by an owner. Typical behaviors included spilling food and drink on a member of the owner's family, breaking equipment, or working inefficiently. Slaves viewed such rebelliousness with equanimity. As one young slave said, "They always tell us it's wrong to lie and steal, but why did the white folks steal my mammy and her mammy?" Other slave practices of self-preservation included the establishment of secret trading groups that exchanged liquor for stolen plantation goods. In addition to providing goods, this secret trading allowed slaves and white traders to discuss matters from family concerns to escape. Any of these interactions was considered an act of disobedience and subject to punishment.

Rarer and more feared by owners were overt acts of physical aggression or sabotage. Among such acts were the 1822 insurrection led by a free slave named DENMARK VESEY and the 1831 insurrection of NAT TURNER. Concerned about curtailing such unrest, political leaders passed laws limiting slave education. In Virginia and North Carolina, slaves were prohibited from learning to read. The just society that reformers and workers were fighting for in the North was far more distant in the South.

Further reading: American Social History Project, *Who Built America: Working People and the Nation's Economy, Politics, Culture, and Society,* Vol. 1 (New York: Pantheon Books, 1989–92); Editors of *American Heritage* and Joseph L. Gardner, *Labor on the March: The Story of America's Unions* (New York: American Heritage Publishing Co., dist. by Harper & Row, 1969); Jacqueline Jones, *A Social History of the Laboring Classes: From Colonial Times to the Present,* rev. ed. (Malden, Mass.: Blackwell Publishers, 1999).

—Melinda Corey

Lafitte, Jean (ca. 1780–ca. 1825)

A notorious pirate and hero of the BATTLE OF NEW ORLEANS (January 8, 1815), Jean Lafitte lived an adventurous life packed with intrigue. Believed to have been born in France, Lafitte eventually made his way to the United States, where he led a group of pirates headquartered on the Baratarian coast, south of New Orleans. Starting around 1810, he and his cohorts frequently targeted Spanish ships, and, with the help of Lafitte's brother Pierre, used New Orleans as a depository for the confiscated goods and slaves that came into their possession.

The WAR OF 1812 (1812–15) interrupted the smuggling and piracy enterprise of Lafitte's operation. In September 1814 he was approached by the British and offered a large sum of money as well as land and a commission in the Royal Navy if he and his men would join with British forces in an assault on New Orleans. Lafitte turned down the offer, and a few days later his ships and headquarters at Barataria were raided by the U.S. Navy. In exchange for a pardon, Lafitte told the Americans about the British offer and agreed to help the United States stop the impending British attack. Indeed, Lafitte and a number of his men served admirably in the Battle of New Orleans, dutifully manning artillery pieces and earning the praise of

General ANDREW JACKSON for bravely contributing to the American victory. After the war, Lafitte received a pardon from President James Madison for attacks on U.S. citizens and property as a reward for his service.

Lafitte took advantage of this new lease on life and almost immediately returned to piracy. With the United States in firm control of Louisiana and the eastern approaches to the Gulf of Mexico, Lafitte and his men moved westward. In 1817 they settled near present-day Galveston, on the southern coast of the province of Tejas, in Spanish territory. From there they engaged in numerous smuggling and piracy operations, and Lafitte's empire expanded. He went from having only a few hundred men to just over a thousand, and for the next three years he successfully attacked American and Spanish ships in the Gulf of Mexico and the Caribbean without any trouble. In 1820, however, the U.S. Navy went in search of Lafitte after some of his men seized American property. Under pressure and fearing capture, he and a band of followers left Galveston in 1821 and probably continued their activities from the coast of newly independent Mexico. The cause of his death is unknown, but he is believed to have died around 1825.

Further reading: J. H. Ingraham, *Lafitte, The Pirate of the Gulf*, 2d ed. (Upper Saddle River, N.J.: Literature House, 1970).

—Sarah Eppler Janda

Lake Erie, Battle of (September 10, 1813)

The Battle of Lake Erie was a pivotal contest during the WAR OF 1812 (1812–15). It gave American forces control of Lake Erie and compelled the British to retreat from western Canada.

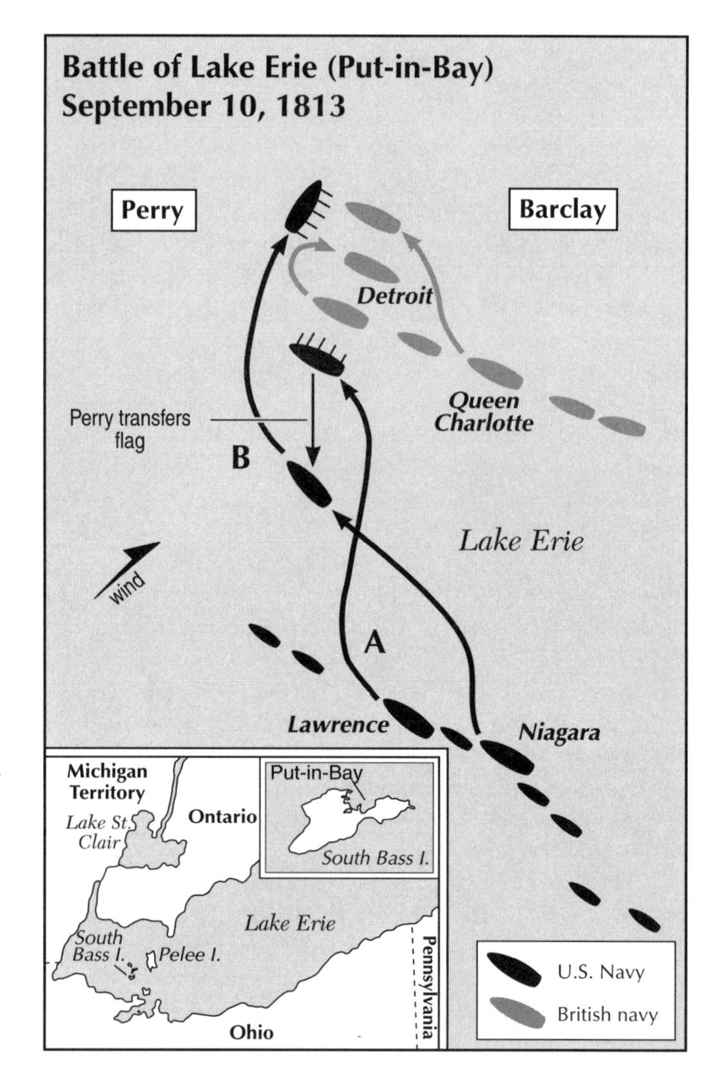

In the early months of the war, the British controlled both Lake Ontario and Lake Erie, enabling them to capture Fort Detroit and supply their troops and Indian allies farther west. The Americans, realizing the need to take control of Lake Erie, assigned the task to Lieutenant Oliver Hazard Perry. Perry was only 27 years old, but he had been in the U.S. Navy since the age of 13. He was the ideal man for the job, with great confidence, excellent administrative skills, and experience in shipbuilding. As commodore, Perry immediately had his men begin constructing ships on the beach near present-day Erie, Pennsylvania. Within a few months, they had produced two brigs and four schooners.

The British commander on Lake Erie was Lieutenant Robert Barclay, who, like Perry, was young, energetic, and ambitious. Although he temporarily held the upper hand, he had a smaller fleet and fewer men and resources. Barclay was unable to convince his superiors to divert men and supplies to Lake Erie from the Lake Ontario region. Eventually he was forced to improvise in equipping his ships. He even stripped local forts of their guns for his squadron. As a result, Barclay's flagship alone had guns of six different calibers, many of dubious effectiveness.

After considerable jockeying for position on the lake and attempting to blockade each other, the two sides met on September 10, 1813. The more heavily armed American force had 10 vessels to the British six. Nevertheless, the battle was a closely fought affair, with each side inflicting severe damage on the other. Perry's flagship the *Lawrence* was disabled, and he was forced to transfer to the *Niagara.* He then daringly sailed straight at the British line and in a matter of minutes was able capture the British flagship and force their squadron to surrender. There were many killed and wounded on both sides, including the seriously wounded Barclay. After the battle, Perry sent the message "We have met the enemy and they are ours" to General WILLIAM HENRY HARRISON.

As a result of his victory Commodore Perry became a national hero, and Congress voted extra pay and generous prize money for him and his crew. The victory gave the Americans a substantial psychological boost and control of Lake Erie. The British general Henry Procter was forced to retreat, and the British relinquished control of Lake Erie to the Americans. This helped to eliminate the danger of British attacks on American forces in the West. Less than a month later, American troops crossed the lake into Canada and won an important victory at the BATTLE OF THE THAMES (October 5, 1813), forcing the British to relinquish their control of the area and cancel their invasion plans. The navy promoted Perry to captain, and he went on to commands in the Mediterranean and the South Atlantic. He never again engaged in combat and died of yellow fever in 1819. Following the War of 1812, there was no more naval warfare on the Great Lakes, and the Canadian-American border was eventually demilitarized.

Further reading: Reginald Horsman, *The War of 1812* (New York: Knopf, 1969); David Curtis Skaggs and Gerard T. Altoff, *A Signal Victory: The Lake Erie Campaign, 1812–1813* (Annapolis, Md.: Naval Institute Press, 1997).

—Robert Lively

Lamy, Jean Baptiste (1814–1888)

Roman Catholic missionary and later archbishop in the American Southwest, Jean Baptiste Lamy was responsible for the establishment of the first school for teaching English in Santa Fe. Lamy was born in 1814 in Lempdes, France, and ordained a priest at Clermont-Ferrand in December 1838. After volunteering for missionary work, he came to the United States to minister to the growing Catholic community in Cincinnati, Ohio.

Under the terms of the TREATY OF GUADALUPE HIDALGO, which ended the MEXICAN-AMERICAN WAR, the United States took the northern third of the Republic of Mexico, a vast area that today includes the states of CALIFORNIA, New Mexico, and Arizona. In response to the new U.S. sovereignty, Lamy was named vicar apostolic of New Mexico. His authority extended over New Mexico, Arizona, and parts of modern Colorado, Nevada, and Utah, a vast area with a then-sparse population mostly Mexican in origin, living in small and widely dispersed villages.

From the beginning, Lamy's new office was a challenging one. He arrived in Santa Fe to find great resentment at the appointment of an outsider to a position of such authority. In 1853 he was named bishop. He worked with Anglo-Americans, Mexicans (Mexican Americans after the treaty), and NATIVE AMERICANS across a vast landscape. In New Mexico he encountered a church that had become self-contained and partly secularized by distance, neglect, and personal choice. Some local priests had married into the most influential families in New Mexico, and Lamy's attempts at reform became closely intertwined with politics. One of the defrocked priests, Jose Manuel Gallegos, became head of an anti-Lamy faction and won election as New Mexico's territorial delegate in 1853. Father Jose Antonio Martinez represented this local authority, and after continuing disagreements, Lamy removed Martinez.

In 1875 Lamy was raised to archbishop. He was again drawn into politics by a bill in the Territorial Assembly that proposed to limit the Catholic Church's influence in the territory's educational system. Lamy actively opposed the bill, and it was defeated. He died at Santa Fe in 1888 after more than 35 years of service to his adopted region. His reforms reshaped the Catholic Church in the American Southwest.

Further reading: Paul Horgan, *Lamy of Santa Fe; His Life and Times* (New York: Farrar, Straus and Giroux, 1975).

Larkin, Thomas Oliver (1802–1858)

Merchant and U.S. consul in Mexican California, Larkin mounted an extended propaganda campaign in favor of the American acquisition of CALIFORNIA. A native of Massachusetts, Larkin moved to California in 1832. Settling in Monterey, he quickly became a powerful commercial force in the town. He used his connections with Boston and the New England merchants to direct the growing trade of California's pastoral economy. With the secularization of the CALIFORNIA MISSIONS after 1833, the region's economy shifted from the missions to the growing number of ranchos. These large pastoral estates, many of them benefiting from the acquisition of mission lands, began to develop a thriving trade in hides and tallow, carried almost exclusively in ships from New England ports. Larkin was at the heart of this growing trade.

Many American merchants who settled in California in the 1830s and 1840s married into the leading Californio families and established roots in the local Mexican community. Larkin, by contrast, remained a citizen of the United States. He married Rachel Hobson Holmes, a widow, and he was proud that his children were the first born in California to U.S. citizens. As an alien resident, he did not participate in politics, but he did discreetly support the activities of Juan Bautista Alvarado to establish an independent California.

In 1844 Secretary of State James Buchanan appointed Larkin American consul in California. In this capacity, Larkin wrote long and detailed letters to the secretary about affairs in Mexican California, ever mindful of the nation's economic and strategic interests there. He came to believe strongly in British designs on naval anchorages along the Pacific coast, especially the harbor at San Francisco. In October 1845 Buchanan gave him an additional appointment as "confidential agent." Buchanan asked Larkin to work for the secession of California from Mexico, with a view to its eventual annexation to the United States. In January 1845, Congress had annexed the Republic of Texas as the 31st state, and this provided a model of the direction in which Buchanan wished to move American policy regarding California. Larkin was to play a vital role in the U.S. plans.

However, these plans were cut short by JOHN C. FRÉMONT's activities, and with the outbreak of the BEAR FLAG REVOLT, Larkin found his diplomatic initiatives superseded. The beginning of the MEXICAN-AMERICAN WAR the next year was President JAMES K. POLK's shortcut to the acquisition of California.

With the discovery of gold in California in January 1848, Larkin became one of the American government's main sources of information about developments in the region. His correspondence with Buchanan offers one of the clearest and most insightful commentaries on the early impact of gold on California's society and economy. In late 1848, Larkin served as a delegate to the California Constitutional Convention. Thereafter, he left public life to concentrate on his business and real estate holdings. He died in 1858.

Further reading: Hammond, George P., ed. *The Larkin Papers,* 10 vols. (Berkeley: University of California Press, 1951–64).

lead mines

The first important lead mines were found in upper Louisiana, in what would become the state of Missouri. Located in St. Francis County, some 70 miles south of St. Louis, these deposits produced some 9 million tons of pig lead, most produced after 1800. The first Europeans to work the surface ores included Sieur de Bienville, one of the founders of French Louisiana. In 1719, Philippe Renaut began systematic mining in the Illinois Country with 200 experienced French miners and 500 slaves purchased in Santo Domingo and brought to the site. Mine La Motte and Mine à Breton produced the first lead for trade. The mines and the trade they fostered were an important part of the French settlements by the 1740s. Still, the Missouri mines remained only marginally productive, as the attention of colonial entrepreneurs shifted to trade in furs. In the years of Spanish rule, MOSES AUSTIN moved from Virginia to Missouri and took an active part in the lead-mining business. With the profits from his mines, he moved his family (including son STEPHEN F. AUSTIN) to St. Louis in 1816.

The second area of lead mineral lay in the upper Mississippi Valley, at the intersection of what would become the states of Illinois, Wisconsin, and Iowa. The area was much larger but less rich than the deposits in Missouri. The earliest leading figure in the region was Julien Dubuque, a French-Canadian entrepreneur who began mining on the Upper Mississippi in 1788, near the site of the present city of Dubuque. Indian peoples knew of these mineral deposits and had mined them sporadically. Dubuque urged the Sauk and Fox to resume work, and he bought lead ore from the Indian miners and shipped it south to St. Louis. By the time of his death in 1810, Dubuque had also begun mining on the Fever River (later renamed the Galena River) and other sites along the Mississippi.

In 1819, after the close of the WAR OF 1812 had established a degree of peace with NATIVE AMERICANS, American miners moved into the region. By the middle of the 1820s, an early mining rush—much like those later to mining sites in the Far West—was underway to the area. Important towns appeared to mark the sites of these mining enterprises: Galena (Illinois), Mineral Point (Wisconsin), and Dubuque (Iowa). Of these towns, Galena was the most important, perhaps because Illinois was early organized as a territory and so offered a degree of institutional structure. Miners here, as later in the Far West, made do with their own rules and regulations. They organized mining districts and adopted local rules for claims and adjudicating disputes, thus laying the foundation for many techniques in mining and organization that would later be used in the CALIFORNIA GOLD RUSH. Lead mining expanded across the three sites through the 1830s, but by 1840 the richest of the deposits had been mined out. With the news of the gold strikes in California, an emigration of lead miners to the West depleted the lead region.

The experiences of lead mining in Missouri and on the upper Mississippi River were important in preparing a foundation for large-scale mining activities in California and eventually across the length and breadth of the West. Underground mining in the lead mines evolved slowly and through trial and error, but it did evolve. Furthermore, many of regulations and procedures that emerged from the lead mines would be transported across the plains with the FORTY-NINERS and reappear in the goldfields. These included the mining claim—namely, how claims would be laid off, recorded, and worked and under what conditions claims might be vacated and sold. The institution of the miner's court first appeared in the lead mines, along with the idea of the mining district as a sovereign body empowered to make and change its rules of conduct.

The lead mines also represented a significant challenge to the orderly distribution of public lands. Since 1785, the nation had evolved a procedure for the survey and sale of acreage to the public. PUBLIC LAND POLICY had consumed much time in Congress, and the continuing advance of settlement to the West had made land sales a necessary part of the frontier's development. In the lead mines of the upper Mississippi, the federal government confronted an awkward variation in its policies. In response to the spread of population and the land system to the upper Mississippi Country, the federal government issued a proclamation reserving lead lands from sale. The policy proved unworkable, and like so many infringements on the public domain, was ignored and reversed.

Further reading: Joseph Schaeffer, *The Wisconsin Lead Region*, (Madison: University of Wisconsin Pess, 1932); James E. Wright, *The Galena Lead District* (Madison: University of Wisconsin Press, 1966).

Liberia

Liberia is a West African nation founded in 1822 by American ex-slaves and subsidized by the AMERICAN COLONIZATION SOCIETY. The circumstances surrounding Liberia's founding reveal the conflicting motivations of Americans, black and white, who were concerned about SLAVERY and the presence of Africans in the young republic. Some whites supported colonization because they wanted to rid the nation of African people, whom they deemed unfit to live in a democracy. Some southern slaveholders advocated the removal of free blacks, whom they considered a threat to their ability to control their slaves. Other whites were more sympathetic to the discrimination experienced by free blacks in the United States; they argued that blacks would be relieved of such racism if they were returned to Africa. Other whites believed that ex-slaves should return to Africa to bring Christianity and European civilization to the continent. All of these groups were skeptical about whether African Americans would ever be accepted by a white populace whose political ideologies were increasingly racist.

Free blacks were also conflicted about the colonization issue. Some shared the view that African Americans would never be treated fairly in the United States, and should therefore return to Africa. Others disagreed, arguing that ex-slaves should stay in the United States to fight for civil rights as citizens and demand the abolition of slavery. Many saw the colonization effort as a cynical plot devised by slave owners to secure domination of their slaves.

Amid this growing debate, the American Colonization Society (ACS) was founded in 1817. As was common practice among reform societies of the time, the ACS raised funds by selling lifetime membership. By 1820, the society had published the first issue of *The African Intelligencer*, a magazine designed to spread the word about colonization. Edited by aspiring missionary Jehudi Ashmun, the journal contained articles about the slave trade, the prospects for founding an African colony, and a copy of the ACS constitution. Support for the cause was meager, however, and publication ceased after the first issue. However, by 1822 the Society was able to purchase land and establish a colony on the West African coast. Ashmun traveled to the new colony that same year, becoming one of the early leaders of the repatriation effort.

By the mid-1820s, support for the ACS had grown, and emigrants began to sail for the new colony, called Liberia. Influential political figures such as HENRY CLAY and former President James Madison were heavily involved in the organization. Sale of lifetime memberships had increased, giving the society the funds needed to continue developing and expanding the venture. Ashmun purchased or leased additional lands along major waterways, establishing the colony as a regional power able to intimidate neighboring tribes. In an 1825 treaty, several native kings agreed (often because Ashmun threatened to use force) to cede land in return for tobacco, rum, gunpowder, and other goods. The colonists established the first Liberian town at Cape Montserado, which they renamed Monrovia after President James Monroe. Members of the ACS continued to promote settlement, sending dispatches back to the United States that told of the emigrants' great success.

By the 1830s, colonization efforts were coming under attack by more radical reform groups working to abolish slavery. Abolitionists such as William Lloyd Garrison criticized the ACS for colluding with slave owners. This new school of abolitionists thought that colonization efforts were an attempt to strengthen slaveholders by removing the members of society most likely to question the slave system: free blacks. Abolitionists believed that colonizationists were undermining efforts to eradicate slavery by removing slave allies and by implicitly arguing that blacks should not be part of American society. The colonization effort continued, however, as free blacks emigrated to Liberia, and the ACS maintained their financial support. The organization even managed to convince some American state legislatures to help finance the effort.

Yet by the 1840s, the ACS could no longer afford to financially support Liberia. The colony was also in political jeopardy because it was not an official colony of the U.S. government, nor was it a sovereign nation. This precarious position endangered its future, because Liberians had no way to repel a political takeover by the British. In 1846, when the U.S. government refused to claim Liberia as an official colony, ACS leaders urged a declaration of independence. Thus, in 1847 the colony became the independent nation of Liberia, with Americo-Liberians (ex-slave emigrants and their descendants) controlling the government.

In the first decades after its founding, Liberian relations with the United States were strained. Because of the worsening American controversy over slavery, the federal government did not recognize Liberia until 1862. African Americans continued to emigrate to Liberia before and after the Civil War, but never in huge numbers. By the

1870s, the American Colonization Society had helped send over about 15,000 emigrants. The nation prospered at first, but it soon experienced economic decline due to competition from European commercial interests. Conflicts between the American-Liberian elite and indigenous tribes also jeopardized political stability. These problems continue to plague the West African nation, which went on to endure civil war and rampant political corruption during the 20th century.

Further reading: Raymond Leslie Buell, *Liberia: A Century of Survival, 1847–1947* (New York: Krause Reprint Company, 1969); Charles Spurgeon Johnson, *Bitter Canaan: The Story of the Negro Republic* (New Brunswick, N.J.: Transaction Books, 1987); Tom W. Shick *Behold the Promised Land: A History of Afro-American Settler Society in Nineteenth-Century Liberia* (Baltimore: Johns Hopkins University Press, 1980).

—Eleanor H. McConnell

Liberty Party

The Liberty Party was the first political party to run on an explicitly antislavery platform, nominating candidates for president in 1840 and 1844. The party, which was dominated by abolitionists, had little to say on issues other than SLAVERY. It generally garnered only scattered support at the polls but helped to lay the foundations for the FREE-SOIL PARTY in 1848 and then the REPUBLICAN PARTY of the 1850s. Members of the Liberty Party, many of whom were evangelical Christians, focused on the sinful nature of slavery and on rights for African Americans. They were also abolitionists who had broken with William Lloyd Garrison over whether they should involve themselves in electoral politics.

The AMERICAN ANTI-SLAVERY SOCIETY, which had been wracked by internal disputes for years, finally collapsed completely in 1839–40. Abolitionists such as Gerret Smith of New York grew disillusioned with the WHIG PARTY when their leader HENRY CLAY came out in support of compromising with slave interests. They therefore began to search for a way to advance their cause in the political arena. The beginning of the Liberty Party as an independent political organization was controversial among many abolitionists, who feared that their efforts would divide their ranks and ultimately benefit the Democrats, the party most associated with slavery. The Liberty Party at its inception drew support from both Whigs and Democrats, but mainly from the former.

James Birney, the party's nominee in both of its presidential elections, was a Democrat. Born in Kentucky, Birney's father was a slaveholder who supported emancipation, as some of that class did at the turn of the 19th century. Birney himself later moved to Alabama, where he became one of the few proabolition members of that state's legislature. An early supporter of colonization, Birney freed his own slaves in 1834 when he moved back to Kentucky. He later moved across the Ohio River to the state of Ohio, where he was indicted for harboring a runaway slave. Having renounced colonization, he embraced abolitionism and subsequently broke with the followers of William Lloyd Garrison in that he wanted a political and constitutional solution to slavery. Birney and others also did not share Garrison's belief that women should have equal voting and officeholding rights with men within abolitionist societies.

Members of the new Liberty Party believed that slaveholders could be persuaded to get rid of their slaves, as Birney had done. He was nominated at the first convention of the Liberty Party in Albany, New York, in 1840, along with Thomas Earle, an abolitionist Democrat from Pennsylvania, as six states sent delegates. He did not conduct anything resembling a campaign; in fact, he was in London attending the World Anti-Slavery Convention throughout the 1840 election season. When the votes were counted, his total was about 7,000, nearly all of them from the New England states as well as New York, New Jersey, Pennsylvania, Ohio, Illinois, and Michigan. Thus, the center of Liberty Party support, such as it was, came from areas strongly influenced by New England Yankee culture. The party ran candidates for state and local office in New England and in other northern states. Among those who supported the Liberty Party were Quakers and Presbyterians, including some from the South who had migrated into the states of the old Northwest.

The debut of the Liberty Party, despite its lack of success at the polls, was significant, as this was the first time there had been a national political party which ran on an avowed antislavery platform. Its weakness in its initial outing was demonstrated by the fact that an estimated 90% of those in abolitionist societies did not vote for the Liberty Party but instead mainly supported the Whigs and their successful candidate, WILLIAM HENRY HARRISON. When Harrison died soon after taking office and was replaced by a southern slaveowner, JOHN TYLER, some Whigs who had hesitated to leave their party for the Liberty Party now joined the ranks of the latter.

In 1844 the Liberty Party nominated Birney once again, this time with Thomas Morris, a former Democratic senator from Ohio, as the vice presidential candidate. That year, Joshua Leavitt, the editor of the *Emancipator,* the Liberty Party newspaper, published a controversial pamphlet, *The Great Duelist,* in which he linked Whig nominee Henry Clay to dueling and slavery. Leavitt portrayed Clay as a violent and sinful man who did not possess sufficient moral character to be president. In the election that year, the Liberty Party garnered 62,000 votes, which represented a nearly ninefold increase over their 1840 results and 2 percent of the national total. In the key northern states of New York and Michigan, Liberty Party voters, most of whom would have otherwise gone to Clay, were a crucial factor in deciding the election in favor of Democratic nominee JAMES K. POLK of Tennessee.

The Liberty Party met again in convention at Buffalo, New York, in late 1847 to nominate a ticket for the next year's election. With Birney became incapacitated from injuries suffered in a fall from his horse, delegates nominated Senator John P. Hale of New Hampshire, an antislavery Democrat. Hale opposed slavery in principle but for constitutional reasons was reluctant to support the Liberty Party goals of abolishing slavery in Washington, D.C., and banning the interstate slave trade. For this reason, he waited almost two months before accepting the nomination. Before the campaign could begin in earnest, however, the Liberty Party dissolved as its members became one of the main groups that formed the new Free-Soil Party. That party had a broader constituency and wider set of goals, including providing settlers in the West with free homesteads and other provisions to draw Democrats and Whigs, than did the single-issue Liberty Party. Nonetheless, the Liberty Party had influenced the outcome of at least one presidential election and forced the nation as a whole to face more squarely the entire question of slavery. The party did fail in that its solution to slavery, that of repentance and peaceful dismantling of the slave system, did not come to pass, but rather its demise came about only after a horrific civil war. Even so, the Liberty Party can be considered one of the more important third parties of the 19th century.

Further reading: Richard H. Sewell, *Ballots for Freedom: Antislavery Politics in the United States* (New York: Oxford University Press, 1976); Vernon L. Volpe, *Forlorn Hope of Freedom: The Liberty Party in the Old Northwest, 1838–1848* (Kent, Ohio: Kent State University Press, 1990).

—Jason K. Duncan

literature

In the years following the Revolutionary War Americans began to develop new forms of political and social life. At the same time, they began to create a new literary culture—one that was influenced by a combination of European sources and North American experience. In the colonial period, Americans were heavily influenced by literature from Britain and western Europe. Novels, poetry, religious tracts, political treatises, and other kinds of literature circulated in the colonies, shaping cultural and political identity. But the exchange was not one-sided. Not only did European works discuss America, Americans increasingly published homegrown literary works in response to conditions in the colonies and Europe. While American writers looked to European models and established writing techniques, they also looked to the frontier world around them to examine new American themes, concerns, and experiences.

In the course of the generation after 1815, new strands appeared in American literature, including writings by Native Americans, African Americans, and a new kind of popular literature, aimed at a more broad-based audience. William Apess (or Apes) (1798–1839) was a Native American whose varied writings made him a literary figure of some influence. Born in Franklin County, Massachusetts, to a Pequot mother and a mixed race father (part Pequot, part Anglo-American), Apess aspired to be a Methodist minister. Denied a license to preach as a Methodist because of his Indian ancestry, Apess left the Methodist Episcopal Church and joined the Methodist Society, which ordained him without reservation in 1829. The same year, Apess published *A Son of the Forest: The Experience of William Apes, a Native of the Forest.* Although this autobiography may have been written as part of a church requirement to document his religious life, its publication was a powerful statement that Native Americans were equal to Euro-Americans in the sight of God, and it called for fair and equitable treatment of these people. Over the next nine years, Apess preached and wrote. He published three other books and a collection of sermons. The message of these works, like his first, was a challenge to the prevalent Euro-American assumptions of racial superiority. He also attacked the uses of European missions to the Indians as an exploitation of Native peoples and he described missionaries as agents of Euro-American imperialism bent on keeping the Indian peoples in an inferior position in American life. These strands came together in the practical arena with Apess's defense of the Mashpee and their lands in Massachusetts.

The 19th century saw the appearance of a broad-based popular literature for the first time. Washington Irving and James Fenimore Cooper were among the first American authors with a wide appeal to an American audience, but others who wrote in an even more popular vein followed them. The most important of these authors was George Lippard. Born on a farm in Chester County, Pennsylvania, Lippard first worked as a lawyer's assistant in Philadelphia, where he encountered the underside of American urban life. In 1842 he left the law to write a satirical column for a Philadelphia newspaper, *The Spirit of the Times.* In 1844 he published his first novel, *The Ladye Annabel; or, The Doom of the Poisoner,* a gothic tale of torture and the grotesque. His friend Edgar Allan Poe praised the inventive nature of the work. The next year, Lippard published the novel that would make him famous and would give him a place in the annals of American literature. *The Quaker City; or, The Monks of Monk-Hall* (1845) was an account of sexual depravity and drunkenness among Philadelphia's upper class. It marked Lippard's transition to social reformer and social commentator as well as gothic novelist. The novel was an instant best-seller, and it sold some 60,000 copies in the first year, the largest sale for an American novel until the publication of Harriet Beecher Stowe's *Uncle Tom's Cabin* (1852). Lippard wrote several other novels that dramatized upper-class depravity and urban corruption. Among the most important were *The Empire City* (1850) and *New York; Its Upper Ten and Lower Million* (1853). Lippard became a popular lecturer, and he worked tirelessly on behalf of labor groups. His novels are noteworthy as among the first products of a popular culture, whose themes had a pointed social message mixed with the gothic formula of the period.

With the emergence of the abolitionist movement in the 1830s came an interest in slave narratives. Written with a striking immediacy, these accounts of life in slavery became an important part of the abolition movement and entered into the life of American literary publications. The most important of these writings was Frederick Douglass's *Narrative of the Life of Frederick Douglass, Written by Himself.* This autobiography, an account of his early life in slavery and his escape, was written in part as exposition of the evils of the institution of slavery and in part as a way to establish the legitimacy of Douglass's early life as a slave. The book sold 30,000 copies in the United States and Britain, and it helped to make Douglass the most important African-American representative in the abolition movement and the most significant African-American author of the day. An accomplished writer and charismatic public speaker, Douglass appeared before northern audiences for 30 years. His autobiography was perhaps the most powerful literary statement in the anti-slavery roster of written accounts. Douglass also founded and edited his own newspaper, *The Northern Star* (1847). In 1852, Douglass published a novel, *The Heroic Slave,* which is generally considered the first major African-American fiction. The novel's central character was the leader of a violent slave revolt, and the book represented Douglass's shift in opposing slavery from moral suasion to activism, including armed rebellion.

The most prominent writers of the early 19th century included Washington Irving and James Fenimore Cooper, members of what became known as the Knickerbocker School. Irving's writings attempted to create a kind of American folk literature, with his satirical stories of early New York told by "Diedrich Knickerbocker." His *Sketch Book* (1819–20) introduced the famous stories "Rip Van Winkle" and "The Legend of Sleepy Hollow." He also published several histories, including his famous *Life of Washington* (1855–59). Irving's characterizations of American life were intended not only to entertain but also to develop his ideas about national identity and his sense of specifically American values.

Cooper's most important works were collectively known as the *Leather-stocking Tales,* some of the first American novels set in the rapidly developing American frontier. In *The Pioneers* (1823), Cooper combines elements of the sentimental and adventure novels to tell the story of life in the frontier town of Templeton (based on Cooperstown, New York, the settlement started by his father in the post-revolutionary years). He continued this story of the struggle between civilization and primitive savagery on the frontier at various points in American history with *The Last of the Mohicans* (1826), *The Prairie* (1827), *The Pathfinder* (1840), and *The Deerslayer* (1841). Cooper also wrote sea-adventure stories and volumes of social criticism that detailed his aristocratic fears about democracy run amok in the Jacksonian era. Other writers in the Knickerbocker School included poet William Cullen Bryant, James Kirke Paulding, and Fitz-Greene Halleck.

In a movement that became known as the "New England Renaissance," writers from this region developed a distinctive literature and philosophy from the 1830s to the Civil War. The transformation of intellectual life in New England could be said to begin with the Unitarian sermons of William Ellery Channing, who challenged religious orthodoxy and promoted a more liberal vision of spiritual life. The critiques raised by Unitarians later influenced the thinking behind the TRANSCENDENTAL MOVEMENT. Transcendentalists like RALPH WALDO EMERSON and HENRY DAVID THOREAU believed in the sanctity of individual experience and the divinity of nature. They promoted self-determination, the primacy of individual experience, and the divine connection between all living things. This philosophy was most apparent in Emerson's *Nature* (1836), *The American Scholar* (1837), and *Poems* (1847). Thoreau's most famous work, *Walden* (1854), detailed his experience living the simple life by Walden Pond in Concord, Massachusetts. In this account and his 1849 essay "Civil Disobedience," Thoreau presented a vision of principled action against the state and the right of individuals to listen to a higher moral law in place of a state law. Other transcendentalists included MARGARET FULLER, George Ripley (founder of the influential but short-lived BROOK FARM), Bronson Alcott, and Orestes A. Brownson. These thinkers were interested not only in realizing individual consciousness but in reshaping society to help people better realize social harmony.

Transcendentalist ideas about the place of the individual in the universe influenced other New England writers, most notably Nathaniel Hawthorne and Herman Melville. Both writers were more pessimistic about human potential

Nathaniel Hawthorne *(Library of Congress)*

than the transcendentalists were, but their singular styles owed a great deal to the ethos of the New England Renaissance. Hawthorne's greatest works examined the interior lives and sins of New Englanders. In *The Scarlet Letter* (1850), he gives his interpretation of the moral and spiritual conflicts of Puritan New England. In *The House of the Seven Gables* (1851), he again uses history as a major theme, showing how the sins of the past are revisited on the present within an old New England family. His other writings include *Twice-Told Tales* (1837) and *The Blithedale Romance* (1852).

Melville began his writing career with sea romances like *Typee* (1846), *Omoo* (1847), *Mardi* (1849), and *Redburn* (1849). These tales derived partly from his own experiences as a sailor, and were well received by the public. His later works, beginning with his masterpiece *Moby-Dick; or The Whale* (1851), transcended the sea-tale genre, developing a completely singular style and a dark sensibility. Indeed, although several of his later works were set at sea, they were more concerned with larger moral questions than in detailing life on the sea. His story "Benito Cereno" (1856) deals with the horrors of slavery, and his novella *Billy Budd* (published posthumously in 1924) describes conflicts between loyalty and justice, love and betrayal. Melville also wrote several works dealing with the dark side of the emerging American urban life, most notably "Bartleby the Scrivener" (1856) and *The Confidence-Man* (1857).

Other major writers examining the emerging urban America were Walt Whitman and Edgar Allan Poe. Whitman's poetry collection *Leaves of Grass* (1855, later expanded) expressed his optimism about human potential, celebrating democracy and the teeming urban life of New York City. Poe's style, in poems and prose, was much darker, dwelling on elements of the romantic, horrific, and grotesque. His major poems include "Annabelle Lee" (1847) and "The Raven" (1845). He published only one novel, the bizarre sea adventure *The Narrative of Arthur Gordon Pym* (1837); and numerous masterful and macabre stories, including "The Gold Bug" (1843), "The Murders in the Rue Morgue" (1843), "The Pit and the Pendulum" (1842), and "The Tell-Tale Heart" (1843). Other important poets of this period include Henry Wadsworth Longfellow and James Russell Lowell.

Probably the most influential and popular literary works of this period were written by women. Writers like Lydia Maria Child, Catharine Maria Sedgwick, Harriet Beecher Stowe, SARAH JOSEPHA HALE, Susan Warner, and Mrs. E.D.E.N. Southworth wrote some of the most loved and esteemed works in the decades before the Civil War. Their writing could be categorized as sentimental and concerned with social and individual reform. These "reform novels" addressed some of the most controversial issues of the day, attempting to reach a wide audience and appeal to their moral conscience. Warner's *The Wide, Wide World* (1850) became the best-selling novel *since Charlotte Temple,* only to be topped two years later by the phenomenal success of Stowe's antislavery novel *Uncle Tom's Cabin* (1852). Stowe continued her attack on SLAVERY and FUGITIVE SLAVE LAWS with *Dred: A Tale of the Great Dismal Swamp* (1856). Her novels are credited as among the most influential forces to bring the conflict over slavery to a head in the 1860s. The rise of professional women writers in America signalled an advance in women's opportunities to become part of the public sphere.

Another important literary development in the antebellum period was the increasing availability of reading materials. Improvements in the printing process triggered the rise in periodicals and the penny press—pulp genre fiction that could be mass-produced and sold cheaply. The establishment of free public education, libraries, and lyceums provided ready access to all types of literature. These institutions and the books they supplied were supposed to promote moral and social improvement through learning. The dissemination of such a diverse American literature reflected and shaped the controversies of the antebellum period, such as slavery, the position of women, the expansion and settlement of the West, and the rapid growth and INDUSTRIALIZATION of cities.

Further reading: Sacvan Bercovitch, ed., *The Cambridge History of American Literature: 1590–1820.* (New York:

Cambridge University Press, 1994); Cathy N. Davidson, *Revolution and the Word: The Rise of the Novel in America* (New York: Oxford University Press, 1986); Ann Douglas, *The Feminization of American Culture* (New York: Noonday Press, 1998); Jane Tompkins, *Sensational Designs: The Cultural Work of American Fiction, 1790–1860* (New York: Oxford University Press, 1985).

—Eleanor H. McConnell

Lovejoy, Elijah (1802–1837)

An abolitionist and editor of several antislavery newspapers, Elijah Lovejoy lost his life while guarding one of his presses. Born in Maine in 1802, he graduated from Colby College in 1826, taught school, and in 1827 moved to St. Louis. In 1832, having made the decision to enter the ministry, Lovejoy enrolled in the Princeton Seminary. After receiving his license to preach, he returned to St. Louis to edit the *St. Louis Observer,* the Presbyterian weekly paper. Gradually over the next few years, his editorials in the paper moved from theology to antislavery and the TEMPERANCE MOVEMENT. The St. Louis area was a hostile one for his new principles. Rather than change the content and tone of his writings, in 1836 Lovejoy moved across the Mississippi River to Alton, Illinois.

Illinois was a free state, but its southern and western boundaries were the Ohio and Mississippi Rivers, and SLAVERY was entrenched on the far side in Kentucky and Missouri. Alton had a strong community of former New Englanders who welcomed Lovejoy's views. It also had a surrounding countryside and a southern reach toward Cairo that supported the institution of slavery and violently opposed any suggestion of greater rights—whether political, economic, or social—for African Americans. Lovejoy changed the name of his paper to the *Alton Observer* and continued to publish his outspoken views on the evils of slavery.

Lovejoy's struggle to express his increasingly radical views and the appearance of a violent resistance against him came to revolve around his printing press. His first press was seized from the wharf in Alton and dumped into the river. A meeting of local citizens deplored this act and pledged support for another press; at the same time, they were careful to distance themselves from the editor's abolitionist ideas. The views of this meeting seemed to express a consensus of the town: Lovejoy was welcome to publish a

This engraving shows the mob attack on the offices of Elijah P. Lovejoy. *(Library of Congress)*

newspaper about Presbyterian Church issues; he was at risk when he ventured into the areas of slavery and abolition.

Lovejoy promised to confine his published views to church issues, but he gradually returned to his abolitionist foundations. On July 4, 1837, he printed an editorial that called for a meeting of antislavery followers in the Alton area to form a branch of the AMERICAN ANTI-SLAVERY SOCIETY. This call reawakened his opposition, and attacks on his newspaper became ever more vehement. The meeting took place, and the new antislavery society was organized in October 1837. As anger and tension rose, Lovejoy's friends urged him to leave Alton, if only temporarily. He refused. The Ohio Anti-Slavery Society promised him another press to continue his work. When the new press arrived on November 7, a riot took place between proslavery and antislavery factions, and in the confusion that followed, Lovejoy was shot and killed. He thus became one of the great martyrs of the ABOLITION MOVEMENT.

Further reading: Merton L. Dillon, *Elijah P. Lovejoy, Abolitionist Editor* (Urbana: University of Illinois Press, 1960).

lyceum movement

The lyceum movement was the first adult-education program in America. It was a major force in American cultural life from the mid-1820s through the 1850s. From its origins in New England, the lyceum concept spread across the nation's northern states and territories, traveling to the West Coast with the movement of the frontier settlers. It influenced the development of public education, fostered such ideas as abolitionism and women's rights, and nurtured the rise of American arts and letters.

Connecticut-born educator Josiah Holbrook (1788–1854) opened the first American lyceum in 1826 in Millbury, Massachusetts. Holbrook aimed to use lectures and debates to bring new ideas—both philosophical and practical—to members of his own community. The name and, to some extent, the concept was based on Aristotle's famous Lyceum in ancient Athens. Holbrook hoped that his lyceum would become a study group that would meet on a regular basis and allow all members to teach one another and share learning experiences. He believed that learning should continue through the course of a lifetime and that no social factor such as class, gender, age, profession, or lack of previous education should be permitted to stop that process.

Holbrook's lyceum was so successful that local lyceums began to spring up throughout Massachusetts. In 1831, he formed the National American Lyceum, which encouraged the development of local lyceum groups, first in New England and later across the country. By 1834, there were an estimated 3,000 lyceums in the United States. Some were set up under the aegis of Holbrook's national organization, but many more were independent groups. The National American Lyceum closed in 1839, but the lyceum movement itself continued to grow. Holbrook toured the country, speaking about and gaining favor for his ideas until his death in 1854.

Many lyceums soon began to offer lectures given by outside speakers, de-emphasizing the mutual learning model envisioned by Holbrook. The speakers initially worked for little or no money, but as demand for their services grew, their fees rose. It was as difficult then as it is now to support oneself by one's pen, and men and women of letters quickly realized that the speaking fees offered by lyceums could make up a crucial component of their income. RALPH WALDO EMERSON, HENRY DAVID THOREAU, Oliver Wendell Holmes, Frederick Douglass, and many more of the leading intellectual lights of the day made lecture tours on the lyceum circuit. It was a common practice for writers to "test-market" their latest poems or philosophical ideas on lyceum audiences before attempting to publish them. Inevitably, booking agencies sprang up to place speakers in the lyceum venues, whose numbers had grown to perhaps 5,000 nationwide by 1839.

The lyceum movement remained forceful throughout the 1850s, but the turmoil brought by the Civil War forced many local lyceums to close. The movement never regained its strength once the war was over, although individual lyceums continued to thrive in subsequent decades. The lyceum movement did raise public expectations for educational opportunities for both adults and youths, and these expectations encouraged communities to establish public schools, libraries, publicly supported museums, endowed lecture series, university extension courses, home-study programs, and the Chautauqua movement of the 1870s.

Further reading: Carl Bode, *The American Lyceum; Town Meeting of the Mind* (New York: Oxford University Press, 1952); Malcolm Knowles, *The Adult Education Movement in the United States* (New York: Holt, Rinehart and Winston, 1962).

—Mary Kay Linge

M

Manifest Destiny

Throughout the first half of the 19th century, it was the ambition of both U.S. citizens and the federal government to expand the nation's borders west to the Pacific, north into present-day Canada, and south to the Rio Grande. In July 1845, John O'Sullivan, editor and publisher of the pro-Democratic Party *United States Magazine and Democratic Review,* gave this American expansionist urge a name and an ideological definition: Manifest Destiny. This was the belief that the United States had the divinely ordained responsibility to expand its borders across the entire North American continent and, in the process, to spread its democratic principle and its Christian civilization to less-developed and unenlightened people.

O'Sullivan represented the pro-expansionist wing of the DEMOCRATIC PARTY, commonly referred to as the "Young America" Movement. In his newspaper he published the works of Walt Whitman, Edgar Allan Poe, and Nathaniel Hawthorne, among others, and trumpeted the Democratic cause. In his 1839 treatise, "The Great Nation of Futurity," O'Sullivan declared that the young republic was "the nation of human progress," and he arrogantly queried, "who will, what can, set limits to our onward march?" Six years later, in "Annexation," a manifesto demanding that the U.S. government annex the independent state of TEXAS, he was even more blatant in his declaration. He argued that it was America's "manifest destiny to overspread the continent allotted by Providence for the free development of our yearly multiplying millions." Yet Texas, according to O'Sullivan, was not enough; CALIFORNIA, he insisted, was also the just right of U.S. conquest.

Inspired by this mission statement, Americans continued to pursue expansion with both impressive zeal and ruthless violence. O'Sullivan and other pro-expansionists found a willing agent to carry out their aims in Democratic president JAMES K. POLK, who was elected to the nation's high office in 1844. Polk echoed O'Sullivan's desires, asserting that "The jurisdiction of our laws and the benefits of our republican institutions should be extended" to American settlers who had staked claims in western territory beyond current U.S. dominion. With Polk as its chief proponent, what Manifest Destiny meant in terms of national policy was a near-war with Great Britain over the Oregon Territory and a two-year war with Mexico.

Although tension existed between the United States and Great Britain over the territory of Oregon since the Americans had acquired portions of it from Russia in the 1820s, both nations had accepted joint occupancy of it. However, in the early 1840s, pressure was brought to bear on the U.S. government to claim the territory for its own by an increasing number of Oregon settlers. After assuming office in 1845, President Polk took up the Oregon cause and sought to claim all of Oregon below the 54th parallel (54° 40') solely of the United States. Despite shouts of "Fifty-four forty or fight" from such extreme expansionists as Missouri senator THOMAS HART BENTON, Polk resisted armed conflict and sought a diplomatic solution. Although negotiations between the two nations were at times thorny and precarious, peace was maintained through the OREGON TREATY OF 1846. The United States agreed to the establishment of the 49th parallel as the permanent U.S.-Canada border. In exchange for this concession, the Americans allowed the British to keep control of Vancouver Island.

Although the situation with Britain was resolved short of war, no such compromise could be reached between the United States and Mexico over Polk's claims for territory that Mexico called its own. His justification for armed conflict was the U.S. annexation of Texas, which the Mexican government bitterly contested. The 1836 defeat of General ANTONIO LÓPEZ DE SANTA ANNA's Mexican army by the forces of SAM HOUSTON secured Texas's independence from Mexico. By 1845 Texans were seeking annexation, and Polk and Congress obliged, disregarding Mexico's protests. The federal government annexed Texas out of expansionist desires; concerns about foreign influence, namely the British; and to further provoke Mexico into a military encounter. This was because Polk had larger designs than Texas. He was determined to acquire, by force if necessary, large portions of northern Mexico, including the territory of California and what would become New Mexico. Although the Mexican government refused to recognize Texas's annexation, it also refused direct military confrontation with its belligerent and aggressive neighbor to the north. Nevertheless, using as provocation the dispute with Mexico over Texas and a dubious act of Mexican military aggression, the United States invaded its southern neighbor in May 1846. After a string of victories, U.S. troops pushed easily down to Mexico City and forced the Mexican government to surrender, ending the MEXICAN-AMERICAN WAR. According to the terms of the TREATY OF GUADALUPE HIDALGO (1848), Mexico ceded to the U.S. two-fifths of its territory (including Texas, California, and New Mexico) for $15 million. Whether they wanted it or not, the inhabitants of these lands were incorporated into the United States.

The victory over Mexico only whetted the American appetite for territory. Bolstered by its success on the southern border, the federal government shifted its manifest-destiny ambitions in other directions. Expansionists began to covet lands beyond the North American continent and turned their attention toward Central America and the Caribbean. CUBA, for example, was, by the 1840s, a sought-after gem for pro-expansionists like O'Sullivan. A like-minded Polk, who was not completely satisfied with the acquisitions from Mexico and Great Britain, offered Spain as much as $100 million for the archipelago in 1848. The Spanish rejected his offer, and France and Britain diplomatically blocked it. President Franklin Pierce made a similar offer to the Spanish government for Cuba and even threatened the use of force to compel the sale. He withdrew this intimidating offer, however, because of negative domestic public reaction. Pierce's successor, President James Buchanan, also supported the acquisition of Cuba and urged Congress to pass a bill for its purchase. Only the election of Abraham Lincoln in 1860 put the issue of Cuba to rest. Lincoln opposed any purchase because he thought it part of a southern states' plot to extend slavery beyond its current borders.

The expansionist lust of some Americans spurred them on to seek territory in the Caribbean and Central America

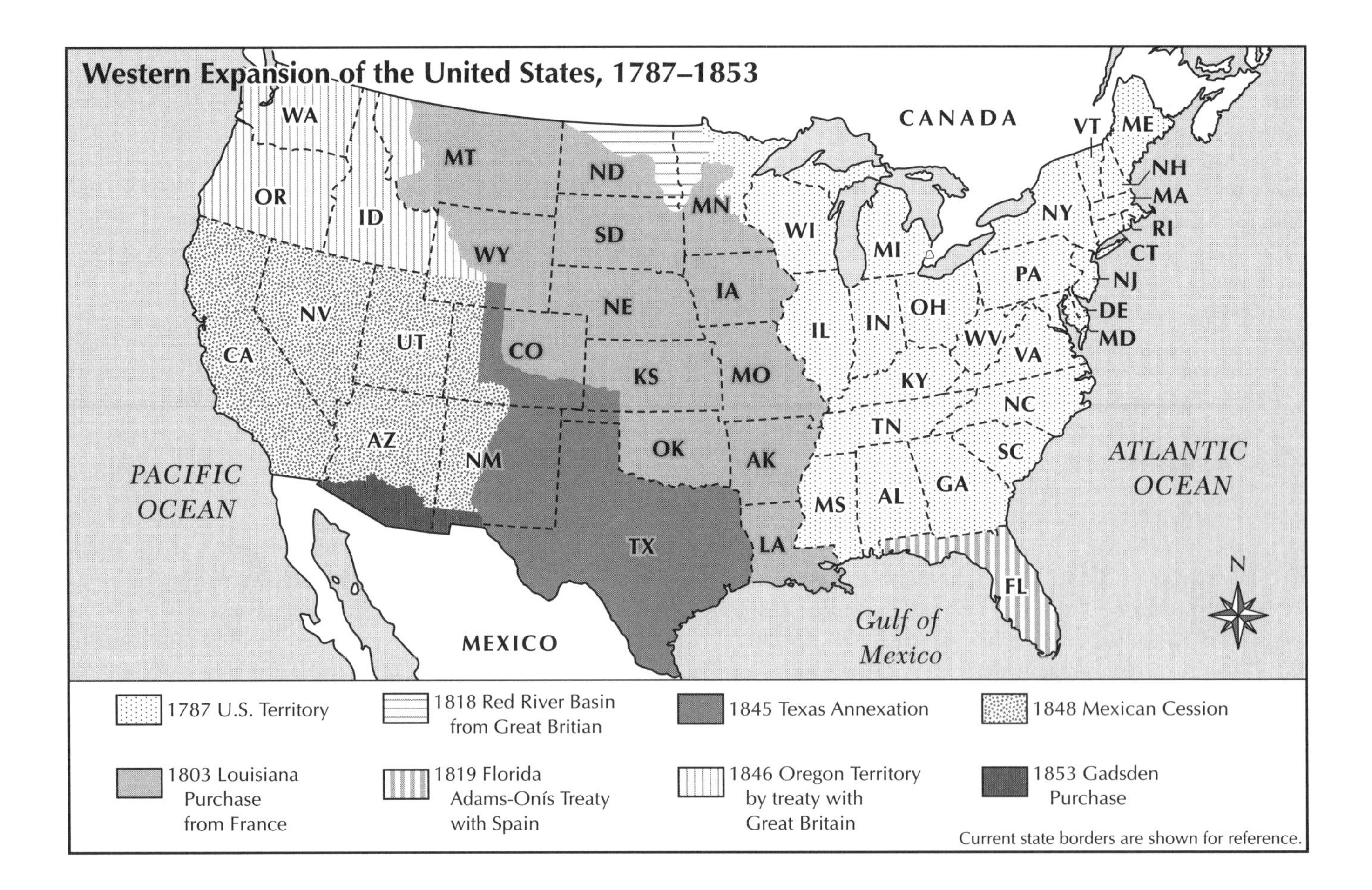

as private enterprises. During the early 1850s, these adventuresome Americans, also called "filibusters," attempted to invade and conquer Cuba, Nicaragua, and even parts of Mexico. Ardent proslavery southerners who professed the doctrine of Manifest Destiny, these filibusters hoped to increase the power and influence of the slave states through conquest. None of the private filibuster expeditions was successful, including an attempted invasion of Cuba in 1850 by, among others, John L. O'Sullivan. The ruthless Tennessean William Walker was able to seize control of and rule the rudderless Nicaragua periodically between 1855 and 1860. In 1856, the Pierce administration even briefly recognized one of Walker's Nicaraguan governments before it collapsed. Four years later, Walker was executed by the government of Honduras for his filibustering. Despite the filibusters' failures to seize new lands and U.S. presidents to buy them, Americans hungered for much of what they saw south of Mexico throughout the remainder of the century.

U.S. expansionist desires and Manifest Destiny was not restricted to the Western Hemisphere. In an effort to establish a presence in the Pacific, promote commerce, find coaling stations and protect shipwrecked American sailors, President Pierce sent U.S. Navy Commodore MATTHEW CALBRAITH PERRY to "open" Japan. In 1853, four U.S. warships, two of them intimidating, steam-powered vessels that belched black smoke, dropped anchor off the coast of Japan. Perry's efforts and determination to fulfill his orders produced a commercial trade treaty with Japan in 1854. The Tokugawa Shogunate rulers of Japan capitulated to Perry's demands because of superior U.S. military power. They also hoped to avoid the humiliating domination several European powers exercised over other Asian nations like India and China. The opening of Japan was only a beginning of direct U.S. interest in Asia and the Pacific.

With the outbreak of the Civil War at Fort Sumter in 1861, U.S. expansionism took secondary importance as Americans became consumed with this costly, bloody, and tragic domestic crisis. However, manifest-destiny sentiments were only temporarily replaced by this more immediate concern. Following the defeat of the Confederacy in 1865, the U.S. government once again returned to an expansionist foreign policy. For the next half-century and beyond, the concept of Manifest Destiny encouraged U.S. commercial and territorial desires well beyond national borders and onto the global stage. It provided the battle cry for the 1898 Spanish-American War, legitimized the seizure of the HAWAIIAN ISLANDS, justified the colonization of the Philippine Islands, and motivated continued economic domination and political manipulation in Latin America. At the close of the 19th century, the pro-expansionist Republican senator Albert J. Beveridge, drawing on the ideas of John L. O'Sullivan, argued for U.S. empire. According to the bellicose senator, "[God] has marked the American people as his chosen nation to finally lead in the regeneration of the world" and "[t]his is the divine mission of America." In 1898, as the United States was embarking on a war with Spain, President William McKinley was more direct in his reference to O'Sullivan, arguing that U.S. expansion into the Pacific and Asia "is manifest destiny."

Further reading: Thomas G. Paterson, J. Garry Clifford, and Kenneth J. Hagen, eds., *American Foreign Policy: A History,* 3d ed. (Lexington, Mass.: D.C. Heath and Company, 1988); Thomas G. Paterson and Dennis Merrill, eds. *Major Problems in American Foreign Relations,* Vol. I, 4th ed. (Lexington, Mass.: D.C. Heath and Company, 1995); Edward L. Widmer, *Young America: The Flowering of Democracy in New York City* (New York: Oxford University Press, 1999).

—Charles Hawley

Mann, Horace (1796–1859)

As an educational reformer, Horace Mann was responsible for improving the educational system in the antebellum United States. He was born on his family farm in Franklin, Massachusetts, on May 4, 1796. The product of a strict Puritan upbringing, his education proved episodic, although he displayed a great aptitude for learning. Mann disliked farming, so he prevailed upon his mother to hire personal tutors to study geometry, Greek, and Latin. Consequently, in 1816 he gained admittance to prestigious Brown University in Providence, Rhode Island. He graduated with honors three years later and, after serving as a tutor and librarian at Brown, subsequently studied law under Tapping Reeve in Litchfield, Connecticut.

Mann was admitted to the Boston bar in 1823 and gained election to the General Court of Massachusetts (the state legislature) four years later. In this capacity he quickly established himself as an activist Whig reformer, championing prison reform and better treatment for the mentally retarded. In concert with DOROTHEA DIX, he created the state's first mental hospital. Mann was also active in promoting the TEMPERANCE MOVEMENT through moral suasion, and in 1831 he sponsored the state's first liquor-licensing regulations. However, it was in the field of EDUCATION reform, an area in which he had previously displayed little interest, that Mann exerted his biggest influence.

As a legislator, Mann had become aware that barely a third of school-age children in Massachusetts received any instruction. The public-school system was in a shambles and generally avoided by families affluent enough to afford private academics. Moreover, the curriculum was either

Horace Mann *(Hulton/Archive)*

outdated or imperfectly taught, and the buildings themselves were usually dilapidated. In 1837, Mann pushed through legislation creating the Massachusetts School Board of Education, for which he resigned from politics to become secretary. It was Mann's belief from the start that common schools, as public institutions, could serve as a great equalizer for all classes, extending positive influences into fields of morality and social mobility. As such, he placed great emphasis on teacher education, creating three of the first normal schools to train teachers in the nation. Moreover, he standardized the curriculum, spent state money on a variety of instructional texts, and doubled the wages of teachers. Mann was also the first educator to recognize the importance of personal hygiene and physical fitness. As a result, Massachusetts students became the first to spend one hour each day either studying or practicing these topics. Most important of all, Mann formally extended the school year to six months and made it compulsory for all Massachusetts children.

Mann toured his state incessantly and lectured public officials on the direct connection between public learning and public morality. As a reflection of his treatment of education as a profession, he compiled and published annual education reports that statistically reflected progress and anticipated problems statewide. He also founded the *Common School Journal*, one of the earliest educational periodicals, and served as its editor for a decade. During his tenure no less than 50 new public schools were founded, replete with new textbooks and school libraries. Through all these expedients, Mann single-handedly revolutionized both the quality and the concept of public education in America. He made an indelible impact on the educational process in Massachusetts for over a decade, with dramatic and sustainable results. His methods were also exported to other states and abroad to other countries, granting him considerable renown.

In 1848 Mann resigned from the educational board to run for the U.S. House of Representatives as a Whig. He was elected and proved a vocal proponent of the extension of slavery. However, Mann was unprepared for the enmity this stance engendered, and in 1852 he declined to run again. That year he made an unsuccessful bid to become governor of Massachusetts as a FREE-SOIL PARTY candidate. Afterwards, he accepted the presidency of Antioch College in Ohio. Mann applied himself vigorously to his charge and was active in creating a curriculum and teaching program. He further distinguished himself among contemporaries by insisting on equal treatment for female students. However, the school failed financially and was ultimately sold.

Mann died of exhaustion in Ohio on August 2, 1858, only two weeks after exhorting Antioch's graduating class to win "some victory for humanity." His strong belief in the virtues of public education, coupled with an unyielding determination to enhance it for the benefit of all citizens, established him as an influential social reformer of the 19th century.

Further reading: Thomas M. Buck, "Horace Mann: Enigmatic Leader in Change and Conflict" (unpublished Ph.D. dis., Marquette University, 1999); Susan-Mary Grant, "Representative Mann: Horace Mann, the Republican Experiment, and the South," *Journal of American Studies* 32 (April 1998): 105–24; Ronald L. Jensen, "A Religious and Social Study of Horace Mann" (unpublished Ph.D. dis., University of Iowa, 1991); Kem K. Sawyer, *Horace Mann* (New York: Chelsea House Publishers, 1993).

—John C. Fredriksen

marriage and family life

Few social institutions were of greater importance to antebellum Americans than marriage and family. Though the United States was comprised of different cultural groups holding different beliefs, the basic family structure was valued by many of these communities.

Several hundred Native American nations existed in North America in the 19th century, and each held a set of culturally specific beliefs about family. Family was defined by reference to the taboos, rights, privileges, and respect owed to members of an individual's household, clan, moiety, or band. Residency patterns emphasized the expansive nature of such kinship systems. While husbands and wives in some northern and western nations maintained their own homes, most Native American households consisted of extended family groups, including married couples and their brothers, sisters, parents, cousins, and children. Some cultures allowed men to marry several wives; a handful permitted women to do the same in reverse. Multiple marriages were usually a sign of a household's high status or rank, indicating the family's wealth as well as its obligation to provide hospitality and support to others in the community. Child care was usually a shared responsibility. Among the nomadic bands of the northern plains, for example, grandparents took particular responsibility for childcare, freeing their own adult sons and daughters to engage in the labor necessary to maintain the economic health of the nation.

Clan membership linked men and women together across household and community lines. Individuals were prohibited from marrying members of their own clan, so each household would contain representatives from at least two. Clan obligation resulted in a network of father and mother figures in every child's life. Among matrilineal societies such as the Hopi of the Southwest, for example, children traced their clan membership through their mother. While their biological father had a significant place in their life, children considered their mother's brothers of equal importance, especially in learning clan-appropriate behavior.

For most Native American groups, kinship was not limited to relationships between humans. The physical world in which communities existed, the animal and plant life found there, elements such as wind and water, and manifestations of the spiritual world were frequently addressed in kinship terms such as father, mother, grandparent, or cousin. Taboos, traditions, and rites governed these relationships as much as those between the human members of an individual's nation.

Kinship practices became a major source of conflict between Euro- and Native Americans as the 19th century progressed. To many non-Indians, the observation of extended kinship, the recognition of obligation beyond the nuclear family, and female-centered households represented moral, economic, and political disorder. Missionaries, government officials, and voluntary organizations all considered the reorganization of family structures to be central to "civilizing" Native Americans. These groups brought pressure to bear on native communities through the establishment of churches and schools, the provision of domestic goods and agricultural equipment in treaty settlements, and the administrative regulations of government agencies. These efforts would culminate in the Dawes Act of 1887, which divided reservations into individual parcels of land to be distributed to households that reflected Euro-American definitions of "family." Many native kinship systems were drastically disrupted by such practices, yet family also became the locus of resistance and cultural continuity. The recognition of extended kinship ties and responsibilities survives among Native communities to this day.

For enslaved men and women, the creation and maintenance of family was a complex endeavor. Anglo-American law classified slaves as property, lacking the legal capacity to enter into contracts. Committed relationships between enslaved men and women were therefore never recognized as marriage by law. Without this legal protection, parents and children could be sold or traded away from one another without any consideration to family ties. Working and living conditions compounded the difficulty of this situation. Many parents lived on neighboring but separate farms and plantations. Enslaved women were often the targets of sexual abuse by the men who owned them, and their children were considered slaves even if the father was free. Poor nutrition and heavy labor during pregnancy caused many women to miscarry, while numerous children died in infancy for want of food and medical care. Those children who survived were put to work at a very young age.

Yet enslaved men and women resisted the attempts of individuals and institutions from outside the slave community to define (or undermine) their idea of family. Enslaved families were variously united through African tradition, Christian belief, and the everyday exchange of neighborly obligation and support. Blood relations, sexual companions, neighbors, and friends could all be counted as family, and kinship traced through mothers as much as fathers. Customs such as "jumping the broom" solemnized marital relationships even as federal or state law denied their legality. Family provided enslaved Americans with the opportunity to forge an identity separate from that ascribed to them by the law. These kinship ties would ultimately survive the rigors of the institution that bound them and sustain the African-American community through the dislocations of the Civil War and the national upheaval that marked Reconstruction.

For free people, Anglo-American common law governed the form and function of family life and prescribed specific responsibilities for husbands and wives. Upon marriage, women surrendered most of their legal capabilities to their husbands. Husbands controlled their wives' property, any income they earned, their ability to sue, their ability to contract, and sexual access to their body. Wives who committed a crime, signed premarital agreements, had trusts created in their name, or appealed to a court with equity jurisdiction could find exceptions to this general rule. In the words of English jurist Sir William Blackstone, however, a wife was ideally considered to be under the legal "wing, protection, and *cover*" of her husband during marriage. Men, in turn, were expected to provide economic support to their wives, and act as their representatives in political matters.

Marriage was meant to be a lifetime contract. While divorce did exist within the American legal system, it was not intended to remedy general unhappiness. Instead, the law's function was to protect "innocent" husbands and wives from moral or physical abuse by their partners. A husband or wife who committed adultery, for example, was considered to have revealed their fundamentally immoral character. As such, it was only proper that their blameless spouse should be able to petition for a divorce, and dissolve the connection between them. Should both partners commit adultery, however, their moral characters were considered equally blemished, and their petition for divorce was likely to be denied. Couples who actively worked together to try and arrange the dissolution of their marriage were similarly penalized. Collusion was one of the primary reasons that legislatures and judges turned down petitions for divorce.

Faced with an inflexible legal system, many husbands and wives chose to separate rather than seek a divorce. Separation was a common occurrence for even the happiest couples in the 19th century, as war, financial crises, and the search for work forced many husbands and wives to spend months, even years, apart. For couples who had come to the conclusion that they could not happily live together, however, separation offered relief where the law could not. Some spouses fled, abandoning their families to move to a different state and begin again. Others did their best to formalize the process through separation agreements, documents that were generally unenforceable at law but laid out the terms and conditions by which unhappy husbands and wives would try to live. Such agreements often contained financial provisions and made custodial arrangements for children.

Over time the American legal system did make room for formal changes in the institution of marriage. From 1839 onward, states and territories passed a series of married women's property acts, allowing women to retain ownership of their property even after marriage. These acts were not intended to equalize the position of men and women within marriage but to offer some relief to families hit hard by the PANIC OF 1837. By allowing a married woman to own property separately from her husband, legislators prevented a wife's assets from being seized to pay for her husband's debts. Over the course of the 19th century, divorce also became easier to obtain, with states such as Indiana and Utah gaining a reputation for allowing couples to divorce on a whim. While the reality was less titillating, many states and territories did add to the grounds on which couples could petition for the dissolution of their marriage. South Carolina, however, did not sanction divorce until 1868.

Anglo-American law dealt with ideals. Marriage was the taking up of specific responsibilities—the knowing adoption of privileges and obligations, one with the other. Wives were ideally dependent on their husbands, husbands ideally provided for their wives, and once married, they were faithful to one another. Marriage was intended to last for a lifetime, and children were meant to be born within its protective bounds. This legal ideal reflected and supported popular Victorian culture, which idealized the domesticity of women and the economic and political accomplishments of men. It remained, however, a model. For the vast majority of free Americans, it did not describe their daily life.

While husbands and wives regularly adopted different responsibilities within marriage, those obligations were not discrete. In rural America, for example, men and women carried out their marital responsibilities in the same physical space. The house in which women cooked, washed, spun cloth, made soap, and raised children was the same house in which men conducted trade and managed the farm. Husbands, wives, and children were also likely to work alongside each other in planting, raising, and harvesting crops. In the cities, factory owners employed men and women in separate spaces for different tasks, but the low wages earned by most working men made it impossible for them to support a wife and family on their own. The work of maintaining the family economy was a collective venture, dependent on the wages earned by wives and children as well as husbands. The comforts of home were unlikely to be a poorer woman's primary concern. Even if she possessed the inclination to attain the standards of housekeeping lauded by Victorian culture, her home was likely to be a space shared with other families, without easy access to water, the benefit of a functioning sewer system, or the most basic concepts of privacy.

For wealthier Americans, especially members of the new industrial middle class, husbands and wives did occupy seemingly separate worlds. It was a mark of prestige for a husband to be able earn enough money for his wife and children to stay out of the workforce. Creating and maintaining social prestige was a joint venture, however, reinforced by the labor of wives within their households. Wives stretched their husbands' financial contributions by their housekeeping skills, and reinforced the reputation of their families as members of the "leisure class" by their modes of dress, fashion, home decoration, and entertainment. While these activities were labor intensive, and helped create and maintain a family's high social status, they were rarely considered "work." As America became more and more industrialized, work became synonymous with earning wages, and the labor of wives within the home was increasingly ignored.

Many journalists, educators, members of religious organizations, and everyday middle-class men and women acknowledged there to be a crisis of the family in the 19th century. Birth rates fell, divorce rates rose, middle-class women agitated for the right to enter professions rather than confine themselves to the home, and the practice of POLYGAMY was adopted by the CHURCH OF JESUS CHRIST OF LATTER-DAY SAINTS in 1843. Despite these fears, however, monogamous marriage continued to be the defining act of adulthood for millions of Americans. Family remained important to every community, defined in different times and places in vastly different ways, but in each instance providing the most basic building block upon which society was founded, both for good and for ill.

Further reading: Nancy F. Cott, *Public Vows: A History of Marriage and the Nation* (Cambridge, Mass.: Harvard University Press, 2000); Hedrik Hartog, *Man & Wife in America: A History* (Cambridge, Mass.: Harvard University Press, 2000); Leslie Schwalm, *"A Hard Fight for We": Women's Transition from Slavery to Freedom in South Carolina* (Urbana: University of Illinois Press, 1997).

—Catherine J. Denial

Massachusetts Emigrant Aid Society

The Emigrant Aid Society was an organization that promoted organized antislavery immigration to the Kansas territory from the Northeast. It was formed shortly before the Kansas-Nebraska Act became law on May 30, 1854. The opening of these territories to white settlement had long been a controversial subject in Congress as the North and South fought to keep a balance of representation in Washington. As a compromise, the doctrine of POPULAR SOVEREIGNTY was included in the new law, which meant that residents of the territories should be allowed to choose for themselves whether SLAVERY would be permitted when the time for statehood arrived.

There was little question that Nebraska would prohibit slavery, for presumably it was too far north for the institution to survive. The South assumed that Kansas was destined for slavery. However, the early activities of northern abolitionists, who were determined not to let Kansas go by default, spurred both the North and South to send in every settler they could.

In the North, one of the organizations created to encourage abolitionist settlement of Kansas was the Massachusetts Emigrant Aid Company. Incorporated under the guidance of Eli Thayer of Worcester in April 1854, the company was a venture designed both for benevolence and moneymaking. Its aims were to secure reduced transportation fares to the West for emigrants traveling in groups organized and directed by the company and to provide temporary accommodations, in the form of boarding or receiving houses, while settlers located and built their own homes. The society also looked to build or buy steam saw and grist mills "and such other machines as shall be of constant service in a new settlement," to aid settlers in building homes and feeding families; and to establish a weekly newspaper in Kansas to act as the voice of the company and be an "index of the love of freedom and of good morals, which it is hoped may characterize the state now to be formed."

In February 1855 a new charter changing the name to the New England Emigrant Aid Company and making organizational improvements was secured. In March the company was reorganized, and business began in earnest as mills were established in Lawrence, Topeka, Manhattan, Osawatomie, Burlington, Wabaunsee, Atchison, Batcheller (now Milford) and Mapleton. In Kansas City, the Gillis House was purchased and renamed the American Hotel. Many other Kansas aid societies were subsequently formed throughout the North (e.g., the Kansas Emigrant Aid Society of Northern Ohio and the New York Kansas League), but the New England group was preeminent in the field, and the name Emigrant Aid Company is associated exclusively with it. Amos A. Lawrence served as treasurer of the company, which, despite its earnest soliciting of the support of clergymen throughout New England, remained in bad financial condition until November 1855, when a notably successful campaign to raise money was launched.

For Thayer, who was vice president of the company, the venture was not only philanthropic but profitable. The company planned to make a profit on its investments by purchasing the land on which its hotels and mills stood and, when settlement had increased and land values correspondingly elevated, selling to the eventual benefit of the stockholders. As stock-subscription agent, he received 10 percent of all the money he collected, provided he gathered $20,000 or more. Thayer easily exceeded that figure, and by May 1856 the company had received over $100,000.

The first party sent to Kansas left Massachusetts even before the company had been completely organized. This pioneer party arrived at the site of Lawrence on August 1, 1854. That summer and fall, five other parties arrived in Kansas, bringing the total of aid-company settlers to about 450. The following spring, seven more groups brought about 800 persons. All told, the company sent out an aggregate of 1,250 settlers under agents such as Charles Robinson, who founded Lawrence and other towns in Kansas. Southerners, at first confident that Kansas was safe for slavery, were moved to organize similar, though proslavery, societies of their own. However, such ill-advised actions by the proslavery societies as the sacking (on May 21, 1856) of the town of Lawrence only stimulated the Kansas aid movement further. Once the territory of Kansas was admitted as a free state, the directors were to dispose of all the company's interests and declare a dividend to the stockholders. The company was then to choose a new area of operation and commence the program again, until another free state had been admitted to the Union.

The backers of the company hoped to raise $5 million and send 20,000 settlers into Kansas. The plan received wide publicity in the newspapers of Horace Greeley, William Cullen Bryant, Thurlow Weed, and others. The company itself issued descriptive pamphlets, and its advocates toured New England lecturing on the benefits to be derived.

As the company's influence waned, some of its agents remained to continue their active roles in Kansas territorial and early state history. Prominent among them were Charles Robinson, who became the state's first governor; Samuel C. Pomeroy, one of its two initial United States senators; and Martin F. Conway, its first representative in Congress.

In spite of the company's initial spurt of activity, there is some question as to its total contribution toward the settling of Kansas. After June 1855, company emigrant parties became smaller and less frequent. Instead of the $5 million it hoped to have, the company actually accumulated only about $190,000. In terms of persons relocated in Kansas, it has been estimated that the company was directly responsible for only about 2,000, of whom perhaps a third returned to the East.

Delegates from 12 states and Kansas convened at Buffalo, New York, in July 1856 and formed a National Kansas Committee. Its goal of establishing Kansas aid committees in every state, county, and town throughout the North was never realized. For one thing, the national committee was divided; one group, in which Amos Lawrence was most conspicuous, advocated peaceful protest against proslavery excesses in Kansas and financial help to the Free Staters; while the other, led by extreme abolitionists such as Gerrit Smith and the Reverend Thomas W. Higginson, urged the creation of state military forces to be used against Union troops in Kansas if necessary. This group also proposed disunion at a convention in Worcester, Massachusetts, in January 1857.

Kansas was admitted to the Union in January 1861, and the following year the stockholders of the New England Emigrant Aid Company ordered that all its properties in Kansas and Missouri be sold. When this was eventually accomplished, the company realized a total of $16,150, which was just about enough to pay outstanding debts.

After 1861 the company transferred its activities to other areas. In 1864 and 1865, it promoted the migration of working women to Oregon; and from 1866 to 1868, it was active in settling northerners in Florida. By 1870, however, the company had fallen idle and never again was active in emigrant aid. No more meetings of the stockholders were held until 1897, when an extension of the charter was requested and granted. That year the company presented its single asset—a claim against the U.S. government for loss of the Free-State Hotel at Lawrence in 1856—to the University of Kansas, and for all practical purposes it ceased to exist thereafter. The extended charter expired on February 19, 1907, and the company was no more.

In spite of its financial failure, the principal stockholders seemed well pleased with the results of the society's operations. Under its influence, several important towns were founded, schools were established, churches were built, and the cause of freedom was served. Indeed, there is some evidence that investors purchased stock knowing full well they would never see their money again. Amos A. Lawrence, a principal stockholder and treasurer of the company, had advised his associates not to invest any more than they felt they could afford to lose.

Further reading: Samuel A. Johnson, *The Battle Cry of Freedom, The New England Emigrant Aid Company in the Kansas Crusade* (Lawrence: University of Kansas Press, 1954).

McCormick, Cyrus Hall (1809–1884)

Cyrus Hall McCormick was the inventor of the world's first effective mechanical reaper, which helped to transform American AGRICULTURE. He was born in Rockbridge County, Virginia, on February 15, 1809. His father owned a large farm and had invented some minor farm machinery, although without commercial success. McCormick, the product of a stern Presbyterian upbringing, enjoyed little formal education, but he proved adept in mechanical tinkering. In 1831, his talents manifested themselves in the creation of a hillside plow for uneven ground. That same year also gave rise to the famous McCormick reaper, a horse-drawn device that allowed wheat and other grains to be harvested mechanically and with greater efficiency. Over the next few years, McCormick continued improving on his device and sold several units to neighboring farms. In 1836, he acquired the Cotopaxi Iron Works and discontinued small-scale manufacturing in favor of other pursuits. However, when the ensuing PANIC OF 1837 drove McCormick's firm into bankruptcy, he resumed perfecting his reaper. This was accomplished over the objection of Obed Hussey, who had invented a similar machine, and resulted in a long series of bitterly disputed court actions. Ultimately, the patent for McCormick's famous device entered into the public domain.

By 1843 McCormick had finally realized that the small-scale farms of Virginia and New England did not represent the optimum market for his product. He then licensed production of his reaper to various subsidiaries in New York and Ohio. However, when these products turned out to be inferior to his own, McCormick decided to centralize production under his personal supervision. In 1847, he relocated his thriving business to Chicago and began catering to the bigger farming interests in Ohio, Illinois, and the Midwest. Chicago—being centrally located, affording greater access to water transport, and on the verge of becoming a major railroad hub—was destined to serve as the center of midwestern agriculture. Accordingly, McCormick established his own factory, adopted a modern mass-production system, and stocked it with the latest time-saving industrial technology to boost productivity. His workforce, which eventually numbered 1,500, were also among the best-trained and most highly paid in the nation.

As the prairies were settled and converted into farmland, the sale of reapers grew exponentially. In 1848, McCormick sold 700 units; by 1860 that number had risen to 5,000 annually. Despite continuous lawsuits, he failed to have his patent secured, and he faced stiff competition from nearly 100 other firms marketing reapers. He countered by developing the best business organization available, completely outpacing his contemporaries. McCormick initially relied upon an extensive series of distributors, who handled sales, repairs, and credit arrangements individually. However, the depression of 1870 forced him to centralize operations, which allowed him to maintain tighter control on subordinates. Moreover, regional offices were established across the country to better coordinate business matters with an extensive network of dealers. In this manner, McCormick pioneered creation of a sales organization to support and monitor dealers, who made the actual sales. The company was also unique in offering generous credit arrangements for customers, and it sponsored one of the first money-back guarantees in business history. The high quality of McCormick's reapers, coupled with consumer satisfaction, made the firm a giant among America's early industrial efforts.

Early on, McCormick tried marketing his revolutionary device in Europe through various farm and trade shows. His reaper won several competitions, but the small size of European farms mitigated against their popular use. Nonetheless, the numerous prizes accrued were subsequently utilized in marketing and advertising campaigns, along with printed testimony from satisfied customers. By the outbreak of the Civil War in 1861, McCormick was uniquely situated to make enormous contributions to national development. At that time, an estimated 80,000–90,000 of his reapers were in use throughout the Midwest. Being very efficient compared to manual labor, they allowed farmers to collect harvests in less time, leading to greater yield and higher profits than before. This, in turn, released large numbers of farm workers from the field, who then transferred their energies to either urban industry or military service. The South, by comparison, was equally agrarian but largely unmechanized, so their quest for sufficient foodstuffs always competed with increasing demands for military manpower. Moreover, the North produced such a surplus that it kept both its population and military victualed, and it also exported food to Europe, which helped to fund the war effort. Simply put, the McCormick reaper was a significant but overlooked factor in the ultimate Union victory of 1865.

Not surprisingly, McCormick, southern-born and bred, was outspoken in his support for the DEMOCRATIC PARTY and the Confederacy. He ran for Congress in 1864 on a peace ticket, but lost. He exerted far greater influence in religious matters through his close association with the Presbyterian Church. McCormick was a devout advocate of the Old School, and he used his great wealth to finance the McCormick Theological Seminary of Chicago. This was an important theological body that sought to curtail expansion of the New School doctrines, which McCormick felt were spiritually unsound. McCormick himself largely personified the strict Calvinistic approach to life, being hard-working and pious and refraining from drinking or smoking. His conservative approach to theology, coupled with a willingness to invest part of his fortune to promote it, renders him a pivotal influence in the history of his church.

McCormick died in Chicago on May 13, 1884, one of the most successful and far-sighted entrepreneurs of his day. His reaper, which he continually updated and improved throughout his life, made possible the rapid settlement of the western frontier and also contributed to the overall accumulation of national wealth. In 1878, he received the Legion of Honor from the prestigious French Academy of Sciences, which extolled him for "having done more for the cause of agriculture than any other living man."

Further reading: Leonard M. Fanning, *Cyrus Hall McCormick: Father of Farm Mechanization* (New York: Mercer Pub., 1950); Lee Grady, "McCormick's Reaper at 100." *Wisconsin Magazine of History* 84, no. 3 (2001): 10–20; Esko Heikkoken, *Reaping the Bounty: McCormick Harvesting Machine Company Turns Abroad, 1878–1902* (Helsinki: Finnish Historical Society, 1995); Charles H. Wendel, *150 Years of International Harvester* (Sarasota, Fla.: Crestline, 1981).

—John C. Fredriksen

Cyrus McCormick, depicted with his factory at Chicago and his mechanical reaper *(Granger Collection)*

McCulloch v. Maryland (*McCulloch v. Maryland,* 1819)

McCulloch v. Maryland was one of the leading early SUPREME COURT DECISIONS establishing the scope of Congress's power to legislate under the Constitution. It was also an important early example of the Court's invalidation of a state statute. The case arose from the State of Maryland's attempt to tax the Bank of the United States. First chartered by Congress in 1791, the bank was a public/private concern tasked with holding and investing the nation's money and issuing national banknotes. Controversial from the start and routinely charged with looking more to the interests of its shareholders than the public good, the bank's charter was allowed to lapse in 1811.

A SECOND BANK OF THE UNITED STATES was chartered in 1816, when the United States's experience with the difficulties of noncentralized finance during the WAR OF 1812 (1812–15) persuaded Congress that even if evil, a national bank was necessary. The Second Bank moved aggressively into a thriving ECONOMY, establishing branches in the various states. Many of these branches engaged in speculation and were run by corrupt officers, a situation brought to light in 1818 when a drop in the cotton market caused a financial panic and many bank customers were unable to get their money out. Several states responded by regulating the bank branches. Maryland imposed a tax on all notes issued by all non-state-chartered banks, including the Bank of the United States. James McCulloch, cashier for the Baltimore branch of the Bank of the United States, refused to pay, and Maryland sued in a case that was argued before the Supreme Court in 1819.

Daniel Webster, William Wirt, and William Pinkney argued the case for the bank; Luther Martin, Joseph Hopkinson and Walter Jones appeared for Maryland. Two issues were foremost: Did Congress have the power to create the bank in the first place? If so, did the state of Maryland have the power to tax it? Resolving the first question required the Court to interpret Article I, Section 8 of the U.S. Constitution, which set forth Congress's powers. Nothing in the section explicitly authorized Congress to create a bank. Nevertheless, the Court found the section did authorize Congress to do a lot of things that would be easier to accomplish with a national bank in place—raise armies and regulate commerce, for example. The existence of the bank made transferring federal funds from one part of the country to another far easier. And Section 8 closed with the "Necessary and Proper Clause," which authorized Congress to exercise powers not listed in Section 8 if the exercise of those additional powers was "necessary and proper" to the exercise of the listed powers. If the words "necessary and proper" were expansively interpreted, they might be held to allow for the creation of the Bank. That is precisely what the Court did.

McCulloch thus saved the bank. More important, it also expanded the permissible scope of Congress's broad power to legislate. The federal government was indeed a government of limited and defined powers, but "[l]et the end be legitimate, let it be within the scope of the constitution, and all means which are appropriate, which are plainly adapted to that end, which are not prohibited, but consistent with the letter and spirit of the constitution, are constitutional." As for the state's imposition of the tax, the Court held it unconstitutional. "The power to tax," Chief Justice Marshall wrote, "involves the power to destroy." The structure of the federal union denied the power of one state to destroy an enterprise constitutionally created by the federal Congress. James McCulloch was therefore not liable for the tax.

Marshall delivered the *McCulloch* opinion for the Court on March 7, 1819, inspiring an immediate hostile backlash. Virginians in particular identified the opinion as a major blow to states' rights. Among other things, the case stood for the proposition that the federal court could decide the constitutional scope of the federal Congress's authority. This doctrine was unpalatable to those who viewed the Constitution as a compact among sovereign states. The debate engendered by *McCulloch* would not go away. In the near term, the Court battled with states throughout the 1820s, staving off, among other threats, efforts by opponents to lodge the ultimate judicial review power in the U.S. Senate. In the longer term, the broader questions raised in *McCulloch* were at the forefront of the constitutional component of the secession debate of the 1850s and 1860s.

Further reading: G. Edward White, *The Marshall Court and Cultural Change, 1815–1835* (New York: Oxford University Press, 1991).

—Lindsay Robertson

McGuffey, William Holmes (1800–1873)

Best known for his popular *Eclectic Readers* for schoolchildren, William Holmes McGuffey was an influential university professor who helped shape American EDUCATION in the 19th century. He was born in 1800 in Washington County, Pennsylvania, to Alexander McGuffey, a former Indian fighter, and Anna Holmes. In 1802 the McGuffeys moved to Connecticut's Western Reserve in what is now northeastern Ohio, settling on a homestead near Youngstown. William spent the next 16 years at his family's farm. Like most rural children at this time, he attended school in fits and starts between the growing and harvesting seasons.

His mother also instructed him at home. When McGuffey was a teenager, his parents sent him to study Latin in Youngstown. His teacher was immediately impressed with his intelligence and his remarkable ability to memorize large portions of the Bible. After his success in Youngstown, McGuffey left home in 1818 to attend the Old Stone Academy in Darlington, Pennsylvania. He then entered Washington College, graduating in 1826. During his college years, he also taught school intermittently, mostly in Kentucky.

In 1826 McGuffey joined the faculty of Miami University in Oxford, Ohio, as a professor of languages. He soon married Harriet Spinning, with whom he had five children. While engaged as a professor, he also received a license to preach in the Presbyterian Church. During the years of his professorship at Miami, he preached every week at a local church.

In 1836 McGuffey became the president of Cincinnati College. After years of teaching and preaching, he was becoming well known for his eloquent lectures on morality and the Bible. He was also heavily involved in the effort to establish a public school system in Ohio. In 1839, he was elected to the presidency of Ohio University in Athens, which he administered until the school temporarily closed in 1843 due to financial disputes. He returned briefly to Cincinnati, teaching at Woodward College until he was elected to a professorship in moral philosophy at the University of Virginia in 1845.

McGuffey continued to promote public education in his new home, persisting in what became his most important endeavor: creating educational readers for children. He began compiling the *Eclectic Readers* while at Miami. The First and Second Readers were published in 1836, the next two in 1837. The Fifth Reader was published in 1844, and the Sixth in 1857. McGuffey's brother, Alexander Hamilton McGuffey, contributed the *Eclectic Spelling Book* in 1846. These volumes were used in all the states, in the kinds of public schools McGuffey worked so hard to establish. Over 122 million copies of his books were eventually sold.

McGuffey's Readers instructed schoolchildren through a simple, effective format. Making use of the "phonic," "word," and "alphabet" educational methods, McGuffey presented morally instructive literary selections designed to gain children's attention. His readers also included appealing illustrations, and dealt with a variety of subjects, including art, philosophy, economics, history, and science. His selections were unabashedly patriotic, promoting virtue, duty, and love of country. The advanced readers contained selections from the most revered English writers, thus introducing millions of students to the classics of world literature. The *Eclectic Readers* became intellectual building blocks for the nation, remaining extremely popular until the end of the 19th century. While his work as a college professor and education advocate was acknowledged during his lifetime, his lasting reputation derives from the elementary textbooks that became a shared experience for millions of American children.

William Holmes McGuffey remained at the University of Virginia for the rest of his life. Harriet Spinning McGuffey died in 1853, and he remarried Laura Howard four years later; the couple had one daughter who died in childhood. During the Civil War, McGuffey was known for his philanthropy toward the poor, both black and white. He continued to teach philosophy in Charlottesville until a few weeks before his death in 1873.

Further reading: Benjamin F. Crawford, *William Holmes McGuffey: The Schoolmaster to Our Nation.* (Delaware, Ohio: Carnegie Church Press, 1963); John H. Westerhoff III, *McGuffey and his Readers: Piety, Morality, and Education in Nineteenth-Century America* (Nashville, Tenn.: Abingdon, 1978).

—Eleanor H. McConnell

McLoughlin, John (1784–1857)

Physician and fur-trade official, John McLoughlin was chief agent of the Hudson's Bay Company in the COLUMBIA RIVER region. He was also one of the most important figures in the FUR TRADE and a towering figure in the early European occupation of the Pacific Northwest. Born in Riviere-du-Loup, Quebec, Canada, McLoughlin was connected on his mother's side to the Frasers, one of Canada's leading fur-trading families. Under the influence of his uncles, Simon and Alexander Fraser, the young John McLoughlin began a career in medicine. After he was licensed to practice in 1803, however, he became interested in employment with the North West Company, a leading company of the fur trade at the turn of the century. McLoughlin first served as resident company physician at Fort William. Even as he performed his duties as physician, he became fascinated with the trading dimension of life at the fort. From his earliest contact, he showed great rapport with Indian peoples, especially in attracting their trust, a necessary dimension of the fur-trade enterprise. These qualities were the more important as the North West Company was engaged in a struggle with the Hudson's Bay Company for the allegiance and trade of Indian groups.

In recognition of his skills, the North West Company made McLoughlin a partner in 1811. He continued in this capacity for another decade, and in 1821, when Parliament forced a merger of the North West Company and the Hudson's Bay Company (taking the latter's name), McLoughlin was made a chief factor, working under Governor George

Simpson. McLoughlin administered the border district from 1822 to 1824 with his usual ability, always mindful of the company's interest in profits. In July 1824, Simpson appointed him superintendent of the huge Columbia District, a domain much larger than Great Britain itself. McLoughlin assumed his responsibilities at FORT VANCOUVER on the Columbia River in early 1825. He remained the most important European figure on the coast of the Pacific Northwest for the next 20 years.

McLoughlin had two main responsibilities. His first allegiance was to the Hudson's Bay Company and his need to support and enhance the profitability of their trading enterprise. But since the Oregon Country was the center of a dispute between the United States and Great Britain, he also needed to keep imperial considerations in mind. His responsibilities in this area were enhanced by the Oregon Joint Occupation Treaty of 1827, which opened the territory to the unrestricted settlement by citizens of both nations. McLoughlin had to manage the Columbia Department to protect both the profits of the company and the national interests of Great Britain. His duties were the more challenging because he had no control over the U.S. citizens within his purview. As he worked to make the Oregon Country a profitable supplier of furs, he supplemented his department's economic prospects by organizing an agricultural enterprise that would also provide profits for the company.

JEDEDIAH STRONG SMITH represented the competition in the fur trade. His generous terms and loose financial arrangements attracted several Hudson's Bay Company employees to his standard. The influence of WILLIAM HENRY ASHLEY and the annual American RENDEZVOUS were among the difficulties McLoughlin faced. He worked with some success to persuade the Hudson's Bay Company to offer more flexible arrangements to its trappers. Under his leadership, the trade of the Columbia Department continued to be profitable through the 1820s and into the 1830s.

The decade of the 1830s brought another challenge in the form of missionaries from the United States. Jason Lee arrived in 1834 with a party of Methodist missionaries, and two years later, Marcus and Narcissa Whitman. Lee's party settled along the Willamette River, an attractive agricultural area removed from McLoughlin's trading operations. The Whitmans settled in Walla Walla on the Columbia, a more central location. McLoughlin freely provided information and supplies to the missionaries, and, in turn, their widely reprinted reports praising the agricultural settlement possibilities of the Oregon Country increased overland immigration to Oregon. Even as the missionaries received reinforcements in the form of people, supplies, and money, the OREGON TRAIL had become the route of growing annual caravans.

McLoughlin continued to believe in the continuing presence of the Hudson's Bay Company on the Columbia, but imperial and company interests increasingly favored evacuation to the north. After 1841, Governor George Simpson himself favored moving the company's base of operations to Vancouver Island. At the same time, the fur-trade revenues had declined in McLoughlin's Columbia Department, as they were declining everywhere. McLoughlin retired in 1845 and died 12 years later.

Further reading: William R. Sampson, *John McLoughlin's Business Correspondence, 1847–1848* (Seattle: University of Washington Press, 1973).

medicine

As the 19th century began, Americans had witnessed many revolutionary changes in their lives, but medicine had not kept pace. Medical practices differed little from those of the 18th century. Citizens of antebellum America were faced with a life filled with DISEASES AND EPIDEMICS, poorly trained doctors, unsafe cures, poor diet, and generally unsanitary living conditions.

Scientific medicine at the beginning of the century was heroic medicine. All diseases resulted from an excess of fluids, and the cure was to relieve the body of the excesses through bloodletting and purging. The basic scientific knowledge necessary to disprove such beliefs was slow to develop in America. The generation of men like Franklin and Jefferson, who dominated the intellectual life of the country from 1750 to 1800 and promoted scientific research, was largely gone by 1800. Besides, the country had little time and little use for such aristocrats as it was swept up in the Age of Common Man. As Alexis de Tocqueville commented, the combination of democracy and economic opportunity in the Jacksonian era placed an emphasis on profitable technology over basic science. As a consequence, medical science based on empirical research suffered too.

Contributing to the stagnation of scientific advances in the 19th century was the philosophical movement that dominated American society: Romanticism. Romanticism came to America from Europe between 1812 and 1861 as a revolt against the Age of Reason. Rather than rational empirical thought, Romanticism emphasized feeling, sensitivity, and the supernatural. As this philosophy mixed with Jacksonian democracy in the 1820s and 1830s, it developed many uniquely American traits, one of them being religious evangelism.

By the mid-1800s, scientific medicine had taken a back seat to quackery. Scientific medicine was hampered by poor training, the continued practice of heroic medicine despite patient protests, and quarreling among the brightest physicians. Proprietary medical schools and their common practice of grave-robbing to obtain dissection specimens did little to improve the public's image of the medical profession.

These factors combined in the 1820s and 1830s with a wave of Jacksonian democracy, producing an egalitarian America with no use for aristocratic physicians. The public came to believe that anyone could cure the ill if they applied the common-sense principles promoted by quack doctors. Physician licensing, once commonplace, was abolished in most states in the 1840s, so anyone was free to practice. Scientific medicine was rapidly replaced by quackery such as hydropathy, patent medicines, phrenology, and mesmerism. When quackery became inextricably linked to the religious revivalism and social reform movements sweeping the country at mid-century, it was unstoppable.

Since the scientific community was doing little to improve medicine, and the public was rebelling against the painful and debilitating treatments of heroics, a void developed in medical treatment. With no organizing body or set of standards for physicians to follow, few could agree to what constituted appropriate practice. Lay health reformers and practitioners, filled with the millennial, democratic spirit, rushed in with theories of their own. Their treatments included water, electricity, manipulation of animal magnetism, and vegetable compounds. Many of the quack theories took on qualities of social reform and religious revivalism to become movements of their own. Each practitioner claimed to be from a specific "school" of medicine. The result was a wide selection of treatments for patients from which to chose. Almost all doctors were "general" practitioners, with very few specializing in one area, such as surgery.

Meanwhile, a new European movement began in Paris. French doctors who caught the spirit of their country's revolution did not feel confined by the writings of the "masters" and instead observed for themselves how patients reacted to disease. Dubbed the French Clinical School, it emphasized both clinical and pathological observations to determine treatments. Doctors collected statistical evidence such as temperatures and pulse rates. Diagnostics were stressed over heroics. Some 700 of the best American doctors traveled to France to study between 1820 and 1860. Yet despite the opposition of those who returned from abroad, heroic medicine continued to be practiced, and eventually the public developed a deep skepticism of doctors and an increased interest in quackery.

The United States produced some of the best surgeons, many of whom studied in France. The rigors of life on the frontier also stimulated the advancement of surgical techniques, as doctors living there often had no alternative to surgery, because they lacked drugs and access to the latest medical advances. Surgery was the last resort because it was often fatal and always painful. Performed with no regard for cleanliness, doctors wore filthy coats—often directly from the autopsy room to the operating room—with pride. This practice spread deadly infections like septicemia or gangrene. The only anesthetics were opium and alcohol. In the 1840s, chloroform, nitrous oxide, and ether began to be used as social drugs by the upper classes, and were eventually applied to surgery. Anesthetics removed the pain of surgery, allowing for longer, more complex and delicate operations.

Three doctors who emphasized diagnostics over heroics were especially influential. Dr. Daniel Drake lived most his life on the frontier rather than on the East Coast, where medical training was centered. Realizing that the frontier lacked adequate facilities to train doctors, he started the Medical College of Ohio in Cincinnati in 1819. He is best known for his exhaustive study *Systematic Treatise on the Principal Diseases of the Interior Valley of North America.* The work not only examined disease but detailed geography, climate, and frontier society. Dr. William Beaumont used an unusual method to study how the digestive system worked. An army doctor at Fort Mackinac, he encountered a patient with a severe stomach wound that would not heal. Beaumont used the opening in the unfortunate victim as a window into the gastrointestinal tract, and his 1833 work *Experiments and Observations on the Gastric Juice and Physiology of Digestion* explained the chemical process of digestion. The work of Dr. Samuel Gross to improve surgical techniques resulted in *A System of Surgery; Pathological, Diagnostic, Therapeutic, and Operative,* used by Gross in his lectures at the Jefferson Medical College in Philadelphia, and by many other medical schools.

This was also the era when women would start to gain a foothold in the medical profession. The prevailing stereotype at the time defined women as sympathetic and nurturing, making them ideally suited to care for children. Women had a long tradition as midwives and lay practioners, but they were not considered suitable for professional medicine, given their irrational and delicate sensibilities. During the 1840s, supporters of the training of female physicians received a boost from a controversy surrounding midwives and childbirth. Male doctors were starting to claim that only they had the medical training and the instruments (namely forceps) that could safely deliver a child. However, many doctors were accused of interfering too much in the process of delivery, sometimes injuring the mother or child (or both). Supporters of female medical training used the resultant backlash to argue that it was immoral for men to be involved in gynecological and obstetric practice. As a result, several schools started to allow women into their programs. In 1849, Elizabeth Blackwell graduated from Geneva Medical College in New York to become the first woman anywhere to receive a

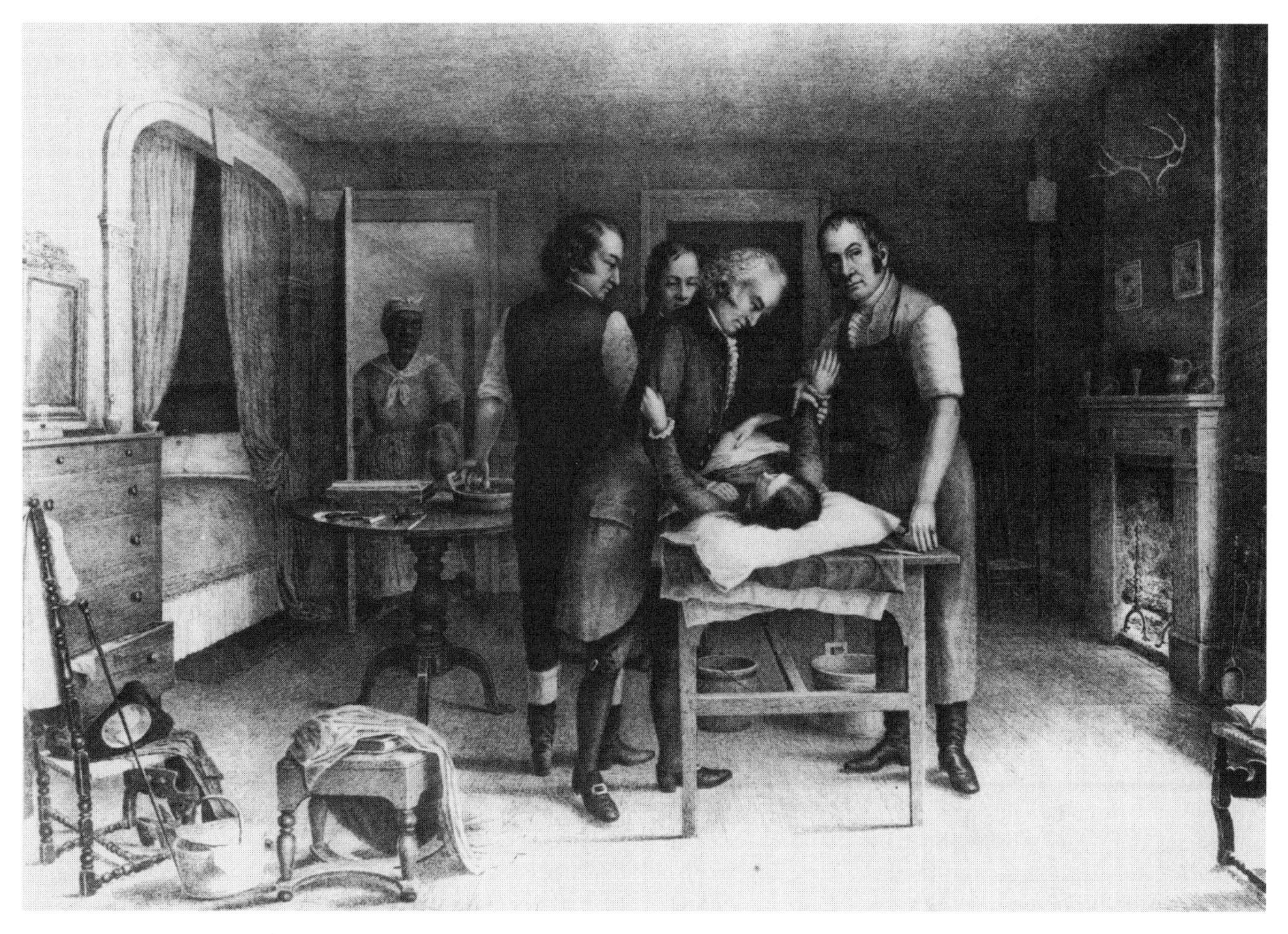

This lithograph depicts the first ovariotomy (removal of an ovary) being performed by Dr. Ephraim McDowell in 1809 in Danville, Kentucky. During the operation, McDowell successfully removed a 20-pound tumor from his 45-year-old patient—without anesthesia. *(National Library of Medicine)*

medical degree. Blackwell's achievement spurred further advances for women in the medical field, such as the establishment of women's medical colleges. The first such institution was the Women's Medical College of Pennsylvania, which opened in Philadelphia in 1850.

In 1847 the American Medical Association (AMA) was established by Nathan Davis Smith, and for the first time a code of medical ethics and educational standards for physicians was published in an effort to improve and standardize medical practice. The AMA also launched an investigation into quack remedies in an effort to enlighten the public in regard to the nature and dangerous tendencies of such remedies. Soon many medical schools were also involved in standardizing medical education, and physicians were now engaged in clinical teaching and research in hospitals. New medical institutions were emerging to provide a more scientific approach to medicine, and new instruments were being developed to assist doctors in treating patients. The 19th century started out with a bleak outlook for American medicine, yet by mid-century it had entered an age of improvement and reform.

Further reading: John Duffy, *From Humors to Medical Science: A History of American Medicine,* 2nd ed. (Urbana: University of Illinois, 1994); Paul Starr, *The Social Transformation of American Medicine* (New York: Basic Books, 1983).

Mexican-American War (1846–1848)

The war between the United States and Mexico, which lasted for less than two years, resulted in the United States gaining a huge swath of territory from the defeated Mexicans. Its origins were based in part on a dispute about the proper boundary between the two nations and the United States's annexation of TEXAS, formerly a state in the Republic of Mexico, in 1845. Texas had broken away from Mexico in 1836, defeating the Mexican army after the siege at THE ALAMO and establishing itself as a republic in its own right. American president ANDREW JACKSON of Tennessee, where many Texans were originally from, immediately recognized Texas, although Mexico did not. Soon thereafter, Texas applied for statehood; most Texans had migrated from the United States, and many of them desired to join the new republic to their former country. However, new president MARTIN VAN BUREN, a northerner, was cool to the idea, believing correctly that northern states might object to admitting another state that permitted slavery, as Texas did. The United States therefore passed on its first opportunity to admit Texas into the Union.

When the WHIG PARTY, which was increasingly opposed to the expansion of slavery, elected its first president, WILLIAM HENRY HARRISON, in 1840, it looked as though any U.S. annexation of Texas would be postponed for some time. However, Harrison died soon after taking office and was replaced by Vice President JOHN TYLER, a southerner and former Democrat. In the United States at that time was a growing belief in the idea of MANIFEST DESTINY, which held that the nation was destined to rule all of North America, including much of Mexico. This idea was tinged with racial and cultural superiority, with some Americans believing that Anglo-Saxons were entitled to lands that the darker-skinned (and Catholic) Mexicans were not using properly: the vast territories of New Mexico and CALIFORNIA. The Mexican government, for its part, continued not to recognize the independence of Texas, although Great Britain and France later did. Mexico itself was struggling as an independent nation and suffered from unstable government, with rule by dictators. It had failed to establish a republican form of government, although this had been its goal when it won independence from Spain in 1821. Few people lived in its northern provinces of California and New Mexico; California had only 15,000 Americans of European ancestry and 24,000 American Indians living on missions. (The total Indian population was much higher.) Many in the United States coveted these territories to complete national expansion. Yet despite its internal problems, Mexico was determined to keep all of its sovereignties intact.

Northern and southern states began to line up on different sides of the question of admitting Texas, due to the problem of SLAVERY. Some proslavery southerners even hoped to divide the massive territory into several smaller slave states so as to increase the power of slaveholders in Congress. South Carolina, the most militantly proslavery and antiabolition state, went so far as to declare that if Texas was not admitted into the United States, then southern states should secede from the Union. There were not enough votes in the Senate, however, to get the needed two-thirds of the votes to ratify a treaty that would result in admitting Texas to the Union. But in the final days of his administration, President Tyler persuaded Congress to pass a joint resolution on the matter, which needed only a simple majority to pass. Tyler promptly extended the offer of statehood to Texas on his last day in office. Opponents of the measure argued that annexation would provoke a war with Mexico. Certainly the Mexican government was outraged; it had stated plainly in 1843 that it would regard any annexation of Texas as a declaration of war by the United States on Mexico. In response to the formal annexation in 1845 that occurred when Texas accepted the American offer of statehood, Mexico broke off diplomatic relations with the United States.

The new president, JAMES K. POLK, had been nominated by the Democrats over Van Buren in 1844 in part because Polk had favored annexation, and the issue contributed to his victory in the general election over Whig candidate HENRY CLAY, who opposed it. Committed to expansionism, Polk was especially interested in acquiring California, which he offered to buy from Mexico. The southern nation refused, however, and also declined to negotiate with the United States about the boundary between the two nations. Mexico had maintained that the proper border was the Nueces River, which had been generally recognized as the boundary of Texas since the 18th century. Polk, pressing his expansionist agenda, contended that it was the river further south, the Rio Grande, which marked the true border between Mexico and the United States. To make the point that he was serious about the matter, in January 1846 he sent an army led by General ZACHARY TAYLOR to occupy the land in question between the Nueces and Rio Grande. The reason he gave to justify the action was that the soldiers were needed there to protect the new American state from a Mexican attack. However, Mexico saw this as a provocation and moved troops of its own into what it believed to be its territory by right.

Almost inevitably, soldiers of the two armies clashed and exchanged fire, with the Americans suffering 16 casualties in winning two encounters with the Mexicans, even though they were outmanned. Polk used the incident to ask Congress for a declaration of war against Mexico, charging that it had "invaded our territory and shed American blood on American soil." Some in Congress, especially Whigs, remained skeptical of the whole business; first-term congressman Abraham Lincoln of Illinois famously asked Polk to specify where exactly U.S. sovereignty had been violated. There was other vocal opposition to war, especially in the Northeast; the Massachusetts legislature passed a resolution opposing it. Nevertheless, led by the Democrats, Congress

went along with the president and declared war on Mexico on May 13, 1846. There was an especially great outcry of support for the decision in the South and West. It was from the states closest to Mexico, including Texas, that most of the military volunteers came—49,000 in all. Along the eastern seaboard, there was much less enthusiasm; the original 13 states contributed only about 13,000 volunteers.

In the conflict that followed, the United States won a series of military victories. Its initial strategy was to launch a two-pronged invasion of Mexico. Zachary Taylor's goal was to invade central Mexico, and on the way he scored some victories in the northeastern part of the country, including capturing the crucial city of Monterrey. The American advance was slowed by severe problems with illness, as many U.S. soldiers fell sick and died from subtropical diseases to which they had no immunity. Taylor also halted progress until his army could receive further supplies, making the American army vulnerable to a Mexican attack. Fortunately for the Americans, though, the Mexican leadership was in chaos, as the government of President Mariano Paredes was overthrown and replaced by one led by the controversial former dictator, ANTONIO LÓPEZ DE SANTA ANNA. He had been in secret negotiations with the Americans and had promised that if he regained control of the Mexican government, he would seek to negotiate a peace treaty under which Mexico would cede territory to the United States.

Polk ordered the American navy and army to let Santa Anna, who had been living in exile in Cuba, pass through a naval blockade. The Mexican general landed and proceeded safely to Mexico City, where he proclaimed himself the new president of Mexico. Having done this, he quickly forgot the promise he had made to the United States and instead began to rally his nation to recommit to the war. He organized a large army of about 20,000 and led them north out of Mexico City toward the American position at Monterrey. Along the way he made the rash statement that he would defeat Taylor's army, march all the way to Washington, and sign his peace treaty there. Many of Taylor's men had been withdrawn from Monterrey and sent to Veracruz to take part in a seaborne landing led by General WINFIELD SCOTT. This left the remaining force under Taylor's command at a 3-1 disadvantage to Santa Anna's army as it took up defensive positions at Buena Vista. A fierce battle ensued with both sides suffering heavy casualties—especially the Mexicans, who were defeated despite their superior size. Among the American soldiers who distinguished themselves in this battle was Mississippi colonel Jefferson Davis, later president of the Confederate States of America.

Meanwhile, a second American force, led by Colonel STEPHEN KEARNY, occupied New Mexico, including Santa Fe, and continued west into California, where it met with American naval forces to complete the conquest of that state. Kearny's expedition was very successful, as he met with only token resistance from the inhabitants of those states, most of whom accepted the American victory.

Determined to capture Mexico City and bring the war to a successful conclusion, Polk ordered the opening of a third front. Winfield Scott led an army of volunteers, including some of Taylor's men, in a coastal landing and proceeded to bombard the city of Veracruz; 1,500 Mexican civilians died in the attack. After inflicting heavy casualties on the Mexican army in street fighting, Scott's forces marched on to Mexico City. The Mexican capital was well defended, and the U.S. Army, which included junior officers such as future Civil War generals Robert E. Lee, Ulysses S. Grant, and George McClellan, regrouped outside of the city to plan their assault. On the approach to Mexico City, the Americans met stiff resistance, but after heavy fighting they captured the Mexican capital in September 1847. Scott and his officers entered the presidential palace, over which the American flag was raised.

One of the Mexican units that inflicted the most punishment on the Americans was the San Patricio battalion, which consisted largely of Irish-American deserters from the U.S. Army. In all, more than 10 percent of American soldiers, many of whom were poor and some of whom were recent immigrants, had deserted from the all-volunteer army.

The American capture of Mexico City effectively ended the war. The relatively swift and decisive U.S. victory was due in large part to some important advantages in the areas of transportation and communications; the Americans had put telegraph, railroads and steamboats to good use in their military effort. In winning the war, the United States had suffered only about 1,700 combat-related deaths, although 11,000 more soldiers died of disease and related health problems.

In the postwar negotiations, the United States was represented by Nicholas Trist. Dealing from a position of strength, Trist persuaded the Mexican government to sign a treaty highly favorable to U.S. interests. Under the provisions of the TREATY OF GUADALUPE HIDALGO, signed in February 1848, the Rio Grande was established as the boundary between Mexico and Texas. Mexico also ceded New Mexico and most of California, recognized Texas as part of the United States, and received about $15 million in compensation. Some expansionist Democrats in the Senate demanded that all of Mexico be brought under the American flag, but Polk rebuffed that idea and was content with the astonishing gains agreed to in the treaty. In all, the United States gained 529,000 square miles from Mexico, including the part of California where the gold rush soon began, bringing people to that territory from around the nation and the world. The victory turned out to be a mixed blessing, however, as northerners and southerners began to disagree strenuously over whether the lands gained from Mexico would be slave or free. It took the Civil War to finally settle the question.

Further reading: Jack Bauer, *The Mexican War: 1846–1848* (New York: Macmillan, 1974); John Eisenhower, *So Far From God: The U.S. War With Mexico, 1846–1848* (New York: Random House, 1989); Robert Johannsen, *To the Hall of the Montezumas: The Mexican War in the American Imagination* (New York: Oxford University Press, 1985).

—Jason Duncan

migration

The era between the American Revolution (1775–88) and the Civil War (1861–65) saw large tracts of territory added to the United States. The country's expansion attracted pioneers and settlers in a westward drive across the continent that became the dominant feature of American migration in the early 19th century—a drive that was encouraged by the U.S. government.

Westward expansion was a spontaneous, disorderly swarming of people along the trails and rivers leading into the interior of the continent and finally to the Pacific coast. This frontier raised basic questions: Who owned the land? How should it be surveyed, sold, and settled? The federal government responded to these questions with policies for Indian removal, land disposal, and the territorial system. The INDIAN REMOVAL ACT of 1830 allowed the government to move NATIVE AMERICANS off large areas of land, thereby making it available to white settlers. The government's PUBLIC LAND POLICY had the greatest impact on the flow of people to the West. Between 1800 and 1860, the federal government enacted a series of laws that were generally advantageous to settler families. This legislation included providing large parcels of land to settlers at very low prices, as long as they agreed to farm the land. Congress also established a system for surveying new territories and organizing governments within them.

This new domain was still not enough to satisfy America's hunger for new lands. Early 19th-century farmers and settlers viewed the unforested plains west of the Mississippi as an uninviting wasteland that lacked timber for building homes and towns, navigable rivers for shipping their goods to markets, and adequate rainfall for the crops they raised. In the first decade of the 19th century, the country was experiencing economic turmoil, and—contrary to what might be assumed—hard times in the East slowed westward movement. Renewed Indian warfare in the Ohio Valley and the WAR OF 1812 further discouraged settlers from heading west. However, the rate of settlement increased rapidly after 1815, as the economy in the Northeast improved and America resumed normal trading relations with England. WILLIAM HENRY HARRISON's triumph over TECUMSEH north of the Ohio River and ANDREW JACKSON's victorious campaigns against the Creek in the South had forced many Native Americans to vacate those territories, opening up millions of acres of land to white settlement. This period of increased settlement is known as the Great Migration.

At first, the major thrust of settlement beyond the Appalachians was heavily concentrated in Kentucky and Tennessee. This was shortly followed by immigrants coming into the Old Northwest, north of the Ohio River, which served as a way into the interior. Although settlers came from every state in the Union, the majority of early pioneers of Indiana, Illinois, and Ohio were southerners from Kentucky and Tennessee. Improved transportation played a major role in bringing on the Great Migration. In 1818, the NATIONAL ROAD stretched from Cumberland, Maryland, to Wheeling in what is now West Virginia. This road, along with other new and improved routes, provided an all-weather pathway for westbound emigrants. Steamboats were another major innovation in transportation, helping spur the rapid development of the region between the Appalachians and the Mississippi. The ERIE CANAL, completed in 1825, opened a new water route to the West.

The impact of the Great Migration was also felt in the southern territories. This region was primarily settled by planters engaged in expanding the COTTON CULTURE. The pressure of soil exhaustion in the southern Atlantic states and the attraction of fertile soil in the Gulf plains combined to produce a swelling westward movement of southerners and cotton production. Settlers poured into the country along the southern Mississippi River region and as far west as western Mississippi and eastern Arkansas territory. Louisiana also saw a great influx of newcomers, most of them wealthier that their northern counterparts, who poured into Louisiana to found new plantations and spread the slave economy of the Southeast.

The PANIC OF 1819 brought a sudden end to the Great Migration. Nevertheless, it had made some tremendous changes in the distribution of the nation's population. According to the 1820 census, there were 1,140,000 more people living west of the Appalachians than had lived there in 1810. Ohio, with 600,000 inhabitants, was the most populous of the trans-Appalachian states. By 1820, roughly one-quarter of the nation's population was living in the West.

By the mid-1820s, great numbers of settlers were advancing into the Lake Plains of the Old Northwest. Settlers from Kentucky and the Northeast sought the fertile land of northern Illinois and present-day southern Michigan and Wisconsin. Migration into the Great Lake plains also came from the South. Farmers of smaller holdings in Georgia, Alabama, and Mississippi, unable to compete with the expanding plantation economy, were attracted by the affordable lands of the public domain. In the South itself, Native Americans found themselves surrounded as settlement advanced into the lands of western Georgia, Florida, Alabama, and Mississippi. In order to clear the way for settlement of these lands, the federal government began enacting legislation such as the Indian Removal Act, which relocated Native Americans to reservations further west, in present-day Kansas and Oklahoma. Contrary to the government's intentions, the establishment of an Indian Country west of the Mississippi did little to stem the nation's rapid westward movement. Instead, it created a two-pronged advance, with the stream of migrating settlers

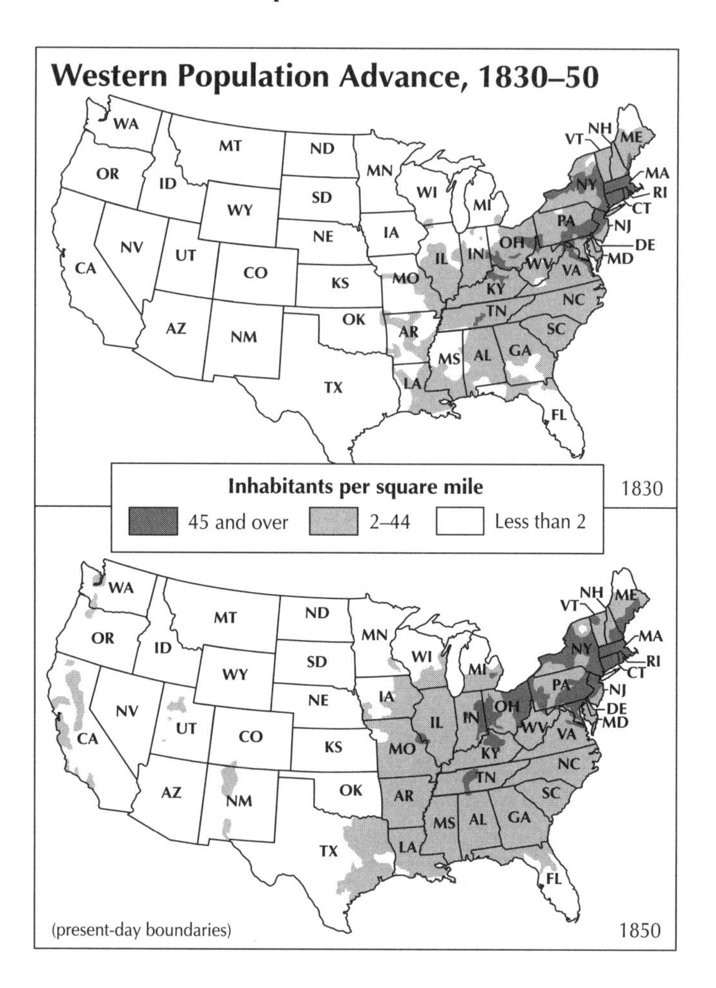

deflected northwestward to the Oregon Country and southwestward into TEXAS.

In 1840 most of Iowa and Wisconsin were still unsettled, and only a few people had advanced into Minnesota. Further south, the westward movement had reached the edge of the PERMANENT INDIAN FRONTIER. Rather than risk entering hostile territory, settlers aimed their sights on Oregon and CALIFORNIA. The overland migrations to the Pacific coast began in 1841, when 69 settlers set out from Missouri along the OREGON TRAIL. In the succeeding years, the volume of migration increased to more than a thousand persons annually. Some went to California, but a majority of them followed the Snake River and COLUMBIA RIVER to the Willamette Valley, which seemed to have a better chance of becoming a part of the United States. By 1845, the American population of the Oregon Country, most of it centered in the Willamette Valley, had grown to more than 6,000. The steady procession of covered wagons into Oregon helped to strengthen American claims to that region, which for a generation had been dominated by the British, specifically the Hudson's Bay Company. To pioneers bound for Oregon and California, the region beyond the Rockies seemed hostile to habitation. Yet this isolated aspect attracted the Mormons, who settled the Salt Lake region of Utah and made a failed attempt to establish their own state along Mormon lines, known as the STATE OF DESERET.

California's rapid transformation from Mexico's sparsely populated northern province in 1847 to its incorporation into the United States in 1850 marked the culmination of half a century of American interest and settlement. Settlement, however, was slow growing, until the discovery of gold in California in 1848, which set off the greatest gold rush in history; thousands headed to the West Coast from all points in the United States and from foreign lands as well. More than 35,000 "Forty-niners" crossed the Great Plains and Rocky Mountains to California, the population of which had exploded from 20,000 to 100,000 by the end of 1849. Within three years, a steady stream of new arrivals, mostly overlanders, would more than double that figure.

The growth of the United States in the first half of the 19th century, propelled by the doctrine of MANIFEST DESTINY, was viewed as a success for white settlers. However, it exacted a human cost. With California, Oregon, and the Southwest as part of the United States, the Permanent Indian Frontier came to be ignored as a geographic boundary; the people it protected were viewed as an inconvenient obstacle. There was a political price as well. Although overland migrations across the Great Plains continued, all pioneers were not headed for the Far West. Public lands newly open to settlement and available at low cost drew thousands of settlers into the eastern prairie regions between the Mississippi and Missouri Rivers. Territories were created to meet the needs of the new population in these areas and also prepare the way for transportation intended to cross the continent. The creation of new territorial governments in the nation's Midwest would reignite the controversy over the spread of SLAVERY. The issue would grow to threaten the survival of the Union.

Further reading: Patricia Nelson Limerick, *The Legacy of Conquest: The Unbroken Past of the American West* (Chicago: W. W. Norton, 1987); Ted Morgan, *A Shovel of Stars: The Making of the American West: 1800 to the Present* (New York: Simon & Schuster, 1996).

Missouri Compromise (1819–1821)

A series of events and debates concerning the admission of Missouri to statehood and the question of whether SLAVERY should be allowed to extend into the western territories resulted in the Missouri Compromise. In 1818, the legislature of Missouri Territory petitioned Congress for statehood. By this time, the territory had gained sufficient population to become a state, with most of its residents hailing from the South. Many of these settlers had brought slaves with them; slavery had also existed in the territory when it was a French colony. Thus, the territorial legislature wanted Missouri to be admitted to the Union as a slave state. In February 1819, Representative James Tallmadge of New York proposed an amendment to the Missouri statehood bill. The Tallmadge amendment banned the importation of slaves to Missouri and called for the gradual emancipation of slaves already living there. Southern opposition to his amendment was immediate and nearly universal. The issue of slavery had not caused such tension since the Constitutional Convention of 1787. As was the case in 1787, the new controversy over slavery centered on a battle for power between free northern states and southern states with slave economies. Northern politicians were still bitter about the constitutional compromise, which allowed southern states to count each slave as three-fifths of a person for the purpose of representation. Because northern politicians already believed the southern states possessed an unfair advantage in representation in Congress, the prospect of Missouri entering the Union as a slave state further threatened northern power.

But the battle over slavery during the Missouri controversy was not only about political representation. On the proslavery side, the increased passion with which southern slaveholders defended the slave system was due to the increasing value of their slaves. After the invention of the cotton gin in 1793 and given the expansion into new territories with a climate ideal for growing cotton, the profitability of the slave system (previously believed to be on the wane) soared. Thus, slaveholders began to respond to any antislavery proposals with increased vehemence. Tallmadge's proposal triggered intense debate in Congress, dividing the North and the South into sectional interests—an early version of the ideological and economic divide that would lead to war four decades later.

The Tallmadge amendment eventually passed in the House but was defeated in the Senate. Southern senators passed another version of the statehood bill, omitting the Tallmadge Amendment. Thus, negotiations began about how to reconcile the two bills. The heated debates centered on two central problems: maintaining a balance of power between slave and free states in Congress and whether the Northwest Ordinance of 1787, which prohibited slavery north of the Ohio River, applied to Missouri. Concerning the first point, by 1819 there were 11 free states and 11 slave states. Northerners were concerned that admitting Missouri as a slave state would upset this balance of power in Congress and give southern interests control over the federal government. The problem of a shift in the balance of legislative power was temporarily solved when Maine petitioned for statehood as a free state in 1820. With the addition of Maine, northerners' fears of a southern-controlled Congress were temporarily allayed.

Confronting the second point of contention proved more difficult. Because Missouri was part of the 1803 Louisiana Purchase and therefore not covered under the Northwest Ordinance, debates arose over whether the 1787 law applied to this territory. (The constitutional compromise had been to allow slavery to continue in the South but ban it from the territories north of the Ohio River through the Northwest Ordinance of 1787.) A settlement was eventually reached in which Missouri would be a slave state, but all other parts of the Louisiana Territory north of the 36°30' line (roughly the extension of the border between Missouri and Arkansas) would be free. Although this element of the compromise is usually attributed to HENRY CLAY, it was actually proposed by Senator J. B. Thomas of Illinois. The admission of Maine as a free state and the designation of Thomas's compromise line seemed to put an end to the conflict, until Missouri proposed a constitution that banned free blacks and mulattoes from the state. This new provision rekindled northern anger. Henry Clay proposed another compromise, offering a vaguely worded resolution stating that this exclusionary clause in the Missouri constitution should never be interpreted so as to violate the rights of any citizen. This resolution implicitly weakened the ability of free blacks to claim the rights of citizenship—a handicap that would become increasingly oppressive in the following decades. But this last compromise resolution succeeded in saving the larger agreement. The compromise legislation finally passed on February 26, 1821. One week later, Missouri was admitted into the Union as a slave state.

This sectional divide over the Missouri question brought to the surface the elemental problem that the founding fathers had failed to resolve in the constitutional debates—namely, how to reconcile the creation of a free republic with a society that relied on and sanctioned slavery. Were the provisions in the Constitution allowing for slavery in the South meant to imply that slavery should expand into new territories or simply be maintained as custom in the places where it was firmly entrenched? Did the Constitution's framers intend to allow slavery to expand or just to exist where it already was? Was society in the newly settling West going to be controlled by slaveholding southerners or by nonslaveholding northerners? These crucial, divisive questions would only temporarily be addressed by the compromises reached in 1820 and 1821. The underlying problems would continue to fester, coming to a head again during the controversies surrounding FUGITIVE SLAVE LAWS and the COMPROMISE OF 1850. The Thomas Proviso prohibiting slavery north of the compromise line was repealed by the Kansas-Nebraska Act of 1854 and by the Supreme Court's decision in the Dred Scott case of 1857. The bitter conflict over the extension of slavery into the West finally exploded in the violent upheaval of the Civil War, which broke out in 1861. While it failed to provide a permanent solution to the conflict over slavery, the Missouri Compromise temporarily eased the tensions between rival states and established a pattern for the future entrance of slave and free states into the Union.

Further reading: George Dangerfield, *The Awakening of American Nationalism, 1815–1828* (New York: Harper and Row, 1965); Don Edward Fehrenbacher, *Sectional Crisis and Southern Constitutionalism* (Baton Rouge: Louisiana State University Press, 1995); Glover B. Moore, *The Missouri Controversy, 1819–1821* (Lexington: University of Kentucky Press, 1953).

—Eleanor H. McConnell and Rita M. Broyles

Missouri Fur Company (1807–1825)

The first of the important St. Louis fur companies, the Missouri Fur Company opened the trade of the upper Missouri River, but throughout its precarious existence, it struggled against hostile Indians and against formidable rival fur companies.

Inspired by the explorations of the Lewis and Clark Expedition (1804–06), Manuel Lisa and his partners—William Morrison and Pierre Menard—founded the St. Louis Missouri Fur Company in 1807. They were all veterans of the fur trade. In that same year, the three partners

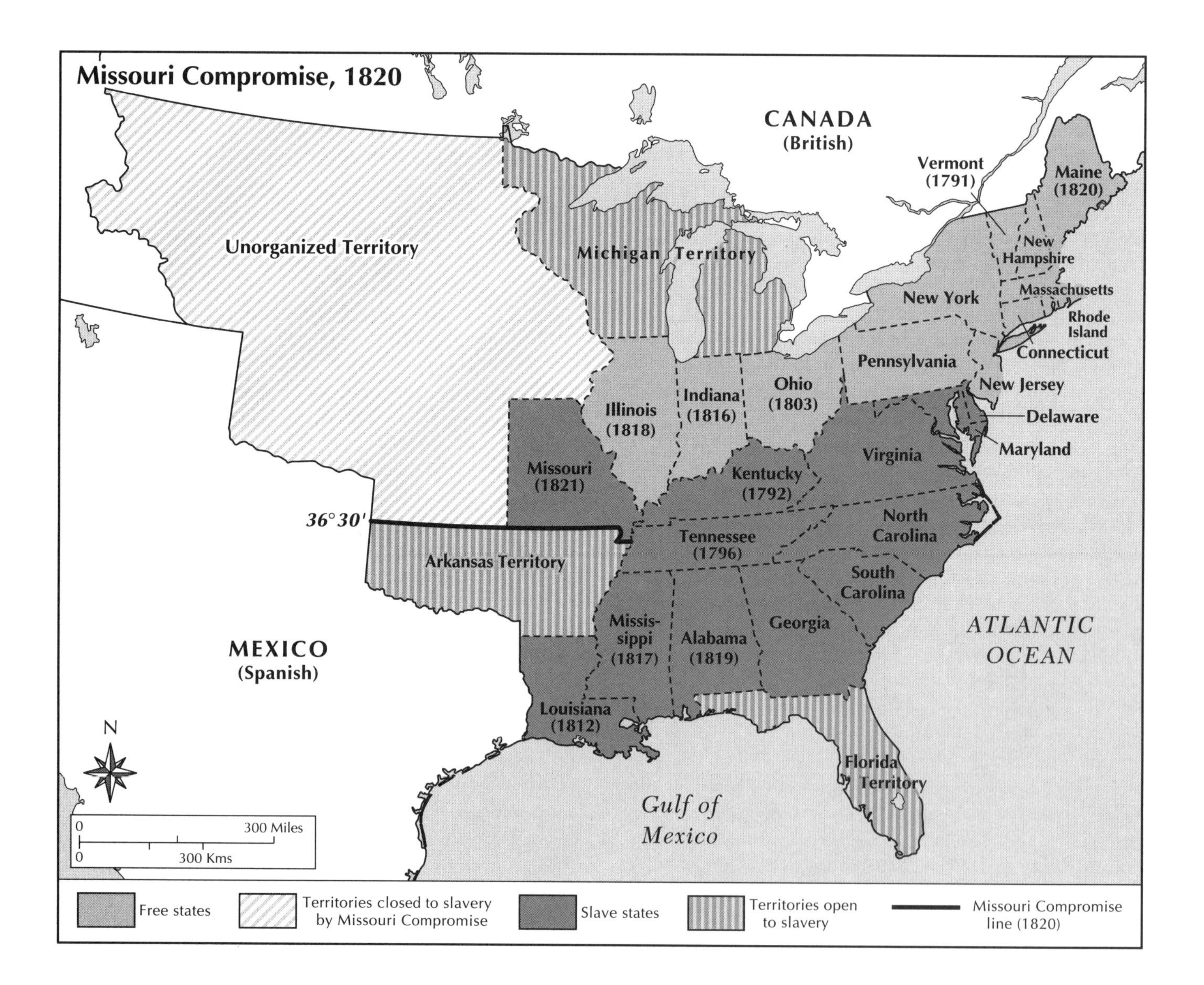

financed a fur-trading expedition by keelboats into the upper Missouri River. The boats and their crews penetrated to the Yellowstone River, where Lisa supervised the construction of a trading post at the mouth of the Bighorn River. From this base of operations, the company sent out several trapping expeditions into the northern Rocky Mountains. In 1809, Lisa and his partners enlarged the company. The fur-trapping and trading ventures made contact with local Indian peoples, but several nations were hostile, and the distances of the trading posts from St. Louis made reinforcement and resupply difficult and expensive. The most important result of the first years of the enterprise was the vastly expanded geographic knowledge of the region. Exploration in these remote areas was always difficult, and the enterprise confronted almost constant hostility from some Indian nations, especially the Blackfeet.

The outbreak of the WAR OF 1812 made the conduct of the fur trade especially dangerous, since it involved NATIVE AMERICANS allied with the Americans and by the British. The company reorganized with three partners—Lisa, Clark, and Sylvestre Labbadie—in 1812, changing its name to the Missouri Fur Company. In 1814, the American government appointed Lisa as Indian subagent, requiring him to use his influence to hold the loyalties of the western tribes. Although Lisa proved useful in this regard, the company was out of business by 1814.

With the close of the war, the rivalries of the fur trade resumed, intensified by the growing reach of the Hudson's Bay Company to the north and the AMERICAN FUR COMPANY on the Pacific coast. In 1819, the Missouri Fur Company reorganized again, in search of new partners and fresh capital. When he died in 1820, Lisa left a legacy of exploration and entrepreneurial activity that had captured the attention of the first generation of American fur traders.

Under the leadership of Joshua Pilcher, the Missouri Fur Company embarked on a new set of expeditions along the upper Missouri. The company initially did well, but a series of attacks by the Blackfeet in 1823 killed several veteran trappers and severely damaged the company's strength. The business threats posed by WILLIAM HENRY ASHLEY and JOHN JACOB ASTOR made the Missouri Fur Company increasingly unprofitable. The company employed some of the foremost veteran trappers of the fur trade, but these men were inexperienced in business at a time when the trade was increasingly competitive and business experience had become as important as skill in the field. Ashley's use of the RENDEZVOUS was an innovative step in the trade's evolution to which the Missouri Fur Company had no answer. Astor's scale of operations further dwarfed the small, almost intimate nature practices of the Missouri Fur Company traders. In 1825, the company failed and went out of business. Pilcher formed another company, but it was never successful, and in 1833 he joined the American Fur Company. In a sense, the failure of the Missouri Fur Company signaled the decline of the fur trade.

Further reading: Abraham P. Nasatir, *Manuel Lisa* (New York: Argosy-Antiquarian, 1964); Richard E. Oglesby, *Manuel Lisa and the Opening of the Missouri Fur Trade* (Norman: University of Oklahoma Press, 1963).

Monroe, James (1758–1831)

A Democratic-Republican and lifelong public servant, James Monroe served two terms as president of the United States from 1817 to 1825 during the ERA OF GOOD FEELINGS. Born in Westmoreland County, Virginia, on April 28, 1758, he was the oldest of four children. His parents, Spence and Elizabeth Jones Monroe, raised their children on a farm in Orange County in the Piedmont region, and Monroe began attending Campbelltown Academy at age 11. He entered the College of William and Mary in June 1774, following the death of his father and his subsequent inheritance of all family property. At 16, he also found himself responsible for his mother and the care of his siblings until they reached maturity.

Caught up in the volatile political climate of Williamsburg, the capital of colonial Virginia, Monroe often allowed his studies to take a back seat to the excitement fostered by the coming of the Revolutionary War (1775–83). With the war in full swing by spring 1776, he enlisted in the Third Virginia Infantry Regiment under the command of Colonel Hugh Mercer to fight for independence from Great Britain. Monroe was trained by General Andrew Lewis, quickly commissioned a lieutenant, and saw his first action at the Battle of Harlem Heights (September 16, 1776) in New York. He later fought in the Battle of Trenton (December 26, 1776), where he was shot in the shoulder while fighting Hessian soldiers after crossing the icy Delaware River; it took three months for him to recover from his wounds. Afterward he was promoted to captain and participated in the Battles of Brandywine (September 11, 1777) and Germantown (October 4, 1777) in Pennsylvania. He then received a promotion to major and served as an aide-de-camp to William Alexander, also known as Lord Stirling.

After suffering through the infamously difficult winter at Valley Forge with George Washington and the rest of the Continental Army in 1777–78, Monroe's final military engagement took place at the Battle of Monmouth Court House (June 28, 1778). Increasingly frustrated in subsequent months because he never received his own command, he left Stirling's staff and the army for good in December. Monroe returned to his academic pursuits in

Virginia and studied law under Thomas Jefferson, who became his lifelong mentor. He took a brief hiatus from his legal studies in 1780 when he was appointed a special military agent for Virginia, and in that capacity he helped establish a communications system to monitor British movement.

The future president began his political career when he was elected to the Virginia legislature in 1782. Between 1783 and 1786, he served in the congress formed under the Articles of Confederation. As a member of the Confederation Congress, he chaired a committee in 1785 that eventually called for the framing of a new constitution, but Monroe did not participate in the Constitutional Convention of 1787. Suspicious of concentrated power, he believed the Constitution gave too much power to the federal government. He did, however, serve as a senator from 1790 to 1794 and remained a vocal opponent of the Federalist Party and many policies of the Washington administration. Despite his political disagreements with President Washington, he served as ambassador to France from 1794 to 1796, until his opposition to the Jay Treaty (1794) led Washington to revoke his appointment. Monroe returned to Virginia and was elected governor, serving from 1799 to 1802. He was politically aligned with his mentor, Thomas

President James Monroe *(Library of Congress)*

Jefferson, who was elected president in 1800. During the Jefferson administration, Monroe helped negotiate the Louisiana Purchase (1803). He also served as minister to France, Spain, and England. His record continued to grow as he was elected for a second time as governor of Virginia in 1811. He resigned the same year when President James Madison appointed him secretary of state, a post he held until 1817. Praised for his foresight when he predicted that the British would assault Washington, D.C., during the WAR OF 1812 (1812–15), Monroe also served as secretary of war between 1814 and 1815.

Monroe's long and distinguished public career culminated in his election as the fifth president of the United States in 1816. As president, he enjoyed great popularity, and he came just one vote short of being unanimously elected to his second term in office in 1820. His two-term presidency is often described as the "Era of Good Feelings" because of the general climate of domestic tranquility and political harmony in the United States. Optimism had swept the nation after the War of 1812, and it marked Monroe's presidency, which lacked serious political opposition due to the demise of the Federalist Party.

A strong nationalist, Monroe supported an economic nationalism that led to the creation of the SECOND BANK OF THE UNITED STATES in 1816. He signed the legislation for the MISSOURI COMPROMISE, although he never quite felt comfortable with the idea of the federal government having the power to limit the expansion of SLAVERY. Other notable accomplishments of his administration include the acquisition of FLORIDA from Spain in 1819 and the issuance of the famous MONROE DOCTRINE in 1823, which warned European powers to stay out of the Western Hemisphere and pledged that the United States would not interfere in European internal affairs.

After leaving office, Monroe served as a regent of the University of Virginia from 1826 to 1830. He passed away at the age of 73 on July 4, 1831. His death marked the end of an era, for he was the last revolutionary war hero to be elected president.

Further reading: Harry Ammon, *James Monroe: The Quest for National Identity* (New York: McGraw-Hill, 1971); Noble E. Cunningham, Jr., *The Presidency of James Monroe* (Lawrence: University of Kansas Press, 1996).

—Sarah Eppler Janda

Monroe Doctrine

The Monroe Doctrine, named after the president who announced it, JAMES MONROE, has been an enduring principle of American FOREIGN POLICY since the 1820s, especially with regard to Central and South America. Its origins lie both in the Old World and the New. Between

1815 and 1822, the weakened Spanish Empire in the Americas all but collapsed, resulting in the creation of several new republics. The United States in 1822 recognized the independence of its new sister republics of Mexico, Chile, Peru, Colombia, and La Plata (later Argentina). Working with his able and experienced secretary of state, JOHN QUINCY ADAMS, President Monroe was anxious to defend and advance American interests, including economic ones, in the face of new political conditions that were emerging in the western hemisphere. One of the origins of the Monroe Doctrine, however, came from an unlikely source: Great Britain. The British, who had just concluded their second war with the United States less than a decade earlier, had benefited economically from the crumbling of the Spanish Empire in the New World. They did not want to see Spain, and possibly its old rival France, rebuild their colonial empires in the western hemisphere. In 1823, France invaded Spain and replaced that nation's liberal government with a more conservative one. This led to speculation that the two nations would combine their military might and undertake an invasion of the Americas in order to reclaim sovereignty over Spain's former colonies. The United States was also concerned that the Holy Alliance, which consisted of Russia, Austria and Prussia, and was based on the shared ideals of Christianity and monarchy between them, would support such a move by Spain and France. The British foreign minister, George Canning, thereby tried to convince the U.S. government that the interests of the two nations were in concert with regards to the Spanish and other continental European powers. Canning suggested that the United States and Britain formulate an official, joint, policy opposing any possible moves by European powers in the Americas. The United States wished to see Britain recognize the independence of the new republics in the western hemisphere, but Britain, not wanting to encourage republicanism in Ireland, refused to do so. Monroe and Adams consulted with former presidents Thomas Jefferson and James Madison, who advised that the United States accept Canning's offer. The president and secretary of state expected, however, that whether or not the United States issued a joint pronouncement with Britain or acted unilaterally, the powerful British navy would back up that policy. They also cooled to Canning's offer when they realized that Britain would not recognize any acquisition of territory by the United States that currently was part of the Spanish Empire. Many in the United States hoped, and indeed expected, that CUBA would at some point become one of the United States, and so it became clear that American and British interests in the New World were not necessarily one and the same. Monroe and Adams further concluded that such a joint U.S.-British policy would not be politically popular with the majority of the American people. The Monroe administration also wanted to maintain the American foreign policy tradition of avoiding formal alliances with European nations if at all possible.

In addition to being concerned about a possible threat from Spain, the United States was also alarmed by an expanding Russian presence in the northwestern part of North America. Russia had an interest in Alaska dating back to the first decades of the 18th century. In 1799, the czar's government had established the Russian-American Company, to which it granted exclusive rights to trade and to make settlements in the parts of northwest North America not claimed by any other nation. American traders, however, did not recognize the rights of the Russian-American Company, and they resisted its mandate from Moscow, trading with the native peoples, and selling them guns and ammunition, among other items. This activity by American citizens generated diplomatic protests from the czar's government to Washington. Russians had begun moving southward from Alaska, their possession; at one point there were Russian settlers in what is now CALIFORNIA, in the vicinity of present-day San Francisco. The U.S. government was concerned that the Russian expansion in the Pacific Northwest might conceivably lead to Americans becoming, at least formally, colonial subjects of the Russian Empire. In 1821, Czar Alexander I, in renewing the monopoly privileges of the Russian-American Company, set their domain at a point further southward than it had been previously, and sent a ship of the Russian navy to protect that claim. When Adams protested in a diplomatic note in 1823, the czar's government responded by dismissing the power of "expiring republicanism." Russian actions in the early 1820s in North America alarmed not just the United States, but Great Britain as well. Even so, the United States decided to reject Britain's offer of formal cooperation and act on its own. As Secretary Adams put it, "it would be more candid, as well as more dignified, to avow our principles explicitly to Russia and France, than to come in as a cockboat in the wake of the British man-of-war."

The actual pronouncement that became known as the Monroe Doctrine was included in the president's message to Congress on December 2, 1823. Although not known for the quality of his mind or breadth of vision in the way that his two Virginia predecessors, Jefferson and Madison, had been, Monroe's own view of the world was a factor in making this policy. He had been a firm advocate of republicanism in his own right, and maintained a strong belief that the institutions of the United States were worthy of emulation by other nations, especially the new republics to the south. From his first year in the White House, 1817, he had expressed a particular solidarity with the struggles of the peoples of America to break free from the Spanish

Empire. He was supported in these views by his secretary of state, who joined Monroe in his dislike for European monarchies and their claims on America.

In his message to Congress, Monroe developed two main points. The first was his assertion that the era of European colonization of the New World was over, and that all of the Americas from that point forward should be considered off limits to the nations of Europe who sought to establish new colonies or claim existing ones. That meant that the United States would not accept any European state transferring one of its colonies to another. His second point involved the general principle of nonintervention. Monroe declared that the United States would not involve itself in general European wars, such as the last of the Napoleonic Wars, which had ended just eight years previously. As the political systems of Republican America differed from those of the European nations, this would be inappropriate. At the same time, Monroe also bluntly warned the European nations that they must respect the sovereignty of the newly independent states of South America and not interfere in the hemisphere with military power. The Monroe Doctrine, as it was stated, did not have the force of law; in fact, European nations were openly skeptical and even contemptuous of it. In retrospect, it is not likely that the European powers would have embarked on any large-scale efforts to lay claim to the former American colonies of Spain. Even so, the nationalist and patriotic overtones of Monroe's message proved to be quite popular within the United States. In real terms it was not binding on any nation, as it was a unilateral declaration and not a treaty. What was more, the United States failed to back up the doctrine with force when Britain acquired some possessions in Central America and as well as the Falkland Islands off the coast of Argentina later in the 19th century. As a result of Monroe's pronouncement, however, Russia agreed not to pursue the acquisition of any territory in northwestern North America below a point satisfactory to the United States. This agreement essentially ended any chance that Russia would emerge as a power, colonial or otherwise, in North America.

The Monroe Doctrine, as it became known in the later 19th century, was not immediately recognized as having long-term significance. It became relevant during the crisis that led to the MEXICAN-AMERICAN WAR of the 1840s. President JAMES K. POLK in 1845 invoked the Monroe Doctrine when criticizing continued British claims to parts of the Oregon Territory that the United States considered to be rightfully theirs. As the United States grew into a world power in the 20th century, it became much easier for it to act in explicit defense of the principles first articulated by Monroe in 1823. Critics of the Monroe Doctrine have labeled it as providing a cover for American economic and military domination of the entire Western Hemisphere. The U.S. government, however, has never revoked the Monroe Doctrine as a general principle, finding occasion to both distance itself from the doctrine, and to invoke it, when it suited its interests in specific instances.

Further reading: George Dangerfield, *The Era of Good Feelings* (New York: Harcourt Brace, 1952); Dexter Perkins, *A History of the Monroe Doctrine,* rev. ed. (Boston: Little Bronx, 1955); Harry Ammon, *James Monroe: The Quest for National Identity* (New York: McGraw-Hill, 1971).

—Jason K. Duncan

Mormon Trail

On their overland emigrations from the towns on the Mississippi and Missouri Rivers to the Mormon settlements in Utah, members of the CHURCH OF JESUS CHRIST OF LATTER-DAY SAINTS followed what came to be known as the Mormon Trail. The first, shortest, and most briefly used segment of the trail ran from Nauvoo, Illinois, to Winter Quarters, Nebraska (near present-day Omaha). In winter 1845–46 the Mormon Community in Nauvoo, under the leadership of BRIGHAM YOUNG, faced the rising hostility of the surrounding countryside. Young had hoped to arrange a truce that would allow the church to emigrate in spring 1846, but armed mobs surrounding the city refused to give him such respite. Instead, as early as late autumn 1845, they began raids on outlying Mormon settlements and soon near the city of Nauvoo itself. Young now directed that the emigrations begin immediately, and in the middle of winter, carefully organized groups of Mormon families crossed the ice on the frozen Mississippi and moved across the Territory of Iowa toward the West.

Advance parties, designated "pioneers," marked the trail, built log cabins for shelter, established a mail service, dug wells, and even planted fields of corn to be harvested by later bands of Mormons. By October 1847 some 12,000 Mormons had reached Winter Quarters, near Omaha on the Missouri River. Winter Quarters was a temporary resting place, but the onset of winter demanded the rapid organization of the community and preparations for the changing season. Work parties built shelter, while others fanned out into the countryside to purchase supplies of food. In spite of the energetic preparations, the winter season was a difficult one. Some 600 Mormons died from exposure and disease.

Even as he struggled to provide for the Mormon encampment in the face of winter, Young and his counselors were planning the emigration to the West. Building on their successful experience in crossing Iowa, he designated pioneers to mark the route and provide support. He

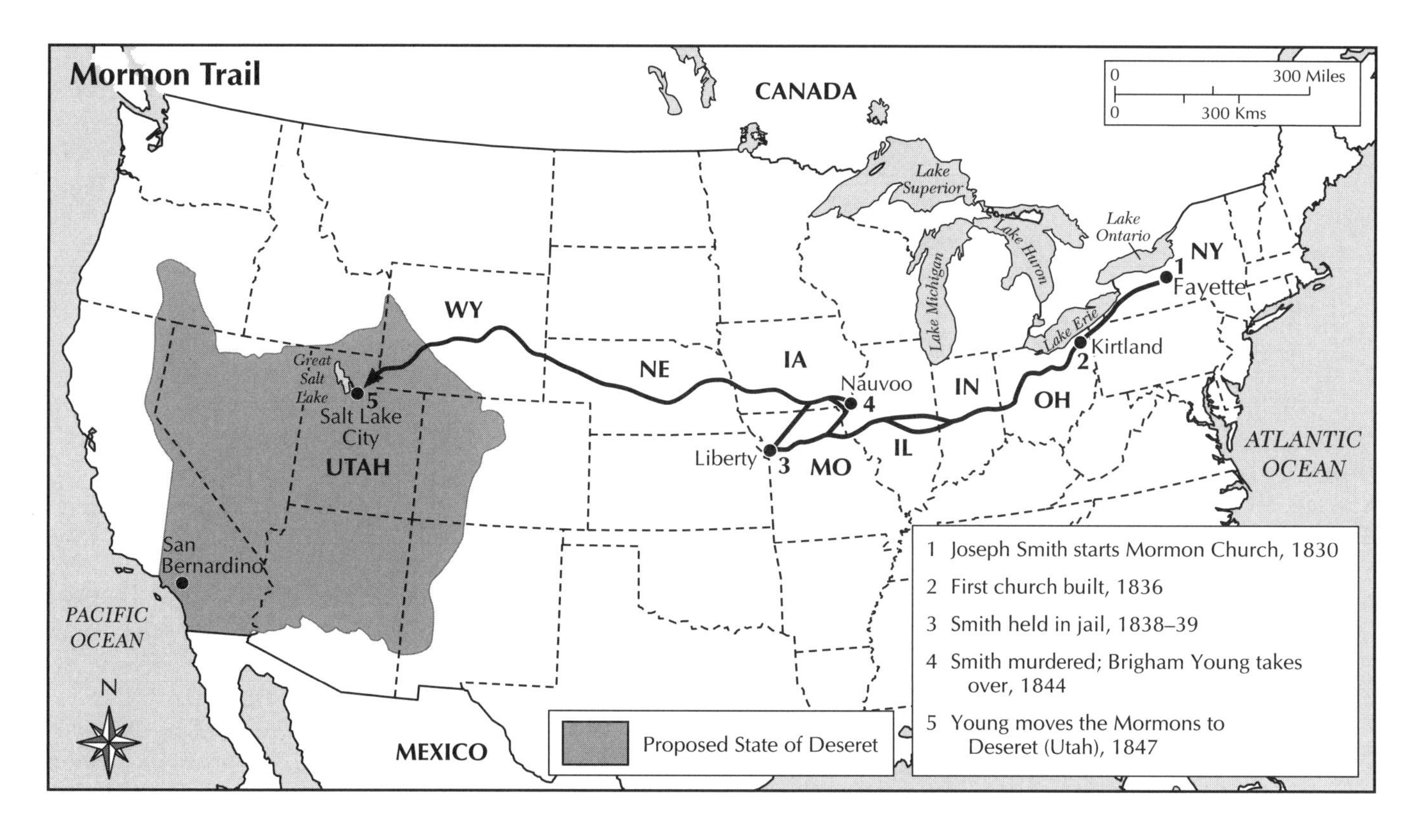

then divided the entire Mormon community into bands of tens, fifties, and hundreds, each group with a designated leader. The chain of command ran up to Young himself. He also issued instructions for driving the wagons, managing the livestock, and maintaining security in camping at night. The Sabbath was to be strictly observed, and in the tradition of looking to the future, Young directed that records of the overland journey to the West be kept and carefully preserved.

In April 1847, the "Pioneer Band" of 148 persons set out from Winter Quarters. The well-marked and well-used OREGON TRAIL followed the south bank of the Platte River, but Young did not follow this trail, probably concluding that any parties encountered would be hostile to the Mormons. Instead, he established a new route along the north bank of the Platte that would become known as the Mormon Trail. The advance party reached FORT LARAMIE in early June, then followed the Oregon Trail for some 400 miles to Fort Bridger. At this point, Young and his party left the Oregon Trail and struck across the Wasatch Range into the Valley of the Great Salt Lake. It was at the entrance to the valley that Young called his party together and announced the site as the future gathering of Zion.

Young now returned east to make preparations for the emigration of the main body of the church to the valley. Using the revised Mormon Trail and supported by the planning of church leaders and the work of the pioneers, the church gradually moved west. Some 1,600 members arrived in 1847, and another 2,500 in 1848. The costs proved daunting, even with the funds acquired from enlisting the Mormon Battalion, a military unit organized by Brigham Young, for the MEXICAN-AMERICAN WAR. In order to economize, Mormon leaders introduced a plan under which emigrants would push handcarts across the plains to the Valley of the Great Salt Lake. The first of the handcart companies departed from Coralville, Iowa, in spring 1856, and over five years, almost 3,000 emigrants pushed or pulled handcarts to the valley. The handcart expeditions were arduous and risky. Two of the first five companies departing in 1856 failed to reach the crest of the mountains before the first major snowfall, and numerous Mormons lost their lives. Eventually the church dispatched supply wagons to accompany the handcart companies. This expedition of the handcart companies was one of the most remarkable stories of the overland migration across the plains.

The Mormon Trail remained in use through the 1860s, although the numbers using it declined steadily. With the completion of the transcontinental railroad in 1869 and its extension into Salt Lake City, railroad travel became the standard means of transportation to the Mormon settlements in Utah. Over its life, approximately 70,000 Mormons followed the trail. It was an important chapter in overland travel to the West.

Further reading: Wallace Stegner, *The Gathering Zion: The Story of the Mormon Trail* (Salt Lake City: Westwater Press, 1964).

Mormon War (1857–1858)

The Mormon War was a conflict between the CHURCH OF JESUS CHRIST OF LATTER-DAY SAINTS and the federal government that led to the invasion and occupation of Utah Territory by the U.S. Army. The war had its origins in 25 years of continuing hostility between the Mormon Church and its neighbors and eventually American society as a whole. These ongoing clashes led to Mormon emigrations from Kirtland, Ohio, to western Missouri; from western Missouri to Nauvoo, Illinois; and, finally, from Nauvoo to the Valley of the Great Salt Lake in Utah.

By the time the main body of the church, under its leader BRIGHAM YOUNG, arrived in Utah in 1847, public distaste for the church had transformed to violent hostility. The original Mormon prophet, JOSEPH SMITH, JR., had been assassinated by a mob in Carthage, Illinois, in 1844. Attacks on Mormons and their property had forced them to move from Nauvoo to the West. The primary causes of the hostility were Mormon growth and prosperity, in-group loyalty and identification at the expense of outsiders, and issues of local and state politics. To these issues were added stories of peculiar Mormon religious rituals and, beginning in 1842, rumors of POLYGAMY among Mormon leaders. These continuing conflicts forced Smith's successor, Brigham Young, and the church to flee west to the Valley of the Great Salt Lake.

Once arrived in the valley, Young organized the landscape and the community to serve the needs of the church. When the U.S. Congress organized Utah Territory as a part of the COMPROMISE OF 1850, Young was appointed governor of the territory; this recognized that the residents of the territory were predominantly Mormon in character. Along with a governor, the Northwest Ordinance, still the organic law for organizing new territories, provided for three judges to be appointed. The judges would form the supreme court of the territory, and the judges and the governor would draft a code of law for the new territory. In company with Young as governor, the president appointed three non-Mormon judges from the East. It would prove to be an awkward mix.

Suspicion of and antagonism toward Mormons experienced a strong revival in 1852 with the public announcement that polygamy, long practiced in secret, was indeed a fundamental belief of the church. To Mormons, polygamy was a holy doctrine, commanded by the Lord through the words of Joseph Smith. To non-Mormons, polygamy was the ultimate proof of the immorality of the church and its leaders, whose real purpose in its promulgation was lust and lawlessness. Certainly adherence to the doctrine of polygamy laid the basis for the revival of conflict that would continue for a half-century.

When the newly appointed federal judges arrived in Utah Territory, they found a large church community organized as a theocracy, with church leaders in control of the natural resources (land and water) of the territory, dominant in political life, and influential in issues of law. Residents were obedient to church doctrine and leaders at every level. Young saw the judges as meddlesome outsiders, distant from and perhaps even hostile to the Mormon community. The judges saw themselves as representatives of the authority of the national government, whose presence was alternately ignored or circumvented. Young and the church leaders actively schemed to bypass the federal courts and handle cases in local courts, where the influence of the church was paramount.

The judges complained to Washington that the authority of the federal government was being undermined and even contravened by the church. As anti-Mormon sentiment rose with the public outcry over polygamy, politicians and parties moved to condemn the Saints. The REPUBLICAN PARTY platform of 1856 singled out for condemnation "those twin relics of barbarism—polygamy and slavery." The DEMOCRATIC PARTY won the election, but the administration of President James Buchanan faced an unending series of insoluble problems associated with sectionalism and SLAVERY. Mormon behavior in the Utah Territory became one of the few issues on which anything like a national consensus could be found. In 1857, Buchanan issued a proclamation accusing the Mormons of rebellion against the constituted authority of the U.S. government. In order to put down this rebellion, the president sent a military expedition to reestablish the American government's authority.

News of the dispatch of an armed expedition heightened the suspicion and hostility of the church and its leaders against non-Mormons. The arrival of an armed expedition produced bombastic rhetoric from church pulpits: Mormons were being subjected to another in a series of persecutions, and the community must defend itself. As war fever swept across the territory, Young and church leaders organized for a spirited armed defense. Soon, however, Young decided in favor of a more passive response. The church leadership went into hiding, and bands of volunteers raided the supply wagons of the advancing federal army. The Mormons burned Fort Bridger, fearing that the outpost would be of assistance to the troops. They also set fire to the grasslands, intent on denying the federal troops the use of forage for livestock.

In late June 1858, the invading army passed through a largely deserted Salt Lake City. It established Camp Floyd some 40 miles away. The two sides now settled down to maintaining a continuing federal presence, while various individuals tried to draft some kind of truce between the two sides. An accommodation of sorts was eventually reached, but armed forces continued to occupy portions of Utah Territory. After much initial suspicion and even hostility, the opposing parties began communicating, and federal officers started buying supplies from Mormon farmers. The federal troops and the Mormon community never entirely accepted one another, but they did meet on a regular basis for mutual benefit. The occupation of Utah as a permanent feature of life in the territory came to an end with the outbreak of the Civil War (1861–65). The elements of the army withdrew.

By this time, Young had been removed as governor of Utah Territory, but discord over authority in Utah Territory continued. In 1862, during the civil conflict over the future of the Union, the government dispatched another armed force to Utah to observe the activities of the church and its leaders. The second expedition was withdrawn later that year, but the conflict between the church and the nation would continue for another 30 years, ending only when the church issued a revised doctrine that outlawed polygamy and Utah was admitted to the Union in 1896.

Further reading: Leonard J. Arrington, *Brigham Young: American Moses* (New York: Knopf, 1985); Newall G. Bringhurst, *Brigham Young and the Expanding American Frontier* (Boston: Little, Brown, 1986).

Morse, Samuel F. B. (1791–1872)

Artist and inventor of the telegraph, Samuel Finley Breese Morse was born in Cambridge, Massachusetts, on April 27, 1791, the eldest son of a Calvinist minister. He was educated at the elite Phillips Academy in Andover before attending Yale College. Morse proved an indifferent student, but while at Yale he displayed considerable artistic talent and painted miniature portraits. This brought him to the attention of noted artist Washington Allston, who convinced him to study at his studio in England. Morse quickly gained renown as a promising painter, winning several awards. However, he had less success following his return home in 1815 and subsequently returned to painting miniatures. Morse married Lucretia Walker in 1818, and eventually settled in New York City, where he helped establish the National Academy of the Arts of Design in 1826.

Morse endured a hardscrabble existence as a painter, talented but lacking sufficient patronage to thrive. Following the deaths of his wife, father, and mother in 1826–28, he spent some time in Europe. While returning home in 1829, he met inventor Charles Thomas Jackson, who convinced him of the practicality of sending messages with electrical impulses. This notion subsequently became the driving force in Morse's life. He eventually found work as a painting and sculpture instructor at the fledgling University of the City of New York (later New York University), investing all of his spare time and money making electromagnetic signals a reality. At length he acquired two partners—Leonard Gale, a chemistry professor; and Alfred Vail, a talented mechanic—in 1837. Together, the three men came up with a viable scheme for sending signals over wire through a transmitter and a receiver. The mechanism employed a system of dots and dashes, combinations of which represented a number or letter, making it possible to decipher messages quickly. This eventually became known as the Morse Code.

Although Morse's telegraph worked and had practical applications, it generated very little enthusiasm. He initially proferred it to the federal government in 1837, but they displayed no interest. Despite his acquisition of a government patent, the telegraph languished from lack of funding. It was not until 1844 that Congress appropriated $30,000 for Morse to lay down a 40-mile telegraph line between Washington, D.C., and Baltimore, Maryland. On May 24, 1844, Morse tapped out the cryptic message "What has God

Samuel F. B. Morse *(Hulton/Archive)*

wrought?"—and a communications revolution began. In fact, the telegraph made an indelible impact on the course of subsequent American history. The device accompanied the railroad lines westward and, through instantaneous transmission of messages, conquered distance. For the first time a network of wires could connect even the remotest frontier settlement with large urban centers on the East Coast, promoting a greater sense of national unity. Telegraphs were also extensively employed by both sides during the Civil War, proving useful for communications and intelligence work.

Morse founded the Magnetic Telegraph Company in 1845, although the company struggled and he ultimately merged with the Western Union Corporation in 1866. Within a few years, telegraphs were being employed throughout the world. Morse eventually retired to his home in Poughkeepsie, New York, to reap a fortune in licensing fees. He died on April 2, 1872, having ushered in the age of global communications.

Further reading: Lewis Coe, *The Telegraph: A History of Morse's Invention and Its Predecessors in the United States* (Jefferson, N.C.: MacFarland, 1993); David P. Hochfelder, "Taming the Lightning: American Telegraphy as a Revolutionary Technology, 1832–1860" (unpublished Ph. D. dis., Case Western Reserve University, 1999); William Kloss, *Samuel F. B. Morse* (New York: H. N. Abrams, 1988); Paul J. Staiti, *Samuel F. B. Morse* (Cambridge, U.K.: Cambridge University Press, 1989).

—John C. Fredriksen

Mott, Lucretia (1793–1880)

Born January 3, 1793, into a Quaker family on Nantucket, Lucretia Coffin Mott was a lifelong activist for abolition and women's rights. The daughter of Anna Folger and Thomas Coffin, Mott credited her childhood with the formation of her independent character. She was surrounded by strong female role models from an early age. Since most men on the island gained their livelihood from the sea, women frequently spent long periods of time alone, raising families and running businesses in the absence of their fathers, husbands, and brothers. "The exercise of women's talents in this line," Mott later wrote, "tended to develop their intellectual powers and strengthen them mentally and physically."

In 1804 the Coffin family left Nantucket for Boston, where she attended a series of public and private schools. At the age of 14, she and a sister left home to attend a coeducational Quaker boarding school near Poughkeepsie, New York. The following year, Lucretia Coffin was asked to become an assistant teacher, and at 16 she joined the staff full-time. It was there that she became friends with another teacher, James Mott, whom she married on April 10, 1811.

Mott remembered the early years of her marriage as a time of considerable difficulty. The WAR OF 1812, her father's death, and general economic uncertainty in the United States presented the couple with a number of financial challenges. To survive, the Motts taught, ran a school for a period of time, and operated a dry-goods business. They welcomed their first child into the world in 1812 and would go on to have five more before 1828. While deeply involved in the raising of her children, Mott confessed later in life that she always read books rather than apply herself to the "unnecessary stitching and ornamental work" that occupied many other women of her class.

At the age of 25, Mott began to take on a more active role within the Society of Friends, becoming a minister in 1821. Following a split in the society in 1827, the Motts became Hicksite Quakers. They believed in a liberal interpretation of the Bible and the power of each individual to understand God on their own terms. Throughout these years, Mott worked diligently on a variety of social issues. She was a devout believer in the TEMPERANCE MOVEMENT, campaigned on a variety of working-class concerns, and became an increasingly vocal participant in the ABOLITION MOVEMENT.

In 1833 Mott organized the Female Anti-Slavery Society of Philadelphia. Early members of the society included ANGELINA GRIMKÉ AND SARAH GRIMKÉ, sisters who would themselves go on to prominent careers as public abolitionists. In 1837, Mott helped to organize the Anti-Slavery Convention of American Women. In 1838, two days after the annual convention had been held at Pennsylvania Hall, Philadelphia, the meeting rooms were burned by opponents of the abolition movement. The protestors tried to attack the Motts' home later the same night.

In 1840 Mott traveled to London with her husband to attend the World Anti-Slavery Convention. Despite attending as an elected delegate of the AMERICAN ANTI-SLAVERY SOCIETY, she was refused entry to the convention because she was a woman. Five other female delegates were also turned away. Mott noted in her diary that she and the other women were treated politely by the organizers of the convention. This did not, however, lessen her offense at having been turned away. Many prominent male delegates to the convention argued that having women in attendance would trivialize their cause and open them up to ridicule. Mott and her allies countered that the same arguments were used in the United States by those who believed black men and women should not attend public meetings.

This was not the first time that Mott had been confronted by prejudice toward her sex. Female teachers at the Quaker boarding school where she had finished her education earned only half the salary of their male colleagues. Later in life, she had established the Female-Anti Slavery Society of Philadelphia because women were initially prohibited from joining William Lloyd Garrison's American Anti-Slavery Society. Mott had also been heckled and threatened for speaking in public and for daring to address mixed crowds, activities considered by many Americans to be improper.

These past experiences were compounded by the situation at the London convention. There Mott met Elizabeth Cady Stanton, the wife of another American delegate, who expressed her sympathies and outrage at the turn of events. In conversation, the two women decided that legal and cultural inequalities suffered by women in the United States must end. They began to plan a convention at which women could meet one another, become educated, and adopt a course of activism to win the rights they had long been denied.

In 1848 the first women's rights convention was held at SENECA FALLS, New York. It was the product of Mott and Stanton's 1840 conversations, their ensuing friendship, and the assistance of many other reform-minded women. The convention was the beginning of a long-term women's rights movement in the United States. It was also the beginning of a new chapter in Mott's life. For the remainder of her years, she worked tirelessly for WOMEN'S STATUS AND RIGHTS. In 1850, she published *Discourses on Women,* a pamphlet that argued there was nothing natural about woman's subordination to man. Instead, argued Mott, the inequities women experienced were created by laws, customs, and a lack of education. All three things, she asserted, needed to be changed.

Throughout the 1850s, Mott lectured and attended women's rights conventions across the United States. Still fiercely abolitionist, she and her husband also opened their home to enslaved men and women escaping the institution of slavery on the Underground Railroad. She remained a devout pacifist and was severely discomforted by the Civil War. Her religious beliefs condemned violence, but she hoped, like many others, that the conflict would bring SLAVERY to a final end. Mott continued to be active in Quaker circles, and she preached regularly for the rest of her life. She died on November 11, 1880.

Further reading: Dana Greene, ed., *Lucretia Mott: Her Complete Speeches and Sermons* (New York: E. Mellon Press, 1980); Nancy Isenberg, *Sex and Citizenship in Antebellum America* (Chapel Hill: University of North Carolina Press, 1998).

—Catherine J. Denial

mountain men

Following the Lewis and Clark expedition (1804–06), fur trappers began moving into the mountains of the West, where they pursued a free and unstructured life. Over time, they became known as mountain men.

The FUR TRADE was among the earliest profitable enterprises for early Europeans in the New World. They traded with Indian peoples who brought them furs; they then took the goods to England and Europe, where there was a ready market. With the development of great European empires, the fur trade took on national as well as economic meaning, and each nation centralized its operations. Eventually the fur trade became dominated by national monopolies. The British government pursued its interests through the Hudson's Bay Company and the upstart North West Company (of Montreal origin); the two companies merged in 1821. The American entrepreneur JOHN JACOB ASTOR and his AMERICAN FUR COMPANY rounded out the field with a few independent traders, such as Manuel Lisa and the CHOUTEAU FAMILY, operating out of St. Louis. Almost all trappers and traders were affiliated with one of these organizations. The fur-trade enterprise involved long journeys over distant uncharted landscapes and interactions with Indian peoples, some of them hostile: while there were great profits, there were also great risks. Therefore the support of a large organization that could provide both safety in numbers and credit was deemed necessary.

After the WAR OF 1812 (1812–15), American fur traders begin to provide stiff competition for the previously dominant British. Mountain men were an important part of the process. In February 1822, WILLIAM HENRY ASHLEY advertised in the *St. Louis Gazette* for "Enterprising Young Men . . . to ascend the Missouri to its source, there to be employed for one, two, or three years." Ashley's first expedition brought together the fur trade's most celebrated figures, those men who would become the most famous of the mountain men. They included JEDEDIAH STRONG SMITH, JAMES BRIDGER, Thomas Fitzpatrick, JIM BECKWOURTH, and Milton and WILLIAM SUBLETTE. These men were independent trappers and traders who functioned within a system established by Ashley known as the RENDEZVOUS. Trappers would assemble annually in the summer at an agreed-upon location, while Ashley came from St. Louis with supplies. In a four-week-long event, the trappers would trade their annual harvest of furs to Ashley for guns, powder, knives, metal tools, and whiskey. An enterprising mountain man might have 400 beaver pelts and perhaps more. The trade would produce a balance sheet that favored both sides: Ashley received the furs, the trapper the necessary supplies to remain in the field for another year.

The rendezvous was more than a market; it was also a social occasion of great importance. Trappers isolated by

American mountain man with his pony laden with luggage *(Hulton/Archive)*

solitary lives in the mountain landscape of the West gathered to meet one another in what amounted to a celebration marked by eating and drinking to excess, contests of skill, gambling, and occasional fights.

Mountain men adopted an identity and mastered the wilderness skills necessary to the life they pursued. In appearance and dress, they were much like the NATIVE AMERICANS in the regions where they lived and trapped. A typical mountain man wore a long hunting shirt, leggings, moccasins, and long shoulder-length hair. Many married Indian women, sometimes to keep peace with their Native American neighbors; some had more than one wife. Observers commented that they often adopted the habits and gait of the Indians with whom they shared the landscape. The mountain man's life was sometimes viewed as romantic, but it was also highly dangerous. Trappers were killed by Indians, mauled by grizzly bears, and frozen to death in the savage winters of the Rocky Mountains.

The long list of mountain men's deaths and injuries emphasized the mortality of the fur trade itself. Independent trappers and contract trappers from the Hudson's Bay Company and the American Fur Company were exceptionally skillful at their trade. Whether individually or in groups called brigades, they trapped the beaver in the most distant reaches of the mountains. As a result the annual harvest of beaver went into a dramatic decline, and it was eventually replaced by trade in buffalo hides. The year 1840 marked the last official rendezvous. Mountain men who still survived settled down to run outfitting stations on the OREGON TRAIL and CALIFORNIA TRAIL, or they became professional guides and explorers.

The exploits of the mountain men helped to open up the West as they found new paths to the Pacific Coast and charted previously unexplored regions. But they represented only a fleeting part of the West's history as their economic enterprise and lifestyle became doomed to extinction.

Further reading: William H. Goetzmann, *Exploration and Empire: The Explorer and the Scientist in the Winning of the West* (New York: Knopf, 1966); James H. Maguire, Peter Wild, and Donald A. Barclay, eds., *A Rendezvous Reader: Tall, Tangled, and True Tales of the Mountain Men, 1805–1850* (Salt Lake City: University of Utah Press, 1997); Robert M. Utley, *A Life Wild and Perilous: Mountain Men and the Paths to the Pacific* (New York: Henry Holt and Co., 1997); David J. Wishart, *The Fur Trade of the American West, 1807–1840* (Lincoln: University of Nebraska Press, 1979).

Murrieta, Joaquín (ca. 1830–1853 or 1878)

A legendary figure from the California goldfields, Joaquín Murrieta (or Murieta) was a Mexican bandit and revolutionary who fought against the U.S. incursion into CALIFORNIA. Murrieta's life was intertwined with myth and fact. The first record of his presence was a baptismal certificate dated 1830 in Sonora, Mexico, identifying him as the son of a laborer in a silver-mining camp. His mother traced her heritage to Cadiz, Spain. The young Murrieta grew up in a world charged with violence. The province of Sonora was in constant turmoil, rebelling against the new, independent Republic of Mexico. The Mayo and Yaqui Indians, laborers in the silver mines, were in revolt against the mine owners.

When he was 13, in about 1843, young Murrieta enrolled in a Jesuit school in Alamos but did not stay long. Leaving the school, he married the daughter of a local laborer and went to work. In 1848, responding to news of the discovery of gold, the young couple joined the CALIFORNIA GOLD RUSH, as thousands of Sonorans migrated north. Indeed, during the early months of the rush, Mexican miners dominated the goldfields of the Sierra Nevada, where their presence was characterized by large numbers and mining skills that they shared with arriving neophyte miners from the United States and, soon, around the world. Murrieta found work on a ranch near Stockton, where he worked with the horses used for transportation of supplies to the mines. In 1850, officials in Stockton arrested him on robbery charges; he was jailed and subsequently released as innocent. Murrieta then moved with his wife to Sonora, the center of the Mexican population in the goldfields. In a gold camp named Saw Mill Flat, he built a cabin and staked a claim.

Murrieta and his wife now fell victim to the growing hostility of American miners toward foreign miners, especially those who did not speak English. The Mexican miners were among the first targets, for they were alien in culture, present in large numbers in the southern mines, and had possession of some of the richest claims. At a time of increased competition in the mines, the Mexicans became the first and most obvious victims of discrimination. The institutional lever was the Foreign Miners Tax of 1850, sometimes called the "Greaser Act" because Mexicans were the acknowledged targets. Passed by the legislature and signed by the governor in 1850, the act soon drove Mexican miners out of the goldfields. However, unlike other foreign nationals—the Chileans, Peruvians, and French, for example—Mexicans always had the option of returning south to home, and most of them did.

At about this time, according to the popular story of Murrieta's life, a band of American miners came to Murrieta's claim, raped his wife, and drove him away. Murrieta now took refuge in the hills and turned to banditry, which was both an economic advantage and an act of revenge for the outrages committed against him and his family. Some came to describe him then and later as a revolutionary, leading an armed insurrection against officials and citizens of the State of California. Whatever the truth, his first attempts at banditry were awkward. But other dispossessed Mexican miners flocked to his standard, along with occasional professional thieves. Within a year, Murrieta commanded a large band, perhaps even several bands, which raided throughout the San Joaquin Valley. In the style of bandits with a political agenda, Murrieta's gang found refuge with the old Californio families in the valley, the group that had been victimized by the arrival of the waves of American miners and lawyers in response to the discovery of gold.

As Murrieta's legend grew, so did demands for his capture and trial. The legislature offered a large reward for him, dead or alive. In July 1853, the California Rangers, a vigilante organization, claimed to have captured, tried, and beheaded Murrieta. His raids ceased about that time, but over the years, his presence reemerged in the California sierra. According to legend, the so-called "Ghost of the Sonora" had escaped his pursuers, and he was ranching in the mountains of Sonora or living in a village. As late as the 1870s, reports of him continued to appear. A final note recorded that he died in 1878 and was buried in an old Jesuit cemetery high in the Sierra Madre.

The political dimension of Murrieta's banditry grew with time, moving him along a path from bandit to rebel to revolutionary. This transition received its fullest statement by a cousin of Murrieta in 1932: "To the Mexicans, he was a great liberator, come out of Mexico to take California back from the hands of the gringos. They did not call his 'looting' and 'killing' banditry. They called it 'war.'" Thus, Murrieta became a rallying cry for a revolution, a war of liberation.

Further reading: Susan Lee Johnson, *Gold Camp: The Social World of the California Gold Rush* (New York: W. W. Norton, 2000); John Rollin Ridge, *The Life and Adventures of Joaquin Murieta 1854* (Norman: University of Oklahoma Press, 1955).

music

Americans in the first half of the 19th century had few musical resources but a great urge to incorporate music into their daily lives. They wanted to hear good tunes and be entertained. This desire, combined with the rapidly increasing population of the United States, created a mass market for music. Consequently, music creators profited from a ready audience, and America began to develop a national musical culture.

The United States in 1813 was a nation of few musical instruments and little formal musical training. A few professional musicians had by then emigrated from Europe, but music-making remained largely an amateur proposition. Amateurs fervently pursued their interest, however, even—or especially—when times did not favor the pursuit. For example, pioneers traveling west of the Mississippi River reported not only the dangers and privations of the journey but also the determined music-making of the travelers. Likewise, miners in the CALIFORNIA GOLD RUSH of 1848–49 eagerly sought sheet music and whatever musical instruments were available—accordions, violins, guitars, flutes, horns—to entertain themselves in camp after each long, tiring day of panning for gold. Throughout the United States, cheap instruments such as Jew's harps could be had and frequently were. Those too remote to buy instruments sometimes fashioned their own, occasionally inventing new kinds of instruments if, due to isolation, they did not know what existing instruments elsewhere looked and sounded like. Music-making was equally ubiquitous in more favorable environments: Saloons everywhere tried to provide music; and singing on trains was so common as to be unavoidable.

The most common form of music to be found in the United States as of 1813 was vocal music. Since the arrival of the first New England settlers, vocal music had been an important form of worship. Hence, sacred songbooks were in demand throughout the United States in the early 19th century. Lowell Mason knew this when he prepared the *Boston Handel and Haydn Society Collection of Church Music,* published in 1821. Yet the degree of demand astounded even him; the collection was an extraordinary success, going through 22 editions and making Mason a very rich man. Competition grew for the sacred music market; in 1836, for example, came *The Billings and Holden Collection of Ancient Psalmody,* which claimed to republish pioneer song "as originally written," in contrast to Mason's versions, which he had "improved" to elevate the public taste. Meanwhile, music had acquired all the trappings of "big business": First, composers could now get rich from sales of their work to the public, a novel development. Second, American mass production and distribution techniques had become sophisticated enough to permit broad dissemination. Finally, sensational advertising and promotion of composers' work propelled sales.

By the 1820s, local manufacture of musical instruments commenced in response to public demand for the means to make music. As the availability of popular sheet music and musical instruments expanded, so did the variety of music performance available in the United States. Half a century before, when professional musicians were especially scarce, the semiprivate subscription concerts of "gentlemen" amateurs had been among the few skilled performances available. By contrast, in the early to mid-19th century, assorted performers toured communities of all sizes. The minister Robert Kemp, for example, tapped into the vogue for "authentically American" music in the 1830s with a series of "Old Folks Concerts," in which singers dressed in 18th-century clothing and sang old-fashioned hymns and ballads; these concerts flourished well in to the 1860s and reached millions, almost throughout America. Family groups such as the famous Hutchinson Family Singers were acclaimed for their republican approach to music: Dressed in ordinary clothes, the three brothers and one sister sang hymns and popular ballads both in concert halls and in common taverns all through the 1840s. The family singers genre became so well-known and successful that it was parodied mercilessly by the end of the decade.

The most successful of all mid-19th-century American entertainments, however, was the minstrel show. This form, which entered northern theaters in about 1840, is believed to be an imitation of the plantation shows mounted by slaves on days when they were not permitted to work. Consisting of singing and dancing by both individuals and groups, plantation shows drew large crowds in the South. The imitation—and later, burlesque—that was the minstrel show was a variety show composed of dancing, singing, and skits. Performers entered ceremonially and seated themselves in a semicircle, with musicians spaced for antiphonal effect. All wore blackface (even black performers) except for the master of ceremonies or "interlocutor," who wore whiteface. The skits borrowed some stock characters—the "Negro type," for example, was a variation of the standard Irish buffoon—and developed some of its own, such as Jim Crow and Zip Coon. Performers sang comic songs and sentimental ballads, known as "Ethiopian songs," in a style imitating African-American idiom. Audiences moved spontaneously to the rhythmic music. By the mid 1840s, the minstrel show was the most popular entertainment in the United States, drawing racially and economically diverse crowds. As time went on, minstrelsy presented increasingly derisive depictions of African Americans before being surpassed in popularity by vaudeville in the 1870s.

Despite Americans' professed admiration for unpretentious performers, snob appeal was effective in drawing crowds, and musical performers and their managers frequently claimed high-class connections. The indefatigable showman P. T. Barnum was a master of such promotional finesse, convincing the public, for example, that the "Swedish nightingale" Jenny Lind was not only as a singer of extraordinary ability but also the personification of womanly virtue. Crowds flocked to see Lind throughout her 1850–52 tour. They were not disappointed. Lind excelled in the art of "descriptive" singing, or dramatically acting out the story of a song while singing it. Such histrionic singing, performance of which often moved audiences to tears of pity, shrieks of terror, or gales of delighted laughter, was in great demand. An earlier master of "descriptive" performance was the English singer Henry Russell, who toured the United States in 1833–41. Russell attributed his inspiration to sing in this style to the politician and orator HENRY CLAY. "Why, if Henry Clay could create such an impression by his distinct enunciation of every word," Russell reported having asked himself, "should it not be possible for me to make music the vehicle of grand thoughts and noble sentiments, to speak to the world through the power of poetry and song!"

Such dramatic performances were not limited to urban centers, and amateur performers likewise attempted to evoke the moods of the songs they sang at home with expression, diction, gesture, and often appropriate costuming. Besides modes of performance, private and public America shared the same tunes everywhere: Although class distinctions were still carefully noted in "republican" America, particularly in the antebellum South, the same melodies were as popular in the parlor as on the minstrel stage.

Popular music was thus a shared point of reference for Americans of diverse backgrounds in the first half of the

19th century. While somewhat anachronistic, better reflecting the tastes of Americans' 18th-century European forebears than the new romantic style then emerging in Europe, American popular music of 1813–55 served as a touchstone of the developing national culture of the United States.

Further reading: Edith Borroff, *Melting Music Round: A History of Music in the United States* (New York: Ardsley House, 1995); Gilbert Chase, *America's Music from the Pilgrims to the Present,* rev. 3d ed. (Urbana and Chicago: University of Illinois Press, 1987); Nicholas E. Tawa, *High-Minded and Low-Down: Music in the Lives of Americans 1800–1861* (Boston: Northeastern University Press, 2000).

—Dorothy Cummings

N

National Road

The National Road refers to a highway constructed with the authorization of the U.S. government in the early 19th century that eventually connected the eastern seaboard with the Ohio River Valley and points west. Also known as the Cumberland Road and the National Pike, it began as a proposal in Secretary of the Treasury Albert Gallatin's plan for the federal government to support INTERNAL IMPROVEMENTS in 1808. Gallatin's plan was comprehensive but controversial, as no clear consensus existed in the government for the federal government to finance public roads. Consequently, state governments paid for the road's construction. Much of the financing came from the state of Ohio, whose 1803 state charter included a stipulation that the federal government and the state would share in the cost of road construction. Five percent of all proceeds from public land sales in Ohio were set aside from the construction of roads. Of this amount, Congress spent two-fifths, while three-fifths was spent by the Ohio legislature.

Construction began in 1811 in Cumberland, Maryland, along an old military road used in the French and Indian War (1754–63). The road connected to the privately built Baltimore Pike, providing a link to coastal roads. By 1818, the National Road cut through western Pennsylvania to Wheeling, Virginia. By 1833, it had reached Vandalia, Illinois. The road spurred western expansion and commerce, improving the ability of pioneers to cut through the Appalachian Mountains to the fertile river valleys and plains to the west. Towns such as Brownsville, Pennsylvania, and Wheeling, Virginia (now West Virginia), boomed with new taverns, blacksmiths, stables, and other businesses to aid travelers.

By 1820 the road had become an important link between the steamboat trade of the Ohio River Valley and the East Coast. It also had significant political implications because of concerns that the federal government did not have constitutional authority to finance its construction. Previously, Thomas Jefferson's initial response to Gallatin's original proposal had been to suggest that it needed a constitutional amendment. Momentum for all internal improvements increased between 1808 and 1825 as a consequence of the Embargo of 1807 and WAR OF 1812 (1812–15). Federal support for internal improvements (including road building) became a pillar of the AMERICAN SYSTEM for economic development pushed from 1816 to 1825 by national political leaders such as HENRY CLAY and JOHN C. CALHOUN. Yet James Madison was a steadfast opponent of federally funded roads and canals on constitutional grounds, and JAMES MONROE also had reservations about the constitutionality of such projects. The issue became prominent in 1817, when Madison vetoed the BONUS BILL, which would have provided federal funds for an array of new roads and canals around the country. In 1822, Monroe expressed his own principles when he vetoed a bill to provide national funding for road repairs. However, in his veto message Monroe also indicated that he would accept federal support for roads as long as the plans met with approval from the states that the roads cut across. Thus, in 1824 he signed the General Survey Act authorizing extensive federal plans for road and canal projects across the nation. Under the General Survey Act, Congress approved plans to extend the National Road across Illinois and the Mississippi River to central Missouri.

The establishment of the National Road saw thousands of travelers heading west over the Allegheny Mountains to settle the rich lands of the Ohio River Valley. Small towns along the road's path began to grow and prosper with the increase in population. Towns such as Cumberland, Maryland; Uniontown, Pennsylvania; Brownsville, Pennsylvania; Washington, Pennsylvania; and Wheeling, West Virginia evolved into commercial centers of business and industry. Uniontown was the headquarters for three major stagecoach lines carrying passengers over the National Road. Brownsville, on the Monongahela River, was a center for steamboat building and river-freight hauling. Many small towns and villages along the road contained taverns,

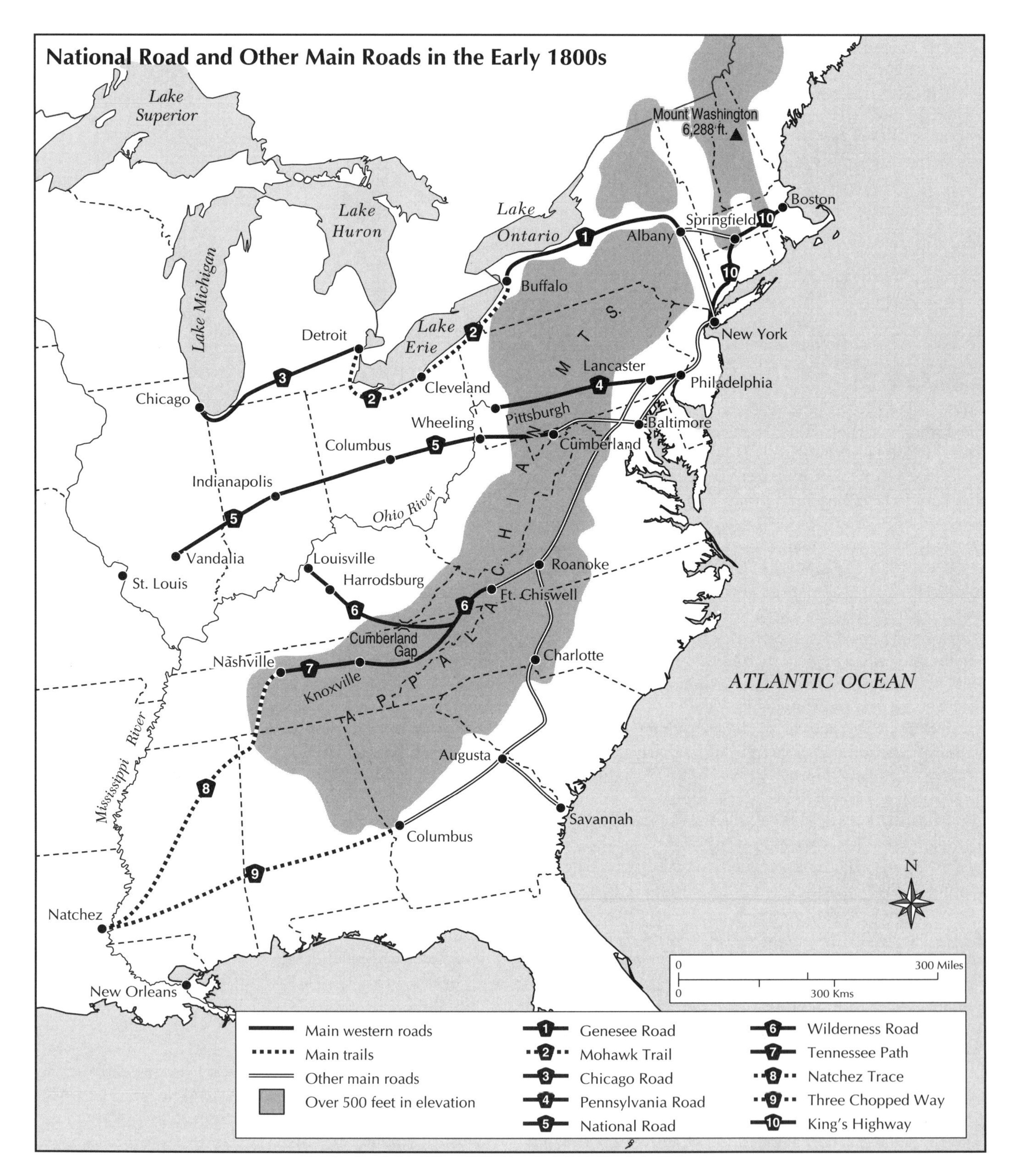

blacksmith shops, and livery stables. During the heyday of the National Road, traffic was heavy throughout the day and into the early evening. Almost every kind of vehicle could be seen on the road. The two most common vehicles were the stagecoach and the Conestoga wagon. Stagecoach travel was designed with speed in mind; stages would average 60–70 miles in one day.

By the early 1850s, technology was changing the way people traveled. The steam locomotive was being perfected, and soon railroads began to cross the Allegheny Mountains. The people of southwestern Pennsylvania fought strongly to keep the railroad out of the area, knowing the impact it would have on the National Road. In 1852, the Pennsylvania Railroad was completed to Pittsburgh and shortly after, the BALTIMORE & OHIO RAILROAD reached Wheeling. This spelled doom for the National Road. As the traffic quickly declined, many taverns went out of business. The National Road became part of U.S. 40 highway in 1926.

Further reading: Charles Sellers, *The Market Revolution: Jacksonian America, 1815–1846* (New York: Oxford University Press, 1991); George Rogers Taylor, *The Transportation Revolution, 1815–1860* (Armonk, N.Y.: M. E. Sharpe, 1989).

—James R. Karmel

Native Americans

At the opening of the 19th century, Native American cultures had already been under assault by disease and displacement for 200 years. The events of the next two generations would accelerate the conflicts between Native and Euro-Americans.

When Meriwether Lewis and William Clark went west in 1804, their mission was to explore the new Louisiana Purchase, find a water route to the Pacific, and make contact with the great nations of the West. At that time, the U.S. government had scant influence over the nations inhabiting its new territory west of the Mississippi River. To the east of the great river, however, the balance between Native Americans and white Americans would be substantially altered by the WAR OF 1812. Up to the WAR OF 1812, the United States's Indian policy had reflected recognition of Indian peoples as strong and independent and treated them as equals in negotiations; after 1815, this policy increasingly treated Indian peoples as dependent on American guidance and authority. This change culminated in their removal from lands east of the Mississippi River. This change received institutional approval in the passage of the INDIAN REMOVAL ACT of 1830, a law identified with the views of ANDREW JACKSON. In the 15 years after the end of the War of 1812, the U.S. population had grown, and its settlers had continued to press to the west with undiminished enthusiasm. The demand for land was intense, and the Native Americans were seen as an obstacle to the white settlers' inevitable progress. Already, the Indians up to the edge of the Appalachians had been effectively expelled from their lands by disease, assimilation, and force. Over the next 30 years, the major nations east of the Mississippi would be removed from their homelands or destroyed altogether, while those of the Plains and Far West found their ways of life increasingly under assault. The Native peoples reacted in varied ways to these attacks on their lands and their cultures.

Active Resistance

The 19th century opened with the leadership of Tecumseh (ca. 1768–1813), the most brilliant Native American leader since Pontiac and a remarkable force for Indian unity amidst the many varied tribal groups at the beginning of the 1800s. Tecumseh, a Shawnee, was to become the main symbol of opposition to white American expansion in this period, determined to keep the Ohio Valley, the traditional Shawnee homeland, in his people's hands. To that end, he was willing to create alliances with other Indian leaders and even with the British.

American settlers had surged into the territory northwest of the Ohio (or the Northwest Territory, as the Ohio-Great Lakes region was called at the time), after the Revolutionary War. The United States had signed various treaties guaranteeing specific tracts to Indian peoples, but in the face of illegal trespassing on Indian lands, the federal government did little or nothing to stop the encroachment. In response, Tecumseh engineered an alliance of the Shawnee, Delaware, Ottawa, Ojibwa, Kickapoo, and Wyandot in 1805. His goal was to create a permanent Indian state in which the members of the confederacy could govern themselves, free of U.S. influence.

WILLIAM HENRY HARRISON, the governor of Indiana Territory became the federal government's representative in making treaties of land cession with representatives of Indian peoples (or factions of tribal groups). He aggressively pursued his mission over a decade, and in his determination to force land cessions by Native Americans, he often made illegal or quasilegal treaties with tribal members not authorized to make agreements for their nations. In this way, between 1803 and 1809 he made treaties that ceded 33 million acres of land to the United States. Despite Tecumseh's repudiation of these treaties and the Shawnee leader's growing outrage at the cession of land and the tactics used to achieve it, Harrison continued to pursue his policies of dividing nations and making treaties of cession with one or more factions. Tecumseh and Harrison finally reached the point where open conflict replaced talk. Encouraged by the British, Tecumseh called for attacks on isolated illegal settlements, even as he pursed his larger vision of a great Indian confederation. When the Shawnee chief went south in 1811 to enlist the support of the numerous and powerful nations there, Harrison organized a force to march on Prophetstown, the main Shawnee village on the Tippecanoe River. The Indian defense was led by Tecumseh's brother Tenskwatawa, known as the Shawnee Prophet. After an inconclusive battle, the Indian force retired from the field, and Harrison and his troops entered the village, burned it to the ground, and declared victory. This fragile military victory, immortalized in the slogan "Tippecanoe and Tyler too," would help Harrison win the presidency in 1840.

In response to the defeat, Tecumseh allied himself with the British. During the War of 1812, he was made a brigadier general and led both whites and Indians into battle. His group helped to capture Fort Detroit in 1813, forcing the surrender of the American force there. But despite the victory, over the next year, the British commander General Henry Procter pulled his forces back into Canada. Harrison pursued with 3,000 men. On October 5, 1813, Tecumseh's warriors, badly outnumbered, stood against Harrison's forces at the BATTLE OF THE THAMES in Ontario, where they were defeated and Tecumseh was killed. With him died much of the Indian resistance in the Northwest Territories. Over the next decades, the Ohio and Great Lakes nations would be confined to small reservations or removed altogether to Indian Territory (present-day Oklahoma).

Among the Creek in Georgia and Florida, Tecumseh's message of resistance had gained a substantial, but not unanimous, following. The Upper Creek, called the Red Sticks for their battle insignia, wanted to forcefully end the creeping American settlement in their lands. The Lower Creek, or White Sticks, wanted peace, even if it meant cultural assimilation. In 1813, the Red Sticks attacked Fort Mims in southern Alabama, killing 350 Americans. The United States' response was massive: A force of 5,000 men under Andrew Jackson, joined by White Stick allies, attacked the Red Sticks at the BATTLE OF HORSESHOE BEND. At least 1,000 Red Sticks were killed. But as punishment, the entire Creek nation—Upper and Lower alike—was forced to cede 20 million acres of land to the United States. In 1832, in the wake of additional treaties of questionable legitimacy, as well as the Indian Removal Act of 1830, the Creek lost all their southeastern lands and were removed to an Indian Territory reservation.

Tecumseh's doctrine of resistance to land cession and illegal white settlement was taken up by Black Hawk, the Sac leader who led the last major Indian resistance effort in the Northwest Territories. But the BLACK HAWK WAR of 1832 was a complete failure, leading to the massacre of Black Hawk's band at the Bad Axe River and the loss of much of the Sac and Fox's assigned reservation lands in the present State of Iowa.

Only the Seminole in northern FLORIDA had any success in resisting the tide of American settlement, and their success was limited. Starting in 1817, the Seminole fought three separate wars against the United States. The first SEMINOLE WAR (1817–18) began with Andrew Jackson's invasion of Florida, which then still belonged to Spain (excepting Western Florida, which had been seized during the War of 1812). The incursion—ostensibly carried out to capture runaway slaves—was part of a scheme to force Spain to cede the remainder of Florida to the United States. This was finally accomplished in 1819, by means of the ADAMS-ONÍS TREATY. With the arrival of the Americans, Seminole resistance intensified. Even though they were forced to leave their farming lands on the Florida-Georgia border, they did not surrender; they merely retreated to the swamps of central Florida. From this base, they conducted the guerrilla operations known as the Second (1835–42) and Third (1855–58) Seminole Wars. The Seminole Wars reflected the alliance between the Seminole peoples and the many escaped African-American slaves, who fled bondage in the Lower South and made their way to the Seminole Nation, where they found acceptance and eventually a common cause against the American army. In some respects, the Second and Third Seminole Wars were as much black as Indian wars. Despite the death of their charismatic leader Osceola (ca. 1803–38) and the removal of most of the nation, a core of Seminole remained in Florida. They never formally surrendered or signed a treaty, and the Seminole Wars are regarded as a costly military failure for the United States.

Alliance and Assimilation

Other nations attempted more subtle resistance strategies. Some, like the Choctaw, believed that native traditions of reciprocity would hold true in their dealings with the Americans. This led them to make alliances with the United States, in the understanding that the relationship would protect their culture and lands from incursion. The Choctaw fought on the American side in the War of 1812, and their help was decisive in Jackson's 1815 victory in the BATTLE OF NEW ORLEANS. Many Choctaw intermarried with whites and adopted Anglo farming methods, housing styles, and modes of dress. But when Jackson, newly elected president, signed the Indian Removal Act into law in 1830, the Choctaw were the first nation to be forced into Indian Territory. Their migration in 1830, in which a third of the nation died, was an ominous sign for the other eastern Native Americans.

The Cherokee hoped to maintain themselves as a nation by succeeding in economic and cultural terms that white America could understand. Many Cherokee willingly adopted American economic practices, opening profitable mills and farming in family groups rather than communally. A large number converted to Christianity. Members of the elite established plantations modeled on those of their neighbors in Georgia and North Carolina, even owning

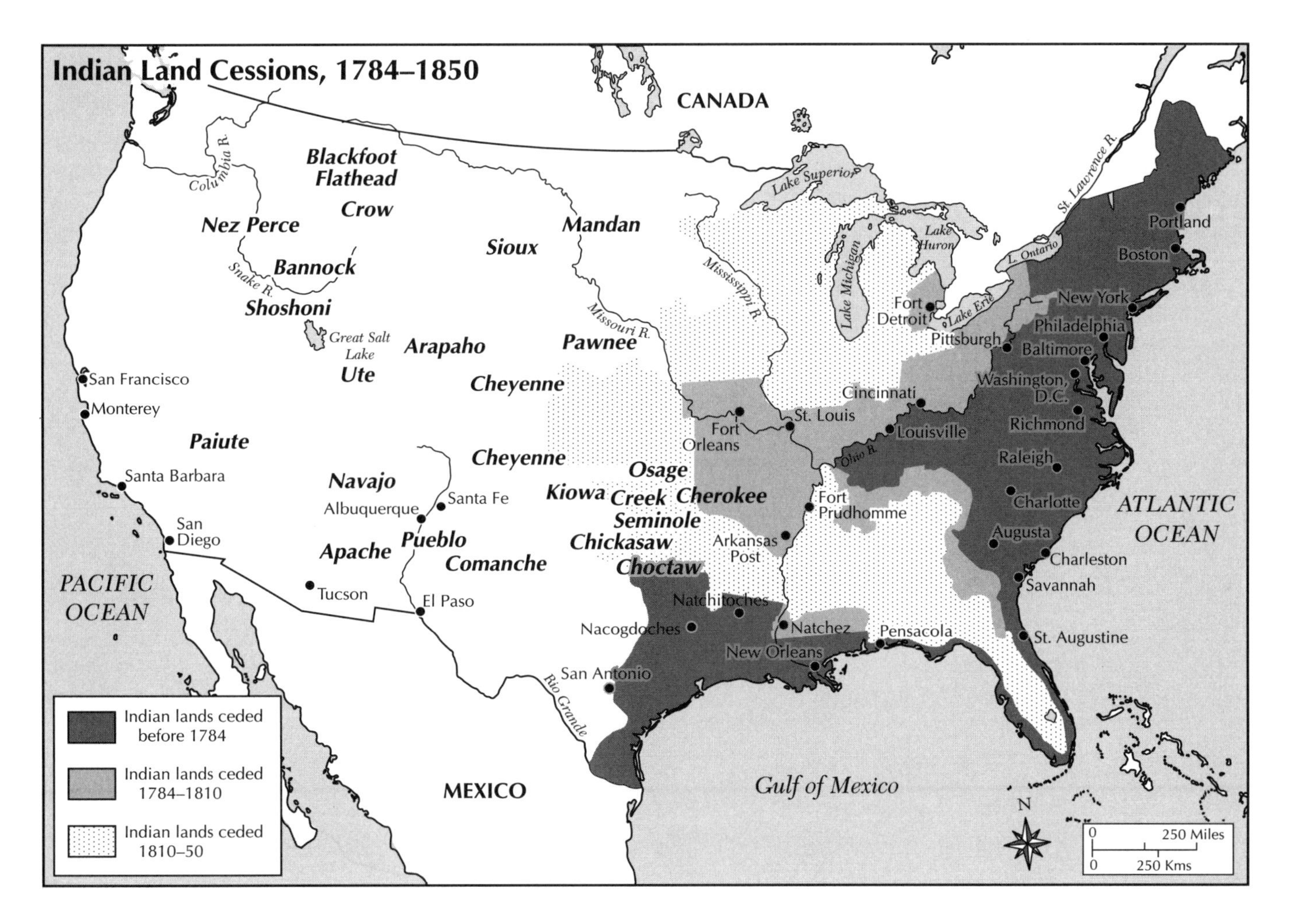

black slaves. The Cherokee could boast of some extraordinarily gifted people, most notably Sequoyah (1776–1843), who invented a Cherokee writing system in 1821; it was so elegantly usable that his people rapidly embraced the written word. By 1828, the Cherokee had their own Bible in translation and their own weekly newspaper.

But while Cherokee life and culture flourished, their homeland was under serious threat. The process began in 1817, when several Cherokee leaders signed a treaty that traded a large area of the nation's traditional land for a tract in Indian Territory. A few thousand Cherokee voluntarily moved to Indian Territory at this time, the first of the eastern peoples to arrive there. Meanwhile, the Cherokee back in Georgia became, in a sense, victims of their own success: the more their farms and businesses thrived, the more permanent they seemed and the more the Georgians coveted their land. In 1828, Georgia asserted authority over the Cherokee lands, nullifying federal authority. When gold was discovered in Cherokee country in 1829, the pressure intensified. The Cherokee sued to overturn the Georgia laws, attempting to use the American legal system to maintain their sovereignty. The U.S. Supreme Court eventually supported their legal position in *Worcester v. Georgia* (1832). But President Jackson refused to enforce the Court's ruling against Georgia. The state held a lottery and parceled the Cherokee lands out from under the nation. In 1838–39, they were forcibly removed in a long and badly managed emigration that became known as the TRAIL OF TEARS. By the time the surviving remnants of the nation had reached Indian Territory, perhaps as many as a quarter of those who started the journey had perished.

The Far West

For most of the first half of the 19th century, few Americans imagined that the native peoples west of the Mississippi would ever be of much concern to them. The removal policies of the 1830s were largely successful by the end of the decade, and the survivors had been placed in a landscape described in many maps as "The Great American Desert," removing them out of the way of American settlement and into a vast and mostly uninhabited and sterile land. But the inexorable westward movement of white

America would not be halted at the Mississippi. By the mid-1840s, wagon trains on the OREGON TRAIL were bringing hundreds, and then thousands, of settlers to the Oregon Territory. The overland migrations of the Mormons to Utah increased traffic across the plains, and with the discovery of gold in CALIFORNIA in 1848, the rising trickle of immigration across the plains and the mountains became a flood.

The Indians of the mountains and coast were experienced traders, with a long history of economic contact with trappers and explorers of many nationalities. Some nations saw the overland migrants and the settlers primarily as a new market. The 1837 smallpox epidemic that destroyed the Mandan nation in North Dakota and the continuing assaults on Indian peoples in California after the arrival of the FORTY-NINERS suggested the hazards associated with any kind of contact with Anglo-Americans. It seemed that Native peoples west of the Mississippi River were no safer in their homelands than those in the East had been. The dangers were particularly acute for those Indian peoples who occupied lands that became the target of mining rushes. The goldfields in California became a killing ground as far as Indians were concerned, as they were systematically hunted down in the most remote reaches of the Sierra Nevada. And later, Indian peoples would come under systematic assault in mining strikes associated with Nevada (1858), Montana (1862), and Colorado (1858).

The federal government attempted to reshape its policies to accommodate immigration across the plains and increasing contact between groups of settlers and Indian peoples. At a large gathering at FORT LARAMIE in 1851, government representatives tried to persuade Plains Indian to accept boundaries to their lands, however vague. In exchange for these lines of maps, signatories solemnly guaranteed large tracts of the plains to the Sioux, Cheyenne, Arapaho, Crow, Arikara, Assiniboine, and Gros Ventre nations. In future years, the government would deal separately with each of these groups for cessions and concessions. Resistance had already begun among certain groups. As early as 1846, the Apache in Arizona began campaigns to keep their lands clear of white settlement. It was a series of military confrontations that would stretch over a half-century and conclude with Geronimo's surrender and exile.

Throughout the century, Americans saw it as their MANIFEST DESTINY to occupy their continent from coast to coast and to use the land in the ways they saw fit. Native Americans stood in the way of that vision, whether they were allies or enemies, Christian or "savage," accommodating or resistant. In the years from 1815 to 1860, the federal government as the representative of the American people used its growing power and authority to remove Indian peoples west of the Mississippi and then to lay the groundwork for expansion onto the plains and into the mountains.

Further reading: Bruce E. Johansen and Donald A. Grinde, Jr., *The Encyclopedia of Native American Biography* (New York: Henry Holt, 1997); Judith Nies, *Native American History* (New York: Ballantine, 1996); Francis Paul Prucha, *The Great Father: The United States Government and the American Indians,* 2 vols. (Lincoln: University of Nebraska Press, 1984); James Wilson, *The Earth Shall Weep* (New York: Atlantic Monthly Press, 1999).

—Mary Kay Linge

Native Americans in the War of 1812

The second war between the United States and Great Britain was the last conflict where the support or opposition of NATIVE AMERICANS played a significant role, though it broke the military power of nations east of the Mississippi River forever. The Indian conflict in the WAR OF 1812 (1812–15) helped to build the reputation of future American presidents such as ANDREW JACKSON, WILLIAM HENRY HARRISON, and ZACHARY TAYLOR.

The republic's expansion after the American Revolution (1775–83) put most Native Americans under pressure. Indian leaders tried a number of different strategies to deal with the ever-increasing demands for more land for white American settlers. Some of the Iroquois sold off their holdings and moved west or north into Canada. The Shawnee, under Tecumseh, wanted to put aside old tribal feuds and unite to stop the advancing Americans. In the South, native peoples tried several solutions. The Creek Confederacy fought among themselves, with those who wanted to accommodate the United States pitted against those who thought they could best protect their people by allying with the British.

Before the United States entered hostilities with Great Britain, an army commanded by William Henry Harrison dispersed many of the warriors based around Prophetstown at the Battle of Tippecanoe (November 7, 1811). Tecumseh and his brother Tenskwatawa, better known as the Shawnee Prophet, had spent the previous few years preaching a political and religious revival to the nations west of the Appalachians. Many native peoples flocked to the town in northwestern Indiana to practice their traditional lifestyles free from the corrupting influence of whiskey and manufactured trade goods.

Harrison used his position as the territorial governor of Indiana to persuade the federal government to allow him to strike at the town. A series of raids on Ohio and Indiana settlements launched from Prophetstown gave Harrison the evidence he needed to convince President James Madison to retaliate. The American government feared that the British in Canada were encouraging the Native Americans to fight, since everybody was sure war was coming. Harrison's victory at Tippecanoe neutralized the threatened alliance between Native Americans and the British. Many warriors lost faith in Tenskwatawa's message and returned to their villages.

When the United States declared war on Great Britain in June 1812, the British quickly seized Mackinac in the northern Michigan Territory. The Americans responded by invading Canada across the narrow straits at Detroit. The American army commanded by General WILLIAM HULL fumbled the opportunity and found itself facing a well-led British and Native American force. Hull and his subordinates were not up to the job and were chased back into Michigan, where the British captured them.

Throughout the winter, the British and their allies raided the southern shores of the Great Lakes. At Fort Dearborn, many American prisoners met their deaths at the hands of their captors. Lurid tales of massacres helped to stir widespread support among the backwoods communities throughout the Ohio Valley and Tennessee. Harrison received a general's commission and raised an army. By spring 1813, the Americans stood ready to push into Canada once more.

Harrison's command was temporarily besieged at Fort Meigs in that spring. The attack was repulsed, and many of the Native Americans who followed Tecumseh during the siege deserted him. In a series of battles around Detroit, Harrison defeated the British forces and pushed them back into Canada. He followed them into British territory and defeated 800 Native Americans and 450 British troops at the BATTLE OF THE THAMES (October 5, 1813). Tecumseh died in the fighting, and the dreams of his great confederacy died with him.

Only a small number of Native Americans fought on for the British in the North after the battle. Some Mohawk led by John Brant (son of Joseph Brant) fought around Fort Niagara. Most other nations stayed out of the conflict or threw their lot in with the Americans. The Iroquois left on American territory followed the advice of Seneca chief Cornplanter and fought for the United States. The nations that had followed Tecumseh left the Indiana Territory and went back home to await the end of the war.

In the South, the War of 1812 sharply divided some of the nations. Many stayed neutral while others supported the United States against Britain. The Spanish in FLORIDA helped the British supply Native Americans who wanted to fight the Americans.

Tecumseh had visited the southern nations in October 1811 (at the same time Harrison was marching on Tippecanoe). He did not succeed in rallying the Choctaw or the Cherokee into supporting the confederation of native peoples. However, he did convince many of the Northern Creek (Muskogee) to take up arms in defense of their homes. Tecumseh was reported to have given red sticks, or rods, to the Creek warriors who followed his advise to resist the Americans. The warriors were to throw away one stick each day until the last stick was gone; the last stick marked the day when they were to attack the white settlers in their part of the country. The practice gave rise to the name "Red Sticks" for those Creeks who took up the hatchet. Most of the southern Creek towns disagreed with Tecumseh and did not go to into battle along with the northerners; this faction was called the "White Sticks."

The northern Creek carried out a series of isolated raids on settlements in lower Tennessee in 1812. The raiders attacked individual homesteads, which often resulted in the deaths of entire families. The American inhabitants of Tennessee reacted with threats to retaliate. Creek leaders caught and executed many of the raiders to keep the white settlers from seeking revenge against the entire nation. Far from solving the problem, though, this enraged the families and friends of the Red Sticks, who threatened to kill the White Stick leaders who had ordered the executions. The Creek Nation soon found itself divided into two camps, those who favored peace with the Americans and those who wanted bloodshed. The situation soon deteriorated into civil war between the two factions. Before long the entire region between the Mississippi and the Appalachians burst into guerrilla warfare.

The Cherokee wanted to stay neutral at first. Although some of their warriors favored siding with the British, most wanted to steer clear of any fighting; memories of the devastating American invasions during the Revolutionary War ran deep. The Cherokee also had a long and bitter rivalry with their neighbors, the Creek, and few wanted to see them grow stronger. When a band of Northern Creek murdered a Cherokee woman, the debate ended and the Cherokee joined the Americans in the Creek War.

Settlers and traders all over the Mississippi Territory feared for their lives. They stockaded themselves into small forts for protection. On the Alabama River, some settlers huddled behind the walls of Fort Mims. On August 31, 1813, more than 1,000 warriors under Creek leaders attacked and took the fort; almost all of the surviving whites were put to death. News of the disaster traveled fast. When Andrew Jackson heard the reports on Fort Mims, he left his sickbed to organize a counterattack. The Choctaw also agreed to fight against the Creek.

In autumn 1813, Jackson attacked the Northern Creek at Tallussahatchie and inflicted heavy casualties on them. Another column of Georgia volunteers under General John Floyd successfully stormed a Creek stronghold at Eccanachaca. Both Jackson and Floyd harassed the Creek for several months. After some inconclusive fighting, Jackson surrounded the Red Stick stronghold at Tohopeka on March 28, 1814, with 2,000 men. General Jackson's force included 500 Cherokees. A thousand Creeks trapped in the fortified town refused to surrender; their religious leaders had assured them they would beat the Americans. Jackson and his men wiped out the entire village, sparing only the women and children in what came to be called the BATTLE OF HORSESHOE BEND.

After Tohopeka, some of the surviving Creek warriors slipped into Florida. The British arranged to help them with the permission of the Spanish government. General Jackson invaded Florida and defeated the British and Spanish at Pensacola. He threatened to make war on the Seminole in the interior of Florida if they dared to help the Creek. Meanwhile, the Americans defeated a British invasion of Mobile Bay aimed at aiding the Creek. The Creek's ability to resist was shattered. After the war, Jackson not only demanded territory from the warring Northern Creek, he also wanted land from his own allies the Southern Creek in order to prevent any more assistance from England or Spain.

The War of 1812 effectively ended the military power of all the native peoples east of the Mississippi except for the Seminole deep in the forests and swamps of Florida. It also set the stage for the removal of all Native Americans to the Indian Territories in the Great Plains.

Further reading: Donald R. Hickey, *The War of 1812: A Short History* (Urbana: University of Illinois Press, 1995).

—George Milne

Nauvoo

Located on the Mississippi River in central-western Illinois, the town of Nauvoo was home to the CHURCH OF JESUS CHRIST OF LATTER-DAY SAINTS (the Mormons) from 1839 to 1846. After moving his persecuted flock from New York to Missouri, violent local opposition in Missouri forced Mormon leader JOSEPH SMITH, JR., and his followers to relocate to Hancock County, Illinois. They purchased a fledgling settlement on the Mississippi called Commerce and renamed it Nauvoo. The new name derived from Biblical sources, and, according to Smith, meant "a beautiful location, a place of rest."

The Illinois legislature initially supported the new Mormon settlement, granting Nauvoo a municipal charter in 1840. The charter allowed the town to be incorporated as a city, with its own university and militia; the latter would prove a much-needed benefit for Mormons fearing mob persecution. Nauvoo grew rapidly, as Mormon missionaries encouraged converts from Canada and England as well as the United States to move to the new town. Though population figures for the era are inexact—reflecting the desires of both Mormon boosters and detractors—it is estimated that Nauvoo was, for a brief time, the biggest city in Illinois, with a population of 20,000 in 1845.

The influx of new residents created a housing shortage as builders struggled to keep up with the rising population. But more important to Joseph Smith than creating housing was constructing the Nauvoo temple, begun in 1841. With a design was inspired by Smith's visions, the temple cost well over $1 million to build. Smith also promoted the construction of the extravagant Nauvoo House hotel, meant to be a monument to Mormon hospitality, but it was never fully completed. Nauvoo's rapid growth seemed to indicate that the Mormon settlement had been unaffected by the economic depression that hit the rest of the United States in the late 1830s and early 1840s. However, it is more likely that the cost of constructing prominent Mormon structures was heavily subsidized by wealthy Mormon leaders and the continuous contributions of church members. Thus, the community seemed prosperous, but the basis of this prosperity was shaky, depending on newcomers' contributions. The everyday local economy was more often based on barter, with tithed church members investing excess income in the church.

Mormon religion spread throughout the region, but non-Mormons were also a significant part of the community. As the Saints' political and economic clout grew, tensions between Mormons and non-Mormons grew. Mormon power over local government seemed almost absolute. The city charter, though not particularly unusual for the time, granted Nauvoo a municipal court. Joseph Smith acted as mayor and also sat as the chief justice, while his city aldermen doubled as associate justices. Thus, Smith served as the mayor, head of the city council, and head of the local court simultaneously. Non-Mormons felt that this blending of government function was antirepublican and caused abuses of power. The existence of the militia, called the Nauvoo Legion, also contributed to the appearance of corruption, since it was commanded by Smith and enlisted about 5,000 Mormon members.

In his efforts to establish a secure settlement for his followers, Smith became an astute follower of state politics. He ably courted both Democrats and Whigs in his attempts to secure self-government and safety from persecution for the Saints. But as a voting bloc, the Mormons had little influence over the state legislature, and Smith resorted to vote-trading to achieve his goals. By 1843, even internal Nauvoo politics involved rowdy conflicts. The following year, many of these conflicts came to a head. Hoping to reestablish a political base, Smith announced his candidacy for president, but dissenting community members established an anti-Smith newspaper, the *Nauvoo Expositor.* After the publication of the first issue, Smith and the city council declared the *Expositor* to be "a public nuisance" and ordered the press and all copies of the paper destroyed. As tempers flared, Smith mobilized the militia and declared martial law. Another Illinois militia arrested

Smith and his brother Hyrum, incarcerating them in the jail at Carthage, about 10 miles away. Soon thereafter, both brothers were killed by an armed mob. Six months later, the Illinois legislature revoked the city charter. The Nauvoo economy was also in trouble, as the boom town's financial conditions deflated and poverty began to rise.

By 1845, with the charter gone and an increase in religious infighting and anti-Mormon mob violence, BRIGHAM YOUNG and the Quorum of the Twelve Apostles began to plan a new westward migration. Plans were made to evacuate the church from Nauvoo just as Smith's cherished temple was near completion. The building was rushed so that the Saints could receive their temple endowments, the financial contributions that had made the edifice possible. In 1846, under the threat of violence, a majority of the Saints left Nauvoo and began their migration to what would become their permanent settlement in Utah. Even without the anti-Mormon violence, Nauvoo was in danger of collapsing economically, and moving on seemed the best way to save the Mormon Church.

After the departure of most of the Saints in 1846, the elaborate temple was vandalized by anti-Mormon mobs. In 1848, the building was heavily damaged by fire, and soon after, the remains were knocked down by a tornado. Although the Mormon settlement at Nauvoo failed, it was an important interlude in the history of the Mormons, providing a key case study of religiously based settlements on the American frontier in the 19th century.

Further reading: Robert B. Flanders, *Nauvoo: Kingdom on the Mississippi* (Urbana: University of Illinois Press, 1965; Annette P. Hampshire, *Mormonism in Conflict: The Nauvoo Years* (New York: E. Mellen Press, 1985).

—Eleanor H. McConnell

Negro Convention movement

The National Negro Convention, which first convened in 1830 under the leadership of Richard Allen (1760–1831), Methodist preacher and founder of the African Methodist Episcopal Church in 1816, was the most successful of three efforts by African-American leaders to form a grand coalition uniting all the major ideological factions in the black community. The Negro Convention, which met off and on from 1830 to 1864, was the most successful because it lasted longer then the subsequent ones in the 1930s and 1970s. The 1830 convention, like the subsequent ones, included proponents of all the major ideological tendencies in African-American politics: conservatives and radicals, integrationists and nationalists, nonviolent "moral suasionists" and advocates of violence. It also attracted the leading African Americans of the time, including Frederick Douglass, Martin Delany, and Henry Highland Garrett. While these diverse personalities and ideologies provided strength to the convention they were also a source of its weakness and its ultimate collapse, since differences over ideology made it difficult for this and other conventions to reach a consensus for a black agenda. Delany and his followers favored emigration and back-to-Africa movements. Douglass was a leader in the ABOLITION MOVEMENT who favored integrationism, and nonviolence, and moral suasion, while Garnett called for violent slave revolts.

In addition to these differences over ideology and strategy, there were other, continuing disagreements, including the controversy over what the race should be called—African, Colored American, Negro, Oppressed Americans; debates over the merits of building separate black-community institutions such as schools, newspapers, and businesses; and arguments over whether whites should be allowed to participate in the convention. (Whites were included for a time, but eventually the convention voted to exclude them based on principles of black nationalism.) There were also class and institutional conflicts between the middle-class black establishment of ministers, teachers, and businesspeople who tended toward conservatism and integration; and the more radical, less well-off persons who tended toward extremism and emigration. In 1854, the radical emigrationists formed their own convention and began to develop plans for emigration to Haiti and other places outside of the United States. Douglass condemned the emigration convention as providing "proof to the enemies of the Negro that they were divided in thought and plans." By 1854, the divisions were plain for all to see, and the Negro Convention could not surmount them. The convention therefore dissolved, although it reconvened one last time in 1864 after the Civil War in order to develop plans for Reconstruction.

Further reading: Howard Bell, "National Negro Conventions of the 1840s: Moral Suasion vs. Political Action," *Journal of Negro History* 22 (1957): 247–60; Bella Gross, "The First National Negro Convention," *Journal of Negro History* 31 (1966): 435–43.

—Robert Smith

New Madrid earthquake

The most powerful earthquake ever recorded within the continental limits of the United States was generally referred to as the New Madrid earthquake, although there were really three separate earthquakes. The first, on December 15, 1811, in New Madrid County, Missouri, was followed by a second on January 23, 1812, and a third on February 7, 1812. Later scientific analysis estimated that the first and greatest of these earthquakes measured between 8.4 and 8.8 on the Richter Scale (the San Francisco earthquake of 1906 was 8.3). These three major earthquakes were followed by more than 1,800 aftershocks. The quakes occurred along the New Madrid fault line, some 40 miles wide and 200 miles in length, running from the Illinois-Missouri border to Memphis, Tennessee.

The physical changes to the landscape were dramatic. In the aftermath of the first quake (1811), the town of New Madrid dropped more than 10 feet, and the Mississippi River swept in to flood the town. In an instant, houses were crushed, forests disappeared, and the course of the river was changed. For several hours after the original earthquake, the river ran north in a temporary channel. After the quakes, river traffic on the most important artery of communication and trade in the West was suspended for several months. Only gradually did the north-south axis reassert itself.

The New Madrid earthquakes were a disaster of enormous proportions for those who lived near the floods. Towns were evacuated as residents fled for their lives, a panic confirmed by the two later earthquakes and the hundreds of aftershocks. The greatest natural disaster of the age called for massive assistance at a time when federal and state/territorial governments were ill-equipped by experience or ideology to give such aid. Finally, in 1815, Congress passed a law that permitted residents of the stricken area to relocate to tracts of equal size in the public domain. It was an appropriate response in an age when federal lands were far more plentiful than federal monies. The New Madrid grants were part of a PUBLIC LAND POLICY that offered land grants for many worthy projects. Speculators hastened to the scene of the disaster, where they bought the entry permits at low prices. As a result, one of the federal government's first large-scale attempts to deal with a natural disaster ended in confusion over land titles and outrage on the part of many earthquake sufferers, now further victimized by unscrupulous land agents. In 1820, Congress passed a second law to disallow the claims transferred from the original victims to third parties, further confusing the issue.

Further reading: William E. Foley, *The Genesis of Missouri: From Wilderness Outpost to Statehood* (Columbia: University of Missouri Press, 1989).

New Orleans, Battle of (January 8, 1815)

Although it took place after the TREATY OF GHENT (1814) officially ended the WAR OF 1812 (1812–15), the Battle of New Orleans gave the United States a clear victory over Great Britain and boosted American national pride. The battle also made the American commander, ANDREW JACKSON, a national hero.

After the defeat of Napoleon Bonaparte in 1814, the British turned their attention to the conflict in North America. The United States remained an enemy and was threatening to invade Canada. With its armies freed from commitments on the European continent, Britain could send its best men to America. Their plan was to invade Louisiana, capture New Orleans, and march up the Mississippi Valley to link up with another force coming south from Canada. The British expected to get help from the NATIVE AMERICANS in the Southeast, particularly the Creek and the Seminole. After the disastrous performance of the American forces outside Washington, D.C., earlier that year, it seemed certain that veteran British troops would easily defeat the U.S. forces.

However, General Jackson's men were not raw militia. He gathered a collection of Kentucky and Tennessee volunteers, experienced soldiers with several years of hard fighting against the Creek and Shawnee to their credit; a regiment of the regular army; pirates under JEAN LAFITTE; some armed slaves; and a band of Choctaw warriors led by the great chief Pushmahata. Although most of Jackson's men did not wear splendid uniforms or perform parade ground drills as well as the British, they were crack shots with their long-range rifles. The English and Scottish regiments, who fought with smoothbore muskets effective only for short distances, counted on discipline and the cold steel of their bayonets.

The British commander, General Edward Pakenham, landed more than 8,000 troops a few miles east of New Orleans in late December 1814. Jackson drew his 4,000 men into an entrenched line between the British and the town of New Orleans on the grounds of Chalmette Plantation. The Mississippi River guarded one side of the position, while the other flank ended in a dense swamp where the Choctaw waited to stop any British soldiers from marching around the line.

After a few skirmishes and an artillery duel, Pakenham launched his main attack on January 8. Regiment after regiment marched forward in perfect ranks. The Americans waited for them behind their fortifications. Cannon balls tore huge gaps in the British ranks, and well-aimed volleys of rifle fire shattered their formations. In a few hours, thousands of British soldiers, including Pakenham, were dead or wounded. When the smoke cleared, it was apparent that the Americans had won a great victory at a very small price. The British suffered between 2,100 and 2,600 killed, wounded, and captured. Only 55 Americans died, with another 278 wounded or missing. A few days later, the British slipped back to their fleet. The United States could now feel that they had defeated their old enemy at last.

Further reading: Robert V. Remini, *The Battle of New Orleans: Andrew Jackson and America's First Military Victory* (New York: Viking, 1999).

—George Milne

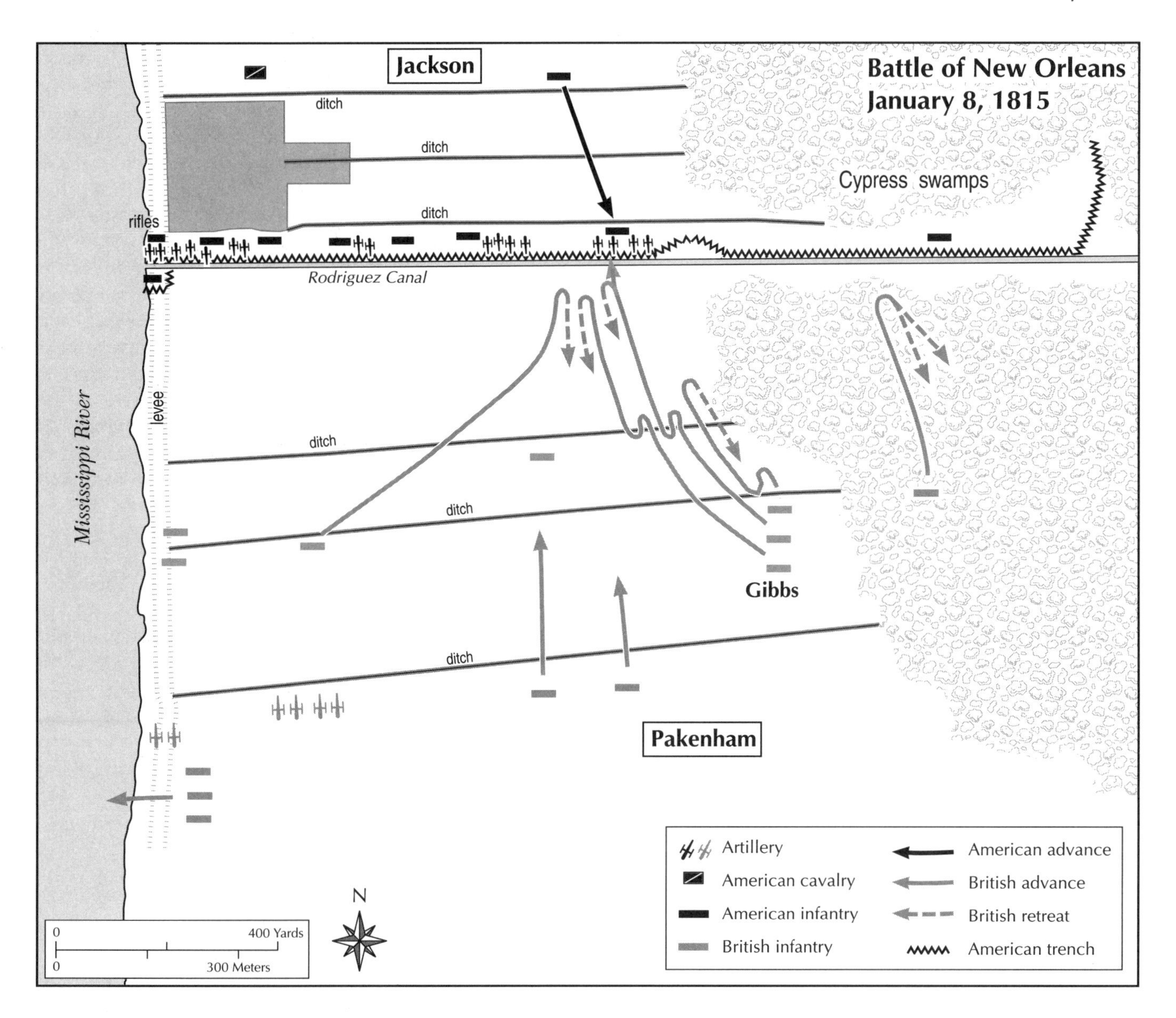

Nullification Controversy

Nullification, in U.S. history, refers to the concept that a state may reject or ignore a federal law or regulation, refusing to allow its enforcement upon its citizens or within its boundaries. In the early decades of the United States, when the federal government and the states were in a continuing battle over sovereignty and power, nullification was central to the arguments of states'-rights advocates. Many of the nation's founders, fearful of tyranny and recognizing the need to check federal power, believed that nullification by the states could be a legitimate way of keeping the government in bounds.

The right of nullification took on significance when the new federal government provided for by the Constitution (drafted 1787, ratified 1789) supplanted the weak, ineffective structure mandated by the Articles of Confederation. Among its leading early proponents were James Madison and Thomas Jefferson, who asserted a state's right to nullify onerous or offensive federal laws in the Kentucky and Virginia resolutions of 1798 and 1799.

At times, nullification movements might be used by officials in the federal government itself to achieve controversial or contested political ends. In 1828, for example, the Georgia state legislature voted to take control of Cherokee tribal lands within the state, directly contravening several federal treaties that guaranteed the territory to the Cherokee. But the land had become extremely attractive to white settlers, since the Cherokee had adopted modern farming methods with great success, and gold had been discovered within the tribal lands in 1827. President ANDREW JACKSON was vigorously pursuing the policy of Indian removal, the frequently forcible moving of native peoples from their traditional homelands in the eastern states to newly carved reservations west of the Mississippi River. The Cherokee were literate and increasingly assimilated; they had more allies in white society than did most nations, and they were stubbornly resistant to removal. Georgia's action, even though it nullified federal policy, coincided neatly with Jackson's own aims, and so he refused to enforce the federal law. Even when the U.S. Supreme Court ruled against Georgia in the matter in 1832, Jackson would not intervene. "[Chief Justice] John Marshall has made his decision," he reportedly said, "now let him enforce it." Georgia parceled the Cherokee lands to white settlers, and the Cherokee were left with little choice but to leave their homeland. Thus, nullification led directly to the enforced removal known as the TRAIL OF TEARS.

The event widely known as the Nullification Controversy occurred in 1832. By this time, the nation was in the throes of continuous change. Industrialization had begun, international and domestic trade was expanding, and the business of individual states was becoming more and more intertwined. Legislators and opinion makers, particularly in the business-oriented northern states, clamored for increased federal power and protections. As the northern states were growing rapidly in population, they had begun to outstrip the South in political representation. In response to this outcry and this political influence, the U.S. Congress passed protective tariffs in 1828 and 1832, giving domestic manufactured products further protection from foreign competition. Of course, the lack of competition meant that southern consumers would often pay higher prices.

This federal intervention, so valued by northern business owners, was anathema to southern agriculturalists. The tariffs at once raised consumer prices of finished goods and depressed the value of cotton and other raw materials produced by southern farms. Southern legislators, aware that the old plantation system was a delicately balanced financial proposition even at the best of times, feared that tariffs would mean its doom. They were also concerned at what they regarded as the blatant economic favoritism made possible by increasing northern political strength, numbers would only grow in the future. Mobilized over what they regarded as a matter of principle, they loudly protested the new fees.

South Carolina's reaction went beyond protest. In November 1832, led by U.S. senator JOHN C. CALHOUN, Governor James Hamilton, Jr., and Robert Barnwell Rheet, the state called a special convention on the tariff matter. Calhoun published two papers in support of his position. The first reaffirmed and analyzed the doctrine of the concurrent majority, by which such divisive issues had to be approved by majorities from each section of the Union, not simply enacted through the majority representation of one section. The second argued that nullification was a legitimate means of redress for acts directed against a state, a means fully recognized by the Constitution. When the convention met in November 1832, the nullifiers (as they were called) were in a decisive majority. They quickly passed an ordinance nullifying the tariff acts of 1828 and 1832. The ordinance prohibited the federal government from collecting tariff duties within the State of South Carolina after February 1, 1833. Furthermore, the ordinance mandated a test oath from all state officeholders to uphold the doctrine of nullification, and it forbade any appeal to the U.S. Supreme Court. Finally, if the federal government used military measures in an attempt to enforce the law, this use would be grounds for secession from the Union. The state legislature then passed laws to provide for raising an armed force and appropriating monies to defend the state against attack by the federal government.

President Jackson's reaction to South Carolina's nullification was as furious as his response to Georgia's had been passive. He denounced the convention's ordinance as treasonous, spurring some South Carolinians to speak openly of secession. While he urged Congress to lower the tariff, Jackson ordered the secretary of war to alert the federal forts in Charleston Harbor to defend themselves. He issued a "Proclamation to the People of South Carolina" in which he characterized nullification as an "impractical absurdity." He went on to assert in clear and direct terms the absolute supremacy of the indivisible federal government. Accordingly, no state could refuse to obey a law of the land and no state would leave the Union. To pursue disunion by armed force was "treason." It was a powerful statement. Jackson also persuaded the U.S. Congress to pass a force bill that would let the government use military action to collect the tariff in the port of Charleston. The debate over the bill produced a notable debate between Calhoun and Senator DANIEL WEBSTER on the nation and the rights of states.

South Carolina replied to Jackson's proclamation with defiance as the legislature adopted a series of hostile resolutions. The new governor, Robert Y. Hayne, called for a convocation of southern states to consider relations between states and the federal government. Responses from the state legislatures generally condemned nullification and refused to consider secession. South Carolina would have to pursue its defiant course alone. While Jackson assumed a strong public posture in defense of federal authority and the Union, he privately reached out to southerners through Kentucky senator HENRY CLAY. With Jackson's support, Clay engineered the Compromise Tariff of 1833 to resolve the matter. When South Carolina learned of the forthcoming tariff compromise, the state suspended its implementation of the nullification ordinance and accepted the reduced tariff rates. Thus the most serious states-rights crisis in the history of the nation was resolved. In order to have the last word on matters of principle, though, the state of South Carolina adopted an ordinance nullifying the Force Bill.

The Nullification Controversy was a forerunner of the crisis over the balance of power between the federal government and individual states that would later lead to a secession movement by South Carolina in December 1860. No compromise would be forthcoming this time, and the state's secession would be followed by others, the establishment of the Confederate States of America, and four years of civil war.

Further reading: William H. Freehling, *Prelude to Civil War: The Nullification Controversy in South Carolina* (New York: Oxford University Press, 1992); James Wilson, *The Earth Shall Weep* (New York: Atlantic Monthly Press, 1999).

—Mary Kay Linge

O

Oregon Trail

From the 1840s to the 1870s, the Oregon Trail was the primary westward route for some 200,000 Americans seeking new lives and opportunities in the West. The trail was generally considered to have begun in Independence, Missouri and ended in Oregon City, Oregon, with a length of about 2,000 miles. In practice, however, emigrants on the trail could join it at any of a number of "jumping-off points," including St. Joseph, Missouri, and Council Bluffs, Iowa. They could also leave the trail to reach individual destinations in Utah, CALIFORNIA, and other spots in the western territories. Since so many settlers used the trail network to get to places other than Oregon, the Oregon Trail is sometimes called the Great Platte River Road, after the river it parallels for much of its length.

Much of the Oregon Trail incorporated routes that had for centuries been used by NATIVE AMERICANS for trade and communications. Other portions were blazed by French and British trappers in an area that had long been a matter of dispute between France and England. Once the United States asserted its own claims to the Oregon Territory, exploration became more systematic. After Thomas Jefferson purchased the Louisiana Territory from the French in 1803, one of his first acts was to dispatch an expedition to explore the vast region. Commanded by Meriwether Lewis and William Clark, the expedition followed rivers and mountain passes to reach the coast of the Pacific Ocean. Their return to St. Louis after 28 months (1804–06) marked the first official exploration of the region by the U.S. government. Within a few short years, American fur traders began moving over the same landscape. The most important of these early fur-trade parties were the overland and seagoing expeditions financed by JOHN JACOB ASTOR, whose employees founded the post of ASTORIA at the mouth of the COLUMBIA RIVER. Over the next 20 years, MOUNTAIN MEN, or independent trappers and traders, explored the region in search of furs, in the process blazing several shortcuts and alternate routes to the West.

In the 1830s the continuing dispute with the British over the ownership of the Oregon Country combined with the activities of Protestant missionaries in the region raised public awareness of Oregon. Adding to information about the routes west were exploring parties sent by the U.S. government. The most important of these was commanded by JOHN C. FRÉMONT, whose 1843 expedition generated favorable publicity for the Oregon Country as a place for settlement. Furthermore, Frémont's report provided for a precise and accurate description of an overland route to Oregon for the first time. His report became the first handbook for immigrants.

The first overland migration of farming families to Oregon took place in spring 1842. Annual migrations followed, with ever-rising numbers. The route was soon known as the Oregon Trail, although the discovery of gold in California in 1848 led to the large immigration of FORTY-NINERS the following year along a variation known as the CALIFORNIA TRAIL.

Beginning in Independence or St. Joseph, the Oregon Trail first followed the Platte River to the west, crossing the river at several points. The first major landmark on the trek was FORT LARAMIE, some 665 miles from the starting point, where travelers paused for rest and resupply. Here too they sent mail to their families in the East and exchanged their fatigued draft animals for fresh stock, at a high price. Once more on the trail, immigrant parties followed the North Platte to the Sweetwater River, and thence by this river to SOUTH PASS. The pass was the level and gradual gateway across the Continental Divide to the interior of the continent. South Pass was about 950 miles from Independence, and it approximately marked the midway point in the overland voyage. Another 100 miles, and the tail came to Fort Bridger, where it turned northwest toward Fort Hall on the Snake River. Pioneers then trekked along the Snake to the valley of the Grande Ronde River, and then across the Blue Mountains to the Columbia River. The trail down the Columbia to FORT VANCOUVER was the final stage. After

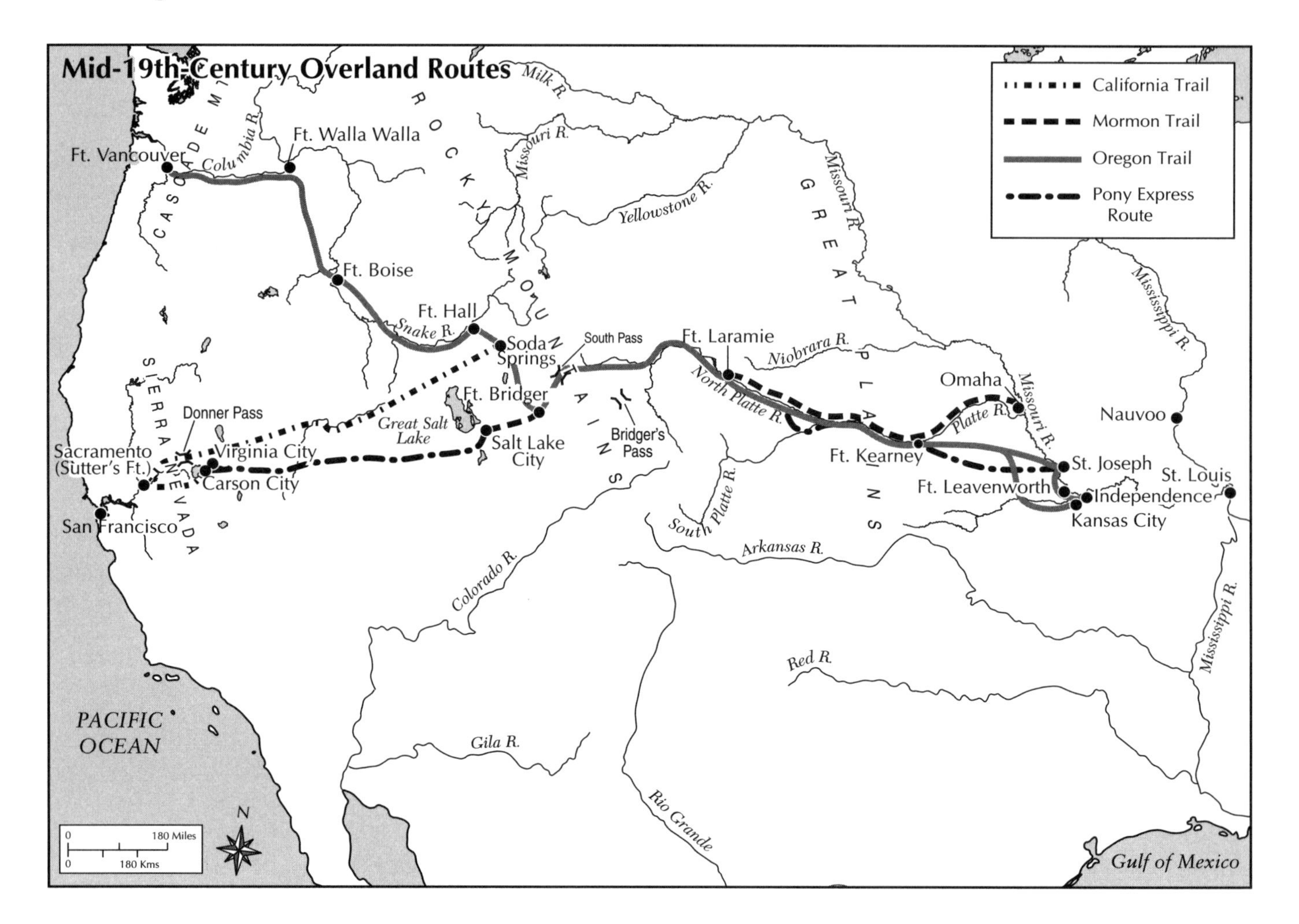

reaching the fort, where they might be welcomed by JOHN MCLOUGHLIN, most of the pioneers traveled south down the Willamette River to the growing agricultural settlements around the Protestant missions.

Initially, the Oregon Trail was difficult to follow, and an experienced guide was a necessity. Within a few years, however, settlers could practically follow the wheel ruts carved by their predecessors' wagons all the way to the Pacific. (These marks can still be seen in places today.) Most emigrants used the Oregon Trail to bring west their entire families and all that they owned, and a special transport system accommodated their needs. The Conestoga wagon, or "prairie schooner," was the method of choice. This was a canvas-covered wooden wagon with a concave bottom, the better to retain its cargo on the bumpy, rutted route. The wagon had to be packed with six months' worth of provisions for each family, along with their tents, blankets, tools, clothing, and all their possessions. The immigrants typically walked the entire way so as not to burden the oxen or mules.

Travel over the Oregon Trail was, in many respects, routine. In confronting the challenges of the western half of the continent, however, the immigrants had to exercise care and judgment. There were few places to find help. To begin with, the travel window was limited. Parties had to depart Independence in May, after grass had begun to appear on the prairie, to support the livestock. They also had to cross the Blue Mountains before the first blizzards of October closed the mountain passes. Therefore the pace on the trail had to be continuous, since the wagon trains could count on only five months to make the journey. Foremost among the priorities was management of the draft animals, and ensuring their continuing health meant that the party needed to travel as lightly as possible.

The great popular danger of the Oregon Trail was always assumed to be Native Americans, but in fact Indian attacks on wagon trains were rare, despite the settlers' fears. Some of the native peoples along the Oregon Trail saw trade opportunities in the newcomers' arrival; others were disturbed by the influx of white settlers in their lands, especially as their numbers grew. But for the overland immigrants on the Oregon Trail, a far greater danger than Indians was disease, for the exhausting trip left migrants vulnerable to many illnesses. Cholera was a particular danger, and epidemics on the trail in some years led to deaths from disease for several weeks after departure. Indeed, given the health dangers associated with river towns, the emigrants probably increased their chances of survival once they had left the towns and were on the trail west.

After 1869, when the Union Pacific Railroad completed its transcontinental line, the Oregon Trail began to fall into disuse. Any settler who could afford it preferred the ease and comfort of a two-week rail journey to a six-month wagon trek. But for the less well-off, the Oregon Trail remained a viable route to the west even into the early part of the 20th century.

Further reading: Francis Parkman, *The Oregon Trail* (New York: Viking, 1849, 1982); Oregon Trail Foundation, "End of the Oregon Trail Interpretive Center" URL: www.endoftheoregontrail.org/index.html. Downloaded 2001; John D. Unruh, *The Plains Across: The Overland Emigrants and the Trans-Mississippi West, 1840–1860* (Urbana: University of Illinois Press, 1979).

—Mary Kay Linge

Oregon Treaty of 1846

The Oregon Treaty of 1846 settled the boundary between British and American claims in the Pacific Northwest. In agreeing on this boundary, which had been unclear since the Louisiana Purchase in 1803, the United States avoided a war with Great Britain at the same time that it was approaching war with Mexico following the annexation of TEXAS in 1845.

Lying between the Rocky Mountains and the Pacific Ocean, the Oregon Country was bounded to the south by Spanish-controlled CALIFORNIA and to the north by Russian-controlled Alaska. In 1819, the ADAMS-ONÍS TREATY established the southern boundary of the U.S. claim on the West Coast at the 42nd parallel (the present-day southern boundary of the state of Oregon), and an 1824 treaty established the border between the U.S. claim in Oregon and Alaska at the line of 54 degrees, 40 minutes (the southernmost point in present-day Alaska) in the north. The other contender for supremacy in Oregon was the British in Canada, with the result that the border between U.S. and British claims required almost 30 years to resolve.

The primary disputed area lay between the COLUMBIA RIVER in the south and the 49th parallel in the north, a region that contained valuable forests, fur-trapping areas, and ports on Puget Sound. The Convention of 1818, which established the 49th parallel as the border between the United States and Canada from the Lake of the Woods (in northern Minnesota) west to the Rocky Mountains, failed to resolve the disputed Oregon boundary. The American negotiator, Richard Rush and Albert Gallatin, were willing simply to extend the line at the 49th parallel to the Pacific Ocean as the Oregon boundary. But the British contingent balked, preferring a boundary following the Columbia River from its mouth to the 49th parallel, then the 49th parallel for the remaining portion of the boundary, leaving the Columbia entirely under British control. Neither side felt much urgency about the Oregon issue in 1818, however. Few American settlers moved to the area at that time, partly because the Lewis and Clark Expedition (1804–06) had reported the territory inhospitable. Furthermore, the British North West Company controlled the fur trade in Oregon, having bought out JOHN JACOB ASTOR's interests in 1813; the North West Company would itself merge with the Hudson's Bay Company in 1821. Accordingly, the negotiators in 1818 agreed to a 10-year, joint American-British occupation of Oregon. As that agreement neared expiration in 1828, the two countries agreed to an indefinite extension of joint control, which could be terminated by either nation with one-year's notice to the other.

In subsequent years, various attempts failed to settle the issue permanently. The United States continued to offer the 49th parallel as a compromise border; the British continued to insist on the Columbia River, sweetening the deal by offering the United States a detached piece of territory on the Olympian peninsula, giving the Americans access to harbors in Puget Sound. However, by the 1840s, conditions had changed, requiring a long-term solution. Most important, several thousand American settlers had made homes in the Willamette Valley south of the Columbia River. This was territory the British never claimed, but clearly it was only a matter of time before American settlers in large numbers crossed into the disputed area. The negotiations that produced the 1842 WEBSTER-ASHBURTON TREATY, which settled other disputed borders between the United States and Canada, made little headway on the Oregon issue. Rumors that DANIEL WEBSTER had offered to trade northern Oregon in exchange for British pressure on Spain to surrender California to the United States caused a firestorm of criticism in the West, where many people believed the Americans should take both California and all of Oregon. The 1840s witnessed the flourishing of ideas of MANIFEST DESTINY, which in its most extreme form asserted that the United States had a divine right to possess the entire North American continent.

Oregon then became one of the important issues in the presidential election of 1844, an election largely contested over questions of expansion. Texas was the most important such question, and former president MARTIN VAN BUREN was denied the Democratic nomination because he opposed annexation of Texas. The nomination instead went to JAMES K. POLK, who ran on a platform favoring both Texas annexation and taking all of Oregon. The WHIG

PARTY and its candidate, HENRY CLAY, were considered generally opposed to expansion, especially in Texas. Expansionists therefore considered Polk's electoral victory to be a mandate for their ideas. Following the election, Senator William "Foghorn Bill" Allen of Ohio coined the phrase "fifty-four forty or fight" to describe U.S. policy in Oregon. In essence, Allen asserted that the United States would go to war rather than surrender any of Oregon to the British. Senators from other western states joined Allen to press Polk to secure all of Oregon by whatever means necessary.

Despite Polk's apparent support for the most belligerent position, upon taking office he directed his secretary of state, James Buchanan, to offer the British the same compromise Americans had been offering since 1818, namely a border to the Pacific at the 49th parallel. When the British again rejected this idea, Polk withdrew the offer and asked Congress to approve the necessary one-year's notice that the United States was terminating joint occupation and preparing to assert its claim to all of Oregon. In the meantime, the settlers in Oregon had established a provisional government and petitioned the United States to take control of the territory; the document creating the provisional government specified that it would expire as soon as U.S. authority was established over the territory. Polk knew, however, that opponents of the "fifty-four forty" position controlled the Senate. Southern Democrats had lost interest in Oregon after the annexation and subsequent admission of Texas as a state before the end of 1845. They no longer had anything to gain by supporting the extreme position in Oregon, and together with the less expansionist Whigs in the Senate, they could block any action on Oregon they did not like. With a fight brewing with Mexico, moreover, both southern senators and the president wished to avoid a simultaneous fight with Great Britain over Oregon. Hence, Polk left the door open for compromise, conveying to the British his willingness to submit any reasonable treaty for Senate approval and to accept any treaty that could gain the Senate's consent.

For their own reasons, the British were ready for a compromise by 1846. For one thing, the strong nationalism

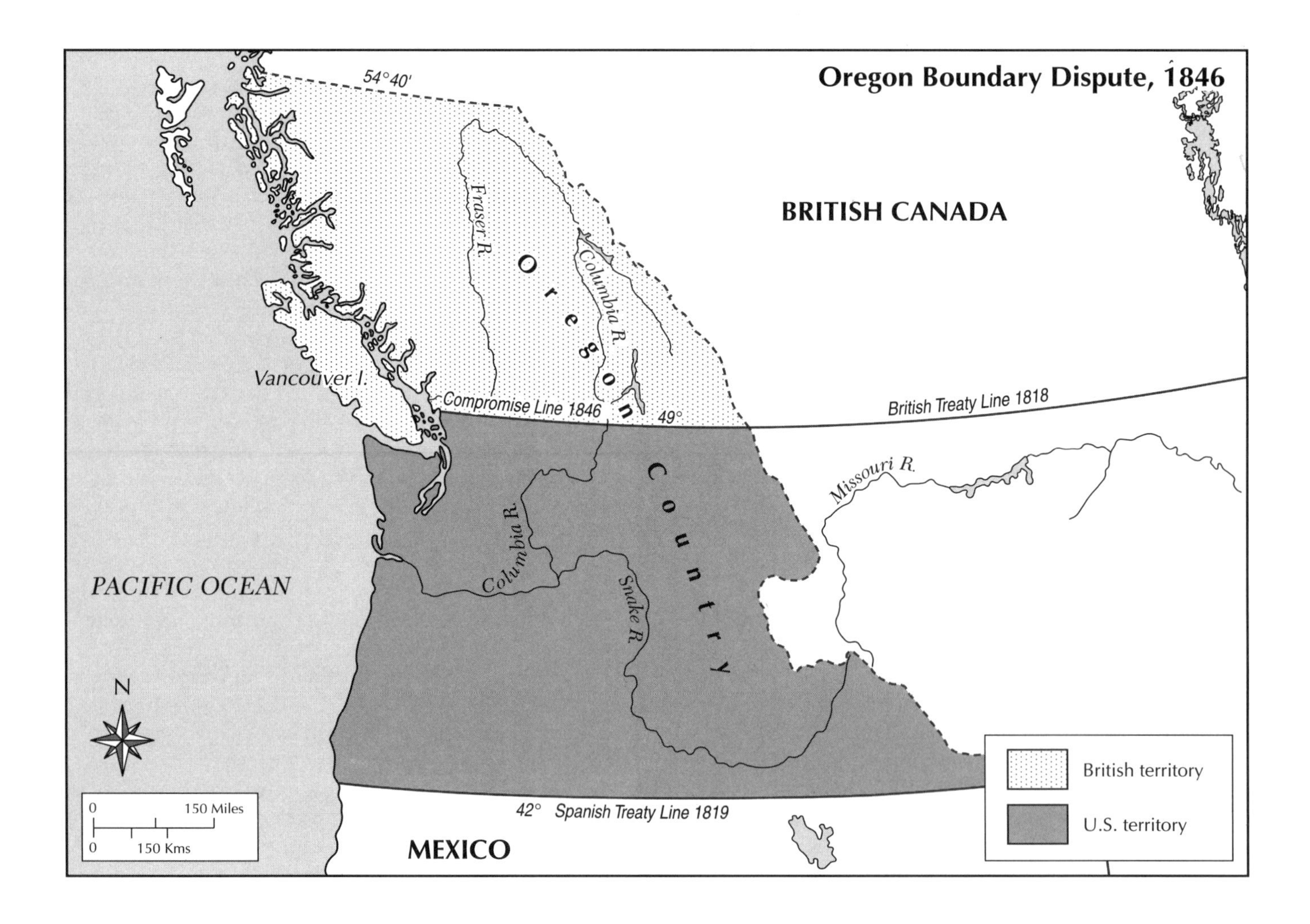

and belligerency expressed during and after the 1844 presidential campaign concerned the British government, which wanted to improve relations. With the Polk administration committed to lowering American tariffs and the Corn Laws limiting food imports in the United Kingdom about to be repealed, Britain sensed opportunities for increased trade that would be disrupted if the Oregon issue came to a crisis point. Further, the fur trade in Oregon had declined substantially, and for that reason and because of increased friction with settlers south of the Columbia River, the Hudson's Bay Company had moved its headquarters northward to Vancouver Island and out of the most hotly disputed area between the Columbia and the 49th parallel. Finally, the British foreign secretary, Lord Aberdeen, believed Oregon to be of little value to England and convinced Prime Minister Robert Peel that compromise was in Britain's interest. Aberdeen thus offered to extend the boundary at the 49th parallel to Puget Sound and thence around the southern end of Vancouver Island to the Pacific Ocean, giving the British control over all of Vancouver Island. Aberdeen also insisted on protection for the property rights of the Hudson's Bay Company and other British subjects in the ceded territory and free navigation of the Columbia River to its mouth.

Though Polk personally rejected the last provision, he submitted the British proposal to the Senate. The Senate approved, and a formal treaty was soon negotiated and ratified by the Senate. The Oregon Treaty became official on August 5, 1846. Polk thus successfully resolved the last outstanding border disagreement with the British in Canada, even though his methods might be considered somewhat clumsy. By initially appearing to support the "fifty-four forty or fight" position, he raised the stakes in Oregon by encouraging extremists in the United States and almost provoking a war with Great Britain. On the other hand, it might also be argued that by raising the stakes, Polk focused British attention on the need to reach a final resolution of the Oregon question. In this view, Polk's diplomacy appears less clumsy than shrewd. While making a show of belligerency in public, behind the scenes he promoted compromise by encouraging the British to make an offer he could get past the United States Senate. In the end, the compromise reached was almost precisely the position the United States had maintained since 1818, minus only the southern tip of Vancouver Island. And with the Oregon dispute settled, the United States could direct its martial resources undividedly to the war with Mexico on its southern border.

See also FOREIGN POLICY.

Further reading: Frederick Merk, *The Oregon Question: Essays in Anglo-American Diplomacy and Politics* (Cambridge: Mass.: The Belknap Press, 1967); David M. Pletcher, *The Diplomacy of Annexation: Texas, Oregon, and the Mexican War* (Columbia: University of Missouri Press, 1973).

—Russell L. Johnson

Ostend Manifesto See Volume V

overland mail

As settlement in the Far West increased in the years following the MEXICAN-AMERICAN WAR, Americans began to call for a regular mail service to the Pacific Coast. In 1857, Congress authorized the creation of an overland mail service, run by private joint stock companies but subsidized by the federal government. The first of these companies, the Overland Mail Company, was founded by individuals already financially connected to express mail companies such as American; National; and Wells, Fargo and Company.

The postmaster general determined the two starting points that would be used for the transcontinental mail service. Routes leading from Memphis and St. Louis would meet at Fort Smith, Arkansas, where the route would extend through Texas, Arizona, Los Angeles, and San Francisco. The service along this route was supposed to be semiweekly, with the round-trip completed in 25 days. This southern route was over 2,500 miles long. Before any mail service could commence, the entire route needed to be surveyed and the road conditions improved. The company needed to position way stations along the route, buy and transport Concord stagecoaches, and stock the route with supplies and horses. Preparing the route took over a year. The first stagecoaches departed in September 1858, successfully completing the journey in only 21 days.

Soon the procedure for transporting people and mail along the line was firmly in place. The company maintained the route very efficiently in the more settled areas but required help from station guards in isolated stretches where Indians were a threat. The road was much rougher in the isolated areas as well, making stagecoach travel a jarring, unpleasant experience. Coaches could carry nine passengers inside, plus a few riding on the outside with the drivers. Mail was stored in the rear of the coach and on top. Passengers who wanted a break from the jolting coach could stop at way stations, some of which had bunks for sleeping. For many passengers, the possibility for stopping did not make up for the poor toilet facilities, overpriced food, and occasionally drunk drivers.

Customers and other commentators complained even more forcefully about the company's inadequate, circuitous route. Critics supported the construction of a new central route that would lead west from Missouri, through Denver, Utah, and on to CALIFORNIA. The Pony Express Company

The overland mail starts from the East. Wood engraving from *Leslie's Illustrated Newspaper,* October 23, 1858 *(Hulton/Archive)*

was created by backers of this new route, who promoted its greater speed and efficiency. Conflicts between Wells, Fargo representatives and Overland Mail Company president John Butterfield prevented the Overland Mail Company from establishing a competing express service along the new central route. The company was reorganized in 1860 with Wells, Fargo shareholders occupying most of the seats on the board of directors.

Conflicts over which route to use were rendered moot with the beginning of the Civil War (1861–65). Because Texas was part of the Confederacy, overland mail operations had to be relocated to the central route. A new contract was awarded in 1861, granting both Pony Express service and stagecoach service to the Overland Mail Company. The company continued as sole operator of the line until 1864, when the contract was divided again between Overland Mail and the Holladay Overland Stage Company. Under the terms of the 1864 contract, only first-class mail and passengers would be carried overland, with newspapers and other documents transported by the much-longer sea route to California. Ownership of the line changed again in 1866, with Wells, Fargo assuming the control of all mail and transport operations in the West.

Stage travel to the West continued to be profitable until the completion of the transcontinental railroad in May 1869. The Wells, Fargo mail contract was canceled with the completion of the railroad line, thus ending the era of the Overland Mail Company. Stage travel continued to be viable for shorter trips for several years, but it eventually died out as railroads flourished. Until this point, the overland mail operation served as a key channel for communication, transport, and settlement across the continent.

Further reading: A. C. Greene, *900 Miles on the Butterfield Trail* (Denton: University of North Texas Press, 1994); Leroy R. Hafen, *The Overland Mail, 1849–1869: Promoter of Settlement, Precursor of Railroads* (Cleveland: A. H. Clark, 1926).

—Eleanor H. McConnell

Owen, Robert (1771–1858)

An industrialist and social reformer known for his radical and unorthodox views of society, Robert Owen was born in Newtown, Wales, on May 14, 1771. Although he attended local schools only through the age of nine, he was nonetheless bright and inquisitive and reputedly borrowed and read a book a day. At the age of 10, Owen left home for Manchester to work in a textile store. By 1791, Britain's Industrial Revolution was starting to develop, and Owen was eager to play his part. That year, despite his youth, Owen became a partner in a small cotton mill. Shortly after, he was hired as the manager of a large cotton-spinning factory. An excellent organizer, his mill became renowned for high-quality work, and in 1795 he advanced to serve as manager and co-owner of the large Chorlton Twist Company. The owner was so pleased by his performance that he offered the 24-year-old Owen annual salary increases and a share of the profits.

In 1799 Owen married the daughter of industrialist David Dale and acquired his factories in New Lanark, Scotland. His wealth and position were now secure, but he became very aware of the dislocation and hardships occasioned by industrialization. Having now acquired the wherewithal, he was determined to address them personally. While at Lanark, he singlehandedly instituted wide-reaching reforms to ameliorate the usually horrid living and working conditions associated with the mills. Long hours and monotonous tasks created great unhappiness and a concomitant rise in alcoholism. Owen countered the drudgery with higher wages, better sanitation, and mandatory temperance. He also invested large sums of money in improving the housing situation for workers and providing schools for their children. Further, he purchased supplies in bulk and sold them to his miniature communities at very reduced prices. Consequently, the happy, healthy workforce at Lanark became one of the most productive in all of Britain. Owen had proved beyond all doubt that contented workers enhanced productivity.

In 1806 when his mills temporarily closed due to the American embargo, Owen furthered his reputation for benevolence by continuing to pay out wages. In 1813, he printed a pamphlet entitled *A New View of Society*, which called for all surplus profit to be spent for the benefit of workers and their children. His political influence crested with the passage of the 1819 Factory Act, which mandated improved working conditions, forbade children younger than 10 from working, and strictly regulated the hours of those under 18.

Owen's reforms garnered him international fame, but his influence as a reformer was marred by a number of radical, seemingly anti-institutional ideas, which were enunciated to promote his vision of a perfect, utopian society. Foremost among them was a determined attack on the existence of organized religion that basically gutted his credibility as a reformer. He also strongly believed that poverty could be eradicated by concentrating the poor in small, self-sustaining villages based on agriculture. For such a strategy to succeed, he insisted, cooperation would have to supplant competition as a guiding human principle. In 1825, Owen acted out his beliefs by purchasing the settlement of New Harmony, Indiana, which he stocked with 900 followers. This was intended as a nonreligious, socialist community but, despite the best of intentions and investment of most of his personal fortune, the experiment failed and closed in 1828. Owen tried implementing a similar scheme in Mexico that year before political instability convinced him to return to England.

Owen returned home somewhat dejected, but he remained a vocal advocate of utopian socialism. Ever attentive to the needs of workers, he was active in the establishment of the Grand National Consolidated Trades Union in 1833, which enjoyed half a million members. He also came to openly promote atheism and oppose the institution of marriage. By 1854, Owen had converted to spiritualism, which placed him even further on the fringes of the reform movement. He died in Newtown on November 17, 1858, a leading pioneer of social reform. Owen's efforts were beset by a tendency toward radicalism that alienated political support, but he functioned simultaneously as one of INDUSTRIALIZATION's greatest practitioners and its most strident critic. His pioneering views subsequently became the basis for socialist and cooperative ideologies of the later 19th century.

See also RELIGION; WARREN, JOSIAH.

Further reading: Charles Burgess, "The Boatload of Trouble: William McClure and Robert Owen, Revisited" (*Indiana Magazine of History* 94, no. 2 (1998): pp. 138–150); Ian Donnachie, *Robert Owen: Owen of New Lanark and New Harmony* (East Linton, Scotland: Tuckwell Press, 2000); J. F. C. Harrison, *Robert Owen and the Owenites in Britain and America: The Quest for the New Moral World* (Aldershot: Gregg Revivals, 1994); Edward Royle, *Robert Owen and the Commencement of the Millennium: A Study of the New Harmony Community* (New York: Manchester University Press, 1998).

—John C. Fredriksen

P

Panic of 1819

The Panic of 1819 is generally considered to be the first major economic depression in the United States, although there had been some distress associated with the Embargo of 1807. After the WAR OF 1812, which the nation had survived intact and independent, there was a burst of patriotism and optimism. The United States enjoyed a postwar economic boom, as farmers sold more of their goods on the world market and trade with Europe opened up after the end of the Napoleonic Wars.

The PUBLIC LAND POLICY helped to fuel this boom as well. Under the Public Land Act of 1800, the federal government has been very generous in extending credit. In the South, many plantation owners left the exhausted soil of the Southeast for fertile lands in Mississippi and Alabama, where they hoped to grow cotton. Cotton prices had risen in these new southern states, and planters paid exorbitant prices for uncleared land in the expectation that prices would remain high. In the western United States, there was much speculation in public lands, as Americans were interested in developing their country but for the most part lacked the capital to do so. In response, many banks, both state and unchartered, sprang into existence. These "wildcat" banks fed the expansionist frenzy by printing enormous amounts of paper money. Western banks were often especially reckless in this regard. As the number of banks grew, so did prices, particularly that of real estate. Much of this apparently booming economy, however, was supported only by paper currency, without much hard currency, or specie, to support it.

Many individuals and businesses fell into heavy debt due to the mania for expansion and growth. For example, in 1819, $22 million was owed to the federal government for debts on public lands. A good number of debtors also owed money to the unregulated wildcat banks. The boom fueled by cheap land, high commodity prices, and easy credit suddenly burst in 1819; one trigger was a collapse in world commodity prices. Part of the problem was that the SECOND BANK OF THE UNITED STATES, which had been chartered in 1816, called in specie from various state banks; those banks could not meet the demands, and thus hard currency dried up. In addition, in 1819, the U.S. Supreme Court, led by Chief Justice John Marshall, ruled that states could not tax the Bank of the United States, which was declared to be constitutional and of more immediate concern. This decision placed further strain on the financial health of the states. Some critics of the bank went so far as to accuse it of causing the Panic of 1819, which is an exaggeration, although it did little to rein in irresponsible state and local banks that contributed to the panic by their liberal lending of paper money. The bank at this point concerned itself primarily with its own financial well-being and was more interested in making profits for its stockholders than it was in regulating the dangerous practices of reckless banks.

As the crisis deepened, much overseas trade and economic growth at home came to a halt. The collapse of wheat prices hurt farmers everywhere. Wheat had sold in some regions for $2.41 a bushel in 1817; four years later, it was getting only 88 cents on the open market. The downturn in prices often made it impossible for indebted farmers to pay off their obligations, and many of them lost their land to the banks. Much economic suffering was also felt in urban areas. Philadelphia, the nation's second largest city, had 75 percent of its people out of work, according to one estimate; nearly 2,000 of its citizens were put in jail for debt. Some cities and towns across the country actually lost population, as people returned to their relatives' homes in the countryside. New England was less affected by the crisis than were other regions, having not experienced so much of a banking-and credit-fueled boom. The West, however, was severely distressed, and several states passed laws suspending debt collection until conditions improved—among them Indiana, Illinois, Tennessee, Kentucky, and Missouri.

In response to the crisis, President JAMES MONROE and the federal government did very little. One measure

Congress did take was to pass a law, which Monroe signed in 1820, lowering the price of public lands. Unlike several of the above-mentioned states, the federal government maintained a strict policy of not interfering in economic matters it thought beyond its constitutional powers. Although their traditional rival, the Federalists, were in disarray and on the verge of formal extinction, Republicans, and especially their supporters in the South, still feared any expansion of the powers of a national government, which might someday threaten slavery.

The economic effects of the panic were felt until at least 1824, with a general prosperity not returning until almost 1830. The political and psychological impact was as important as the economic consequences, however. Much of the optimism that swept the nation following the BATTLE OF NEW ORLEANS and the end of the War of 1812 ended with the panic. This doubt over whether an economy increasingly based on market values was in the nation's best interest coincided with the congressional dispute between North and South in 1819–21. In that controversy, the debate was whether Missouri should be admitted to the Union as a free or slave state. It combined with the anxieties that came with the panic to produce some genuine concern over the future of the republic. There were proposals for keeping the country largely agricultural, while others continued to point the finger of blame at the Bank of the United States and called for a government vigorous enough to contest its powers. The economic distress sparked a renewed interest in politics, as farmers, merchants, workers, and others began to think of what type of government might be needed to avoid a repeat of the hard times that erupted in 1819. One possible remedy was higher tariffs that would protect infant American industries from overseas competition; a major step in that direction was taken with the Tariff of 1824, which raised duties considerably on imports. In the 1820s and beyond, voters would begin to demand more of their elected officials as the American economy become more complex and diversified and the threats of panics remained.

Further reading: George Dangerfield, *The Era of Good Feelings* (New York: Harcourt, Brace, 1952); Murray Rothbard, *The Panic of 1819* (New York: Harcourt, Brace & World, 1963).

—Jason Duncan

Panic of 1837

The Panic of 1837 brought to an end an extended economic boom, one of the most productive in the history of the United States. It began in the 1820s, when British investors poured large amounts of capital into American canals in the North, as well as into Southern cotton, and basic commodities tripled in price. The nation's economy was undergoing a transformation that had accelerated in the decades since the WAR OF 1812, one marked by the development of an interconnected market and a workforce characterized more and more by wage labor. During the boom, there was a rage for speculation and credit, and it began to spin out of control.

One effort by the federal government to discourage speculation, which was blamed by some for rising inflation, was to issue the so-called Specie Circular in 1836. Drawn up by Senator THOMAS HART BENTON of Missouri and issued as an executive order by President ANDREW JACKSON over the objections of the WHIG PARTY, the Specie Circular mandated that only specie—i.e., gold and silver—would be acceptable payment for public lands. This was essentially an effort to end speculation with banknotes and allow ordinary people a better chance to buy land. The result, however, was that specie became harder to come by, especially in the Northeast, and it went west to pay for lands.

Another potential economic problem was rooted in the Bank War of 1832, which had resulted in the expiration of the charter of the SECOND BANK OF THE UNITED STATES in 1836. This took away a major force against runaway credit, and therefore inflation had increased because state and local banks were issuing too many notes.

The boom reached its peak between 1834–37, but some saw danger in all of the speculation and easy credit. One skeptic famously asked "When Will the Bubble Burst?" One of the first signs of trouble on the economic horizon was a series of crop failures in the United States, beginning in 1835; as a result, farmers could not repay their bank loans. As agriculture began to decline, the international balance of trade began to work against the United States. In the South, cotton firms began to fail and agricultural production in general slipped. Overexpansion had led to great amounts of debt and bad currency. Overtrading on Wall Street had led to a real-estate boom that also began to bust.

Although these domestic factors all played a role in the onset of the panic, it appears that its most important causes originated overseas. There came to be concern in London over the increased export of specie, especially gold, from their vaults to the United States. The Bank of England therefore decided to restrict the outflow of specie to the United States and demand the payment of specie that was owed to them. It also rather suddenly ceased granting credit to English firms doing business with their American counterparts. At the same time, a poor harvest in England caused a dip in the demand for American cotton, probably the most important commodity in the United States. These developments in England, which was the center of the Western world's financial system, contributed to a collapse of world prices that affected many sectors of the U.S. ECONOMY. Banks began to suspend specie payments in spring 1837, meaning they would not redeem any paper notes for gold or silver. This helped to create a panic, as investors were fearful of losing their savings and rushed to withdraw them from the banks. As paper money became devalued, the notes in which workers were paid lost much of their purchasing power.

By early 1837, business failures had begun to mount. The distress was especially devastating in northern cities. Commerce and transportation declined; most construction, an important source of jobs, ceased; and goods went unsold. Wage-dependent workers in the new economy were especially vulnerable. Some of them were thrown out of their homes when they could not pay rent, and moved into cellars and basements. There were food riots that were reminiscent of colonial times. As the number of unemployed and food prices both soared, there was looting of bakeries and shops. In the South, cotton plantations were sold on the market for only 10 percent of their original price. To make matters even worse, hopes for economic recovery and a relatively brief panic were dashed in 1839, as another wave of business failures, unemployment, and general economic suffering hit the nation.

In response to the crisis, radical antibank Democrats, known as the Locofocos, began to call for hard currency so that workers and farmers could pay their debts, while Whigs and conservative Democrats called for paper money to ease the panic. There were many accusations in Washington over who was responsible for the panic. Whigs cried "Locofocoism" and blamed Democrats and their economic policies during the Jackson presidency; the Democrats pointed the finger at the now-defunct Bank of the United States. The initial response of President MARTIN VAN BUREN, who had taken office in 1837 just as the crisis was deepening, was that the panic was a healthy corrective to an overheated economy. He steadfastly refused to provide federal funds to relieve the distress caused by panic. Van Buren did eventually propose a policy known as the independent treasuries, or subtreasury. It called for the federal government to take its funds out of the banking system altogether and place them in government vaults. The idea behind this policy was that it would keep the federal government out of reach of economic elites and eliminate government-backed speculation in public lands. There was much opposition to this plan, both among the Whigs and the more business-minded Democrats, but Congress eventually passed it in 1840.

The impact of the panics of the late 1830s was such that general economic prosperity did not return until about 1844. Among the long-range consequences of the economic crisis was that labor organizations, which had begun to form in the late 1820s and early 1830s, essentially collapsed in the face of a massive loss of bargaining power and would not return in force until after the Civil War. The DEMOCRATIC PARTY, which lost the White House in 1840 because the Whigs were able to blame them for the nation's economic troubles, in the future would be reluctant to pursue antibank and anticredit policies which, rightly or wrongly, had cost them so much politically. Debates over these issues would also soon be supplanted by the growing controversy brought by expansion, as the United States once and for all confronted the question of SLAVERY.

Further reading: Peter Temin, *The Jacksonian Economy* (New York: W. W. Norton, 1969); Richard H. Timberlake, Jr., "The Specie Circular and the Distribution of the Surplus." *Journal of the Political Economy,* 1980; Sean Wilentz, *Chants Democratic: New York City and the Rise of the American Working Class, 1788–1850* (New York: Oxford University Press, 1984).

—Jason Duncan

Panic of 1857 See Volume V

penitentiary movement

Historians have argued about the origins of the penitential reform movement. Enlightenment thought, urbanization, the Industrial Revolution, and bourgeois fear of social disorder have all been suggested as causes of this historical development. Historians can all agree that in the late 18th and early 19th centuries, liberal republics shifted their major form of state punishment from public displays such as whippings to the incarceration of criminals in institutions.

The social movement to end public displays as the state's primary form of punishment may have originated in 18th-century philosophical thought. Age of Enlightenment penal theorists influenced reformers and state officials in late 18th-century America. Cesare Beccaria, who wrote *An Essay on Crimes and Punishments* (1764), advocated the consistency of punishment through a standard criminal code and the eradication of arbitrary punishment. Whipping, stocks, and other public humiliations had been effective methods in small, close-knit communities, but in rapidly growing urban areas with rising crime rates, developing a uniform punishment system was more efficient and manageable.

These new theories and the increasing level of disorder in urban centers influenced city officials to eradicate public punishments and build a new kind of system for dealing with crime. Philadelphia, for example, ceased public whipping for punishments in 1786 and instituted penal labor as the primary punishment for crime. When Philadelphia officials decided that chain-gang labor on public works did not properly reform the criminals to lead virtuous lives as good citizens, the idea of placing criminals in institutions began to gain support. The noted physician Benjamin Rush, for example, advocated the cessation of all public punishment, believing that this interaction with the citizenry would contaminate the public morals. In 1787, he published a pamphlet, *An Enquiring into the Effects of Public Punishments upon Criminals and upon Society,* which criticized current state punishments. He believed that public executions and punishments degraded both the criminal and the spectators. Social reformers like Rush supported the institutionalization of criminals, believing that a highly structured program of organized activity could encourage repentance and develop the virtue needed for citizens in the new republic.

Prison reformers adopted the practice of social isolation as a technique for the moral rehabilitation of inmates. Early jails tended to be lightly monitored, with the prisoners largely governing themselves; they could often mingle freely, and their families could visit them regularly. Because the penitential reformers viewed the origins of criminal behavior as arising from corrupting social influences, the movement's proponents insisted on separating criminals from society and isolating them from their families and friends. For reformers who believed that virtue was rooted in individual responsibility and religious devotion, the goals of the penitential movement were ideologically appealing. Americans involved in this movement included such well-known reformers as DOROTHEA DIX and Louis Dwight.

As states with growing cities and populations, New York and Pennsylvania would lead the nation in developing new ways to punish criminals. The prison reforms adopted by these two states were later embraced by other states with some modifications. The Jacksonian era introduced the construction of large penitentiaries. In 1829, Pennsylvania opened the Eastern State Penitentiary, the first large institution designed by supporters of penitential reformers. This institution aimed to inculcate virtue through isolation, silence, and religious instruction. The architects who designed Eastern State carefully arranged the structure to facilitate this separation of prisoners, even during exercise and eating periods.

A debate emerged between social reformers who advocated the Pennsylvania system of incarceration and those who supported the treatment of prisoners in New York institutions. This debate centered around the degree of solitude institutions should require of prisoners. The New York system allowed prisoners to labor outside of their cells in workshops with other inmates, although prison regulations still required silence. The Pennsylvania system, in contrast, advocated as much separation as possible, including solitary confinement. Both systems embodied the belief that prisoner isolation would lead criminals to atone for their past vices and absorb a new sense of morality. Letters from family and friends were carefully censored, and the prisoners were only allowed

This detail rendering of an iron gag is an attack on the cruelty in Pennsylvania's Eastern Penitentiary, a prison notorious for its abuses and atrocities against prisoners, 1835. *(Library of Congress)*

reading material that could be depended upon to teach them moral behavior. This carefully controlled environment and lack of communication with the outside world was supposed to both produce repentance and teach the inmate the steady work habits necessary to a successful American citizen.

The expense of separating prisoners and keeping the institutions carefully regulated was often difficult for other states to reproduce; most adopted only some aspects of the New York or Pennsylvania system. But the general model of incarceration and separation was implemented throughout the country and remains a basic characteristic of the American criminal justice system to this day. The penitentiary reformers' disciplinary strategies spurred the building of all sorts of other institutions, including asylums for the poor and the insane. The construction of these new kinds of institutions signified an expansion of the state's power to control social behavior and punish those who deviated from established norms.

See also CITIES AND URBAN LIFE.

Further reading: Adam Jay Hirsch, *The Rise of the Penitentiary: Prisons and Punishment in Early America* (New Haven, Conn.: Yale University Press, 1992); Michael Meranze, *Laboratories of Virtue: Punishment, Revolution and Authority in Philadelphia, 1760–1835* (Chapel Hill: Published for the Institute of Early American History and Culture by the University of North Carolina Press, 1996).

—Sharon E. Romeo

Permanent Indian Frontier (1840)

A policy for permanently separating NATIVE AMERICANS from white settlers, the Permanent Indian Frontier had its roots in earlier plans suggested by presidents Thomas Jefferson and JAMES MONROE for dealing with conflicts between Indians and whites. Jefferson had proposed in 1803 that these conflicts could be solved by persuading nations to trade their lands east of the Mississippi for lands west of the river. Clearly dividing Indian and white lands would, he hoped, eliminate the violent confrontations on the frontier that were making western expansion difficult. He assumed that the amount of land east of the Mississippi would satisfy white demand for many generations. In 1825, Monroe officially proposed the concept of a permanent dividing line west of Missouri. He asserted that this policy would protect the Indians, who could form and administer their own separate government.

President ANDREW JACKSON supported removal to the West but opposed treating Native Americans as an independent nation. His concept of permanent relocation was passed in the INDIAN REMOVAL ACT (1830). After this policy was initiated in the 1830s, almost all eastern Native Americans were forced to move west of the Mississippi River. However, violent conflict between Indians and whites persisted, as American settlers continued to encroach on Indian lands. The U.S. government began looking for a way to defuse the conflict between Indians and white settlers for good. In an effort to establish the boundaries of settlement, the government proposed the creation of a "permanent Indian frontier" at about the 95th meridian (near the present-day western boundaries of Arkansas, Missouri, and Iowa). Officials hoped that by setting aside this large area for Native Americans, further conflicts with white settlers could be avoided. This frontier would, in essence, be a single large reservation for Indians.

But before this new policy had been implemented, white emigrants were already crossing the line on overland trails to CALIFORNIA and trespassing onto the Indian territory itself in an attempt to settle there. The Permanent Indian Frontier was difficult to enforce, and within 10 years the federal government had caved in to pressure from white settlers, abandoning the idea of one large Indian reservation. After the 1850s, government policy was to relocate Indian nations to many smaller, isolated reservations. Indian leaders were forced by economic necessity and intimidation into signing land cession treaties. They accepted goods, annuities, and small reservations in exchange for the large tracts needed to quench the white thirst for new lands. The new small-reservation plan was the latest in a string of policies that rendered Native Americans increasingly dependent on white traders and government officials in order to survive. The annuity money did not go far and was often not even paid, and soon Indians in the West were suffering from disease, malnutrition, and alcoholism.

Trapped on reservations, Indian nations were less and less able to support themselves through their traditional means of hunting and agriculture. On small reservations, they were supposed to learn Euro-American farming practices and live like whites. Most continued to resist this pressure to adopt white ways, and open conflict between the United States and Native Americans continued in scattered pockets until the 1890s. The fate of the Permanent Indian Frontier embodies the general trend of U.S. Indian policy throughout the 19th century: Indian rights to land were consistently discarded because white Americans would not accept limits on their own settlement rights.

Further reading: Francis Paul Prucha, *The Great Father: The United States Government and the American Indians,* 2 vols. (Lincoln: University of Nebraska Press, 1984); Robert A. Trennert, Jr., *Alternatives to Extinction: Federal Indian Policy and the Beginnings of the Reservation System, 1846–1851* (Philadelphia: Temple University Press, 1975).

—Eleanor H. McConnell

Perry, Matthew Calbraith (1794–1858)

Commander of the naval expedition that established U.S. relations with Japan, Matthew Calbraith Perry was born on April 10, 1794, in South Kingstown, Rhode Island, the brother of Oliver Hazard Perry. He began his naval career as midshipman at the age of 15, advancing to lieutenant in 1813 and to commander in 1826. Perry supervised the construction of the first naval steamship, the *Fulton,* and upon its completion in 1837, he took command with the rank of captain. He was promoted to commodore in 1842. In 1846–47, he commanded the Gulf squadron during the MEXICAN-AMERICAN WAR.

As commander of U.S. naval forces in the China seas, Perry was a staunch expansionist. In 1852, he warned President MILLARD FILLMORE that the British, who had already taken control of Hong Kong and Singapore, would soon control all trade in the area. Perry recommended that the

United States take "active measures to secure a number of ports of refuge" in Japan. Fillmore agreed with Perry, and in 1853 he ordered the commodore to open negotiations with the emperor of Japan.

American ships had long been active in the Pacific, as New England whaling fleets scoured the ocean in search of their prey. The China trade had been enriching Yankee merchants since 1784. Japan, however, had effectively closed its doors to outsiders, and it restricted foreign ships to a small part of Nagasaki. For more than 200 years, a strict feudal system operated, and no foreigner was allowed to enter Japan at all. Even shipwrecked sailors were forced to remain so that no information about the country could leak out. The Dutch had established trading relations with the Japanese in the early 1600s, but were then forced, in 1641, to remove themselves and all future trading via an artificial island called Decima.

On July 8, 1853, Perry led a squadron of four ships into Tokyo Bay and presented representatives of the emperor with the text of a proposed treaty for commerce and friendship. To give the reluctant Japanese time to consider the offer, he then sailed for China. With an even more powerful fleet, he returned to Tokyo in February 1854 and came ashore to meet with representatives of the ruling shogun. He was accompanied by 600 men and a naval band. The Japanese signed the Treaty of Kanagawa on March 31, 1854, providing that humane treatment be extended to sailors shipwrecked in Japanese territory, that U.S. ships be permitted to buy coal in Japan, and that the ports of Shimoda and Hakodate be opened to U.S. commerce. Perry's mission ended Japan's isolation, a prerequisite for its subsequent development into a modern nation. Matthew Calbraith Perry died in New York City on March 4, 1858.

Further reading: John Schroeder, *Matthew Calbraith Perry: Antebellum Soldier and Diplomat* (Annapolis: Naval Institute Press, 2001).

personal liberty laws

Personal liberty laws were statutes passed by northern U.S. states to counter the FUGITIVE SLAVE LAWS. Article IV, Section 2 of the Constitution called for states to surrender escaped slaves to their owners, but as the ABOLITION MOVEMENT had grown, northern states not only refused to extradite runaway slaves but protected them from their owners and from hired slave catchers. Several northern states responded by passing so-called "personal liberty" laws aimed at thwarting the federal requirements. Among other things, these laws guaranteed the writ of habeas corpus, the right to a jury trial, and other procedural devices that protected the runaways, made it difficult for slave owners to prove their case in court, and made it costly for them to do so. Indiana and Connecticut, for example, passed liberty laws that assured fugitives the right to a jury trial and provided them with attorneys. In 1842, the U.S. Supreme Court, in *Prigg v. Pennsylvania,* ruled that obstructing the rights of slave owners to reclaim their slaves was unconstitutional. This ruling crippled the liberty laws that were currently in effect.

Several states responded by taking new approaches. Massachusetts passed a new liberty law in 1843 that prohibited the use of state resources to catch fugitive slaves. This required slave owners to rely on federal officials, who were in short supply, or hire their own slave catchers. As part of the COMPROMISE OF 1850 designed to reduce tensions between North and South, Congress passed a new and tougher fugitive slave law that so one-sidedly favored slave owners that it became a major propaganda weapon for the abolitionists. The Fugitive Slave Act called for all citizens to help apprehend fugitives, or face stiff penalties. However, the North continued to pass laws intended to help fugitive slaves, while the South cited these laws as an assault on states' rights and a justification for secession.

Further reading: Paul Finkelman, *An Imperfect Union: Slavery, Federalism, and Comity* (Union, N.J.: Lawbook Exchange, 2000); Thomas D. Morris, *Free Men All: The Personal Liberty Laws of the North, 1780–1861* (Union, N.J.: Lawbook Exchange, 2001).

Phillips, Wendell (1811–1884)

As an abolitionist, Wendell Phillips was considered one of the great orators of the antislavery movement. He was born in Boston, Massachusetts, on November 29, 1811, into one of the state's oldest and most distinguished families. He was educated at the Boston Latin School, where he already displayed unusual ability as an orator, and subsequently studied at Harvard under the noted jurist Joseph Story. Phillips received his law degree in 1833 and set up a successful practice in Boston. By dint of his patrician lineage and background, he was expected to enjoy an accomplished career in law and a pursuit of public office. However, his life reached an important crossroads in 1835 when he witnessed a mob accost William Lloyd Garrison, the outspoken Massachusetts abolitionist, and drag him through the streets by a rope. Phillips was so outraged by the event that he adopted the protection of civil liberties as a personal cause.

Two years later, in 1837, the death of abolitionist editor Elijah Lovejoy in Illinois prompted Phillips to issue the first of his celebrated public ripostes that praised Lovejoy as a martyr to the cause of liberty. Hereafter, he became a vocal proponent of free speech for abolitionists, whose movement he had yet to embrace. Another turning point in Phillips's life occurred in 1837 when he met and fell in love with Ann Terry Greene, the wealthy daughter of a prominent merchant and an active member of the Boston Female Anti-Slavery Society. They married in December 1837. Through her influence, he formally abandoned his legal practice altogether to become active in the ABOLITION MOVEMENT. Within a few years, he gained national renown as one of abolition's most eloquent and outspoken proponents after Garrison. He also began to champion the rights of Irish Catholics, whom he viewed as another exploited class.

Being in great demand, Phillips toured the country widely as a speaker, earning considerable fees for his lectures. He also spoke on a number of nonpolitical issues; one speech, "The Lost Arts," was rendered more than 2,000 times. A dynamic, vigorous orator, Phillips captivated and entertained his audiences through clever use of invective, which simultaneously demonized and insulted the opposition. Throughout his career, he also relied heavily on his wife Ann's advice, and he freely admitted that she was usually ahead of him with respect to social issues. By deft use of his acerbic wit and thunderous delivery, Phillips found his niche as the nation's most sought-after political agitator.

The onset of the Civil War in 1861 further enhanced Phillips' image as a social and political radical. He forcefully advocated having the Union be dissolved rather than compromise its moral integrity by remaining associated with the slave-owning South. He also attacked the Constitution for becoming the legal basis for SLAVERY. Phillips refused to support Abraham Lincoln during the war years, regarding the president as essentially accommodating toward the "peculiar institution."

After 1865, Phillips ended his long association with Garrison, who withdrew from politics, and succeeded him as head of the AMERICAN ANTI-SLAVERY SOCIETY. Using this organization as a pulpit, he agitated for the civil rights of African Americans and for WOMEN'S STATUS AND RIGHTS. Toward the end of his long career, Phillips also espoused labor rights, including an eight-hour workday. He died in Boston on February 2, 1884, one of the most memorable orators of American history and a strident advocate for change.

Further reading: Irving H. Bartlett, *Wendell Phillips: Brahmin Radical* (Westport, Conn.: Greenwood Press, 1973); Timothy Messer-Kruse, "Eight Hours, Greenbacks, and Chinamen: Wendell Phillips, Ira Steward and the Fate of Labor Reform in Massachusetts," *Labor History* 42, no. 2 (2001): 133–158; James B. Stewart, *Wendell Phillips, Liberty's Hero* (Baton Rouge: Louisiana State University Press, 1998).

—John C. Fredriksen

Pike, Zebulon Montgomery (1779–1813)

Army officer and explorer, Zebulon Pike led expeditions through lands acquired in the Louisiana Purchase. Born in Trenton, New Jersey, in 1779, Pike enlisted in the army in 1794 at the age of 15 and participated in the campaigns in the Old Northwest under General Anthony Wayne. In 1799, at 20, he was commissioned a lieutenant and went on to serve in various forts on the trans-Appalachian frontier, including Fort Washington and Fort Knox. His formal education was limited, and Pike determined to make the most of his career opportunities in the army by a vigorous program of self-study. He read widely on military tactics, mathematics, and science, and he also studied the French and Spanish languages. Brave and a natural leader, Pike was ideally suited to serve on the frontier of the late 18th and early 19th centuries.

In 1805 General James Wilkinson ordered Pike to make a reconnaissance of the upper Mississippi River. Thomas Jefferson's recent purchase of the Louisiana Territory had turned the attention of the nation to its western possessions. With 20 soldiers, Pike left St. Louis in August 1805 in a 70-foot keelboat. Wilkinson had directed him to explore to the headwaters of the Mississippi and to do so before the onset of winter. Pike was given a list of items to observe: furs and minerals, the Indian peoples of the territory, and the population (Indian and European), among other things. He was also given authority to purchase sites for future military posts and to invite important Indian leaders to St. Louis to meet Wilkinson personally. Pike eventually left the keelboat at Prairie du Chien (then part of Michigan Territory and later Wisconsin), and he proceeded with his command upriver in small boats. With the onset of winter, he determined that his work was not yet finished and so decided to make a winter camp with his men at the present site of Little Falls, Minnesota. From this spot, he moved by sled up the Mississippi to what he thought was the river's source. In fact he had failed to find the real source, which lies in Lake Itasca.

Pike returned to St. Louis in late April 1806. Throughout the course of the expedition, he had displayed the highest qualities of leadership through a difficult winter in one of the most remote regions of the nation. The more practical aspects of the trip were less successful. Few Indian leaders accepted his invitation to visit St. Louis, and the U.S. Senate declined to ratify the treaty he had negotiated with the Sioux. His map and journal were of lasting importance, however, as they provided the first picture of the upper Mississippi Country.

Within three months, by July 15, 1806, Pike had received further orders from Wilkinson. This time he accompanied 50 Osage Indian captives to their homes in western Missouri; then he swung north to the Pawnee villages in Nebraska, where he presided over a treaty of peace among the nations of the region. From here, he headed west, eventually exploring the headwaters of the Arkansas River in present-day Colorado. While on this leg of his trip, he and his men tried without success to climb the peak that would bear his name. Pike then moved south across the Sangre de Cristo range and eventually reached the Rio Grande. Although the boundary line of the recent Louisiana Purchase was not yet mapped, Pike had clearly passed into Spanish territory. In February 1807, a Spanish patrol captured him at a stockade they had constructed on the Rio Grande. Pike and his men were first taken to Santa Fe, then to Chihuahua, and finally released near Natchitoches, Louisiana. They returned to American territory on June 30, 1807.

In subsequent debate about the expedition, there was a consensus that Pike had been lost. At the same time, his journey had been a voyage of exploration. What was important was that he saw new places and could report on them. In this part of his mission, he was eminently successful. Furthermore, his capture and incarceration by the Spanish allowed him to see many Spanish towns and fortifications that would otherwise have been closed to him as an officer representing the U.S. Army. In 1810, Pike published his travel narrative, which later appeared in British, German, French, and Dutch editions. Pike had established something of an international reputation as an explorer, but this fame had little effect on his military career.

The expedition to the West enhanced Pike's reputation as an excellent officer. At the outbreak of the WAR OF 1812, he was promoted to the rank of brigadier general. In April 1813, he was killed while leading an attack on Toronto. A brave officer and effective troop leader, Pike is remembered now for his expeditions to the West and for the peak in the Rocky Mountains that bears his name.

Further reading: Eugene W. Hollen, *The Lost Pathfinder; Zebulon Montgomery Pike* (Norman: University of Oklahoma Press, 1949); Donald Jackson, *The Journals of Zebulon Montgomery Pike* (Norman: University of Oklahoma Press, 1966).

"Pike's Peak or Bust"

In 1858, the discovery of gold in Cherry Creek, Colorado, near the site of present-day Denver, triggered a large overland migration known as the COLORADO GOLD RUSH. The CALIFORNIA GOLD RUSH had provided the original model for a mass migration across the continent. The discoveries in Colorado a decade later produced many of the same outbursts of enthusiasm.

The first parties to go west headed for Pike's Peak, under the mistaken impression that this was the site of the strikes. The immigration to Colorado of as many as 100,000 miners in the summer of 1859 was based on better information, and most of these overlanders headed to Cherry Creek. Nevertheless, Pike's Peak retained a prominent place in the gold rush as the site, however erroneously identified, of the original strikes. In addition, the peak itself was, from a distance, the most prominent and visible sign of the Rocky Mountains. That it could be seen some 40 miles distant on a clear day gave the eager argonauts of '59 their first glimpse of what they hoped would be the New El Dorado, the new CALIFORNIA. Consequently, many of the prospective miners who headed west in the summer of 1859 painted "Pike's Peak or Bust" on the sides of their wagons. After the original enthusiasm had spent itself in disappointment, Pike's Peak had another life as a familiar landmark for the flood of gold seekers moving through the area to the Continental Divide.

Further reading: Elliott West, *The Contested Plains: Indians, Gold Seekers, and the Rush to Colorado* (Lawrence: University Press of Kansas, 1997).

Polk, James K. (1795–1849)

The 11th president of the United States, James Knox Polk served only one term in office but is generally credited with accomplishing all of his major goals. Born in Mecklenburg County, North Carolina, into a Presbyterian family of Scottish ancestry, Polk later attended school in Tennessee. He returned to North Carolina to attend the state university at Chapel Hill, graduating from there in 1818 with a reputation for hard work and achievement. After moving back to Tennessee to study law, he was admitted to the bar in 1820 and went on to practice law for three years.

In 1823, Polk was elected to the Tennessee legislature, serving for two years and establishing a friendship with ANDREW JACKSON, the state's most prominent political figure. During that time, he married Sarah Childress. In 1825, he was elected to the U.S. Congress, where he opposed the policies of President JOHN QUINCY ADAMS and was a strong Jackson supporter, a political alliance that continued after Jackson was elected president in 1828. From his position as chairman of the influential Ways and Means Committee, Polk pursued the Jacksonian line of opposition to the SECOND BANK OF THE UNITED STATES. He also supported the president when he issued his controversial veto of the Maysville Road Bill. Polk served a total of 14 years in Congress, rising to become speaker of the House in 1835, a position he held for four years. While in Congress, Polk became a target of criticism from the new WHIG PARTY, which alleged he was nothing more than Jackson's errand boy.

Although a powerful member of Congress, Polk was drafted by his party to run for governor in Tennessee after the Whigs had captured the state's highest office. He was elected governor in 1839, serving ably during his two-year term. He was subsequently defeated for reelection in 1841, however, and lost again two years later when he tried to regain the governorship. The second defeat seemed to end any serious political future for him, but Polk stubbornly continued to remain active, both in Tennessee and nationally.

The DEMOCRATIC PARTY was determined to regain the White House, and most assumed they would nominate former president MARTIN VAN BUREN in 1844. Polk's name was circulated early on as a possible candidate for vice president. The main issue of that year's campaign was the annexation of the Republic of Texas, where SLAVERY was legal, to the United States. Van Buren hurt his hopes for nomination by coming out in opposition to annexation, which he did to head off protests from northern Democrats opposed to the influence of slaveholders within the party. With that stroke, Van Buren opened up the door for another candidate, especially one agreeable to the South. Former president Andrew Jackson was upset with Van Buren's stance on TEXAS, and he began to search for another candidate, eventually throwing his support behind his old protégé, James Knox Polk. The party as a whole remained divided, with Van Buren retaining significant support as the Democratic convention opened in Baltimore in May of 1844. After deadlocking between Van Buren and LEWIS CASS of Michigan, the convention finally turned to Polk, who did support annexation, as a compromise "dark horse" candidate. In accepting the nomination, Polk pledged himself to a single term as president, in an effort to heal the divisions within the party. Polk and running mate George M. Dallas of Pennsylvania, running on an expansionist platform that called for American sovereignty over Texas and the disputed Oregon territory, then defeated Whig stalwart HENRY CLAY of Kentucky in a close election. Polk had been a consistent critic over the years of Clay's AMERICAN SYSTEM. The LIBERTY PARTY candidate, James Birney, had drawn antislavery votes away from Clay that were crucial in a few states, including the key one of New York.

The 49-year-old Polk took office in 1845 as the youngest man to that point to serve as president. Although hampered somewhat by his one-term pledge, he proved to be an extraordinarily hard-working, focused, and in many ways successful president in terms of carrying out his program. He saw his four major goals in office as reducing the tariff; supporting an independent treasury, an institution by which the government kept its deposits separate from private banking interests; settling the Oregon boundary dispute with Britain; and acquiring the huge territory of California from Mexico. Thus, foreign affairs occupied much of his time, to a greater extent than it had most of his predecessors.

President James K. Polk *(Library of Congress)*

Although the United States and Britain had been negotiating over the Oregon territory and what should be the boundary between the United States and Canada, Polk forced the issue to a conclusion. He did so despite some disagreement within his own party on the issue, with Democrats from the Old Northwest favoring expansion and southern Democrats wary of war with Britain and skeptical of adding what was certain to be non-slave territory to the Union. The prospect of armed conflict with Britain ended when the two nations signed the OREGON TREATY OF 1846, with the United States gaining most of the territory in question and Britain retaining Vancouver Island.

Relations with Mexico, however, continued to be strained and had been made worse when the United States annexed Texas shortly before Polk took office. Polk pursued the acquisition of CALIFORNIA by offering to buy it from Mexico, which also owed the United States unpaid debts. When Mexico refused to repay its debts by selling California, Polk planned to ask Congress to declare war on that basis. In the meantime, however, American troops in a disputed area were fired on and killed by the Mexican army. Polk claimed that Mexican forces had actually invaded the United States and attacked its soldiers, which was arguable. In any event, Congress declared war on Mexico, and the United States successfully prosecuted the war, conquering the enemy in a series of spectacular victories and capturing much territory in doing so. The MEXICAN-AMERICAN WAR was not without its critics, with some decrying it as "Mr. Polk's War" and condemning it as a conflict of aggression and expansionism. Polk proved to be a capable wartime leader, as the partisan Democrat was able to work with Whig generals such as WINFIELD SCOTT. Determined to both win the peace and secure California, the Polk administration negotiated with Mexico from a position of strength. Under the TREATY OF GUADALUPE HIDALGO, which formally ended the war, the United States gained title to the huge territory of California and New Mexico. However, the victory contained within it the seeds of civil war, as North and South clashed sharply in the aftermath of the conflict about whether slavery should be allowed in the new territory.

Polk also succeeded politically on the domestic front. At his urging, Congress lowered the tariff, with the new rates remaining in effect for 11 years. As a consistently antibank Democrat, Polk threw his support behind the idea of an independent treasury as well. Overshadowed by the tariff question and the war with Mexico, the independent treasury did not generate the controversy or interest it had in the late 1830s; Polk himself paid minimal attention to it. Nonetheless, the measure became law.

Another important domestic issue which Polk tackled as president was that of INTERNAL IMPROVEMENTS. As befitting a staunch Jacksonian Democrat, he had consistently opposed efforts to use federal funds to build transportation networks, finding such plans to be beyond the constitutional boundaries of the federal government. In vetoing a bill that called for improvements in several western rivers and harbors, Polk said that federal funds for local projects would "produce a disreputable scramble for the public money." Congress failed to override this particular veto, and when Polk later vetoed a similar piece of legislation, he again placed himself firmly in the Jacksonian tradition as he cited Jackson's Maysville Road veto in his own message to Congress. Not only was the Constitution at stake, but the treasury and financial stability of the nation itself would be threatened by federal expenditures for so many projects, he warned.

Having kept his pledge to not run for reelection, Polk left office at the end of his term in 1849. He lived only a few months more, having exhausted himself through his hard work as president. One of the leading examples of a Jacksonian Democrat, Polk has generally received high marks from historians for having set out a specific set of goals as president and then proceeding to achieve them. While not quite as charismatic as his mentor, Polk, who was sometimes called "Little Hickory," is generally considered to have been the most able president between Jackson and Lincoln. He died on June 15, 1849, and was buried in Nashville.

Further reading: Paul H Bergeron. *The Presidency of James K. Polk* (Lawrence: The University Press of Kansas, 1987); Charles Grier Sellers, *James K. Polk, Continentalist* (Princeton, N.J.: Princeton University Press, 1966).

polygamy

In 19th-century America, jurisdiction for the regulation of marriage was a state concern. This resulted in variations in marital law, particularly with regard to the age at which single individuals could marry and which races could marry one another. Under Euro-American law, however, marriage was, universally, a contract entered into by a single man and single woman. Upon marriage, women surrendered most of their legal rights and capabilities to their husbands. Husbands controlled their wives' property, any income they earned, their ability to sue, their ability to contract, and sexual access to their bodies. Wives who committed a crime, signed premarital agreements, had trusts created in their name, or appealed to a court with equity jurisdiction could find exceptions to this general rule. In the words of English jurist Sir William Blackstone, however, a wife was ideally considered to be under the legal "wing, protection, and *cover*" of her husband during marriage. Since women could not vote or be elected to public office, their husbands became their civic representatives. Marriage was the cornerstone of orderly government, prescribing ideal roles for men and women in civil society.

Polygamy, the practice of one man having several wives, was therefore the antithesis of orderly government. From the revolutionary period on, polygamy had been linked with the worst abuses of imperial rule. A husband who took several wives, argued theorists, was akin to a political despot whose power was predicated on the negation of other people's liberty. Bigamy and polygamy were abuses of the roles and responsibilities inherent within the marriage contract—the equal exchange of obligation and privilege between one man and one woman.

Polygamy was a moral and political issue to 19th-century Americans, who looked upon its practice in certain Native American communities as a sign of the latter's uncivilized state of being. Transforming Indian marital practices to mirror those of Euro-Americans was a central priority of the government and of missionary organizations throughout the 19th century. By transforming MARRIAGE AND FAMILY LIFE, they hoped to transform tribal culture. Since Euro-American marriage was weighted with civic meaning, replacing polygamy with monogamy was a stepping-stone to replacing tribal government with a democratic civil order.

It was the practice of polygamy in Utah's Mormon communities, however, that gave many Americans their greatest concern. While settled in Illinois in 1843, JOSEPH SMITH, JR., the leader of the CHURCH OF JESUS CHRIST OF LATTER-DAY SAINTS, received a vision in which Mormons were instructed to practice polygamy. It was nine more years before the revelation was widely known, by which time the Saints had migrated to Utah and Smith had died. While only the wealthiest Mormon men could afford to have several wives, the fact remained that polygamy was being practiced in a U.S. territory. Many Americans were outraged.

For the Mormons, the issue was one of states' rights. The regulation of marriage was of state concern, and the territorial government of Utah resisted attempts to force it to outlaw the practice. As a states' rights issue, the Mormons theoretically should have enjoyed southern support, as the right of a state to regulate domestic law was central to the South's defense of SLAVERY. Southern members of Congress, however, rejected such comparisons, preferring to paint polygamy as northern liberalism run amok. They were aided in this decision by northern arguments that compared slavery and polygamy. Slaveholders were, argued many northern politicians, no better than polygamous husbands themselves, since their female slaves were under their sexual control as much as their wives. To northerners, slavery and polygamy were both breakdowns of democratic social order. Despite the public outcry and moral outrage on all sides, however, Congress did not outlaw the practice of polygamy until well after the Civil War (1861–65).

Further reading: Nancy F. Cott, *Public Vows: A History of Marriage and the Nation* (Cambridge, Mass.: Harvard University Press, 2000); Michael Grossberg, *Governing the Hearth: Law and the Family in Nineteenth Century America* (Chapel Hill: University of North Carolina Press, 1985).

popular sovereignty

Popular sovereignty was put forth in the late 1840s as the moderate answer to the question of whether or not SLAVERY should be extended into the territories. It offered a deceptively simple solution: let the settlers of a territory decide for themselves if they wished to enter the Union as a slave or a free state, without the interference, for or against, of the federal government.

Significantly, northern Democrats first developed the concept as an alternative to the Wilmot Proviso (1846), which would have unilaterally banned slavery from the territories acquired in the MEXICAN-AMERICAN WAR. The proviso was alarmingly popular in the North among both Democrats and Whigs, but deeply repugnant to the southern wing of the DEMOCRATIC PARTY. Popular sovereignty seemed to offer a middle way between the extremes of the proslavery advocates and free-labor positions that were threatening the harmony of the Union. It would also preserve the strength of the national Democratic Party.

First introduced in Congress by New York's Democratic senator Daniel S. Dickinson, popular sovereignty received its most important early support in 1847 from LEWIS CASS, a Democratic senator from Michigan and presidential hopeful. Cass declared that the doctrine should become a policy of the Democratic Party. He denied that Congress had the constitutional right to exclude slavery from the territories, and emphasized the pleasing but ambiguous notion that such decisions were best left to the people themselves. Voters of both sections could support the doctrine, but among other flaws, popular sovereignty left wide open the question of when settlers should make this decision.

Northerners wanted territorial legislatures to make the decision before applying for statehood. They worried that by the time a territory became a state, it would be too late to vote slavery out. This was because the legal structure supporting slavery would already exist and would in turn promote the continued settlement of slaveholders. Southerners assumed the exact opposite and were adamant that neither Congress nor territorial governments had the right to exclude slavery from a territory. To the contrary, they believed that slavery could not be voted in or out until after the territory drafted its constitution in the process of applying for statehood.

Popular sovereignty was included in the COMPROMISE OF 1850, which allowed territorial legislatures in New Mexico and Utah to pass slave codes before filing their state constitutions. The key test of the doctrine of popular sovereignty, however, came in its application to the organization and settlement of land that was not acquired from the Mexican-American War, but rather the last parcel of unorganized land from an earlier land purchase.

In order to get the Kansas-Nebraska Act of 1854 passed with southern support, Senator Stephen A. Douglas of Illinois agreed to abolish the 1820 MISSOURI COMPROMISE line that divided free and slave states in the Louisiana Territories. This act set off a firestorm of protest in the North that led to the "little civil war" in the Kansas territory. It was the beginning of the end for popular sovereignty, which was now in danger of being rejected by both northerners and southerners. As the Kansas fiasco unfolded, the newly elected president James Buchanan hoped that the Supreme Court would decide once and for all the question of slavery in the territories.

In December 1857, the Court's verdict against Dred Scott dealt popular sovereignty and the Missouri Compromise the final blow. The decision in *Dred Scott v. Sandford* asserted that Congress had no power to exclude slavery from the territories, which alarmed many northerners. The decision went further to state that no one, not even the territorial legislatures, could properly exclude slave property from the territories, popular will or not. This part of the opinion was problematical for Democrats. Ever the optimist, Stephen A. Douglas asserted that while *Dred Scott* guaranteed the slaveholder's constitutional rights, slavery could not exist without protective laws voted on by a majority of settlers, whom he assumed would be antislavery. Douglas failed to revive the doctrine in any meaningful fashion, and popular sovereignty faded from the political arena as a viable compromise position to deciding the fate of slavery in the territories.

Further reading: Eric Foner, *Free Soil, Free Labor, Free Men: The Ideology of the Republican Party Before the Civil War* (New York: Oxford University Press, 1995); Kenneth Stampp, *America in 1857: A Nation on the Brink* (New York: Oxford University Press, 1990).

—Chad Vanderford

public land policy

In 1800, as the new American nation began two generations of the greatest expansion in its history, the guidelines for public land policy reflected the Ordinance of 1785. The Land Ordinance (as it was known) embodied certain lasting principles that would continue to guide the evolution of land policy throughout the new century. These fixed principles included: (1) The federal government would acquire title to Indian lands through honorable negotiations; (2) the government would then survey the land before sale based on rectangular divisions of land into townships of six miles square, with the townships divided into 36 sections, or one mile square; (3) section 16 would be set aside to maintain public schools; (4) the government would sell the surveyed lands in minimum lots of 640 acres at the price of $1 per acre; (5) the title would pass in fee simple, that is to say, absolutely, without other annual dues.

Under the Land Act of 1796, the Congress of the new national government under the Constitution of 1789 confirmed the rectangular survey system. The new law raised the minimum price of public land from $1 to $2 an acre with credit of one year. Alternate tiers of townships would be sold in quarter-township lots (5,760 acres) at the national capital, and the other townships would be sold in sections of 640 acres at the newly established land offices at Cincinnati and Pittsburgh. Sales under the new law were few because of the high price, the short period of credit, and the large minimum size of salable tracts. Furthermore, the designated land offices were great distances from settler families. But Congress had begun its first adjustment of terms and the size of tracts; there would be many others. Between 1800 and 1860, Congress would enact more than 3,000 laws dealing with the public domain, but the basic principles of rectangular survey before sale, public auction, and title in fee simple issued by the federal government would remain constant.

The first major change in the land system was the Land Law of 1800 (sometimes known as the Harrison Law for its sponsor, WILLIAM HENRY HARRISON, territorial delegate from the Northwest Territory). Within the broad guidelines of the Land Ordinance, the Land Law of 1800 offered several important modifications to the advantage of individual settler families. It retained the price of $2 an acre but offered four years of credit; the minimum size of a tract to be purchased was reduced from 640 to 320 acres; and it provided for establishing four district land offices in the Northwest Territory, making it more convenient for settler families to transact their land business. Tracts of land would first be sold at public auction held at the district land offices; after the individual tracts had been offered for sale, these lands would be open for private entry at the minimum price. The easier terms and more convenient access encouraged sales, and settlers and speculators alike responded. The credit provisions, however, produced a continuing administrative nightmare of payment calculations. In 1804, Congress further reduced the minimum tract that might be purchased to 160 acres. The sales of the public domain immediately increased.

With the close of the WAR OF 1812, a great surge of immigration to the West began. Settler families moved down the Ohio River and up tributaries into the Old Northwest, across the mountains and into the new southwest of Alabama and Mississippi Territories. Land sales surged; competitive bidding, especially on cotton lands in the South, rose to unheard-of levels of $40 an acre and, in a few cases, to $70 an acre. The credit system encouraged cultivators and speculators to bid and to acquire beyond their means. With the collapse of the ECONOMY in the PANIC OF 1819, a reckoning was at hand. That year, the secretary of the Treasury, William H. Crawford, reported that since 1789, the government had sold lands for $44 million, but only half that sum had been paid, while the other half was still owed. Congress eventually passed 12 relief acts to retire these debts incurred in optimistic times. For the future, and to ensure that the system would never again produce a large land debt owed by the nation's citizens, Congress enacted the Land Law of 1820. This new law abolished the credit system, requiring that all land be paid for in cash (hereafter known as "land office money"). The price was reduced to $1.25 an acre, and the minimum tract was fixed at 80 acres. A family could now buy a farm for $100.

Land legislation over the next generation reflected several threads of settlement patterns and sectional politics. Congress had to pass numerous laws to deal with land claims dating from French and Spanish grants, attempting to meld the two legal and land traditions. The purchase of Louisiana in 1803 and the subsequent organization of the Territory of Orleans (later the state of Louisiana) and the Territory of Louisiana (later the state of Missouri) came to involve the large-scale examination of earlier land grants in these territories west of the Mississippi River. The acquisition of FLORIDA in 1819 would raise the same issues in this new territory. Congress also made numerous gifts of land to individuals and special interests, ranging from veterans of the War of 1812 to educational institutions to cultivators of the vine and the olive. The rising sectional issues reflected the emergence of the West as a distinctive section with its representatives and senators in the Congress and its own special interests. Among these interests was the liberalization of land laws. Whatever the differences that emerged between the Northwest and the Southwest over the issue of SLAVERY, they would agree that liberal access to land would serve the interests of the nation's frontier peoples.

The first major issue was preemption. The principle of preemption affirmed that settlers who made improvements as evidence of their serious intention to occupy and cultivate the land should be entitled to purchase their tracts, up to 160 acres, for the minimum price without competitive bidding. Eastern representatives in Congress argued that preemption rewarded trespassing and illegal settlement, and they were right. But whatever their feelings, it was not possible for the federal government to evict illegal settlers, for no elected official who had hope for a future in politics would use force to eject settler families from the public domain.

While the Congress in Washington debated the merits of preemption, settlers on the frontier fashioned their own remedy. The CLAIM CLUBS brought together settlers in a land district to protect their holdings against bidding by speculators at public auctions. Settlers thus agreed to bid only the minimum, and they physically threatened competitors who might bid against them. Although an extralegal institution, most state, territorial, and local governments accepted claim clubs.

In 1830, the West mustered sufficient support to enact a temporary preemption act. It provided that settlers who had cultivated land on the public domain might purchase their improvements and as many as 160 acres at the minimum price of $1.25 an acre. The act was approved for a year, and Congress renewed the law annually until a permanent preemption law was enacted on 1841. The Pre-emption Act of 1841 reflected a shift in principle that dated back to the Ordinance of 1785 by making settlement by individuals and families a priority over revenue. Henceforth, the land laws of the nation would reflect an increasing liberalization and an acknowledgement that the public domain was to be distributed as widely and generously as possible to actual settler families. Legislation would reflect both the liberalization of terms and attempts to benefit individuals and families as opposed to large-scale speculators.

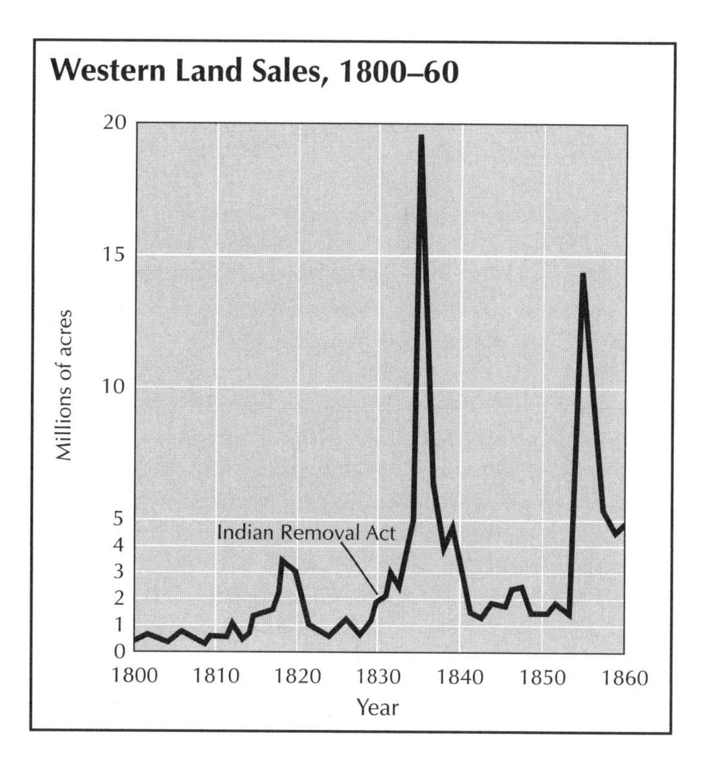

In 1854, in the next landmark law, Congress enacted the principle of graduation. This act provided that lands unsold on the market for long periods would be offered at graduated prices. Lands available on the market for more than 10 years would be sold at $1 an acre; more than 15 years, 75 cents an acre; more than twenty years, 25 cents an acre; more than 30 years, 12½ cents an acre. The law represented a political alliance between East and West (with the South opposed), coming as it did in the midst of a decade characterized by growing sectional feeling. Millions of acres were sold as a result of this liberal law, which was repealed in 1862.

This same East-West alliance worked to enact a Homestead Law that would give free homesteads of 160 acres to settler families. In 1860, President James

Buchanan vetoed a homestead law passed by both houses of Congress. In response, the REPUBLICAN PARTY inserted a strong homestead plank in its platform for the presidential election of 1860. It was a promise that spoke in the strongest terms to western voters.

After Abraham Lincoln's victory in November 1860, the South seceded from the Union, and the Civil War began. Amidst the chaos and confusion of a nation at war, the Republican Congress passed a Homestead Act in 1862, fulfilling an important election promise. The law offered any citizen of the republic—or any immigrant who intended to become a citizen, was head of a family, and was over 21 year of age—a tract of 160 acres in the public domain after five years of residence. The entrant had to pay registration fees and administrative costs, but the idea of "free land" to settlers was as much a reality as Congress and the president could make it. As an added benefit, the homestead was exempt from attachment for debt.

With the passage of the Homestead Law, an era in the history of the public domain had ended. This 60-year period was characterized by adherence to the basic principles of the Ordinance of 1785; by the continuous liberalizing of terms under which the public domain might be acquired; and by the gradual acceptance of the principle that the public domain was not a source of revenue but, instead, a resource to be distributed to the citizens of the republic on the most liberal terms possible. The public land system had provided guidelines for the greatest physical expansion in the nation's history, and it had offered to the citizens of the republic generally fertile and well-watered lands. If it was true that some had benefited more than others in the sense of acquiring larger tracts, it was also true that almost everyone who had sought lands had acquired something. The opportunities for landownership under this system were unique in the history of the world.

In the next generation, from the close of the Civil War to the end of the century, the nation would continue its expansion at an unparalleled pace into the distant lands of the trans-Mississippi West and then to the shores of the Pacific. In so doing, settlers and speculators would find new landscape and new climates that would dramatically transform the ways that Americans thought about the public domain. It would gradually dawn on citizens, pioneer families, and officials alike that the old land laws were inapplicable to the challenges of the new, distant West.

Further reading: Vernon Carstensen, *The Public Domain* (Madison: University of Wisconsin Press, 1963); Paul Wallace Gates, *History of Public Land Law Development* (Washington, D.C.: U.S. Government Printing Office, 1968); Malcolm J. Rohrbough, *The Land Office Business* (New York: Oxford University Press, 1968).

R

race and race relations

The United States in the 19th century was a nation composed of a rapidly growing and racially diverse population. It was also a nation in which social, economic, and political power and legal status were determined by race. Despite the 1776 pronouncement in the Declaration of Independence that the fledgling nation was to be one founded on the principle that "all men are created equal," race, racism, and racial inequality would, by 1865, be deeply woven into the U.S. legal, societal, and cultural fabric. Throughout the century, members of the so-called white race (also referred to commonly as the Anglo-Saxon or European race) dominated over those deemed members of different, and allegedly inferior, racial groups. Prior to the Civil War (1861–65), three processes—SLAVERY, expansion, and IMMIGRATION—that were fundamental to the development of the nation also fostered and structured its system of race relations. The precedents these processes set for racial interaction during the first half of the 19th century would persist well into the 20th century.

Americans did not invent "race" and "racism," but these concepts determined life in the 19th-century United States as a nation of political power and privilege for white males. After the U.S. Constitution was ratified in 1788, the nascent federal government passed the Naturalization Act in 1790. According to this act, only "free white persons" were entitled to become U.S. citizens. Even more significant than the laws governing who could become citizens were the laws that defined which citizens could vote. Initially, these were only white, male property owners and taxpayers. This initial restriction on democratic participation was directed not only toward nonwhite and female populations but toward landless and poor white males. However, by the 1850s, most states lifted economic requirements, and suffrage became universal—but only for white men. Although the laws for citizenship and voting were modified several times prior to the Civil War, it was not until after the passage of the Fourteenth Amendment in 1868 and the Fifteenth Amendments in 1870 that voting and citizenship were extended to freed slaves and people of African descent. It would be several more decades before other non-whites, and women generally, were granted eligibility to citizenship and enfranchisement.

Nothing shaped racial thinking and race relations more than the institution of slavery. By the middle of the 19th century, to be a slave meant to be black, to be of African heritage, and to be burdened with the weight of dehumanizing negative racial stereotyping. Almost from the beginning of British and European settlement, various colonies, particularly those with slave-labor economies, established laws demarcating lines between slave and the white populations. The colony of Virginia, for example, passed laws in the 1670s prohibiting free blacks from owning white servants or striking or physically harming white persons. Laws were promulgated in various colonies that denied slaves the right to vote, prohibited their testimony in court, and prevented them from holding any public office.

Yet the laws that were designed to separate the races were those that prohibited miscegenation, or interracial relationships. Whites were greatly troubled by such relationships for numerous reasons, including the general fear of interracial sexual unions, the blurring of a child's status as a slave or free person, and a child's inheritance rights. Miscegenation made clear the malleability of racial classification. In 1691, Virginia passed the first antimiscegenation law "for the prevention of that abominable mixture and spurious issue." Other colonies followed suit. Most of these laws targeted "Negroes" and "mulattoes" (mixed-race people), but Native Americans were usually included in the list of those prohibited from romantic or sexual relations with whites. These laws also uniformly barred such relations only with regard to white women. White men were not legally prevented from entering into relationships with slave women or other nonwhite women. However, their children, should paternity be proved, would be considered slaves and nonwhite. Because determining a person's racial lineage was so difficult and the anxieties about racial separation so great, many laws were later adopted stating that even "one drop" of nonwhite blood meant a person was nonwhite.

Laws that limited the political activity of slaves and prevented interracial marriage were designed, in part, to reenforce racial attitudes and the notion that blacks were less than human and, as slaves, were to be considered property. The U.S. Constitution did not recognize a slave as a whole person but only as three-fifths of a person. In 1850, the federal government passed the Fugitive Slave Law, which empowered slaveholders to retrieve their slaves, as private property, in free states and territories. The notion that slaves were merely chattel was reenforced by the U.S. Supreme Court in *Dred Scott v. Sandford* (1857). The Court ruled that black people, slave or free, were not U.S. citizens and therefore could not sue in federal courts and that U.S. government could not interfere with a slave owner's right to his property.

What made the Supreme Court's ruling in the *Dred Scott* case unsurprising was a U.S. culture greatly influenced by theories about race and racial difference. In order to defend slavery, an institution that denied slaves their freedom and humanity, southern slave owners and proslavery advocates from the 17th century onward propounded theories based on racial difference that set slaves apart from free people. These racial theories defined people of African descent as suitable only for slavery and servitude. Although proslavery thinking differed and at times conflicted, it always relied on an assumption of racial distinction between "black" slaves and "white" free people. Slavery was defended on biblical grounds as well as on outward physical difference. Some proslavery advocates believed in monogenesis, having one origin, and argued that differing environmental conditions promoted racial variation. A superior environment enabled white people to emerge as a superior race. Other proslavery Christians maintained that black people were the children of Ham, the disgraced son of Noah, and therefore condemned to a life of servitude. Those who believed in polygenesis, or having many sources, defended slavery and maintained that black people were a completely separate species and therefore excluded from the rules governing white humanity. Proslavery advocates explained that slavery was a positive good either because it regulated slaves, who were subhuman and dangerous, or paternalistically cared for slaves, who were childlike and helpless.

In the 1820s, "scientific" studies of race first appeared in numbers. These studies and their authors were to have a growing influence on how Americans saw race and racial groups. The following half-century was a period of growing study of science and the impact of science on American life. Among the most important figures were Louis Agassiz (1807–73) and Arnold Henry Guyot (1807–84), who represented the gradual separation of science from theology, and the efforts on the part of men like Guyot to reconcile the growing scientific discoveries of the 19th century with the Bible.

Issues of race and the racial dimension of scientific theories had its first important scientific spokesman in Samuel George Morton (1799–1851). Like other scientific figures of the period, Morton trained as a doctor and began his professional career practicing medicine. While Morton's career as a doctor developed gradually over time, he used his spare time to pursue scientific interests. Among his early pursuits were a study in paleontology that analyzed the fossils collected by MERIWETHER LEWIS and WILLIAM CLARK on their celebrated expedition to the West. But Morton's most important study, begun in 1830, focused on the study of human skulls, or craniology. His work eventually encompassed the scientific measurement of more than 1,000 skulls. Through a wide correspondence network that stretched around the world, Morton had access to specimens from all over the globe, from which he deduced capacity of the skulls' interior. In 1839 he published *Carnia Americana* (1839), a study that confirmed the division of humankind into five races: American, Caucasian, Ethiopian, Malay, and Mongolian. In this study, Morton argued that the American race was one species that included groups from South America to the Canadian border, and that the physical characteristics of different races were independent of external causes. Many scientists praised Morton's theories, including Agassiz, but they were particularly popular among southern supporters of slavery, who energetically proposed and defended the theory that human races had different origins and did not belong to the same family. Morton's work was so important that scientists at the time referred to an "American school" of physical anthropology.

The most important racial theorist of the first half of the 19th century was Josiah Clark Nott (1804–73). Also trained as a medical doctor, Nott was first associated with the growing independence of scientific research from theologians and religion. In 1843, he published an article on mulattoes that began his work on race, which would lead to an international reputation. He became a leader in the American School of Ethnology, a group that included Samuel George Morton. Nott came to be regarded as a friend and respected scientist by many northern men of science, including Louis Agassiz. Nott believed that wide differences in innate capacity marked the different races; these differences were especially marked between blacks and whites. Like others, Nott argued that blacks and whites belonged to separate species without a common origin. Because of these innate differences, blacks were suitable to slavery because their limited capacity prevented them from competing against superior races. In the long run, American Indians and the colored races were doomed to extinction unless they had a protected role in slavery. An important corollary of these theories was the central role of the superior races in human progress over the centuries, and to continue this progress, the superior races should be kept pure, hence the fear of racial amalgamation. Nott brought these theories together in his *Types of Mankind* (jointly written with George R. Gidden). Published in 1854, this work was regarded as the accepted account of racial origins in the 1850s, and it was republished in several editions over the next 20 years.

Even opponents of slavery, primarily northern abolitionists who argued for the abolishment of the institution on biblical grounds and believed in the slaves' basic humanity, viewed African Americans as racially different and inferior. Most abolitionists were neither egalitarians nor integrationists. They shared the same attitudes as proslavery paternalists. In fact, during the first half of the 19th century, many abolitionists and moderate critics of slavery, including Harriet Beecher Stowe and Abraham Lincoln, supported recolonization of slaves and free blacks to Africa. Such a plan was actively pursued by the AMERICAN COLONIZATION SOCIETY. Only William Lloyd Garrison and fellow radicals argued in favor of racial equality and integration, but they were on the distant fringe of the ABOLITION MOVEMENT.

Racial animus was directed not just at black slaves but at free blacks as well. Even in liberal northern states, such as Massachusetts, free blacks suffered from racial discrimination in the larger society and culture, particularly among the growing white working-class population, who saw free blacks as a challenge to their employment. Despite the prominent role free black Americans like Fredrick Douglass and Sojourner Truth played in the abolition movement, the majority of white Americans viewed slaves and free blacks as being a distinct and lesser race.

By the outbreak of the Civil War in 1861, the debates over slavery and theories of race were largely inseparable. Slavery proponents and critics not only marshaled existing race ideologies for their causes, they also refined and altered such ideologies to fit their needs. Even those who condemned slavery and demanded immediate emancipation considered blacks to be a separate race, and, consequently, saw themselves as the superior race because of their white skins. In 1859, British scientist Charles Darwin published *Origin of Species.* Although Darwin's theories of evolution and natural selection were popularized too late to help the cause of slavery on the eve of the Civil War, these theories would add scientific legitimacy to racial thinking and racism during the second half of the 19th century.

Race thinking and racism were as integral to U.S. expansionism in the 19th century as they were to slavery. Proexpansionist Americans used racial difference, primarily that between American Indian peoples and white settlers, to justify their quest for territory. From the beginning of European colonization of North America, whites encountered indigenous people. Most white settlers viewed the Native American population as a dangerous obstacle occupying valuable territory. They constructed their struggles with indigenous people in racial terms. Whites cast Native Americans as "uncivilized" and "savages" in order to validate the breaking of treaties and the use of violence to seize land. More charitable white Americans did not see Native Americans as inherently "savage." In fact, in a racial hierarchy that was developing over the course of the 19th century, Native Americans were placed above slaves. However, they were still considered by most whites as racially subordinate. Thomas Jefferson, for example, held such views, and as president offered Native American people incorporation into U.S. society and good treatment if they agreed to surrender their lands and assimilate white behaviors. For those who refused this option, Jefferson offered them lands west of the Mississippi.

Jefferson's views, however, were not predominant in the United States. President ANDREW JACKSON, a Tennessee slave owner, who gained his reputation as a violent "Indian Fighter" against the Creek and Seminole peoples during the War of 1812, rejected the notion that Indians were assimilable. As president, he won the passage of the INDIAN REMOVAL ACT in 1830, which forcibly pushed all Indian peoples west. Native Americans were thus presented with the miserable choices of evacuation, assimilation, or extinction. White Americans justified this harsh treatment with race ideologies.

Over the course of the 19th century, race thinking and racism would continue to bolster white Americans' expansionism. The notion of MANIFEST DESTINY characterized the U.S. domestic, expansionist policy. According to Manifest Destiny, white Americans, specifically Anglo-Saxons, were preordained to expand across the North American continent. Anglo-Saxons were to rule over, "Christianize" and "civilize" nonwhites, including black slaves, the Indian peoples, and Mexicans, who were incorporated into the United States after the MEXICAN-AMERICAN WAR (1846–48). This racially charged expansionism would lead to more violent clashes with Native Americans and other nonwhite peoples following the Civil War. It would also be used as a rationale for overseas expansion at the century's conclusion.

Ironically, President Jackson's term in office was also called the period of "Jacksonian Democracy" and the celebration of equality among Americans. However, this democracy was open only to white American men. It stressed the unity of white people at a time when even "whiteness" was not necessarily racially uniform. From the 1830s through the Civil War period, the United States witnessed a dramatic increase in immigration from famine-stricken Ireland and politically turbulent Germany. In 1854, the number of immigrants entering the country was nearly 500,000. For the majority population of Protestant Americans, this influx of new immigrants, who were primarily poor, uneducated, and Catholic, was threatening. Irish immigrants in particular drew the ire of Anglo-Saxon Americans, who initially characterized them as a substandard race. Such anti-immigrant sentiment spawned pride in Anglo-Saxonism and the formation of short-lived, but dramatic nativist politics at mid-century.

Although white Protestant Americans were concerned about the increasing immigration of non-Protestant Europeans, the influx of Chinese immigrants created even greater anxiety. The Chinese came to the United States during the CALIFORNIA GOLD RUSH of 1849. Full-blown anti-Asian racism would not develop until the late 19th century, but white Americans, especially those on the West Coast, began establishing early barricades against Chinese immigration and integration into U.S. society. In the 1850s, white state legislatures passed laws that taxed only Chinese miners. Naturalization laws prevented Chinese immigrants, defined as nonwhite, from becoming citizens. Even the U.S. Supreme Court denied Chinese the right to testify in court in the *People v. Hall* decision (1854). As with slavery and expansionism, race and racial difference justified the white American response to and regulation of immigration.

By the time the Civil War concluded in 1865, race thinking and racism were well-entrenched in U.S. culture, society, and law. Although the post–Civil War amendments to the Constitution ended slavery, gave free slaves citizenship, and enfranchised black men, this did not usher in an alteration in race relations. In fact, race became a more significant factor in U.S. life and politics as white Americans confronted a newly freed black population, a more intransigent Native American population, and an ever-increasing non-Protestant, nonwhite immigrant population. In their struggle to maintain supremacy, white Americans would rely on race and race theories, especially scientific theory, to legitimize the use of violence and terror, segregation, race-based immigrant exclusion, and war to maintain their hold on power. It would not be until World War II that the United States would see a gradual liberalization in racial thinking, a rollback of racist policies, and the recognition of nonwhite peoples' civil rights.

Further reading: George Fredrickson, *The Black Image in the White Mind: The Debate on Afro-American Character and Destiny, 1817–1914* (Hanover, N.H.: Wesleyan University Press, 1987); Matthew Frye Jacobson, *Whiteness of a Different Color: European Immigrants and the Alchemy of Race* (Cambridge, Mass.: Harvard University Press, 1999); Ronald Takaki, *Iron Cages: Race and Culture in 19th-Century America* (New York: Oxford University Press, 1990); Ronald Takaki, *Strangers from a Different Shore: A History of Asian Americans* (New York: Penguin Books, 1989).

—Charles V. Hawley

railroads

By 1815 there were few nations in the world with a greater need for an effective transportation system than the United States. With the uncertainties of national survival overcome, Americans were beginning to move west over the Allegheny Mountains. Although most of the nation's population lived near the seaboard, and the rivers draining into the ocean provided adequate local transportation, the need to travel inland was increasing, and the lack of transportation across the mountains was a major hindrance.

The first idea of a railroad in the United States had been advanced before the Revolutionary War when the great American inventor Oliver Evans suggested the construction of a steam-powered railroad between Philadelphia and New York. Evans, who was not adequately appreciated by his contemporaries, had been experimenting with steam engines to power millstones. By 1801, he had constructed an amphibious steam carriage that chugged around Philadelphia, convincing people that Evans was deranged. Unfortunately, his inventions were ahead of their time, and he was unable to secure funds to perfect them. He died in 1819, convinced that future steam locomotives would pull passenger trains up to 300 miles per day. Most of his contemporaries continued to derive great mirth from Evan's predictions, but many of them lived to see him vindicated.

Probably the first known transportation system to actually use rails in the United States was constructed in 1795 to transport rock and cement in the Boston area. In 1807, another railway was constructed in Boston by Silas Whitney. Two years later, Thomas Leiper built a railroad to a stone quarry near Philadelphia, and in May 1827 a nine-mile line was constructed to a coal mine in Pennsylvania. The longest early railroad was the Delaware & Hudson (D&H) Canal Company's 29-mile gravity railroad from its Honesdale, Pennsylvania, coal mines to the D&H canal at Roundout, New York. All of these railroads, however, used wooden rails and horse or mule power. Most of the lines were gravity lines, where cars coasted downgrade with loads and were drawn back up to the mine or oven by animal power. With the exception of the D&H line, they were also quite short. These lines were designed to haul a single cargo to the point where it was to be used or to haul it to a better-developed and more efficient source of water transportation.

The first incorporated railroad in the United States was the Granite Railway Company of Massachusetts,

This engraving depicts a race between Peter Cooper's locomotive Tom Thumb and a railcar pulled by a horse. *(Hulton/Archive)*

which was chartered by the state on March 4, 1826. Its purpose, hauling blocks of granite for the construction of the Bunker Hill Monument, was similar to that of the earliest railroads. The Granite Railway was only three miles long and was powered by horses. It was also the first railroad to utilize wooden rails overlaid with iron. The line eventually became part of the New York, New Haven & Hartford Railroad.

The first known charter for an intercity railroad in the United States was granted to New Jersey in 1815 to Colonel John Stevens. Stevens had been attempting to secure this charter since 1811, and in 1812 he petitioned Congress to support a national railroad. Since Colonel Stevens was not as eccentric as Evans, he was regarded more seriously. In 1825, he operated one of the first live-steam model railroads—a locomotive that ran around a loop of track on his lawn.

One of the major reasons people were unwilling to back Stevens was that most Americans believed an effective transportation system had already been developed. The same year Stevens first operated his live-steam model, the great engineering marvel of the new nation, the ERIE CANAL, had been opened. The canal opened the west to New York City and, furthermore, provided a laboratory for the training of many American civil and mechanical engineers, such as John Jervis. Until the 1840s, canals remained competitive with railroads in the question over which could provide better transportation. Eventually, the high initial cost of canals, the fact that they froze over in the winter in many parts of the country, and the slow speed of the boats allowed the railroad to win out. Canals continued, however, to transport bulk commodities, such as coal, that did not require speedy or timely delivery. Canals never were able to overcome their problem dealing with mountainous terrain. Railroads proved to be more adaptable to the severe grades faced by projects moving to the West.

Thus, by the late 1820s, railroads clearly promised to be one facet of a transportation system that the new nation could utilize to, in the words of JOHN C. CALHOUN, "bind the Republic together with a perfect system of roads and canals." Although railroads were in their infancy when Calhoun made his statement in 1817, by 1830 they were already looming as a major factor in interstate transportation. Two major factors combined in the 1820s to increase the need for all forms of transportation. One was the tremendous population growth of the states west of the original 13 states (Kentucky, Tennessee, Ohio, Louisiana, Indiana, Mississippi, Illinois, Alabama, and Missouri). In 1810, these states or territories contained 15 percent of the total U.S. population, but by 1830 this figure had grown to 28 percent. Trade with this increasingly populous region was extremely important for the East. The topography of the Midwest provided adequate river transportation down the Ohio and Mississippi Rivers to New Orleans. Early efforts were made to improve transportation by connecting the Great Lakes and the Ohio River by canal. If the East did not develop an effective transportation link with these western states, those in the West would be forced to trade primarily with New Orleans. By 1825, a significant number of steamboats were already competing to make the best time to and from New Orleans.

The second major factor was the rivalry that developed between the major eastern cities for dominance in the western trade. There were five major American coastal cities in the early 19th century: Boston, New York, Philadelphia, Baltimore, and Charleston. New York and Philadelphia had the initial edge for the western trade because of their size and huge financial resources. Baltimore's convenient and strategically placed harbor allowed it to join the "big two." Both Boston and Charleston gradually fell behind in the battle for the western trade, Boston because it was located farther from the western states than the other

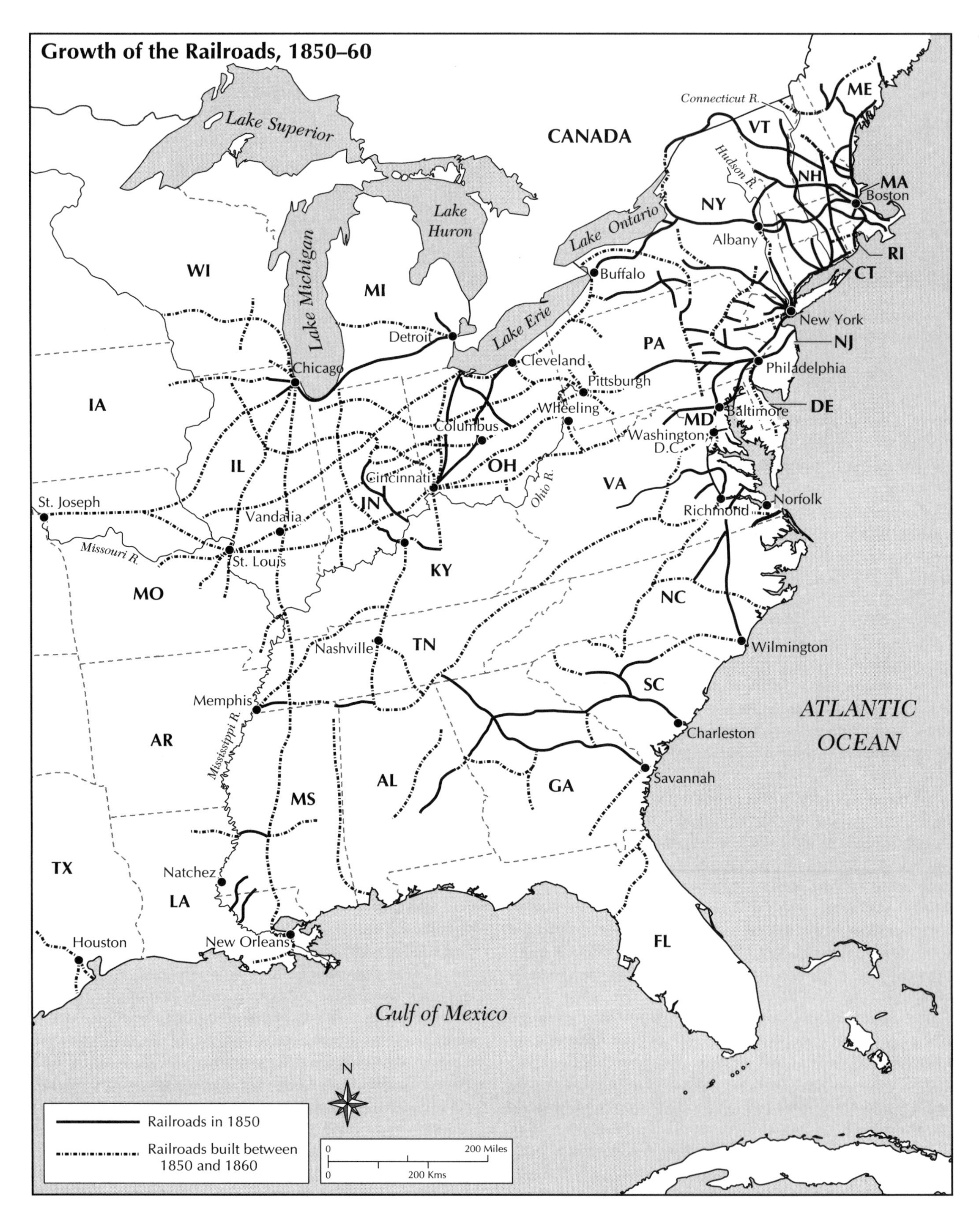
Growth of the Railroads, 1850–60
Lake Superior
CANADA
Connecticut R.
ME
VT
Hudson R.
NH
MA
Boston
Lake Huron
Lake Michigan
NY
Albany
RI
CT
Lake Ontario
WI
MI
Buffalo
New York
NJ
Lake Erie
Detroit
PA
Chicago
Cleveland
Philadelphia
Pittsburgh
IA
Wheeling
Baltimore
DE
MD
Columbus
Washington, D.C.
OH
IL
Cincinnati
Ohio R.
VA
St. Joseph
IN
Richmond
Norfolk
Vandalia
Missouri R.
St. Louis
KY
MO
NC
Nashville
TN
Wilmington
Memphis
SC
ATLANTIC OCEAN
Charleston
AR
Mississippi R.
AL
GA
Savannah
MS
TX
Natchez
LA
Houston
New Orleans
FL
Gulf of Mexico
N
Railroads in 1850
Railroads built between 1850 and 1860
0
200 Miles
0
200 Kms

cities, and Charleston because it did not have the capital base of the merchant-oriented northern cities. Boston, in particular, still attempted to gain its share of the western trade indirectly by trading with New Orleans, but the city was less and less successful as the century progressed.

Early railroads had one of three purposes. First, there were the short lines, like the Granite Railway of Massachusetts, whose major purpose was to carry a single product a short distance. Second, there were the intercity railroads or western lines that attempted to link up cities or markets in a linear fashion, the BALTIMORE & OHIO RAILROAD being a primary example. Finally, there were railroads designed to provide transportation to local markets in a major city. Such cities usually had lines radiating out from them like the spokes on a wheel. Boston was the leading example of this type of railroad system, with lines running to Lowell, Fitchburg, and Worcester, Massachusetts; Norwich, Connecticut; and Providence, Rhode Island.

With the success of such railroads as the Baltimore & Ohio, the South Carolina, and the Mohawk & Hudson, a type of "railroad fever" swept many parts of the nation. Opposition to the railroads came from people who stood to lose business and money because of their introduction. Sometimes railroad workers were shot at and beaten up, sections of railroad were torn up, and locomotives and rolling stock were damaged. But such opposition did not last long. Railroads were infinitely superior to canals and turnpikes, and the feared displacement of workers did not occur.

The Baltimore & Ohio was not the first railroad to reach the western waters from one of three competing eastern cities; rail service between the Hudson River and the Great Lakes had been available since the 1840s. About 10 short connecting railroads, including the Mohawk & Hudson, constituted an unincorporated "Central Line," but the trip from New York to Albany had to be made by riverboat until 1852, when it was possible to travel from New York to Lake Erie by rail. Philadelphia businessmen began a western railroad late compared to Baltimore, but, once started, they pushed its construction across Pennsylvania with vigor. The Pennsylvania Railroad was incorporated in 1846, and by 1852, also a little ahead of the B&O, the line was completed to Pittsburgh. Until 1854, this line had to use inclined planes to reach over the Allegheny Mountains. Thus, rail lines from all three cities reached western waters at Buffalo, Pittsburgh, and Wheeling at about the same time.

Another early railroad associated with Philadelphia and New York was the Camden & Amboy (C&A), built by Robert L. and Edwin A. Stevens, the sons of Colonel John Stevens. After acquiring a charter in 1830, the C&A was constructed from Camden, New Jersey, across the river from Philadelphia, to South Amboy, New Jersey, on the ocean 30 miles south of New York City. Final connections to both cities involved ferry boats. Direct connections on rails leased or owned by the Pennsylvania Railroad from west of Philadelphia to New York were not obtained until after the Civil War. From the 1850s to 1863, New York-bound traffic from Pennsylvania had to be turned over to Philadelphia & Reading at Harrisburg. The C&A dominated transportation between Philadelphia and New York for over 30 years.

Railroad construction in New England did not lag behind that in the Middle Atlantic states merely because Boston appeared to be out of the race for western trade. Eventually the railroads radiating out of Boston made efforts to connect with key markets in three specific directions. First, a series of lines, including the Fitchburg and the Vermont Central, attempted to link Boston with eastern Canada, thus directing Canadian trade to and from Boston. Second, attempts were made, primarily through the Western Railroad of Massachusetts, to link Boston with Albany and the "Central Line" to Buffalo and the western trade. Third, via predecessors of the Boston & Maine and the New York, New Haven & Hartford, efforts were made to link Boston with New York. All of these efforts succeeded to some degree, but they were unable to restore Boston to the economic preeminence it enjoyed in the 18th century.

Until the 1850s, the financing of railroads involved a combination of private and public capital. The coal-mine lines were low-cost affairs financed by the owners of the mines and quarries themselves. The Baltimore & Ohio and the South Carolina Railroad were essentially city projects, and most of the money came in the form of municipal bonds or other forms of public support. Exceptions such as the Camden & Amboy were financed primarily by individual investors, who also played a minor early role in the B&O and the South Carolina Railroad. The Pennsylvania Railroad, during the late 1840s and early 1850s, was heavily financed by state and local commitments; in 1857, however, an amendment to the Pennsylvania state constitution made it illegal for counties, municipalities, or townships to invest public funds in railway construction. Thereafter, the issuance of stocks and bonds formed the basis for financing Pennsylvania's railroads. Several other states developed similar prohibitions on using public money to support what were frequently dubious railroad construction projects. Prior to the Civil War, little capital to support railroad construction came from outside the United States.

In 1830, 23 miles of railroad were in operation. This figure grew to 2,818 miles in 1840 and to 9,021 miles in 1850. The year in which the greatest mileage was put into service was 1850, with 1,261 miles added. By 1860, 30,626 miles of railroad were in operation. Part of the reason for the success of railroads was the speed and relatively low cost of the transportation. In 1853, the cost of moving a ton of freight one mile by turnpike was approximately $15, while the rate on most railroads ranged between $1 and $2.

River transportation, costing about 37 cents, was the least expensive, but rivers did not always flow where the freight had to go.

By the time of the Civil War, an extensive network of railroads covered New England, the Middle Atlantic states, Ohio, Indiana, Illinois, and the southern Michigan and Wisconsin. Lines in the South were less numerous, but all states had at least one rail line. In states like Texas, Florida, Louisiana, and Alabama, many of the lines were isolated with no outside connections, which was seldom the case in the North. The South had little of what could be termed a railroad system, but the North had already progressed a long way toward developing such a system.

Further reading: Sarah Gordon, *Passage to Union: How the Railroads Transformed American Life* (Chicago: Ivan R. Dee, 1996); John F. Stover, *American Railroads* (Chicago: University of Chicago Press, 1997).

religion

The early 19th century was a time of great religious ferment in the United States. Most Americans were Christians, but the unity of this background disguised great variety. New forms of Christianity, such as Mormonism, were being born; old denominations were undergoing revival, change, conflict, and fragmentation. IMMIGRATION was changing religious demographics, as Roman Catholics arrived in large numbers. Religious ideas inspired social reform, utopian experiments, and movements as varied as transcendentalism and spiritual communication with the dead.

Religious revivals swept the nation from the 1790s to the 1830s in a movement called the SECOND GREAT AWAKENING; this commemorated the Great Awakening in the thirteen colonies in the 1730s and 1740s. The Second Great Awakening was marked by Evangelicalism, an enthusiastic way of spreading the Gospel that deemphasized reason and learning in favor of emotional, personal acceptance of God's offer of grace. Coming into being at the end of the 18th century, the movement sprang forward from two areas. In Kentucky, Presbyterian pastor James McGready started the tradition of outdoor revivals called camp meetings. In Connecticut, Congregationalist Timothy Dwight, president of Yale College from 1795 to 1817, sought to correct the irreligion of Yale students by heartfelt preaching and common-sense application of religious truths to life.

One of Dwight's students, Presbyterian Lyman Beecher, furthered the Second Great Awakening with revival services in Boston beginning in 1826. CHARLES GRANDISON FINNEY left his law practice in 1821 to make upstate New York a hotbed of revivalism. Methodist bishop Francis Asbury used revivalistic preaching to spread Methodism in western frontier areas and in settled regions of the East. Tirelessly crisscrossing the country on horseback, Asbury set an example for other circuit riders, Methodist preachers who covered a large territory through regular travel.

Women found opportunities to testify and preach at revival meetings, though usually without being ordained as clergy. A prominent woman preacher was Phoebe Palmer, who in the 1830s began to preach a message of holiness later promoted through her periodical *Guide to Holiness* (1864–74).

The printing of Bibles and a growing interest in religious education were indicators of the spiritual fervor of the times. In 1816, the American Bible Society was founded to distribute English-language Bibles to Americans; it was soon publishing 300,000 copies a year. In 1824, the American Sunday School Union was formed to provide general and religious instruction. The spread of missions and the formation of missionary societies were other signs of widespread zeal. Congregationalist missionaries brought the Gospel to the Sandwich Islands, now Hawaii, in 1819. Other American missionaries were venturing as far as Burma and Africa by the 1820s. Closer to home, missionaries, with federal government aid, proselytized and educated Native Americans, particularly the Five Civilized Tribes (Cherokee, Choctaw, Creek, Chickasaw, and Seminole). This mission effort was severely disrupted by the forced removal of Native Americans from the Southeast in the 1830s.

Evangelical Christianity was linked to reform movements such as temperance, the movement against alcohol consumption; and abolitionism, the movement to end SLAVERY. Christians were involved in founding the Society for the Promotion of Temperance in 1826 and the American Temperance Union in 1836. Christian teaching about human equality before God was an important spur to the antislavery activists who founded the AMERICAN COLONIZATION SOCIETY (1819), which was aimed at resettling freed slaves in Africa; and the AMERICAN ANTI-SLAVERY SOCIETY (1833). Harriet Beecher Stowe, author of the antislavery novel *Uncle Tom's Cabin* (1852), was a daughter of the revivalist preacher Lyman Beecher. Some Christians, particularly Quakers, took grave risks to participate in the Underground Railroad, a clandestine network that transported fugitive southern slaves to free regions in the northern United States and Canada.

Although Christians in the North were increasingly likely to oppose slavery, those in the South, where slavery was concentrated, were increasingly likely to justify it, often on Biblical grounds. From the 1760s to about the 1820s, southern Methodists and Baptists had opposed slavery, but by the 1830s they had largely joined the South's defense of its "peculiar institution." Differences about slavery led to schisms in many denominations, including Presbyterians, Methodists, and Baptists. The Southern Baptist Convention, which would become the largest body of Baptists,

Engraving showing a preacher and his audience on a southern plantation *(Billy Graham Center Museum)*

formed in 1845 to distinguish itself from northern Baptists who forbade missionaries to own slaves.

African Americans, whether slave or free, sometimes worshiped with whites during this period (usually in separate sections) and sometimes formed churches of their own. Baptist and Methodist preachers in the early 19th century converted a growing number of southern slaves to evangelical Christian worship. Black Christians formed their own meeting houses and developed distinctive spirituals, folk hymns indebted both to African tradition and to the white spirituals sung at revivalist camp meetings. Some blacks kept alive the religious traditions of West Africa, often mingled with Christianity. Voodoo or vodun, practiced in Louisiana, was a blend of Roman Catholicism and West African religion.

African-American preaching often contained references to Moses and Exodus, drawing an analogy between black slaves and the Hebrew slaves whom God had freed from bondage in Egypt. Sometimes the radical implications of this imagery went beyond preaching. In the South, Christian teaching, with its message of equality before God, was sometimes used to justify slave rebellions, such as Denmark Vesey's in Charleston, South Carolina, in 1822; and Nat Turner's in Southampton County, Virginia, in 1831.

Black churches took shape in the North as well as the South. The African Methodist Episcopal (A.M.E.) Church, an independent Methodist denomination, was founded in Philadelphia in 1816 by former slave Richard Allen, who became its first bishop. Allen started the church after being outraged by enforcement of segregation rules in a white-controlled Methodist church. The African Methodist Episcopal Zion (A.M.E.Z.) Church, another black Methodist denomination, was established as a national body in 1821.

With all the changes underway, it was no wonder that religious demographics shifted. In 1800, the Congregationalists were the nation's largest denomination, followed in order by Presbyterians, Baptists, Episcopalians, Methodists, and Roman Catholics. But by 1850, Roman Catholics and Methodists were vying for first place, followed by Baptists, Presbyterians, and Congregationalists. Episcopalians were no longer in the top five, and the wholly new Disciples of Christ were in sixth place.

Congregationalism, a denomination descended from New England's Puritans, was split by the secession of Unitarianism. Rejecting the Trinity and preaching human perfectibility and universal salvation, Unitarians had been active in the United States since the late 18th century, drawing on roots that dated to the 16th century in Switzerland and Poland. Many Congregationalists, particularly the intellectual and social elite, quietly embraced Unitarian belief, but the sect did not fully come into its own until after William Ellery Channing's influential sermon "Unitarian Christianity," delivered in Baltimore in 1819. In the 1820s, the American Unitarian Association formed, with Channing as its first president, attracting many Congregational churches.

Unitarians shifted in the early 19th century from emphasizing scripture to stressing reason and service to humankind. This shift gathered force in New England in the 1830s and 1840s under the influence of Unitarian minister Theodore Parker and essayist RALPH WALDO EMERSON. Universalism, a denomination with tenets similar to Unitarianism, spread about this time in rural and small-town areas of the Midwest, particularly Ohio, Indiana, and Illinois.

Those churches that remained Congregationalist retained the Calvinist orthodoxy inherited from 16th-century Protestant theologian John Calvin, but exhibited tensions between liberals and conservatives. Nathaniel W. Taylor, first professor of theology at Yale Divinity School, created a schism when he questioned the doctrine of election and other Calvinist tenets. "Taylorism," as it was known, was so detested by conservatives as to prompt the formation of a pastoral Union for the suppression of heresy (1833). Horace Bushnell, Congregational minister, author of *Christian Nurture* (1847) and *God in Christ* (1849), stressed the presence of divinity in nature and humanity and spoke against the traditional severity of Calvinism.

Among Protestant denominations, Methodists and Baptists made the greatest gains in antebellum America; by the 1850s, about 70 percent of all Protestants were Methodists and Baptists. Methodism spread thanks to the efforts of the circuit riders. Baptists, who advocated baptism of believers by total immersion, spread their emotionally charged faith throughout frontier areas by entrusting the Gospel to individual farmers who became licensed preachers in their local congregations.

After a period as a small minority, Roman Catholicism was on its way to becoming the country's single largest denomination, as it is to this day. The great increase in Catholic numbers before the Civil War was due largely to Irish immigrants. Driven from Ireland by poverty and oppression, these devoted Catholics began migrating to America in large numbers in the 1820s. Immigration rose to a new height in the 1840s, when the Irish potato famine of 1845–46 forced many to either leave home or starve. Between 1845 and 1854 alone, about 1.3 million Irish emigrated to America. Catholic immigrants from Germany, another major source of immigration during this period, also swelled the numbers of Catholics in America. The U.S. acquisition of CALIFORNIA and major parts of the Southwest from Mexico in the 1840s brought in still more Catholics, as the Mexican population in that region was absorbed into the U.S. citizenry.

With the growing numbers of Catholics came a growing anti-Catholic movement among Protestants who saw the new immigrants as a threat. Tracts denouncing Catholicism proliferated, and in the 1854 local and state elections, the anti-Catholic KNOW-NOTHING PARTY scored numerous victories.

To a much smaller degree, immigration during this period also increased the numbers of Jews in America. They came mainly from Germany, beginning in the 1820s. In the 1850s, Cincinnati rabbi Isaac Mayer Wise spearheaded the development of Reform Judaism, a liberal form of the faith that incorporated Enlightenment ideals. The CALIFORNIA GOLD RUSH, which began in 1849, brought still other groups of believers, this time from China. The Chinese imported to America Buddhism, Taoism, Confucianism, and various traditional beliefs.

Some wholly new forms of belief sprouted in the United States during this period. One of the most successful was Mormonism, or the CHURCH OF JESUS CHRIST OF LATTER-DAY SAINTS. This religion was established in 1830 in Fayette, New York, by JOSEPH SMITH, JR. That year Smith published the Book of Mormon, which he said he had translated from gold plates given to him by an angel. Smith regarded his faith as a restored version of Christianity, but it was different enough in its teachings to be regarded by outsiders as a new religion. Mormonism taught that Jesus Christ had visited the New World to preach to ancient peoples of Hebrew descent; claimed that the Second Coming would take place in America; advocated POLYGAMY; and established a centralized church structure with a strong emphasis on communal activity. The Mormon church grew rapidly but was persecuted for its beliefs, with Smith murdered in 1844. Seeking refuge, the Mormons under BRIGHAM YOUNG began migrating to Utah in 1847, where they established a distinctive community they called the STATE OF DESERET.

Another new denomination in this period was the Disciples of Christ, or Christian Churches. This group grew out of what was called the Restoration Movement, which sought to unite all Christian churches by restoring what it viewed as the simple Christianity of the New Testament. In Kentucky in 1803, Presbyterian minister Barton Warren Stone and like-minded colleagues founded a group who called themselves "Christians." In Pennsylvania in 1809, Presbyterian minister THOMAS CAMPBELL and his son Alexander formed the Christian Association of Washington, Pennsylvania, which temporarily joined forces with the

Baptists. The Stoneites and the Campbellites (as they were sometimes called) merged in 1832, united around such principles as the autonomy of congregations and the importance of individual interpretation of scripture.

Around the same time, another new Christian movement, Adventism, was making its mark. In 1831, New York farmer William Miller began preaching his interpretation of scripture, according to which Christ's second coming would occur on March 21, 1843. Through periodicals, tracts, camp meetings, and lectures, Miller developed a large following of tens of thousands of Millerites or Adventists (from Latin *advent,* coming). When the second coming did not take place in 1843, the date was shifted to 1844, but again Christ failed to appear as scheduled. Miller and other true believers remained convinced that Christ would come soon, and they formed several Adventist churches to prepare. The largest of these, the Seventh-Day Adventists, adopted Saturday, not Sunday, as the Sabbath in 1844.

Still another new denomination was the Christadelphians (Greek, "Brothers of Christ"), founded by John Thomas in 1848. It also emphasized belief in Christ's Second Coming, but it had distinctive touches, including pacifism, nonparticipation in government, and rejection of the doctrines of the Trinity and hell.

Some spiritual movements of the time were not so much sects or denominations as intellectual currents. Most prominent among these was transcendentalism, a philosophical and literary movement that called for the individual to encounter God directly. Influenced by German Romanticism, the TRANSCENDENTAL MOVEMENT celebrated the presence of divinity in nature, encouraged self-reliance, and belittled organized religion. Its greatest spokesperson was Ralph Waldo Emerson, who had been trained as a Unitarian minister. In 1838, at Harvard Divinity School, Emerson delivered his "Divinity School Address" marking the beginning of transcendentalism and drawing controversy for his criticism of traditional Christianity. HENRY DAVID THOREAU's *Walden* (1854), based on his experiment in living simply and "deliberately" at Walden Pond near Concord, Massachusetts, further developed transcendentalist ideas.

SPIRITUALISM, a religious movement focused on contact with the spirits of the dead, emerged in the 1840s. In 1848, Margaret, Leah, and Catherine Fox of New York claimed to hear rappings that were messages from spirits. Paying audiences flocked to theaters to see the Fox sisters communicate with the dead. Spiritualism drew much skepticism but also many followers, including newspaper editor Horace Greeley. A leading spiritualist was Andrew Jackson Davis, clairvoyant and author of *Nature's Divine Revelations* (1847).

Utopian experiments attempting to reestablish society on a sounder basis were characteristic of this period of spiritual fervor. New Harmony, Indiana, was founded in 1814 by the Harmony Society, a German Separatist group espousing communal ownership and celibacy. (They were also known as Harmonists or Rappites, for their leader George Rapp.) New Harmony was sold in 1825 to British socialist reformer ROBERT OWEN, who turned it into a communistic colony that quickly broke up due to internal dissension. The Shakers, or the United Society of Believers in Christ's Second Appearing, also espoused communal ownership and celibacy. Founded in the 18th century, the movement established 18 Shaker communities in eight states by 1826. In decline after 1860, the Shakers left a legacy of fine furniture and handcrafts.

At Putney, Vermont, in 1839, John Humphrey Noyes founded a society that sought to carry out his perfectionist teachings of Biblical communism. Forced to flee when neighbors became outraged at the colony's polygamy, Noyes moved to Oneida, New York, in 1848, where his experiments in communal living continued until the 1870s. At BROOK FARM near Boston, several transcendentalists tried an experiment in communal living (1841–47). And in Iowa, the Amana Church Society, a group of seven colonies, was founded by a German Pietist group called the Ebenezer Society in 1855. Known for their fine woolens and expert farming, the cooperative villages would survive into the 20th century.

Further reading: Sydney E. Ahlstrom, *A Religious History of the American People* (New Haven, Conn.: Yale University Press, 1972); Martin E. Marty, *Pilgrims in Their Own Land: 500 Years of Religion in America* (New York: Penguin Books, 1985); Grant Wacker, *Religion in Nineteenth Century America* (New York: Oxford University Press, 2000).

—George Ochoa

rendezvous

The rendezvous, an annual gathering of independent fur traders at a prearranged site in the Rocky Mountains, was held for the first time in 1825 and for the last time in 1840. From the beginnings of the fur trade, traders often worked in groups for ease of operation in handling tasks requiring more than a single individual and, increasingly, for mutual protection. The system of contracted allegiance to a large-scale employer became more common over time as the trade increasingly became controlled by a few large companies. The most influential of these—the Hudson's Bay Company, the AMERICAN FUR COMPANY, and the North West Company—signed on large numbers of trappers and other fur-trade personnel. At the same time that these large companies provided credit and protection, they also paid minimal prices for furs and contracted with trappers who could sell only to them. As the fur trade became more competitive in the early 19th century, the great companies tried to hire trappers away from competitors.

Amidst this consolidation of fur-trading companies came the reemergence of the individual fur trader. The person most responsible for this change was WILLIAM HENRY ASHLEY, a trader from St. Louis. The difficulty for Ashley and others was purchasing furs from the trappers in the field and resupplying them on a regular basis. Ashley proposed to do both by freighting supplies to a designated point in the Rocky Mountains on an annual basis. (One of the unusual features of Ashley's plan was that he freighted the supplies overland rather than up the Missouri River). Trappers would then bring their winter harvest of furs to this site, where Ashley would purchase the furs and sell them supplies for the coming year.

This annual gathering came to be called the "rendezvous." It was a week of commercial transactions, but it also served as a social occasion. The trappers ate, drank, gambled, sometimes fought, and engaged in contests of skill. The first rendezvous was held at Henry's Fort on the Green River in spring 1825. Although Ashley sold out his interests and left the fur trade for land speculation and politics after the second rendezvous in 1826, it continued annually until 1840.The rendezvous provided an occasion for bringing together some of the most famous MOUNTAIN MEN associated with the frontier of the West. Its passing marked the decline of the fur trade.

Further reading: Richard M. Clokey, *William H. Ashley* (Norman: University of Oklahoma Press, 1968); Dale L. Morgan, *The West of William H. Ashley* (Denver, Colo.: Old West Publishing Company, 1964).

Republican Party

The modern Republican Party has its roots in a northern, antislavery party of the 1850s. The Republicans emerged rather suddenly and came to play a major role in events preceding the Civil War. Most historians agree that the party's origins stem from northern outrage over Congress's passage of the Kansas-Nebraska Act, which Democratic President Franklin Pierce signed into law in 1854. That act, whose most prominent champion was Senator Stephen Douglas of Illinois, essentially overturned the MISSOURI COMPROMISE of 1820 and permitted SLAVERY in the Nebraska Territory north of the line that the compromise had set as its limit. Under the Kansas-Nebraska Act, POPULAR SOVEREIGNTY, i.e., the desires of the people who settled a territory, would now determine whether or not it would enter the Union as a slave or free state. Northerners believed that the Kansas Territory, which was carved out from the Nebraska Territory under the act's provisions, was being targeted by southerners who wanted to bring their slaves there.

Even before Congress passed the controversial bill, the beginnings of what was to become the Republican Party were apparent when a group of Whigs, Democrats, and Free-Soilers opposed to the Nebraska bill met in Ripon, Wisconsin in 1854. Other anti-Nebraska gatherings were held in Illinois and in Jackson, Michigan. American politics was in a period of great change in 1854 and 1855. The WHIG PARTY had tried to keep its members at arm's length from the ABOLITION MOVEMENT, but the storm of protest that was forming as the "anti-Nebraska" movement made this task much more difficult. The American Party, more commonly referred to as the KNOW-NOTHING PARTY, included a diverse number of Nativists united by their fear and mistrust of immigrants, especially Catholics, who had entered the United States in recent years. The Know-Nothings showed great strength in elections in 1854 in states such as Massachusetts. That party, however, was in danger of splitting because of differing views on slavery.

Across the North, the anti-Nebraska movement quickly became a political force. Its adherents at first called themselves anti-Nebraska Whigs or anti-Nebraska Democrats. In the 1854 election, the DEMOCRATIC PARTY, which voters identified with the Kansas-Nebraska Act, lost badly in northern states. Some Whigs were not yet ready to give up on their party, and its supporters ran candidates under the old name in New York as well as other states. The existence of the Whig Party was threatened by a deep and growing split over the slavery issue, and it finally collapsed altogether.

Abolitionists sensed that they had a significant opportunity to organize a new antislavery party that might attract former Whigs, Know-Nothings, and disaffected northern Democrats. The new movement first met to organize itself on a national basis in Pittsburgh in early 1856. Proposed names for the fledgling party included the People's and Union Party, but no formal name was adopted at that time. Later that year, however, the movement began to call itself the Republican Party, after Thomas Jefferson's party of the same name at the turn of the 19th century. In summer 1856, the Republicans had their inaugural convention, nominating JOHN C. FRÉMONT, a former Democrat from California, for president. Frémont had some Catholic roots; his father had been a Catholic, and the candidate himself had been married by a Catholic priest. This bothered some of the nativists and Know-Nothings in the emerging Republican coalition.

Slavery was now becoming the defining issue in American politics, and the Republicans were poised to take advantage of this shift in focus away from other issues. The new party was building a coalition that included those who had supported the antislavery LIBERTY PARTY and FREE-SOIL PARTY of the 1840s; former nativists and Know-

Nothings; and former Whigs of New England origin, many of whom now lived in the states of the Ohio and Mississippi River valleys and others who had been active in the various reform movements that arose during the SECOND GREAT AWAKENING. From the beginning, Republicans also attracted the votes of Protestant immigrants from Britain and Scandinavia, although Catholics remained for the most part loyal to the Democratic Party. In addition, the Republican ranks included those who were committed to free-market economics and capitalist development. At its birth, then, the Republican Party was very much a sectional party. Its 1856 convention had been attended by a few delegates from Upper South slave states, but it had no hope of winning any southern states. Its platform called for a Kansas free of slavery and opposed Democratic plans of annexing CUBA as a slave territory. Its first slogan in 1856 stated clearly what the party stood for, and who it hoped to represent: "Free Soil, Free Labor, Free Men and Frémont."

In the election, the new Republican Party did very well across the North, winning 45 percent of the popular vote there (former president MILLARD FILLMORE was running as the American Party nominee) and capturing 11 of the 16 free states. Democrat James Buchanan, largely on the strength of the solid South, was elected president, but the Republican Party had shown impressive strength in its first national election. One danger sign for the party and the future of the union was that their ticket appeared on the ballot in only four slave states, all in the Upper South, and the party did not approach even 1 percent of the vote in any of them. Democrats would charge over the course of the next four years that a national victory by the "Black Republicans" (so called for their antislavery views) would mean the dissolution of the union.

In 1857 the case of *Dred Scott v. Sandford* galvanized much of the North around Republican antislavery principles. The U.S. Supreme Court, in a decision written by Jacksonian Democrat Roger Taney, declared that Dred Scott, a slave attempting to claim his freedom based on his residence in the North, had "no rights which the white man was bound to respect," due to Scott's race. The Scott decision essentially overruled the Missouri Compromise and appeared to make the expansion of slavery easier by insisting that African Americans could not be citizens of the United States. While the decision was met with enthusiastic approval in the slave states, and with cheers from some northern Democrats as well, Republicans denounced it in the most bitter terms. They were most outraged by the Taney Court's contention that Congress had no authority to exclude slavery from the territories, as it had done in the Missouri Compromise. Republicans now attracted to their party former Democrats and others who began to see, for the first time in some cases, a conspiracy by the slavery supporters to extend their "peculiar institution" across the country. Abraham Lincoln of Illinois said that the next step could well be a decision by the Supreme Court "declaring that the Constitution of the United States does not permit a state to exclude slavery from its limits."

In the late 1850s, the Republicans continued to show impressive strength across the North. Political blame for the PANIC OF 1857 was placed on the floundering Buchanan administration. There were still many Democrats in the North, however, who remained wary of the Republicans on a range of issues, including slavery. Then the Kansas question boiled again, as President Buchanan put his support behind a contested state constitution written by proslavery advocates. He went so far as to declare that Kansas was "as much a slave state as Georgia or South Carolina." Although the Senate approved a bill granting Kansas entrance into the Union as a slave state, the House rejected the measure. Leading Senate Democrat Stephen A. Douglas of Illinois broke with his party on this crucial issue, earning him the enmity of southern Democrats and presaging the splitting of the country along sectional lines.

The question of slavery continued to roil the nation as abolitionist John Brown led a band of his followers on a raid on the federal arsenal at Harpers Ferry, Virginia. Although the attempt failed badly and Brown was captured, tried, and executed, many in the North, especially those who were already in or moving toward the Republican Party, looked on him as a hero and martyr.

In its second attempt to win the presidency, the Republicans in 1860 turned to Abraham Lincoln, who had lost a Senate seat to Douglas in Illinois just two years earlier. Although not an outright abolitionist by any means, Lincoln was firmly opposed to the further expansion of slavery. He was a relative newcomer on the national political scene, and Republicans were determined to win the crucial state of Illinois, which they had lost in 1856. A former Whig who was acceptable to all wings of the new party, Lincoln and his running mate Hannibal Hamlin of Maine, a former Democrat, faced the same difficulty as did Frémont: Their party's political support remained entirely in the North. The difference in 1860 was that the Democrats had fractured into northern and southern wings, with Stephen Douglas as the regular nominee and John Breckinridge as the southern Democrat. There was a fourth candidate, John Bell of Tennessee, who was nominated by the Constitutional Union Party, which drew its support in the Upper South from former Whigs. Lincoln campaigned on a platform of Free Soil, which would stop slavery's expansion, but he and the Republicans were careful to distance themselves from abolitionists, especially the radical wing as personified by John Brown.

Although there was increasing talk of secession by the South if Lincoln won, the Republican nominee was elected the 16th president on the strength of his showing in the

North, as he won the electoral votes in every free state except for New Jersey, where he split them with Douglas. As Lincoln prepared to assume office, South Carolina and several other slave states seceded from the Union as a direct result of the Republican triumph, and North and South lurched toward a civil war.

Further reading: Eric Foner, *Free Soil, Free Labor, Free Men: The Ideology of the Republican Party before the Civil War* (New York: Oxford University Press, 1970).

—Jason Duncan

Rocky Mountain Fur Company

A latecomer to the North American fur-trading business, the Rocky Mountain Fur Company was the fourth such business to operate within the Pacific Northwest. It was organized in St. Louis in 1823 by Andrew Henry and WILLIAM HENRY ASHLEY. Henry had already gained fame for having built Fort Henry in what is now southern Idaho. Ashley was described as a "little man who always had a stomach ache," but this did not prevent him from earning $50,000–$60,000 a year during the first four years of the company's life.

In 1826, JEDEDIAH STRONG SMITH, Milton and WILLIAM SUBLETTE, and David Jackson bought the Rocky Mountain Fur Company, and for the next seven years it continued to prosper. Unlike its competitors (such as the AMERICAN FUR COMPANY), the company did not build forts or trading houses. This meant that trappers had no home base but lived independently, fending for themselves. They caught their own food, found their own shelter, and fought off wild animals and hostile Indians. These independent trappers, who were known as MOUNTAIN MEN, led exciting but lonely lives and in time became the subject of many a dime novel. In addition to Smith and the Sublettes, some of these men included JAMES BRIDGER, JIM BECKWOURTH, Joe Meek, Robert Newell, and KIT CARSON. Every summer the mountain men and traders for the Rocky Mountain Fur Company would gather at a RENDEZVOUS to trade pelts and purchase supplies. It was a chance to relax and enjoy themselves after a long season in the mountains, so there was much drinking, gambling, and dancing.

The Rocky Mountain Fur Company was constantly challenging the domain of the Hudson's Bay Company. Their rendezvous were consistently located near a Hudson's Bay Company post in an attempt to draw off some of the Indian trade. A number of the mountain men went into the Snake River region of Oregon, where they competed with the Hudson's Bay's Snake River brigade for trade with the Indians. They also penetrated the Umpqua and Rogue River Valley, which was considered the domain of the Hudson's Bay Company.

In 1826, Jedediah Smith pioneered a trail from the Bear Lake rendezvous to a Spanish mission in southern California. After a trapping expedition into northern California, he made his way back to Bear Lake. In 1827, he led a party of 20 men over the northern California mountains into Oregon country. This expedition proved to be a disaster. Not only did they suffer terrible hardship in crossing the mountains, they were attacked by Indians in the Umpqua River region and all but three of the party were massacred. Smith was out scouting at the time of the attack and survived.

After the attack, Smith traveled north to the COLUMBIA RIVER and FORT VANCOUVER, which was under the control of the Hudson's Bay Company. While there, he was able to obtain firsthand knowledge about the fort. He reported in letters to the East that the fort looked like a permanent establishment, with its many inhabitants, its gardens, livestock, and shops. He complained to the American government that the British were trying to keep Americans out of the Oregon Territory. Smith subsequently realized that the future of the fur trade lay in the Southwest region, and he organized an expedition in late May 1831. While on that expedition, he was killed by some Comanche Indians near the Cimarron River in present-day southwestern Kansas.

One of the biggest factors in the demise of the Rocky Mountain Fur Company was the campaign of opposition that the AMERICAN FUR COMPANY mounted after 1830. The expansion of the American Fur Company from the upper Missouri into the Rocky Mountains was part of JOHN JACOB ASTOR's ambition to monopolize the U.S. fur trade. This competition produced a temporary inflation, forcing the fur traders to bear the brunt of the increase. The American Fur Company could bear the short-term losses. The Rocky Mountain Fur Company, on the other hand, simply did not have the financial resources to compete, and in 1833 it was bought out by Astor.

Further reading: Hiram Martin Chittenden, *The American Fur Trade of the Far West: A History of the Pioneer Trading Posts and Early Fur Companies of the Missouri Valley and Rocky Mountains, and of the Overland Commerce with Santa Fe* (Stanford, Calif.: Academic Reprints, 1954).

S

Santa Anna, Antonio López de (1794–1876)

A leading military and political figure in the history of Mexico for more than half a century, Antonio López de Santa Anna was born in Veracruz. In 1810, at the age of 16, he joined a Veracruz regiment of the Royal Spanish Infantry, where he initially fought against the Mexican independence movements. As the rebels became stronger and Spanish resistance in Mexico and elsewhere in the New World declined, Santa Anna moved to the side of the rebels, fighting in the final struggles to establish an independent Republic of Mexico. In 1821, he allied himself with Agustín de Iturbide, a self-appointed leader of the revolution, who soon crowned himself Emperor Agustín I of Mexico. Augustín's reign was characterized by growing discontent over his excesses, as a result of which Santa Anna turned against the emperor and joined with others to overthrow him.

Mexico became a republic and drafted a constitution in 1824. Santa Anna retired from public life, living as a country squire while remaining in touch with his military friends. In 1829, King Ferdinand of Spain mounted a military expedition to regain control of his former colony. Santa Anna returned to lead the Mexican army in resisting the invasion. The Spanish military force attempted a landing at Tampico that was plagued by poor organization and bad luck. The Mexican army's victory was overwhelming, and Santa Anna was proclaimed the "hero of Tampico." Now tremendously popular, he went to Mexico City, deposed the president, and installed his friend, Anastasio Bustamante, as president.

After Bustamante had governed for three years, Santa Anna overthrew him in 1832 and chose Valentín Gómez Farías as the new president before again retiring to his estate. Gómez Farías was a reformer whose policies alienated the Catholic Church, the large landholders, and the military. Once more, Santa Anna stepped in to remove the president, but this time he assumed the office himself. In 1833 he was elected president in a popular election, and he began to consolidate his power in a series of campaigns to destroy his opposition. He extended his presidential term to eight years and abolished the constitution of 1824. His authority was now absolute, but there was much opposition to him in liberal circles in Mexico.

In 1835 Santa Anna turned his army toward TEXAS, which he found in a state of rebellion. Since the late 1820s, factions in Texas had long talked of secession and independence from Mexico, followed by union with the United States. STEPHEN F. AUSTIN, the voice of moderate loyalty to Mexico, opposed this policy. Santa Anna's abolition of the constitution and his invasion of Texas in 1835 strengthened the hand of the rebels. That same year, under the leadership of SAM HOUSTON, Texans called a convention that issued a declaration of independence. Angered by this expression of disloyalty, Santa Anna intended to crush the revolution and force Texans to accept their former status within the nation of Mexico.

The advance guard of Santa Anna's army crossed the frontier into Texas on October 2, 1835. The first serious objective was the old Spanish mission at THE ALAMO in San Antonio. Rebellious Texans had seized the mission, and in spite of orders to evacuate, they fortified the place, convinced that they could defeat a force several times larger than their own. Santa Anna would give them the opportunity. After a prolonged artillery bombardment, he ordered a frontal assault, which overwhelmed the Alamo's defenders. Santa Anna ordered that no survivors should be taken alive. None were, and the handful of prisoners was immediately executed. Next, he ordered the execution of prisoners recently taken at Goliad. These brutal tactics confirmed him in his belief that the TEXAS REVOLUTION could be put down by ruthless force.

For Texans, Santa Anna's actions offered conclusive proof that they must come together, appoint a commander, train an army, and defeat him in the field. The commander was Sam Houston, and he quickly assembled and trained a small force of some 800 men. Houston retreated up the coast, and Santa Anna followed with an army three times the size. On April 21, Santa Anna confronted

Drawing showing Texan leader and soldier Sam Houston accepting the surrender of General Santa Anna and Perfecto de Cos after the Battle of San Jacinto during the Texan War of Independence *(Hulton/Archive)*

Houston at the San Jacinto River, and in a brief and savage battle, the Texans routed his Mexican army. Although disguised, Santa Anna was recognized and taken prisoner. After he had signed the Treaty of Velasco that recognized Texas independence, and against the advice of many who wished to execute Santa Anna for his treatment of prisoners, Houston permitted him to leave for Veracruz. In Mexico, Santa Anna immediately repudiated the treaty of Texas independence, and the two sides faced one another for nine years in an uneasy truce across the Rio Grande.

With the outbreak of the MEXICAN-AMERICAN WAR in 1846, Santa Anna offered his service to his nation once again. With an army of some 20,000, he attacked General ZACHARY TAYLOR at Buena Vista. In one of the bloodiest engagements of the war, Taylor defeated Santa Anna after two days of hard fighting. He then engaged the American army under General WINFIELD SCOTT at the Battle of Cerro Gordo, where he was defeated. The TREATY OF GUADALUPE HIDALGO, signed in February 1848, set the boundaries of the State of Texas and added the northern third of Mexico to the expanding American continental empire. Santa Anna's long campaign to preserve Mexico's North had failed.

With the close of the war, Santa Anna went into self-imposed exile. The Conservative Party recalled him in 1853, and he was once again appointed president. To support his empty treasury, he sold 45,000 acres (the GADSDEN PURCHASE) to the United States for $10 million. Two years later, the Liberal Party overthrew his government, and Santa Anna was forced into exile. Forbidden to return to Mexico, he traveled, including one trip to the United States. He continually petitioned the government to return to his native land, and his request was granted in 1874. Santa Anna died at the age of 82.

Further reading: Oakah L. Jones, *Santa Anna* (New York: Twayne Publishers, 1968).

Santa Fe Trail

The Santa Fe Trail was an overland commercial route between Independence, Missouri, and Santa Fe, New Mexico. It was used from the establishment of the Republic of Mexico in 1821 until railroads put it out of business in the years following the Civil War.

For 300 years, Spain had protected her empire in the Americas by forbidding the visits or residence of foreigners. After the United States achieved independence from Great Britain in 1783, American traders or explorers who ventured into Spanish territory in the Southwest were routinely arrested and confined. However, after gaining independence from Spain in 1821, the new republic of Mexico pursued a policy of trade and open access. One dimension of this new direction was the law that STEPHEN F. AUSTIN used to colonize TEXAS. Another was the opening of the southwest of New Mexico to trade. When WILLIAM BECKNELL, the first Missouri trader to visit under the new policy, returned to Missouri in 1822 with bags of Spanish silver, others were anxious to follow his example. In summer that year, Becknell returned to Santa Fe with a wagon train of goods, pioneering a route across the Cimarron desert that avoided the hazardous Raton Pass across the Raton Mountains linking southeast Colorado and northern New Mexico. As subsequent trading expeditions began using this route, Becknell became known as the "Father of the Santa Fe Trade."

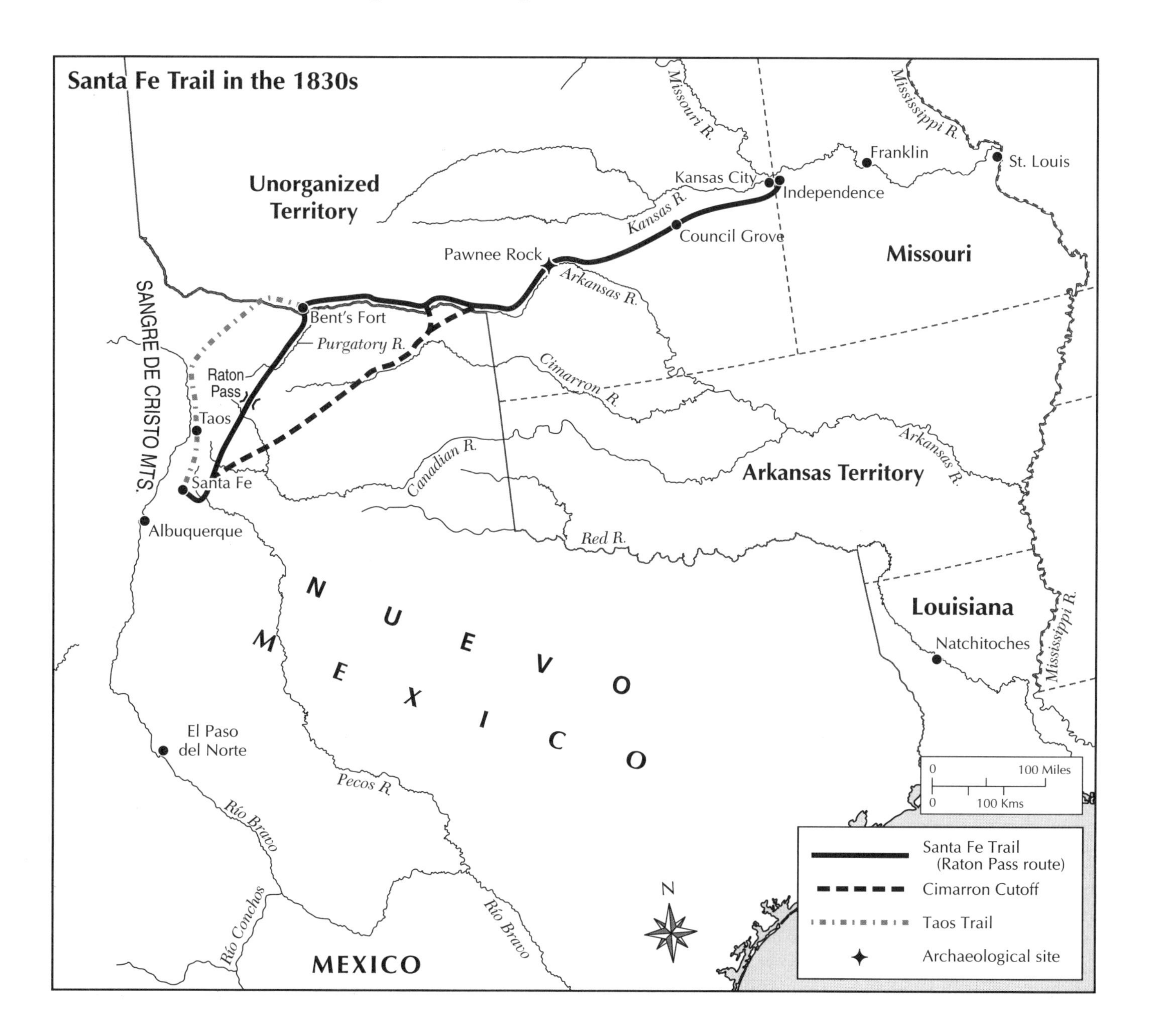

By 1824 Becknell and other merchants had established a regular trade with Santa Fe, with gross returns that year on the order of $200,000. With the appearance of regular caravans on the trail, the Indian peoples adjacent to the passage—mostly Kiowa and Comanche—began regular raids on the wagon trains. The combination of profits for Missouri traders and Indian raiders brought the trail and its trade to the attention of the U.S. government. Senator THOMAS HART BENTON of Missouri introduced legislation to mark the trail and protect the traders. In 1825 one law provided for an official survey of the Santa Fe Trail and a second appropriated $20,000 to negotiate with the Indians for a right of way. Beginning in 1828, military escorts accompanied the wagons, but this protection ended after two years; thereafter, the traders had to defend themselves.

As William Becknell was from Franklin, Missouri, for the first few years, this town marked the beginning of the trail. By 1830, though, the starting point had become Independence, a town at the bend of the Missouri River that had become the staging place for overland travel to the West. From Independence, the trail ran south and west to Council Grove, across the Arkansas and Canadian Rivers to San Miguel on the Pecos. From this point, the wagons moved directly to Santa Fe over Glorietta Pass. An alternate route from the Arkansas River ran west to BENT'S FORT and thence south over Raton Pass to Santa Fe. The second trail was longer and steeper, but it avoided most of the Indian dangers and the 60-mile Cimarron desert. Many chose the alternate trail because of Bent's Fort (completed in 1832), the most permanent and secure outpost on the southern plains. Whatever the southern route of the trail, the end of the 800-mile journey was Santa Fe. With a full load of wagons, the trip from Missouri to Santa Fe took three months. The return trip with empty wagons took perhaps half that time.

Arriving at Santa Fe with the trail and its dangers behind them, the American traders now had to deal with customs duties and the officials who collected them. The entrance into the town could be a frustrating and sometimes expensive exercise. Taxes levied on the Santa Fe trade were arbitrary and inconsistent. Mexican officials charged with enforcing the customs laws were virtually independent of oversight and far removed from Mexico City. Little of what was actually collected found its way into the national treasury. Sometimes powerful individuals levied their own duties. For some time, Governor Manuel Armijo levied his personal tax of $500 on each wagon. Faced with such an array of officials and charges, the American traders evaded them at every turn. Sometimes they used little-known trails. They also tried to sneak into town in the middle of the night, a difficult feat in view of the warm welcome accorded them by the Mexican population.

The arrival of a wagon train in Santa Fe was a moment of universal enthusiasm. The Mexican peoples lined the street to celebrate. The business of the day transacted, the drives and the local population met at a fandango, a raucous public dance that provided a suitable end to the privations of three months on the trail and often ended in personal confrontations of various kinds. Whatever the social occasions, the business of the trail and its trade was good for Santa Fe. Leading town merchants had stores on the square, and the Mexican merchants sometimes traveled to Independence to choose their goods. Even with the vagaries of customs duties and officials, the 1830s was a time of mutual accommodation and prosperity for the Santa Fe Trail and for its twin terminals of Independence and Santa Fe.

Beginning about 1840, the Mexican government became less welcoming. The TEXAS REVOLUTION had showed the dangers of American immigration and commercial connections. The independent Republic of Texas claimed boundary lines to include the upper Arkansas River, placing Santa Fe within its territory. Although Texas was never able to extend its authority over Santa Fe, its presence and expansionist policies disturbed Mexican officials. In 1841 the Republic of Texas mounted an invasion of New Mexico. Although the enterprise failed, it added to the uneasiness that seemed to surround the regular arrival of caravans of trade goods and traders from Missouri.

In 1846 the outbreak of the MEXICAN-AMERICAN WAR confirmed the Mexican view of American designs on Mexican territory in the Southwest. In the summer of that year, General STEPHEN WATTS KEARNY occupied Santa Fe and claimed New Mexico as part of the United States. In 1848 the TREATY OF GUADALUPE HIDALGO confirmed the cession of New Mexico to the continental American empire.

The Santa Fe Trail now assumed a new and expanded form. Mexican officials and customs duties disappeared with American sovereignty. The U.S. Army constructed a series of forts along the trail to protect wagon trains, and traffic expanded to include mail and stagecoach service. The discovery of gold in California in 1848 and the subsequent CALIFORNIA GOLD RUSH further enlarged the business of the Santa Fe Trail. By 1855 the volume of trade reached $5 million annually.

Trade along the Santa Fe Trail continued during the Civil War (1816–65), enlarged by supplies sent to Union military forces assembled to meet a perceived Confederate threat in the West. With the arrival of the Southern Pacific Railroad in Santa Fe, the trail vanished as a trade route. Having served the Republic of Mexico and the United States for a half-century it was a symbol of the significance of trade in the opening of the Southwest.

Further reading: Josiah Gregg, *Commerce of the Prairies,* edited by Milo Milton Quaife (Lincoln: University of

Nebraska Press, 1967); David Lavender, *Bent's Fort* (Gloucester, Mass.: P. Smith, 1968).

science and technology

In the period of 1813–55, the United States was not known for achievements in pure science. Most of the major advances in physics, chemistry, biology, and other sciences had been taking place in Europe. In Britain, Michael Faraday researched electromagnetism and Charles Darwin began to develop his theory of evolution; in Germany, Friedrich Wöhler made the first synthetic organic compound; in France, Jean-Bernard-Léon Foucault constructed a pendulum that demonstrated the rotation of the Earth. Americans of this period showed an interest in such investigations, but, as pragmatic citizens of a young and growing nation, they were more prone to distinguish themselves as inventors and adapters of practical technology. American innovations of the period included the telegraph, the mechanical reaper, the six-shooter, and ether anesthesia. In the meantime, through the foundation of professional societies and journals, the nation took steps toward establishing itself as the scientific power it would become in the 20th century.

An important example of American ingenuity was the electromagnetic telegraph, patented by SAMUEL F. B. MORSE in 1837. This device for transmitting messages via wire greatly increased humanity's capacity to communicate swiftly over long distances. Morse and his assistant Alfred Vail also developed Morse code, a system for encoding messages to be telegraphed. In 1844, Morse demonstrated the practicality of his invention by sending the telegraph message "What hath God wrought!" from Washington, D.C., to Baltimore, Maryland. Morse was indebted to earlier scientists and rivaled by contemporaries, notably Charles Wheatstone and W. F. Cooke in England. But his business sense and his system's practical advantages soon made it the world's standard.

In 1831 CYRUS HALL McCORMICK invented a mechanical, horse-drawn reaper that greatly improved the efficiency of harvesting. For McCormick, as it had been for Morse, business acumen was key to supplanting rivals and making his machine the leader in its market. In 1835–36, another skillful entrepreneur, SAMUEL COLT, patented his six-shooter, a pistol with six revolving chambers. The Colt revolver would become popular worldwide and became identified in folklore with the nation's "Wild West."

Some inventors were better at inventing than at profiting from their technology. In 1839, Charles Goodyear discovered a process for vulcanizing rubber, through which it kept its elasticity in all weather. Previously, rubber had tended to become sticky in warm weather and brittle in cold. Goodyear's process made rubber a much more practical material for industrial and consumer uses, but it did not make him rich. What with debts and failure to keep control of his patents, he died in poverty.

In 1852, Elisha Graves Otis patented an automatic safety device to prevent an elevator from falling. His safety elevator would become vital to the spread of multistory buildings, but not until after his death in 1861.

A technology with more immediate uses was anesthesia. Previously, surgery and dental work had been accompanied by unavoidable pain. In 1846, dentist William Thomas Morton publicly demonstrated the effectiveness of ether as an anesthetic, or pain-deadening agent, in tooth extraction. That same year, collaborating with surgeon John Warren, Morton also used ether for the first time in surgery, during an operation to remove a neck tumor.

Americans were resourceful adapters of existing technology. The steam engine had been invented in Britain in 1769, but it was American engineer Robert Fulton who, in 1807, used it to launch the first commercially viable steamboat, the *Clermont*. Throughout the years 1813–55, the steamboat was improved and adapted for many purposes, including war: Fulton introduced the first steam warship in 1814–15. In 1819, the USS *Savannah*, traveling from Georgia to Liverpool, England, completed the first transatlantic trip powered by a combination of sail and steam. With the steamboat's spread, canals became increasingly important. In 1819, Rome and Utica, New York, were joined in the opening of the first part of the ERIE CANAL. In 1825, the full length of the canal, spanning over 300 miles, opened for business, linking the Hudson River to the Great Lakes and inspiring other canal projects.

Steam locomotives had been operating on RAILROADS in Britain since 1804, but American engineers added refinements. In 1830, Robert Livingston Stevens invented the T-rail, which would become standard equipment on rail lines. That same year, the first U.S.-built locomotive, the Tom Thumb, was introduced, and the BALTIMORE & OHIO RAILROAD (B&O) began using steam locomotives for rail service. Based in Baltimore, the B&O steadily extended its reach, to St. Louis, Missouri, by 1857.

During the early years of American railroads, locomotives were imported from England, but these imported engines proved poorly adapted to the uneven rails, sharp curves, and heavy grades of the early American railroads. American locomotive designs and manufacture soon developed engines to meet the American needs, with headlights, cowcatchers, and the Baldwin "flexible beam" truck to hold locomotives and cars on the track in sharp curves. The American locomotive builders Matthias Baldwin and William Norris of Philadelphia began as jewelers and then shifted to machine shops. The Baldwin Locomotive Works, first in Philadelphia and then in Eddystone, Pennsylvania, became the largest builder in the nation and Norris's railroad engines were exported around the world. The two companies produced a sizable portion of all the locomotives that carried freight and passengers in South America, Australia, Russia, Africa, and the Middle East.

Another important step in transportation technology was the wire-cable suspension bridge, which German-American engineer John Augustus Roebling pioneered in the 1840s in Pittsburgh, Pennsylvania, and Wheeling, Virginia (later West Virginia).

American innovations of the period were as varied as Americans themselves. Dentist Anthony Plantson introduced the dental plate in 1817–18. A few years later, in 1824, Shakers in Hancock, New York, built the first round barn, a design that became popular with dairy farmers. Other inventions included the platform scale or Fairbanks scale, produced by Thaddeus Fairbanks, 1830; a compression machine for cooling water, a precursor of modern refrigerators, Jacob Perkins, 1834; a corn harvester, Henry Blair (the first African American to receive a patent, 1836); a steam-powered thresher, John and Hiram Pitts, 1837; a safety pin, Walter Hunt, 1849; prefabricated homes, James Bogardus, 1849; and a process for condensing milk, Gail Borden, 1855.

Despite the emphasis on technology, the young United States did produce some advances in pure science. In 1831, American physicist Joseph Henry and British physicist Michael Faraday independently discovered the principle of electromagnetic induction. In the course of doing so, they invented the dynamo, or electric generator, which would make possible the widespread use of electric power from the late 19th century onward. Henry also improved the electromagnet, built one of the first electric motors, and was important in institutionalizing and stimulating scientific research in America. He was a professor at Princeton (1832–46), the first secretary and director of the Smithsonian Institution (1846–78), and a founder of the American Association for the Advancement of Science (AAAS) in 1847. At the Smithsonian, he set up a weather-reporting system that led to the creation of the U.S. Weather Bureau.

Medical science was advanced by physician Oliver Wendell Holmes, father of the Supreme Court justice of the same name. In 1843, the elder Holmes demonstrated, based on many case studies, that puerperal fever, or childbed fever, was contagious, a finding supported four years later by the studies of Hungarian physician Ignaz P. Semmelweis.

More generally during this period, science was being transformed from the hobby of amateurs, known as natural philosophers, to the profession of specialized scholars called scientists (a word coined at this time by British philosopher William Whewell). The founding of the AAAS was a key step in that direction, as was the founding of other scientific and professional societies, including the American Medical Association, established in 1847; and the American Psychiatric Association, started in 1844. Earlier, in 1818, chemist Benjamin Silliman had founded the *American Journal of Science and Arts,* which prided itself on publishing serious scientific research, even when too arcane for the general public. Silliman also became important in the 1850s for his distillation of crude oil and his report of the many uses to which it could be put—a prescient view, given that the invention of the petroleum-driven internal combustion engine was still years away.

Despite the growing shift toward professional science, there was still ample scope for the dedicated amateur in early 19th-century America, particularly when it came to natural observation and collection rather than theory and experiment. Astronomy, paleontology, geology, botany, and zoology were all areas in which gentlemen could dabble, whether they were clergymen, lawyers, doctors, merchants, or planters. Sometimes the results were astonishing. From 1827 to 1838, one-time storekeeper JOHN JAMES AUDUBON published his landmark, multivolume collection of ornithological drawings, *Birds of America.* In the Connecticut Valley in 1818, Solomon Ellsworth, Jr., and Nathan Smith discovered fossil bones of the dinosaur *Anchisaurus* without understanding the significance of their find. From 1818 to 1858, no fewer than 13 academies of science were founded in the Middle West alone, from Ohio to Wisconsin. Most of their members were amateur natural scientists.

Despite their more restricted opportunities, women too could achieve impressive results. Maria Mitchell, librarian and amateur astronomer, established the orbit of a newly discovered comet in 1847. For this feat, she became the first woman admitted to the American Academy of Arts and Sciences.

Archaeology and oceanography were fields of growing interest. Ephraim George Squier and Edwin H. Davis made the first major exploration of the earthworks of the Native American Mound Builders in Ohio in 1845–47. In 1854, naval officer Matthew Fontaine Maury discovered Telegraph Plateau, a shallow section of the Atlantic Ocean, while searching for an undersea route for the transatlantic cable. Maury charted the Gulf Stream and wrote *Physical Geography of the Sea* (1855), the first textbook of modern oceanography.

In *Democracy in America* (1835), French visitor Alexis de Tocqueville devoted a chapter to the subject "Why Americans Prefer the Practice Rather Than the Theory of Science." Tocqueville was probably right that Americans were more interested in practical inventions than in theoretical findings, yet there was popular interest in loftier matters. Through newspapers, books, and popular lectures (often in a local lyceum), Americans learned about findings in astronomy, botany, chemistry, physics, and other areas. The passage of the Great Comet of 1843 was eagerly followed. Much of this popular science was confined to "curiosities" and "wonders" rather than deep inquiry into the causes of phenomena. But it showed that Americans at this time were not averse to scientific learning. In fact, many viewed it as morally uplifting. Naturalist Increase A. Lapham, lecturing in Milwaukee in 1840, said: "Teach young persons to relish the pure and simple beauties of nature—excite in their bosoms an ardent and enthusiastic love of the wonderful works of the Great Creator and you have one of the surest safeguards against immorality and vice."

Further reading: Donald Cardwell, *The Norton History of Technology* (New York: W. W. Norton & Co., 1995); George Ochoa and Melinda Corey, *The Wilson Chronology of Science and Technology* (New York: H. W. Wilson, 1997); Nathan Reingold, ed., *Science in America Since 1820* (New York: Science History Publications, 1976).

—George Ochoa

Scott, Winfield (1786–1866)

U.S. Army general and Whig politician, Winfield Scott's victories during the MEXICAN-AMERICAN WAR made him a national hero. Scott was born in Petersburg, Virginia, on June 13, 1786, the son of a Revolutionary War veteran. He attended William and Mary College briefly in 1806, but dropped out the following year to study law. Scott joined the U.S. Army as a captain in 1808. He proved himself a studious and capable individual, but extremely sensitive about matters concerning personal honor. In 1810, for publically denouncing his superior, General James Wilkinson, Scott was court-martialed and suspended for a year. More determined than ever to be a good officer, he spent that interval reading and mastering several European manuals on the art of war. He reemerged as one of the most promising young officers in the American army.

When the WAR OF 1812 commenced in June 1812, Scott was a lieutenant colonel of the Second U.S. Artillery. In October that year, he fought with great bravery at the debacle at Queenston Heights on the Niagara frontier and was captured. Exchanged the following year, and promoted to full colonel, he accompanied General Henry Dearborn's amphibious expedition against Fort George in May 1813 and was conspicuous in its capture. Scott pursued the defeated enemy vigorously and would have taken them prisoner but for Dearborn's premature order to withdraw. He spent the balance of the year along the Niagara Frontier before joining General Wilkinson's ill-fated St. Lawrence expedition that fall.

As one of several junior officers to acquire distinction in service, in March 1814 Scott became the youngest brigadier general in the army. He was then assigned to the Left Division under General Jacob Brown at Buffalo, New York, where he instituted the first systematized training

Winfield Scott *(National Archives)*

regimen for American troops. On July 5, 1814, his intense drilling paid dividends when his brigade won an overwhelming victory over a larger British force at Chippawa Creek, Canada. This was the first time in the War of 1812 that American troops had defeated their professional adversaries in an open field and proof of their growing professionalism. Three weeks later, Scott commanded the American front line at the Battle of Lundy's Lane. The battle was a draw, and Scott was seriously wounded. Sent to Baltimore to convalesce, he saw no further fighting, but he had acquired a military reputation second only to ANDREW JACKSON.

After the war, Scott convinced the War Department to send him to Europe to study military institutions there. Thus began a 50-year quest for promoting and sustaining military professionalism in the U.S. Army. In this capacity, Scott authored several widely read drill manuals and regulations, some of which remained in use until 1861. However, he remained stubbornly opinionated about personal affairs and publicly quarreled with General Edmund P. Gaines over seniority. This row resulted in the selection of

Alexander Macomb as commanding general of the army in 1828. Such was Scott's insistence on military protocol that he was widely derided as "Old Fuss and Feathers."

Scott continued to function effectively as a soldier, and he was actively involved in the Second Seminole War, the Cherokee removal, and border disputes with Canada. He became the army's senior military leader in 1841, and six years later he led the decisive campaign of the Mexican-American War. Landing at Veracruz, he bested a series of larger Mexican armies in a brilliant campaign of maneuvers that included cutting off his own lines of communication. Mexico City was subsequently taken, and the government of General ANTONIO LÓPEZ DE SANTA ANNA sued for peace.

As a national hero, Scott tried to secure the WHIG PARTY's nomination for president in 1848, but lost to ZACHARY TAYLOR. He achieved his quest in 1852, but badly lost the election that year to Franklin Pierce. He was nonetheless honored the following year by being elevated to lieutenant general, the first officer to hold such a distinction since George Washington.

Scott remained the nation's senior military figure until the outbreak of the Civil War in April 1861, when he was succeeded by General George McClellan. Before retiring, he promulgated the so-called Anaconda Plan for defeating the Confederacy. This entailed establishment of a naval blockade coupled with a series of western advances down the Mississippi River that carved up enemy territory methodically and slowly strangled the South. The strategy brought him into direct conflict with younger officers like McClellan, who sought to attack immediately before the army was properly trained. Much lampooned at first, Scott's strategy eventually triumphed. The old soldier died at West Point on 29 May 1866, having bequeathed to the U.S. Army traditions of professionalism and victory that it heretofore had not possessed.

Further reading: Richard V. Barbuto, *Niagara, 1814: America Invades Canada* (Lawrence: University Press of Kansas, 2000); John S. D. Eisenhower, *Agent of Destiny: The Life and Times of Winfield Scott* (Norman: University of Oklahoma Press, 1997); John C. Fredriksen, "Niagara, 1814: The United States Army Quest for Tactical Parity in the War of 1812 and Its Legacy" (unpublished dissertation, Providence College, 1993); Timothy D. Johnson, *Winfield Scott and the Quest for Military Glory* (Lawrence: University Press of Kansas, 1998).

—John C. Fredriksen

Second Great Awakening

Beginning in the 1790s, a wave of revivalism swept across the United States that ultimately transformed the religious and social landscape. The revival reflected tremendous faith in the ability of an individual to affect his own salvation. In an age when the clarion of equality was gaining in tempo, suddenly every men was equal before God. All a person had to do, so many revivalists declared, was open his or her heart up to Jesus, and the individual would be saved. Harsh Calvinism was shunted aside, and the learned minister was no longer needed to guide the layman. Evangelicals did not write formal and reasoned sermons. Instead, they preached as the Lord moved them, threatening sinners with fire and brimstone and speaking in an impassioned voice.

Camp meetings, such as the one shown here, helped to spread Protestantism to the scattered frontier population. *(Library of Congress)*

While regular church services might be a part of the revival, the camp meeting became its special tool. In rural areas where population was dispersed, the camp meeting provided a reason for hundreds, sometimes thousands, to assemble together in both a social and religious setting. In summer 1801, over 12,000 people attended the Cane Ridge camp meeting in Kentucky. Similar gatherings occurred throughout the early 19th century. The behavior of the participants at such camp meetings could border on the bizarre, with some individuals barking like dogs, others shouting and screaming for the glory of God, and still others sobbing in the recognition of their own sin.

The enthusiastic RELIGION associated with this revival had its greatest impact on the frontier both in the North and the South. Kentucky and Tennessee were particularly responsive to the revival. Western upstate New York, recently occupied by European Americans, experienced so many revivals that it was known as the "burned over district," because the fires of religion had repeatedly burned over the area. Charismatic and imposing preachers such as CHARLES GRANDISON FINNEY would draw large crowds. In newly settled regions, Americans were looking for some order in an unstructured social environment. The Awakening, even with some of its extravagant behavior, provided individuals with reassurance that they were guaranteed salvation and had a special relationship with God. Many evangelical denominations also emphasized the need for personal discipline and attacked drinking, gambling, and other forms of misbehavior.

The implications of the revival on society were profound. The Awakening brought an ever-increasing number of Americans into church attendance. It was also at this time that many African-American slaves became Christians, responding to the evangelical currents swirling about them. Denominations like the Methodists and Baptists swelled in numbers, quickly becoming the predominant religious groups in many sections of the nation. Eventually, after 1820, new denominations like the Mormons and the Church of Christ appeared. The call for self-discipline also helped to spawn a host of reform movements in the United States. With the emphasis on an individual's personal relationship with God, the need to spread the gospel led to Bible and Sunday school societies. In turn, other groups emerged to help the poor and disadvantaged and to reform society. While these reform movements gained their fullest expression in the 1830s and 1840s, it is in the opening decades of the 19th century that they began. Ultimately, however, the greatest impact of the revival was the further impetus it gave to the developing central creed of the American nation. In the face of this massive religious upheaval, it became increasingly difficult to sustain social distinctions and oppose the rise of equality.

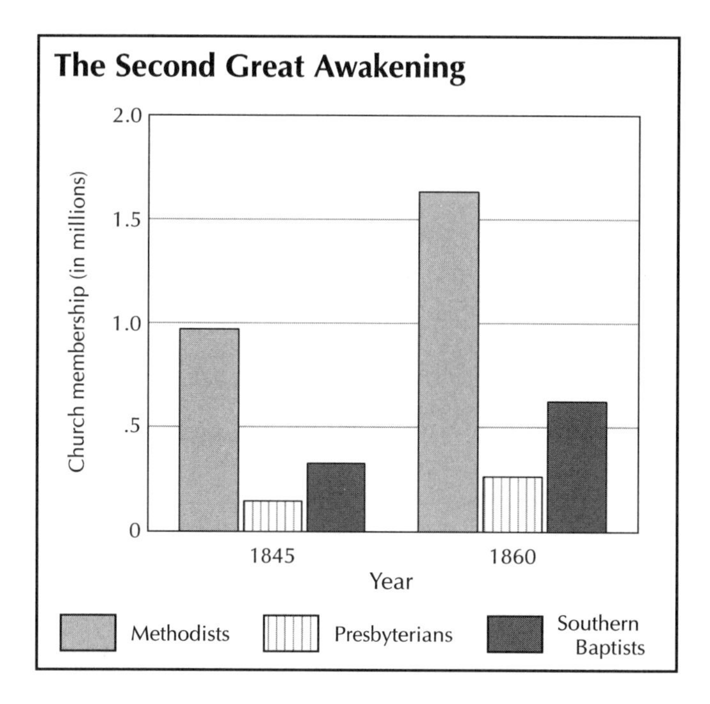

Further reading: Whitney R. Cross, *The Burned-Over District: The Social and Intellectual History of Enthusiastic Religion in Western New York, 1800–1850* (New York: Octagon Books, 1981); Nathan O. Hatch, *The Democratization of American Christianity* (New Haven, Conn.: Yale University Press, 1989); Christine Leigh Heyrman, *Southern Cross: The Beginnings of the Bible Belt* (New York: A. A. Knopf, 1997).

Seminole War, First and Second (1817–1818), (1835–1842)

The history of the Seminole Indians begins with the early 18th-century conflicts between English and Spanish interests in what is now northern Florida. After Creek and English incursions destroyed the Spanish mission system and the Indians associated with it, the Spanish wanted protection from their enemies in order to rebuild their strength. They invited groups of Lower Creek Indians to move into northern Florida, hoping their presence would act as a shield against the English settlements to the north. By the mid-18th century, these Lower Creek had developed a distinct society and were known as the Seminole, a corruption of the Spanish word "cimarron," or "runaway." The Seminole fought on the Loyalist side in the Revolutionary War, and when Spain resumed control of the Floridas from Great Britain in 1783, they continued to act as important strategic partners.

Over time the Seminole became what is known as a "triracial isolate" because they welcomed runaway slaves and others escaping from established colonial society. Their willingness to welcome escaped slaves would prove pivotal in the First Seminole War. American slaveholders resented the presence of havens for runaway slaves in Florida and pushed the government to roust out fugitives. Seminole were known to be hostile to the Americans, a position that led to violence in 1817. The previous year, the United States had built Fort Scott on the border between Florida and Georgia in Spanish territory, near the Seminole village of Fowlstown. This village was a hotbed of anti-American sentiment, and its chief, Neamathla, used the area to stage raids on Georgia. Runaway slaves were also known to congregate in Fowlstown. By 1817, the Seminole's hostility in Fowlstown induced General Edmund P. Gaines, commander of Fort Scott, to attack the Indian settlement. The Seminole were forced to retreat and join forces with another band further south.

In 1818, General ANDREW JACKSON invaded West Florida, partly to assert U.S. jurisdiction over the territory, partly to capture escaping Red Stick Creek and partly to recover fugitive slaves. Jackson and his troops pushed the Seminole eastward, destroying their villages along the way. This aggressive American behavior induced the Spanish to cede EAST AND WEST FLORIDA to the United States, which they did through the ADAMS-ONÍS TREATY of 1819. All of Florida, including Seminole lands, now officially belonged to the United States.

In 1830 Congress passed the INDIAN REMOVAL ACT, which required Indians east of the Mississippi River to be removed from their lands and relocated to the West. Seminole resistance to Indian removal led to the Second Seminole War. In 1835, their leader Osceola ordered the killing of an Indian agent and two companies under Major Francis L. Dade. Indian forces achieved major victories in attacks on northeastern Florida. Joining the Seminole in battle were escaped slaves who had become part of the nation. The presence of these former slaves among the Indians angered American southerners, who continued to pressure the federal government to stamp out the rebellions.

Following Osceola's victories, President Andrew Jackson sent military hero General WINFIELD SCOTT to lead the fight against the Seminole. Scott's troops were stymied by the Indians' guerrilla tactics, and his campaign failed. Jackson replaced Scott with General Thomas S. Jesup, who used a more ruthless approach for battling the Seminole, violating the rules of war and using torture and execution. In 1837, Jesup captured Osceola, even though a truce was supposedly in effect; the Seminole leader died in captivity a few months later. That same year, a major battle was fought at Lake Okeechobee, with American troops commanded by General ZACHARY TAYLOR. By 1838, 100 Indians had been killed and over 2,500 captured and transported to Oklahoma. Among those transported were former slaves who had fought for their freedom alongside the Indians.

The fighting continued, the combatants locked in a stalemate. Jesup lost his command, and the cast of American generals would continue to change over the next four years. The Seminole also fought under the leadership of various men after Osceola's death, but no single leader emerged. As the war advanced, both sides used Indian fighting tactics—the only viable method for fighting in the subtropical environment.

By 1842 only about 300 Seminole remained in Florida. The last American commander, General William J. Worth, proposed that the United States cease fighting in Florida and strike an agreement with the Seminole holdouts. In August, the Seminole agreed with Worth to stay in the region south of Pease Creek and west of Lake Okeechobee. This agreement was not an official treaty, but it did end seven years of fighting, the longest and most expensive war ever fought by Indians against the United States.

Florida Territory petitioned for statehood in 1845 and was admitted as a slave state. Soon state officials were demanding the removal of the remaining Seminole in order to make white settlement safe. Military forces provoked a confrontation by destroying the property of Seminole leader Billy Bowlegs. The Indians retaliated in 1855, starting a smaller conflict that became known as the Third Seminole War (1855–58). By 1858, Billy Bowlegs and 165 others had agreed to go to Oklahoma; he later convinced another 75 to join the migration. After all the bloodshed, 125 Seminole resistors remained in the remote swampland of Florida. They were never removed. The Seminole who moved to Oklahoma lived on the Creek reservation until 1856, when they were given their own reservation. The nation's alliances were divided during the Civil War, and those in Indian Territory continued to be isolated from the remaining Florida Seminole. The nation strove to regain a unified identity after the war. Like other Native Americans in the last half of the 19th century, the Seminole were plagued by poverty, disease, and the indifference of the U.S. government. By the beginning of the 20th century, the nation had traded its reserved land for allotments, and their tribal government provided less and less protection for the most resistant eastern nation.

Further reading: Virginia Peters Bergman, *The Florida Wars* (Hamden, Conn.: Archon Books, 1979); John K. Mahon, *History of the Second Seminole War, 1835–1842* (Gainesville: University of Florida Press, 1967); Kenneth W. Porter, *The Black Seminoles: History of a Freedom-Seeking People* (Gainesville: University of Florida Press, 1996).

—Eleanor H. McConnell

Seneca Falls

On July 19 and 20, 1848, nearly 300 men and women gathered at the Wesleyan Chapel in Seneca Falls to attend a women's rights convention. Considered by many historians to mark the beginning of an organized movement for WOMEN'S STATUS AND RIGHTS in the United States, the convention built on decades of political activism by women devoted to the causes of abolitionism, temperance, and religious reform. The convention broadened and sometimes redirected women's political action. It used familiar language to articulate new political goals. Most of all, however, it gave notice that the legal and cultural identity of women in American could not and would not remain the same.

While the American Revolution severed the former colonies' ties to Great Britain, it did little to alter the balance of power between women and men. Denied equal access to education, prohibited from joining professions, and without the benefit of apprenticeships in profitable trades, most women of the new republic were forced into economic dependency on men. Young women were taught the business of home management and child care, skills with their own economic worth that were nevertheless rarely sufficient to provide a woman with financial independence. Marriage was therefore a largely economic transaction, in which women and men exchanged their financial skills in order to form a household. Marriage also wrought another transformation on women. Upon marriage, women became "civilly dead"—that is, their legal identities were largely suspended in those of their husbands, who controlled their property, earnings, ability to contract and sue, sexual access to their bodies, and custody of their children. In general, only men were allowed to vote, serve on juries, enter the legal profession, or become elected officials. Women relied on men to act on their behalf in each of these arenas.

This left women on the civic fringes of the new republic forged during the Revolutionary War. What would their stake be in the perpetuation of the state? What role should the women who had upheld economic sanctions, worked on battlelines, and run households in the absence of their husbands be expected to shoulder now that the war was done?

The answer was a political identity rooted in motherhood. For the republic to flourish, it was necessary that the sons and daughters of the revolutionary generation understand the civic identity they had inherited. Who better to instill this in the youngest generation of Americans than their mothers? Seized upon by women as well as men as a means to channel their political expression, "Republican Motherhood" became the very definition of a woman's political role.

It was as mothers (and for young women, mothers-to-be) that women made the majority of their political claims in the early 19th century. Early temperance activists used the rhetoric of motherhood to urge politicians to protect women against drunken husbands, financial ruin, and physical violence. Many women who lobbied state legislatures for the better protection of married women's property rights did so with the argument that mothers and children needed protection from the wasteful financial habits of neglectful men. Rarely did anyone argue that women deserved equal legal rights with men out of basic justice. Those who did ran the risk of alienating the politicians they hoped to sway, opening themselves to ridicule or scaring their constituents with the possibility of a radically changed social order.

Yet the women at Seneca Falls did not make their claims to political activism on the basis of motherhood. The lasting impact of the convention was their plainspoken demand to be considered the equals of men and to be understood as citizens in their own right. The resolutions of the convention did not suggest that women deserved rights because they deserved protection from a harsh and violently male world. Instead, the organizers and attendees argued that the business begun by the American Revolution was not finished and could not be until the laws of the land recognized that "all men and women were created equal."

The evolution of this particular brand of women's activism owed much to the influence of Quakerism in the United States. More egalitarian than many religious groups, the Quakers encouraged women to speak at religious meetings and allowed them to become ministers. Members often considered social activism indistinguishable from spiritual responsibility. As a group, Quakers were fiercely opposed to SLAVERY, and many of the most prominent women's rights activists of the 19th century learned their organizing and public speaking skills as Quaker advocates of abolitionism. ANGELINA AND SARAH GRIMKÉ, for example, became Quakers after moving to Philadelphia in the 1820s and were outspoken abolitionists throughout the 1830s. The public condemnation of their lectures to mixed-sex crowds propelled them to defend a woman's right to political action.

LUCRETIA MOTT was another Quaker abolitionist who became an advocate for women's rights. In her youth, she had worked as a teacher and was paid only half the salary of her male colleagues. As an adult, she had hoped to join William Lloyd Garrison's AMERICAN ANTI-SLAVERY SOCIETY but was denied membership because of her sex. In response, she formed the Female Anti-Slavery Society of Philadelphia and organized a series of conventions for women abolitionists. In 1839, after fierce debate, the American Anti-Slavery Society admitted women to its ranks, causing many who opposed this development to break with the organization and form their own society. Mott joined Garrison's organization and was elected as a delegate to the 1840 World Anti-Slavery Convention in London.

Mott, along with five other women delegates, was refused entrance to the convention because of her sex. The occurrence compounded her earlier experiences with prejudice and persuaded her that a movement to advance women's rights was as necessary as the ABOLITION MOVEMENT. Many of her ideas were honed in conversation with Elizabeth Cady Stanton, the young wife of another American delegate to the convention, who was staying at the same boardinghouse as Mott. Stanton possessed only a fraction of Mott's experience with reform movements, but she was nevertheless appalled by the treatment of the women delegates to the convention. The two agreed that a women's rights convention should be organized in the United States as soon as possible.

It was eight more years before the convention would take place. Mott returned to Philadelphia, where she remained active in abolitionist circles and continued to preach as a Quaker minister. Stanton was absorbed by the birth and care of her children—three before 1847—and the management of her homes, first in New York, then in Boston. Everywhere reformists continued to press for changes in American society. Persistent lobbying eventually secured the passage of a married women's property act in New York in April 1848. Antislavery petitions continued to pour into Congress, and the TRANSCENDENTAL MOVEMENT was flourishing in the Northeast. Within the ranks of Hicksite Quakerism, the pressure brought to bear by many liberals who wanted greater equality for women and a deeper commitment to secular activism resulted in a split in the movement. It was a time replete with the possibility of change.

In 1847 Stanton moved with her husband and children to Seneca Falls, New York. Close to the Quaker community in Waterloo and populated by many abolitionists, Henry Stanton hoped the town would offer him the opportunity to launch a political career. Elizabeth Cady Stanton, however, disliked her new home. She felt cut off from the intellectual circles of Boston and New York, could find no hired help, and found her children hard to control and frequently sick. As her husband began to travel, Stanton felt increasingly isolated. The home that had once been her solace began to feel like her jail.

In July 1848 Lucretia Mott traveled to Seneca Falls to visit her sister, Martha Wright. On July 13, Wright invited Stanton to join the sisters in a visit to their friends Mary Ann McClintock and Jane Hunt. The five women conversed, and in the course of the day, Stanton confessed her discontent with her life at home. The women sympathized and began to talk of the connections between domestic unhappiness and political dependency. By the end of the day, the five had resolved to call the convention that Mott and Stanton had proposed eight years before. The five sent announcements to local newspapers for a convention to be held in six days, on July 19.

It was harvest season around Seneca Falls, and the organizers expected only a few people to attend. Confounding their expectations, some 300 people flocked to the Wesleyan Chapel for the two-day conference, most from the local area, some from great distances, all from upstate New York. Almost everyone in attendance had experience in reform work, whether as Quakers, abolitionists, temperance workers, lawyers, writers, or newspaper editors. Some, such as Mott and Frederick Douglass, were already well known. Others, such as Stanton and AMELIA BLOOMER, would gain their greatest notoriety after the event. Unprepared for such a turnout, the organizers asked James Mott, Lucretia's husband, to chair the event. (Within two weeks, another women's rights convention was held in Rochester, New York; it was chaired by a woman.)

The centerpiece of the Seneca Falls convention was the "Declaration of Sentiments," a list of political grievances generated by the five organizers and written by Stanton. Using the Declaration of Independence as a model, Stanton claimed that "[t]he history of mankind is a history of repeated injuries and usurptions on the part of man toward woman, having in direct object the establishment of an absolute tyranny over her." The document then listed the grievances the women felt most keenly. Women were, they argued, prohibited from voting, from making laws, from securing elected office, from entering profitable employment, from gaining a useful education, and from gaining positions of authority in church. Women had no legal claim to their property, their earnings, or their children, were forced into unnatural obedience to their husbands before the law, were oppressed by divorce laws that favored men, forced to pay taxes without gaining representation, and subject to a moral double standard. In short, charged the women, man had "usurped the prerogative of Jehovah himself, claiming it as his right to assign for [woman] . . . a sphere of action, when that belongs to her conscience and to God." Worthy women, they argued, lacked the rights that men, regardless of character, enjoyed.

The Declaration of Sentiments was both shrewd and revolutionary. It was shrewd because it used the language on which the republic was formed to demonstrate the failings of government toward half of those it governed. It was revolutionary because it removed husbands, fathers, brothers, and children from a woman's claim to citizenship. Women did not ask for the opportunity to serve others more faithfully. Instead, they demanded the right to serve themselves.

For two days, the men and women in attendance at the convention debated the declaration. Thirteen resolutions were offered and passed, 12 of them unanimously. One passed by majority vote—a resolution offered on the second day by Elizabeth Cady Stanton in which she called for a campaign for woman's suffrage. It was a controversial resolution, not because the idea was new but because many activists feared that the idea would garner so much negative attention that it would make their other goals impossible to achieve. There were also Quaker women in attendance who did not want the vote, as it would make them party to a political system that approved of war.

At the end of the second day, 68 women and 32 men signed the Declaration of Sentiments. They ranged in age from 14 to 68 and came from a variety of backgrounds. Under immense pressure from their families and friends, many—including Elizabeth Cady Stanton's sister Harriet—would later recant their support for the declaration. The principles and ideas it contain continued to spread, however, communicated through family and reform networks across the country. Women's rights conventions were held in numerous states for years to come. The political and social demands of women became impossible to ignore.

Further reading: Gerda Lerner, "The Meaning of Seneca Falls, 1848–1898," *Dissent* Fall (1998): 35–41; Judith Wellman, "The Seneca Falls Women's Rights Convention: A Study of Social Networks," *Journal of Women's History* 3 (1991): 9–37.

—Catherine J. Denial

Seton, Elizabeth Ann (1774–1821)

The first American-born Roman Catholic saint, Elizabeth Ann Seton founded the Catholic order known as the Sisters of Charity, the first American-based community of Roman Catholic women. She is also regarded as the mother of the parochial school system in the United States.

Seton was born into the prominent Bayley family of New York City. Her father, physician Richard Bayley, was an educator and a public servant who served as Columbia University's first professor of anatomy and New York City's first public-health officer. Her mother, the daughter of an Episcopalian minister, saw that their children were reared in the Protestant faith. Elizabeth would often accompany her father as he cared for the desperately sick Irish immigrants in the city's quarantine on Staten Island. She was struck by both their poverty and their strong, sustaining Catholic faith.

In 1794 Elizabeth Bayley married William Magee Seton, a prosperous financier. They had five children, but as she raised her young family, she found herself drawn toward religious contemplation and charity. Early each morning, she left her fashionable house on the Bowery with a basket filled with medicines and food for the poor. Though pregnant, she ministered to the quarantined immigrants by her father's side and nursed him through the course of the yellow fever he contracted from his patients. He died of the illness in 1801.

At the same time, her own family's financial and physical health declined. William Seton had inherited his father's troubled banking and shipping businesses, and they continued to founder. Meanwhile, a lingering tubercular condition left him a near-invalid. By 1803, William was convinced that only a sojourn in Italy, where he had lived for a time as a young man, would cure him. The couple set off with their eldest child, but to no avail; William died in Italy.

Elizabeth Seton found herself in a strange country, widowed, separated from her children, and without funds, but she was unbowed by all this hardship. Instead, she made many friends, all of whom were Roman Catholics. Again, she was fascinated by their faith. She began to study Catholicism in earnest, returned to New York in 1804, and there was confirmed a Catholic in 1805.

Her new faith made her very nearly an outcast in the New York of the day. Catholics were a distinct minority, made up largely of working-class immigrants. Seton found work as a teacher, but her notoriety and several incidents

Elizabeth Ann Seton *(Library of Congress)*

of anti-Catholic violence soon made life in New York impossible.

In 1808, the Archdiocese of Baltimore came to the rescue. Seton was invited to come, children and all, and open the first Catholic elementary school in America. Her school for girls was an immediate success—Catholics were a majority in Maryland, not the oddity they were in New York—and "Mother Seton," as she soon became known, attracted four postulants, or nuns-in-training, within a year of her arrival. The women took vows, chose a habit, and lived, studied, taught, and worshipped together. The first American religious order had been born.

When a tract of land in Emmitsburg, Maryland, was donated to Mother Seton in 1809, she established the Sisters of Charity's motherhouse there. During the next several decades, the sisters opened schools and hospitals in cities throughout the Northeast and as far west as Cincinnati. The order's rule was influenced by St. Vincent de Paul and was organized along the lines of his Daughters of Charity in France. More than 150 of the sisters would serve as nurses in the Civil War.

Mother Seton was the order's superior until her death in 1821. In 1975, she was canonized as a saint of the Catholic Church.

Further reading: Leonard Feeney, *Saint Elizabeth of New York* (Still River, Mass.: Ravengate Press, 1975.)

—Mary Kay Linge

slavery

An economic, political, and cultural institution lasting for more than two centuries, slavery affected every man, woman, and child in the 19th century United States. In broad terms, American slavery could be considered a labor system in which enslaved men and women, overwhelmingly of African descent, were owned by free men and women, overwhelmingly white. Yet such a definition obscures the complexity of the system and the ways in which it was shaped by those who participated in it, whether by coercion or by choice. Slavery varied by industry, by region, through personal relationships, and by the actions of owners and enslaved men and women themselves. Often defined in total opposition to liberty, slavery was in fact a complicated cultural system in which enslaved men and women actively negotiated and fought for multiple freedoms on the road to their emancipation. While the institution of slavery ended with the Civil War and Reconstruction, this fight for freedom continued well into the 20th century.

Politically, slavery was a contentious issue with the power to divide the United States. All of the original 13 colonies had permitted slavery before the Revolutionary War, although the highest concentration of enslaved people was in the South. Less dependent on slave labor to support its more diversified economy, the North was able to move cautiously toward abolition after the war. Historians have debated the reasons for this shift. Some contend that the rhetoric of the American Revolution, with its emphasis on personal liberty and the natural rights of man, convinced individuals that it was hypocritical to own slaves. Others contend that the shift was motivated purely by economics or religious conviction. Whatever combination of motivations spurred northern states toward abolition, slavery came to a slow end in the late 18th and early 19th centuries.

Northern abolition was neither uniform nor immediate. Many states chose to free enslaved men and women once they reached adulthood or if they accepted Christianity. Others legislated that existing slaves would live in bondage, but their children would be born free. This gradual emancipation meant that a significant number of slaves existed in the North well into the 19th century, although their numbers dropped steadily with time. Congress had endeavored to make new northern territories free as early as 1787. The Northwest Ordinance, passed in that year to govern the expansion, settlement, and government of the Ohio region and beyond, prohibited "involuntary servitude" in the territory. Slaves accompanying their owners on travel or to military service in the northern territories remained enslaved despite these legislative developments.

In the South, slavery was so firmly entrenched in the region's culture and so central to its economic health that abolition was widely opposed. There had been efforts during the revolutionary period to relax the grounds on which owners might manumit their slaves, but these were not widespread. They were further scaled back after events like the aborted Prosser Slave Rebellion in 1800 outside Richmond, Virginia, convinced many southerners that their lives were at risk. Unlike most slave regimes in South America, the slave population of the American South grew through natural reproduction, sometimes through consensual sex, sometimes through abuse and rape, often at the hands of slave owners. This natural increase in the slave population made slavery especially profitable for whites. After a one-time investment in slaves, slaveholders expected them to increase in number and value with only a moderate additional investment of food and shelter. Since slaves were considered property that could be willed and inherited, many individuals became slave owners without buying a slave themselves. The entire economic structure of slaveholding was based on the idea of free labor. Paying slaves a wage, argued the slaveholders, would completely undermine the region's economy.

Southerners did not argue that slavery was a purely economic necessity. Many argued that it was a moral blessing. Proponents of slavery contended that conditions in the factories of the North were far worse than those in the slave communities of the South. They suggested that northerners should turn their reformist zeal toward their own poor rather than demanding an end to slavery, an institution which they argued provided food, clothing, and shelter to those within its bounds. Conditioned by racial prejudice, proponents of slavery often argued that AFRICAN AMERICANS lacked intelligence, common sense, and a work ethic, making them incapable of supporting themselves outside the confines of the institution. Southerners also defended the long workdays imposed on slaves as well as the prohibition of education and noninstitutional religious meetings. Too much education, too little work, and the unsupervised practice of religion, they argued, would make slaves a danger to white citizens across the South.

Slavery was also bound up with the issue of states' rights. From its inception, the republic had struggled with the issue of slavery and the right of the federal government to govern its existence. Article One of the Constitution, which decreed that slaves would be counted as three-fifths of a person for the purpose of census counts (thus allowing southern states to gain a greater number of Congressional representatives than if free-born men had been counted alone) recorded such struggle and compromise. By 1819, as Missouri and Maine both applied to become states in the Union, the struggle had become particularly severe. Eleven free states and 11 slave states existed in the Union, with the free states supporting 105 delegates to the House of Representatives, as opposed to the South's 81. Several antislavery delegates offered amendments to the legislation making Missouri a state, demanding that the slavery be prohibited within the region. A bitter debate ensued in which the arguments for and against slavery—political, economic, and cultural—were all aired. At the crux of the matter lay the Constitution. Antislavery delegates insisted that Congress's power to set the terms by which new states entered the Union gave the federal government the power to prohibit slavery. Proponents of slavery argued that the government possessed no such power, and that the Constitution protected state and personal liberties. A compromise

This illustration idealizes slavery; the reality was that picking cotton for long hours, six days a week, was grueling work. *(Library of Congress)*

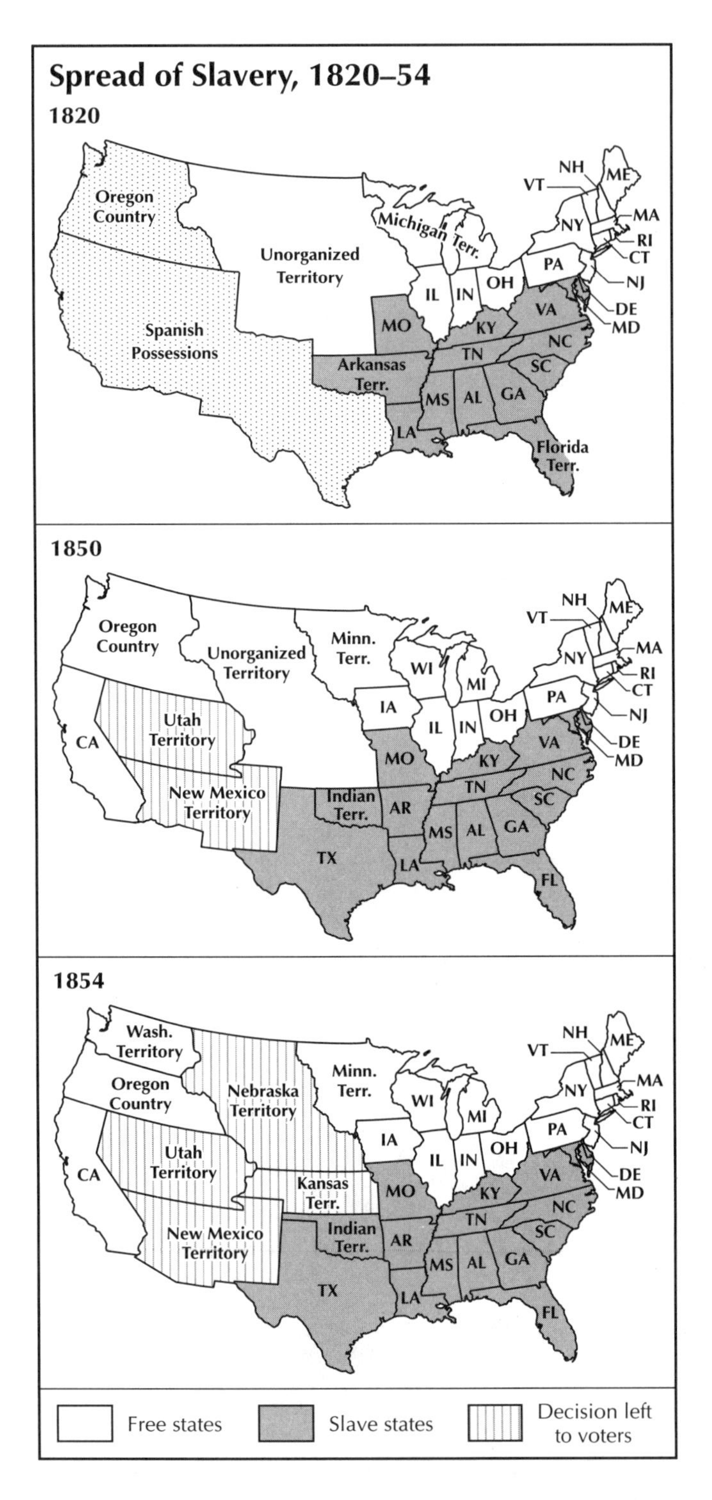

was eventually forged in which Maine entered the Union as a free state, Missouri as a slave state, and slavery was prohibited in all remaining territories of the Louisiana Purchase, north of 30°36'.

This was not the end of sectional difficulties, however, nor a permanent answer to the question of which rights legitimately belonged to the states. The issue was revisited with the Kansas-Nebraska Act of 1854 and the decision in *Dred Scott v. Sandford* (1857), both of which undermined the federal government's ability to regulate slavery in the states. In December 1860, South Carolina seceded from the Union, believing that the election of Abraham Lincoln to the presidency would result in a concerted attempt to limit states' rights. Ten other southern states followed suit, and within the year a civil war had begun.

Yet slavery was much more than a political question. For millions of Americans, it was a way of life. At the outbreak of the Civil War, an estimated 4 million African Americans were held as slaves in the southern and western territories of the United States. Despite sharing a common legal identity, their experiences differed widely depending on the type of labor they were expected to perform.

The vast majority of slaves lived in rural areas. Contrary to popular imagination, few lived on sprawling plantations but instead lived and worked on small farms. The most popular crops grown by slave labor were cotton, rice, sugar, and tobacco, with smaller investments in corn and indigo. Field labor was notoriously harsh no matter what was grown, but each crop demanded a specific cycle of cultivation and harvest. While tobacco required constant attention, it facilitated a steady pace of work and was relatively safe to grow, harvest, and process. Rice, on the other hand, grew in water, and slaves were easy prey for waterborne diseases. Rice cultivation required relentless labor, and while workdays might be short, they were exhausting. In order to turn rice into a viable product for market, it had to be watered, harvested, dried, buried, stacked, threshed, winnowed, and pounded by hand. Accidents were common from the complexity of the work and the fatigue that accompanied production. Cotton cultivation required physical strength and endurance since workdays were always long, especially in picking season. An average enslaved man or woman was expected to pick between 150 and 200 pounds of cotton a day. All slaves had a supervisor, whether their owner, an overseer, or the head of their field gang. The level of supervision varied, from task systems where enslaved men or women were allowed a degree of control over how long it took to complete a job to oppressive regimes where the work pace was enforced by whippings or beatings.

Even in rural areas, not all enslaved men and women worked in the fields. Many slave owners used slave labor in their homes where women worked as housekeepers, cooks, nursery maids, and laundresses; and men were employed as blacksmiths, wheelwrights, valets, and stable hands. These positions often offered physically comfortable working conditions when compared to field labor, but they required slaves to work under the direct supervision of their owners. The result was too often the physical and sexual abuse of slaves by slaveholders and their families.

A sizeable number of slaves worked in urban communities during the antebellum period. Urban slavery generally offered enslaved men and women greater freedom of movement, the chance to earn money from their labor, and the opportunity to acquire and perfect a marketable skill. As well as employing slaves in their homes, many urban slave owners allowed enslaved men and women to hire themselves out for wages in return for paying a fee every week. Such opportunities were more plentiful for men than for women. Men could work in construction, in skilled trades such as carpentry, at railroad terminals, and on docks. Women were more limited in their options; the most skilled profession open to them was midwifery, and their more usual choices included dressmaking, laundry, and market work. This inequality of opportunity also existed in rural slave communities, where skilled positions were most likely given to men. Inequalities spilled over into the home lives of slaves, where the burdens of housekeeping, laundry, cooking, and child care fell heavily on the shoulders of women.

In all aspects of their lives, slaves fought to maintain and protect their own traditions and communities, even in the face of opposition from white society. At work, slaves engaged in slowdowns and sabotage to regulate the pace of work imposed on them by overseers and owners. Some slaves offered physical resistance to their ill-treatment, and many ran away in the hopes of reuniting with loved ones or escaping the harsh conditions under which they worked. Widespread revolts such as NAT TURNER's rebellion of 1831 testified to the fierce desire of enslaved men and women to be free, regardless of southern platitudes about the benevolence of slavery as an institution.

On a day-to-day level, enslaved men and women worked hard to create a meaningful life away from work. Men and women entered into marriage, solemnizing their relationships through customs such as "jumping the broom" even as Anglo law denied the legality of such ceremonies. Blending African tradition, neighborly obligation, and friendship, enslaved men and women observed extended kinship networks that stretched beyond individual farms to surrounding counties, even as slave owners wielded the power to divide families and sell individuals far from home. Despite frequent bans on unorganized religious activity, slaves interpreted the Bible for themselves, practiced multiple African religions, and often blended these to create wholly new expressions of spirituality. Despite the widespread prohibition of slave education, literate slaves and sympathetic free whites and blacks did teach others to read and write. Often barely sustained by rations of food and clothing from their owners, enslaved men and women supplemented their lot by hunting and raising gardens where possible. For many slaves, these activities represented a measure of freedom, hard won amid an oppressive system of exploitation.

Further reading: Frederick Douglass, *The Life and Times of Frederick Douglass, An American Slave, Written by Himself* (1845; reprint, Boston: Bedford Books, 1993); Elizabeth Fox-Genovese, *Within the Plantation Household: Black and White Women of the Old South* (Chapel Hill: University of North Carolina Press, 1988); Eugene Genovese, *Roll, Jordan, Roll: The World the Slaves Made* (New York: Random House, 1974); Harriet Jacobs, *Incidents in the Life of a Slave Girl, Written By Herself*, ed. Jean Fagan Yellin (1861; reprint, Cambridge: Harvard University Press, 1987); Leslie A. Schwalm, *"A Hard Fight for We": Women's Transition from Slavery to Freedom in Lowcountry South Carolina* (Urbana: University of Illinois Press, 1997).

—Catherine J. Denial

slave trade, internal

Although increasingly confined to the South, American SLAVERY underwent massive expansion in the antebellum period. From some 700,000 in 1790, the number of slaves had more than quintupled to almost 4 million in 1860. The African slave trade was stopped in 1808, only to be supplanted by an equally horrific domestic slave trade. Hundreds of thousands of black Americans were taken west in irons to sustain the growth of a vast southern empire based on slave labor. By 1860, slavery had spread to nine new states and extended more than halfway across the continent into Texas.

In the half-century after the legal termination of the African slave trade, the slave population of the United States first surpassed that of any other country in the New World and then went on to exceed that of all the other American countries combined. This growth was due almost entirely to natural increase, as the number of slaves smuggled into the United States roughly equaled the number gaining freedom through manumission or escape.

There are several reasons for the much higher growth rate in the United States. The generally healthy and mild climate of the South kept slaves from succumbing to the kinds of diseases more prevalent in the tropics. Work as a field hand was an unremitting ordeal, but the cultivation of cotton and tobacco was less physically demanding than that of sugar or coffee. Most important, though, was that slaves themselves became the crop.

Cotton cultivation, which required a minimum growing season of 200 frostless days, was confined to the Lower South. The rapid expansion of cotton plantations across the Deep South created an intense demand for slave labor. Slave owners in the Upper South quickly realized that their "surplus" slaves were a valuable commodity. With the decline in tobacco production, it was a commodity the Chesapeake states, particularly Virginia, had in abundance. By 1800 a domestic slave trade had developed, with slave traders purchasing excess slaves in non-cotton-producing states and then moving them to cotton-producing areas for sale. This domestic commerce had already reached the point in 1808 where it could readily replace the newly closed African slave trade as the regular source of slaves.

The Deep South's cotton boom, combined with the ban on slave importations, kept the domestic slave trade a lucrative business throughout the antebellum period. The price of a field hand eventually rose from about $300 in 1795 to between $1,200 and $1,800 in 1860. It was not unusual for the average trader's annual rate of return to reach 30 percent. Such profits bound the South together in a slave economy.

As the COTTON CULTURE moved westward into Alabama, Mississippi, Louisiana, and Texas, so did the domestic slave trade. It is estimated about 1 million slaves were taken west between 1790 and 1860. Many accompanied masters who left home in search of new opportunities. This was the case with the majority of the early black migrants into Kentucky and Tennessee, as many of the states' first settlers were slave owners from Virginia and North Carolina. Later in the Deep South, entire plantation staffs would be moved westward by slave-owning families relocating or expanding their holdings.

After 1815, the domestic slave trade predominated in the forced internal migration of slaves. Eventually, the commerce accounted for as much as 70 percent of the massive transfer of slaves westward. In doing so it replicated many of the horrors of the African slave trade; it also created new ones. One of these was the virtual breeding of slaves. Almost all the blacks relocated by the domestic slave trade came from the more northern slave states and almost all went to the cotton-producing tier of states along the Gulf of Mexico. Maryland, North Carolina, and Kentucky all had active slave markets, but Virginia was by far the biggest provider, sending roughly 300,000 slaves to the Gulf states between 1830 and 1860.

To ensure a steady supply of slaves, slave owners in the Upper South took to guaranteeing the constant replenishment of their slave populations through the most basic means of human reproduction. Some chose mates for young slaves and forced them to live together. More often, owners would encourage slaves to marry, and thus to procreate, at an early age.

When it came time to sell, however, there was little or no respect for slave marriages, much less the slave families. In many cases, slaves were sold and moved without regard for family ties. In the Upper South, about one in three marriages was broken by the slave trade, and close to half of all children were sold away from at least one parent. Most sellers kept children with their mothers until about age 13, at which point they were deemed capable of work and thus ready for market.

Slaves were normally bought and sold at auction like cattle. Most in demand, not surprisingly, were prime field hands, ranging in age from 15 to 30. Next in order of value were slaves capable of household and industrial tasks. A disproportionate share of the slaves sent west were young adults between the ages of 15 and 25. Both men and women toiled as field hands. Except to Louisiana, where the premium was on young men for the backbreaking work in the sugar fields, slave merchants shipped roughly equal numbers of males and females.

It was not uncommon for a young female slave in Virginia to find herself suddenly torn from her family and transported hundreds of miles to a strange new plantation in Mississippi. Separation from relatives and friends was probably the most devastating experience endured by slaves. The physical ordeal of the journey west was made even worse by the psychological cruelty involved in the permanent forced parting from loved ones.

Most of the domestic slave trade moved overland. Slaves were formed into coffles, or chain gangs, and marched under guard into boats that plied the coastal waters from Virginia to Texas. Major marketing and distribution points included Richmond, Norfolk, and Louisville in the slave-sending Upper South and Charleston, Mobile, and New Orleans in the slave-receiving Lower South. The trade was relentless, with at least 100,000 slaves taken west every decade between 1810 and 1860.

Further reading: Michael Tadman, *Speculators and Slaves: Masters, Traders and Slaves in the Old South* (Madison: University of Wisconsin Press, 1989).

Smith, Jedediah Strong (1799–1831)

Fur trader and explorer who opened up trails and territory that were followed by settlers of the West, Jedediah Strong Smith was born in Bainbridge, New York, in 1799. As a young man, he had a good basic education by the standards of the day. At 13, he found a job as a clerk on a Lake Erie commercial vessel and gained experience in business transactions. He may also have met fur trappers and traders from the Great Lakes and southern Canada. He left the Lake Erie trade for St. Louis, perhaps as early as 1816 but certainly by the end of the decade. There he saw WILLIAM HENRY ASHLEY's notice in the *St. Louis Gazette,* with a call to "Enterprising Young Men . . . to ascend the Missouri to its source, there to be employed for one, two, or three years." Smith responded to the appeal and discovered the opportunities associated with the FUR TRADE.

In 1822, Smith joined Ashley's first expedition up the Missouri River. The following year, he was once again on the upper Missouri when his party was attacked by the Arikara and suffered several casualties. He next led an overland party to the Black Hills, where he was badly injured in an encounter with a grizzly bear. From this point, Smith and his group went west, wintering in Wyoming. From encounters with Native Americans, he learned of an easy gateway through the Rocky Mountains. Expeditions from Fort ASTORIA had used SOUTH PASS as a gateway to the West in 1811, but Smith's rediscovery of it in 1824 made it a vital part of transcontinental travel. Over the next generation, South Pass would become the access route by way of the Platte and Sweetwater Rivers through the mountains used by overlanders on both the CALIFORNIA TRAIL and the OREGON TRAIL. Not only was South Pass a gentle slope, it was also wide enough to allow the use of wagons.

In 1824, still in Ashley's employ, Smith met the Hudson's Bay Company expedition to the Snake River Country, and he visited the HBC post at Flathead Lake. Based on his observations, he wrote a report for Ashley on the outfitting and trading policies of their chief rival. The following year, Ashley made Smith a full partner and placed him in charge of field operations. At the second great RENDEZVOUS in 1826, Smith (with David Jackson and WILLIAM SUBLETTE) bought out Ashley, who retired to St. Louis and politics.

As a managing partner in his own company, Smith and a few chosen companions now set out to explore the West in search of new fur-trapping and trading opportunities. They went from the rendezvous to the south, past the Great Salt Lake, along the Colorado River, and through the

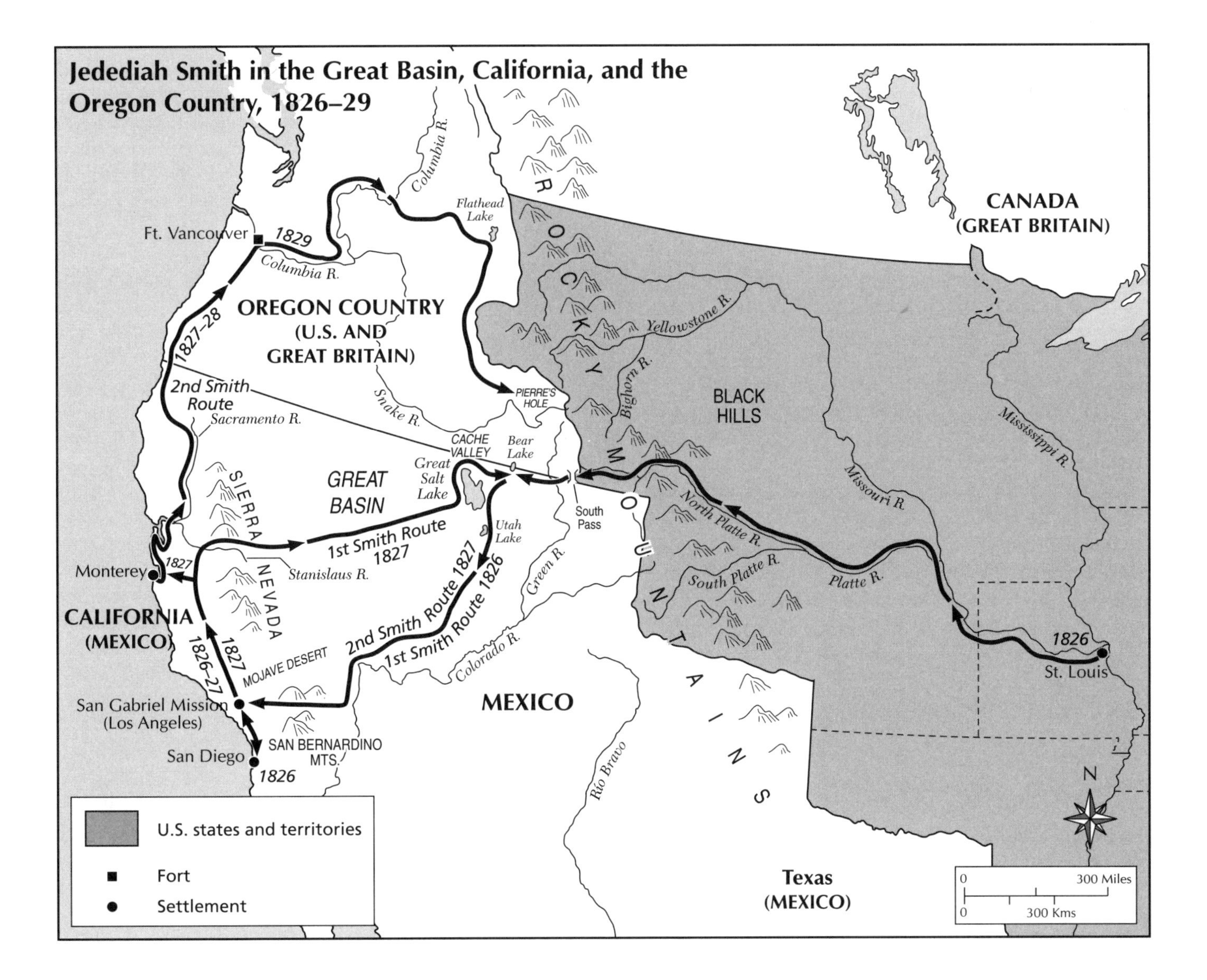

Mohave Desert, crossing into California and coming to the San Gabriel Mission in late November 1826. The Americans' presence aroused the suspicion of the Mexican governor of California, and Smith soon departed north through the San Joaquin Valley. In spite of repeated attempts in the face of difficult conditions, Smith failed to find a passage through the Sierra Nevada, and he and his company had to winter in the valley. The following spring, they crossed the mountains and made their way back to the Rockies by way of the Great Salt Lake to the annual rendezvous, arriving in July 1827. In making this journey, Smith and his companions were the first Americans to cross the Sierra Nevada from west to east.

In late summer 1827, Smith set out to retrace his earlier year's route, but this time he and his party were attacked by the Mohave Indians. Ten members of the party were killed, and Smith led the eight survivors across the mountains into California and the mission at San Gabriel. Although he had only just survived the Indian assault, Smith's second appearance in California intensified the suspicion of Mexican officials. Eventually permitted to leave, he made his way by San Francisco and the San Joaquin Valley north to Oregon. In July 1828, Indians attacked Smith and his party on the Umpqua River. Of 18 men in the party, only Smith and three others escaped to find refuge at FORT VANCOUVER. There, JOHN MCLOUGHLIN gave Smith assistance, including the recovery of some of his furs seized at the Umpqua River. The meeting of Smith and McLoughlin at Fort Vancouver brought together two of the most important figures in the fur trade, and each represented the separate lines associated with the enterprise: McLoughlin the savvy administrator for the Hudson's Bay Company, who ran his empire from a fort; Smith, the explorer constantly on the move, who represented the independent trader.

Based on his stay at Fort Vancouver, Smith wrote a report for the secretary of war assessing the British presence in the Oregon Country. In 1828, he once again attended the annual rendezvous, when he decided to retire from the fur-trading business. In 1830, however, he was persuaded to enter the Santa Fe trade. Like CHARLES BENT and WILLIAM BENT, Smith recognized that the future of the trade lay in the Southwest. He organized and captained a caravan of goods headed for the New Mexican capital of Santa Fe. As he scouted ahead to find a water hole, he was attacked and killed by Comanche Indians on the Cimarron River.

When Smith died in 1831 at the age of 32, he was one of the nation's most accomplished fur traders and explorers. Modern scholars have acknowledged his many accomplishments; transcontinental travelers were indebted to him for identifying South Pass as the universal route to the west; and his fellow trappers and traders widely admired him for his modesty, faithfulness, and kindness.

Further reading: Dale L. Morgan, *Jedediah Smith and the Opening of the West* (Indianapolis: Bobbs-Merrill, 1953); Alson Jesse Smith, *Men Against the Mountains: Jedediah Smith and the Southwest Expedition of 1826–1829* (New York: John Day Company, 1965).

Smith, Joseph, Jr. (1805–1844)

Founder, prophet, and first president of the CHURCH OF JESUS CHRIST OF LATTER-DAY SAINTS, Joseph Smith, Jr., was born in Sharon, Vermont. He was the fourth of nine children in a family with marginal economic prospects, and his father failed at a variety of enterprises, most of them associated with farming and storekeeping. The young Smith moved with his family several times across northern New England and finally in 1816 to Palmyra, New York. Like other children in similar circumstances, Joseph had little formal schooling, and from an early age, he sought employment to assist the family's marginal circumstances. In this capacity, he worked as a hired laborer on neighboring farms. As others in that time sometimes did, he looked for buried treasure, and he claimed to have special powers to find hidden riches.

Smith's family bequeathed him a heritage of intense religious introspection. His mother joined the Presbyterian Church, but his father remained outside any religious denomination and maintained a belief in dreams and revelations. The surrounding countryside and indeed the whole of upstate New York was caught up in religious feelings and disputations that gave it the name "burned-over district." It was in this context that Smith claimed to be visited by God and Jesus Christ in the spring of 1820. On this occasion, according to Smith, these divine personages indicated to him that he had been chosen for a special task that would be revealed subsequently. Three years later, according to Smith, he was visited by the Angel Moroni and informed that he had been chosen to translate a text from golden plates. The text was the history of pre-Columbian inhabitants of the Western Hemisphere. According to Smith's account, between 1823 and 1827 he made periodic visits to the site of the hidden plates, and he received instructions that would make him the modern prophet of a new religion. Completed in 1830, the publication of the *Book of Mormon* provided the text for the new religion, and Joseph Smith, Jr., was its prophet. On April 6, 1830, Smith incorporated the new church under New York law and revealed a revelation that designated him "a seer, a translator, a prophet, and apostle of Jesus Christ."

Smith's first converts were members of his own family, but he soon recruited others, including Heber C. Kimball and BRIGHAM YOUNG. Smith's continuing revelations—on subjects ranging from heaven and hell to the economy and banking—kept the church in turmoil. But whatever the day-to-day confusion, the church grew, from perhaps 300 at the close of 1830 to 700 at the close of 1831. With the conversion of Sidney Rigdon and his congregation of the Christian Church (Disciples of Christ), Smith moved the church to Kirtland, Ohio. At the same time, he established a strong missionary presence in western Missouri, near the frontier town of Independence. The church grew and prospered in Kirtland, and by 1835 its numbers exceeded 8,500, although exact numbers are unknown. In Kirtland, Smith directed the construction of a temple, the first of what would become several Mormon temples. Just as the Mormon community in Kirtland prospered in the boom times of the early 1830s, so it suffered with the onset of the PANIC OF 1837 and the subsequent depression. The situation was especially serious because the church had become involved in the banking business, and when the bank failed, the church was confronted by furious non-Mormon creditors.

Smith and his church fled Kirtland for the Mormon settlements in western Missouri, although apostasy thinned the ranks of the faithful. In Missouri, the church soon found itself in escalating conflict with its surrounding neighbors. As the membership continued to expand, so did the church's need for land, and aggressive, expansionist Mormons made neighbors uneasy. Furthermore, the Mormons were a closed and self-righteous group, openly proclaiming their virtues as a "chosen people" and denouncing the sins of the rest of the world. They were eastern in their cultural characteristics, alien to the frontier environment of western Missouri, and sympathetic to the plight of slaves and Indians alike. These views made their presence unwelcome to other settlements in western Missouri. Conflicts escalated in the late 1830s, especially after the arrival of the church members from Kirtland. Missourians raided Mormon settlements, and Smith, tired of turning the other cheek, organized a quasi-military body known as "the Danites" to protect the church and its leadership. The church and Joseph Smith now became an issue in state politics. Missouri governor Lilburn Boggs apparently saw the Mormons and their prophet as a useful political target, and, speaking of them as threats to domestic order, he issued what became known as an "order of extermination," ordering Mormons to leave the state or face expulsion.

What became known as the Mormon War of 1838–39 cost Smith and his church severe losses. Men and women were killed, property destroyed, and when Boggs called up the state militia to enter the war, Smith's position was hopeless. He agreed to surrender, and he and other Mormon leaders were jailed for five months without formal charges. While they were incarcerated, Brigham Young took command and organized the emigration of the Mormon community from Missouri to Illinois, where, they took over a small village, Commerce, on the upper Missouri River. Smith, released from a Missouri jail in April 1839 and once more leader of the church, renamed the town NAUVOO. Here, beginning in 1839, the church and its leader began another cycle of prosperity and growth. Bolstered by numbers of converts from aggressive missionary activities and natural increase, the population of Nauvoo grew steadily, and by 1845 Mormons claimed 12,000 people in the city, numbers that rivaled Chicago as the most rapidly growing and progressive in the state.

Joseph Smith, Jr. *(Library of Congress)*

Smith's plans for Nauvoo were three-dimensional. To begin with, alarmed by the Missouri experience and its threat to the Mormon community, he sought political and military power. He found political influence by bargaining with the state's Whig and Democratic parties, almost equally balanced in numbers. Using his leverage to deliver a bloc of votes, Smith received the concessions of independence and security that he sought. The state legislature passed, and the governor signed, the so-called "Nauvoo Charter," which gave specific rights to the Mormon community. These included the authority to establish a university (founded but never organized) and its own court system. Smith was elected mayor of Nauvoo under the charter in 1842, and at the same time, the governor made him a major general in the Illinois state militia. Smith organized the Nauvoo Legion, a training body of men armed with guns from the state arsenals who were the answer to his search for military security.

In spring 1844, Smith announced himself a candidate for president of the United States, confirming Mormon views of his destiny to lead the nation and non-Mormon views that he was a danger to the nation. He also embarked on religious growth that paralleled the secular prosperity of Nauvoo. He ordered the construction of a large temple, which would become the center of church life and rituals, and experienced a series of religious revelations that laid the basis for the church's future. Included among these were the ordinance sealing husbands and wives for eternity and his declaration that men could become godlike. But the most important of these revelations for the immediate future of the church was the one sanctioning POLYGAMY, under which a chosen church leader would have more than one wife. Smith may have taken his first plural wife as early as 1841, but the revelation on polygamy is dated 1843, and within a year, other prominent church leaders had secretly married plural wives. When the practice became known, deep divisions within the church developed over it. Smith at first publicly disavowed the practice of polygamy. Some of those who left the church (or were expelled) wrote vivid accounts, quite horrifying to a 19th-century Protestant America that saw marriage based on monogamy.

In the face of this controversy, various church leaders remained loyal to the church itself but agitated for the removal of Smith as president. Consequently, Smith surrounded himself with a personal bodyguard to insure his office. In spring 1844, a group of dissident church leaders published a newspaper, the *Nauvoo Expositor,* which exposed the doctrine of polygamy and called Smith "a fallen prophet." He now used his authority to condemn the press as a danger to the public and ordered the destruction of the press. The dissidents fled Nauvoo in fear of their lives, and they swore out a warrant for Smith's arrest, charging him with disorderly conduct. Assured by the governor of his personal safety, Smith surrendered and was lodged in the Carthage jail. On June 27, 1844, a mob broke into the jail and assassinated Joseph Smith and his brother Hyrum. The Mormon prophet was 38 years old.

In his short life, Joseph Smith became one of the most charismatic American religious leaders of the 19th century. Indeed, in terms of the lasting influence of his church, no other religious leader compares to his presence over almost two centuries. Smith established a church with great appeal to Americans in his time, one that spoke to men and women of small means (like the family from which he came), that condemned the rich and powerful, and that praised success in economic ventures. Furthermore, if the church was male-dominated through the priesthood, so was every other church at the time, and Smith made the perfection of the church and the godlike stature of its members available to all men, women, and children. By opening salvation to families through conversion, ancestors could gain this exalted status. With continuing prophecies, Smith could meet the changing conditions faced by the church, and he did so. Tall, distinguished, commanding, and articulate, he seemed to embody physically the prophets that he spoke of, wrote about, and represented.

Further reading: Fawn M. Brodie, *No Man Knows My History: The Life of Joseph Smith* (New York: Knopf, 1945); Jan Shipps, *Mormonism: The Story of a New Religious Tradition* (Urbana: University of Illinois Press, 1985).

South Pass

South Pass is a route across the Continental Divide, between the northern and southern Rocky Mountains. Part of the OREGON TRAIL, CALIFORNIA TRAIL, and MORMON TRAIL, it was used by overland immigrants from the 1830s to the late 1860s.

Although Native Americans had known of South Pass for centuries, the first Euro-American to use it was Robert Stuart and a group of Astorians, who were returning eastward from ASTORIA on the Oregon Coast in 1812. Stuart's discovery was ignored, since trading companies at that time viewed transcontinental travel as more difficult than travel by sea. In opening up the trade of the Pacific Coast, JOHN JACOB ASTOR primarily used sea vessels. With the close of the WAR OF 1812, fur traders and explorers resumed overland travel. In spring 1824, JEDEDIAH STRONG SMITH and a party of trappers used the pass, apparently after being informed by a Crow Indian of the easy route across the Continental Divide. Smith recognized the significance of the pass for the FUR TRADE: Furs and supplies could be moved this way across the Rocky Mountains and in so doing avoid the dangerous route via the upper Missouri River. WILLIAM HENRY ASHLEY subsequently used South Pass to bring supplies to the RENDEZVOUS in 1825.

South Pass, as used by the fur traders and later overland travelers, was a gentle slope at the southern end of the Wind River Mountains. A broad, high plain, some 20 miles wide, it in no way resembled the image of a jagged gap in a mountain range. Travelers followed the Sweetwater River to its source and then continued up the gradual rise, to a height of 7,550 feet; a few miles later, the waters flowed west. Overland travelers confided in their journals that they found the "pass" something of a disappointment, although they came to appreciate its easy access across a formidable mountain barrier.

In 1830, Jedediah Smith and his trading partners informed the secretary of war that South Pass offered easy access to the Oregon Country. At a time when the issue of Oregon was still a contentious one (later settled by the OREGON TREATY OF 1846), South Pass provided an important means to move settlers and supplies into this contested region. In 1832, Captain Benjamin Bonneville brought wagons through the pass, thus demonstrating the trail's usefulness for settler families traveling to Oregon and CALIFORNIA. Four years later, Narcissa Whitman and Eliza Spaulding, going west as the wives of missionaries, were the first white women to cross South Pass.

By the late 1830s and early 1840s, annual wagon trains of several hundred settler families went overland to Oregon by way of South Pass. In 1843, the federal government dispatched JOHN C. FRÉMONT to explore routes to the West, but Frémont's well-publicized expedition added nothing to the accepted consensus that South Pass was the best route to Oregon and the Pacific Northwest. It soon also became the standard route to California.

With the discovery of gold in 1848, California became a national obsession, and the numbers on the overland trail grew in like proportion. In 1849, some 75,000 FORTY-NINERS crossed the pass in a single season, and annual numbers thereafter remained high. The large number of diaries and travel accounts of the gold-seekers and the numbers of published accounts established South Pass—along with FORT LARAMIE, Independence Rock, the Humboldt River, and Sutter's Fort—as a landmark in the great overland pioneering experience. Mormons, who also used the trail to the Utah settlement of the CHURCH OF JESUS CHRIST OF LATTER-DAY SAINTS, joined the argonauts on the way west. Although the Mormons continued to use the overland trail, with its variations to Salt Lake City, until the completion of the transcontinental railroad in 1869, by the middle of 1850s, many California-bound migrants had shifted to the sea route. Between 1836 and 1853, some 160,000 overland migrants used South Pass.

Further reading: John D. Unruh, *The Plains Across* (Urbana: University of Illinois Press, 1979).

spiritualism

The central tenet of spiritualism, a 19th-century American religious movement, is that spirits of the dead can communicate with the living through mediums. The spiritualist movement began in 1845 when two sisters, Kate and Margaret Fox, heard knocks on walls and tables in their upstate New York home. Amy and Isaac Post, well-known Quaker activists in Rochester, New York, publicized the Fox sisters' experiences and invited many progressive friends to view the young girls' preternatural abilities. The sisters toured the United States in the 1850s, spreading the spiritualist ideology to such far-reaching sites as Philadelphia, Ohio, New York City, and Washington, D.C. This tour helped spread spiritualism in the Midwest and along the eastern seaboard.

Spiritualists believed that humans could communicate with the souls of the dead. Séances and the use of ouija boards (known as planchettes) aided them in their quest to speak to their dead loved ones. The desire to contact the dead reflected the anxieties of a rising middle class, for whom family life centered on sentimental affection rather than economic survival. Thus, spiritualists were drawn to the idea that they could stay connected to the loved ones they had relied upon for emotional comfort. Spiritualists strove to be effective mediums, possessing the powerful sensory and spiritual abilities necessary to reach the deceased. Famous spiritualist converts included many individuals from radical and socially active families. William Lloyd Garrison, ANGELINA AND SARAH GRIMKÉ, and Isabella Beecher Hooker were all attracted to the spiritualist faith.

The so-called burned-over district (see RELIGION) of upstate New York had been the center of several popular religious movements. Quakerism, which had supported the antislavery activity organized in western New York, merged with the new spiritualism movement. The spiritualist concept of individuals having direct connections to the beyond echoed the Quaker doctrine of the inner light, which declared that every individual held the divinity of God within themselves and formal authority should not outweigh this divine source of inspiration and thought. Quaker meetings allowed those moved by the divine light to stand and testify to the congregation. Likewise, in spiritualist circles, ordinary people were encouraged to speak out in public about their communications with the dead.

The belief that all individuals possessed the divine spirit granted authority to women and provided them with opportunities to speak at religious gatherings. Like the Fox sisters, mediums were often young women, supposedly innocent and pure and thus the ideal vessels for transmitting messages from beyond. Those who were identified as spiritualists often belonged to religious denominations with liberal dogmas, such as the Quakers, Unitarians, and Universalists. Spiritualists rejected the orthodoxy of Calvinism and conservative evangelical doctrines. Those who were identified as spiritualists often doubted the divinity of Jesus and were skeptical of the Bible as a literal translation of God's will. The Universalist church drew the most interest in spiritualism from its members, since the Universalist faith declared that all souls would be saved, and their rejection of Hell and damnation fed into the spiritualist rejection of Protestant orthodoxy. Politically and socially, spiritualists tended to support a variety of both progressive and radical causes, such as marriage reform, the ABOLITION MOVEMENT, religious freedom, WOMEN'S STATUS AND RIGHTS, and the TEMPERANCE MOVEMENT. The social and theological ideologies followed by spiritualists supported their individualistic and heterodox belief systems.

Spiritualists viewed the family and the home as the true center of religious life. They subscribed to no official doctrines and were not organized nationally. Because there was no official affiliation required to be a spiritualist and no group theological consensus, the spiritualists' main sources of linkage were conferences and the dissemination of journals, newspapers, and books. A well-known spiritualist newspaper was the *Banner of Light*, published in Boston. The popularity of the movement can be seen in the many books and pamphlets sold in the second half of the 19th century. Spiritualist bookstores appeared throughout the United States, and more than 50,000 books on spiritualism were sold in 1871.

Spiritualists strongly supported the 19th-century women's rights movement. Radical, "ultraist" women's rights supporters were often attracted to the spiritualist faith. They promoted women's self-ownership of both body and soul and believed that orthodox religions oppressed women as a group. In an era when women were not supposed to speak in public gatherings, spiritualist gatherings allowed them to assert a powerful public presence, even if they were technically only supposed to be mediums for the dead. Thus, spiritualist meetings helped remove the stigma from women in the public sphere, making women's rights activities gradually more acceptable. These activists also criticized the legal and social restrictions that marriage placed on women. Their criticism included calling attention to the potential for sexual coercion in marriage, and they accepted divorce as a reasonable solution for unhappy marriages. Spiritualist beliefs promoted spiritual attraction as a necessary basis for a loving relationship. Spiritualists believed this affinity of souls would then produce a "true" marriage of body, mind, and spirit. Their beliefs about marriage resulted in critics labeling spiritualists as promiscuous and supporters of "free love." Victoria Woodhull, a supporter of woman's suffrage and a practicing spiritualist, popularized the criticisms of free love as a result of sensational newspaper reports about her. Spiritualists often had to fight their stereotype as promiscuous sex radicals in the popular mind due to their promotion of "true marriages."

By the 1890s, the spiritualist movement was in decline in terms of membership and popularity. But during the height of its influence, spiritualism provided a forum wherein many reform-minded people gathered and formulated radical new ideas about the capacities of the living and the dead.

Further reading: Ann Braude, *Radical Spirits: Spiritualism and Women's Rights in Nineteenth-Century America* (Boston: Beacon Press, 1989).

—Sharon E. Romeo

Stanton, Elizabeth Cady See Volume V

Stearns, Abel (1798–1871)

Abel Stearns was a pioneer merchant in CALIFORNIA. Born in Lunenburg, Massachusetts, on February 9, 1798, Stearns went to sea at an early age. He acquired his own ship by 1822, and for many years he plied the trade routes to China, the West Indies, and South America. Four years later, he relocated to Mexico City and became a naturalized citizen.

In 1828, Stearns migrated to Monterey, California, where he spent two years trying to obtain a land grant. He subsequently enjoyed better luck in Los Angeles, where he was operating a mercantile house by 1831. Stearns quickly acquired great wealth as part of the local hide and tallow trade then prevalent in Mexican California. He also cemented many friendships among the ruling elite, gained election to the Los Angeles *ayuntamiento* (town council), and later functioned as its *sindico procurador* (treasurer/tax collector). In 1835, he experienced an unfortunate brawl with a Kentucky mountain man that left him disfigured facially and suffering from a permanent speech impairment. Nonetheless, Stearns's popularity remained undiminished, and in 1836 and 1844 he wielded sufficient influence to assist two uprisings against unpopular Mexican governors who were then replaced by native Californians more sympathetic to the popular will.

Stearns proved himself a successful businessman, but his physical demeanor was so grotesque that he acquired the sobriquet of *Cara de Caballo* (horse face). Looks notwithstanding, he married into the local nobility, which also boosted his reputation and popularity among neighboring *rancheros*. He also built an impressive home, El Palacio, which served as a social center to facilitate his many transactions.

When the MEXICAN-AMERICAN WAR broke out in 1846, California was invaded by American forces. Stearns, as a Mexican national, maintained a studious neutrality. Afterwards, he retained all his property under the new regime, and in 1849 he participated in the state constitutional convention at Monterey. The following year, Stearns gained election to the new state assembly first as a WHIG PARTY candidate and, after 1860, as a member of the REPUBLICAN PARTY. He also amassed a considerable fortune by buying up the property of dispossessed *rancheros;* by 1858, he owned an estimated 450,000 acres. However, between 1856 and 1865, declining cattle prices, coupled with flood and droughts, severely impacted his holdings, and Stearns liquidated most of his assets to pay off his debts. He subsequently reentered the real-estate market, then enjoying a postwar boom, and regained most of his wealth. By the time Stearns died in San Francisco on August 23, 1871, he ranked as one of the richest individuals in that state. His life personified the first generation of Anglo settlers to California who prospered under Mexican rule and then assisted its transition to self-government.

Further reading: Philip C. Fedewa, "Abel Stearns in Transitional California, 1848–1871" (unpublished Ph.D. dis., University of Missouri, Columbia, 1970); Ronald C. Woolsey, "A Capitalist in a Foreign Land: Abel Stearns in Southern California Before the Conquest," *Southern California Quarterly* 72, no. 2 (1993): 101–118; Doris M. Wright, *A Yankee in Mexican California: Abel Stearns, 1798–1848* (Santa Barbara, Calif.: W. Hebberd, 1977).

—John C. Fredriksen

Stewart, Maria (1803–1879)

Maria Stewart was one of the first African-American female abolitionists and feminists. She was born Maria Miller in Hartford, Connecticut, in 1803. Orphaned at an early age, she matured in the home of an African-American clergyman and subsequently worked as an indentured servant. She had previously attended Sabbath school, showing an aptitude for literacy and theology. In 1826, she married James W. Stewart, a black merchant and WAR OF 1812 veteran from Boston, and adopted his middle initial and family name. She resided in Boston in relative comfort until 1829, when her husband died and she was cheated from her inheritance by dishonest executors. In despair, she experienced a religious conversion in 1830 and thereafter dedicated her life to proselytizing religion and civil rights.

Over the next few years, Stewart gained notoriety as the first African American to lecture publicly on national issues. Drawing on her religious background, she heartily condemned SLAVERY in biblical terms, but white northern communities were also castigated for their systematic discrimination against people of color. She therefore exhorted the free African-American community to band together, educate themselves, and demand their civil rights. She also distinguished herself by calling out for women's rights with concomitant larger roles in civic and political affairs. Stewart's stridency brought her to the attention of abolitionist William Lloyd Garrison, and the two struck up a fruitful association. In January 1832, when he printed several of Stewart's remarks in his newspaper, *The Liberator,* she became one of the first African-American woman to be published. This was followed up by several radically tinged pamphlets containing harsh language and open criticism of men, the first from a woman of any race, which brought her acrimony and resistance from her own community. At length, Stewart decided she accomplished little by remaining in Boston, so she resettled in New York City in 1833. Intent on becoming a teacher, she sought further enlightenment by joining the Female Literary Society there.

Stewart successively taught in New York, Baltimore, and Washington, D.C., until the advent of the Civil War in 1861. She then organized a school for poor black students and also gained appointment as matron of the Freedman's Hospital. Ever conscious of the need for educating children, in 1871 she opened another school near the newly founded Howard University and called on the faculty there to assist her. In March 1879, Stewart received a government pension based on her late husband's military service, and with the proceeds she published a second edition of her *Meditations from the Pen of Mrs. Maria W. Stewart* (1879), now featuring supporting letters from Garrison and other leading abolitionists. Stewart died in Washington on December 17, 1879, generally regarded as the first African-American feminist.

Further reading: Jami L. Carlacio, "In Their Own Words: The Rhetorical Practices of Maria Stewart and Sarah Grimke" (unpublished Ph.D. dis., University of Wisconsin–Madison, 2001); Lora Romero, *Home Fronts: Domesticity and Its Critics in the Antebellum United States* (Durham, N.C.: Duke University, 1997); Rodger Streitmatter, "Maria W. Stewart: The First Female African-American Journalist," *Historical Journal of Massachusetts* 21, no. 2 (1993): 44–49.

—John C. Fredriksen

Still, William (1821–1902)

An abolitionist and businessman, William Still personally sheltered most of the slave fugitives who made it as far as Philadelphia. He was born in Medford, New Jersey, on October 7, 1821, the youngest of 18 children. His parents were both former slaves who either purchased their freedom or escaped. Barely educated and largely self-taught, Still worked on his father's farm until the age of 20, then left home to work as a laborer. In 1844, he arrived in Philadelphia, site of the largest community of free African Americans in the country. He worked at numerous odd jobs until 1847, when he joined the Anti-Slavery Society office. This was a front organization of the famous "underground railroad," which smuggled slaves to northern cities and Canada. Still performed well, and in 1852 he gained appointment as secretary and chairman of the society's General Vigilance Committee. He was then tasked with raising money for the effort and keeping accurate records. At this time, the Fugitive Slave Law of 1850 made it a federal offense not to aid in the recovery of escaped slaves, but Philadelphia nonetheless thrived as an important station in the underground railroad. Still became directly responsible for assigning shelter to fugitives, feeding them, and sending them north to Canada. He also carefully interviewed each escaped slave to record their individual experiences. In this manner, Still inadvertently encountered his long-lost brother, who had been abandoned by his mother 40 years earlier. In 1855 Still also ventured to Canada to report favorably on the progress of fugitive slaves settling there.

When the Civil War erupted in 1861, Still left the ABOLITION MOVEMENT to concentrate on business matters. After opening a lucrative coal yard, he was called on to service Camp William Penn outside the city, where African-American soldiers were stationed. Postwar emancipation further intensified Still's social activism. He subsequently initiated a drive to fight the prohibition against African Americans' using the city's streetcars, and in 1867 the state legislature complied, forbidding such discrimination. He also gained a measure of national attention through publication of his eloquent book *The Underground Railroad* (1872), which related the experience through the eyes of the fugitives. This landmark publication went through three editions, with several thousand copies sold.

Still further enhanced his reputation for philanthropy by providing material assistance to the African-American community of Philadelphia. He remained a longtime member of the Freedmen's Aid Commission as well as a number of charitable and welfare agencies. Despite his advanced years, Still was active in founding a YMCA for black youth and the Home for Aged and Infirm Colored Persons. Still died in Philadelphia on July 14, 1902, a leading African-American reformer and civil rights champion of the 19th century.

Further reading: William C. Kashatus, "Two Stationmasters on the Underground Railroad: A Tale of Black and White," *Pennsylvania Heritage* 27 (Fall 2001): 5–11; Lurey Khan, *One Day, Levin . . . he be free: William Still and the Underground Railroad* (New York: E. P. Dutton, 1972); William Still, *The Underground Railroad* (New York: Arno Press, 1968); William J. Switala, *The Underground Railroad in Pennsylvania* (Mechanicsburg, Pa.: Stackpole Books, 2001).

—John C. Fredriksen

Stockton, Robert Field (1795–1966)

Commodore Robert Field Stockton was an American naval officer who commanded the Pacific squadron during the MEXICAN-AMERICAN WAR (1846–48). With a small naval force, he occupied southern CALIFORNIA, fought two battles, and broke Mexican resistance by early 1847.

Stockton was born in Princeton, New Jersey, on August 20, 1795, the grandson of Richard Stockton, one of the signers of the Declaration of Independence. He left the College of New Jersey (now Princeton) to enter the U.S. Navy at the age of 16. Commissioned a midshipman on September 5, 1811 he served under Commodore John Rodgers aboard the USS *President* during the WAR OF 1812. Promoted to lieutenant, Stockton sailed to the Mediterranean aboard the USS *Guerrière* and took part in the campaign against the Barbary pirates.

Stockton was selected by President JOHN TYLER to bring a proposal for annexation to TEXAS in 1845. Following the outbreak of the Mexican-American War, in July 1846, he sailed around Cape Horn to take command of the Pacific squadron, arriving in Monterey to relieve Commodore John Sloat as commander. Stockton proceeded to occupy the ports of Southern California, capturing Santa Barbara on August 4, 1846 and Los Angeles several weeks later with the aid of Colonel JOHN C. FRÉMONT's California Battalion. He declared California a territory of the United States and named himself the governor of the new civil and military government.

While Stockton was in the north, Mexican loyalists recaptured most of the southern California towns. In January 1847, he joined forces with Brigadier General STEPHEN WATTS KEARNY in recapturing Los Angeles and ending Mexican resistance in California. Stockton and Kearny feuded over who had U.S. governmental authority in California. Kearny's position was upheld, and Stockton returned to the East Coast. He retired from the navy in May 1850 and became a U.S. senator from New Jersey for a brief time (1851–53). While in the Senate, he urged the abolition of flogging as punishment in the U.S. Navy. Stockton retired to Princeton, New Jersey, where he died on October 7, 1866.

Further reading: K. Jock Bauer, *Surfboats and Horse Marines: U.S. Naval Operations in the Mexican War, 1846–48* (Annapolis, Md.: U.S. Naval Institute, 1969); Samuel John Bayard, *A Sketch of the Life of Commodore Robert F. Stockton* (New York: Derby & Jackson, 1856).

Stowe, Harriet Beecher See Volume V

Strang, James Jesse (1813–1856)

James Jesse Strang was the founder and self-proclaimed king of a religious colony in Michigan. Born in Scipio, New York, in 1836, he married and became postmaster and editor of the *Randolph Herald* in western New York. In 1843, he moved to Wisconsin, where he became interested in Mormonism, converting in 1844. The following year, after the murder of JOSEPH SMITH, JR., Strang announced that he was the new prophet. He was cast out of the Mormon church and subsequently established a colony in Wisconsin called Voree, which attracted Mormons disaffected by BRIGHAM YOUNG's rule.

The community lasted until 1847, when Strang decided to move his followers to Beaver Island in Lake Michigan. Although he sought to establish a benevolent theocracy, in reality he ruled as a harsh despot, which caused friction between the native inhabitants and the "Strangites," as they were called. The public outcry eventually became so great that the federal government brought charges against Strang, but he successfully defended himself. His influence grew, and in 1850 he crowned himself "king" of the island. He was later elected to the Michigan House of Representatives. The conflict between the colony and the surrounding population increased, finally resulting in a raid on the island in July 1853, which the Strangites repelled. However, Strang's autocratic rule made him enemies, and he was assassinated in 1856 by some of his own followers. The colony disbanded soon after, and the land was reclaimed by its original inhabitants.

Further reading: Roger Van Noord, *Assassination of the Michigan King: The Life of James Jesse Strang* (Ann Arbor: University of Michigan Press, 1997).

Strauss, Levi (1829–1902)

Clothier to the American West and later to the nation, Levi Strauss made his fortune selling dry goods to the gold-rush miners who flooded into CALIFORNIA after 1848. Born Loeb Strauss in Buttenheim, Bavaria, Strauss immigrated to the United States with his family in 1847. Two of his older brothers were already in the dry-goods business in New York City, and Levi Strauss (as he would be called) joined them. In 1850, he established Levi Strauss and Company, and three years later, he moved to San Francisco to join his brother-in-law, David Stern, in a business there. The CALIFORNIA GOLD RUSH was underway, and tens of thousands of new miners arrived annually. Every miner needed tools, food, and clothing. Stores in San Francisco and smaller emporia in the towns and mining camps did a booming business. Strauss and Company supplied miners with a strong canvas and denim pants that were ideal for work in the streams of the sierra. The Strauss brothers in New York manufactured the pants and shipped them to California, where Levi Strauss and David Stern sold pants as rapidly as they could be unpacked and shelved. Mining ran in seasonal cycles, but whatever their luck on the streams, miners had to have good clothing. The Levi Strauss and Company pants quickly established a reputation for protection and durability.

In 1872, Jacob Davis, a tailor in Nevada and sometime customer of Strauss, made an important advance in work clothing. He perfected a way to reinforce the pocket seams and long seams of work trousers with copper rivets. This reinforcement made the durable pants even more durable. In May 1873, Strauss and Davis became partners in patenting the new clothing idea. Strauss immediately established a factory on Fremont Street, San Francisco, to manufacture the new pants. He later carried the new reinforcing technique over to work shirts, hunting coats, and other outdoor wear. In all these enterprises, the company continued to prosper.

As the century ended, Strauss gradually left the business in the hands of his four nephews. He was a bachelor, and David Stern had died in 1874. Strauss had a remarkable reputation for fairness to customers and employees alike. He served on the board of directors of many of San Francisco's most important companies. He was also known for his philanthropy. The University of California at Berkeley was one of the greatest beneficiaries of his financial support. Strauss died in San Francisco in 1902. He left an estate of more than $6 million, with beneficiaries ranging from the university to orphans. His nephews continued to operate the company on his principles, rebuilding the factory and the business after the devastating earthquake that leveled San Francisco in 1906. An entrepreneur who formed a bridge from the California gold rush to the modern city, Levi Strauss produced a quality product for sale at a reasonable price, and the public responded with its continuing patronage.

Further reading: Ed Cray, *Levi's* (Boston: Houghton Mifflin, 1978).

Sublette, William (1799–1845)

Fur trader and mountain man, William Sublette was one of the major figures of the American FUR TRADE. Born in Kentucky in 1799, Sublette was the eldest of five brothers, all associated with the fur trade; the others were Milton, Andrew, Pinckney, and Solomon. In 1816–17, the entire Sublette family moved to Missouri Territory. In 1823, William Sublette joined the second expedition of WILLIAM HENRY ASHLEY to the upper Missouri River, where they were attacked by the Arikara. Sublette, JEDEDIAH STRONG SMITH, and Ashley were among the few that escaped. Sublette joined Colonel Henry Leavenworth's force in the hunt for the Indians involved, but they were not successful. Still, the presence of the troops, whatever their numbers, did bring a degree of calm to the vast region of the upper Missouri.

As Ashley and other traders resumed trading operations, Sublette joined Smith's overland trek in search of new routes of communication and new sites for trapping. It was this party that reopened SOUTH PASS as a route of access across the Rocky Mountains. For the next 15 years, overland caravans would use the South Pass route, which became part of the CALIFORNIA TRAIL and the OREGON TRAIL. For Sublette and his fellow trappers, South Pass opened up access to the rich fur-trapping region of the Green River.

In 1826 Sublette joined Smith and David Jackson in purchasing Ashley's fur company. Four years later, he sold his interest in the ROCKY MOUNTAIN FUR COMPANY, whose other partners now included JAMES BRIDGER, Thomas Fitzpatrick, and Milton Sublette, one of William's younger brothers. Sublette himself continued to play a strong role in the fur business, building FORT LARAMIE in eastern Wyoming (which he later lost to the AMERICAN FUR COMPANY). Throughout these years, from 1830 to 1836, he continued to attend the annual RENDEZVOUS, where he was a major supplier and trader.

In 1836 Sublette retired from the fur trade, one of the most revered of the original MOUNTAIN MEN, and went into the mercantile business in St. Louis. He bought a country estate near Sulphur Springs, complete with racetrack and hotel, and stayed in close touch with his younger brothers, who were still active in the fur trade. A vigorous supporter of Senator THOMAS HART BENTON and the Missouri Democratic Party, his main interest in retirement was politics. In 1844, he married Frances Hereford. The last years of his life were a continuing struggle against tuberculosis. He died at a hotel in Pittsburgh while on his way east to convalesce on the New Jersey shore.

Further reading: John E. Sunder, *Bill Sublette: Mountain Man* (Norman: University of Oklahoma Press, 1959).

Supreme Court decisions

The United States Supreme Court was created by the Judiciary Act of 1789, in conformity with Article III of the Constitution. As the highest tribunal in the nation, the Court's decisions on various issues of law have shaped American life and concepts of justice throughout the history of the United States. During its first 70 years, the Supreme Court ruled on dozens of landmark cases with far-reaching consequences for American society.

During its first years, the Court considered several cases in which it clarified the constitutional roles of the states, the federal government, and the three branches of government. In *Chisholm v. Georgia* (1793) the Court ruled that federal judicial power could, among other things, extend to controversies between two or more states. This decision was later overturned by the passage of the Eleventh Amendment (1798), which declared that the judicial power of the United States would not extend to cases in which a person in one state files a suit in equity law against another state. *Marbury v. Madison* (1803) concerned the validity of a judicial appointment. In this case, Chief Justice John Marshall first introduced the concept of "judicial review," or the power of the Supreme Court to determine the constitutionality of a law or statute passed by Congress. Although judicial review was not mentioned in Article III of the Constitution as a power of the Supreme Court, Marshall and his associate justices ruled that the Court did possess this power. This seminal decision instituted a powerful and specific role for the judiciary branch, and Americans ever since have assumed the principles in the case: that in a conflict between the Constitution and a federal or state law, the Constitution is paramount, and that it is the Supreme Court's ultimate responsibility to interpret American laws.

In *Fletcher v. Peck* (1810) the Court ruled that a contract in which Indian lands were sold to Georgia speculators was valid, even though the land sale was later revoked by the Georgia legislature because of fraud and bribery in the original transaction. This decision invalidated the state law, upholding a contract despite the shady circumstances of the agreement. In other words, the Court held that the Constitution does not permit state legislatures to pass laws voiding contracts made by previous legislatures. After *Fletcher*, there were many other key cases decided on issues of contract and land titles. This was a primary concern in the early republic, because contracts concerning property affected the ability of Americans to purchase frontier lands. In *Martin v. Hunter's Lessee* (1816), another case concerning land title, the Court ruled that state courts must obey the Constitution, reaffirming the supremacy of the Supreme Court and the uniformity of federal law from state to state. In *Dartmouth College v. Woodward* (1819), the Court ruled that Dartmouth's private corporate charter was protected from any state law that aimed to change the nature and purpose of the original contract. Here again, the Court sided with the individual right to contract over the state's legislative power. The same year, in *McCULLOCH V. MARYLAND*, the Court decided that the Bank of the United States was not subject to state taxation, and that a bank legitimately established by Congress should be regulated and taxed by Congress. Again, the Court addressed the relationship between the rights of states, individuals, and the federal government.

The Court also decided several commerce cases in this period. In *Cohens v. Virginia* (1821), a case concerning the sale of lottery tickets in a state where lotteries were illegal, the justices reaffirmed the judicial supremacy of the Supreme Court over state laws. In *Gibbons v. Ogden* (1824), the Court ruled that a New York law prohibiting vessels licensed by the U.S. from navigating in state waters was unconstitutional. These vessels were commercial and conducted trade with vessels from other states; therefore the New York law was void. This decision reaffirmed that Congress alone had the power to regulate all aspects of interstate commerce, and states only had the power to regulate commerce that was entirely internal.

In the *Charles River Bridge* case (1837) the Court reconsidered the purposes of contract. Marshall's recently appointed successor as chief justice, Roger B. Taney, ruled that the Constitution was primarily responsible for fostering "the happiness and prosperity of the community," not simply protecting the right to property. The proprietors of the Charles River Bridge sought to enjoin the Warren Bridge Company from constructing a bridge that would compete with their own. The Charles River Bridge proprietors argued that their exclusive contract for bridge transport prevented Warren from erecting a competing bridge. Taney ruled in favor of Warren, arguing that in a prosperous young nation, exclusive contracts dampened competition and slowed down the economic expansion of the nation. This decision implied that the interests of developers building new roads and other improvements would take precedence over established companies with exclusive contracts. The case had far-reaching consequences, since it connected "happiness and prosperity" with the right of capitalists to develop new structures and industries.

With the passage of the INDIAN REMOVAL ACT of 1830 and the increasing conflict over Indian lands came cases concerning the sovereignty of Indian nations and the powers of states to pass laws affecting those nations. In *Cherokee Nation v. Georgia* (1831), the Court decided that it did not have jurisdiction to rule on a case where a state enforced its laws upon the Cherokee. This decision seemed to contradict the previous efforts of the Court to assert its supremacy. In *Worcester v. Georgia* (1832), another Cherokee case concerning state powers and tribal sovereignty, the Court ruled that Indian tribes were "dependent domestic nations." As such, they retained rights to any lands they had not voluntarily ceded to the United States. Marshall's ruling in this case did not prevent the administration of President ANDREW JACKSON from forcing eastern nations to isolated reservations in the West. Clearly, the Court's authority would be sacrificed to popular opinion in the case of Native American removal.

The relationship between nonwhite peoples and American law would arise again with the *AMISTAD* INCIDENT (1841) and the first Supreme Court case that dealt with the issue of slavery. Ostensibly an issue of international law, the fate of the Africans who mutinied on the *Amistad* became a high-profile public referendum on SLAVERY. Justice Joseph Story in his majority opinion upheld a lower-court ruling that the Africans had been kidnapped and thus were not the legitimate property of the Spanish traders who had captured them. The Court ordered the Africans returned to their own land. Notably, the justification for this ruling was not that slavery was unlawful but that the *Amistad* Africans were not lawfully slaves.

The Taney Court's position on the legality of slavery became clearer in *Dred Scott v. Sandford* (1857). Scott, a slave, was transported to northern (free) territory by his owner, John Sandford. Scott believed that by entering free territory, he had been freed. When he and Sandford returned to St. Louis, he sued for his freedom. At issue in the case was whether slaves were citizens of the United States with the right to sue in court. In this case, the Court emphasized the rights of the owner, Sandford, over the rights of his black slave. Slaves were property, not citizens, and thus could not use the courts for redress. As Taney famously remarked in his opinion, black people had no rights that white people were bound to respect. Freeing Scott would violate Sandford's Fifth Amendment right to due process. In this case, unlike *Charles River Bridge,* Taney upheld the rights to property. Taney added that Congress had no power to prohibit slavery in the territories, which rendered the MISSOURI COMPROMISE unconstitutional. This controversial decision infuriated abolitionists and was one of the main factors contributing to the outbreak of the Civil War four years later.

Throughout the history of the United States, the Supreme Court has been a visible and powerful mediator between the federal and state governments and between the three branches of the federal government. Like any other institution, the Court has reflected the priorities and anxieties of the nation. During the first half of the 19th century, the Court often took a conservative position on matters of individual liberties while adopting a more liberal stance on economic matters like contracts and property rights. As the *Dred Scott* case shows, Supreme Court decisions often reflected the self-interest of the judges in establishing the supremacy of the Court. Many of the cases described also demonstrate the Court's unwillingness to apply judicial powers to what they saw as legislative responsibilities.

Further reading: Peter Irons, *A People's History of the Supreme Court: The Men and Women Whose Cases and Decisions Have Shaped Our Constitution* (New York: Viking, 1999); Bernard Schwartz, *A History of the Supreme Court* (New York: Oxford University Press, 1993); Charles Warren, *The Supreme Court in United States History* (Boston: Little, Brown, 1926).

—Eleanor H. McConnell

Sutter, John (1803–1880)

Intimately associated with the discovery of gold in CALIFORNIA in 1848 and the European colonization of the Sacramento River Valley, John Sutter was also a victim of the CALIFORNIA GOLD RUSH. He was born Johann Augustus Sutter near Basel, Switzerland (the German-speaking part of trilingual nation), in 1803. After elementary, schooling, he married and became a dry-goods merchant, but both ventures failed. To escape the prospect of debtor's prison, Sutter abandoned his wife and traveled to America. On the frontier of settlement in Missouri, he gave himself the military title of captain and engaged in trade over the SANTA FE TRAIL. His ventures failed here as well, and he traveled overland to Oregon and then to Hawaii before arriving in California in 1839.

That year Sutter petitioned the Mexican governor, Juan Bautista Alvarado, for a grant of land. Alvorado gave him 11 square leagues (nearly 50,000 acres) in the Sacramento River Valley and also authorized him to serve as a local justice and law officer. With his large landholdings and official status, Sutter was soon the most important Euro-American in central California. As the command post of his new empire, which he named New Helvetia, Sutter built a fort on the site of the present city of Sacramento. He soon made his fort the center of a series of economic enterprises that included AGRICULTURE, grazing, trapping, and the FUR TRADE. He traded extensively and supplied the trappers who had visited the region for a decade before his arrival. This expansive enterprise was created in substantial part through the use of Indian labor. Native Americans worked his fields under conditions that varied from debt peonage to slavery. He also recruited an Indian army, which he armed and used to enforce order and his own style of justice in the interior of California.

Sutter also befriended arriving American immigrants, and his warm welcome at Fort Sutter symbolized the end of the CALIFORNIA TRAIL. Some of the immigrant families settled on his lands; others were employed in his various economic enterprises. As the largest economic force in central California, he assisted the immigrants while enriching himself at the same time. Sutter held a commission and lands from the republic of Mexico, but he distrusted Mexicans and favored the Americans. With the outbreak of the MEXICAN-AMERICAN WAR in 1846, he openly sided with the Americans, and he was enthusiastic about the prospect of an American victory and California's annexation to the United States.

As part of the expansion of his many enterprises, Sutter employed a carpenter, James W. Marshall, to build a sawmill on the American River. It was in the race of the mill that Marshall discovered gold on January 24, 1848. Marshall shared his news with his employer, but Sutter (like so many others) did not sense the immense implications of the discovery, and he asked Marshall to keep the news quiet so that the mill could be completed. However, the news began to circulate through the interior valleys and then to San Francisco, and soon the California gold rush was under way. From within California, from Monterey and San Francisco, from Oregon and the HAWAIIAN ISLANDS, from the East Coast, from Chile and Peru, and eventually from all over the world, men and women by the tens and eventually hundreds of thousands swarmed over the watercourses of central California. By far the largest numbers were the Americans from the East Coast. Several thousand came by sea in the late 1848 and the first half of 1849, but they began flooding into California in the summer of 1849. Sutter's New Helvetia was at the center of this uncontrollable rush. His workers, including the Indians, deserted him for the gold that seemed to lie everywhere. Prospective miners invaded his property, destroyed his crops, stole his livestock, and took the gold from his lands as their own. Sutter could not stop them; no individual could, and eventually the federal government simply threw up its hands and let the gold rush proceed.

The California gold rush ruined Sutter. Although by proximity he was the individual best placed to profit from it, his vantage point was too close. When he tried to hold on to part of his claim, he found himself without the abundance of paper records that the American land commissioners demanded. By 1852, the great empire of New Helvetia was in ruins. In 1865, Sutter abandoned any attempt to claim part of his grant, and he moved to Pennsylvania, bankrupt. For the rest of his life, he petitioned the federal government on an annual basis for compensation. He asked for damages for the losses he suffered during the Mexican-American War and for the losses that he sustained during the gold rush. He was never successful. In a final blow to his prospects, the Supreme Court denied his land claims in the Sacramento River Valley.

Further reading: Richard Dillon, *Fool's Gold: The Decline and Fall of Captain John Sutter of California* (New York: Coward-McCann, 1967).

T

Tappan, Arthur (1786–1865), **and Tappan, Lewis** (1788–1863)

Two of the most influential abolitionists in the antebellum United States, Arthur and Lewis Tappan were born in Northampton, Massachusetts. Growing up in a devoutly Calvinistic family, both were deeply influenced by their parents' evangelical beliefs. The PANIC OF 1837 caused the family's dry-goods business to fail, but the brothers quickly started another venture, founding America's first credit-rating service (later to be known as Dun & Bradstreet). The brothers accumulated enough wealth to found a newspaper, the *New York Journal of Commerce,* and to fund various humanitarian causes ranging from abolition to temperance.

The Tappans' concern for the abolition of SLAVERY dates from the early 1830s, a dangerous period for public expression of antislavery sentiment. At that time, the ABOLITION MOVEMENT had not made much progress because many businessmen saw it as a threat to law and order. This feeling repeatedly incited mob action against the abolitionists and free blacks in the Northeast and in the Midwest.

It took courage to speak out, but in 1833 Lewis and Arthur Tappan and Theodore Weld formed the AMERICAN ANTI-SLAVERY SOCIETY. That same year, the Tappan brothers founded Oberlin College, open to blacks and whites alike. Lewis Tappan financially backed the *Emancipator,* the most widely circulated antislavery journal. To his brother Benjamin, a U.S. senator from Ohio, Lewis wrote that slavery "was the worm at the tree of liberty. Unless killed, the tree will die."

The Tappans' public statements against slavery brought about public reaction on July 4, 1834, when a mob trashed Lewis's home and burned his furniture in the street. Tappan wrote to Weld that he wanted his house to remain "this summer as it is, a silent anti-slavery preacher to the crowds who will see it." The next year, a church built by the Tappans was set on fire when it was rumored that they intended to promote racial "amalgamation."

Undeterred, the Tappans continued their efforts to bring about a peaceful end to slavery. Like many abolitionists, they proposed reforming the system from within and worked tirelessly to win over churches and missionary societies to their views. Lewis was more fully committed than his brother Arthur, who stopped short of associating with blacks. Lewis tried to eliminate the "black pew" in New York churches and caused a furor in upstate New York when he and his family sat in the pews reserved for black communicants. On another occasion, members of the American Anti-Slavery Association blocked his proposal to invite a black minister to speak to the association.

In the *AMISTAD* incident, Lewis Tappan recognized the opportunity not only to help the captured Africans but also to dramatize the evils of the slave trade. He had been handed a "Providential occurrence," he admitted when the district court opened proceedings. Ultimately, he hoped to use the opportunity to strike at slavery itself, "the *market* that invites the *supply,*" he concluded, in suitably businesslike fashion.

He assumed major responsibility for mapping out the strategy for the court trials, raised money in "the voice of humanity and liberty," visited the imprisoned Mendian captives, located Africans who could talk with them, and wrote letters to the *New York Journal of Commerce* presenting the Africans' side of the mutiny. In company with Ellis Gray Loring, John Quincy Adams's friend of many years, Tappan pleaded eloquently with Adams to join Roger Sherman Baldwin in arguing the case for the defense before the U.S. Supreme Court. Adams did so, and on hearing the Court's decision, he wrote to Tappan, "The captives are free . . . 'Not unto us, not unto us!' but thanks, thanks, in the name of humanity and justice to you."

In the year following the release of the Mendians, Lewis Tappan devoted his energy to arranging for their transportation home to Sierra Leone, and he very likely helped spirit away Antonio (the *Amistad's* slave cabin boy) to freedom in Canada. Lewis Tappan's participation in the

Amistad case may be considered the high point of his career as an abolitionist. At Adams's suggestion, he attended an antislavery convention in London in 1843, and in 1846 he was instrumental in merging the *Amistad* committee with other missionary groups to form the American Missionary Society (1846).

In the 1840s, the Tappan brothers split with abolitionist William Lloyd Garrison, who wanted to branch off into other kinds of reform, including WOMEN'S STATUS AND RIGHTS. Arthur Tappan continued to work for abolition, helping to found the American and Foreign Anti-Slavery Society (1840). With the passage of the Fugitive Slave Act of 1850, he declared himself now willing to disobey the law and actively supported the efforts of the underground railroad to help slaves escape to freedom. He lived long enough to witness the emancipation of slaves and died as the Civil War ended, in 1865. His brother Lewis had predeceased him by two years.

Further reading: Lawrence J. Friedman, *Gregarious Saints: Self and Community in American Abolitionism, 1830-1870* (New Rochelle, N.Y.: Cambridge University Press, 1982); Bertram Wyatt-Brown, *Lewis Tappan and the Evangelical War against Slavery* (Cleveland, Ohio: Press of Case Western Reserve University, 1966).

Taylor, Zachary (1784–1850)

Zachary Taylor, 12th president of the United States, was a career soldier who never voted, and he served fewer than 500 days in the White House. Nevertheless, he significantly influenced political developments during the first half of 1850, when there was a domestic crisis and a grave possibility of civil war. Although long a slaveholder, Taylor was as much a westerner as a southerner. He was nationalistic in his orientation, seeking, above all, to preserve the Union.

Born in Virginia on November 24, 1784, Taylor was taken as an infant to Kentucky and raised on a plantation. By 1800, his family owned 10,000 acres in Kentucky and a number of slaves. In 1808, he received his first commission as an army officer, commanding the garrison at Fort Pickering, site of modern-day Memphis. Two years later, he married Margaret Mackall Smith of Calvert County, Maryland. As a captain in the WAR OF 1812, Taylor won distinction in September 1812 for his defense of Fort Harrison in Indiana Territory against an Indian attack. For this achievement, the young officer became the first brevet major in the U.S. Army. In 1814, Taylor led U.S. troops against British and Indians at Credit Island in Illinois Territory. Outnumbered three to one, he scored temporary successes before withdrawing. In 1815, he was promoted to the lineal grade of major.

After a year as a civilian, Taylor reentered the army in 1816. At various times, he served in the states or future states of Wisconsin, Minnesota, Missouri, Mississippi, Louisiana, Arkansas, and Oklahoma. Commissioned a colonel in 1832, he fought in the BLACK HAWK WAR that year, participating in the climactic Battle of Bad Axe River. Taylor acquired his nickname, "Old Rough and Ready," while fighting the Seminole Indians in FLORIDA Territory from 1837 to 1840. His victory at the Battle of Okeechobee in 1837 was the single most successful U.S. effort of the protracted SECOND SEMINOLE WAR. Breveted a brigadier general in 1838, he commanded all U.S. troops in Florida. He emerged from the struggle with the reputation of a determined, resourceful leader.

There followed five placid years, 1840–45, during which Taylor remained in the army but also gave careful attention to his plantation in Mississippi. The annexation of TEXAS, however, enabled him to receive his most important military assignment. In August 1845 he was in command of a small army of regulars near the mouth of the Nueces River at Corpus Christi, Texas. Both the United States and Mexico claimed the region between this river and the Rio Grande, and because Mexican military activity was rumored, Taylor augmented his troops and awaited specific instructions before moving through the disputed region. President JAMES K. POLK ordered Taylor and his troops into the contested area. After winning two decisive encounters, Taylor triumphed against overwhelming odds in a battle with the Mexican general ANTONIO LÓPEZ DE SANTA ANNA at Buena Vista. When the smoke cleared, Taylor's army of 6,000 had defeated a Mexican force of 20,000, and Zachary Taylor, "Old Rough and Ready," was a national hero.

Although Taylor had never divulged his political preferences, clubs sprang up after his victory to support his presidential candidacy. He was by then a wealthy slaveowner, and the South hoped he would support states' rights and the expansion of SLAVERY into the new areas won from Mexico. The North pointed to his service on the nation's behalf and hoped fervently that he was a Union man. In fact, Taylor thought of himself as an independent. He differed with the DEMOCRATIC PARTY over the concept of a strong national bank and opposed the extension of slavery into areas where neither cotton nor sugar could be grown. He also had problems with the WHIG PARTY's support of strong protective tariffs. Most important, he passionately opposed secession as a means of resolving the nation's problems. In the end, he announced that he was a Whig. At their 1848 nominating convention, the party named Taylor for president, adding New York's MILLARD FILLMORE to the ticket to appease those who opposed the nomination of a slaveowner.

November 7, 1848, was the first time the entire nation voted on the same day. Taylor and Fillmore narrowly

Zachary Taylor *(Library of Congress)*

defeated the Democratic ticket, headed by Michigan's LEWIS CASS, and that of the FREE-SOIL PARTY, led by former president MARTIN VAN BUREN.

Slavery had been the driving issue of the campaign, and it was to be the central challenge of Taylor's brief presidency as well. The nation was polarized over the question of whether to extend the institution to the new western territories. Taylor believed that the people of California, New Mexico, and Texas should be allowed to decide for themselves whether to permit slavery. In this way, the issue could be decided without a national debate. Many in the South feared that the addition of three free states would upset the delicate North-South balance in the Senate.

Some southern Democrats called for a secession convention, and Taylor's reaction was a bristling statement that he would hang anyone who tried to disrupt the Union by force or conspiracy. In this heated atmosphere, HENRY CLAY, DANIEL WEBSTER, and others began to cobble together a compromise. To placate the South, they proposed the enactment of a second FUGITIVE SLAVE LAW that would mandate the return of escaped slaves apprehended anywhere in the nation. Such a plan would, in essence, force the federal government to recognize the interstate slave trade. This effort would become the COMPROMISE OF 1850.

The compromise legislation did not prohibit slavery in the western states. It admitted CALIFORNIA as a free state, and it allowed for the organization of Utah and New Mexico as states, without any federal restrictions on slavery. This left open the possibility that they would admit slavery in those states as well as the possibility that other western states would be admitted as "slave states." This was the issue that pushed the country even closer to civil war.

At a time when strong leadership and party politics were absolutely essential, Taylor probably damaged his cause by refusing to engage directly with Congress or to pull together a functional coalition. He held on to his belief that the president should stand above party politics. On July 4, 1850, after attending celebrations in Washington, he contracted a virulent stomach ailment that may have been cholera. He died on July 9, and more than 100,000 people lined the funeral route to see the hero laid to rest.

Taylor left behind a country sharply divided, and a vice president, Millard Fillmore, who supported the Compromise of 1850, which specifically prohibited slavery in the new western states. In the end, Taylor had little personal impact on the presidency, and his months in office did little to slow the approach of the great national tragedy of the Civil War.

Further reading: K. Jack Bauer, *Zachary Taylor: Soldier, Planter, Statesman of the Old Southwest* (Baton Rouge: Louisiana State University Press, 1985); Elbert B. Smith, *The Presidencies of Zachary Taylor and Millard Fillmore* (Lawrence: University Press of Kansas, 1988).

Tecumseh See Volume III

temperance movement

Using tactics as varied as moral suasion, strict licensing, and outright prohibition, the temperance movement aimed to eradicate the use of alcoholic beverages throughout American society. While local groups had been advocating abstinence from alcohol since the turn of the 19th century, temperance societies with a broader reach began to emerge in 1813. That year, the Massachusetts Society for the Suppression of Intemperance (MSSI), was founded in Boston. An elitist group seeking to control the behavior of those lower in the social hierarchy, the MSSI focused its efforts on moderation rather than abstinence. But the drinking culture proved too powerful for a group with such limited appeal, and its efforts soon failed.

Boston would later give rise to the national organization responsible for temperance's widespread influence. It was there that, in 1826, the American Society for the Promotion of Temperance was born. This group later changed its name to the American Temperance Society (ATS). The ATS had a radically different approach from that of the MSSI, seeking mass appeal on a grassroots level. Founded by evangelical ministers who had emerged from a culture of religious revivalism, the ATS used the same tactics to spread the gospel of abstinence from distilled spirits. By distributing printed materials such as vivid tracts and weekly newspapers and sending itinerant organizers to far-flung communities, the ATS grew rapidly. By 1835, the society claimed over 1.5 million members in more than 8,000 auxiliaries, nearly 20 percent of the free adult population.

The success of the temperance movement was possibly due to the overall climate of progressive reform during this period. Many historians have dubbed the years between 1830 and 1850 as an "age of reform." Religious revivalism, the ABOLITION MOVEMENT, pacifism, WOMEN'S STATUS AND RIGHTS, intentional communities, and universal EDUCATION were only a few of the causes embraced by segments of the American public. INDUSTRIALIZATION, westward expansion, and urbanization contributed to the notion of inevitable American progress. Within these contexts, religious and moral reform could be seen as intrinsic to the new nation's future.

Evangelical clergy, businessmen, and farmers were at the forefront of this economic and social change. Although they operated within divergent spheres, these men found common cause in seeking to improve society as a whole by urging their parishioners and employees to improve themselves.

Intellectual elites also took part in temperance reform. The movement spread rapidly on college campuses as administrators, faculty, and students sponsored revivals and built reform networks. Doctors soon followed suit, as the 19th-century drive to professionalize MEDICINE depended on distinguishing it from midwifery and other folk-healing practices. Adopting a view of alcohol as harmful helped solidify the role of physicians as experts in health-related matters.

Temperance reform attracted women for a variety of reasons. The mid-19th century ideology casting men and women as belonging to separate spheres valued women as moral gatekeepers of the home in what historians describe as the "cult of true womanhood." The growing market ECONOMY brought about an increase in female dependence on male wages earned outside the home. Excessive drunkenness among men could thus imperil women's financial stability.

Initially, the temperance movement was less grounded in political activism than in moral suasion; as such, women were encouraged to participate within a seemingly nonpolitical sphere of activity. However, that distinction would later break down as moral reform gave way to the drive for prohibition. By 1852, prominent female activists such as Elizabeth Cady Stanton, Susan B. Anthony, and AMELIA BLOOMER began to link the temperance crusade to broader campaigns for women's rights.

The first temperance pledges, which members would sign, vowed abstinence from distilled spirits but allowed for the continued consumption of fermented beverages such as beer, wine, and cider. These were considered to contain some elements of alcohol but not alcohol itself. A new pledge rose during the 1830s, known as the "long" and "teetotal" pledge, which included both distilled and fermented beverages. The teetotal movement came about from the earlier reform movement's success and sense of progress, as well as from changing scientific knowledge about the alcohol content of fermented beverages. The discovery by a chemist during the 1820s that alcohol was also present in wine, beer, and cider became widely publicized, changing the popular view of fermented beverages as essentially harmless.

Teetotalism marked a major shift in temperance activism, one that was not universally adopted by reformers. Some found it too radical, especially wealthy elites who were not eager to abandon wine. Wine also became a subject of controversy within organized religion due to the practice of distributing fermented wine for communion. Many mainstream clergy, who had been central to the temperance movement, withdrew their support.

During the 1830s, temperance advocates began to shift their efforts from moral suasion to more coercive methods, including legal reform. Initial legal efforts by temperance activists were designed to be symbolic. Various states adopted no-license laws in order to send a moral message to their constituents that the sale of liquor was no longer a respectable profession; their intention was not to use the law to prevent people from drinking. Regardless of the law's intent, liquor became hard to come by in these areas. As a result, illegal sales proliferated much as they would under nationwide prohibition during the 1920s. Prohibition activity continued throughout the 1840s, until the landmark passage of the Maine Law in 1851 banning the manufacture of liquor and restricting its sale to agents of the state for medicinal and industrial users.

The success of the Maine Law spurred other states to implement prohibition. Between 1851 and 1855, 13 states and territories passed legislation forbidding the manufacture and sale of alcohol. Other states passed narrower laws restricting sales to a specific amount or location. Such efforts met with strong opposition from liquor manufacturers, who formed liquor leagues to finance and organize repeal efforts. Some drinkers became vehemently opposed to prohibition as well, sparking violence in cities like

Chicago and New York. Repeal efforts were successful in many states, to the dismay of temperance advocates.

This groundswell of public opposition, combined with growing sectional strife and the approaching Civil War, caused the temperance movement to founder. Its revival did not take place until the formation of the Women's Christian Temperance Union in the 1870s. The new temperance movement, unlike earlier male-driven ones, proved a formidable platform for a broader women's rights agenda.

Further reading: Jack S. Blocker, *American Temperance Movements: Cycles of Reform* (Boston: Twayne Publishers, 1989); Jessy Randall and Nicole Ketcham, "Ardent Spirits: The Origins of the American Temperance Movement," *Journal for Multimedia History* URL: http://www.albany.edu/jmmh/vol2no1/spirits.html. Downloaded 2001.

—Eva Pendleton

Texas

The largest of the continental U.S. states, Texas has a widely varied landscape and a long history of diverse human occupation. The geographic boundaries of Texas are defined by the Gulf of Mexico on the east, the Rio Grande to the south and west, the Sabine River to the east, and the Red River to the north. The geography extends from a part of the Gulf Coast plains associated with Louisiana and Arkansas in the East across the Great Plains to the arid peaks in the West. The coastal plain, first occupied by American settler families in the 1820s and 1830s, included grazing and the COTTON CULTURE (with slave labor) at that time. This area includes the present cities of Dallas/Fort Worth, San Antonio, and Austin. To the west lies the southern extension of the Great Plains. Here, grazing was the basis of the ECONOMY of this vast landed area stretching north to the panhandle. The western part of Texas is the high plains, an extension of the southern Rockies, with a landscape reflecting a climate that is semiarid. The climate in Texas is as varied as its topography. While the east and areas along the gulf are wet and humid, the west and north are dry. Texas is home to dramatic storms, hurricanes from the Gulf Coast, and winter blizzards in the west and north.

The first Native American peoples probably appeared in what is now Texas some 15,000 years ago. The variations in these peoples reflected the size and varied landscape of the region. In the east were the Caddo, forest dwellers related to the Indian peoples of Louisiana. To the south were the Jumano, who pursued AGRICULTURE. The Apache, the essence of the mounted raiders associated with the Indians of the Great Plains, were in the west.

The Spanish were the first of the European explorers and colonizers to reach the area, having already conquered the region that is now Mexico. Spanish explorers had visited the mouth of the Rio Grande in 1520, and Álvar Núñez Cabeza da Vaca and the survivors of Pánfilo de Narváez's expedition to Florida crossed Texas beginning in 1528. Of these, only Cabeza da Vaca and a black Moroccan slave named Esteban survived to reach Mexico. Their reports prompted others to set out in search of golden cities, most notably the expedition led by Francisco Vásquez de Coronado.

At the end of the 17th century, Spain established its first settlements at the sites of El Paso and Santa Fe (now New Mexico). Spanish officials occasionally dispatched small expeditions to Texas, but it lay at the far northern edge of an empire that was already in decline. Still, the Spanish took note of the ill-fated expedition of Sieur de la Salle, who sought the mouth of the Mississippi River and landed instead at Matagorda Bay. LaSalle and his men almost all perished, but his presence indicated an expanded French interest in the area. LaSalle's expedition and the founding of Mobile and New Orleans as the southern anchor of the French empire galvanized the Spanish into action, and they settled what is today eastern Texas by a series of missions that ran from Laredo on the Rio Grande to Nacogdoches on the Louisiana border. The most important center of Spanish influence was San Antonio, founded in 1718. Although the French were ineffectual in opposing Spanish expansion, the Indians were a continuing obstacle, especially the Apache and, in the 17th century, the Comanche, who expanded from the mountains out onto the plains. As Native Americans acquired horses, they became even more warlike and nomadic, forcing the Spanish to confine themselves to the missions and settlements in the eastern part of Texas.

Although opposed by the French, the Comanche, and the Apache, Spanish settlements and missions in east Texas grew throughout the first half of the 18th century. With the expulsion of the French under the Treaty of Paris in 1763, the Spanish position in Texas seemed secure, with the French gone and the victorious English far distant along the East Coast. This security was short-lived. With the success of the American Revolution and the recognition of American independence in another Treaty of Paris in 1783, the Spanish found a new, expansionist neighbor. Under the terms of the treaty, the American boundary on the west was the Mississippi River. The desire of Americans for Spanish possessions was first felt in Florida but soon moved closer to Texas. At the turn of the century, Spain retroceded Louisiana to the French as part of the endless imperial trading characteristic of Europe at the time. In 1803, in an astonishing act of national self-interest and intrigue, Napoleon Bonaparte sold Louisiana to the United States. Although the western boundary of the Louisiana Purchase was in dispute, the ADAMS-ONÍS TREATY of 1819, in which Spain ceded Florida to the United States, also established the Sabine River as the border. Texas was now on the edge of an expanding American nation looking to the west and the south.

Spain's empire in the Americas was already under assault from national independence movements. In Mexico, isolated revolutionary outbreaks began in 1811; Spain finally recognized Mexican independence in 1821. In a last desperate attempt to colonize American settlers in Texas, the Spanish government had experimented with a system of contracted immigration under the direction of an individual who would serve as an intermediary between the Spanish government and the new settlements. The original contact was with MOSES AUSTIN, a St. Louis entrepreneur who had failed in the PANIC OF 1819 and subsequent depression. Upon his death in 1821, Austin's project was taken over by his son, STEPHEN F. AUSTIN. The success of the Mexican Revolution intervened to delay the younger Austin's plans, but the new, independent government of the Republic of Mexico finally agreed to proceed with the policy of contracted immigration.

Between 1820 and 1830, Austin and other "empresarios" brought hundreds of American families into Texas. Austin's settlements, by far the largest, were in the Brazos and Colorado River valleys. Other immigrant groups settled along the coast. The very success of the republic of Mexico's contracted immigration policy soon created innumerable problems for Mexican officials in Texas and in Mexico City. By 1830, the American population of Texas was 20,000, all arrived within the last 10 years. Texan residents of Hispanic descent were approximately 4,000, the same as in 1820.

Austin was intensely loyal to the Republic of Mexico, but the settler families, in spite of the generous grants of land given to them, remained American. They were impatient with the local state government of Coahuila-Texas and inclined to pursue the American frontier doctrine of taking collective action rather than calling on the government for assistance. To the American settlers in Texas, this was an appropriate solution to their complaints about local government, the court system, and protection against the Indians. To officials of the Republic of Mexico in Texas and in Mexico, such actions were tantamount to rebellion against constituted authority. That Americans in the age of MANIFEST DESTINY often looked on Mexicans as inferior and incompetent increased the tensions.

Austin counseled patience and forbearance, but his imprisonment in Mexico City for 18 months in 1834 and 1835 removed from Texas the most important voice of compromise. In autumn 1835, scattered armed clashes took place between Texans and Mexican authorities. The fact that numbers of armed Texans had gathered together in pursuit of political freedom only confirmed the view of Mexican officials that an armed rebellion was imminent. General ANTONIO LÓPEZ DE SANTA ANNA, to consolidate his authority and suppress a rebellion, led a large army into Texas in early 1836. The Texans suffered disastrous defeats at Goliad and at THE ALAMO, but SAM HOUSTON organized the scattered volunteers into something like an army and defeated Santa Anna at the Battle of San Jacinto. Santa Anna signed a treaty recognizing Texan independence, and the Republic of Texas was established.

The leaders of the new Republic of Texas had always assumed that they would seek annexation to the United States. With the republic established, however, several issues caused a distinctly cool response on the part of the government in Washington to the suggestion of annexation. Within the international community, the United States had been heavily criticized for what was perceived as its partisan attitude during the TEXAS REVOLUTION. That Americans individuals and collectively should support the Texas cause was understandable, but as a government, the United States was bound to pursue a policy of neutrality. Nevertheless, large quantities of men, arms, supplies, and financial support made their way from American soil to Texas—much of it through southern ports, especially New Orleans, with little or no attempt at interdiction on the part of Washington. In view of such lax enforcement of neutrality laws, it was awkward for the United States to hastily annex a state so recently a part of the Republic of Mexico.

Sam Houston, the victorious commander at San Jacinto, was elected president of the Republic of Texas. His successors were Mirabeau B. Lamar and Anson Jones. Although vigorously committed by public oratory to independence, the Republic of Texas had many problems to overcome. Among these were a continuing war with Mexico, an ongoing conflict with many Native Americans, and uncertain financial policies. . The prevailing philosophy of government was based on the policies of ANDREW JACKSON: minimal intrusion on the part of government into the lives of individual citizens. As a result, Texas had no taxes and minimal import duties. The free-trade posture delighted Great Britain and France but left the republic with an empty treasury. Indians on the Texas frontier fought the expansion of a growing population. That Texas grew from 40,000 in 1836 to 120,000 in 1846 meant continuing conflict with Native Americans. Elements of the Mexican army periodically sent expeditions into Texas, raising cries of alarm among the civil population and confusion among elements of the Texas militia. A Texan military expedition against Santa Fe, to confirm Texas's claim to the upper Rio Grande watershed, ended in disaster. As annexation to the United States became the focus of diplomatic efforts on both sides, the issue became embroiled in domestic American politics. SLAVERY was legal in Texas, and elements in Congress opposed to slavery and its expansion into the new territory organized to oppose Texas annexation. Finally, in 1845, Texas was brought into the Union by a resolution of annexation in both houses, a parliamentary maneuver that required only a simple majority rather than the two-thirds required by a treaty. Under terms of the annexation, Texas was admitted as a state and retained its public lands to retire its debt.

At almost the same time as annexation came the MEXICAN-AMERICAN WAR, which began in spring 1846. One of the causes was conflict over the boundary line between Mexico and Texas. Although Texas and its relations with Mexico—the republic of Mexico still regarded Texas as a state in rebellion—was important in the opening of the war, most of the military campaigns were to the south in Mexico or west in California. The close of the war, with the signing of the TREATY OF GUADALUPE HIDALGO in early 1848, confirmed Texas annexation to the United States and included the cession of California, New Mexico, and Arizona to the American nation. The resolution of the territories acquired during the war was the subject of an extended national debate, eventually resolved by the COMPROMISE OF 1850. Under the terms of the agreement, Texas gave up its claims to portions of Colorado and New Mexico and received $10 million to settle the state's long-standing debt.

Texas resumed its rapid growth, from 300,000 in 1850 to 600,000 in 1860, with the densest population living along the Gulf Coast, where Texas had a cotton/slave economy like the Deep South. By 1860 the state had a large slave population, some 20 percent of its enumerated population. Cattle ranching was also important in the hill country and farther inland, where ranchers grazed large herds. The only substantial town was San Antonio, with 8,000 inhabitants. With the rise of sectional feeling in the 1850s, Texas was in the proslavery camp. Although Sam Houston, who supported the Union, was elected governor in 1860, Texas nevertheless seceded from the Union in 1861. Houston, who would not take an oath to support the Confederacy, was forced to resign.

Further reading: Seymour V. Connor, *Texas: A History* (New York: Crowell, 1971); Mark E. Nackman, *A Nation Within a Nation: The Rise of Texas Nationalism* (Port Washington, N.Y.: Kennikat Press, 1975); Walter Prescott Webb, ed., *Handbook of Texas* (Austin: Texas State Historical Association, 1952–76).

Texas Revolution (1835–1836)

The Texas Revolution is the name given to the series of events that led to the independence of Texas from Mexico and the subsequent establishment of the Republic of Texas. Texas had long been the northern extension of the Spanish Empire in the Americas. Although sparsely settled from the opening of the 17th century, the region was an important outpost of Spanish imperial policy, at the same time forming a barrier against the French advance from Louisiana to the West and a line of defense against Indian raiders on the plains. As Spanish colonies turned toward independence at the close of the 18th century, Mexico joined those who sought independence. The success of the Mexican Revolution and the establishment of an independent republic of Mexico in 1821 began a new chapter in the history of Texas.

As part of a plan to settle its northern states, Mexico established a system of contracted immigration. MOSES AUSTIN had first proposed the scheme in 1820 to Spanish officials in Mexico City. Upon Austin's death the following year, his proposal was taken over by his son, STEPHEN F. AUSTIN. After the establishment of Mexican independence, the younger Austin spent a year in Mexico City, lobbying officials to accept his father's proposal. His persistence paid off when Mexico agreed to permit Austin to settle 300 families on a large tract of land in Texas. Austin eventually chose the Brazos and Colorado River valleys as the site of his settlement. Under the terms of the arrangement, Austin would receive a large land grant from Mexico, and he would choose the settler families to whom he would make substantial grants of land. He would have enormous authority not only in making land grants but also in maintaining order, establishing a court system, providing a defense against Indians, and deciding other issues that confronted every new settlement on the frontier. The Mexican government eventually passed a law embodying the outlines of Austin's scheme, which became a national policy. Hundreds of immigrant families from the United States—Austin eventually brought in some 700 families under three contracts—settled in the Mexican state of Texas. This policy of supervised immigration appeared to be a great success. Enterprising pioneer families settled portions of

The flag of the Republic of Texas, the "Lone Star" state *(Library of Congress)*

coastal Texas and the river valleys under the leadership of designated "empresarios."

But the success of the enterprise made for problems. By 1830, the American population of Texas—all arrived within the decade of the 1820s—had reached 20,000. Officials in Mexico City found themselves confronted with a numerous and increasingly unsettled population that was more American than Mexican. Under the terms of the contracted immigration, in exchange for generous land grants, Americans agreed to become citizens of the Republic of Mexico and to become Roman Catholics. That the predominantly Protestant settlers from the lower Mississippi Valley did neither was indicative of their attitudes toward their new nation. That Stephen F. Austin remained intensely loyal to the Republic of Mexico was a stabilizing influence, but the growing numbers of Americans invariably led to talk of separation from Mexico and occasional plots to foment an uprising against Mexican authority. The uneasiness of the Americans was increased by the attachment of Coahuila to Texas, creating a united state of Coahuila-Texas, which American Texans saw as a way of minimizing their political influence.

Mexican officials were aware of the difficulties posed by the preponderance of Americans in Texas, and in 1830 Mexico passed a law forbidding further immigration from the United States. For Austin, the new law threatened a successful system of contracted immigration, and it was, among other things, unenforceable. For the Americans in Texas, the 1830 law confirmed their views that Mexican officials intended to infringe on their liberties, including the right to immigrate. The Americans in Texas now organized to give voice to their grievances. They did so in a traditionally American way, by electing delegates to meet in a convention, drafting petitions to explain their views, and conveying these petitions to the proper authority. The most important Texan, Stephen F. Austin, took the petitions to Mexico City in 1833.

Changes in the political situation in Mexico City made Austin's mission more difficult. Mexico's political world had always been somewhat unstable, mitigated by the consistency of a federal bureaucracy. In 1832, General ANTONIO LÓPEZ DE SANTA ANNA overthrew the constitutional government in Mexico. The next year, after Santa Anna won a popular mandate, he embarked on a series of military campaigns to subdue rebellions in parts of the Republic of Mexico. Texans observed Santa Anna's campaigns throughout the southern portion of Mexico with growing uneasiness. As for Santa Anna, with the south pacified, he intended to turn his attention to Texas, long considered disloyal because of its increasingly dominant American population.

In this atmosphere of growing uneasiness on both sides, Austin appeared in Mexico City with his petitions. He found a generally cordial reception. The Santa Anna government agreed to his requests with one exception. The petition for separate statehood for Texas was denied, as Mexican authorities saw a separate state of Texas as a prelude to secession. As Austin was returning from what he regarded as a successful mission, he was arrested. Jailed in Mexico City for almost two years, his absence accelerated the increasingly radical stance of the new Texan leaders, of whom the most noteworthy newcomer was SAM HOUSTON, who had immigrated to Texas in 1832.

As Texans began to consider their relations with the Republic of Mexico, several common issues came into focus. One faction pointed to RELIGION and the requirements of marriage associated with the Roman Catholic Church, since only Catholics could inherit. As Anglo-Texans had more to inherit, the issue was more pressing. The question of local government and the court system was also an issue; hence the request to create a separate state of Texas that could more effectively meet the needs of the immigrants from the North. Throughout these debates, Texans clung to the traditional American frontier institution of a local armed militia for protection, especially against the Indians, and raised questions of public schools and language. In addition, they continued to insist on their rights as citizens under the constitution of 1824 at a time when it was increasingly irrelevant under the new presidency of Santa Anna.

Mexican officials were also uneasy about the situation in Texas. To begin with, they saw Texas as Mexican and the newly arrived settlers as ungrateful Norte Americanos. In exchange for generous land grants, the settlers had sworn allegiance to the Republic of Mexico, and it was to their new nation that they owed allegiance. As citizens of the Republic of Mexico, they were bound to follow the laws of the republic, whether these laws suited them or not. If they objected to laws or officials, they should not convene conventions but instead initiate a correspondence through the hierarchy of officials, beginning with the state of Coahuila-Texas. The idea of Anglo-Texans forming an armed militia seemed little less than a prelude to armed rebellion. Loyal Texans should have recourse to the Mexican army. Above all, Texans must be taught to respect and obey Mexican laws. Mexican officials were, understandably, sensitive to what they regarded as ethnic slights and ethnic slurs. Relations between the two groups were further inflamed by two recent considerations: Santa Anna's campaigns to reduce opposition to his rule and the presence of Mexican troops in garrisons in Texas ports, which would invariably lead to confrontations between Mexican forces intent on upholding the honor of the republic of Mexico and Anglo-Texans who saw such garrisons as an alien occupying force.

In 1835, Austin returned after two years in prison to find Texas split into two factions. One favored peace overtures to the Republic of Mexico and a continuing search for an alliance with Santa Anna's liberal political opponents. The second supported a revolution in favor of independence. Austin soon allied himself with the first group; Houston headed the second. Military clashes between the two sides had begun to sharpen hostility between Mexicans and Anglo-Texans. When, in June 1835, some 30 Texans forced the garrison at Anahuac to surrender, many communities in Texas repudiated the action, but Mexican officials saw the confrontation as part of a Texas revolt. Although the Texan force surrendered its arms, local officials did not turn the 30 rebels over to Mexican officials to stand trial.

Santa Anna was now determined to pacify Texas by military force as he had other parts of the Republic of Mexico. In so doing, he disavowed any observance of the Constitution of 1824 so sacred to many Texans, and he also threatened to force observance of Mexico's ban on slavery. In late 1835, as Santa Anna dispatched an army to put down what he saw as a rebellion, even Austin realized that the time for mediation had passed. Instead, he urged Texans to resist the invasion and bring Texas finally into the United States. In his own words: "War is our only recourse. There is no other remedy." When Texas communities convened in November 1835 to consider the future, they strongly supported loyalty to Mexico under the Constitution of 1824. Deferring independence did win some Tejano support, but most Tejanos—Texans of Spanish and Mexican origin—were distant from the Anglo-Texans, whom they regarded as brash and aggressive.

Sam Houston led the movement to armed insurrection. At first, Texan attempts at military activity were uncoordinated and reflected individual leaders. In December 1835, a contingent of Texans coordinated an attack in San Antonio that laid siege to the Mexican garrison in THE ALAMO and eventually forced its surrender. Houston counseled the evacuation of the Alamo; he favored a retreat toward the center of Anglo-Texas settlement with a continuing guerrilla war. He therefore sent JIM BOWIE to San Antonio with orders to remove the Alamo's guns, blow up the old mission, and evacuate the Texan garrison. When Bowie arrived at the Alamo, however, he did not carry out his orders. Instead, he and others decided that the Alamo was a key position and must be defended. When Santa Anna reached San Antonio, he had some 2,000 troops ready for the field; Bowie and the garrison at the Alamo numbered 100, perhaps a quarter of them soldiers and the rest volunteers. Bowie's appeal for reinforcements, ignored by the provisional government of Texas, was answered by Colonel WILLIAM BARRET TRAVIS, a leader of the war party; and DAVY CROCKETT, a former congressman from Tennessee. They and their companions raised the defenders of the mission to perhaps 187.

On February 25, 1835, Santa Anna and his army arrived at San Antonio. Bowie offered to surrender on condition of safe conduct for combatants; Santa Anna demanded unconditional surrender. The siege began. After a long period of Mexican bombardment that was largely ineffective, Santa Anna launched a frontal assault by 1,800 soldiers on March 6, 1835. Sheer numbers carried the day. After 90 minutes of combat, some of it hand-to-hand, Santa Anna was in control of the old mission. He had lost 600 men; most of the Texan defenders were dead. Santa Anna executed the handful of prisoners, including Davy Crockett, as a warning to others who remained in revolt against the Mexican government. Although Santa Anna had won a military victory, he had given the Texans' cause a company of martyrs and a reason for a declaration of independence. Henceforth, the battle cry of the infant Republic of Texas would be: "Remember the Alamo!"

The disaster at the Alamo was followed by another military and human defeat. As the Texans retired north in the face of Santa Anna's advance, Colonel James Fannin delayed his withdrawal from Goliad's fort for so long that he and his force were captured by advance troops of the Mexican army. Santa Anna ordered the execution of the 300 prisoners. He was convinced that he had overwhelmed Texan resistance to his force, and the panicked retreat of thousands of refugees to the north, including the provisional government, seemed to confirm his view.

In the face of this hysteria mixed with a burning desire for revenge, Houston recruited and trained an army. It was not a large force, perhaps 800 men, but it had a degree of discipline and training that other Texas forces had lacked. Houston and his army met a Mexican army about twice as large under Santa Anna on a plain west of the San Jacinto River (near Galveston Bay). On April 21, 1836 Houston ordered a frontal charge, and in 20 minutes, the Texans had won the field. The slaughter of the retreating Mexican army went on for several hours, at the end of which 630 Mexican soldiers were dead.

After the battle, Santa Anna was captured while trying to escape. Many favored his execution for his crimes against prisoners, but Houston forced him to sign a treaty recognizing Texas independence. Under the terms of the Treaty of Velasco, Santa Anna ordered all Mexican soldiers to evacuate Texas and recognized the independence of the former state. Although signed under duress and later repudiated by the government of Mexico, this treaty of independence was generally recognized abroad. The revolution was over; the Republic of Texas was established.

Further reading: Paul D. Lack, *The Texas Revolutionary Experience: A Political and Social History, 1835–1836* (College Station: Texas A&M University Press, 1992); David J. Weber, *The Mexican Frontier, 1821–1846: The American*

Southwest Under Mexico (Albuquerque: University of New Mexico Press, 1982).

Thames, Battle of the (October 5, 1813)

The overwhelming American victory at the Battle of the Thames broke the back of the last organized Native American resistance east of the Mississippi. The leader of the movement to unite the nations, Tecumseh, died in the encounter.

The Thames River flows through Canada near the U.S. border at Detroit, Michigan. During the WAR OF 1812 (1812–15), Great Britain feared the Americans would launch an invasion into the region around it to seize control of the Great Lakes and possibly annex the entire colony. Americans made several failed attempts to conquer the area in 1812 and 1813.

On September 27, 1813, WILLIAM HENRY HARRISON and 3,000 Americans crossed uncontested into Canada. Tecumseh and his warriors had fallen back into British territory in the hopes that they would defeat the Americans and reclaim their homes in the Michigan and Indiana territories. The British commander, Major General Henry Proctor, wanted to retreat to a more defensible spot further away from the border. Tecumseh convinced Proctor to face the enemy along a narrow stretch of road between the Thames River and a swampy thicket. However the 450 British troops ran from their positions at the road after a brief assault by the powerful American forces. Americans quickly crushed the remaining 800 Native American warriors who had stayed to cover the retreat. Tecumseh died in the fighting, and his body was never recovered.

After the battle, most of the Native Americans south of the Great Lakes accepted that the United States was too strong for them to stop. Within two decades, the government forced most of the remaining nations to move west of the Mississippi.

Further reading: R. David Edmunds, *Tecumseh and the Quest for Indian Leadership* (Boston: Little, Brown, 1984).

—George Milne

Thoreau, Henry David (1817–1862)

Essayist, poet, naturalist, educator, and lecturer, Henry David Thoreau was born on July 12, 1817, in Concord, Massachusetts. His father, John Thoreau, was a pencil manufacturer. The young Thoreau attended Concord Academy and Harvard College, graduating in 1837. He then worked as a public-school teacher to supplement his family's income and pay for his college EDUCATION. Later, he opened a day and boarding school from the family home. Shortly after returning from Harvard to Concord, Thoreau met fellow intellectual RALPH WALDO EMERSON. They soon began a remarkable relationship based on their work in the important literary movement of transcendentalism.

The new TRANSCENDENTAL MOVEMENT was mainly comprised of young men and women from New England who rejected formal RELIGION for what they called "The Transcendental Law." This was the moral law through which man discovers for himself the nature of God. Transcendentalists like Thoreau believed that God was embodied in a spirit whose essence could never be defined or contained by tedious, learned texts or rules. Rather, transcendentalists advised looking to the fluid, energetic, and "transcendental" unity of life. They celebrated a somewhat vaguely defined, but nonetheless liberating, "truth" whose essence could only be discovered through the natural world. The simple life was celebrated, although few adherents to the movement took that as far as Thoreau.

Thoreau began publishing poetry and essays regularly in the transcendentalist magazine *The Dial.* From 1845 to 1847, he formed the basis for 18 more essays, collectively entitled *Walden; or My Life in the Woods,* when he moved to a cabin on Emerson's property near Walden Pond in Concord in order to live as simply and as close to nature as possible. Midway through his stay there, Thoreau refused to pay the local poll tax because of his opposition toward a government that condoned SLAVERY and had launched what he considered an imperialist war against Mexico. Thoreau's one night in jail as well as his thoughts on the subject fueled the essay *Resistance to Civil Government,* or *Civil Disobedience* (1849), in which he espoused the need to live up to higher ideals than those of civil society—even if this meant breaking laws in the process. "The law will never make men free," he declared, "it is men who have got to make the law free."

Thoreau continued his own private form of social activism after he moved out of the woods. He wrote essays and delivered lectures such as "Slavery in Massachusetts" (1854) in support of the ABOLITION MOVEMENT. He explained his ideas on the role of the state: "There will never be a really free and enlightened state until the state comes to recognize the individual as a higher and independent power . . . and treats him accordingly." Following John Brown's failure to incite a slave revolt with his raid on Harpers Ferry, Thoreau delivered "A Plea for Captain Brown" (1859) in order to exonerate Brown in the eyes of the law for living up to a higher ideal. Brown was hanged, however, and it is believed that the incident shocked Thoreau so much as to hasten his own death.

After spending a few years beginning a study of the plight of NATIVE AMERICANS, Thoreau, who had suffered from tuberculosis for many years, finally died of its effects on May 6, 1862. His final works, *The Maine Woods* (1864) and *Cape Cod* (1865) were published posthumously.

WALDEN;

OR,

LIFE IN THE WOODS.

BY HENRY D. THOREAU,

AUTHOR OF "A WEEK ON THE CONCORD AND MERRIMACK RIVERS."

I do not propose to write an ode to dejection, but to brag as lustily as chanticleer in the morning, standing on his roost, if only to wake my neighbors up. — Page 92.

Title page of *Walden,* by Henry David Thoreau *(Library of Congress)*

Further reading: Walter Roy Harding, *The Days of Henry Thoreau: A Biography* (Princeton, N.J.: Princeton University Press, 1992); Robert Richardson, *Henry Thoreau: A Life of the Mind* (Berkeley: University of California Press, 1996); Henry David Thoreau, *Walden and Other Writings of Henry David Thoreau,* edited by Brooks Atkinson (New York: Modern Library, 1992).

—Lee Ashley Smith

Trail of Tears

Between 1830 and 1839, the Choctaw, Chickasaw, Creek, Cherokee, and Seminole nations—who collectively came to be known as the Five Civilized Tribes—were removed under varying degrees of coercion from their homes in the Southeast to new lands west of the Mississippi River. Their relocation was the culmination of a decades-old dispute between southeastern Indian nations and the white settlers who wanted their lands.

White Americans had long coveted the fertile soil of the Southeast and the lucrative possibility of expanding cotton production there. Many considered Native Americans to be undeserving stewards of such lands, falsely characterizing them as lazy and nomadic. These stereotypes were especially egregious when applied to the southeastern nations. By the 1820s, many of them had made a series of cultural adaptations that responded to the presence of so many whites in the region and the failure of military resistance early in the century to prevent the same. By 1828, the Cherokee nation boasted a bicameral legislature, a Cherokee alphabet, a bilingual newspaper, their own network of schools and churches, and the flourishing practice of cash-crop AGRICULTURE. Yet such adaptations only convinced whites that it was imperative to remove Native Americans from the Southeast. It was clear that the vast majority of American Indian people would not surrender their lands voluntarily, and the southern states rejected the idea that self-governing Indian nations could constitutionally exist within their borders. Amid a tangle of arguments about state vs. federal rights, land hunger, and racial prejudice, overwhelming white pressure for the removal of Indian people from the East to the West was born. The long and painful process of Cherokee removal became known as the Trail of Tears.

On May 28, 1830, Congress passed the INDIAN REMOVAL ACT. Approved and signed by President ANDREW JACKSON the act authorized the exchange of Indian lands in the East for new territories west of the Mississippi. It promised that the new western lands offered to American Indian nations would remain theirs forever, and they would be protected against encroachment from other nations or settlers. Native Americans were to be compensated for any improvements they had made on their eastern lands, and the government was authorized to provide financial assistance with the process of removal. While the act was used to relocate American Indian communities across the United States, it was in the Southeast that it was used to its most devastating effect. As a result, the peoples of the Choctaw, Chickasaw, Creek, and Cherokee nations would suffer tremendous material and physical losses in the process of removal.

The Indian Removal Act stipulated that any east-west land exchange was to be voluntary, open to "such tribes or nations of Indians as may choose" to be part of the process. In reality, however, coercion was used at every turn to facilitate removal. Annuities owed to nations from past treaties were doled out to individuals instead of tribal leaders, undermining the ability of chiefs to maintain their leadership positions or to provide for the needs of their communities. States extended their laws over tribal lands, nullifying the legal and judicial systems of each nation, making Native Americans liable for taxes and withholding their right to vote or testify in court. States took no action to protect Indians from squatters encroaching on their lands, and the federal government likewise ignored the problem. Federal officials purposely negotiated removal treaties with the most disaffected members of nations, and often bribed Indian representatives into agreeing to sign.

The Choctaw were the first to be relocated under the provisions of the Indian Removal Act. The Treaty of Dancing Rabbit Creek was signed between a handful of Choctaw and the federal government in 1830, sealing the removal of the nation to lands in present-day Oklahoma. Their experience was miserable. Two thousand men, women, and children set out from Mississippi in autumn 1830. Only 400–500 reached their new homeland after battling extreme cold, starvation, and disease. More Choctaw emigrated over the next two years, their experience largely the same. Forced to cover enormous distances of the trek on foot, the Choctaw saw hundreds of their horses die, while they themselves battled cholera and malnutrition. It is estimated that approximately 9,000 Choctaw relocated to Indian Territory, 7,000 stayed in Mississippi (often in hiding), and over 4,000 died during removal.

The removal of the Creek nation was equally cruel. In 1832, those Creek who had not already emigrated west signed a treaty with the United States that ostensibly left the option of removal up to each individual family. Creek lands in Alabama were to be divided into individual allotments and protected by the federal government from intrusion for up to five years. These lands could be sold and the family removed to Indian Territory, or they could wait and receive the deed to their land after a five-year period.

The plan fell apart almost immediately. Squatters encroached on Indian lands, often forcing families out of their homes. Land companies committed massive fraud, engaging individual Indians to pretend to be landowners, illegally selling the same plot of land to a multitude of bidders. Tension between squatters and the increasing number of dispossessed Creek built into outbreaks of violence, resulting in military intervention in the region in 1836. Over the next two years the Creek, whether "peaceful" or "hostile," were removed to Indian Territory under deplorable conditions. Thousands died from starvation and exposure along the way.

For the Chickasaw, the experience of removal was less harsh, although just as fraught with difficulty. After signing a removal treaty in 1832, the Chicksaw were forced to wait five years for the federal government to resolve where in Indian Territory they might live. In those five years, Chickasaw lands were sold from under them and overrun with squatters. It was not until 1837 that the Choctaw agreed to cede part of their new land to the Chickasaw, who migrated with better supplies, protection, and transportation than either of their predecessors to Indian Territory.

The removal of the Cherokee was the last in the series because of the vigorous opposition of Indian peoples and a group of American reformers. When the state of Georgia extended its jurisdiction over Cherokee lands within the state in 1828, the Cherokee nation sued the state to void the state law. In 1831 the SUPREME COURT ruled in *Cherokee Nation v. State of Georgia* that the suit was null and void because Indian tribes could not sue. In a subsequent case brought in the name of Samuel Worcester, a Congregational missionary, the Court declared in 1832 that the Cherokee Nation was a separate and distinct community with its own territory within the state. President Andrew Jackson refused to enforce the decision.

The most important Cherokee chief, John Ross, refused to negotiate a treaty of cession. In 1835, after months of unsuccessful talks, the federal government ordered the entire nation to appear at the town of New Echota. Those Cherokee who refused to appear would be considered in support of any treaty negotiated at the meeting. The enormous pressure applied by the United States government divided the Cherokee Nation. After weeks of threats and behind-the-scenes discussions, the Treaty of New Echota was signed between representatives of the federal government and John Ridge, who sought to save the tribe from threats of internal and external violence. Perhaps as few as 500 of the 17,000 Cherokee people favored the agreement.

While some groups emigrated almost immediately, the majority of the Cherokee nation stayed in Georgia. They refused to acknowledge the legality of the treaty or the May 23, 1838, deadline for voluntary removal. After the deadline had passed, however, the Cherokee were rounded up at bayonet point and held in temporary camps. They were not allowed to gather personal possessions or make preparations for the journey ahead of them. While around 5,000 Cherokee were immediately dispatched to Indian Territory, the rest were held in camps under military guard through the summer of 1838, suffering from disease and food shortages. Approximately 3,000 Cherokee died in the camps, and those who survived were forced to trek some 800 miles to their new lands west of the Mississippi. The march was carried out in two trips in 1838–39, and the journey killed another thousand people. Even once they had reached Oklahoma, disease and lack of food further reduced their population. Such were the devastating effects of the removal that the Cherokee called their route "Nunna daul Tsuny" ("the Trail Where They Cried"). In time, the "Trail of Tears" came to apply to the combined experience of all Indian Nations removed from the Southeast.

Further reading: Theda Perdue and Michael D. Green, eds., *The Cherokee Removal: A Brief History with Documents* (Boston: Bedford Books, 1995); Anthony F. C. Wallace, *The Long Bitter Trail: Andrew Jackson and the Indians* (New York: Hill and Wang, 1993).

—Catherine J. Denial

transcendental movement

American transcendentalism was a New England-based philosophical and literary movement that began with the 1836 founding of the Transcendental Club in Concord, Massachusetts. The movement's members included RALPH WALDO EMERSON (1803–82), HENRY DAVID THOREAU (1817–62), MARGARET FULLER (1810–50), Nathaniel Hawthorne (1804–64), and Bronson Alcott (1799–1888).

The transcendentalists believed in the inherent goodness of humanity and all of nature. They were strongly influenced by the German idealists, including Immanuel Kant, and the romantic movement in England. Emerson was inspired to form the Transcendental Club on his return from a trip to Europe, where he met William Wordsworth, Samuel Taylor Coleridge, Thomas Carlyle, and other important romantic writers. The transcendentalists explicitly rejected rationalism and the Puritan attitudes they had inherited as New Englanders. Instead, they expressed near-religious fervor for nature, intuition, and the creative process. They believed that God (or, as they called it, the Over-Soul) permeated all of creation, living and nonliving things alike, and that an individual's highest potential could only be achieved through complete awareness of the truth and beauty of the natural world.

The Transcendental Club's magazine, *The Dial*, was published from 1840 to 1844 and was an influential literary journal of the day. Edited by Fuller in its first two years of publication, it introduced many of Emerson's best-known essays.

The transcendentalists were known for their experiments in alternative modes of living. Thoreau, most famously, lived alone and largely off the land for a time. His book about his solitary experience, *Walden, or Life in the Woods* (1854), remains one of the most widely read of the transcendentalists' works. The idea that intellectual work and physical labor must go hand in hand appealed to the transcendentalists, whose philosophy after all compelled them to seek a complete awareness of and union with nature. Communal living and cooperative farming were attempted at BROOK FARM in West Roxbury, Massachusetts, where a number of the transcendentalists, including Hawthorne, lived in a socialist society from 1841 to 1847. Alcott's cooperative vegetarian farm, Fruitlands, in Harvard, Massachusetts, endured for only a few months in 1843. Neither of the farms were financial successes, and in fact their members had to endure much monetary hardship. But these utopian communities did allow their residents to attempt to live in harmony with the land and in accordance with their transcendental ideals. They were also an important inspiration for the communes, organic farms, and cooperatives of later generations of idealists, especially in the 1960s.

It is for their writings that the transcendentalists are best remembered. Emerson's book *Nature* (1836) and his essay "Self-Reliance" (1841) both focus on important aspects of transcendentalist philosophy. Fuller's *Woman in the Nineteenth Century* (1845) is a major early feminist work that grew out of the women-only philosophy seminars she held in Boston between 1839 and 1844. Hawthorne's novels and short stories remain important; *The Blithedale Romance* (1852) was based on his experience as part of the Brook Farm community, and his masterworks *The Scarlet Letter* (1850) and *The House of the Seven Gables* (1851) criticize the values and legacy of Puritanism. Along with *Walden*, Thoreau is best known for his essay "Civil Disobedience" (1849), which was a powerful influence on 20th-century thinkers and activists including Martin Luther King, Jr., and Mohandas K. Gandhi.

Further reading: Charles Capper and Conrad Edick Wright, eds. *Transient and Permanent: The Transcendentalist Movement and Its Contexts* (Boston: Northeastern University Press, 1999); Perry Miller, *The Transcendentalists* (Cambridge, Mass.: Harvard University Press, 1960).

—Mary Kay Linge

Travis, William Barret (1809–1836)

A lawyer and Texas military leader, William Barret Travis was an ardent supporter of American expansion into Mexican territory. He was born in Edgefield, South Carolina, in 1809. In 1818, the Travis family joined the great migration to the opening of new lands in the South, moving to Conecuh County, Alabama. The young Travis received a fair education at the local school. Like other ambitious young men in this frontier environment, he decided to read law. He pursued his study in the office of Judge James Dellett in Claiborne, Alabama. In 1819, just before his 20th birthday, he was admitted to the bar. Travis set up a legal practice in a new state whose prospects were immediately blighted by the economic crisis of 1819. To supplement his income, he taught school. In 1828, he married Rosanna Cato, one of his students.

In 1831, Travis left his wife (they were divorced in 1835) and two children and moved to TEXAS, where he settled in Anahuac, on Galveston Bay. This was also the site of the Mexican military garrison, commanded by Colonel John Bradbury, a Kentucky native now in the service of

Mexico. Bradbury was an arbitrary officer, and Travis quickly rose to the leadership of an American faction in opposition to Mexican authority. The newly arrived immigrants from the United States aggressively defended their rights in the Republic of Mexico, viewing their position from the perspective of a different frontier tradition and generally ignoring their responsibilities as recipients of Mexican land grants. On every issue, Travis took a radical position, asserting that settlers' rights must be upheld, if necessary, by force. Almost immediately on his arrival in Texas, he offended the authorities and was arrested. When an armed force gathered to demand his release, Mexican officials complied. The issue was settled peacefully, but hard feelings remained on each side. In October 1832, Travis moved to San Felipe, where he set up a thriving legal practice and soon became involved in local politics, once again as a vigorous defender of the rights of new settlers from the United States.

When General ANTONIO LÓPEZ DE SANTA ANNA ascended to power in Mexico City, alarm bells sounded for Travis and other Texans. Heretofore, the issues of rights and obligations, while hotly debated, had been largely abstract matters of principle. With Santa Anna's decision to march north with his army and subdue dissident factions in Texas, these issues had become immediate. Travis was at the forefront of those determined to take vigorous action. In 1835, when Santa Anna sent soldiers to regarrison the fort at Anahuac, Travis raised a volunteer company, disarmed the Mexican soldiers, and seized the fort. The surrounding countryside was electrified by his actions. Many Texans repudiated his radical steps, but Travis and others pressed the issue of Texan rights and forced Santa Anna toward a campaign to subjugate the rebels. His aggressive actions at the head of an invading army validated Travis's position that Texans must take up arms in defense of their rights.

When a convention convened at San Felipe to prepare a defense, Travis was commissioned a lieutenant colonel in the cavalry. In autumn 1835, he participated actively in the siege of San Antonio. In December that year, he was appointed to command the artillery, and soon thereafter, he transferred to the cavalry, once again with the rank of lieutenant colonel. In early February 1836, with 25 men, he reinforced the small garrison at THE ALAMO. On February 13, he was appointed joint commander (with JAMES BOWIE) of the force, Travis to command the regulars and Bowie to lead the volunteers. Travis and Bowie disagreed on almost every aspect of the command, and they were still sorting out their views when Santa Anna's army arrived at the gates of the Alamo. Bowie was soon felled by typhoid fever, and Travis assumed overall command. When Santa Anna launched his frontal assault on March 6, Travis was killed along with the other defenders, including Bowie and DAVY CROCKETT. He was 26 years old. Officials and citizens alike remembered him as a staunch defender of principle and a Texas patriot.

Further reading: William C. Binkley, *The Texas Revolution* (Baton Rouge: University of Louisiana Press, 1952); T. R. Fahrenbach, *Lone Star: A History of Texas and Texans* (New York: Macmillan, 1968).

Truth, Sojourner See Volume V

Tubman, Harriet See Volume V

Turner, Nat (1800–1831)

Born in Southampton County, Virginia, on October 2, 1800, Nat Turner became one of the most infamous enslaved men and insurrectionists of the 19th century. The child of African-born parents, Nat was owned first by Benjamin Turner and then his son Samuel. Nat's father was a recurrent runaway who succeeded in escaping slavery and emigrating to LIBERIA. His mother Nancy was also a slave at the Turner plantation. Nat learned to read early in his childhood, and claimed that he did so through a natural and inexplicable gift rather than instruction. His intelligence was widely discussed within his community.

Turner grew up to become a fieldhand, entering adulthood just as the PANIC OF 1819 marked the beginning of a four-year depression in the United States. In an effort to maintain his plantation's profitability, Samuel Turner instructed his overseer to work his slaves particularly hard. After a whipping from the overseer during this period, Nat Turner ran away to the nearby Flat Swamps. He remained free for 30 days, before returning to the Turner plantation of his own free will, convinced by a series of religious visions that it was the right course of action. Few of his fellow slaves understood his choice.

Sometime within the next two years, Nat married Cherry, another slave on the Turner plantation. In 1823, Samuel Turner died, and the couple were sold to different planters—Nat to Thomas Moore and Cherry to Giles Reese. Although separated, the couple worked on neighboring plantations and were able to see each other from time to time. Together they had three children.

During the mid-1820s, Turner became increasingly convinced that his life had a special religious purpose. From his childhood, adults around him had suggested that he was meant for great things, and visions throughout his life had strengthened his own conviction of the same. In 1825, Turner began to preach, traveling to Cross Keys, Jerusalem, and Bethlehem Crossroads in Southampton

County on different Sundays. Turner spoke to whites and blacks in his travels, and most famously baptized Etheldred T. Brantley, a white overseer in the county who had been shunned by his own church. The baptism came after Brantley had confessed unnamed sins to Turner and subsequently had been cured of an outbreak of bleeding boils through fasting and prayer.

It was a vision experienced on May 12, 1828, that would most significantly change Turner's life. Remembering the moment as he sat in jail in 1831, Turner recalled that "the Spirit instantly appeared to me and said the Serpent was loosened, and Christ had laid down the yoke he had borne for the sins of men, and that I should take it on and fight against the Serpent, for the time was fast approaching, when the first should be last and the last should be first." Turner took the vision to mean that at a given sign he should rise up against the institution of SLAVERY and kill those he considered his enemies "with their own weapons."

The sign did not come for another three years. In the interim, Thomas Moore died, and his slaves became the property of his widow. One year later, Moore's widow married Joseph Travis, a wheelwright in the county, who moved his business and his own slaves to the Moore plantation. The slave community at the plantation numbered 17 in February 1831, when Turner received the sign he'd been waiting for in the shape of a solar eclipse. Keeping the details of his plan to himself, Turner alerted his closest allies—Sam Francis, Henry Porter, Hark Travis, and Nelson Williams—that an important event would take place on July 4. When Turner fell ill, the plans were postponed, but on August 13 more solar disturbances convinced Turner that the time was again ripe for revolt.

On Sunday, August 21, Turner's four allies, plus Jack Reese and Will Francis, met at Cabin Pond to await instruction. While there, the men ate wild pig and drank brandy, joined eventually by Turner, who had been keeping religious solitude in preparation for the night ahead. At

Cartoon illustrating Nat Turner's uprising against southern whites *(Library of Congress)*

around 2 A.M. on the morning of August 22, the group broke into the Travis home and killed Joseph, his wife, and their children. The plan was to kill whites in the county without reference to age or sex, thereby scaring other whites into submission. The ultimate goal of the rebels was to seize Jerusalem, the county seat, where there was an arsenal they hoped to use. Armed, and with their brutalities widely known, the group believed that it would be a mere matter of time before slavery would come to an end. Indiscriminate killing would be unnecessary beyond the early example they hoped to make in the homes of the planter families around them.

The men worked steadily through their corner of Southampton County, killing between 55 and 65 white men, women, and children as their numbers swelled. By the evening of August 22, Nat Turner's band had grown to between 60 and 70 slaves, armed with guns, swords, pikes and axes. Despite repelling the local militia once during the day, the band was attacked again at nightfall as they rested and regrouped at the Ridley plantation. Swelled with reinforcements the militia succeeded in ending the revolt, slaughtering many of the men involved and placing at least a dozen severed heads on poles as an example to other slaves. Turner escaped into the swamps, but he was captured on October 30. Put on trial on November 5, Turner was found guilty of "making insurrection, and plotting to take away the lives of divers [sic] free white persons." He was executed by hanging on November 11, 1831.

The ramifications of the rebellion were wide-ranging. To enslaved men and women, Turner was a hero. To whites, he was an example of what religion, education, and leniency from owners could create in the slave population, causing a crackdown on all three of the same. Badly scared by the incident, the Virginia state legislature briefly considered abolition, coupled with the deportation of all African Americans in the state. The measure died, and slavery was practiced in the state for more than 30 additional years.

Further reading: John B. Duff and Peter M. Mitchell, eds., *The Nat Turner Rebellion: The Historical Event and the Modern Controversy* (New York: Harper and Row, 1971); Kenneth S. Greenberg, ed., *The Confessions of Nat Turner and Related Documents* (Boston: Bedford Books, 1996).

—Catherine J. Denial

Tyler, John (1790–1862)

An antebellum president and Confederate congressman, John Tyler was born and raised in Charles City County, Virginia. At the age of 12, he entered William and Mary College, graduating five years later. In 1809 he was admitted to the bar, and two years after that he became involved in politics, serving terms in the Virginia legislature, the U.S. House of Representatives, and as Virginia's governor. While serving in the House of Representatives (1816–21), Tyler voted against most nationalist legislation and opposed the MISSOURI COMPROMISE.

In 1827 Tyler was elected to the U.S. Senate, where he became one of its leading figures. As a southern planter, Tyler opposed tariffs, a standing army, and extending the right to vote to men without property. He vehemently opposed President ANDREW JACKSON's threat to use federal force against South Carolina when the state renounced federal tariffs, and he frequently condemned what he saw as Jackson's abuse of executive power. In 1834 he censured the president's removal of federal funds from the national bank. In February 1836 the Jacksonian-controlled Virginia legislature instructed Tyler to vote to expunge the Senate censure resolution against the president on this matter. He refused, resigned his seat, and severed his Democratic ties. Tyler's disgust with Jackson drove him to join forces with HENRY CLAY and DANIEL WEBSTER to form the new WHIG PARTY.

In 1840 the Whigs nominated WILLIAM HENRY HARRISON for president and added Tyler to the ticket to balance it out. Though both men were Whigs, Harrison and Tyler had little in common politically. Running under the slogan "Tippecanoe and Tyler Too," the Whig ticket easily captured the White House.

Senator Henry Clay was the real power behind the Whig Party, and he expected to be able to control President Harrison from behind the scenes. However, much to Clay's dismay, the popular and genial Harrison contracted pneumonia and died one month after taking office. Tyler succeeded to the presidency, becoming the first vice president ever to do so. He spent his first few months in office establishing that he was legitimately the president and not just the "acting president." Tyler also made clear that he would not be Clay's puppet and, in so doing he effectively alienated the party that had elected him. Fearing that he would alienate Harrison's supporters, Tyler decided to keep Harrison's entire cabinet, enough though some were openly hostile to him. Following his core belief in states' rights led Tyler to veto a bill for a federal Bank of the United States, a bill that the Whig majority in Congress favored. His entire cabinet resigned in protest, with the exception of Daniel Webster.

Tyler was able to score some FOREIGN POLICY successes, most notably the signing of a trade pact with China. His domestic agenda, however, ground to a halt over the issue of TEXAS's annexation. In 1842 South Carolina senator JOHN C. CALHOUN negotiated a treaty that allowed the Republic of Texas, then independent, to become the Union's 28th state. Many congressmen opposed the treaty because they did not want another slave state to be added

President John Tyler *(Library of Congress)*

to the Union, or because they did not wish to antagonize Mexico, from which Texas had won her independence six years earlier. Tyler tried repeatedly to force the treaty through Congress.

The 1844 presidential election came down to a three-way race between Tyler, JAMES K. POLK, and Henry Clay. Fearing that he and Polk might split the vote, thereby handing the election to Clay, Tyler withdrew from the race, and Polk was elected. Tyler, nearly bankrupt, retired to his plantation. When Abraham Lincoln was elected president, Tyler tried to help broker a compromise between northern authorities and southern secessionists. After his proposals were rejected, in April 1861, Tyler went to Virginia's secession convention and voted in favor of the state's withdrawal from the Union. He was elected to the Confederate House of Representatives but died on January 18, 1862, in Richmond before he could take his seat. His death marked the only time that the United States completely ignored the death of a former president.

Further reading: Norma Lois Peterson, *The Presidencies of William Henry Harrison & John Tyler* (Lawrence: University Press of Kansas, 1989); Robert Seager, *And Tyler Too: A Biography of John and Julia Gardiner Tyler* (New York: McGraw Hill, 1963).

—Christopher Bates

V

Van Buren, Martin (1782–1862)

Eighth president of the United States, Martin Van Buren was born on December 5, 1782, in Kinderhook, New York. Van Buren was the first president not born a British subject or even of British ancestry. The Van Burens were a large, struggling Dutch family. Martin's father, Abraham Van Buren, ran a tavern where politicians would often gather as they traveled between New York City and Albany. This environment gave the young Martin a taste for politics. Though the Van Burens could not afford to send him to college, he managed to get a job as a clerk in a law office, where he began studying law independently. After he became a lawyer, Van Buren joined the Democratic-Republicans and began his climb up the political ladder, starting at the very bottom as a minor county official.

Immediately, Van Buren began showing the qualities that earned him such nicknames as "The Red Fox" and "The Little Magician." Unfailingly polite but thoroughly wily, he earned recognition from friends and enemies alike for his ability to land on the winning side of a controversial issue. Gradually, he moved from the New York State Senate to the New York attorney general's office and then to the U.S. Senate—always working within the New York political network known as the Albany Regency. Unhappy with the stuffy and aloof President JOHN QUINCY ADAMS, Van Buren aligned himself instead with ANDREW JACKSON, the immensely popular war hero who wanted a return to the Jeffersonian policies of minimalist government.

When Jackson became president, he rewarded Van Buren by making him secretary of state. Van Buren also chose wisely when he decided to befriend Peggy O'Neil Eaton, wife of a cabinet secretary and a woman all of Washington had chosen to snub because she had remarried too quickly after the death of her first husband. Andrew Jackson had no tolerance for such snobbery, since his own wife, Rachel, had been subjected to the same treatment. Toward the end of his first term, Jackson dismissed much of his cabinet, including Vice President JOHN C. CALHOUN, and in Jackson's second term Van Buren became vice president.

Van Buren went on to win the presidential election of 1836, beating WILLIAM HENRY HARRISON of the newly formed WHIG PARTY while promising to carry on the policies of Andrew Jackson. Historians generally agree that the country's support for Van Buren was actually an expression of esteem for his predecessor. Unfortunately, Jackson had left a terrible legacy for the new president. His intense opposition to the Bank of the United States had led him to divest its holdings in favor of state banks. This destabilized

President Martin Van Buren *(Library of Congress)*

the economy, and by the time of Van Buren's election, the United States, was in the grip of a dangerous cycle of inflation. Interest rates skyrocketed, cotton prices spiraled, and food price riots erupted in New York City. The so-called PANIC OF 1837 was followed by the worst depression yet faced by the young nation. Van Buren failed to act decisively to remedy the situation, and the economic storm raged on. To make matters worse, the president, whose family had been poor, loved to dress in fancy clothes and travel through the streets of Washington in an elegant coach pulled by matched horses and attended by footmen in regal uniforms. The public was outraged and quickly turned against him.

Van Buren lost additional support by opposing statehood for TEXAS, fearing that it would upset the balance of slave and free states in the Union. He also had problems in the area of foreign policy. In 1837, a small separatist movement in Canada sought independence from England. When some Americans supported the rebels by supplying them with guns and supplies, England attacked the American ship being used, set it ablaze, and pushed it over Niagara Falls. Van Buren ignored calls for another war with England; his position of neutrality in the Canadian independence issue made him appear weak in the eyes of many Americans.

With a depression at home and perceived humiliation by Britain abroad, William Henry Harrison was able to defeat Van Buren in the election of 1840. The Whigs manipulated Harrison's image as the rough and tumble "Log Cabin and Hard Cider" candidate, a sharp contrast to Van Buren's fussy, aristocratic, and unmanly image. They also made the election fun, bombarding the public with sewing boxes, cigar tins, whiskey bottles, and pennants with the catchy slogan, "Tippecanoe and Tyler Too." There was little truth in all the hoopla; in reality, it was Van Buren who came from a modest background, while Harrison was from a ruling-class Virginia family and had made himself wealthier through unethical land deals with NATIVE AMERICANS. Nevertheless, Van Buren lost the election, failing to carry even his home state of New York.

Martin Van Buren rose to power on the new wave of machine politics and fell from it as victim of another—i.e., politics as entertainment. Like several other troubled presidents, he was better at securing power than at using it. His hesitation during the early stages of the Panic of 1837 had a ruinous effect on the ECONOMY, and it took nearly a decade for the nation to recover. Unable to right the nation's course, Van Buren was replaced by the populist hero William Henry Harrison, as the Whigs won their first presidential election.

Further reading: John Niven, *Martin Van Buren: The Romantic Age of American Politics* (New York: Oxford University Press, 1983); Major L. Wilson, *The Presidency of Martin Van Buren* (Lawrence: University Press of Kansas, 1984).

Vanderbilt, Cornelius (1794–1877)

Born on May 27, 1794, in Staten Island, New York, Cornelius Vanderbilt was one of nine children of Cornelius Vanderbilt, a farmer, and Phebe Hand Vanderbilt. He received almost no schooling and began working full-time with his father at the age of 11. Described as a rugged, headstrong, untamable, illiterate youth who at the age of 12 could scarcely write his own name, Vanderbilt showed an early instinct for making and manipulating money. At the age of 16, with $100 borrowed from his mother, he bought a small sailing vessel and began ferrying passengers and farm produce across New York Bay to Manhattan. Diligent and efficient, he made the business pay, and the WAR OF 1812 brought him a government contract to supply the island forts. By then he owned three boats that operated as far south as the Carolinas. In 1813 he married Sophia Johnson, with whom he had 13 children, of whom 11 survived him.

Vanderbilt quickly recognized the advantage of steam over sail. In 1818 he sold his schooners and took a job as captain of a steamboat to familiarize himself with the craft. The vessel traveled between New York and New Brunswick, New Jersey, where he made his home and where his wife supplemented the family income by running a tavern. By 1829 the family had saved enough to permit him to leave his job and establish his own steamboat service on the Hudson River. His business strategy was characteristic of the ruthless methods of the time: He exacted maximum labor for minimum wages, bribed city officials to give him exclusive docking privileges, and reduced his fares and freight rates until he forced his competitors into bankruptcy and then raised his prices to exorbitant levels. Regarded as the prime buccaneer of the shipping world, by the middle 1830s Vanderbilt was the largest steamboat owner and builder in the country. His vessels, numbering more than 100, served many cities on the coast, and newspapers began referring to him as Commodore. In 1847, in response to the CALIFORNIA GOLD RUSH, he organized a steamship line to San Francisco across Nicaragua.

During the 1850s the Commodore recognized the limitations of maritime shipping and the dangers of privateers preying on mercantile vessels, and he turned his attentions to railroads. In 1855 his fortunes were estimated at $1.5 million; within the next 10 years, his railroad interests multiplied that sum more than tenfold and made him, in Burton J. Hendrick's words, "the symbol that links the old industrial era with the new." He took control of the Harlem Railroad in 1857, the Hudson River Railroad in

Cornelius Vanderbilt *(Library of Congress)*

1865, and the New York Central in 1867. By the time of his death 10 years later on January 2, 1877, his railroad empire covered 4,300 miles and extended to Chicago; and his estate amounted to more than $104 million, the first of the colossal American fortunes that were destined to astound the world.

Unbending in business, Vanderbilt was known for his arrogance and truculence. When reminded that one of his transactions was contrary to law, he was reported as sneering, "What do I care about the law? Hain't I got the power?" Although he left $1 million to found Central University of Nashville, Tennessee (later renamed Vanderbilt University), he left the bulk of his money to his son William Henry, initiating America's first great dynasty of wealth and power.

Further reading: Wheaton J. Lane, *Commodore Vanderbilt: An Epic of the Steam Age.* (New York, A. A. Knopf, 1942).

—Dennis Wepman

Vesey, Denmark (c.1767–1822)

Probably born on St. Thomas in the Virgin Islands, Denmark Vesey, the future advocate of slave rebellion, was purchased by Captain Joseph Vesey on his way from Charleston, South Carolina, to Cap-Français, Santo Domingo (later, Haiti) in 1781. Impressed by the 14-year-old slave's intelligence and ability, the captain made him the ship's mascot and nicknamed him Telemaque, for the Greek mythological hero Telemachus. He eventually became known as Denmark, a name possibly derived from Telemaque, or perhaps a reference to his origin in the Virgin Islands, then a colony of Denmark. The captain's mascot was sold along with the other slaves on board when the ship reached Cap-Français.

Returning to Cap-Français a year later, Captain Vesey was forced to buy back Denmark from his master, who claimed that the young man suffered from seizures which made him unfit to work. The captain kept him as his own slave. Because no mention is made of his seizures after leaving Santo Domingo, some have speculated that Denmark faked epileptic fits in order to escape the grinding labor that awaited him on the Caribbean sugar plantations. When Joseph Vesey settled in Charleston, Denmark Vesey (as he was now commonly known) learned carpentry and became one of the many highly skilled slaves whose labor was rented out by their masters in this urban seaport.

In 1799 Denmark Vesey won $1,500 in the East Bay Street lottery and purchased his freedom from Joseph Vesey for $600. He continued to work as a master carpenter in Charleston, establishing a good reputation and owning a respectable house on Bull Street. Unlike many ambitious free blacks in Charleston, he rejected the idea of acquiring slaves as a way to bolster his own social status. For the most part, he distrusted and avoided the free blacks (often light-skinned mulattos) who attempted to cultivate favor in white society by living like white slave owners. A charismatic leader who spoke several languages, Vesey became a powerful voice in the Charleston slave community. He married at least one slave woman, possibly several. He believed in the equality of blacks and whites, and, while free himself, resented that his children were still classified as slaves because their mothers were slaves.

Vesey used his economic power and relative mobility to organize within the community of slaves and free blacks. In 1817 he joined the Second Presbyterian Church and later joined the newly established African Methodist Church. His charisma and literacy made him a leader in the congregation, to which he argued that Scripture advocated the delivery of Africans from SLAVERY. Threatened by the autonomy of the African Methodist congregation, white Charlestonians attempted to stop their activities by having hundreds of congregants arrested for disorderly conduct and ordering that black churches could not educate slaves. This religious oppression, combined with the national controversy surrounding the MISSOURI COMPROMISE and the lingering example of the successful slave revolution in Haiti impelled Vesey to begin organizing for a slave revolt in Charleston.

After several years of heightening tensions, Vesey began planning action with the five men who would become his main partners in the insurrection: Peter Poyas, Ned Bennett, Rolla Bennett, Monday Gell, and Gullah Jack Pritchard. Like Vesey, his comrades were effective organizers because of their unusual mobility and their knowledge of different segments of the African community in Charleston and the surrounding countryside. Indeed, Vesey's rebellion strategy was the first North American insurrection to emphasize pan-Africanism: the unification of disparate African and African-American communities, free and slave, in order to challenge white racism and the oppression of black people. Vesey and his lieutenants appealed to skilled urban laborers, recently arrived slaves on the Gullah-speaking sea islands and slaves from the inland agricultural areas. As many as 9,000 slaves would be involved.

Vesey's plan called for attacking Charleston from six different areas. The organized companies would seize important government buildings such as the U.S. arsenal, the governor's mansion, and the city's guardhouse. The surprise attack was to take place at midnight on Sunday, July 14, 1822—a moonless night in the hot and sluggish middle of summer, while many white Charlestonians would be vacationing away from the city. Sunday was also the only day of the week when large numbers of rural slaves could enter the city without triggering suspicion.

In late May, however, word of the planned insurrection fell into the wrong hands when one of Vesey's supporters, William Paul, told mulatto slave Peter Prioleau Desverney about the plot. On the advice of a free mulatto slave owner, Desverney told his master, Colonel Prioleau. William Paul was arrested and interrogated, eventually giving police the names of other conspirators, but not Vesey. When brought in for questioning, the accused maintained their composure and denied the charges. Authorities were left with rumors but no real proof, and the anxiety level among whites began to rise. Vesey and the other undetected conspirators continued to plan for the attack, moving the date up to June 16.

Promising him his freedom, white authorities hired George Wilson to spy on potential conspirators and infiltrate meetings in local churches. Wilson brought them solid proof of a continuing conspiracy, providing names, dates, and strategies. After learning of their betrayal, Vesey and his men sent word to the rural slave companies to postpone their march, but the word came too late. When Vesey's soldiers arrived on June 16, they found Charleston occupied by federal troops. Authorities convened a secret court to begin hearings, and the police began arresting the leaders. Vesey was arrested on June 20. By early July, all of the principal leaders were in custody at the Charleston Work House, the prison for slaves.

With the exception of Monday Gell, all of the conspirators maintained silence while incarcerated in an attempt to protect their followers. Vesey urged his lieutenants to "die in silence." The secret court found them guilty, and Vesey and his inner circle were executed on July 2, 1822, in a desolate part of Charleston known as Blake's Lands. By the end of July, 35 men had been executed. Twenty-two of them were publicly hanged on the main thoroughfare in Charleston, their bodies left hanging for three days as a grisly warning to would-be insurrectionists.

In the aftermath of the failed insurrection, white authorities tightened their grip on free and enslaved blacks in Charleston. Legislators passed laws restricting the movements of free blacks and their ability to organize gatherings. These new legal restrictions—especially the Negro Seaman's Act of 1823, which required the incarceration of free black sailors while their ships where in Charleston—helped trigger the constitutional battle between the federal government and South Carolina that resulted in the Ordinance of Nullification and, later, the Civil War (1861–65). Thus, Vesey's conspiracy and the violent response to it embodied the tensions that continued to intensify in the slave society of the South in the first half of the 19th century. While Vesey's revolutionary plan was unsuccessful, his efforts left a deep impression among both fearful whites and hopeful blacks, who remembered him as a heroic leader in the struggle against slavery. Recent scholarship has raised questions about the nature and extent of Vesey's conspiracy, but the vigorous reaction of the white population in Charleston confirms its powerful influence at the time.

Further reading: Michael P. Johnson et al., "The Making of a Slave Conspiracy," *William and Mary Quarterly* 59 (2002); Edward A. Pearson, ed., *Designs Against Charleston: The Trial Record of the Denmark Vesey Slave Conspiracy of 1822* (Chapel Hill: University of North Carolina Press, 1999); David Robertson, *Denmark Vesey* (New York: Knopf, 1999); Lois A. Walker and Susan R. Silverman, eds., *A Documented History of Gullah Jack Pritchard and the Denmark Vesey Slave Insurrection of 1822* (Lewiston, N.Y.: E. Mellen Press, 2000).

—Eleanor H. McConnell

W

War Hawks

In 1812, about 20 young Democratic-Republican members of Congress from western and southern states actively favored war with Britain, hoping to conquer Canada, end impressment, and guarantee free trade. The group was given its name, War Hawks, by John Randolph of Roanoke, Virginia. They included future cabinet members HENRY CLAY of Kentucky and JOHN C. CALHOUN of South Carolina and several less well known members of congress.

Examinations of congressional votes leading up to the WAR OF 1812 (1812–15) reveal what at first seems a puzzling pattern. British attacks had the greatest impact on New England, yet those states were largely against war. In contrast, the areas represented by the War Hawks, the farming regions of the West and South, were in favor of aggressively defending the national honor. The fact that New Englanders, in the time-honored manner, continued to make money despite the annoyance of British deprivations may partially explain this. It was also true that the farming regions suffered when the price of goods increased due to British interference with trade. However, other concerns motivated the War Hawks and their constituents.

Conflict with Indian nations often disrupted life in the backcountry. Such conflict posed real dangers to settlers and interfered with the lucrative business of land speculation by limiting the amount of secure land available for sale. Westerners blamed the British for instigating Indian raids and supplying the Native Americans with weapons from their safe haven in Canada. Driving the British from Canada therefore promised to remove the threat to the frontier while opening large areas of Canadian land for speculation. The violation of neutral rights was indeed an important factor in the decision to go to war. However, for the War Hawks and their backcountry constituents, the desire for Canadian land appears to have been an equally powerful motivation. The prowar campaign of the War Hawks was successful in increasing war fever among the public and helped prepare popular support for the declaration of war.

Further reading: Reginald Horsman, *The War of 1812* (New York: Knopf, 1969); Julius W. Pratt, *Expansionists of 1812* (New York: Macmillan, 1925); Norman K. Risjord, *The Old Republicans* (New York: Columbia University Press, 1965).

—Robert Lively

War of 1812 (1812–1815)

The War of 1812 marked the culmination of a bankrupt foreign policy and demonstrated both the weaknesses and the strengths of the American republic. When Great Britain and France went to war in 1793, the United States had a problem: how to remain neutral in a major European war while reaping the benefits of trade and commerce. Repeatedly the United States came to the brink of war, first with one power and then the other. At times, some politicians cried out for a declaration of war against both Great Britain and France. Such fanciful assertions reflected a degree of unreality that many Americans displayed in the area of FOREIGN POLICY. During the opening decade of the 19th century, with the ascendancy of Thomas Jefferson and the Democratic-Republican Party, foreign policy assumed an Anglophobe caste. While both France and Great Britain increased their efforts to influence American trade, the government generally looked on Britain as the villain. When Napoleon Bonaparte hinted that he would repeal his Berlin and Milan decrees putting restraints on neutral trade, James Madison's administration seized the opportunity to reinstate a trade ban with Great Britain, following Macon's Bill No. 2 (1810). This action created a new crisis with the British that ultimately led to Madison asking Congress for a declaration of war on June 1, 1812. Madison signed a Declaration of War passed by Congress on June 18, 1812. Ironically, Great Britain had decided to end its blockade of Europe and ease its restrictions on the United States the day before. But since transatlantic communication took weeks and sometimes months, no one was aware of these concessions as the United States entered the war.

Many Federalists, especially in New England, objected to the war. These opponents wanted to maintain their commercial contacts with Great Britain and saw little reason for fighting. Many of them continued to trade illegally with Britain and even flirted with secession. The HARTFORD CONVENTION (1814) gave the greatest form and substance to the Federalist complaints just as the hostilities were ending.

If the Federalists were right and there was no immediate reason to fight the War of 1812, there were many long-term causes for the conflict. First, there was the issue of neutral rights that had plagued the United States since 1793. Americans insisted that neutral ships carried neutral goods and believed that the profits of the carrying trade should be theirs. Second, there was the question of impressment. For almost two decades, the British Navy had forced Americans to serve on its ships. This violation of the integrity of the United States was not only a diplomatic affront, it also affected the lives of thousands of American seamen who found themselves trapped—virtually enslaved—aboard British men of war for years and sometimes decades. Third, many Americans believed that British agents encouraged NATIVE AMERICANS to fight against the United States. Americans blamed British agitation for Tecumseh's pan-Indian movement that led to the Battle of Tippecanoe (November 7, 1811). Fourth, led by WAR HAWKS, expansionist fever swept many parts of the United States. War with Great Britain would allow Americans not only to fight Indians and gain control of more land, but potentially promised the addition of Canada and even FLORIDA (which was Spanish). Finally, many Americans believed that if a republic was ever to be taken seriously on the world stage, the United States had to defend its honor and demonstrate that it could successfully fight a war.

Success was elusive, and the national government was so ineffective, it almost proved its critics right. However, the same traits that made the country appear weak also saved the republic from complete disaster. Jefferson's policies had been dismantling the strong central government created by the Federalists. Instead of a capital that would be the new Rome, as the Federalists had hoped, Washington, D.C., became a mere shadow of a city. Its destruction might be humiliating, but it had little real impact on the ability to wage war. Allowing the First Bank of the United States to expire in 1811 removed an area of central finance, but it encouraged banking to spread elsewhere. The army was not extensive, but thousands of men were in the militia and could be called upon in a time of invasion. Finally, the nation was spread out over millions of square miles. Such a territory might be hard to defend, but it was also almost impossible to conquer. These conditions made it difficult to win the war, but it was equally hard to lose it.

The war began badly on land. In 1812, there were three major campaigns along the Canadian border: the west, the Niagara River, and the Lake Champlain corridor. Each ended in failure. The biggest disaster occurred in the west. The British captured Fort Mackinac which guarded the straits between Lakes Huron, Michigan, and Superior by the end of July. The evacuation of Fort Dearborn (now Chicago) ended in an Indian massacre on August 15, and the inept general WILLIAM HULL surrendered Fort Detroit on August 16. The American effort on the Niagara Frontier was little better. An invasion across the Niagara River ended in a costly defeat at the Battle of Queenstown (October 11, 1812) when the militia refused to cross into Canada, arguing that they were a defensive force only. The thrust into Canada at Lake Champlain was only a mild setback. The American army got a late start, reached the border, and when the militia refused to enter Canada, the whole force simply retreated into winter quarters.

By comparison, the U.S. Navy began the war in a spectacular fashion, experiencing a series of single-ship victories that stunned the British. On August 19, 1812, the American super frigate USS *Constitution* pummeled the HMS *Guerriere* so heavily that the British ship had to be scuttled after it surrendered. On October 15, the USS *United States* handled the HMS *Macedonian* in a similar fashion, but managed to bring its prize to an American port. Then, on December 29, the *Constitution* sank the HMS *Java* off the coast of Brazil. Along with some smaller ship actions, these victories gave Americans something to boast about.

The war on land improved slightly for the Americans in 1813. There was a major turnaround in the situation in the west. Oliver Hazard Perry built a fleet of ships on Lake Erie, then defeated a British squadron in the BATTLE OF LAKE ERIE (September 10, 1813). This victory compelled the British to abandon Detroit. General WILLIAM HENRY HARRISON, the hero of Tippecanoe, pursued the British, defeating a combined Native American and British force at the BATTLE OF THE THAMES (October 5, 1813), thus ending the threat to the northwest during the war. Tecumseh was killed in this battle, eliminating that threat as well.

Further south, Andrew Jackson began his campaign against the Creek Indians with devastating effect. He and his army pursued the Creek with vigor, winning the BATTLE OF HORSESHOE BEND (March 27, 1814). The Niagara campaign began well, with an American victory at Fort George (May 24, 1813), where the Niagara meets Lake Ontario. The Americans did not immediately seize the initiative that this victory had opened. The result was that the British and Canadian forces were able to rally, and, under

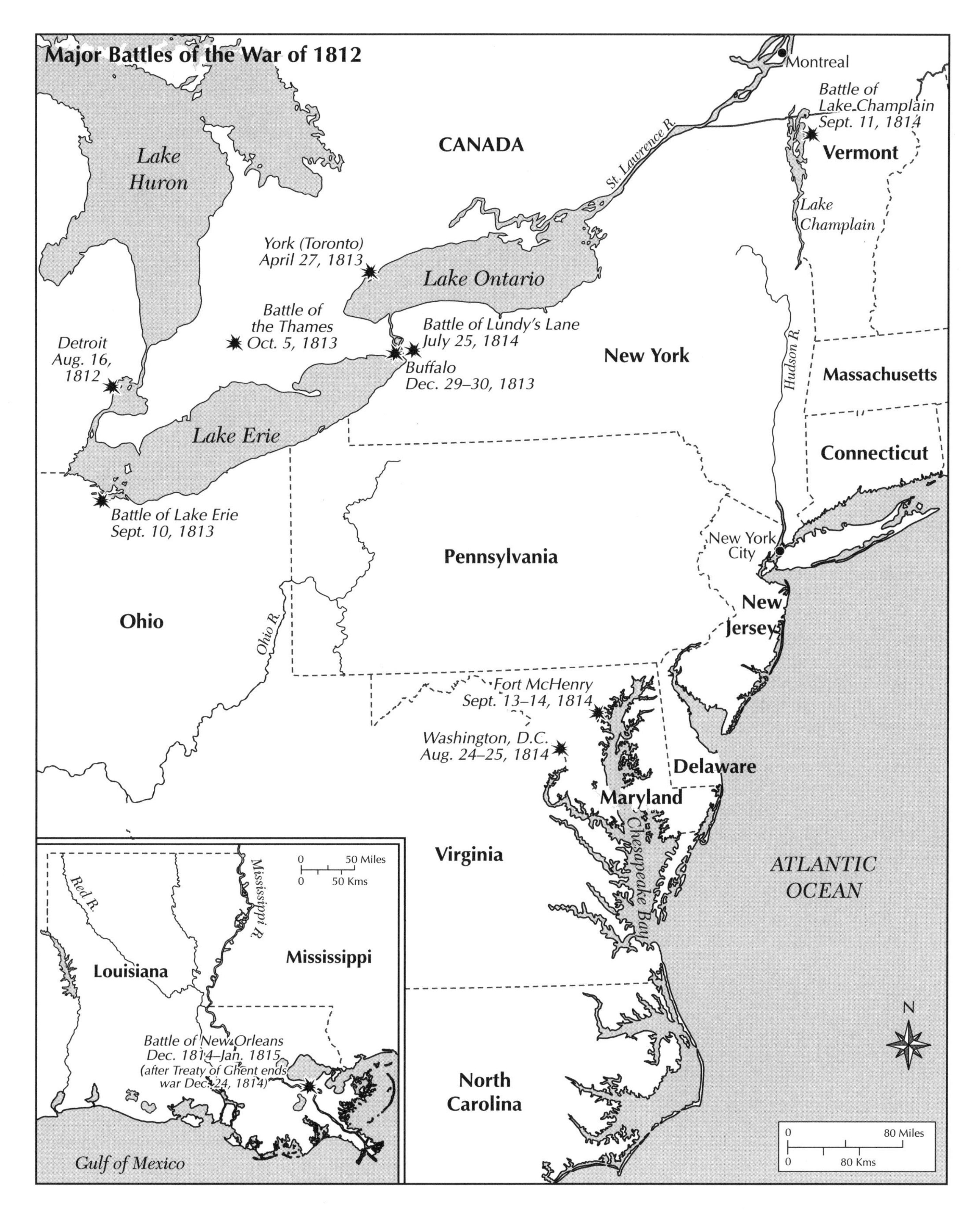
Major Battles of the War of 1812
Montreal
Battle of Lake Champlain Sept. 11, 1814
CANADA
Lake Huron
St. Lawrence R.
Vermont
Lake Champlain
York (Toronto) April 27, 1813
Lake Ontario
Battle of the Thames Oct. 5, 1813
Battle of Lundy's Lane July 25, 1814
Detroit Aug. 16, 1812
Buffalo Dec. 29–30, 1813
New York
Hudson R.
Massachusetts
Lake Erie
Connecticut
Battle of Lake Erie Sept. 10, 1813
New York City
Pennsylvania
Ohio
Ohio R.
New Jersey
Fort McHenry Sept. 13–14, 1814
Washington, D.C. Aug. 24–25, 1814
Delaware
Maryland
Chesapeake Bay
Virginia
ATLANTIC OCEAN
0 50 Miles
0 50 Kms
Red R.
Mississippi R.
Louisiana
Mississippi
Battle of New Orleans Dec. 1814–Jan. 1815 (after Treaty of Ghent ends war Dec. 24, 1814)
Gulf of Mexico
North Carolina
N
0 80 Miles
0 80 Kms

effective military leadership (something the Americans lacked), the British won a series of victories in the summer, fall, and winter. They not only recaptured Fort George but also took Fort Niagara (December 18, 1813) on the American side of the river. By the beginning of 1814, the situation along this front had deteriorated into almost a complete debacle. The war further north remained a stalemate. Two invasions, one from Lake Ontario, the other along Lake Champlain, ran into some minor resistance and were quickly abandoned.

If the United States was unable to generate much offensive firepower and seemed to be spinning its wheels, the British also were getting nowhere. Victories in the west in 1812 and on the Niagara in 1813 did little good. In both cases the occupation of forts barely dented the huge territorial expanse of the United States, and the British armies remained hundreds of miles from the American population centers. In 1813, the British finally won a single frigate action—the HMS *Shannon* captured the ill-fated USS *Chesapeake* (June 1, 1813)—and had effectively blockaded most of the American navy. But American privateers continued to wreak havoc on British shipping. Moreover, Native American power had been broken in both the North and the South.

In Europe, Napoleon's armies were in retreat and his defeat was almost certain. Despite war weariness (the war with France had been waged almost without interruption since 1793), Britain was able to turn greater attention to the United States in 1814. Although reinforcements brought British North American forces to approximately 40,000, the war continued to be a stalemate in 1814. The Americans launched two initiatives that accomplished little, while the British seized the offensive in four areas that led to mixed results. Hoping to further stabilize the northwestern frontier, an American force was sent against the British-occupied Fort Mackinac. A combined British and Indian attack (August 4) surprised and defeated the advancing Americans. Having regained some strength on the Niagara River over the winter, American forces launched yet another invasion of Canada, winning the Battle of Chippewa (July 5), fighting the Battle of Lundy's Lane (July 25) to a draw, and successfully defending Fort Erie (August 15). The entire Niagara campaign saw little net change. The British planned a major invasion along Lake Champlain. With a vastly superior force, they advanced on Plattsburgh (New York). But when Lieutenant Thomas Macdonough defeated the British fleet in the Battle of Lake Champlain (September 11), the British army was compelled to retreat despite success on land in the Battle of Plattsburgh (September 11).

The British were able to occupy most of eastern Maine almost unopposed in the summer of 1814. They also launched a combined army and naval operation in the Chesapeake, winning the Battle of Bladensburgh (August 24) and burning the American capital of Washington, D.C. However, when the British attempted to extend this success at the BATTLE OF BALTIMORE (September 12–14), they were repulsed and withdrew from the area. The final British campaign ended in disaster after the TREATY OF GHENT (1814). An experienced army under General Edward Packenham fought General ANDREW JACKSON at the BATTLE OF NEW ORLEANS (January 8, 1815), with tremendous casualties for the British. Packenham was killed and lost over 2,000 men.

The peace treaty that ended the war settled nothing. The outstanding issues of free trade, impressment and boundaries were left untouched. Yet with Napoleon defeated, impressment and free trade became moot, while the United States had other areas in which it could seek expansion. The war also marked an important watershed in American history. Native American power east of the Mississippi was nearly crushed. A new nationalism emerged from the war that would help propel the United States across a continent. And, although seriously challenged, the republic showed that it could viably defend itself.

See also FREE TRADE AND SAILOR'S RIGHTS.

Further reading: Harry L. Coles, *The War of 1812* (Chicago: University of Chicago Press, 1965); Donald R. Hickey, *The War of 1812: A Forgotten Conflict* (Urbana: University of Illinois Press, 1989); Reginald Horsman, *The War of 1812* (New York: Knopf, 1969).

Warren, Josiah (1798–1874)

Firmly rooted in the American experience was a long native tradition of hostility to the authority of the state. Strong elements of anarchism can be found in some early American religious sects, in such groups as the abolitionists, and in individuals like HENRY DAVID THOREAU. But the most systematic philosophy of native American anarchism originated with Josiah Warren.

Like most of the other adherents of this variety of anarchism, Warren came from an old New England family. He was a highly inventive and practical-minded individual who in the course of his life worked as a musician and orchestra leader, invented and manufactured a lard-burning lamp, contributed to the improvement of the printing press, and devised an original system of musical notation. In 1826, he moved to ROBERT OWEN's community at New Harmony, Indiana, where he lived for over a year. In what was perhaps the earliest anarchist critique of socialism, he attributed the failure of New Harmony to its communal property arrangements and system of authority. He concluded that the true principle of social organization lay in voluntary association, with each individual owning property equal to the value of his own labor.

Never content merely to propound a theory, Warren proceeded to test its validity in practice. His first experiment was the "time store." As described later by his son George:

> The time store was started by my father for the purpose of illustrating the labor-for-labor system. The goods he bought principally of Evansville merchants. The customers would come in and ask for what was wanted. The time dial was set to correspond with the minute hand of the clock and when the customer was through with his purchase, the time required in waiting on him was figured up; this labor was paid by the customer in labor notes and the cost of the goods was paid in cash. There was no profit added to the first cost of the goods, except the amount expended in freight, bills, and other incidentals. The labor notes, of course, represented all classes—merchants, farmers, doctors, and every description of laborer, and the rates per hour were regulated by the cost to the person of having to spend the time in learning the business in which he was engaged.

Some years later, Warren opened another store utilizing a somewhat more refined system of labor notes (an idea originally conceived by Owen). In addition, he made several attempts to implement his theories on a larger scale by founding an anarchist colony. The first of these, the Village of Equity in Ohio, soon came to grief. The other two, Utopia, located not far from Cincinnati, and Modern Times, on Long Island, were more enduring and at least for a time followed Warren's principles of social organization and used labor notes as a medium of exchange. Modern Times, the most ambitious of Warren's efforts, was founded in 1851, changing its name after a few years to Brentwood, which it remains today. Warren himself left the colony in 1863, and even within his lifetime it lost much of its unique character and began to settle into more conventional patterns. Nevertheless, Warren looked upon it as a success and as a vindication of his principles. He spent the last year of his life in Massachusetts, dying at Charlestown in 1874.

Further reading: William Bailie, *Josiah Warren: The First American Anarchist* (Boston: Small, Maynard & Co., 1971); George Warren. Labadie Collection, University of Michigan, in "Josiah Warren (1781–1984): Reformer, Inventor, Musician, Writer." URL: www.2.evansville.edu/ck6/bstud/warren.html. Downloaded 2002.

Webster, Daniel (1782–1852)

As a senator and statesman, Daniel Webster was his era's foremost advocate of American nationalism. Webster also argued several of the most important constitutional law cases in U.S. history before the Supreme Court. He was born in 1782 in Salisbury, New Hampshire, the youngest son in a family of 10 children. Born into a farming family, young Daniel preferred to work in his father's tavern, where the regulars nicknamed him "Black Dan" for his dark hair and complexion. After going to local schools, Webster attended Philips Exeter Academy and then graduated from Dartmouth College in 1801, followed by a legal apprenticeship. In 1807, he opened a legal practice in Portsmouth, New Hampshire, and a year later married Grace Fletcher. He developed an early interest in politics and rose quickly as a lawyer and Federalist party leader.

In 1812 Webster was elected to the U.S. House of Representatives because of his opposition to the WAR OF 1812, which had crippled New England's shipping trade. After two terms in the House, he left Congress in 1816 and moved to Boston and his law practice. Over the next six years, he won major constitutional cases before the U.S. Supreme Court (most notably, *Dartmouth College v. Woodward* [the DARTMOUTH COLLEGE CASE], *Gibbons v. Ogden*, and *MCCULLOCH V. MARYLAND*), establishing himself as the nation's leading lawyer and an outstanding orator. In 1823

Daniel Webster *(Library of Congress)*

Webster was returned to Congress from Boston, and in 1827 he was elected senator from Massachusetts.

New circumstances enabled Webster to become a champion of American nationalism. With the Federalist Party dead, he joined the National Republican Party, allying himself with westerner HENRY CLAY and endorsing federal aid for roads in the West. In 1828, the dominant economic interests of Massachusetts having shifted from shipping to manufacturing, Webster backed the high-tariff bill of that year. Angry southern leaders condemned the tariff, and South Carolina's JOHN C. CALHOUN argued that his state had the right to nullify the law. Replying to South Carolina's Robert Hayne in a Senate debate in 1830, Webster triumphantly defended the Union. His words "Liberty and Union, now and forever, one and inseparable!" won wide acclaim.

Webster and President ANDREW JACKSON joined forces in 1833 to suppress South Carolina's attempt to nullify the tariff. But Webster and members of the recently formed WHIG PARTY battled Jackson on other issues, including his attack on the SECOND BANK OF THE UNITED STATES. Webster ran for the presidency in 1836 as one of three Whig candidates but carried only Massachusetts. For the remainder of his career, he aspired in vain to the presidency.

In 1841 President WILLIAM HENRY HARRISON named Webster his secretary of state. Harrison's death in April that year brought JOHN TYLER to the presidency, and in September 1841 all the Whigs but Webster resigned from the cabinet. Webster remained to settle a dispute with Great Britain involving the Maine-Canada boundary, successfully concluding the WEBSTER-ASHBURTON TREATY in 1842. Whig pressure finally induced him to leave the cabinet in May 1843.

The annexation of TEXAS in 1845 and the resulting MEXICAN-AMERICAN WAR (1846–48), both opposed by Webster, forced the country to face the issue of the expansion of SLAVERY. Webster opposed such expansion but feared even more a dissolution of the Union over the dispute. In a powerful speech before the Senate on March 7, 1850, he supported the COMPROMISE OF 1850, denounced southern threats of secession, and urged northern support for a stronger law for the recovery of fugitive slaves. In July 1850, President MILLARD FILLMORE named Webster secretary of state, in which capacity he supervised the strict enforcement of FUGITIVE SLAVE LAWS. Webster's stand alienated antislavery forces and divided the Whig Party, but it helped to preserve the Union. He died in 1852.

Further reading: Maurice G. Baxter, *One and Inseparable: Daniel Webster and the Union* (Cambridge, Mass.: Harvard University Press, 1984); Merrill D. Peterson, *The Great Triumvirate: Webster, Clay, and Calhoun* (New York: Oxford University Press, 1987).

Webster-Ashburton Treaty (1842)

The Webster-Ashburton Treaty, signed on August 9, 1842, resolved two boundary issues between the United States and the English in Canada left over from the Revolutionary War. The first was the boundary between the state of Maine and the Canadian provinces of New Brunswick and Quebec. The second was the boundary from Lake Superior to the Lake of the Woods in the old Northwest Territory. The treaty is significant both for eliminating potential trouble spots with the British and for paving the way for further expansion in Oregon and in the Southwest. When the United States turned to settling the disputed Oregon boundary and approached war with Mexico later in the 1840s, it did not have to deal simultaneously with problems in the old Northwest Territory and in the Northeast.

The Treaty of Paris in 1783 left unclear the intended boundaries in the Northwest and Northeast, since the two countries could not agree on the identity of rivers specified in the treaty. In its early years, the United States asserted a boundary in the Northeast that would carry American territory northward, close to the St. Lawrence River. This boundary would give the United States control of the headwaters of the St. John River while leaving the mouth of the river in Canada. It would also cut across a planned military road between Quebec and New Brunswick, leaving the latter vulnerable to American expansionism. The British, on the other hand, asserted a boundary placing the entire St. John River, as well as the smaller Aroostock River, in Canada. In all, the disputed territory comprised a little more than 12,000 square miles, much of it covered in valuable timber resources.

In 1818, under terms established in the TREATY OF GHENT at the end of the WAR OF 1812, American representatives in England negotiated a treaty fixing the boundary between the United States and Canada at the 49th parallel from the Lake of the Woods to the Rocky Mountains. Attempts to resolve the northeastern boundary and the boundary from Lake Superior to the Lake of the Woods in the same treaty, however, failed. In 1836, the Senate rejected a compromise line for the northeastern boundary suggested by the king of the Netherlands, the key obstacle being the reluctance of the states of Maine and Massachusetts (which controlled Maine until 1820) to surrender the territory north of the St. John River. Two years later, lumberjacks from Maine occupied and began cutting timber in the disputed area, prompting a crisis. General WINFIELD SCOTT was sent to the area and settled what became known as the AROOSTOCK WAR (1838–39) by getting the citizens of Maine and New Brunswick to agree to stay in the areas they currently occupied, pending a final disposition of the disputed land.

In 1842 conditions were ripe for a settlement. A new Tory government in Great Britain appointed Lord Ashbur-

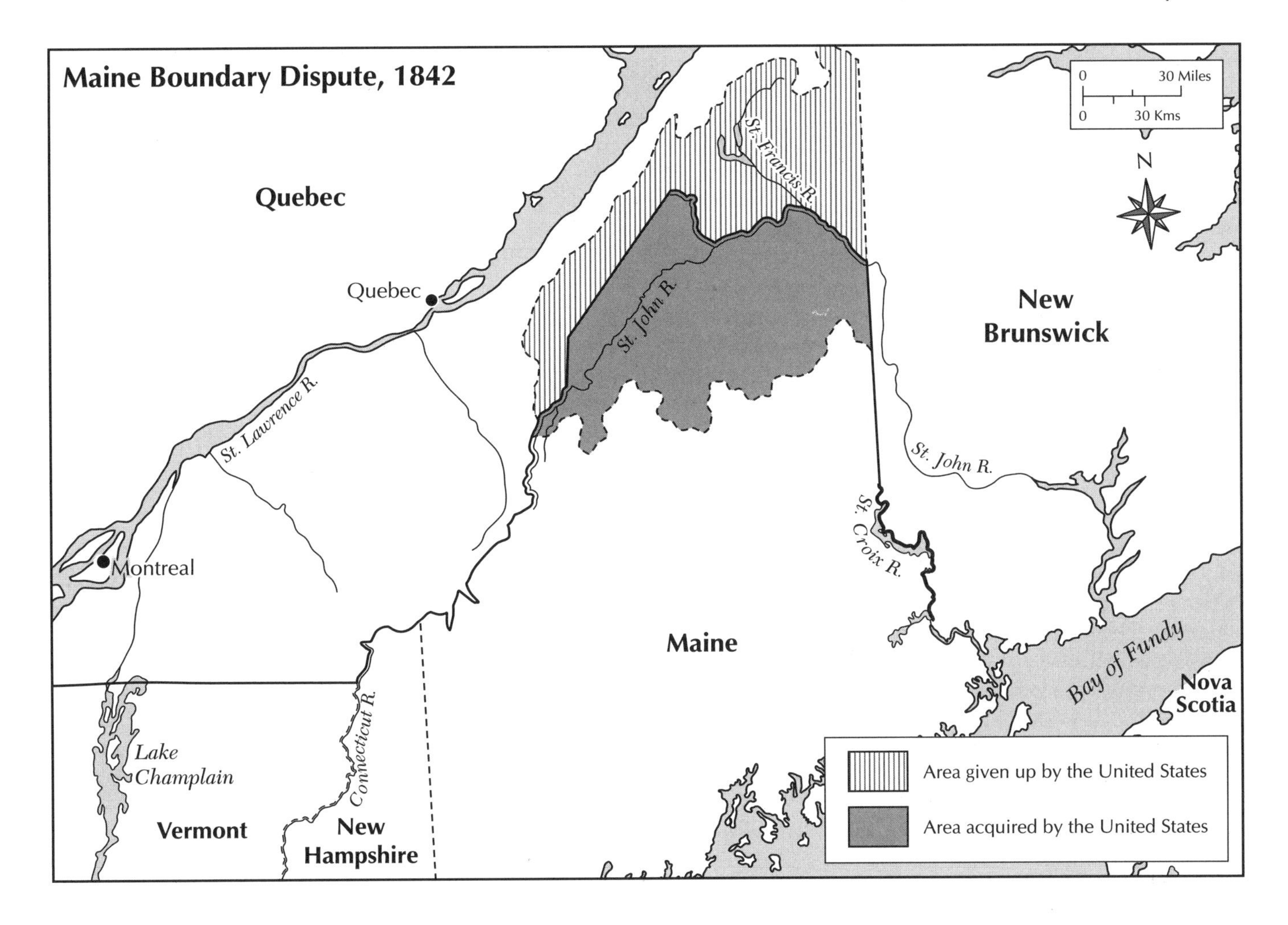

ton its representative in negotiations with the United States. Ashburton, who had an American wife, had spent much of his career seeking improved relations with the United States, and the British government gave him wide latitude for making concessions to settle the boundary dispute. The American secretary of state, DANIEL WEBSTER, was equally ready for a settlement. Webster wanted better relations with England, and for this reason he had remained in the cabinet after the death of President WILLIAM HENRY HARRISON in 1841; the rest of Harrison's cabinet had resigned rather than serve under his successor, JOHN TYLER. The states of Maine and Massachusetts dropped their objections to a settlement after being offered $150,000 each by the federal government.

In his eagerness to deal, however, Webster received less territory in the Northeast than the United States would have received under the compromise proposed by the king of the Netherlands and, more important, less overall than Ashburton might have given. Webster might also have been able to get the British to pay the compensation made to Maine and Massachusetts. But if Webster lost territory in the Northeast, securing the entire Mesabi region in the Old Northwest meant the United States controlled its rich iron ore deposits, of which Ashburton may have been only vaguely aware. The Mesabi iron deposits more than compensated the United States for the loss of timberland in the Northeast.

In the ratification process, both countries produced old maps that seemed to show the other country's full claim was the more just and hence the compromise represented a victory. Still, the Webster-Ashburton Treaty received unqualified acceptance in neither country. Although only nine senators voted against ratification in the U.S. Senate, the Webster-Ashburton treaty seemed to represent a retreat at a time when Americans were feeling particularly expansionist. Further, the treaty left the thorniest problem between the United States and Great Britain—Oregon—untouched.

Further reading: Howard Jones, *To the Webster-Ashburton Treaty* (Chapel Hill: University of North Carolina Press, 1977); Bradford Perkins, *The Creation of a Republican*

Empire, vol. 1 of *The Cambridge History of American Foreign Relations, 1776–1865,* gen. ed. Warren I. Cohen (New York: Cambridge University Press, 1993).

—Russell L. Johnson

Weld, Theodore Dwight (1803–1895)

A leading northern abolitionist and perhaps the most effective of all antislavery speakers, Theodore Dwight Weld was born in Connecticut and raised near Utica, New York. He studied at Hamilton College, where he met revivalist CHARLES GRANDISON FINNEY, whose financial support permitted Weld to enter Oneida Institute in 1827 to study for the ministry. While still at college, Weld was influenced by Charles Stuart, an early abolitionist organizer, to get involved in the antislavery cause.

When ARTHUR AND LEWIS TAPPAN of New York organized an antislavery society in 1831, Weld attended the early meetings. After several years of lecturing and leading revivals, he was commissioned by the Tappans to select a theological seminary in the West for them to endow. Weld chose Lane Seminary at Cincinnati and persuaded many of students there to join the ABOLITION MOVEMENT. When the AMERICAN ANTI-SLAVERY SOCIETY was formed, it began a pamphlet campaign which met resistance in both North and South. Weld returned to Lane Seminary to study in 1833 and organized a debate on slavery that converted a large number of students to the abolitionist cause. Although the Lane Seminary trustees expelled Weld and his followers, they moved on to Oberlin College, where they were able to continue their work without interference. Many of Weld's followers were persuaded to become itinerant lecturers for emancipation. With Weld, they preached the sinfulness of slavery and dwelt on emancipation as a revival in benevolence. Their work firmly established the movement in Ohio, Michigan, Pennsylvania, New York, and western Massachusetts.

The success of Weld's agents caused the American Anti-Slavery Society to abandon its pamphlet campaign and sponsor these local volunteers. With Henry B. Stanton and John Greenleaf Whittier, Weld chose many new agents and trained them in a conference meeting in 1836. These lecturers consolidated the antislavery movement throughout the North, and under Weld's direction they deluged Congress with antislavery petitions. The drive for signatures was bolstered by the publication of tracts, with Weld writing three of the four most popular ones. The consequent rise of numerous local antislavery societies and the controversial activities of William Lloyd Garrison led to the dissolution of the national society in 1840. Garrison packed the last American Anti-Slavery Society convention with his delegates and won the society's name for his own group of reformers in New England. The original Tappan group subsequently formed the American and Foreign Anti-Slavery Society.

During the 1836 training conference Weld met ANGELINA AND SARAH GRIMKÉ, daughters of a distinguished slaveholding family of Charleston, South Carolina. The Grimké sisters had become convinced of the evil of slavery and had moved to Philadelphia to join the Society of Friends. They wrote and lectured for the antislavery cause and for WOMEN'S STATUS AND RIGHTS, becoming the first American women to publicize the movement. Weld married Angelina in 1838, and they had three children.

In 1841 Weld went to Washington and for two years served as a lobbyist for the insurgents trying to form an antislavery bloc in the Whig party. After 1844, with his wife and Sarah, Weld retired from public life and founded a school, Eaglewood, near Raritan, New Jersey. Weld turned his energy to writing, publishing his most famous book, *American Slavery As It Is,* in 1839. This work, said to be a strong influence on Harriet Beecher Stowe's *Uncle Tom's Cabin,* won many supporters to the cause of black emancipation. Theodore Dwight Weld died at Hyde Park, Massachusetts, on February 3, 1895.

Further reading: Robert H. Abzug, *Passionate Liberator: Theodore Dwight Weld and the Dilemma of Reform* (New York: Oxford University Press, 1980).

Whig Party (1834–1856)

The political party known as the Whigs was formed during the second quarter of the 19th century to oppose President ANDREW JACKSON and the DEMOCRATIC PARTY. HENRY CLAY of Kentucky and DANIEL WEBSTER of Massachusetts were its leading organizers and proponents. In U.S. politics, the term *Whig* came into common use in 1834 and persisted until the disintegration of the party after the presidential election of 1856.

The name of Whig originally came into use during the 1680s in England when Protestants became threatened by the establishment of a line of Catholic Kings, starting with James II. These Protestants, who held that Parliament could prevent such a succession, came to be called Whigs after a radical Presbyterian group in Scotland, the Whigamores. During the American Revolution, many on the revolutionary side identified with the English Whigs, which continued to be the party in favor of Parliament's keeping the king in check.

The 19th-century Whig Party in the United States was primarily concerned with promoting INTERNAL IMPROVEMENTS, such as roads, canals, RAILROADS, deepening of rivers, etc. This was of interest to many westerners in this period, isolated as they were and in need of markets. Abraham Lincoln was a Whig for most of this period.

A deepening economic recession in 1834 caused the country to become more politically polarized. It was during this period that the National Republicans assumed the name Whigs. This conjured up ghosts of the antiroyal, pro-Parliament, English factions of the 17th and 18th centuries. Consequently, Jackson was labeled "King Andrew I" and depicted as a tyrant in political cartoons; he was, for example, drawn as a king holding a scepter labeled "Veto."

The Whigs did not exist as a political party before 1834, but it had its beginnings in 1824 when supporters of JOHN QUINCY ADAMS and Henry Clay joined forces against Andrew Jackson. This coalition, which later called itself the National Republican Party, increased in strength after Jackson's election in 1828 and was joined in opposition to the president by other smaller parties, the most notable being the Anti-Masonic Party. The National Republicans advocated a nationalistic economic policy known as the AMERICAN SYSTEM, much of which could be traced back to Alexander Hamilton's Federalist economic policy of 1791, but were stymied by the rising power of the Jacksonians, who were thereafter called Democrats. Jackson's inauguration in 1829 began the period of National Republican opposition and the catalyst for the coalition of political forces leading to the formation of the Whig Party. Henry Clay and Daniel Webster became the party's leading figures.

Webster was more of a nationalist than Clay, as he demonstrated in his famed defense of national constitution authority against Robert Hayne's doctrine of states' rights (January 26–27, 1830). But both men urged a program of tariff protection, federally sponsored communication projects (internal improvements), continuation of the national bank, and a conservative public land sales policy—the American System. This program had an especially strong appeal for merchants and manufacturers whose business operations went beyond state lines. Clay made the president's veto of a bill to recharter the SECOND BANK OF THE UNITED STATES the key issue of the 1832 election, but Jackson easily won reelection.

By 1832 Jackson had also earned the enmity of such diverse groups as states' rights advocates in the South, proponents of internal improvements in the West, and businessmen and friends of the Bank of the United States in the East. This opposition had been fostered and nurtured by Henry Clay in the election that year. Two years later, in 1834, all the various groups were combined in a loose alliance.

State sovereignty, not economic nationalism, was the idea that brought a significant addition to the ranks of those opposing Jackson. JOHN C. CALHOUN of South Carolina broke his alliance with Jackson when he realized that he would not be the next Democratic president, and the split widened during South Carolina's attempt to nullify federal tariff laws. Jackson reacted sternly to this defiance, giving Clay an opportunity to introduce a compromise tariff bill in February 1833. Calhoun approved the compromise and for several years acted in uneasy association with other anti-Jacksonians.

Another source of recruits was the Anti-Masonic Party, particularly strong in New York and Pennsylvania. The stated purpose of this strange phenomenon in American history was to combat the supposed threat of Masonic power over judicial and political institutions. It also provided younger politicians with a convenient means for advancement. Among those Anti-Masons who became important Whig leaders were William H. Seward and Thurlow Weed of New York, and Thaddeus Stevens of Pennsylvania. With the addition of two more groups—antinullification states' rights southerners and the so-called Democratic Conservatives, who opposed their party's financial policies after 1836—the Whig coalition was complete but hardly united.

In the 1836 presidential election, the Whigs were not unified or strong enough to join behind a single presidential candidate; instead, several Whig candidates ran for office. The most prominent were Daniel Webster in New England, WILLIAM HENRY HARRISON in the Northwest, and Hugh Lawson White in the Southwest. The election went to the Democrat MARTIN VAN BUREN, but the Whigs grew steadily stronger.

Hard times following the PANIC OF 1837 and the popularity of the Whig candidate, William Henry Harrison, brought the party victory in 1840 over Jackson's successor, Martin Van Buren. The new Whig managers stole a turn from the Democrats by outdoing them in raucous electioneering during the "Log Cabin" campaign—the most tumultuous presidential campaign the nation had yet seen. (This was the formula for the only other Whig victory, that of ZACHARY TAYLOR in 1848). Harrison's death on April 4, 1841 (one month after assuming office), resulting in John Tyler's succession to the presidency, was especially disastrous for the party.

A definite break ensued between Tyler and the Whig leaders in Congress, a development that illustrated the Whig philosophy of government. The Whigs had originated in objection to what they considered the excessive power of the executive branch under Andrew Jackson. To them the legislative branch of the government represented the wishes of the people, and the task of the executive was to serve as the enforcing agent of the legislative branch. When Tyler ignored the counsel of his cabinet and vetoed bills that sought to reestablish the Bank of the United States, about 50 Whig congressmen met in caucus and read Tyler out of the party. With this the last pre–Civil War opportunity for passage of a modified American System had slipped by.

In 1844 the Whig Party nominated Henry Clay for president. However, Clay refused to take a definite stand on the TEXAS annexation issue, provoking northern abolitionists, who opposed its admission as a slave state, to support the LIBERTY PARTY candidate. The Whig split ensured a victory for the Democrat JAMES K. POLK. Once the MEXICAN-AMERICAN WAR (1846–48) had been declared, controversy over admitting or excluding SLAVERY from territory gained in the war further splintered the party. Antislavery Whigs known as Conscience Whigs opposed the Cotton Whigs in the proslavery states.

In 1848 the nomination slipped away from Webster and Clay and went to ZACHARY TAYLOR, who had gained wide popularity as a victorious general in the Mexican-American War. This move temporarily prevented a division of the party, and Taylor was elected. The nation had become deeply divided by the issues of slavery and national expansion. With disunion threatening, the aged Whig leaders Clay and Webster tried, in January and March 1850, to formulate a series of laws designed to resolve the main points of sectional friction. President Taylor opposed their moves, but his death on July 9, 1850, made MILLARD FILLMORE, a Whig Party loyalist from New York, president. Fillmore supported the efforts of Clay and Webster, and the COMPROMISE OF 1850 was enacted. While the Compromise of 1850 was not solely a Whig accomplishment, the party's leadership had been prominent in its passage. Webster, now Fillmore's secretary of state, dreamed of capturing the presidency at the head of a Union movement in 1852. But both major parties accepted the Compromise, and on June 16, 1852, the Whigs reverted to form in nominating another general, WINFIELD SCOTT, for president. Two weeks later, Clay was dead; Webster died in October. The Whig Party never recovered from the loss of its two greatest figures.

The passing of Clay and Webster heralded the Whig disaster of 1852. The party's call for moderation and union, by now far more prominent than the national economic policy, became even more ineffective as the Civil War neared. Southern Whigs, fearful of northern encroachment on slaveholding rights, thought the Democrats more receptive to their interests; and a key number of northern Whigs had already moved into the antislavery FREE-SOIL PARTY, which had been formed on the eve of the 1848 election.

The rise of the REPUBLICAN PARTY and the anti-immigrant KNOW-NOTHING PARTY completed the Whig downfall. Defections to Republicanism were numerous, while the former Whig president, Fillmore, accepted the Know-Nothing nomination. A Whig national convention met in 1856, but it simply endorsed the Fillmore ticket. Thus, the party of unionism came to an end, a victim of sectional controversy. In 1860, a feeble remnant of the Whig party organized the Constitutional Union Party, a last-ditch attempt to prevent disruption of the Union. They fared badly in the election; their constitutional conservatism was politically dead, and with it had perished the Whig Party.

It is difficult to speak of Whig doctrine in a party of such diverse elements. Politically, the opposition to Jackson had dictated an attack on excessive presidential energy. Whigs believed Congress should initiate policy, not the president. Whig views of the Constitution ranged from Webster's nationalism to Tyler's states' rights views, with the nationalistic view predominating. But its national economic policy best characterized the Whigs, although not all those calling themselves Whigs accepted it. Politically, this was a premature nationalism at a time when the effective power of government remained to a large extent with the states. The Democrats, through their generally superior state political organizations and greater identification with popular interests, were usually able to maintain their ascendancy. The absence of true nationalism before the Civil War meant that the party with a national economic policy had to depend on political trumpery and war heroes for its two national victories. With no southerners in Congress during the Civil War and with a former Illinois Whig, Abraham Lincoln, in the White House, the Republican Party finally passed much of the economic legislation on tariff and banking that the Whigs had long advocated.

Further reading: Thomas Brown, *Politics and Statesmanship: Essays on the American Whig Party* (New York: Columbia University Press, 1985); Michael F. Holt, *The Rise and Fall of the American Whig Party: Jacksonian Politics and the Onset of the Civil War* (New York: Oxford University Press, 1999).

—Richard L. Friedline

Willard, Emma (Hart) (1787–1870)

Born in Berlin, Connecticut, the ninth child of Captain Samuel and Lydia (Hinsdale) Hart, Emma Willard spent her life teaching and advocating improvement in women's EDUCATION. From an early age, her father included her in family discussions about politics, philosophy, RELIGION, and morality. She was encouraged to learn on her own and think independently. In addition to her father's progressive teachings, she attended the local public school and later entered the Berlin Academy, one of the first academies established in Connecticut. In an era when girls attended school sporadically, if at all, and when educating girls was generally considered useless, or even potentially damaging, Willard's interest in learning (and the encouragement she received from her father) made her experience exceptional. She also proved to be an exceptionally gifted teacher and was asked to run the Berlin village school when she was only 17. To improve her knowledge as a teacher, she continued her own education, attending the Misses Patten's school in Hartford. She was then asked to run the winter school at the Berlin Academy and soon took over summer duties as well. In the spring and fall, she continued her learning at Mrs. Royse's school in Hartford. In 1807, she went to Middlebury, Vermont, to oversee all aspects of the Female Academy. She excelled in this role, winning the trust of Middlebury's leading citizens. In 1809, she left her position to marry John Willard, a local politician and physician. They had one child, John Hart Willard, in 1810.

John Willard supported his wife's continued interest in learning, encouraging her to study his medical and scientific books. One of her nephews, then attending neighboring Middlebury College, showed her his course of study. She was intrigued by what was being taught to young men in college and asked her nephew if she could study along with him. She mastered his coursework and asked him to test her on it. Her excellent performance encouraged her to continue studying the material that, she was beginning to see, had been closed off from her and other young women. Always motivated to learn and urged to do so, she began to see that the educational experience of most women was quite different from that of men. While boys and young men were offered a comprehensive plan of study, women and girls were mostly given bits and pieces of intellectual matter. Female education emphasized music, French, embroidery, and other skills meant to display refinement and grace, not mental acumen. Realizing through her own experiences that women could learn about the higher or more difficult subjects just as well as men, Willard began to ponder how the disparity between men's and women's education might be remedied.

Obliged to teach once again because of her husband's financial difficulties, Willard began to think more seriously about ways to promote women's education. To that end, in 1814 she founded the Middlebury Female Academy, where she combined traditionally female subjects with traditionally male subjects such as mathematics and history. Barred from sitting in on classes at Middlebury to bolster her own ability to teach these subjects, she was left to teach herself and devise her own techniques for teaching these topics to her students. Her experiences in Vermont led her to think that her ideas might meet with more success in New York. In 1818, she sent an appeal to New York governor DeWitt Clinton, asking for more public funding for girls' schools. She argued that better education for women would not undermine male and female roles, but rather it would improve the prospects of the young republic by ensuring that children raised by educated mothers would be more virtuous citizens. Her *Plan for Improving Female Education* (1819) received some support when she addressed groups of New York legislators, but most of her listeners still believed that educating women would interfere with their God-given duties as helpmates for men.

Emma Willard *(Hulton/Archive)*

Willard established another female academy in Waterford, New York, hoping the legislature would provide state funds for her endeavor. When this assistance failed to appear, the academy was saved by the intervention of prosperous citizens in nearby Troy, a booming canal town with progressive and ambitious ideas about education. Willard moved her school to Troy, where it survived and began to prosper, even without state aid. Students at the Troy Female Academy learned a combination of the lighter traditional subjects and the more rigorous intellectual subjects previously reserved for men. Always looking for better ways to teach, Willard thought the existing textbooks were inadequate and off-putting to students. With typical vigor and creativity, she began writing her own texts: *A System of World Geography* (1824); *History of the United States, or Republic of America* (1828); and *A System of Universal History in Perspective* (1835). These were hailed as more accessible tools for educating about these subjects and were some of the best-selling textbooks of the 19th century. Always zealous in promoting her cause, Willard continued to write about education reform and publicized her ideas energetically. She encouraged her students to serve their country by becoming teachers themselves, hoping to send her pupils out to the newly settled West to provide the schooling so lacking on the frontier. She traveled far herself, promoting the cause of education reform around the nation and in Europe.

In 1838, Willard retired from active teaching at the Troy Female Academy, but she continued to be a powerful figure at the school until her death. Her first husband, John Willard, died in 1825. After retirement and a brief, unhappy second marriage, she returned to her work, proposing ways to improve the common schools in Connecticut and other states. She continued to write, publishing books in her later years on subjects ranging from physiology to history to astronomy. While Willard opposed women's suffrage as unnecessary and politically counterproductive to the cause of women's education, she continued to advocate for women's financial independence and the liberating effects of rigorous education. She continued on as an inspiring, charismatic presence at the Troy Female Academy until her death in 1870. The academy was renamed the Emma Willard School as a tribute to the vision of its founder, the first American woman to publicly advocate better education for women. Her school became a model for other academies, seminaries, and colleges for women in the United States and around the world.

Further reading: Stephen Mintz, *Moralists and Modernizers: America's Pre–Civil War Reformers* (Baltimore: Johns Hopkins University Press, 1995).

Williams, Peter, Jr. (ca. 1780–1840)

Born in New Jersey sometime around 1780, Peter Williams, Jr., moved to New York at an early age and became one of New York City's leading African-American clergymen and activists. The son of an enslaved man (and Revolutionary War veteran) and a black indentured woman, he was educated at one of the abolitionist schools for free blacks. As an activist, Williams published some of the earliest pamphlets by an African American against racial injustice. His first such essay, entitled *An Oration on the Abolition of the Slave Trade,* was published in 1808. While celebrating the recent congressional ban on slave imports, Williams also attacked continued racial oppression.

Throughout his life, Williams worked passionately for such issues as black EDUCATION, community uplift, and the ABOLITION MOVEMENT. He was a member of the African Society for Mutual Relief; a supporter of the first black-run newspaper, *Freedom's Journal* (inaugurated in New York City in 1827); and, later in his life, a founder of two educational groups, the African Dorcas Association (1828) and the Phoenix Society (1833). In addition, Williams joined the new generation of immediate abolitionists rising in American culture during the 1830s. As the editors of *The Black Abolitionist Papers* put it, "Williams firmly established his credentials as a leading black abolitionist by the 1830s." From 1833 to 1836, he served on the American Anti-Slavery Society's Board of Managers and was one of its very few black Executive Committee members.

Williams also gained fame for starting St. Phillips Episcopal Church in New York City. After a period of tutelage under a white Episcopal theologian, and after having led a group of black Episcopalians in worship, Williams organized St. Phillips 1819. The congregation expanded to more than 200 families during the next several years, making St. Phillips one of the city's leading African-American churches. Williams became an ordained Episcopal priest in 1826. According to *The Black Abolitionist Papers,* Williams encountered hardship during the 1830s when "rumors that he had conducted an interracial marriage provoked a white mob to destroy his church and Rectory." Told by a bishop in 1834 to formally resign his station in antislavery societies promulgating racial equality, Williams did so but remained at the head of his congregation. He continued to work as an abolitionist, however, attending antislavery meetings and promoting his activist views. One of Williams's last acts in this regard came in 1836 when he received a passport for a trip to England. Although he endured discrimination during his travels, he also claimed American citizenship through the passport, thereby justifying many black abolitionists' claims to equality.

Further reading: C. Peter Ripley, et al., eds., *The Black Abolitionist Papers,* vol. 3 (Chapel Hill: University of North Carolina Press, 1985–1992).

—Richard Newman

Wilmot Proviso See Volume V

women's status and rights

In the Antebellum United States, a woman's status and rights depended on the law, economics, culture, custom, EDUCATION, ethnicity, and race. By 1860, the efforts of reformers had begun to expand the boundaries of women's concerns, challenge the cultural prejudices that limited their experiences, and set them on the road toward suffrage.

The most basic element of a woman's status was whether she was free or enslaved. Legally, enslaved women were considered the property of their owners and counted as three-fifths of a person for the purpose of the census. As property, enslaved women could not contract and therefore could not marry in the eyes of the law. While many enslaved men and women did engage in fulfilling, consensual relationships that constituted marriage by any other name, the law did not recognize them as such, allowing owners to separate husbands and wives on a whim. An enslaved woman's children were not hers to keep, but rather the property of her owner, who could sell them or remove them at any time. Conception itself was often out of an enslaved woman's control, as sexual abuse was common and her right to seek legal redress often nil. An enslaved woman's status in American society was further compromised by stereotypes. Young women were painted as sly, sexual predators who could not be trusted, while older women were represented as slow, unfeminine, and devoted to their owner's family. These stereotypes suggested that enslaved women did not have or care for families of their own, that they had no relationships within the slave community that were as important as those they had with whites, and that they were intrinsically unsuited for freedom.

These marks of status were imposed from outside the slave community and did not encompass an enslaved woman's own sense of self. Enslaved men and women engaged in sexual, romantic, and emotional relationships with one another, regardless of the law's opinion of the same. Extended family networks were created and maintained through blood ties and friendship, despite the separations imposed by the institution under which they lived. Enslaved men and women engaged in slowdowns, outright disobedience, and rebellion, and sometimes they ran away. Each of these acts spoke of their own sense of identity and status, pushing back against the expectations of white culture.

A free woman's legal status depended most significantly on whether she was married or not. An unmarried single woman over the age of 18 was able to contract, sue, be charged with criminal activity, own property, make wills, run a business in her own name, and keep her earnings. Once married, however, a woman's legal identity was suspended in that of her husband. He gained control of all property she brought to the marriage, any she gained afterward, her earnings, her ability to contract and sue, and sexual access to her body. A wife could not testify against her husband since the two were legally one, and their children were considered to be in his custody. There were exceptions to these rules, brokered by courts of equity, by some criminal matters, and by premarital trusts. For the majority of women, however, marriage made them the legal dependents of their spouse.

Divorce did exist in the early 19th-century United States, but it was difficult to obtain. Originally judged by state and territorial legislatures, and later by the courts, successful divorce petitions had to demonstrate that one party was guilty of a moral offense against the other and that the latter had remained blameless. A woman whose husband had committed adultery, for example, might be successful in obtaining a divorce. A couple who had both committed adultery and were unhappy together, however, would rarely be able to divorce, since there was no innocent party in the marriage for the courts or legislatures to protect. The most common grounds for divorce were adultery or impotence. Many states and territories would allow couples to legally separate if there were evidence of extreme violence in the marriage, a failure of the husband to provide, or if one or the other spouse had been abandoned. The rules of divorce varied from state to state, causing some husbands and wives to move in order to benefit from more liberal laws. Indiana and Utah gained reputations as "divorce-mills," churning out divorces as if they were products for sale, yet South Carolina refused to allow any divorce until 1868.

A free woman's choice to marry or stay single, however, was conditioned by the economic opportunities available to her. Women were prohibited from most professions, trades, and apprenticeships during the early 19th century, leaving few women with the personal or familial wealth to be able to support themselves without getting married. Even if they possessed such wealth, they were legally prohibited from engaging in sexual relationships outside the bonds of matrimony. A woman who wanted such a relationship, therefore, was forced to marry or face the fierce moral and cultural disapproval of her family and peers.

Wealth had always provided individuals with a certain status in America, but as the 19th century progressed, industrialization changed and heightened the link between the two. In preindustrial America, almost everyone worked in or around their home. Goods and services were bartered and traded for one another, and few items were bought or sold for cash. With the advent of industrialization, however, many families moved to cities, and work became synonymous with laboring for wages outside the home. For women, the change had two repercussions. The first was that labor inside the home—the business of housekeeping for your own family, for example—ceased to be recognized as work. The second was that working for wages became a mark of your low social rank.

For many social critics, journalists, editors, preachers, and politicians, the social changes unleashed by INDUSTRIALIZATION were disruptive and often frightening. Stability quickly became associated with the actions of women, whose role as mothers provided a constant amid a sea of change. A woman's role in the home was lauded by popular culture, identified as a vital balance to the struggles of the working world. It quickly became a mark of status for a man to make enough money to afford to keep his wife at home, whether he managed a factory or worked in the fields.

Women who did stay at home were not, as popular culture suggested, ladies of leisure. Housekeeping, even with the aid of hired help, required constant attention, a situation complicated further by the standards of decoration and entertainment that became associated with maintaining a high social rank. Elaborate furniture required meticulous dusting, while the fashion for embroidered chairs and wall hangings demanded creativity, planning, and time. Women communicated their status to others by their dress and appearance; such dress-making and hair styling were time-consuming affairs. High-ranking women produced status through their labor in the home just as much as their husbands did through their work outside it.

Most working families became stigmatized by these cultural ideals. Men who could not support their families were considered unmasculine. Women were castigated for failing themselves and their children by working outside the home. Health problems, poverty, domestic violence, and illiteracy were all at some time or another blamed on the "problem" of the working wife. Yet working women often faced a bitter choice: work outside the home or face the possibility of hunger and homelessness.

The theory that women were domestic nurturers spilled over into other areas of their lives. Since the American Revolution, the idea that women should be educated in order to raise properly patriotic sons and daughters had smoothed the way for the foundation of a number of female-oriented schools. While the rich had easier access to education than the poor, literacy rates for women rose steadily throughout the 19th century, and many went on to become teachers. Lauded by reformers such as Catharine Beecher, teaching was considered an extension of motherhood and therefore a fitting profession for women to enter. School boards and districts also paid women less than men (rationalizing that they had no families to support), making female teachers a cost-effective way to expand the provision of education.

It was also as mothers (and mothers-to-be) that many women became involved in social reform. The TEMPERANCE MOVEMENT of the early 19th century was particularly noteworthy in this respect. Women argued that wives needed protection from the violence and wastefulness of drunken husbands. As concerned mothers, they lobbied politicians, circulated petitions, and held public lectures to raise social awareness about their cause. The earliest changes in a woman's legal status also relied on the rhetoric of motherhood. The married women's property acts of the early 19th century, first passed in Mississippi in 1839, allowed women to regain control of their property after marriage in order to protect them against their husbands' debts. The reforms had little to do with equality, but rather with protecting women and children from neglect.

The same qualities presumed to make women excellent mothers and guardians of the home lent themselves to the suggestion that women were, generally, morally superior to men. So rose the concept of "public housekeeping"—the idea that women were the guardians of a society's morals and that the talents they used at home made them invaluable beyond its bounds. Abolitionist women made particular use of this argument. In 1836, for example, Angelina Grimké wrote *An Appeal to the Christian Women of the South,* in which she argued that southern women had a particular responsibility to sway their husbands, fathers, brothers, and sons to the ABOLITION MOVEMENT. While such rhetoric allowed many women to gain acceptance as public reformers, they still faced opposition. Grimké's pamphlet was burned in the South, and her lectures were condemned by the clergy of Massachusetts as improper and unfeminine.

By the mid-19th century, however, such rhetoric began to change. In 1848, a women's rights convention was held at SENECA FALLS, New York. The brainchild of abolitionist and Quaker minister LUCRETIA MOTT and reformer Elizabeth Cady Stanton, the convention brought together around 300 men and women who believed that women's rights needed direct and urgent redress. The participants at the convention debated and signed "The Declaration of Sentiments," a document penned by Stanton and based on the Declaration of Independence. "We hold these truths to be self evident," claimed the convention goers, "that all men and women are created equal."

The document claimed specific grievances. It lamented the exclusion of women from the electoral, legislative, and judicial process and argued that marriage reduced them to legal infants. The women of Seneca Falls opposed paying taxes to a government that did not represent them, and they demanded control over their property, contracts, and deeds. They charged society at large with limiting them through a moral double standard and abhorred the prejudice that kept them out of higher education, professions, and business. Man had no right to limit woman's desires or achievements, they argued. Such a prerogative belonged solely to God.

The convention-goers did not ask for rights so that they might be better wives and mothers. Instead, they asked for the rights due to them as citizens of the United States. The convention launched an organized women's rights movement in the nation that would span decades. This movement often clashed with traditional women's reform because of its unapologetic claim that women deserved the same legal and social rights as men without qualification or concession to cultural norms.

Both branches of reform were culturally specific. Enormous problems arose, for example, when reformers turned their attention to Native American women. Rather than seeking to understand the complexity of American Indian cultures, reformers compared the role of men and women in various tribal societies to their own understanding of appropriate gender behavior and rights. The result was an effort to remake Native American societies in the image of Euro-America. This effort spanned the entire 19th century, and involved education, missionary work, and legal reform. The result, however, was often the impoverishment of tribal communities and the disruption of their traditions, sparking massive resistance from many American Indian women and men.

Further reading: Jeanne Boydston, *Home and Work: Housework, Wages, and the Ideology of Labor in the Early Republic* (New York: Oxford University Press, 1990); Nancy F. Cott, *Public Vows: A History of Marriage and the Nation* (Cambridge, Mass.: Harvard University Press, 2000); Lori Ginzberg, *Women and the Work of Benevolence: Morality, Politics, and Class in Nineteenth Century United States* (New Haven, Conn.: Yale University Press, 1990); Nancy Isenberg, *Sex and Citizenship in Antebellum America* (Chapel Hill: University of North Carolina Press, 1998).

—Catherine J. Denial

Wright, Fanny (1797–1852)

Frances (Fanny) Wright was born in Dundee, Scotland, on September 6, 1797. By the age of two, she had lost both her parents and was sent with her sister to be raised by relatives in London, England. There she stayed until the age of 21, when she returned to Scotland to live with James Milne, her great-uncle and a professor at Glasgow College. Fanny used the time to her advantage, studying in the college's vast library. A year later, armed with a keen mind and the fortune left to her by her parents, she journeyed to the United States. Wright was favorably impressed by what she saw, considering American society to be extremely progressive compared to the Europe she had left behind. On her return to England, Wright published her thoughts in *Views of Society and Manners in America.* The book caught the attention of the Marquis de Lafayette, the French hero of the American Revolution, and the two became friends. Wright accompanied Lafayette on his 1824 trip to the United States, where she had the opportunity to meet Thomas Jefferson and James Madison, among others.

Wright's travels throughout the United States brought her into close contact with the institution of SLAVERY. The brutality of the system appalled her, and she became an increasingly vocal proponent of gradual emancipation. Wright believed that abolition should be the concern of the federal government and advocated that Congress set aside land on which slaves could be relocated, trained for freedom, and allowed to work to purchase their liberty. In the hopes of convincing others of her ideas, Wright purchased 640 acres of land in western Tennessee in 1825, naming the property Nashoba. There she settled a community of enslaved men and women, promising them their eventual freedom. The experiment was plagued with difficulties from the outset, including sensational reporting in the press and outbreaks of swamp fever. By 1830, Wright was forced to admit that her plan had failed, and she freed the slaves, arranging for their transportation to Haiti.

The failure of the Nashoba experiment did nothing to dampen Wright's commitment to the ABOLITION MOVEMENT or a variety of other social causes. During this period, Wright became friends with ROBERT OWEN and went to live at his utopian community in New Harmony, Indiana. There she became editor of the New Harmony *Gazette* and later of the New York *Free Enquirer,* a newspaper particularly well known for its advocacy of public EDUCATION and working-class activism. At the same time, she entered the lecture circuit, arguing for changes in popular and legal conceptions of marriage, more lenient divorce laws, the safe and widespread practice of birth control, abolition, and the education of women. She also spoke against the practice of capital punishment. Wright published these ideas in two volumes of *Courses of Popular Lectures* in 1829 and 1836. Many Victorians considered her lectures to be scandalous. Not only did Wright speak publicly about issues of sexuality and women's rights, she also spoke to mixed audiences of men and women, defying polite convention.

In 1830 Wright traveled to France, where she met Guillaume Sylvan Casimi Phiquepal D'Arusmont. The pair were married in 1831, and Wright divided much of her time in the 1830s between France and the United States. She campaigned for the DEMOCRATIC PARTY in 1836 and 1838 and continued to give periodic lectures on social issues for the remainder of her life. She and her husband divorced in 1850, and Wright died two years later in Cincinnati, Ohio. Her ideas exerted a lasting influence on women's rights activists throughout the 19th century.

Further reading: Elizabeth Ann Bartlett, *Liberty, Equality, Sorority: The Origins and Interpretation of American Feminist Thought: Frances Wright, Sarah Grimke, and Margaret Fuller* (Brooklyn, N.Y.: Carlson Publishing Company, 1994); Celia Morris Eckhardt, *Fanny Wright: Rebel in America* (Cambridge, Mass.: Harvard University Press, 1984).

—Catherine J. Denial

Y

Young, Brigham (1801–1877)

Second president of the CHURCH OF JESUS CHRIST OF LATTER-DAY SAINTS, Brigham Young was also one of the most important colonizers in the American West in the 19th century. He was born in Whittingham, Vermont, and, like the Mormon prophet JOSEPH SMITH, JR., grew up in a poor, rural environment. The family moved constantly, eventually setting in upstate New York. Young's large family—he was the ninth of 11 surviving children—was intensely moral and religious. Like others in his rural and isolated world, he had little formal EDUCATION, and he apprenticed himself as a carpenter and painter. In 1824, he married his first wife, Miriam Works.

Originally a Methodist, Young came into contact with the Mormon Church in 1830, the year Joseph Smith published the Book of Mormon and incorporated the church under New York State law. Young gradually became converted to the millennialist core of the church, its moralist beliefs, and, above all, the magnetism and presence of its founder and prophet, Joseph Smith, Jr. Perhaps Young was also attracted to the idea of a lay priesthood in which male members of the church came to exercise authority and influence. Whatever his reasons, Young and his family joined the church in 1832.

From the beginning, Young labored full-time on behalf of his new church, going on several missions and fulfilling other ministerial tasks. The church had become both a route to salvation and an avenue to worldly advancement. In 1835, Smith appointed him to the Council of Twelve, the ruling body of the church. After the Mormon community in Missouri disintegrated under the pressure of casual violence and official condemnation, Young, as the senior member at large (Smith and other church leaders were then in a Missouri jail) took charge of the Mormon immigration from Missouri to Illinois. He would later demonstrate this organizational skill in directing other Mormon migrations. When Smith established the Mormon settlements at NAUVOO, he sent Young to head missionary activities in England, where he was enormously successful.

In 1841 Young returned to Nauvoo, where he was quickly initiated into the new Mormon rituals. The most dramatic was the doctrine of POLYGAMY, or plural wives, which was secret, publicly disavowed by the church, and practiced by only a few leaders. Young immediately embraced the new policy; he would eventually marry 55 women. In 1844, Smith announced himself a candidate for

Brigham Young *(Library of Congress)*

president of the United States, and Young journeyed east to work on behalf of the Mormon prophet's candidacy.

Young was in Boston when he received news of Smith's assassination in June 1844. He immediately returned to Nauvoo, where he was elected as the church's leader. His first duty was to arrange a truce with the neighboring mobs, and in this he was partially successful. His refusal to seek revenge for Smith's death won him a period of quiet, but he could not make a lasting peace. In 1845, attacks on outlying Mormon settlements began again, and the entire Mormon community around Nauvoo was in danger. Young rapidly organized the emigration of the entire church to the West. The first party left in the middle of winter and crossed the Mississippi on the ice, moving across Iowa to a camping site near Omaha. Young directed that a series of outfitting stations be established along the route to serve subsequent parties. "Winter Quarters," as it came to be known, was an elaborate community of some 12,000 governed by a theocracy, but it was only temporary. In spring 1847, Young led a pioneer company to the West, and when he reached the Great Salt Lake Valley, he pronounced it the site of the future gathering of Zion. On his return, he called a meeting of church leaders and had himself declared "prophet, seer, and revelator." He was now the absolute leader of the church, with the same powers of the original prophet Joseph Smith.

The Great Basin was an ideal location for the church. It was possessed of enough natural resources to make a thriving community possible, and it was sufficiently remote to keep it distant from other settlers. Young sought to insure the safety of the church by laying out a vast territory that he called the STATE OF DESERET. The limits of the territory included some of present-day Idaho, Nevada, and CALIFORNIA. In order to ease the migration of converts from Europe (especially England), he established a warm-weather route of access through Southern California, by way of San Bernadino to St. George, and thence to the Great Salt Lake Valley. Young established numerous settlements in Nevada to protect his Southern California connection. He laid out numerous towns along the base of the Wasatch Range, including (in addition to Salt Lake City) Provo, Utah, and Lemhi, Idaho.

Young established a structure of government in the form of a theocracy. The church and its leaders, principally Young himself, made all the important decisions, with the church at the head. The church, in the person of its leader Brigham Young, granted land and water rights to chosen settlers. He brought together in himself the branches of the executive, legislature, and judiciary. When Congress organized Utah Territory in 1850, the president appointed Young governor of the territory, recognizing the reality of the Utah settlement. But the judges appointed to serve the territory were non-Mormons. They quickly found themselves ostracized and their authority circumscribed by the activities of the church bishops in referring legal cases to the church courts. The relations of the federal government with Young and the Mormons were further strained by Young's public announcement of the doctrine of polygamy in 1852.

Conflict between Young and the U.S. government grew throughout the 1850s, in the midst of a growing sectional violence over SLAVERY in the East and a rising strain of anti-Mormon feeling, rising to a fever pitch over the issue of polygamy. In 1857, President James Buchanan declared the Mormons and their leader in rebellion against the nation and ordered U.S. troops to Utah Territory, an action known as the MORMON WAR. After much deliberation, Young decided not to oppose the invasion by force. Instead, he and other church leaders went into hiding, and an army of occupation settled into Utah Territory for two years. This period of occupation was characterized by a degree of accommodation on both sides, but Young never compromised what he regarded as the will of the church. He was eventually removed as governor of the territory, and the troops retired to the East with the coming of the Civil War (1861–65).

The war provided a prolonged period for Young to direct the affairs of the church without interference. Although the federal government had reduced the size of the State of Deseret to the boundary of the present state of Utah (Young had sold the ranch in San Bernadino), he continued to supervise the founding of settlements throughout the limits of the territory. He also laid the foundations of a self-sufficient ECONOMY through the Zion's Cooperative Mercantile Institution and several other cooperatives. Young finally had to come to terms with the growing proximity and influence of American society into the affairs of his church domain, as exemplified by the arrival of the transcontinental railroad at Promontory Point, Utah, in 1869. That he was able to make these transitions and expand the scope and influence of the Mormon church throughout the American West was a final tribute to his genius.

Young was not an important figure in Mormon doctrine, as he built on the dogma and rituals of Joseph Smith and vigorously defended unpopular practices such as polygamy. He is perhaps best known in the modern age for his pronouncement in 1847 that black men could not hold the office of the priesthood, a condition of participation in the affairs of the church open to all men. (This ban on AFRICAN AMERICANS as priests in the church remained in effect until 1978.) But as an organizer and colonizer, Young proved himself a remarkable leader, presiding over church expansion in area and numbers. When he died in 1877, the Mormon population in Utah numbered 125,000, and its settlements more than 200.

In his personal life, Young had at least 55 wives (some historians say more); and 16 of his wives would bear him 57 children. Young was also a successful pioneer businessman in the Great Basin. Among his various business enterprises were a ferryboat company, a wagon-express company, and later interest in a railroad. He also owned extensive valuable real estate and operated a number of successful early manufacturing businesses. His estate exceeded $600,000, making him the wealthiest member of the church at the time.

Further reading: Leonard J. Arrington, *Brigham Young: American Moses* (New York: Knopf, 1985); Leonard J. Arrington, *Great Basin Kingdom: An Economic History of the Latter-Day Saints, 1830–1900* (Cambridge, Mass.: Harvard University Press, 1956).

Chronology

1812
In response to British attacks on American shipping, the United States declares war on Great Britain; the conflict is known as the War of 1812.

Indian leaders Tecumseh and Black Hawk ally their forces with the British.

1813
British forces seize Washington, D.C., and burn the White House and the Capitol.

James Madison begins his second term as president.

1814
The Treaty of Ghent, negotiated largely by Albert Gallatin and John Quincy Adams, ends the War of 1812.

1815
Unaware that the War of 1812 has ended, British troops instigate the Battle of New Orleans; they are defeated by an American army led by General Andrew Jackson.

Red Jacket becomes a powerful leader of the Seneca Indian nation.

1816
Democratic-Republican James Monroe is elected president over Federalist Rufus King.

Martin v. Hunter's Lessee affirms the U.S. Supreme Court's right to review the decisions of state courts in all cases involving U.S. laws, treaties, and the Constitution.

Jim P. Beckwourth, one of the first mountain men, becomes a scout for the Ashley fur trading expedition.

1817
The First Seminole War, between the United States and the Seminole Indians of Florida, begins; many runaway slaves support the Native Americans in battle.

DeWitt Clinton, governor of New York, authorizes the construction of the Erie Canal.

Davy Crockett serves as a scout in the conflict between western settlers and the Creek Indians.

The American Colonization Society is founded to send former slaves back to Africa.

Great Britain and the United States agree to the mutual demilitarization of the Great Lakes and Lake Champlain in the Rush-Bagot Agreement of 1817.

1818
The Convention of London resolves U.S.-British disputes over the northern boundary of the Louisiana Purchase and the settlement of the Oregon Territory.

1819
Spain cedes all of Florida to the United States in the Adams-Onís Treaty after being defeated in the First Seminole War.

In *Dartmouth College v. Woodward,* the U.S. Supreme Court upholds the sanctity of the college charter as a contract under the Constitution. The decision encourages business growth by limiting state control over charters or private corporations.

The U.S. Supreme Court finds in *McCullough v. Maryland* that the state of Maryland's imposition of a tax on the Bank of the United States is unconstitutional.

1820
While on a sailing voyage in the South Atlantic, Captain Nathaniel Brown Palmer discovers the continent of Antarctica.

The U.S. Congress adopts the Missouri Compromise, or the Missouri Enabling Act, which aims for a balance between free and slave states. The compromise eases tensions between the increasingly industrial North and the agricultural, slaveholding South by prohibiting slavery in the Louisiana Purchase north of the 36°30' latitude.

The Land Act of 1820 abolishes the purchase of land through the system established in the Land Act of 1796.

1821

Chancellor of Columbia College James Kent's "Universal Suffrage" speech argues against the proposal to abolish the property ownership requirement for voter eligibility.

James Monroe assumes his second term as president.

1822

Denmark Vesey's plan for revolt, involving 9,000 slaves, is foiled in Charleston, South Carolina. Vesey and his aides are hanged.

Sequoyah, a Cherokee Indian, begins teaching his alphabet to his people, thereby creating the first Native American written language.

1823

The Monroe Doctrine is announced. The doctrine warns European powers that the United States will not tolerate intervention in the newly independent nations of the Western Hemisphere.

1824

Thomas L. McKenney is appointed the first chief of the Bureau of Indian Affairs.

The Tariff Act of 1824 increases protective duties on wool, iron, lead, glass, silk, linens, cutlery, hemp, and cotton bagging.

The U.S. Supreme Court decision *Gibbons v. Ogden* establishes the federal government's jurisdiction over interstate commerce.

Democratic-Republican John Quincy Adams wins a close presidential race over three other candidates: Henry Clay, William H. Crawford, and Andrew Jackson.

1825

Native American leaders of Wisconsin settle land claims with the U.S. government at the Council of Prairie du Chien.

The Erie Canal opens; it links the Great Lakes with the Atlantic Ocean, thus greatly increasing trade between the East and the West.

1826

John B. Russwurm, one of the first African Americans to earn a college degree, graduates from Bowdoin College.

James Fenimore Cooper publishes *The Last of the Mohicans.*

1827

The first black-owned newspaper is published by Samuel Cornish and John B. Russwurm.

The Massachusetts High School Law mandates the establishment of high schools throughout the state. It is the first such law enacted in the United States.

The Constitution of the Cherokee Nation is drafted.

Publication of *The Birds of America* by John Audubon begins.

1828

Construction of the Baltimore & Ohio (B&O) Railroad, the first U.S. passenger railroad, begins.

The Tariff Act of 1828 imposes duties on foreign manufactured goods and imported raw materials.

John C. Calhoun's South Carolina Exposition voices strong opposition to the Tariff Act of 1828 and legitimizes North Carolina's authority to nullify the law.

John Quincy Adams runs for reelection but is defeated by Democrat Andrew Jackson.

The "tariff of abominations" is passed.

1829

David Walker, a freeborn merchant in Boston, publishes *Appeal to the Colored Citizens of the World,* an antislavery pamphlet in which he urges slaves to kill their masters.

1830

The Indian Removal Act is signed into law, ordering the Five Civilized Tribes of the Southeast to relocate west of the Mississippi.

Senators Daniel Webster of Massachusetts and Robert Y. Hayne of South Carolina debate the importance of states' rights versus nationalism.

The first covered wagons cross the Rocky Mountains.

Dan Rice popularizes "Jim Crow" minstrel acts.

Joseph Smith, Jr., founds the Mormon Church.

1831

Cyrus Hall McCormick invents the mechanical reaper.

The U.S. Supreme Court decides in *Cherokee Nation v. Georgia* that it does not have jurisdiction to rule on a case where a state enforces its laws on the Cherokee.

William Lloyd Garrison publishes the first issue of the *Liberator,* a radical abolitionist newspaper.

Nat Turner leads a slave rebellion in Southampton County, Virginia.

1831–1861

Approximately 75,000 slaves escape from the South using the underground railroad, a network of antislavery activists.

1832
The Tariff Act of 1832 lowers the high protective duties of the Tariff Act of 1828, but is labeled as a sectionalist measure that benefits the northern industrialized states.

The Seminole Treaty is signed. The Seminole people agree to cede lands in Florida and relocate west of the Mississippi.

The Black Hawk War, a conflict in Wisconsin between settlers and Native Americans, ends with the defeat of Chief Black Hawk.

Andrew Jackson is reelected president over Henry Clay of the Whig Party.

Archduke Maximilian of Germany and Karl Bodmer travel among the Plains Indians.

Crisis over states' rights and the doctrine of nullification develops.

1833
William Lloyd Garrison founds the American Anti-Slavery Society.

The U.S. Supreme Court decision *Barron v. Baltimore* holds that the Bill of Rights is binding upon the federal government, but not upon state governments.

The Tariff Act of 1833 resolves the national dispute over tariff laws passed in 1828 and 1832.

President Jackson and Attorney General Roger Taney remove federal deposits from the Bank of the United States.

1834
The Currency Act of 1834 sets standards for the weight and quantity of metal in gold coins minted in the United States.

1835
A severe smallpox epidemic almost wipes out the Mandan, Hidatsa, and Arikara nations along the Missouri River.

Alexis de Tocqueville's *Democracy in America* is the Frenchman's analysis of the American political system.

The Texas Rangers are formed, primarily to protect white settlers against Comanche raids in Texas.

Antislavery pamphlets are removed from the U.S. mails and burned in public.

Seminole chief Osceola leads the Indians of Florida in the Second Seminole War (1835–42), resisting the federal government's order to relocate.

George McDuffie's "On the Question of Slavery" speech defends slavery and denounces antislavery campaigners for stirring insurrection and endangering the lives of white families.

In the Treaty of New Echota, the Cherokee nation relinquishes claim to its capital city, New Echota, and over 7 million acres of land.

1836
American settlers in the Mexican province of Texas rebel against Mexican rule. Texan defeats at Goliad and the Alamo are followed by a decisive victory at San Jacinto, and Texas becomes an independent republic under the leadership of Sam Houston.

President Jackson's Specie Circular of 1836 requires the U.S. Treasury to accept only specie (gold or silver), not paper money, as payment in the sale of public lands.

Democrat Martin Van Buren defeats Whig candidate William Henry Harrison in the presidential election.

Ralph Waldo Emerson's first volume of essays, *Nature,* is hailed as a landmark in transcendentalist literature.

Henry Blair invents a corn harvester and becomes the first African American to receive a patent.

1837
Elijah P. Lovejoy, a white owner of an abolitionist newspaper, is killed in a proslavery riot.

Osceola, leader of the Seminole Indians in Florida, is captured.

School reformer Horace Mann leads the Massachusetts Board of Education, which becomes a national model for public school administration.

1838
The first African-American magazine, *The Mirror of Liberty,* is published by abolitionist David Ruggles in New York City.

Charles Lenox Remond, a freeborn African American from Massachusetts, is hired as the first black lecturer for an antislavery society.

General Winfield Scott commands the removal of the Cherokee Indians from the southern states to the Indian Territory (now the state of Oklahoma) west of the Mississippi River.

1839
Samuel F. B. Morse invents the telegraph.

Joseph Cinqué and about 50 enslaved Africans revolt aboard a Spanish ship, the *Amistad,* and kill the captain and crew.

The Liberty Party, the first political party built around the antislavery cause, is organized in Warsaw, New York.

1840
In a tough presidential race, William Henry Harrison defeats incumbent Martin Van Buren by a small margin.

1841
Frederick Douglass, an escaped slave from Maryland, begins lecturing for the Massachusetts Anti-Slavery Society.

U.S. Congress establishes prices of public lands in the western territories and further provides for their organization.

The Oregon Trail opens.

William Henry Harrison dies in office; John Tyler succeeds him as president.

Edgar Allan Poe publishes *The Murders in the Rue Morgue,* the first American detective story.

1842

U.S. secretary of state Daniel Webster and British minister Alexander Baring, Lord Ashburton, negotiate the Webster-Ashburton Treaty of 1842 to settle heated border disputes between the United States and Great Britain.

Rhode Islanders wage the Dorr Rebellion to protest discriminatory property laws.

John C. Frémont and Kit Carson explore the Pacific Northwest; Frémont's writings encourage emigration to Oregon.

1843

Dorothea Dix delivers an influential report to the Massachusetts legislature in which she criticizes the cruel treatment of the mentally ill in state institutions.

Sojourner Truth, a former slave, begins her career as a lecturer; she denounces slavery and promotes women's rights.

1844

The Treaty of Wanghia opens selected Chinese ports to trade with the United States.

Painter George Caleb Bingham begins portraying life on the western frontier.

Democrat James Knox Polk is elected president over Whig Henry Clay.

1845

The U.S. Congress enacts the joint resolution that makes possible the annexation of Texas by the United States; Mexico refuses to accept Texan independence.

1846

The Independent Treasury Act of 1846 establishes an independent treasury separate from the national banking and financial system.

The House of Representatives proposes the Wilmot Proviso to deal with the status of slavery in lands conquered in the Mexican-American War.

The Walker Tariff Act of 1846 establishes a moderate protective and revenue-generating tariff.

Three Cherokee political factions settle reimbursement issues from the Treaty of 1835 in a treaty with the Cherokee nation.

In the Bidlack Treaty between the United States and New Granada (Colombia and Panama), the United States gains rights of transit across the isthmus of Panama.

The Senate ratifies the Oregon Treaty of 1846, which sets the U.S.-Canadian border at the 49th parallel.

U.S. and Mexican troops clash on the disputed Texas-Mexico border, starting the Mexican-American War; General Zachary Taylor and his forces move into Mexico.

1847

An American force under General Winfield Scott lands at Veracruz, Mexico, marches inland, and captures Mexico City.

Henry Ward Beecher, pastor of the Plymouth Church in Brooklyn, New York, begins to advocate publicly for woman suffrage and abolition.

Evangeline by Henry Wadsworth Longfellow is published.

1848

The Treaty of Guadalupe Hidalgo ends the Mexican-American War; the United States gains the territory that will become the states of California, Nevada, and Utah, and most of the land that will make up New Mexico, Colorado, and Arizona. The southwestern Indians, including the Navajo, are now under U.S. jurisdiction.

The women's rights convention at Seneca Falls, New York, is led by Elizabeth Cady Stanton, Lucretia Mott, and Lucy Stone; the meeting marks the beginning of the women's rights movement.

The New York Married Women's Property Act grants women the right to their own property once married, control of their own wages, and custody of their children.

Zachary Taylor, the Whig candidate, is elected president, defeating Democrat Lewis Cass.

1849

Henry David Thoreau's essay "Civil Disobedience" advocates civil disobedience as a means for an individual to protest governmental actions that he considers unjust.

Escaped slave Harriet Tubman begins the first of her 19 underground railroad trips.

Amelia Jenks Bloomer begins editing the *Lily,* a newspaper concerned with women's rights, abolition, and temperance.

The California gold rush sends thousands of prospectors across the country, hoping to get rich.

Cornelius Vanderbilt establishes a company to transport miners to California by way of Central America; the company becomes the basis of his great fortune.

Elizabeth Blackwell graduates from Geneva Medical College, becoming the first American woman to earn an M.D.

1850

President Zachary Taylor dies in office; Millard Fillmore succeeds him.

U.S. and British diplomats negotiate the Clayton-Bulwer Treaty of 1850 to guarantee the strict neutrality of any interoceanic canal opened in Nicaragua or elsewhere in Central America.

Nathaniel Hawthorne publishes his novel *The Scarlet Letter.*

Amid bitter debate, the U.S. Congress enacts the Compromise of 1850; the bill repeals much of the Missouri Compromise and requires northern states to assist in the capture of escaped slaves.

As part of the Compromise of 1850, the Fugitive Slave Act of 1850 requires U.S. marshals to seize runaway slaves and imposes severe penalties on anyone who aids fugitives.

Senator John C. Calhoun denounces abolitionist activity and voices his opposition to the Compromise of 1850 in his final address delivered to U.S. Congress.

1851

In Sojourner Truth's *"A'n't I a Woman?"* speech, the abolitionist argues in favor of women's equality.

At a conference at Camp Traverse de Sioux, the Santee Sioux cede large portions of land in the Minnesota Territory to the United States.

William C. Nell publishes the first historical treatment of African Americans, titled *Services of Colored Americans in the Wars of 1776 and 1812.*

1852

Harriet Beecher Stowe denounces slavery in *Uncle Tom's Cabin, or Life Among the Lowly.* A best-seller, it rouses antislavery sentiment and increases the tension between the North and South.

Anthony Burns, the last fugitive slave to be returned from Massachusetts, is escorted out of Boston by 2,000 U.S. troops.

1853

Clotel, or The President's Daughter, by William Wells Brown, is published in England; it is the first novel by an African American.

Franklin Pierce is elected 14th president of the U.S., defeating Mexican-American War hero Winfield Scott.

Commodore Matthew Calbraith Perry of the U.S. Navy leads a mission that "opens" Japan to the western world.

In the Gadsden Treaty of 1853, the United States buys a strip of land from Mexico in order to build a transcontinental railroad.

Mrs. Douglass, a Virginia schoolteacher, is arrested in Norfolk for violating the state law against teaching black children to read.

1854

Stephen A. Douglas introduces the Kansas-Nebraska Act of 1854, which grants "popular sovereignty" to territorial governments in decisions involving slavery.

The modern Republican Party is formed.

Henry David Thoreau's *Walden* is published. His transcendentalist work communicates a reverence for nature.

1855

Tribal leaders from the Washington Territory cede 60,000 square miles of land to the United States at a conference in Walla Walla.

Free-Soilers in the Kansas Territory adopt their own state constitution.

Walt Whitman publishes his controversial book of poetry *Leaves of Grass.*

Documents

War Message (1812)
President James Madison

In Gaillard Hunt, ed. *The Writings of James Madison*, Vol. 8 (New York: G. P. Putnam's Sons, 1900–1910), pp. 192–200

Washington, D.C.
June 1, 1812

To the Senate and House of Representatives of the United States:

I communicate to Congress certain documents, being a continuation of those heretofore laid before them on the subject of our affairs with Great Britain.

Without going back beyond the renewal in 1803 of the war in which Great Britain is engaged, and omitting unrepaired wrongs of inferior magnitude, the conduct of her Government presents a series of acts hostile to the United States as an independent and neutral nation.

British cruisers have been in the continued practice of violating the American flag on the great highway of nations, and of seizing and carrying off persons sailing under it, not in the exercise of a belligerent right founded on the law of nations against an enemy, but of a municipal prerogative over British subjects. British jurisdiction is thus extended to neutral vessels in a situation where no laws can operate but the law of nations and the laws of the country to which the vessels belong, and a self-redress is assumed which, if British subjects were wrongfully detained and alone concerned, is that substitution of force for a resort to the responsible sovereign which falls within the definition of war . . .

The practice, hence, is so far from affecting British subjects alone that, under the pretext of searching for these, thousands of American citizens, under the safeguard of public law and of their national flag, have been torn from their country and from everything dear to them; have been dragged on board ships of war of a foreign nation and exposed, under the severities of their discipline, to be exiled to the most distant and deadly climes, to risk their lives in the battles of their oppressors, and to be the melancholy instruments of taking away those of their own brethren.

Against this crying enormity, which Great Britain would be so prompt to avenge if committed against herself, the United States have in vain exhausted remonstrances and expostulations, and that no proof might be wanting of their conciliatory dispositions, and no pretext left for a continuance of the practice, the British Government was formally assured of the readiness of the United States to enter into arrangements such as could not be rejected if the recovery of British subjects were the real and the sole object. The communication passed without effect.

British cruisers have been in the practice also of violating the rights and the peace of our coasts. They hover over and harass our entering and departing commerce. To the most insulting pretensions they have added the most lawless proceedings in our very harbors, and have wantonly spilt American blood within the sanctuary of our territorial jurisdiction. The principles and rules enforced by that nation, when a neutral nation, against armed vessels of belligerents hovering near her coasts and disturbing her commerce are well known. When called on, nevertheless, by the United States to punish the greater offenses committed by her own vessels, her Government has bestowed on their commanders additional marks of honor and confidence.

Under pretended blockades, without the presence of an adequate force and sometimes without the practicability of applying one, our commerce has been plundered in every sea, the great staples of our country have been cut off from their legitimate markets, and a destructive blow aimed at our agricultural and maritime interests. In aggravation of these predatory measures they have been considered as in force from the dates of their notification, a retrospective effect being thus added, as has been done in other important cases, to the unlawfulness of the course pursued. And to render the outrage the more signal these mock blockades have been reiterated and enforced in the face of official communications from the British Government declaring as the true definition of a legal blockade "that particular ports must be actually invested and previous warning given to vessels bound to them not to enter."

Not content with these occasional expedients for laying waste our neutral trade, the cabinet of Britain resorted at length to the sweeping system of blockades, under the name of orders in council, which has been molded and managed as might best suit its political views, its commercial jealousies, or the avidity of British cruisers . . .

Abandoning still more all respect for the neutral rights of the United States and for its own consistency, the British Government now demands as prerequisites to a repeal of its orders as they relate to the United States that a formality should be observed in the repeal, of the French decrees nowise necessary to their termination nor exemplified by British usage, and that the French repeal besides including that portion of the decrees which operates within a territorial jurisdiction, as well as that which operates on the high seas, against the commerce of the United States should not be a single and special repeal in relation to the United States, but should be extended to whatever other neutral nations unconnected with them may be affected by those decrees. And as an additional insult, they are called on for a formal disavowal of conditions and pretensions advanced by the French Government for which the United States are so far from having made themselves responsible that, in official explanations which have been published to the world, and in a correspondence of the American minister at London with the British minister for foreign affairs such a responsibility was explicitly and emphatically disclaimed.

It has become, indeed, sufficiently certain that the commerce of the United States is to be sacrificed, not as interfering with the belligerent rights of Great Britain; not as supplying the wants of her enemies, which she herself supplies; but as interfering with the monopoly which she covets for her own commerce and navigation. She carries on a war against the lawful commerce of a friend that she may the better carry on a commerce with an enemy—a commerce polluted by the forgeries and perjuries which are for the most part the only passports by which it can succeed . . .

In reviewing the conduct of Great Britain toward the United States our attention is necessarily drawn to the warfare just renewed by the savages on one of our extensive frontiers—a warfare which is known to spare neither age nor sex and to be distinguished by features peculiarly shocking to humanity. It is difficult to account for the activity and combinations which have for some time been developing themselves among tribes in constant intercourse with British traders and garrisons without connecting their hostility with that influence and without recollecting the authenticated examples of such interpositions heretofore furnished by the officers and agents of that Government.

Such is the spectacle of injuries and indignities which have been heaped on our country, and such the crisis which its unexampled forbearance and conciliatory efforts have not been able to avert. It might at least have been expected that an enlightened nation, if less urged by moral obligations or invited by friendly dispositions on the part of the United States, would have found its true interest alone a sufficient motive to respect their rights and their tranquillity on the high seas; that an enlarged policy would have favored that free and general circulation of commerce in which the British nation is at all times interested, and which in times of war is the best alleviation of its calamities to herself as well as to other belligerents; and more especially that the British cabinet would not, for the sake of a precarious and surreptitious intercourse with hostile markets, have persevered in a course of measures which necessarily put at hazard the invaluable market of a great and growing country, disposed to cultivate the mutual advantages of an active commerce.

Other counsels have prevailed. Our moderation and conciliation have had no other effect than to encourage perseverance and to enlarge pretensions. We behold our seafaring citizens still the daily victims of lawless violence, committed on the great common and highway of nations, even within sight of the country which owes them protection. We behold our vessels, freighted with the products of our soil and industry, or returning with the honest proceeds of them, wrested from their lawful destinations, confiscated by prize courts no longer the organs of public law but the instruments of arbitrary edicts, and their unfortunate crews dispersed and lost, or forced or inveigled in British ports into British fleets, whilst arguments are employed in support of these aggressions which have no foundation but in a principle equally supporting a claim to regulate our external commerce in all cases whatsoever.

We behold, in fine, on the side of Great Britain, a state of war against the United States, and on the side of the United States a state of peace toward Great Britain.

Whether the United States shall continue passive under these progressive usurpations and these accumulating wrongs, or, opposing force to force in defense of their national rights, shall commit a just cause into the hands of the Almighty Disposer of Events, avoiding all connections which might entangle it in the contest or views of other powers, and preserving a constant readiness to concur in an honorable re-establishment of peace and friendship, is a solemn question which the Constitution wisely confides to the legislative department of the Government. In recommending it to their early deliberations I am happy in the assurance that the decision will be worthy the enlightened and patriotic councils of a virtuous, a free, and a powerful nation . . .

Treaty of Ghent (1814)

Landmark Documents in American History. CD-ROM (New York: Facts On File, 1998)

December 24, 1814

Treaty of Peace and Amity

Between his Britannic Majesty and the United States of America.

His Britannic Majesty and the United States of America, desirous of terminating the war which has unhappily subsisted between the two countries, and of restoring, upon principles of perfect reciprocity, peace, friendship, and good understanding between them, have, for that purpose, appointed their respective plenipotentiaries, that is to say: His Britannic Majesty, on his part, has appointed the right honorable James Lord Gambier, late admiral of the white, now admiral of the red squadron of His Majesty's fleet, Henry Goulburn Esquire, a member of the Imperial Parliament, and under Secretary of State, and William Adams, Esquire, Doctor of Civil Laws:—And the President of the United States, by and with the advice and consent of the Senate thereof, has appointed John Quincy Adams, James A. Bayard, Henry Clay, Jonathan Russell and Albert Gallatin, citizens of the United States, who, after a reciprocal communication of their respective full powers, have agreed upon the following articles:

Article the First

There shall be a firm and universal peace between His Britannic Majesty and the United States, and between their respective countries, territories, cities, towns, and people, of every degree, without exception of places or persons. All hostilities, both by sea and land, shall cease as soon as this treaty shall have been ratified by both parties, as hereinafter mentioned. All territory, places, and possessions whatsoever, taken by either party from the other, during the war, or which may be taken after the signing of this treaty, excepting only the islands hereinafter mentioned, shall be restored without delay, and without causing any destruction, or carrying away any of the artillery or other public property originally captured in the said forts or places, and which shall remain therein upon the exchange of the ratifications of this treaty, or any slaves or other private property. And all archives, records, deeds, and papers, either of a public nature, or belonging to private persons, which, in the course of the war, may have fallen into the hands of the officers of either party, shall be, as far as may be practicable, forthwith restored and delivered to the proper authorities and persons to whom they respectively belong. Such of the islands in the Bay of Passama quoddy as are claimed by both parties, shall remain in the possession of the party in whose occupation they may be at the time of the exchange of the ratifications of this treaty, until the decision respecting the title to the said islands shall have been made in conformity with the fourth article of this treaty. No disposition made by this treaty, as to such possession of the islands and territories claimed by both parties, shall, in any manner whatever, be construed to affect the right of either.

Article the Second

Immediately after the ratifications of this treaty by both parties, as hereinafter mentioned, orders shall be sent to the armies, squadrons, officers, subjects and citizens, of the two powers, to cease from all hostilities. And to prevent all causes of complaint which might arise on account of the prizes which may be taken at sea after the said ratifications of this treaty, it is reciprocally agreed, that all vessels and effects which may be taken after the space of twelve days from the said ratifications, upon all parts of the coast of North America, from the latitude of twenty-three degrees north, to the latitude of fifty degrees north, and as far eastward in the Atlantic ocean, as the thirty-sixth degree of west longitude from the meridian of Greenwich, shall be restored on each side: That the time shall be thirty days in all other parts of the Atlantic ocean, north of the equinoctial line or equator, and the same time for the British and Irish channels, for the Gulf of Mexico and all parts of the West Indies: Forty days for the North seas, for the Baltic, and for all parts of the Mediterranean: Sixty days for the Atlantic ocean south of the equator, as far as the latitude of the Cape of Good Hope: Ninety days for every other part of the world south of the equator: And one hundred and twenty days for all other parts of the world, without exception.

Article the Third

All prisoners of war taken on either side, as well by land as by sea, shall be restored as soon as practicable after the ratifications of this treaty, as hereinafter mentioned, on their paying the debts which they may have contracted during their captivity. The two contracting parties respectively engage to discharge, in specie, the advances which may have been made by the other for the sustenance and maintenance of such prisoners.

Article the Fourth

Whereas it was stipulated by the second article in the treaty of peace, of one thousand seven hundred and eighty-three, between His Britannic Majesty and the United States of America, that the boundary of the United States should comprehend all islands within twenty leagues of any part of the shores of the United States, and lying between lines to be drawn due east from the points where the aforesaid boundaries, between Nova Scotia, on the one part, and East Florida on the other, shall respectively touch the bay of Fundy, and the Atlantic ocean, excepting such islands as now are, or heretofore have been, within the limits of Nova Scotia; and whereas the several islands in the Bay of Passamaquoddy, which is part of the Bay of Fundy, and the island of Grand Menan in the said Bay of Fundy, are claimed by the United States as being comprehended within their aforesaid boundaries, which said islands are claimed as belonging to his Britannic Majesty, as having been at the time of, and previous to, the aforesaid treaty of one thousand seven hundred and eighty-three, within the limits of the province of Nova Scotia: In order, therefore, finally to decide upon these claims, it is agreed that they shall be referred to two commissioners to be appointed in the following manner, viz: one commissioner shall be appointed by his Britannic Majesty, and one by the president of the United States, by and with the advice and consent of the Senate thereof, and the said two commissioners so appointed shall be sworn impartially to examine and decide upon the said claims according to such evidence as shall be laid before them on the part of his Britannic Majesty and of the United States respectively. The said commissioners shall meet at Saint Andrews, in the province of New Brunswick, and shall have power to adjourn to such other place or places as they shall think fit. The said commissioners shall, by a declaration or report under their hands and seals, decide to which of the two contracting parties the several islands aforesaid do respectively belong, in conformity with the true intent of the said treaty of peace of one thousand seven hundred and eighty-three. And if the said commissioners shall agree in their decision, both parties shall consider such decision as final and conclusive. It is further agreed, that in the event of the two commissioners differing upon all or any of the matters so referred to them, or in the event of both or either of the said commissioners refusing, or declining, or wilfully omitting, to act as such, they shall make jointly or separately, a report or reports, as well to the Government of his Britannic majesty as to that of the United States, stating in detail the points on which they differ, and the grounds upon which their respective opinions have been formed, or the grounds upon which they, or either of them, have so refused, declined, or omitted to act. And his Britannic majesty, and the government of the United States, hereby agree to refer the report or reports of the said commissioners, to some friendly sovereign or state, to be then named for that purpose, and who shall be requested to decide on the differences which may be stated in the said report or reports, or upon the report of one commissioner, together with the grounds upon which the other commissioner shall have refused, declined, or omitted to act, as the case may be. And if the commissioner so refusing, declining, or omitting to act, shall also wilfully omit to state the grounds upon which he has so done, in such manner that the said statement may be referred to such friendly sovereign or state, together with the report of such other commissioner, then such sovereign or state shall decide ex parte upon the said report alone. And his Britannic Majesty and the government of the United States engage to consider the decision of such friendly sovereign or state to be final and conclusive on all the matters so referred.

Article the Fifth

Whereas neither that point of the high lands lying due north from the source of the river St. Croix, and designated in the former treaty of peace between the two powers as the northwest angle of Nova- Scotia, nor the northwesternmost head of Connecticut river, has yet been ascertained; and whereas that part of the boundary line between the dominions of the two powers which extends from the source of the river St. Croix directly north to the abovementioned northwest angle of Nova-Scotia, thence along the said highlands which divide those rivers that empty themselves into the river St. Lawrence from those which fall into the Atlantic ocean to the northwesternmost head of Connecticut river, thence down along the middle of that river to the forty-fifth degree of north latitude; thence by a line due west on said latitude until it strikes the river Iroquois or Cataraguy, has not yet been surveyed: it is agreed, that for these several purposes two commissioners shall be appointed, sworn, and authorized to act exactly in the manner directed with respect to those mentioned in the next preceding article, unless otherwise specified in the present article. The said commissioners shall meet at St. Andrews, in the province of New-Brunswick, and shall have power to adjourn to such other place or places as they shall think fit. The said commissioners shall have power to ascertain and determine the points abovementioned, in conformity with the provisions of the said treaty of peace of one thousand seven hundred and eighty three, and shall cause the boundary aforesaid, from the source of the river St. Croix to the river Iroquois or Cataraguy, to be surveyed and marked according to the said provisions. The said commissioners shall make a map of the said boundary, and annex to it a declaration under their hands and seals, certifying it to be the true map of the said boundary, and particularizing the latitude and longitude of the northwest angle of Nova-Scotia, of the northwesternmost head of Connecticut river, and of such other points of the said boundary as they may deem proper. And both parties agree to consider such map and declaration as finally and conclusively fixing the said boundary. And in the event of the said two commissioners differing, or both, or either, of them, refusing, declining, or wilfully omitting to act, such reports, declarations, or statements, shall be made by them, or either of them, and such reference to a friendly sovereign or state, shall be made, in all respects, as in the latter part of the fourth article is contained, and in as full a manner as if the same was herein repeated.

Article the Sixth

Whereas, by the former treaty of peace that portion of the boundary of the United States from the point where the forty-fifth degree of north latitude strikes the river Iroquois or Cataraguy to the lake Superior, was declared to be "along the middle of said river into lake Ontario, through the middle of said lake until it strikes the communication by water between that lake and lake Erie, thence along the middle of said communication into lake Erie, through the middle of said lake until it arrives at the water communication into the lake Huron, thence through the middle of said lake to the water communication between that lake and lake Superior." And whereas doubts have arisen what was the middle of the said river, lakes and water communications, and whether certain islands lying in the same were within the dominions of his Britannic majesty or of the United States: In order, therefore, finally to decide these doubts, they shall be referred to two commissioners, to be appointed, sworn, and authorized to act exactly in the manner directed with respect to those mentioned in the next preceding article, unless otherwise specified in this present article. The said commissioners shall meet, in the first instance, at Albany, in the state of New-York, and shall have power to adjourn to such other place or places as they shall think fit: The said commissioner shall, by a report or declaration, under their hands and seals, designate the boundary through the said river, lakes, and water communications, and decide to which of the two contracting parties the several islands lying within the said rivers, lakes, and water communications, do respectively belong, in conformity with the true intent of the said treaty of one thousand seven hundred and eighty-three. And both parties agree to consider such designation and decision as final and conclusive. And in the event of the said two commissioners differing, or both, or either of them, refusing, declining, or wilfully omitting to act, such reports, declarations or statements, shall be made by them, or either of them, and such reference to a friendly sovereign or state shall be made in all respects as in the latter part of the fourth article is contained, and in as full a manner as if the same was herein repeated.

Article the Seventh

It is further agreed that the said two last-mentioned commissioners, after they shall have executed the duties assigned to them in the preceding article, shall be, and they are hereby authorized, upon their oaths impartially to fix and determine, according to the true intent of the said treaty of peace, of one thousand seven hundred and eighty-three, that part of the boundary between the dominions of the two powers, which extends from the water communication between lake Huron, and lake Superior, to the most north-western point of the lake of the Woods, to decide to which of the two parties the several islands lying in the lakes, water communications, and rivers, forming the said boundary, do respectively belong, in conformity with the true intent of the said treaty of peace, of one thousand seven hundred and eighty-three; and to cause such parts of the said boundary, as require it, to be surveyed and marked. The said commissioners shall, by a report or declaration under their hands and seals, designate the boundary aforesaid, state their decision on the points thus referred to them, and particularize the latitude and longitude of the most north-western point of the lake of the Woods, and of such other parts of the said boundary as they may deem proper. And both parties agree to consider such designation and decision as final and conclusive. And, in the event of the said two commissioners differing, or both, or either of them refusing, declining, or wilfully omitting to act, such reports, declarations, or statements, shall be made by them, or either of them and such reference to a friendly sovereign or state, shall be made in all respects, as in the latter part of the fourth article is contained, and in as full a manner as if the same was herein repeated.

Article the Eighth

The several boards of two commissioners mentioned in the four preceding articles, shall respectively have power to appoint a secretary, and to employ such surveyors or other persons as they shall judge necessary. Duplicates of all their respective reports, declarations, statements and decisions, and of their accounts, and of the journal of their proceedings, shall be delivered by them to the agents of his Britannic majesty, and to the agents of the United States, who may be respectively appointed and authorized to manage the business on behalf of their respective governments. The said commissioners shall be respectively paid in such manner as shall be agreed between the two contracting parties, such agreement being to be settled at the time of the exchange of the ratifications of this treaty. And all other expenses attending the said commissions shall be defrayed equally by the two parties. And in the case of death, sickness, resignation, or necessary absence, the place of every such commissioner, respectively, shall be supplied in the same manner as such commissioner was first appointed, and the new commissioner shall take the same oath or affirmation, and do the same duties. It is further agreed between the two contracting parties, that in case any of the islands mentioned in any of the preceding articles, which were in the possession of one of the parties prior to the commencement of the present war between the two countries, should, by the decision of any of the boards of commissioners aforesaid, or of the sovereign or state so referred to, as in the four next preceding articles contained, fall within the dominions of the other party, all grants of land made previous to the commencement of the war, by the party having had such possession, shall be as valid as if such island or islands had, by such decision or decisions, been adjudged to be within the dominions of the party having had such possession.

Article the Ninth

The United States of America engage to put an end, immediately after the ratification of the present treaty, to hostilities with all the tribes or nations of Indians with whom they may be at war at the time of such ratification; and forthwith to restore to such tribes or nations, respectively, all the possessions, rights, and privileges, which they may have enjoyed or been entitled to in one thousand eight hundred and eleven, previous to such hostilities: *Provided always,* That such tribes or nations shall agree to desist from all hostilities, against the United States of America, their citizens and subjects, upon the ratification of the present treaty being notified to such tribes or nations, and shall so desist accordingly. And his Britannic majesty engages, on his part, to put an end immediately after the ratification of the present treaty, to hostilities with all the tribes or nations of Indians with whom he may be at war at the time of such ratification, and forthwith to restore to such tribes or nations, respectively, all the possessions, rights, and privileges, which they may have enjoyed or been entitled to, in one thousand eight hundred and eleven, previous to such hostilities:

Provided always, That such tribes or nations shall agree to desist from all hostilities against his Britannic majesty, and his subjects, upon the ratification of the present treaty being notified to such tribes or nations, and shall so desist accordingly.

Article the Tenth

Whereas the traffic in slaves is irreconcileable with the principles of humanity and justice, and whereas both his Majesty and the United States are desirous of continuing their efforts to promote its entire abolition, it is hereby agreed that both the contracting parties shall use their best endeavors to accomplish so desirable an object.

Article the Eleventh

This treaty, when the same shall have been ratified on both sides, without alteration by either of the contracting parties, and the ratifications mutually exchanged, shall be binding on both parties, and the ratifications shall be exchanged at Washington, in the space of four months from this day, or sooner, if practicable. In faith whereof, we, the respective plenipotentiaries, have signed this treaty, and have thereunto affixed our seals.

Done, in triplicate, at Ghent, the twenty-fourth day of December, one thousand eight hundred and fourteen.

Gambier, (L. S.) Henry Goulburn, (L. S.) William Adams, (L. S.) John Quincy Adams, (L. S.) J. A. Bayard, (L. S.) H. Clay, (L. S.) Jona. Russell, (L. S.) Albert Gallatin. (L. S.)

Adams-Onís Treaty (1819)

Landmark Documents in American History.
CD-ROM (New York: Facts On File, 1998)

Washington, D.C.
February 22, 1819

Treaty of Amity, Settlement, and Limits

Between the United States of America and his Catholic Majesty.

The United States of America and his Catholic Majesty, desiring to consolidate, on a permanent basis, the friendship and good correspondence which happily prevails between the two parties, have determined to settle and terminate all their differences and pretensions, by a Treaty, which shall designate, with precision, the limits of their respective bordering territories in North America.

With this intention, the President of the United States has furnished with their full powers John Quincy Adams, Secretary of State of the said United States; and his Catholic Majesty has appointed the most excellent Lord Don Luis De Onís, Gonzales, Lopez y Vara, Lord of the town of Rayaces, perpetual Regidor of the Corporation of the City of Salamanca, Knight Grand-Cross of the Royal American Order of Isabella the Catholic, decorated with the Lys of La Vendee, Knight Pensioner of the Royal and distinguished Spanish Order of Charles the Third, Member of the Supreme Assembly of the said Royal Order, of the Council of his Catholic Majesty; his Secretary, with Exercise of Decrees, and his Envoy Extraordinary and Minister Plenipotentiary near the United States of America.

And the said Plenipotentiaries, after having exchanged their powers, have agreed upon and concluded the following articles:

Article 1
There shall be a firm and inviolable peace and sincere friendship between the United States and their citizens, and his Catholic Majesty, his successors and subjects, without exception of persons or places.

Article 2
His Catholic Majesty cedes to the United States, in full property and sovereignty, all the territories which belong to him, situated to the eastward of the Mississippi, known by the name of East and West Florida. The adjacent islands dependent on said provinces, all public lots and squares, vacant lands, public edifices, fortifications, barracks, and other buildings, which are not private property, archives and documents, which relate directly to the property and sovereignty of said provinces, are included in this article. The said archives and documents shall be left in possession of the commissaries or officers of the United States, duly authorized to receive them . . .

Article 5
The inhabitants of the ceded territories shall be secured in the free exercise of their religion, without any restriction; and all those who may desire to remove to the Spanish dominions, shall be permitted to sell or export their effects, at any time whatever, without being subject, in either case, to duties.

Article 6
The inhabitants of the territories which his Catholic Majesty cedes to the United States, by this Treaty, shall be incorporated in the Union of the United States, as soon as may be consistent with the principles of the Federal Constitution, and admitted to the enjoyment of all the privileges, rights, and immunities, of the citizens of the United States. . .

Article 11
The United States, exonerating Spain from all demands in future, on account of the claims of their citizens to which the renunciations herein contained extend, and considering them entirely cancelled, undertake to make satisfaction for the same, to an amount not exceeding five millions of dollars. To ascertain the full amount the validity of those claims, a Commission, to consist of three Commissioners, citizens of the United States, shall be appointed by the President, by and with the advice and consent of the Senate . . .

Article 15
The United States, to give to his Catholic Majesty a proof of their desire to cement the relations of amity subsisting between the two nations, and to favour the commerce of the subjects of his Catholic Majesty, agree that Spanish vessels, coming laden only with productions of Spanish growth or manufactures, directly from the ports of Spain, or of her colonies, shall be admitted, for the term of twelve years, to the ports of Pensacola and St. Augustine, in the Floridas, without paying other or higher duties on their cargoes, or of tonnage, than will be paid by the vessels of the United States. During the said term, no other nation shall enjoy the same privileges within the ceded territories. The twelve years shall commence three months after the exchange of the ratifications of this Treaty.

Article 16
The present Treaty shall be ratified in due form, by the contracting parties, and the ratifications shall be exchanged in six months from this time, or sooner, if possible. In witness whereof, we, the under written Plenipotentiaries of the United States of America and of his Catholic Majesty, have signed, by virtue of our powers, the present Treaty of Amity, Settlement, and Limits, and have thereunto affixed our seals, respectively.

Done at Washington, this twenty-second day of February, one thousand eight hundred and nineteen.
John Quincy Adams, (L. S.) Luis De Onís, (L. S.)

The Missouri Compromise (1819–1821)

Tallmadge Amendment (1819)

Henry Steele Commager and Milton Cantor, eds.
Documents of American History, 10th ed.
(Englewood Cliffs, N.J.: Prentice Hall, 1988), p. 225

And provided also, That the further introduction of slavery or involuntary servitude be prohibited, except for the punishment of crimes, whereof the party shall be duly convicted; and that all children of slaves, born within the said state, after the admission thereof into the Union, shall be free but may be held to service until the age of twenty-five years.

Taylor Amendment (1820)

Henry Steele Commager and Milton Cantor, eds.
Documents of American History, 10th ed.
(Englewood Cliffs, N.J.: Prentice Hall, 1988), p. 225

The reading of the bill proceeded as far as the fourth section; when Mr. Taylor, of New York, proposed to amend the bill by incorporating in that section the following provision: Section 4, line 25, insert the following after the word "States"; "And shall ordain and establish, that there shall be neither slavery nor involuntary servitude in the said State, otherwise than in the punishment of crimes, whereof the party shall have been duly convicted: Provided, always, That any person escaping into the same, from whom labor or service is lawfully claimed in any other State, such fugitive may be lawfully reclaimed, and conveyed to the person claiming his or her labor or service as aforesaid: *And provided, also*, That the said provision shall not be construed to alter the condition or civil rights of any person now held to service or labor in the said Territory."

Thomas Amendment (1820)

Henry Steele Commager and Milton Cantor, eds. *Documents of American History*, 10th ed. (Englewood Cliffs, N.J.: Prentice Hall, 1988), p. 225

And be it further enacted, That, in all that territory ceded by France to the United States, under the name of Louisiana, which lies north of thirty-six degrees and thirty minutes north latitude, excepting only such part thereof as is included within the limits of the State contemplated by this act, slavery and involuntary servitude, otherwise than in the punishment of crimes whereof the party shall have been duly convicted, shall be and is hereby forever prohibited. *Provided always,* That any person escaping into the same, from whom labor or service is lawfully claimed in any State or Territory of the United States, such fugitive may be lawfully reclaimed, and conveyed to the person claiming his or her labor or service, as aforesaid.

Missouri Enabling Act (1820)

Henry Steele Commager and Milton Cantor, eds. *Documents of American History*, 10th ed. (Englewood Cliffs, N.J.: Prentice Hall, 1988), p. 226

An Act

To authorize the people of the Missouri territory to form a constitution and state government, and for the admission of such state into the Union on an equal footing with the original states, and to prohibit slavery in certain territories.

Be it enacted That the inhabitants of that portion of the Missouri territory included within the boundaries hereinafter designated, be, and they are hereby, authorized to form for themselves a constitution and state government, and to assume such name as they shall deem proper; and the said state, when formed, shall be admitted into the Union, upon an equal footing with the original states, in all respects whatsoever.

Sec. 2. That the said state shall consist of all the territory included within the following boundaries, to wit: Beginning in the middle of the Mississippi river, on the parallel of thirty-six degrees of north latitude; thence west, along that parallel of latitude, to the St. Francois river; thence up, and following the course of that river, in the middle of the main channel thereof, to the parallel of latitude of thirty-six degrees and thirty minutes; thence west, along the same, to a point where the said parallel is intersected by a meridian line passing through the middle of the mouth of the Kansas river, where the same empties into the Missouri river, thence, from the point aforesaid north, along the said meridian line, to the intersection of the parallel of latitude which passes through the rapids of the river Des Moines, making the said line to correspond with the Indian boundary line; thence east, from the point of intersection last aforesaid, along the said parallel of latitude, to the middle of the channel of the main fork of the said river Des Moines; thence down and along the middle of the main channel of the said river Des Moines, to the mouth of the same, where it empties into the Mississippi river; thence, due east, to the middle of the main channel of the Mississippi river; thence down, and following the course of the Mississippi river, in the middle of the main channel thereof, to the place of beginning: . . .

Sec. 3. That all free white male citizens of the United States, who shall have arrived at the age of twenty-one years, and have resided in said territory three months previous to the day of election, and all other persons qualified to vote for representatives to the general assembly of the said territory, shall be qualified to be elected, and they are hereby qualified and authorized to vote, and choose representatives to form a convention: . . .

Sec. 8. That in all that territory ceded by France to the United States, under the name of Louisiana, which lies north of thirty-six degrees and thirty minutes north latitude, not included within the limits of the state, contemplated by this act, slavery and involuntary servitude, otherwise than in the punishment of crimes, whereof the parties shall have been duly convicted, shall be, and is hereby, forever prohibited: *Provided always,* That any person escaping into the same, from whom labour or service is lawfully claimed, in any state or territory of the United States, such fugitive may be lawfully reclaimed and conveyed to the person claiming his or her labour or service as aforesaid.

Constitution of Missouri (1820)

Henry Steele Commager and Milton Cantor, eds. *Documents of American History*, 10th ed. (Englewood Cliffs, N.J.: Prentice Hall, 1988), pp. 226–227

Sec. 26. The general assembly shall not have power to pass laws—

1. For the emancipation of slaves without the consent of their owners; or without paying them, before such emancipation, a full equivalent for such slaves so emancipated; and,
2. To prevent *bona-fide* immigrants to this State, or actual settlers therein, from bringing from any of the

United States, or from any of their Territories, such persons as may there be deemed to be slaves, so long as any persons of the same description are allowed to be held as slaves by the laws of this State.

They shall have power to pass laws—

1. To prevent *bona-fide* immigrants to this State of any slaves who may have committed any high crime in any other State or Territory;

2. To prohibit the introduction of any slave for the purpose of speculation, or as an article of trade or merchandise;

3. To prohibit the introduction of any slave, or the offspring of any slave, who heretofore may have been, or who hereafter may be, imported from any foreign country into the United States, or any Territory thereof, in contravention of any existing statute of the United States; and,

4. To permit the owners of slaves to emancipate them, saving the right of creditors, where the person so emancipating will give security that the slave so emancipated shall not become a public charge.

It shall be their duty, as soon as may be, to pass such laws as may be necessary—

1. To prevent free negroes end [and] mulattoes from coming to and settling in this State, under any pretext whatsoever; and,

2. To oblige the owners of slaves to treat them with humanity, and to abstain from all injuries to them extending to life or limb.

Resolution for the Admission of Missouri (1821)

Henry Steele Commager and Milton Cantor, eds. *Documents of American History*, 10th ed. (Englewood Cliffs, N.J.: Prentice Hall, 1988), p. 227

Resolution *providing for the admission of the State of Missouri into the Union, on a certain condition.*

Resolved, That Missouri shall be admitted into this union on an equal footing with the original states, in all respects whatever, upon the fundamental condition, that the fourth clause of the twenty-sixth section of the third article of the constitution submitted on the part of said state to Congress, shall never be construed to authorize the passage of any law, and that no law shall be passed in conformity thereto, by which any citizen, of either of the states in this Union, shall be excluded from the enjoyment of any of the privileges and immunities to which such citizen is entitled under the constitution of the United States: *Provided,* That the legislature of the said state, by a solemn public act, shall declare the assent of the said state to the said fundamental condition, and shall transmit to the President of the United States, on or before the fourth Monday in November next, an authentic copy of the said act; upon the receipt whereof, the President, by proclamation, shall announce the fact; whereupon, and without any further proceeding on the part of Congress, the admission of the said state into this Union shall be considered as complete.

Monroe Doctrine (1823)

James D. Richardson, ed. *A Compilation of Messages and Papers of the Presidents, 1789–1897,* Vol. 2 (Washington, D.C.: 1998), pp. 207–220

Washington
December 2, 1823.

Fellow-Citizens of the Senate and House of Representatives:

Many important subjects will claim your attention during the present session, of which I shall endeavor to give, in aid of your deliberations, a just idea in this communication. I undertake this duty with diffidence, from the vast extent of the interests on which I have to treat and of their great importance to every portion of our Union. I enter on it with zeal from a thorough conviction that there never was a period since the establishment of our Revolution when, regarding the condition of the civilized world and its bearing on us, there was greater necessity for devotion in the public servants to their respective duties, or for virtue, patriotism, and union in our constituents.

Meeting in you a new Congress, I deem it proper to present this view of public affairs in greater detail than might otherwise be necessary. I do it, however, with peculiar satisfaction, from a knowledge that in this respect I shall comply more fully with the sound principles of our Government. The people being with us exclusively the sovereign, it is indispensable that full information be laid before them on all important subjects, to enable them to exercise that high power with complete effect. If kept in the dark, they must be incompetent to it. We are all liable to error, and those who are engaged in the management of public affairs are more subject to excitement and to be led astray by their particular interests and passions than the great body of our constituents, who, living at home in the pursuit of their ordinary avocations, are calm but deeply interested spectators of events and of the conduct of those who are parties to them. To the people every department of the Government and every individual in each are responsible, and the more full their information the better they can judge of the wisdom of the policy pursued and of the conduct of each in regard to it. From their dispassionate judgment much aid may always be obtained, while their approbation will form the greatest incentive and most gratifying reward for virtuous actions, and the dread of their censure the best security against the abuse of their confidence. Their interests in all vital questions are the same, and the bond, by sentiment as well as by interest, will be proportionably strengthened as they are better informed of the real state of public affairs, especially in difficult conjunctures. It is by such knowledge that local prejudices and jealousies are surmounted, and that a national policy, extending its fostering care and protection to all the great interests of our Union, is formed and steadily adhered to.

A precise knowledge of our relations with foreign powers as respects our negotiations and transactions with each is thought to be particularly necessary. Equally necessary is it that we should form a just estimate of our resources, revenue, and progress in every kind of improvement connected with the national prosperity and public defense. It is by rendering justice to other nations that we may expect it from them. It is by our ability to resent injuries and redress wrongs that we may avoid them.

The commissioners under the fifth article of the treaty of Ghent, having disagreed in their opinions respecting that portion of the boundary between the Territories of the United States and of Great Britain the establishment of which had been submitted to them, have made their respective reports in compliance with that article, that the same might be referred to the decision of a friendly power. It being manifest, however, that it would be difficult, if not impossible, for any power to perform that office without great delay and much inconvenience to itself, a proposal has been made by this Government, and acceded to by that of Great Britain, to endeavor to establish that boundary by amicable negotiation. It appearing from long experience that no satisfactory arrangement could be formed of the commercial intercourse between the United States and the British colonies in this hemisphere by legislative acts while each party pursued its own course without agreement or concert with the other, a proposal has been made to the British Government to regulate this commerce by treaty, as it has been to arrange in like manner the just claim of the citizens of the United States inhabiting the States and Territories bordering on the lakes and rivers which empty into the St. Lawrence to the navigation of that river to the ocean. For these and other objects of high importance to the interests of both parties a negotiation has been opened with the British Government which it is hoped will have a satisfactory result.

The commissioners under the sixth and seventh articles of the treaty of Ghent having successfully closed their labors in relation to the sixth, have proceeded to the discharge of those relating to the seventh. Their progress in the extensive survey required for the performance of their duties justifies the presumption that it will be completed in the ensuing year.

The negotiation which had been long depending with the French Government on several important subjects, and particularly for a just indemnity for losses sustained in the late wars by the citizens of the United States under unjustifiable seizures and confiscations of their property, has not as yet had the desired effect. As this claim rests on the same principle with others which have been admitted by the French Government, it is not perceived on what just ground it can be rejected. A minister will be immediately appointed to proceed to France and resume the negotiation on this and other subjects which may arise between the two nations.

At the proposal of the Russian Imperial Government, made through the minister of the Emperor residing here, a full power and instructions have been transmitted to the minister of the United States at St. Petersburg to arrange by amicable negotiation the respective rights and interest of the two nations on the northwest coast of this continent. A similar proposal had been made by His Imperial Majesty to the Government of Great Britain, which has likewise been acceded to. The Government of the United States has been desirous by this friendly proceeding of manifesting the great value which they have invariably attached to the friendship of the Emperor and their solicitude to cultivate the best understanding with his Government. In the discussions to which this interest has given rise and in the arrangements by which they may terminate the occasion has been judged proper for asserting, as a principle in which the rights and interests of the United States are involved, that the American continents, by the free and independent condition which they have assumed and maintain, are henceforth not to be considered as subjects for future colonization by any European powers. . . .

It was stated at the commencement of the last session that a great effort was then making in Spain and Portugal to improve the condition of the people of those countries, and that it appeared to be conducted with extraordinary moderation. It need scarcely be remarked that the result has been so far very different from what was then anticipated. Of events in that quarter of the globe, with which we have so much intercourse and from which we derive our origin, we have always been anxious and interested spectators. The citizens of the United States cherish sentiments the most friendly in favor of the liberty and happiness of their fellowmen on that side of the Atlantic. In the wars of the European powers in matters relating to themselves we have never taken any part, nor does it comport with our policy so to do. It is only when our rights are invaded or seriously menaced that we resent injuries or make preparation for our defense. With the movements in this hemisphere we are of necessity more immediately connected, and by causes which must be obvious to all enlightened and impartial observers. The political system of the allied powers is essentially different in this respect from that of America. This difference proceeds from that which exists in their respective Governments; and to the defense of our own, which has been achieved by the loss of so much blood and treasure, and matured by the wisdom of their most enlightened citizens, and under which we have enjoyed unexampled felicity, this whole nation is devoted. We owe it, therefore, to candor and to the amicable relations existing between the United States and those powers to declare that we should consider any attempt on their part to extend their system to any portion of this hemisphere as dangerous to our peace and safety. With the existing colonies or dependencies of any European power we have not interfered and shall not interfere. But with the Governments who have declared their independence and maintained it, and whose independence we have, on great consideration and on just principles, acknowledged, we could not view any interposition for the purpose of oppressing them, or controlling in any other manner their destiny, by any European power in any other light than as the manifestation of an unfriendly disposition toward the United States. In the war between those new Governments and Spain we declared our neutrality at the time of their recognition, and to this we have adhered, and shall continue to adhere, provided no change shall occur which, in the judgment of the competent authorities of this Government, shall make a corresponding change on the part of the United States indispensable to their security.

The late events in Spain and Portugal shew that Europe is still unsettled. Of this important fact no stronger proof can be adduced than that the allied powers should have thought it proper, on any principle satisfactory to themselves, to have interposed by force in the internal concerns of Spain. To what extent such interposition may be carried, on the same principle, is a question in which all independent powers whose governments differ from theirs are interested, even those most remote, and surely none more so than the United States. Our policy in regard to Europe, which was adopted at an early stage of the wars which, have so long agitated that quarter of the globe, nevertheless remains the same, which is, not to interfere in the internal concerns of any of its powers; to consider the government *de facto* as the legitimate government for us; to cultivate friendly relations with it, and to preserve those relations by a frank, firm, and manly policy, meeting in all instances the just claims of every power, submitting to injuries from none. But in regard to those continents circumstances are eminently and conspicuously different. It is impossible that the allied powers should extend their political system to any portion of either continent without endangering our peace and happiness; nor can anyone believe that our southern brethren, if left to themselves, would adopt it of their own accord. It is equally impossible, therefore, that we should behold such interposition in any form with indifference. If we look to the comparative strength and resources of Spain and those new Governments, and their distance from each other, it must be obvious that she can never subdue them. It is still the true policy of the United States to leave the parties to themselves, in the hope that other powers will pursue the same course.

If we compare the present condition of our Union with its actual state at the close of our Revolution, the history of the world furnishes no example of a progress in improvement in all the important circumstances which constitute the happiness of a nation which bears any resemblance to it. At the first epoch our population did not exceed 3,000,000. By the last census it amounted to about 10,000,000, and, what is more extraordinary, it is almost altogether native, for the immigration from other countries has been inconsiderable. At the first epoch half the territory within our acknowledged limits was uninhabited and a wilderness. Since then new territory has been acquired of vast extent, comprising within it many rivers, particularly the Mississippi, the navigation of which to the ocean was of the highest importance to the original States. Over this territory our population has expanded in every direction, and new States have been established almost equal in number to those which formed the first bond of our Union. This expansion of our population and accession of new States to our Union have had the happiest effect on all its highest interests. That it has eminently augmented our resources and added to our strength and respectability as a power is admitted by all. But it is not in these important circumstances only that this happy effect is felt. It is manifest that by enlarging the basis of our system and increasing the number of States the system itself has been greatly strengthened in both its branches. Consolidation and disunion have thereby been rendered equally impracticable. Each Government, confiding in its own strength, has less to apprehend from the other, and in consequence each, enjoying a greater freedom of action, is rendered more efficient for all the purposes for which it was instituted. It is unnecessary to treat here of the vast improvement made in the system itself by the adoption of this Constitution and of its happy effect in elevating the character and in protecting the rights of the nation as well as of individuals. To what, then, do we owe these blessings? It is known to all that we derive them from the excellence of our institutions. Ought we not, then, to adopt every measure which may be necessary to perpetuate them?
James Monroe

The Indian Removal Act (1830)
U.S. Congress

United States Statutes at Large (21st Cong., 1st sess., chap. 148), pp. 411–412

An Act to provide for an exchange of lands with the Indians residing in any of the states or territories, and for their removal west of the river Mississippi.

Be it enacted by the Senate and House of Representatives of the United States of America, in Congress assembled, That it shall and may be lawful for the President of the United States to cause so much of any territory belonging to the United States, west of the river Mississippi, not included in any state or organized territory, and to which the Indian title has been extinguished, as he may judge necessary, to be divided into a suitable number of districts, for the reception of such tribes or nations of Indians as may choose to exchange the lands where they now reside, and remove there; and to cause each of said districts to be so described by natural or artificial marks, as to be easily distinguished from every other.

Sec. 2. *And be it further enacted,* That it shall and may be lawful for the President to exchange any or all of such districts, so to be laid off and described, with any tribe or nation of Indians now residing within the limits of any of the states or territories, and with which the United States have existing treaties, for the whole or any part or portion of the territory claimed and occupied by such tribe or nation, within the bounds of any one or more of the states or territories, where the land claimed and occupied by the Indians, is owned by the United States, or the United States are bound to the state within which it lies to extinguish the Indian claim thereto.

Sec. 3. *And be it further enacted,* That in the making of any such exchange or exchanges, it shall and may be lawful for the President solemnly to assure the tribe or nation with which the exchange is made, that the United States will forever secure and guaranty to them, and their heirs or successors, the country so exchanged with them; and if they prefer it, that the United States will cause a patent or grant to be made and executed to them of the same: *Provided always,* That such lands shall revert to the United States, if the Indians become extinct, or abandon the same.

Sec. 4. *And be it further enacted,* That if, upon any of the lands now occupied by the Indians, and to be exchanged for, there should be such improvements as add value to the land claimed by any individual or individuals of such tribes or nations, it shall and may be lawful for the President to cause such value to be ascertained by appraisement or otherwise, and to cause such ascertained value to be paid to the person or persons rightfully claiming such improvements. And upon the payment of such valuation, the improvements so valued and paid for, shall pass to the United States, and possession shall not afterwards be permitted to any of the same tribe.

Sec. 5. *And be it further enacted,* That upon the making of any such exchange as is contemplated by this act, it shall and may be lawful for the President to cause such aid and assistance to be furnished to the emigrants as may be necessary and proper to enable them to remove to, and settle in, the country for which they may have exchanged; and also, to give them such aid and assistance as may be necessary for their support and subsistence for the first year after their removal.

Sec. 6. *And be it further enacted,* That it shall and may be lawful for the President to cause such tribe or nation to be protected, at their new residence, against all interruption or disturbance from any other tribe or nation of Indians, or from any other person or persons whatever.

Sec. 7. *And be it further enacted,* That it shall and may be lawful for the President to have the same superintendence and care over any tribe or nation in the country to which they may remove, as contemplated by this act, that he is now authorized to have over them at their present places of residence: *Provided,* That nothing in this act contained shall be construed as authorizing or directing the violation of any existing treaty between the United States and any of the Indian tribes.

Sec. 8. *And be it further enacted,* That for the purpose of giving effect to the provisions of this act, the sum of five hundred thousand dollars is hereby appropriated, to be paid out of any money in the treasury, not otherwise appropriated.

Liberator Editorial, First Issue (January 1, 1831)

William Lloyd Garrison

Writings and Speeches of William Lloyd Garrison, (Boston: R. F. Walcott), pp. 62–64

Commencement of the Liberator

In the month of August, I issued proposals for publishing 'The Liberator' in Washington city; but the enterprise, though hailed approvingly in different sections of the country, was palsied by public indifference. Since that time, the removal of the 'Genius of Universal Emancipation' to the Seat of Government has rendered less imperious the establishment of a similar periodical in that quarter.

During my recent tour for the purpose of exciting the minds of the people by a series of discourses on the subject of slavery, every place that I visited gave fresh evidence of the fact, that a greater revolution in public sentiment was to be effected in the free States—and particularly in New England—than at the South. I found contempt more bitter, opposition more active, detraction more relentless, prejudice more stubborn, and apathy more frozen, than among slave owners themselves. Of course, there were individual exceptions to the contrary. This state of things afflicted, but did not dishearten me. I determined, at every hazard, to lift up the standard of emancipation in the eyes of the nation, within sight of Bunker Hill, and in the birth-place of liberty. That standard is now unfurled; and long may it float, unhurt by the spoliations of time or the missiles of a desperate foe; yea, till every chain be broken, and every bondman set free! Let Southern oppressors tremble; let their secret abettors tremble; let their Northern apologists tremble; let all the enemies of the persecuted blacks tremble.

Assenting to the 'self-evident truths' maintained in the American Declaration of Independence, 'that all men are created equal, and endowed by their Creator with certain inalienable rights—among which are life, liberty, and the pursuit of happiness,' I shall strenuously contend for the immediate enfranchisement of our slave population. In Park Street Church, on the Fourth of July, 1829, in an address on slavery, I unreflectingly assented to the popular but pernicious doctrine of gradual abolition. I seize this opportunity to make a full and unequivocal recantation, and thus publicly to ask pardon of my God, of my country, and of my brethren, the poor slaves, for having uttered a sentiment so full of timidity, injustice and absurdity. A similar recantation, from my pen, was published in the 'Genius of Universal Emancipation,' at Baltimore, in September, 1829. My conscience is now satisfied.

I am aware, that many object to the severity of my language; but is there not cause for severity? I will be as harsh as truth, and as uncompromising as justice. On this subject, I do not wish to think, or speak, or write, with moderation. No! no! Tell a man, whose house is on fire, to give a moderate alarm; tell him to moderately rescue his wife from the hands of the ravisher; tell the mother to gradually extricate her babe from the fire into which it has fallen; but urge me not to use moderation in a cause like the present! I am in earnest. I will not equivocate—I will not excuse—I will not retreat a single inch—and I will be heard. The apathy of the people is enough to make every statue leap from its pedestal, and to hasten the resurrection of the dead.

It is pretended, that I am retarding the cause of emancipation by the coarseness of my invective, and the precipitancy of my measures. The charge is not true. On this question, my influence, humble as it is, is felt at this moment to a considerable extent, and shall be felt in coming years—not perniciously, but beneficially—not as a curse, but as a blessing; and posterity will bear testimony that I was right. I desire to thank God, that he enables me to disregard 'the fear of man which bringeth a snare,' and to speak his truth in its simplicity and power. And here I close with this fresh dedication:— 'Oppression! I have seen thee, face to face, And met thy cruel eye and cloudy brow; But thy soul-withering glance I fear not now—For dread to prouder feelings doth give place, Of deep abhorrence! Scorning the disgrace Of slavish knees that at thy footstool bow, I also kneel—but with far other vow Do hail thee and thy herd of hirelings base:—I swear, while life-blood warms my throbbing veins, Still to oppose and thwart, with heart and hand, Thy brutalizing sway—till Africa's chains Are burst, and Freedom rules the rescued land, Trampling Oppression and his iron rod:—Such is the vow I take—so help me, God!'
Boston, January 1, 1831.

Texas Declaration of Independence (1836)

Henry Steele Commager and Milton Cantor, eds.
Documents of American History, 10th ed.
(Englewood Cliffs, N.J.: Prentice Hall, 1988), pp. 281–283

Washington, Texas
March 2, 1836

When a government has ceased to protect the lives liberty and property of its people, from whom its legitimate powers are derived, and for the advancement of whose happiness it was instituted, and so far from being a guarantee for the enjoyment of those inestimable and inalienable rights, becomes an instrument in the hands of evil rulers for their oppression: When the Federal Republican Constitution of their country, which they have sworn to support, no longer has a substantial existence, and the whole nature of their government has been forcibly changed without their consent, from a restricted federative republic, composed of sovereign states of a consolidated central military despotism in which every interest is disregarded but that of the army and the priesthood—both the eternal enemies of civil liberty, the ever-ready minions of power, and the usual instruments of tyrants:

When, long after the spirit of the constitution has departed, moderation is at length so far lost by those in power that even the semblance of freedom is removed, and the forms, themselves, of the constitution discontinued; and so far from their petitions and remonstrances being regarded, the agents who bear them are thrown into dungeons; and mercenary armies sent forth to force a new government upon them at the point of the bayonet: When, in consequence of such acts of malfeasance and abdication, on the part of the government, anarchy prevails, and Civil Society is dissolved into its original elements. In such a crisis, the first law of nature, the right of self-preservation—the inherent and unalienable right of the people to appeal to first principles and take their political affairs into their own hands in extreme cases enjoins it as a right towards themselves and a sacred obligation to their posterity to abolish such government and create another in its stead, calculated to rescue them from impending dangers, and to secure their future welfare and happiness.

Nations, as well as individuals, are amenable for their acts to the public opinion of mankind. Statement of a part of our grievance is, therefore, submitted to an impartial world, in justification of the hazardous but unavoidable step now taken of severing our political connection with the Mexican people, and assuming an independent attitude among the nations of the earth.

The Mexican government, by its colonization laws, invited and induced the Anglo-American population of Texas to colonize its wilderness under the pledged faith of a written constitution that they should continue to enjoy that constitutional liberty and republican government to which they had been habituated in the land of their birth, the United States of America. In this expectation they have been cruelly disappointed, in as much as the Mexican nation has acquiesced in the late changes made in the government by General Antonio Lopez de Santa Anna, who, having overturned the constitution of his country, now offers as the cruel alternative either to abandon our homes, acquired by so many privations, or submit to the most intolerable of all tyranny, the combined despotism of the sword and the priesthood.

It has sacrificed our welfare to the State of Coahuila, by which our interests have been continually depressed through a jealous and partial course of legislation carried on at a far distant seat of government by a hostile majority, in an unknown tongue; and this to, notwithstanding we have petitioned in the humblest terms, for the establishment of a separate state government, and have, in accordance with the provisions of the national constitution presented to the General Congress a republican constitution which was, without just cause, contemptuously rejected.

It incarcerated in a dungeon, for a long time, one of our citizens, for no other cause but a zealous endeavor to procure the acceptance of our constitution and the establishment of a state government.

It has failed and refused to secure on a firm basis, the right of trial by jury, that palladium of civil liberty, and only safe guarantee for the life, liberty, and property of the citizen. It has failed to establish any public system of education, although possessed of almost boundless resources (the public domain) and although it is an axiom in political science, that unless a people are educated and enlightened it is idle to expect the continuance of civil liberty, or the capacity for self-government.

It has suffered the military commandants stationed among us to exercise arbitrary acts of oppression and tyranny; thus trampling upon the most sacred rights of the citizen and rendering the military superior to the civil power.

It has dissolved by force of arms, the State Congress of Coahuila and Texas, and obliged our representatives to fly for their lives from the seat of government; thus depriving us of the fundamental political right of representation.

It has demanded the surrender of a number of our citizens and ordered military detachments to seize and carry them into the interior for trial; in contempt of the civil authorities, and in defiance of the laws and the constitution.

It has made piratical attacks upon our commerce, by commissioning foreign desperadoes, and authorizing them to seize our vessels, and convey the property of our citizens to far distant ports for confiscation.

It denies us the right of worshipping the Almighty according to the dictates of our own conscience, by the support of a national religion calculated to promote the temporal interest of its human functionaries rather than the glory of the true and living God. It has demanded us to deliver up our arms, which are essential to our defence, the rightful property of freemen, and formidable only to tyrannical governments.

It has invaded our country by sea and by land, with intent to lay waste our territory and drive us from our homes, and has now a large mercenary army advancing to carry on against us a war of extermination.

It has, through its emissaries, incited the merciless savage, with the tomahawk and scalping knife, to massacre the inhabitants of our defenceless frontiers.

It hath been, during the whole time of our connection with it, the contemptible sport and victim of successive military revolutions, and hath continually exhibited every characteristic of a weak, corrupt, and tyrannical government.

These, and other grievances, were patiently borne by the people of Texas until they reached that point at which forbearance ceases to be a virtue. We then took up arms in defence of the national constitution. We appealed to our Mexican brethren for assistance. Our appeal has been made in vain. Though months have elapsed, no sympathetic response has yet been heard from the interior. We are, therefore, forced to the melancholy conclusion that the Mexican people have acquiesced in the destruction of their liberty and the substitution therefore of a Military Government—that they are unfit to be free and incapable of self-government.

The necessity of self-preservation, therefore, now decrees our eternal political separation. We therefore, the delegates with plenary powers, of the people of Texas, in solemn convention assembled, appealing to a candid world for the necessities of our condition, do hereby resolve and declare that our political connection with the Mexican Nation has forever ended; and that the people of Texas do now constitute a free sovereign and independent republic, and are fully invested with all the rights and attributes which properly belong to independent nations; and conscious of the rectitude of our intentions, we fearlessly and confidently commit the issue to the decision of the Supreme Arbiter of the destinies of Nations.

Richard Ellis, *President*

From "Appeal to the Christian Women of the South," (September, 1836)
Angelina Grimké

In Kathryn Cullen-DuPont. *Encyclopedia of Women's History*, 2d ed. (New York: Facts On File, Inc., 2000), pp. 306–309

I have thus, I think, clearly proved to you seven propositions, viz.: First, that slavery is contrary to the declaration of our independence. Second, that it is contrary to the first charter of human rights given to Adam, and renewed to Noah. Third, that the fact of slavery having been the subject of prophecy, furnishes *no* excuse whatever to slave dealers. Fourth, that no such system existed under the patriarchal dispensation. Fifth, that *slavery never* existed under the Jewish dispensation; but so far otherwise, that every servant was placed under the *protection of law,* and care taken not only to prevent all *involuntary* servitude, but all *voluntary perpetual* bondage. Sixth, that slavery in America reduces a *man* to a *thing*, a "chattel personal," *robs him of all* his rights as a *human being,* fetters both his mind and body, and protects the *master* in the most unnatural and unreasonable power, whilst it *throws him out* of the protection of law. Seventh, that slavery is contrary to the example and precepts of our holy and merciful Redeemer, and of his apostles.

But perhaps you will be ready to query, why appeal to *women* on this subject? *We* do not make the laws which perpetuate slavery. *No* legislative power is vested in *us*; *we* can do nothing to overthrow the system, even if we wished to do so. To this I reply, I know you do not make the laws, but I also know that *you are the wives and mothers, the sisters and daughters of those who do;* and if you really suppose *you* can do nothing to overthrow slavery, you are greatly mistaken. You can do much in every way: four things I will name. 1st. You can read on this subject. 2d. You can pray over this subject. 3d. You can speak on this subject. 4th. You can *act* on this subject. I have not placed reading before praying because I regard it more important, but because, in order to pray aright, we must understand what we are praying for; it is only then we can "pray with the understanding and the spirit also."

1. Read then on the subject of slavery. Search the Scriptures daily, whether the things I have told you are true. Other books and papers might be a great help to you in this investigation, but they are not necessary, and it is hardly probable that your Committees of Vigilance will allow you to have the other. The *Bible* then is the book I want you to read in the spirit of inquiry, and the spirit of prayer. Even the enemies of Abolitionists, acknowledged that their doctrines are drawn from it. In the great mob in Boston, last autumn, when the books and papers of the Anti-Slavery Society, were thrown out of the windows of their office, one individual laid hold of the Bible and was about tossing it out to the ground, when another reminded him that it was the Bible he had in his hand. *"O! 'tis all one,"* he replied, and out went the sacred volume, along with the rest. We thank him for the acknowledgment. Yes, *"it is all one,"* for our books and papers are mostly commentaries on the Bible, and the Declaration. Read the *Bible* then, it contains the words of Jesus, and they are spirit and life. Judge for yourselve whether *he sanctioned* such a system of oppression and crime.

2. Pray over this subject. When you have entered into your closets, and shut to the doors, then pray to your father, who seeth in secret, that he would open your eyes to see whether slavery is *sinful,* and if it is, that he would enable you to bear a faithful, open and unshrinking testimony against it, and to do whatsoever your hand find to do, leaving the consequences entirely to him, who still says to us whenever we try to reason away duty from the fear of consequences, *"What is that to thee, follow thou me."* Pray also for that poor slave, that he may be kept patient and submissive under his hard lot, until God is pleased to open the door of freedom to him without violence or bloodshed. Pray too for the master that his heart may be softened, and he made willing to acknowledge, as Joseph's brethren did, "Verily we are guilty concerning our brother," before he will be compelled to add in consequence of Divine judgment, "therefore is all this evil come upon us." Pray also for all your brethren and sisters who are laboring in the righteous cause of Emancipation in the Northern States, England and the world. There is great encouragement for prayer in these words of our Lord. "Whatsoever ye shall ask the Father *in my name,* he *will give* it to you"—Pray then without ceasing, in the closet and the social circle.

3. Speak on this subject. It is through the tongue, the pen, and the press, that truth is principally propagated. Speak then to your relatives, your friends, your acquaintances on the subject of slavery; be not afraid if you are conscientiously convinced it is *sinful,* to say so openly, but calmly, and to let your sentiments be known. If you are served by the slaves of others, try to ameliorate their condition as much as possible; never aggravate their faults, and thus add fuel to the fire of anger already kindled, in a master and mistress's bosom, remember their extreme ignorance, and consider them as your Heavenly Father does the *less* culpable on this account, even when they do wrong things. Discountenance *all* cruelty to them, all starvation, all corporal chastisement; these may brutalize and *break* their spirits, but will never bend hem to willing, cheerful obedience. If possible, see that they are comfortably and *seasonably* fed, whether in the house or the field; it is unreasonable and cruel to expect slaves to wait for their breakfast until eleven o'clock, when they rise at five or six. Do all you can, to induce their owners to clothe them well, and to allow them many little indulgences which would

contribute to their comfort. Above all, try to persuade your husband, father, brothers and sons, that *slavery is a crime against God and man,* and that it is a great sin to keep *human beings* in such abject ignorance; to deny them the privilege of learning to read and write. The Catholics are universally condemned, for denying the Bible to the common people, but, *slaveholders must not* blame them, for *they* are doing the *very same thing,* and for the very same reason, neither of these systems can bear the light which bursts from the pages of that Holy Book. And lastly, endeavour to inculcate submission on the part of the slaves, but whilst doing this be faithful in pleading the cause of the oppressed.

> "Will *you* behold unheeding,
> Life's holiest feelings crushed,
> Where *woman's* heart is bleeding,
> Shall *woman's* voice be hushed?"

4. Act on this subject. Some of you *own* slaves yourselves. *If* you believe slavery is *sinful,* set them at liberty, "undo the heavy burdens and let the oppresed go free." If they wish to remain with you, pay them wages, if not let them leave you. Should they remain, teach them, and have them taught the common branches of an English education; they have minds and those minds, *ought to be improved.* So precious a talent as intellect, never was given to be wrapt in a napkin and buried in the earth. It is the *duty* of all, as far as they can, to improve their own mental faculties, because we are commanded to love God with *all our minds,* as well as with all our hearts, and we commit a great sin, if we *forbid or prevent* that cultivation of the mind in others, which would enable them to perform this duty. Teach your servants then to read &c, and encourage them to believe it is their *duty* to learn, if it were only that they might read the Bible.

But some of you will say, we can neither free our slaves nor teach them to read, for the laws of our state forbid it. Be not surprised when I say such wicked laws *ought to be no barrier* in the way of your duty, and I appeal to the Bible to prove this position. What was the conduct of Shiphrah and Puah, when the king of Egypt issued his cruel mandate, with regard to the Hebrew children? "*They* feared *God,* and did *not* as the King of Egypt commanded them, but saved the men children alive." Did these *women* do right in disobeying that monarch? "*Therefore* (says the sacred text,) *God dealt well* with them, and made them houses" Ex. i. What was the conduct of Shadrach, Meshach, and Abednego, when Nebuchadnezzar set up a golden image in the plain of Dura, and commanded all people, nations, and languages to fall down and worship it? "Be it known, unto thee, (said these faithful *Jews*) O king, that we will not serve thy gods, nor worship the image which thou hast set up." Did these men *do right in disobeying the law* of their sovereign? Let their miraculous deliverance from the burning fiery furnace, answer; Dan. iii. . . .

But some of you may say, if we do free our slaves, they will be taken up and sold, therefore there will be no use in doing it. Peter and John might just as well have said, we will not preach the gospel, for if we do, we shall be taken up and put in prison, therefore there will be no use in our preaching. *Consequences,* my friends, belong no more to *you,* than they did to these apostles. Duty is ours and events are God's. If you think slavery is sinful, all *you* have to do is to set your slaves at liberty, do all you can to protect them, and in humble faith and fervent prayer, commend them to your common Father. He can take care of them; but if for wise purposes he sees fit to allow them to be sold, this will afford you an opportunity of testifying openly, wherever you go, against the crime of *manstealing.* Such an act will be *clear robbery,* and if exposed, might, under the Divine direction, do the cause of Emancipation more good, than any thing that could happen, for, "He makes even the wrath of man to praise him, and the remainder of wrath he will restrain."

I know that this doctrine of obeying *God,* rather than man, will be considered as dangerous, and heretical by many, but I am not afraid openly to avow it, because it is the doctrine of the Bible; but I would not be understood to advocate resistance to any law however oppressive if, in obeying it, I was not obliged to commit *sin.* If for instance, there was a law, which imposed imprisonment or a fine upon me if I manumitted a slave, I would on no account resist that law, I would set the slave free, and then go to prison or pay the fine. If a law commands me to *sin I will break it;* if it calls me to *suffer,* I will let it take its course *unresistingly.* The doctrine of blind obedience and unqualified submission to *any human* power, whether civil or ecclesiastical, is the doctrine of despotism, and ought to have no place among Republicans and Christians.

But you will perhaps say, such a course of conduct would inevitably expose us to great suffering. Yes! my christian friends, I believe it would, but this will *not* excuse you or any one else for the neglect of *duty.* If Prophets and Apostles, Martyrs, and Reformers had not been willing to suffer for the truth's sake, where would the world have been now? If they had said, we cannot speak the truth, we cannot do what we believe is right, because the *laws of our country or public opinion are against us,* where would our holy religion have been now? . . .

But you may say we are *women,* how can our hearts endure persecution? And why not? Have not women stood up in all the dignity and strength of moral courage to be the leaders of the people, and to bear a faithful testimony for the truth whenever the providence of God has called them to do so? Are there no *women* in that noble army of martyrs who are now singing the song of Moses and the Lamb? Who led out the women of Israel from the house of bondage, striking the timbrel, and singing the song of deliverance on the banks of that sea whose waters stood up like walls of crystal to open a passage for their escape? It was a *woman:* Miriam, the prophetess, the sister of Moses and Aaron. Who went up with BArak to Kadesh to fight against Jabin, King of Canaan, into whose hand Israel had been sold because of their iniquities? It was a *woman!* Deborah, the wife of Lapidoth, the judge, as well as the prophetess of that backsliding people; Judges iv, 9. Into whose hands was Sisera, the captain of Jabin's host delivered? Into the hands of a *woman.* Jael he wife of Heber! Judges vi, 21. Who dared to *speak the truth* concerning those judgments which were coming upon Judea, when Josiah, alarmed at finding that his people "had not kept the word of the Lord to do after all that was written in the book of the Law," sent to enquire of the Lord concerning these things? It was a *woman.* Huldah the prophetess, the wife of Shallum; 2, Chron. xxxiv, 22. Who was chosen to deliver the whole Jewish nation from that murderous decree of Persia's King, which wicked Haman had obtained by calumny and fraud? It was a *woman;* Esther the Queen; yes, weak and trembling *woman* was the instrument appointed by God, to reverse the bloody mandate of the eastern monarch, and save the *whole visible church* from destruction. What human voice first proclaimed to Mary that she should be the mother of our Lord? It was a *woman!* Elizabeth, the wife of Zacharias; Luke i, 42, 43. Who united with the good old Simeon in giving thanks publicly in the temple, when the child, Jesus, was presented there by his parents, "and spake of him to all them that looked for redemption in Jerusalem?" It was a *woman!* Anna the prophetess. Who first proclaimed Christ as the true Messiah in the streets of Samaria, once the capital of the ten tribes? It was a *woman!* Who ministered to the Son of God whilst on earth, a despised and persecuted Reformer, in the humble garb of a carpenter? They were *women!* Who followed the rejected King of Israel, as his fainting footsteps trod the road to Calvary? "A great company of people and of *women;*" and it is remarkable that to *them alone,* he turned and addressed the pathetic language, "Daughters of Jerusalem, weep not for me, but weep for yourselves and your children." Ah! who sent unto the Roman Governor when he was set down on the judgment seat, saying unto him, "Have thou nothing to do with that just man, for I have suffered many things this day in a dream because of him?" It was a *woman!* the wife of Pilate. Although "*he knew* that for envy the Jews had delivered Christ," yet *he* consented to surrender the Son of God into the hands of a brutal soldiery, after having himself scourged his naked body. Had the *wife* of Pilate sat upon that judgment seat, what would have been the result of the trial of this "just person?" . . .

And what, I would ask in conclusion, have *women* done for the great and glorious cause of Emancipation? Who wrote that pamphlet which moved the heart of Wilberforce to pray over the wrongs, and his tongue to plead the cause of the oppressed African? It was a *woman,* Elizabeth Heyrick. Who labored assiduously to keep the sufferings of the slave continually before the British public? They were *women.* And how did they do it? By their needles, paint brushes and pens, by speaking the truth, and petitioning Parliament for the abolition of slavery. And what was the effect of their labors? Read it in the Emancipation bill of Great Britain. Read it, in the present state of her West India Colonies. Read it, in the impulse which has been given to the cause of freedom, in the United States of America. Have English women then done so much for the negro, and shall American women do nothing? Oh no! Already are there sixty female Anti-Slavery Societies in operation. These are doing just what the English women did, telling the story of the colored man's wrongs, praying for his deliverance, and presenting his kneeling image constantly before the public eye on bags and needle-books, card-racks, pen-wipers, pin-cushions, &c. Even the children of the north are inscribing on their handy work, "May the points of our needles prick the slaveholder's conscience." Some of the reports of these Societies exhibit not only considerable talent, but a deep sense of religious duty, and a determination to persevere through evil as well as good report, until every scourge, and every shackle, is buried under the feet of the manumitted slave.

The Ladies' Anti-Slavery Society of Boston was called last fall, to a severe trial of their faith and constancy. They were mobbed by "the gentlemen of property and standing," in that city at their anniversary meeting, and their lives were jeoparded by an infuriated crowd; but their conduct on that occasion did credit to our sex, and affords a full assurance that they will *never* abandon the cause of the slave. The pamphlet, Right and Wrong in Boston, issued by them in which a particular account is given of that "mob of broad cloth in broad day," does equal credit to the head and the heart of her who wrote it. I wish my Southern sisters could read it; they would then understand that the women of the North have engaged in this work from a sense of *religious duty,* and that nothing will ever induce them to take their hands from it until it is fully accomplished. They feel no hostility to you, no bitterness nor wrath; they rather sympathize in your trials and difficulties; but they well know that the first thing to be done to help you, is to pour in the light of truth on your minds, to urge you to reflection, and pray over the subject. This is all *they* can do for you, *you* must work out your own deliverance with fear and trembling, and with the direction and blessing of God, *you can do it.* Northern women may labor to produce a correct public opinion as the North, but if Southern women sit down in listless indifference and criminal idleness, public opinion cannot be rectified and purified at the South. It is manifest to every reflecting mind, that slavery must be abolished; the era in which we live, and the light which is overspreading the whole world on this subject, clearly show that the time cannot be distant when it will be done. Now there are only two ways in which it can be effected, by moral power or physical force, and it is for *you* to choose which of these you prefer. Slavery always has, and always will produce insurrections wherever it exists, because it is a violation of the natural order of things, and no human power can much longer perpetuate it . . .

The *women of the South can overthrow* this horrible system of oppression and cruelty, licentiousness and wrong. Such appeals to your legislatures would be irresistible, for there is something in the heart of man which *will bend under moral suasion.* There is a swift witness for truth in his bosom, which *will respond to truth* when it is uttered with calmness and dignity. If you could obtain but six signatures to such a petition in only one state, I would say send up that petition, and be not in the least discouraged by the scoffs and jeers of the heartless, or the resolution of the house to lay it on the table. It will be a great thing if the subject can be introduced into your legislatures in any way, even by *women,* and *they* will be the most likely to introduce it there in the best possible manner, as a matter of *morals* and *religion,* not of expediency or politics. You may petition, too, the different ecclesiastical bodies of the slave states. Slavery must be attacked with the whole power of truth and the sword of the spirit. You must take it up on *Christian* ground, and fight against it with Christian weapons, whilst your feet are shod with the preparation of the gospel of peace. And *you are now* loudly called upon by the cries of the widow and the orphan, to arise and gird yourselves for this great moral conflict, with the whole armour of righteousness upon the right hand and on the left.

United States v. Libellants and Claimants of the Schooner Amistad, (1841)
United States Supreme Court

40 U.S. 518 (1841)

APPEAL FROM THE CIRCUIT COURT
OF CONNECTICUT

Opinions

STORY, J., Opinion of the Court

Mr. Justice STORY delivered the opinion of the Court.

This is the case of an appeal from the decree of the Circuit Court of the District of Connecticut, sitting in admiralty. The leading facts, as they appear upon the transcript of the proceedings, are as follows: On the 27th of June, 1839, the schooner L'Amistad, being the property of Spanish subjects, cleared out from the port of Havana, in the island of Cuba, for Puerto Principe, in the same island. On board of the schooner were the captain, Ransom Ferrer, and Jose Ruiz, and Pedro Montez, all Spanish subjects. The former had with him a negro boy, named Antonio, claimed to be his slave. Jose Ruiz had with him forty-nine negroes, claimed by him as his slaves, and stated to be his property, in a certain pass or document, signed by the Governor General [p*588] of Cuba. Pedro Montez had with him four other negroes, also claimed by him as his slaves, and stated to be his property, in a similar pass or document, also signed by the Governor General of Cuba. On the voyage, and before the arrival of the vessel at her port of destination, the negroes rose, killed the captain, and took possession of her. On the 26th of August, the vessel was discovered by Lieutenant Gedney, of the United States brig Washington, at anchor on the high seas, at the distance of half a mile from the shore of Long Island. A part of the negroes were then on shore at Culloden Point, Long Island; who were seized by Lieutenant Gedney, and brought on board. The vessel, with the negroes and other persons on board, was brought by Lieutenant Gedney into the district of Connecticut, and there libelled for salvage in the District Court of the United States. A libel for salvage was also filed by Henry Green and Pelatiah Fordham, of Sag Harbour, Long Island. On the 18th of September, Ruiz and Montez filed claims and libels, in which they asserted their ownership of the negroes as their slaves, and of certain parts of the cargo, and prayed that the same might be "delivered to them, or to the representatives of her Catholic majesty, as might be most proper." On the 19th of September, the Attorney of the United States, for the district of Connecticut, filed an information or libel, setting forth, that the Spanish minister had officially presented to the proper department of the government of the United States, a claim for the restoration of the vessel, cargo, and slaves, as the property of Spanish subjects, which had arrived within the jurisdictional limits of the United States, and were taken possession of by the said public armed brig of the United States; under such circumstances as made it the duty of the United States to cause the same to be restored to the true proprietors, pursuant to the treaty between the United States and Spain: and praying the Court, on its being made legally to appear that the claim of the Spanish minister was well founded, to make such order for the disposal of the vesel, cargo, and slaves, as would best enable the United States to comply with their treaty stipulations. But if it should appear, that the negroes were persons transported from Africa, in violation of the laws of the United States, and brought within the United States contrary to the same laws; he then prayed the Court to make such order for their removal to the coast of Africa, pursuant to the laws of the United States, as it should deem fit.

On the 19th of November, the Attorney of the United States [p*589] filed a second information or libel, similar to the first, with the exception of the second prayer above set forth in his former one. On the same day, Antonio G. Vega, the vice-consul of Spain, for the state of Connecticut, filed his libel, alleging that Antonio was a slave, the property of the representatives of Ramon Ferrer, and praying the Court to cause him to be delivered to the said vice-consul, that he might be returned by him to his lawful owner in the island of Cuba.

On the 7th of January, 1840, the negroes, Cinque and others, with the exception of Antonio, by their counsel, filed an answer, denying that they were slaves, or the property of Ruiz and Montez, or that the Court could, under the Constitution or laws of the United States, or under any treaty, exercise any jurisdiction over their persons, by reason of the premises; and praying that they might be dismissed. They specially set forth and insist in this answer, that they were native born Africans; born free, and still of right ought to be free and not slaves; that they were, on or about the 15th of April, 1839, unlawfully kidnapped, and forcibly and wrongfully carried on board a certain vessel on the coast of Africa, which was unlawfully engaged in the slave trade, and were unlawfully transported in the same vessel to the island of Cuba, for the purpose of being there unlawfully sold as slaves; that Ruiz and Montez, well knowing the premises, made a pretended purchase of them: that afterwards, on or about the 28th of June, 1839, Ruiz and Montez, confederating with Ferrer, (captain of the Amistad,) caused them, without law or right, to be placed on board of the Amistad, to be transported to some place unknown to them, and there to be enslaved for life; that, on the voyage, they rose on the master, and took possession of the vessel, intending to return therewith to their native country, or to seek an asylum in some free state; and the vessel arrived, about the 26th of August, 1839, off Montauk Point, near Long Island; a part of them were sent on shore, and were seized by Lieutenant Gedney, and carried on board; and all of them were afterwards brought by him into the district of Connecticut.

On the 7th of January, 1840, Jose Antonio Tellincas, and Messrs. Aspe and Laca, all Spanish subjects, residing in Cuba, filed their [p*590] claims, as owners to certain portions of the goods found on board of the schooner L'Amistad.

On the same day, all the libellants and claimants, by their counsel, except Jose Ruiz and Pedro Montez, (whose libels and claims, as stated of record, respectively, were pursued by the Spanish minister, the same being merged in his claims,) appeared, and the negroes also appeared by their counsel; and the case was heard on the libels, claims, answers, and testimony of witnesses.

On the 23d day of January, 1840, the District Court made a decree. By that decree, the Court rejected the claim of Green and Fordham for salvage, but allowed salvage to Lieutenant Gedney and others, on the vessel and cargo, of one-third of the value thereof, but not on the negroes, Cinque and others; it allowed the claim of Tellincas, and Aspe and Laca with the exception of the above-mentioned salvage; it dismissed the libels and claims of Ruiz and Montez, with costs, as being included under the claim of the Spanish minister; it allowed the claim of the Spanish vice-consul for Antonio, on behalf of Ferrer's representatives; it rejected the claims of Ruiz and Montez for the delivery of the negroes, but admitted them for the cargo, with the exception of the above-mentioned salvage; it rejected the claim made by the Attorney of the United States on behalf of the Spanish minister, for the restoration of the negroes under the treaty; but it decreed that they should be delivered to the President of the United States, to be transported to Africa, pursuant to the act of 3d March, 1819.

From this decree the District Attorney, on behalf of the United States, appealed to the Circuit Court, except so far as related to the restoration of the slave Antonio. The claimants, Tellincas, and Aspe and Laca, also appealed from that part of the decree which awarded salvage on the property respectively claimed by them. No appeal was interposed by Ruiz or Montez, or on behalf of the representatives of the owners of the Amistad. The Circuit Court, by a mere pro forma decree, affirmed the decree of the District Court, reserving the question of salvage upon the claims of Tellincas, and Aspe and Laca. And from that decree the present appeal has been brought to this Court.

The cause has been very elaborately argued, as well upon the [p*591] merits, as upon a motion on behalf of the appellees to dismiss the appeal. On the part of the United States, it has been contended, 1. That due and sufficient proof concerning the property has been made to authorize the restitution of the vessel, cargo, and negroes to the Spanish subjects on whose behalf they are claimed pursuant to the treaty with Spain, of the 27th of October, 1795. 2. That the United States had a right to intervene in the manner in which they have done, to obtain a decree for the restitution of the property, upon the application of the Spanish minister. These propositions have been strenuously denied on the other side. Other collateral and incidental points have been stated, upon which it is not necessary at this moment to dwell.

Before entering upon the discussion of the main points involved in this interesting and important controversy, it may be necessary to say a few words as to the actual posture of the case as it now stands before us. In the first place, then, the only parties now before the Court on one side, are the United States, intervening for the sole purpose of procuring restitution of the property as Spanish property, pursuant to the treaty, upon the grounds stated by the other parties claiming the property in their respective libels. The United States do not assert any property in themselves, or any violation of their own rights, or sovereignty, or laws, by the acts complained of. They do not insist that these negroes have been imported into the United States, in contravention of our own slave trade acts. They do not seek to have these negroes delivered up for the purpose of being transported to Cuba as pirates or robbers, or as fugitive criminals against the laws of Spain. They do not assert that the seizure, and bringing the vessel, and cargo, and negroes into port, by Lieutenant Gedney, for the purpose of adjudication, is a tortious act. They simply confine themselves to the right of the Spanish claimants to the restitution of their property, upon the facts asserted in their respective allegations.

In the next place, the parties before the Court on the other side as appellees, are Lieutenant Gedney, on his libel for salvage, and the negroes, (Cinque, and others,) asserting themselves, in their answer, not to be slaves, but free native Africans, kidnapped [p*592] in their own country, and illegally transported by force from that country; and now entitled to maintain their freedom.

No question has been here made, as to the proprietary interests in the vessel and cargo. It is admitted that they belong to Spanish subjects, and that they ought to be restored. The only point on this head is, whether the restitution ought to be upon the payment of salvage or not? The main controversy is, whether these negroes are the property of Ruiz and Montez, and ought to be delivered up; and to this, accordingly, we shall first direct our attention.

It has been argued on behalf of the United States, that the Court are bound to deliver them up, according to the treaty of 1795, with Spain, which has in this particular been continued in full force, by the treaty of 1819, ratified in 1821. The sixth article of that treaty, seems to have had, principally, in view cases where the property of the subjects of either state had been taken possession of within the territorial jurisdiction of the other, during war. The eighth article provides for cases where the shipping of the inhabitants of either state are forced, through stress of weather, pursuit of pirates, or enemies, or any other urgent necessity, to seek shelter in the ports of the other. There may well be some doubt entertained, whether the present case, in its actual circumstances, falls within the purview of this article. But it does not seem necessary, for reasons hereafter stated, absolutely to decide it. The ninth article provides, "that all ships and merchandise, of what nature soever, which shall be rescued out of the hands of any pirates or robbers, on the high seas, shall be brought into some port of either state, and shall be delivered to the custody of the officers of that port, in order to be taken care of and restored entire to the true proprietor, as soon as due and sufficient proof shall be made concerning the property thereof." This is the article on which the main reliance is placed on behalf of the United States, for the restitution of these negroes. To bring the case within the article, it is essential to establish, First, That these negroes, under all the circumstances, fall within the description of merchandise, in the sense of the treaty. Secondly, That there has been a rescue of them on the high seas, out of the hands of the pirates and robbers; which, in the present case, can only be, by showing that they [p*593] themselves are pirates and robbers; and, Thirdly, That Ruiz and Montez, the asserted proprietors, are the true proprietors, and have established their title by competent proof.

If these negroes were, at the time, lawfully held as slaves under the laws of Spain, and recognised by those laws as property capable of being lawfully bought and sold; we see no reason why they may not justly be deemed within the intent of the treaty, to be included under the denomination of merchandise, and, as such, ought to be restored to the claimants: for, upon that point, the laws of Spain would seem to furnish the proper rule of interpretation. But, admitting this, it is clear, in our opinion, that neither of the other essential facts and requisites has been established in proof; and the onus probandi of both lies upon the claimants to give rise to the causes foederis. It is plain beyond controversy, if we examine the evidence, that these negroes never were the lawful slaves of Ruiz or Montez, or of any other Spanish subjects. They are natives of Africa, and were kidnapped there, and were unlawfully transported to Cuba, in violation of the laws and treaties of Spain, and the most solemn edicts and declarations of that government. By those laws, and treaties, and edicts, the African slave trade is utterly abolished; the dealing in that trade is deemed a heinous crime; and the negroes thereby introduced into the dominions of Spain, are declared to be free. Ruiz and Montez are proved to have made the pretended purchase of these negroes, with a full knowledge of all the circumstances. And so cogent and irresistible is the evidence in this respect, that the District Attorney has admitted in open Court, upon the record, that these negroes were native Africans, and recently imported into Cuba, as alleged in their answers to the libels in the case. The supposed proprietary interest of Ruiz and Montez, is completely displaced, if we are at liberty to look at the evidence of the admissions of the District Attorney.

It, then, these negroes are not slaves, but are kidnapped Africans, who, by the laws of Spain itself, are entitled to their freedom, and were kidnapped and illegally carried to Cuba, and illegally detained and restrained on board of the Amistad; there is no pretence to say, that they are pirates or robbers. We may lament the dreadful acts, by which they asserted their liberty, and took possession of the Amistad, and endeavoured to regain their native [p*594] country; but they cannot be deemed pirates or robbers in the sense of the law of nations, or the treaty with Spain, or the laws of Spain itself; at least so far as those laws have been brought to our knowledge. Nor do the libels of Ruiz or Montez assert them to be such.

This posture of the facts would seem, of itself, to put an end to the Whole inquiry upon the merits. But it is argued, on behalf of the United States, that the ship, and cargo, and negroes were duly documented as belonging to Spanish subjects, and this Court have no right to look behind these documents; that full faith and credit is to be given to them; and that they are to be held conclusive evidence in this cause, even although it should be established by the most satisfactory proofs, that they have been obtained by the grossest frauds and impositions upon the constituted authorities of Spain. To this argument we can, in no wise, assent. There is nothing in the treaty which justifies or sustains the argument. We do not here meddle with the point, whether there has been any connivance in this illegal traffic, on the part of any of the colonial authorities or subordinate officers of Cuba; because, in our view, such an examination is unnecessary, and ought not to be pursued, unless it were indispensable to public justice, although it has been strongly pressed at the bar. What we proceed upon is this, that although public documents of the government, accompanying property found on board of the private ships of a foreign nation, certainly are to be deemed prima facie evidence of the facts which they purport to state, yet they are always open to be impugned for fraud; and whether that fraud be in the original obtaining of these documents, or in the subsequent fraudulent and illegal use of them, when once it is satisfactorily established, it overthrows all their sanctity, and destroys them as proof. Fraud will vitiate any, even the most solemn transactions; and an asserted title to property, founded upon it, is utterly void. The very language of the ninth article of the treaty of 1795, requires the proprietor to make due and sufficient proof of his property. And how can that proof be deemed either due or sufficient, which is but a connected, and stained tissue of fraud? This is not a mere rule of municipal jurisprudence. Nothing is more clear in the law of nations, as an established rule to regulate their rights, and duties, [p*595] and intercourse, than the doctrine, that the ship's papers are but prima facie evidence, and that, if they are shown to be fraudulent, they are not to be held proof of any valid title. This rule is familiarly applied, and, indeed, is of every-days occurrence in cases of prize, in the contests between belligerents and neutrals, as is apparent from numerous cases to be found in the Reports of this Court; and it is just as applicable to the transactions of civil intercourse between nations in times of peace. If a private ship, clothed with Spanish papers, should enter the ports of the United States, claiming the privileges, and immunities, and rights belonging to bona fide subjects of Spain, under our treaties or laws, and she should, in reality, belong to the subjects of another nation, which was not entitled to any such privileges, immunities, or rights, and the proprietors were seeking, by fraud, to cover their own illegal acts, under the flag of Spain; there can be no doubt, that it would be the duty of our Courts to strip off the disguise, and to look at the case according to its naked realities. In the solemn treaties between nations, it can never be presumed that either state intends to provide the means of perpetrating or protecting frauds; but all the provisions are to be construed as intended to be applied to bona fide transactions. The seventeenth article of the treaty with Spain, which provides for certain passports and certificates, as evidence of property on board of the ships of both states, is, in its terms, applicable only to cases where either of the parties is engaged in a war. This article required a certain form of passport to be agreed upon by the parties, and annexed to the treaty. It never was annexed; and, therefore, in the case of the Amiable Isabella, 6 Wheaton, 1, it was held inoperative.

It is also a most important consideration in the present case, which ought not to be lost sight of, that, supposing these African negroes not to be slaves, but kidnapped, and free negroes, the treaty with Spain cannot be obligatory upon them; and the United States are bound to respect their rights as much as those of Spanish subjects. The conflict of rights between the parties under such circumstances, becomes positive and inevitable, and must be decided upon the eternal principles of justice and international law. If the contest were about any goods on board of this ship, to which American citizens asserted a title, which was [p*596] denied by the Spanish claimants, there could be no doubt of the right of such American citizens to litigate their claims before any competent American tribunal, notwithstanding the treaty with Spain. A fortiori, the doctrine must apply where human life and human liberty are in issue; and constitute the very essence of the controversy. The treaty with Spain never could have intended to take away the equal rights of all foreigners, who should contest their claims before any of our Courts, to equal justice; or to deprive such foreigners of the protection given them by other treaties, or by the general law of nations. Upon the merits of the case, then, there does not seem to us to be any ground for doubt, that these negroes ought to be deemed free; and that the Spanish treaty interposes no obstacle to the just assertion of their rights.

There is another consideration growing out of this part of the case, which necessarily rises in judgment. It is observable, that the United States, in their original claim, filed it in the alternative, to have the negroes, if slaves and Spanish property, restored to the proprietors; or, if not slaves, but negroes who had been transported from Africa, in violation of the laws of the United States, and brought into the United States contrary to the same laws, then the Court to pass an order to enable the United States to remove such persons to the coast of Africa, to be delivered there to such agent as may be authorized to receive and provide for them. At a subsequent period, this last alternative claim was not insisted on, and another claim was interposed, omitting it; from which the conclusion naturally arises that it was abandoned. The decree of the District Court, however, contained an order for the delivery of the negroes to the United States, to be transported to the coast of Africa, under the act of the 3d of March, 1819, ch. 224. The United States do not now insist upon any affirmance of this part of the decree; and, in our judgment, upon the admitted facts, there is no ground to assert that the case comes within the purview of the act of 1819, or of any other of our prohibitory slave trade acts. These negroes were never taken from Africa, or brought to the United States in contravention of those acts. When the Amistad arrived she was in possession of the negroes, asserting their freedom; and in no sense could they possibly intend to import themselves here, as [p*597] slaves, or for sale as slaves. In this view of the matter, that part of the decree of the District Court is unmaintainable, and must be reversed.

The view which has been thus taken of this case, upon the merits, under the first point, renders it wholly unnecessary for us to give any opinion upon the other point, as to the right of the United States to intervene in this case in the manner already stated. We dismiss this, therefore, as well as several minor points made at the argument.

As to the claim of Lieutenant Gedney for the salvage service, it is understood that the United States do not now desire to interpose any obstacle to the allowance of it, if it is deemed reasonable by the Court. It was a highly meritorious and useful service to the proprietors of the ship and cargo; and such as, by the general principles of maritime law, is always deemed a just foundation for salvage. The rate allowed by the Court, does not seem to us to have been beyond the exercise of a sound discretion, under the very peculiar and embarrassing circumstances of the case.

Upon the whole, our opinion is, that the decree of the Circuit Court, affirming that of the District Court, ought to be affirmed, except so far as it directs the negroes to be delivered to the President, to be transported to Africa, in pursuance of the act of the 3d of March, 1819; and, as to this, it ought to be reversed: and that the said negroes be declared to be free, and be dismissed from the custody of the Court, and go without day.

This cause came on to be heard on the transcript of the record from the Circuit Court of the United States, for the District of Connecticut, and was argued by counsel. On consideration whereof, it is the opinion of this Court, that there is error in that part of the decree of the Circuit Court, affirming the decree of the District Court, which ordered the said negroes to be delivered to the President of the United States, to be transported to Africa, in pursuance of the act of Congress, of the 3d of March, 1819; and that, as to that part, it ought to be reversed: and, in all other respects, that the said decree of the Circuit Court ought to be affirmed. It is therefore ordered adjudged, and decreed by this Court, that the decree of the said Circuit Court be, and the same is hereby, affirmed, except as to the part aforesaid, and as to that part, that it be reversed; and that the cause be remanded to the Circuit Court, with directions to enter, in lieu of that part, a decree, that the said negroes be, and are hereby, declared to be free, and that they be dismissed from the custody of the Court, and be discharged from the suit and go thereof quit without day. This cause came on to be heard on the transcript of the record from the Circuit Court of the United States, for the District of Connecticut, and was argued by counsel. On consideration whereof, it is the opinion of this Court, that there is error in that part of the decree of the Circuit Court, affirming the decree of the District Court, which ordered the said negroes to be delivered to the President of the United States, to be transported to Africa, in pursuance of the act of congress of the 3d of March, 1819; and that, as to that part, it ought to be reversed: and in all other respects, that the said decree of the [p*598] Circuit Court ought to be affirmed. It is therefore ordered adjudged, and decreed by this Court, that the decree of the said Circuit Court be, and the same is hereby, affirmed, except as to the part aforesaid, and as to that part, that it be reversed; and that the cause be remanded to the Circuit Court, with directions to enter, in lieu of that part, a decree, that the said negroes be and are hereby, declared to be free, and that they be dismissed from the custody of the Court, and be discharged from the suit and go thereof quit without day.

Annexation of Texas (1845)

United States Statutes at Large (29th Cong., 1st sess., chap. 1), pp. 1–2

March 1, 1845

An Act

To extend the Laws of the United States over the State of Texas, and for other Purposes. Be it enacted by the Senate and House of Representatives of the United States of America in Congress assembled, That all the laws of the United States are hereby declared to extend to and over, and to have full force and effect within, the State of Texas, admitted at the present session of Congress into the Confederacy and Union of the United States.

Sec. 2. *And be it further enacted,* That the said State of Texas shall constitute one judicial district, to be called the District of Texas, for which one judge shall be appointed, who shall reside therein, and who shall receive a salary of two thousand dollars per annum, and who shall hold the first term of said court at Galveston, on the first Monday of February next, and at such other times and places in said district as may be provided by law, or as said judge may order; and that said court shall have and exercise the same powers and jurisdiction as have been conferred by law on the District Courts of the United States; and, also, shall have and exercise the powers and jurisdiction of a Circuit Court of the United States; and appeals and writs of error shall lie from the decisions of said District and Circuit Courts for the District of Texas to the Supreme Court of the United States, in the same cases as from a Circuit Court of the United States to said Supreme Court, and under the same regulations.

Sec. 3. *And be it further enacted,* That there shall be appointed in and for said district a person learned in the law, to act as attorney of the United States for said district, and also a person to act as marshal of the United States for said district, each of whom shall receive an annual salary of two hundred dollars, and also such compensation and fees for official services as have been or may be provided by law for United States district attorneys and marshals; and the judge of said court shall appoint a clerk therefor, who shall receive like compensation and fees as have been or may be allowed by law to clerks of the District and Circuit Courts of the United States. Approved, December 29, 1845.

Oregon Boundary Treaty (1846)

U. S. Statutes at Large 9 (1845–51), pp. 869–870

June 15, 1846

Treaty with Great Britain

In Regard to Limits Westward of the Rocky Mountains.

The United States of America and her Majesty the Queen of the United Kingdom of Great Britain and Ireland, deeming it to be desirable for the future welfare of both countries that the state of doubt and uncertainty which has hitherto prevailed respecting the sovereignty and government of the territory on the northwest coast of America, lying westward of the Rocky or Stony Mountains, should be finally terminated by an amicable compromise of the rights mutually asserted by the two parties over the said territory, have respectively named plenipotentiaries to treat and agree concerning the terms of such settlement—that is to say: the President of the United States of America has, on his part, furnished with full powers James Buchanan, Secretary of State of the United States, and her Majesty the Queen of the United Kingdom of Great Britain and Ireland has, on her part, appointed the Right Honorable Richard Pakenham, a member of her Majesty's Most Honorable Privy Council, and her Majesty's Envoy Extraordinary and Minister Plenipotentiary to the United States; who, after having communicated to each other their respective full powers, found in good and due form, have agreed upon and concluded the following articles:—

Article I

From the point on the forty-ninth parallel of north latitude, where the boundary laid down in existing treaties and conventions between the United States and Great Britain terminates, the line of boundary between the territories of the United States and those of her Britannic Majesty shall be continued westward along the said forty-ninth parallel of north latitude to the middle of the channel which separates the continent from Vancouver's Island, and thence southerly through the middle of the said channel, and of Fuca's Straits, to the Pacific Ocean: *Provided, however,* That the navigation of the whole of the said channel and straits, south of the forty-ninth parallel of north latitude, remain free and open to both parties.

Article II

From the point at which the forty-ninth parallel of north latitude shall be found to intersect the great northern branch of the Columbia River, the navigation of the said branch shall be free and open to the Hudson's Bay Company, and to all British subjects trading with the same, to the point where the said branch meets the main stream of the Columbia, and thence down the said main stream to the ocean, with free access into and through the said river or rivers, it being understood that all the usual portages along the line thus described shall, in like manner, be free and open. In navigating the said river or rivers, British subjects, with their goods and produce, shall be treated on the same footing as citizens of the United States; it being, however, always understood that nothing in this article shall be construed as preventing, or intended to prevent, the government of the United States from making any regulations respecting the navigation of the said river or rivers not inconsistent with the present treaty.

Article III

In the future appropriation of the territory south of the forty-ninth parallel of north latitude, as provided in the first article of this treaty, the possessory rights of the Hudson's Bay Company, and of all British subjects who may be already in the occupation of land or other property lawfully acquired within the said territory, shall be respected.

Article IV

The farms, lands, and other property of every description, belonging to the Puget's Sound Agricultural Company, on the north side of the Columbia River, shall be confirmed to the said company. In case, however, the situation of those farms and lands should be considered by the United States to be of public and political importance, and the United States government should signify a desire to obtain possession of the whole, or of any part thereof, the property so required shall be transferred to the said government, at a proper valuation, to be agreed upon between the parties.

Article V

The present treaty shall be ratified by the President of the United States, by and with the advice and consent of the Senate thereof, and by her Britannic Majesty; and the ratifications shall be exchanged at London, at the expiration of six months from the date hereof, or sooner, if possible.

In witness whereof, the respective Plenipotentiaries have signed the same, and have affixed thereto the seals of their arms.

Done at Washington, the fifteenth day of June, in the year of our Lord one thousand eight hundred and forty-six. James Buchanan. [L. S.] Richard Pakenham. [L. S.]

Treaty of Guadalupe-Hidalgo (1848)

Charles I. Bevans, ed., *Treaties and Other International Agreements of the United States, 1776–1947* (Washington, D.C.: Dept. of State, 1968–), pp. 791–806

Guadalupe-Hidalgo, Mexico
February 2, 1848

In the name of Almighty God:

The United States of America, and the United Mexican States, animated by a sincere desire to put an end to the calamities of the war which unhappily exists between the two Republics, and to establish upon a solid basis relations of peace and friendship, which shall confer reciprocal benefits upon the citizens of both, and assure the concord, harmony and mutual confidence, wherein the two Peoples should live, as good Neighbours, have for that purpose appointed their respective Plenipotentiaries: that is to say, the President of the United States has appointed Nicholas P. Trist, a citizen of the United States, and the President of the Mexican Republic has appointed Don Luis Gonzaga Cuevas, Don Bernardo Couto, and Don Miguel Atristain, citizens of the said Republic; who, after a reciprocal communication of their respective full powers, have under the protection of Almighty God, the author of Peace, arranged, agreed upon, and signed the following

TREATY OF PEACE, FRIENDSHIP, LIMITS AND SETTLEMENT BETWEEN the United States of America and the Mexican Republic

Article I

There shall be firm and universal peace between the United States of America and the Mexican Republic, and between their respective Countries, territories, cities, towns and people, without exception of places or persons . . .

Article V

The Boundary line between the two Republics shall commence in the Gulf of Mexico, three leagues from land, opposite the mouth of the Rio Grande, otherwise called Rio Bravo del Norte, or opposite the mouth of it's deepest branch, if it should have more than one branch emptying directly into the sea; from thence, up the middle of that river, following the deepest channel, where it has more than one to the point where it strikes the Southern boundary of New Mexico; thence, westwardly along the whole Southern Boundary of New Mexico (which runs north of the town called *Paso*) to it's western termination; thence, northward, along the western line of New Mexico, until it intersects the first branch of the river Gila; (or if it should not intersect any branch of that river, then, to the point on the said line nearest to such branch, and thence in a direct line to the same;) thence down the middle of the said branch and of the said river, until it empties into the Rio Colorado; thence, across the Rio Colorado, following the division line between Upper and Lower California to the Pacific Ocean . . .

Article VII

The river Gila, and the part of the Rio Bravo del Norte lying below the southern boundary of New Mexico, being, agreeably to the fifth Article, divided in the middle between the two Republics, the navigation of the Gila and the Bravo below said boundary shall be free and common to the vessels and citizens of both countries; and neither shall, without the consent of the other, construct any work that may impede or interrupt, in whole or in part, the exercise of this right: not even for the purpose of favoring new methods of navigation . . .

Article VIII

Mexicans now established in territories previously belonging to Mexico, and which remain for the future within the limits of the United States, as defined by the present Treaty, shall be free to continue where they now reside, or to remove at any time to the Mexican Republic, retaining the property which they possess in the said territories, or disposing thereof and removing the proceeds wherever they please; without their being subjected, on this account, to any contribution, tax or charge whatever. . .

Article XII
In consideration of the extension acquired by the boundaries of the United States, as defined in the fifth Article of the present treaty, the Government of the United States engages to pay to that of the Mexican Republic the sum of fifteen Millions of Dollars . . .

Article XIII
The United States engage moreover, to assume and pay to the claimants all the amounts now due them, and those hereafter to become due, by reason of the claims already liquidated and decided against the Mexican Republic, under the conventions between the two Republics, severally concluded on the eleventh day of April eighteen hundred and thirty-nine, and on the thirtieth day of January eighteen hundred and forty three: so that the Mexican Republic shall be absolutely exempt for the future, from all expense whatever on account of the said claims.

Article XIV
The United States do furthermore discharge the Mexican Republic from all claims of citizens of the United States, not heretofore decided against the Mexican Government, which may have arisen previously to the date of the signature of this treaty: which discharge shall be final and perpetual, whether the said claims be rejected or to be allowed by the Board of Commissioners provided for in the following Article, and whatever shall be the total amount of those allowed.

Article XV
The United States, exonerating Mexico from all demands on account of the claims of their citizens mentioned in the preceding Article, and considering them entirely and forever cancelled, whatever their amount may be, undertake to make satisfaction for the same, to an amount not exceeding three and one quarter millions of dollars . . .

Article XXI
If unhappily any disagreement should hereafter arise between the Governments of the two Republics, whether with respect to the interpretation of any stipulation in this treaty, or with respect to any other particular concerning the political or commercial relations of the two Nations, the said Governments, in the name of those Nations, do promise to each other, that they will endeavour, in the most sincere and earnest manner, to settle the differences so arising, and to preserve the state of peace and friendship, in which the two countries are now placing themselves: using, for this end, mutual representations and pacific negotiations. And if, by these means, they should not be enabled to come to an agreement, a resort shall not, on this account, be had to reprisals, aggression or hostility of any kind, by the one Republic against the other, until the Government of that which deems itself aggrieved, shall have maturely considered, in the spirit of peace and good neighbourship, whether it would not be better that such difference should be settled by the arbitration of Commissioners appointed on each side, or by that of a friendly nation. And should such course be proposed by either party, it shall be acceded to by the other, unless deemed by it altogether incompatible with the nature of the difference, or the circumstances of the case.

Declaration of Women's Rights (1848)

Henry Steele Commager and Milton Cantor, eds.
Documents of American History, 10th ed.
(Englewood Cliffs, N.J.: Prentice Hall, 1988) pp. 315–317

July 19, 1848

1. Declaration of Sentiments

When, in the course of human events, it becomes necessary for one portion of the family of man to assume among the people of the earth a position different from that which they have hitherto occupied, but one to which the laws of nature and of nature's God entitle them, a decent respect to the opinions of mankind requires that they should declare the causes that impel them to such a course.

We hold these truths to be self-evident: that all men and women are created equal; that they are endowed by their Creator with certain inalienable rights; that among these are life, liberty, and the pursuit of happiness; that to secure these rights governments are instituted, deriving their just powers from the consent of the governed. Whenever any form of government becomes destructive of these ends, it is the right of those who suffer from it to refuse allegiance to it, and to insist upon the institution of a new government, laying its foundation on such principles, and organizing its powers in such form, as to them shall seem most likely to effect their safety and happiness. Prudence, indeed, will dictate that governments long established should not be changed for light and transient causes; and accordingly all experience hath shown that mankind are more disposed to suffer while evils are sufferable, than to right themselves by abolishing the forms to which they are accustomed. But when a long train of abuses and usurpations, pursuing invariably the same object, evinces a design to reduce them under absolute despotism, it is their duty to throw off such government, and to provide new guards for their future security. Such has been the patient sufferance of the women under this government, and such is now the necessity which constrains them to demand the equal station to which they are entitled.

The history of mankind is a history of repeated injuries and usurpations on the part of man toward woman, having in direct object the establishment of an absolute tyranny over her. To prove this, let facts be submitted to a candid world.

He has never permitted her to exercise her inalienable right to the elective franchise.

He has compelled her to submit to laws, in the formation of which she had no voice.

He has withheld from her rights which are given to the most ignorant and degraded men—both natives and foreigners.

Having deprived her of this first right of a citizen, the elective franchise, thereby leaving her without representation in the halls of legislation, he has oppressed her on all sides.

He has made her, if married, in the eye of the law, civilly dead.

He has taken from her all right in property, even to the wages she earns.

He has made her, morally, an irresponsible being, as she can commit many crimes with impunity, provided they be done in the presence of her husband. In the covenant of marriage, she is compelled to promise obedience to her husband, he becoming, to all intents and purposes, her master—the law giving him power to deprive her of her liberty, and to administer chastisement.

He has so framed the laws of divorce, as to what shall be the proper causes, and in case of separation, to whom the guardianship of the children shall be given, as to be wholly regardless of the happiness of women—the law, in all cases, going upon a false supposition of the supremacy of man, and giving all power into his hands.

After depriving her of all rights as a married woman, if single, and the owner of property, he has taxed her to support a government which recognizes her only when her property can be made profitable to it.

He has monopolized nearly all the profitable employments, and from those she is permitted to follow, she receives but a scanty remuneration. He closes against her all the avenues to wealth and distinction which he considers most honorable to himself. As a teacher of theology, medicine, or law, she is not known.

He has denied her the facilities for obtaining a thorough education, all colleges being closed against her.

He allows her in Church, as well as State, but a subordinate position, claiming Apostolic authority for her exclusion from the ministry, and, with some exceptions, from any public participation in the affairs of the Church.

He has created a false public sentiment by giving to the world a different code of morals for men and women, by which moral delinquencies which exclude women from society, are not only tolerated, but deemed of little account in man.

He has usurped the prerogative of Jehovah himself, claiming it as his right to assign for her a sphere of action, when that belongs to her conscience and to her God.

He has endeavored, in every way that he could, to destroy her confidence in her own powers, to lessen her self-respect and to make her willing to lead a dependent and abject life.

Now, in view of this entire disfranchisement of one-half the people of this country, their social and religious degradation—in view of the unjust laws above mentioned, and because women do feel themselves aggrieved, oppressed, and fraudulently deprived of their most sacred rights, we insist that they have immediate admission to all the rights and privileges which belong to them as citizens of the United States.

In entering upon the great work before us, we anticipate no small amount of misconception, misrepresentation, and ridicule; but we shall use every instrumentality within our power to effect our object. We shall employ agents, circulate tracts, petition the State and National legislatures, and endeavor to enlist the pulpit and the press in our behalf. We hope this Convention will be followed by a series of Conventions embracing every part of the country.

2. Resolutions

Whereas, The great precept of nature is conceded to be, that "man shall pursue his own true and substantial happiness." Blackstone in his Commentaries remarks, that this law of Nature being coeval with mankind, and dictated by God himself, is of course superior in obligation to any other. It is binding over all the globe, in all countries and at all times; no human laws are of any validity if contrary to this, and such of them as are valid, derive all their force, and all their validity, and all their authority, mediately and immediately, from this original; therefore,

Resolved, That all laws which prevent woman from occupying such a station in society as her conscience shall dictate, or which place her in a position inferior to that of man, are contrary to the great precept of nature, and therefore of no force or authority.

Resolved, That woman is man's equal—was intended to be so by the Creator, and the highest good of the race demands that she should be recognized as such.

Resolved, That the women of this country ought to be enlightened in regard to the laws under which they live, that they may no longer publish their degradation by declaring themselves satisfied with their present position, nor their ignorance, by asserting that they have all the rights they want.

Resolved, That inasmuch as man, while claiming for himself intellectual superiority, does accord to woman moral superiority, it is pre-eminently his duty to encourage her to speak and teach, as she has an opportunity, in all religious assemblies.

Resolved, That the same amount of virtue, delicacy, and refinement of behavior that is required of woman in the social state, should also be required of man, and the same transgressions should be visited with equal severity on both man and woman.

Resolved, That the objection of indelicacy and impropriety, which is so often brought against woman when she addresses a public audience, comes with a very ill-grace from those who encourage, by their attendance, her appearance on the stage, in the concert, or in feats of the circus.

Resolved, That woman has too long rested satisfied in the circumscribed limits which corrupt customs and a perverted application of the Scriptures have marked out for her, and that it is time she should move in the enlarged sphere which her great Creator has assigned her.

Resolved, That it is the duty of the women of this country to secure to themselves their sacred right to the elective franchise.

Resolved, That the equality of human rights results necessarily from the fact of the identity of the race in capabilities and responsibilities.

Resolved, That the speedy success of our cause depends upon the zealous and untiring efforts of both men and women, for the overthrow of the monopoly of the pulpit, and for the securing to women an equal participation with men in the various trades, professions, and commerce.

Resolved, therefore, That, being invested by the creator with the same capabilities, and the same consciousness of responsibility for their exercise, it is demonstrably the right and duty of woman, equally with man, to promote every righteous cause by every righteous means; and especially in regard to the great subjects of morals and religion, it is self-evidently her right to participate with her brother in teaching them, both in private and in public, by writing and by speaking, by any instrumentalities proper to be used, and in any assemblies proper to be held; and this being a self-evident truth growing out of the divinely implanted principles of human nature, any custom or authority adverse to it, whether modern or wearing the hoary sanction of antiquity, is to be regarded as a self-evident falsehood, and at war with mankind.

"Civil Disobedience" (1849)

Henry David Thoreau

Brooks Atkinson, ed., *Walden and Other Writings of Henry David Thoreau* (New York: The Modern Library, 1965)

I heartily accept the motto,—"That government is best which governs least;" and I should like to see it acted up to more rapidly and systematically. Carried out, it finally amounts to this, which also I believe,—"That government is best which governs not at all;" and when men are prepared for it, that will be the kind of government which they will have. Government is at best but an expedient; but most governments are usually, and all governments are sometimes, inexpedient. The objections which have been brought against a standing army, and they are many and weighty, and deserve to prevail, may also at last be brought against a standing government. The standing army is only an arm of the standing government. The government itself, which is only the mode which the people have chosen to execute their will, is equally liable to be abused and perverted before the people can act through it. Witness the present Mexican war, the work of comparatively a few individuals using the standing government as their tool; for, in the outset, the people would not have consented to this measure.

This American government,—what is it but a tradition, though a recent one, endeavoring to transmit itself unimpaired to posterity, but each instant losing some of its integrity? It has not the vitality and force of a single living man; for a single man can bend it to his will. It is a sort of wooden gun to the people themselves. But it is not the less necessary for this; for the people must have some complicated machinery or other, and hear its din, to satisfy that idea of government which they have. Governments show thus how successfully men can be imposed on, even impose on themselves, for their own advantage. It is excellent, we must all allow. Yet this government never of itself furthered any enterprise, but by the alacrity with which it got out of its way. *It* does not keep the country free. *It* does not settle the West. *It* does not educate. The character inherent in the American people has done all that has been accomplished; and it would have done somewhat more, if the government had not sometimes got in its way. For government is an expedient by which men would fain succeed in letting one another alone; and, as has been said, when it is most expedient, the governed are most let alone by it. Trade and commerce, if they were not made of India-rubber, would never manage to bounce over the obstacles which legislators are continually putting in their way; and, if one were to judge these men wholly by the effects of their actions and not partly by their intentions, they would deserve to be classed and punished with those mischievous persons who put obstructions on the railroads.

But, to speak practically and as a citizen, unlike those who call themselves no-government men, I ask for, not at once no government, but *at once* a better government. Let every man make known what kind of government would command his respect, and that will be one step toward obtaining it.

After all, the practical reason why, when the power is once in the hands of the people, a majority are permitted, and for a long period continue, to rule is not because they are most likely to be in the right, nor because this seems fairest to the minority, but because they are physically the strongest. But a government in which the majority rule in all cases cannot be based on justice, even as far as men understand it. Can there not be a government in which majorities do not virtually decide right and wrong, but conscience?—in which majorities decide only those questions to which the rule of expediency is applicable? Must the citizen ever for a moment, or in the least degree, resign his conscience to the legislator? Why has every man a conscience, then? I think that we should be men first, and subjects afterward. It is not desirable to cultivate a respect for the law, so much as for the right. The only obligation which I have a right to assume is to do at any time what I think right. It is truly enough said, that a corporation has no conscience; but a corporation of conscientious men is a corporation *with* a conscience. Law never made men a whit more just; and, by means of their respect for it, even the well-disposed are daily made the agents of injustice. A common and natural result of an undue respect for law is, that you may see a file of soldiers, colonel, captain, corporal, privates, powder-monkeys, and all, marching in admirable order over hill and dale to the wars, against their wills, ay, against their common sense and consciences, which makes it very steep marching indeed, and produces a palpitation of the heart. They have no doubt that it is a damnable business in which they are concerned; they are all peaceably inclined. Now, what are they? Men at all? or small movable forts and magazines, at the service of some unscrupulous man in power? Visit the Navy-Yard, and behold a marine, such a man as an American government can make, or such as it can make a man with its black arts,—a mere shadow and reminiscence of humanity, a man laid out alive and standing, and already, as one may say, buried under arms with funeral accompaniments, though it may be,—

> "Not a drum was heard, not a funeral note,
> As his corse to the rampart we hurried;
> Not a soldier discharged his farewell shot
> O'er the grave where our hero we buried."

The mass of men serve the state thus, not as men mainly, but as machines, with their bodies. They are the standing army, and the militia, jailors, constables, posse comitatus, etc. In most cases there is no free exercise whatever of the judgment or of the moral sense; but they put themselves on a level with wood and earth and stones; and wooden men can perhaps be manufactured that will serve the purpose as well. Such command no more respect than men of straw or a lump of dirt. They have the same sort of worth only as horses and dogs. Yet such as these even are commonly esteemed good citizens. Others—as most legislators, politicians, lawyers, ministers, and office-holders—serve the state chiefly with their heads; and, as they rarely make any moral distinctions, they are as likely to serve the Devil, without *intending* it, as God. A very few, as heroes, patriots, martyrs, reformers in the great sense, and *men*, serve the state with their consciences also, and so necessarily resist it for the most part; and they are commonly treated as enemies by it. A wise man will only be useful as a man, and will not submit to be "clay," and "stop a hole to keep the wind away," but leave that office to his dust at least:—

> "I am too high-born to be propertied,
> To be a secondary at control,
> Or useful serving-man and instrument
> To any sovereign state throughout the world."

He who gives himself entirely to his fellow-men appears to them useless and selfish; but he who gives himself partially to them is pronounced a benefactor and philanthropist.

How does it become a man to behave toward this American government to-day? I answer, that he cannot without disgrace be associated with it. I cannot for an instant recognize that political organization as *my* government which is the *slave's* government also.

All men recognize the right of revolution; that is, the right to refuse allegiance to, and to resist, the government, when its tyranny or its inefficiency are great and unendurable. But almost all say that such is not the case now. But such was the case, they think, in the Revolution of '75. If one were to tell me that this was a bad government because it taxed certain foreign commodities brought to its ports, it is most probable that I should not make an ado about it, for I can do without them. All machines have their friction; and possibly this does enough good to counterbalance the evil. At any rate, it is a great evil to make a stir about it. But when the friction comes to have its machine, and oppression and robbery are organized, I say, let us not have such a machine any longer. In other words, when a sixth of the population of a nation which has undertaken to be the refuge of liberty are slaves, and a whole country is unjustly overrun and conquered by a foreign army, and subjected to military law, I think that it is not too soon for honest men to rebel and revolutionize. What makes this duty the more urgent is the fact that the country so overrun is not our own, but ours is the invading army.

Paley, a common authority with many on moral questions, in his chapter on the "Duty of Submission to Civil Government," resolves all civil obligation into expediency;

and he proceeds to say, "that so long as the interest of the whole society requires it, that is, so long as the established government cannot be resisted or changed without public inconveniency, it is the will of God that the established government be obeyed, and no longer. . . . This principle being admitted, the justice of every particular case of resistance is reduced to a computation of the quantity of the danger and grievance on the one side, and of the probability and expense of redressing it on the other." Of this, he says, every man shall judge for himself. But Paley appears never to have contemplated those cases to which the rule of expediency does not apply, in which a people, as well as an individual, must do justice, cost what it may. If I have unjustly wrested a plank from a drowning man, I must restore it to him though I drown myself. This, according to Paley, would be inconvenient. But he that would save his life, in such a case, shall lose it. This people must cease to hold slaves, and to make war on Mexico, though it cost them their existence as a people . . .

I meet this American government, or its representative, the state government, directly, and face to face, once a year—no more—in the person of its tax-gatherer; this is the only mode in which a man situated as I am necessarily meets it; and it then says distinctly, Recognize me; and the simplest, most effectual, and, in the present posture of affairs, the indispensablest mode of treating with it on this head, of expressing your little satisfaction with and love for it, is to deny it then. My civil neighbor, the tax-gatherer, is the very man I have to deal with,—for it is, after all, with men and not with parchment that I quarrel,—and he has voluntarily chosen to be an agent of the government. How shall he ever know well what he is and does as an officer of the government, or as a man, until he is obliged to consider whether he shall treat me, his neighbor, for whom he has respect, as a neighbor and well-disposed man, or as a maniac and disturber of the peace, and see if he can get over this obstruction to his neighborliness without a ruder and more impetuous thought or speech corresponding with his action. I know this well, that if one thousand, if one hundred, if ten men whom I could name,—if ten *honest* men only,—ay, if *one* honest man, in this State of Massachusetts, *ceasing to hold slaves*, were actually to withdraw from this copartnership, and be locked up in the county jail therefor, it would be the abolition of slavery in America. For it matters not how small the beginning may seem to be: what is once well done is done forever. But we love better to talk about it: that we say is our mission. Reform keeps many scores of newspapers in its service, but not one man. If my esteemed neighbor, the State's ambassador, who will devote his days to the settlement of the question of human rights in the Council Chamber, instead of being threatened with the prisons of Carolina, were to sit down the prisoner of Massachusetts, that State which is so anxious to foist the sin of slavery upon her sister,—though at present she can discover only an act of inhospitality to be the ground of a quarrel with her,—the Legislature would not wholly waive the subject the following winter.

Under a government which imprisons any unjustly, the true place for a just man is also a prison. The proper place to-day, the only place which Massachusetts has provided for her freer and less desponding spirits, is in her prisons, to be put out and locked out of the State by her own act, as they have already put themselves out by their principles. It is there that the fugitive slave, and the Mexican prisoner on parole, and the Indian come to plead the wrongs of his race should find them; on that separate, but more free and honorable ground, where the State places those who are not *with* her, but *against* her,—the only house in a slave State in which a free man can abide with honor. If any think that their influence would be lost there, and their voices no longer afflict the ear of the State, that they would not be as an enemy within its walls, they do not know by how much truth is stronger than error, nor how much more eloquently and effectively he can combat injustice who has experienced a little in his own person. Cast your whole vote, not a strip of paper merely, but your whole influence. A minority is powerless while it conforms to the majority; it is not even a minority then; but it is irresistible when it clogs by its whole weight. If the alternative is to keep all just men in prison, or give up war and slavery, the State will not hesitate which to choose. If a thousand men were not to pay their tax-bills this year, that would not be a violent and bloody measure, as it would be to pay them, and enable the State to commit violence and shed innocent blood. This is, in fact, the definition of a peaceable revolution, if any such is possible. If the tax-gatherer, or any other public officer, asks me, as one has done, "But what shall I do?" my answer is, "If you really wish to do anything, resign your office." When the subject has refused allegiance, and the officer has resigned his office, then the revolution is accomplished. But even suppose blood should flow. Is there not a sort of blood shed when the conscience is wounded? Through this wound a man's real manhood and immortality flow out, and he bleeds to an everlasting death. I see this blood flowing now...

The authority of government, even such as I am willing to submit to,—for I will cheerfully obey those who know and can do better than I, and in many things even those who neither know nor can do so well,—is still an impure one: to be strictly just, it must have the sanction and consent of the governed. It can have no pure right over my person and property but what I concede to it. The progress from an absolute to a limited monarchy, from a limited monarchy to a democracy, is a progress toward a true respect for the individual. Even the Chinese philosopher was wise enough to regard the individual as the basis of the empire. Is a democracy, such as we know it, the last improvement possible in government? Is it not possible to take a step further towards recognizing and organizing the rights of man? There will never be a really free and enlightened State until the State comes to recognize the individual as a higher and independent power, from which all its own power and authority are derived, and treats him accordingly. I please myself with imagining a State at last which can afford to be just to all men, and to treat the individual with respect as a neighbor; which even would not think it inconsistent with its own repose if a few were to live aloof from it, not meddling with it, nor embraced by it, who fulfilled all the duties of neighbors and fellow-men. A State which bore this kind of fruit, and suffered it to drop off as fast as it ripened, would prepare the way for a still more perfect and glorious State, which also I have imagined, but not yet anywhere seen.

The Compromise of 1850
Henry Clay

Calvin Colton, ed. *The Life, Correspondence and Speeches of Henry Clay,* vol. 3 (1855; reprint, New York: G. P. Putnam's Sons, 1904), pp. 301–302

"On the Compromise of 1850" (1850)

January 29, 1850

Resolutions Introduced in the Senate of the United States by Mr. Clay

Preamble.—It being desirable for the peace, concord, and harmony of the Union of these States, to settle and adjust amicably all questions of controversy between them arising out of the institution of Slavery, upon a fair equality and just basis, therefore—

1st. *Resolved,* That California, with suitable boundaries, ought, upon her application, to be admitted as one of the States of this Union, without the imposition by Congress of any restriction to the exclusion or introduction of slavery within those boundaries.

2d. *Resolved,* That as slavery does not exist by law, and is not likely to be introduced into any of the territory acquired by the United States from the Republic of Mexico, it is inexpedient for Congress to provide, by law, either for its introduction into, or its exclusion from, any part of the said territory; and that appropriate territorial Governments ought to be established by Congress, in all of the said territory not assigned as the boundaries of the proposed State of California, without the addition of any restriction or condition on the subject of slavery.

3d. *Resolved,* That the western boundary of the State of Texas ought to be fixed on the Rio del Norte, commencing one marine league from its mouth, and running up that river to the southern line of New Mexico, thence with that line eastwardly, and continuing in the same direction, to the line as established between the United States and Spain, excluding any portion of New Mexico, whether lying on the east or west of that river.

4th. *Resolved,* That it be proposed to the State of Texas that the United States will provide for the payment of all that portion of all the legitimate and bona fide public debts of that State, contracted prior to its annexation to the United States, and for which the duties on foreign imports were pledged by the said States to its creditors, not exceeding the sum of—dollars, in consideration of the duties, as pledged, having been no longer applicable to that object after the said annexation, but having thenceforward become payable to the United States, and upon the condition also that the said State shall, by some solemn and authentic act of her Legislature, or of a convention, relinquish to the United States any claim which it has to any part of New Mexico.

5th. *Resolved,* That it is inexpedient to abolish slavery in the District of Columbia, while that institution continues to exist in the State of Maryland, without the consent of that State, without the consent of the people of the District, and without just compensation to the owners of slaves within the District.

6th. *Resolved,* That it is expedient to prohibit within the District the trade in slaves brought into it from States or places beyond the limits of the District, either to be sold therein, as merchandise, or to be transported to other markets without the District of Columbia.

7th. *Resolved,* That more effectual provision ought to be made by law according to the requirements of the Constitution, for the restitution and delivery of persons bound to service or labor, in any State, who may escape into any other State or Territory of this Union.

8th. *Resolved,* That Congress has no power to prohibit or obstruct the trade in slaves between the slaveholding States, and that the admission or exclusion of slaves brought from one into another of them, depends exclusively upon their own particular law.

Texas and New Mexico Act (1850)

U.S. Statutes at Large 9 (1845–51), pp. 446–452

An Act Proposing to the State of Texas the Establishment of her Northern and Western Boundaries, the Relinquishment by the said State of all Territory claimed by her exterior to said Boundaries, and of all her Claims upon the United States, and to establish a territorial Government for New Mexico.

Be it enacted by the Senate and House of Representatives of the United States of America in Congress assembled, That the following propositions shall be, and the same hereby are, offered to the State of Texas, which, when agreed to by the said State, in an act passed by the general assembly, shall be binding and obligatory upon the United States, and upon the said State of Texas: *Provided,* The said agreement by the said general assembly shall be given on or before the first day of December, eighteen hundred and fifty:

First. The State of Texas will agree that her boundary on the north shall commence at the point at which that meridian of one hundred degrees west from Greenwich is intersected by the parallel of thirty-six degrees thirty minutes north latitude, and shall run from said point due west to the meridian of one hundred and three degrees west from Greenwich; thence her boundary shall run due south to the thirty-second degree of north latitude; thence on the said parallel of thirty-two degrees of north latitude to the Rio Bravo del Norte, and thence with the channel of said river to the Gulf of Mexico.

Second. The State of Texas cedes to the United States all her claim to territory exterior to the limits and boundaries which she agrees to establish by the first article of this agreement.

Third. The State of Texas relinquishes all claim upon the United States for liability of the debts of Texas, and for compensation or indemnity for the surrender to the United States of her ships, forts, arsenals, custom-houses, custom-house revenue, arms and munitions of war and public buildings with their sites, which became the property of the United States at the time of the annexation.

Fourth. The United States, in consideration of said establishment of boundaries, cession of claim to territory, and relinquishment of claims, will pay to the State of Texas the sum of ten millions of dollars in a stock bearing five per cent, interest, and redeemable at the end of fourteen years, the interest payable half-yearly at the treasury of the United States...

Sec. 2. *And be it further enacted,* That all that portion of the Territory of the United States bounded as follows: Beginning at a point in the Colorado River where the boundary line with the republic of Mexico crosses the same; thence eastwardly with the said boundary line to the Rio Grande; thence following the main channel of said river to the parallel of the thirty-second degree of north latitude; thence east with said degree to its intersection with the one hundred and third degree of longitude west of Greenwich; thence north with said degree of longitude to the parallel of thirty-eight degree of north latitude; thence west with said parallel to the summit of the Sierra Madre; thence south with the crest of said mountains to the thirty-seventh parallel of north latitude; thence west with said parallel to its intersection with the boundary line of the State of California; thence with said boundary line to the place of beginning—be, and the same is hereby, erected into a temporary government, by the name of the Territory of New Mexico: Provided, That nothing in this act contained shall be construed to inhibit the government of the United States from dividing said Territory into two or more Territories, in such manner and at such times as Congress shall deem convenient and proper, or from attaching any portion thereof to any other Territory or State: *And provided, further,* That, when admitted as a State, the said Territory, or any portion of the same, shall be received into the Union, with or without slavery, as their constitution may prescribe at the time of their admission.

Utah Act (1850)

U.S. Statutes at Large 9 (1845–51), pp. 453-458

An Act to establish a Territorial Government for Utah.

Be it enacted by the Senate and House of Representatives of the United States of America in Congress assembled, That all part of the territory of the United States included within the following limits, to wit: bounded on the west by the State of California, on the north by the Territory of Oregon, and on the east by the summit of the Rocky Mountains, and on the south by the thirty-seventh parallel of north latitude, be, and the same is hereby, created into a temporary government, by the name of the Territory of Utah; and, when admitted as a State, the said Territory, or any portion of the same, shall be received into the Union, with or without slavery, as their constitution may prescribe at the time of their admission: *Provided,* That nothing in this act contained shall be construed to inhibit the government of the united States from dividing said Territory into two or more Territories, in such manner and at such times as Congress shall deem convenient and proper, or from attaching any portion of said Territory to any other State or Territory of the United States . . .

Fugitive Slave Act (1850)

U.S. Statutes at Large 9 (1845–51), pp. 462–463

September 18, 1850

An Act

To amend, and supplementary to, the Act entitled "An Act respecting Fugitives from Justice, and Persons escaping from the Service of their Masters," approved February twelfth, one thousand seven hundred and ninety-three.

. . . Sec. 5. *And be it further enacted,* That it shall be the duty of all marshals and deputy marshals to obey and execute all warrants and precepts issued under the provisions of this act, when to them directed; and should any marshal or deputy marshal refuse to receive such warrant, or other process, when tendered, or to use all proper means diligently to execute the same, he shall, on conviction thereof, be fined in the sum of one thousand dollars, to the use of such claimant, on the motion of such claimant, by the Circuit or District Court for the district of such marshal; and after arrest of such fugitive, be such marshal or his deputy, or whilst at any time in his custody under the provisions of this act, should such fugitive escape, whether with or without the assent of such marshal or his deputy, such marshal shall be liable, on his official bond, to be prosecuted for the benefit of such claimant, for the full value of the service or labor of said fugitive in the State, Territory, or District whence he escaped: and the better to enable the said commissioners, when thus appointed, to execute their duties faithfully and efficiently, in conformity with the requirements of the Constitution of the United States and of this act, they are hereby authorized and empowered, within their counties respectively, to appoint, in writing under their hands, any one or more suitable persons, from time to time, to execute all such warrants and other process as may be issued by them in the lawful performance of their respective duties; with authority to such commissioners, or the persons to be appointed by them, to execute process as aforesaid, to summon and call to their aid the bystanders, or *posse comitatus* of the proper county, when necessary to ensure a faithful observance of the clause of the Constitution referred to, in conformity with the provisions of this act; and all good citizens are hereby commanded to aid and assist in the prompt and efficient execution of this law, whenever their services may be required, as aforesaid, for that purpose; and said warrants shall run, and be executed by said officers, any where in the State within which they are issued.

Sec. 6. *And be it further enacted,* That when a person held to service or labor in any State or Territory of the United States, has heretofore or shall hereafter escape into another State or Territory of the United States, the person or persons to whom such service or labor may be due, or his, her, or their agent or attorney, duly authorized, by power of attorney, in writing, acknowledged and certified under the seal of some legal officer or court of the State or Territory in which the same may be executed, may pursue and reclaim such fugitive person, either by procuring a warrant from some one of the courts, judges, or commissioners aforesaid, of the proper circuit, district, or county, for the apprehension of such fugitive from service or labor, or by seizing and arresting such fugitive, where the same can be done without process, and by taking, or causing such person to be taken, forthwith before such court, judge, or commissioner, whose duty it shall be to hear and determine the case of such claimant in a summary manner; and upon satisfactory proof being made, by deposition or affidavit, in writing, to be taken and certified by such court, judge, or commissioner, or by other satisfactory testimony, duly taken and certified by some court, magistrate, justice of the peace, or other legal officer authorized to administer an oath and take depositions under the laws of the State or Territory from which such person owing service or labor may have escaped, with a certificate of such magistracy or other authority, as aforesaid, with the seal of the proper court or officer thereto attached, which seal shall be sufficient to establish the competency of the proof, and with proof, also by affidavit, of the identity of the person whose service or labor is claimed to be due as aforesaid, that the person so arrested does in fact owe service or labor to the person or persons claiming him or her, in the State or Territory from which such fugitive may have escaped as aforesaid, and that said person escaped, to make out and deliver to such claimant, his or her agent or attorney, a certificate setting forth the substantial facts as to the service or labor due from such fugitive to the claimant, and of his or her escape from the State or Territory in which such service or labor was due, to the State or Territory in which he or she was arrested, with authority to such claimant, or his or her agent or attorney, to use such reasonable force and restraint as may be necessary, under the circumstances of the case, to take and remove such fugitive person back to the State or Territory whence he or she may have escaped as aforesaid. In no trial or hearing under this act shall the testimony of such alleged fugitive be admitted in evidence; and the certificates in this and the first [fourth] section mentioned, shall be conclusive of the right of the person or persons in whose favor granted to remove such fugitive to the State or Territory from which he escaped, and shall prevent all molestation of such person or persons by any process issued by any court, judge, magistrate, or other person whomsoever.

Sec. 7. *And be it further enacted,* That any person who shall knowingly and willingly obstruct, hinder, or prevent such claimant, his agent or attorney, or any person or persons lawfully assisting him, her, or them, from arresting such a fugitive from service or labor, either with or without process as aforesaid, or shall rescue, or attempt to rescue, such fugitive from service or labor, from the custody of such claimant, his or her agent or attorney, or other person or persons lawfully assisting as aforesaid, when so arrested, pursuant to the authority herein given and declared; or shall aid, abet, or assist such person so owing service or labor as aforesaid, directly or indirectly, to escape from such claimant, his agent or attorney, or other person or persons legally authorized as aforesaid; or shall harbor or conceal such fugitive, so as to prevent the discovery and arrest of such person, after notice or knowledge of the fact that such person was a fugitive from service or labor as aforesaid, shall, for either of said offences, be subject to a fine not exceeding one thousand dollars, and imprisonment not exceeding six months, by indictment and conviction before the District Court of the United States for the district in which such offence may have been committed, or before the proper court of criminal jurisdiction, if committed within any one of the organized Territories of the United States; and shall moreover forfeit and pay, by way of civil damages to the party injured by such illegal conduct, the sum of one thousand dollars, for each fugitive so lost as aforesaid, to be recovered by action of debt, in any of the District or Territorial Courts aforesaid, within whose jurisdiction the said offence may have been committed. . .

Sec. 9. *And be it further enacted,* That, upon affidavit made by the claimant of such fugitive, his agent or attorney, after such certificate has been issued, that he has reason to apprehend that such fugitive will be rescued by force from his or their possession before he can be taken beyond the limits of the State in which the arrest is made, it shall be the duty of the officer making the arrest to retain such fugitive in his custody, and to remove him to the State whence he fled, and there to deliver him to said claimant, his agent, or attorney. And to this end, the officer aforesaid is hereby authorized and required to employ so many persons as he may deem necessary to overcome such force, and to retain them in his service so long as circumstances may require. The said officer and his assistants, while so employed, to receive the same compensation, and to be allowed the same expenses, as are now allowed by law for transportation of criminals, to be certified by the judge of the district within which the arrest is made, and paid out of the treasury of the United States.

Sec. 10. *And be it further enacted,* That when any person held to service or labor in any State or Territory, or in the District of Columbia, shall escape therefrom, the party to whom such service or labor shall be due, his, her, or their agent or attorney, may apply to any court of record therein, or judge thereof in vacation, and make satisfactory proof to such court, or judge in vacation, of the escape aforesaid, and that the person escaping owed service or labor to such-party. Whereupon the court shall cause a record to be made of the matters so proved, and also a general description of the person so escaping, with such convenient certainty as may be; and a transcript of such record, authenticated by the attestation of the clerk and of the seal of the said court, being produced in any other State, Territory, or district in which the person so escaping may be found, and being exhibited to any judge, commissioner, or other officer authorized by the law of the United States to cause persons escaping from service or labor to be delivered up, shall be held and taken to be full and conclusive evidence of the fact of escape, and that the service or labor of the person escaping is due to the party in such record mentioned. And upon the production by the said party of other and further evidence if necessary, either oral or by affidavit, in addition to what is contained in the said record of the identity of the person escaping, he or she shall be delivered up to the claimant. And the said court, commissioner, judge, or other person authorized by this act to grant certificates to claimants of fugitives, shall, upon the production of the record and other evidences aforesaid, grant to such claimant a certificate of his right to take any such person identified and proved to be owing service or labor as aforesaid, which certificate shall authorize such claimant to seize or arrest and transport such person to the State or Territory from which he escaped: *Provided,* That nothing herein contained shall be construed as requiring the production of a transcript of such record as evidence as aforesaid. But in its absence the claim shall be heard and determined upon other satisfactory proofs, competent in law.
Approved, September 18, 1850.

Act Abolishing the Slave Trade in the District of Columbia (1850)

U.S. Statutes at Large 9 (1845–51), pp. 467-468

September 20, 1850

An Act to Suppress the Slave Trade in the District of Columbia.

Be it enacted by the Senate and House of Representatives of the United States of America in Congress assembled, That from and after the first day of January, eighteen hundred and fifty-one, it shall not be lawful to bring into the District of Columbia any slave whatever, for the purpose of being sold, or for the purpose of being placed in depot, to be subsequently transferred to any other State or place to be sold as merchandize. And if any slave shall be brought into the said District by its owner, or by the authority or consent of its owner, contrary to the provisions of this act, such slave shall thereupon become liberated and free.

Sec. 2. *And be it further enacted,* That it shall and may be lawful for each of the corporations of the cities of Washington and Georgetown, from time to time, and as often as may be necessary, to abate, break up, and abolish any depot or place of confinement of slaves brought into the said District as merchandize, contrary to the provisions of this act, by such appropriate means as may appear to either of the said corporations expedient and proper. And the same power is hereby vested in the Levy Court of Washington county, if any attempt shall be made, within its jurisdictional limits, to establish a depot or place of confinement for slaves brought into the said District as merchandize for sale contrary to this act.

Approved, September 20, 1850.

Bibliography

Abzug, Robert H. *Cosmos Crumbling: American Reform and the Religious Imagination.* New York: Oxford University Press, 1994.

Aron, Stephen. *How the West Was Lost: The Transformation of Kentucky from Daniel Boone to Henry Clay.* Baltimore: Johns Hopkins University Press, 1996.

Arrington, Leonard J. *Brigham Young: American Moses.* New York: Knopf, 1985.

Arrington, Leonard J. and Davis Bitton. *The Mormon Experience: A History of the Latter-Day Saints.* Urbana: University of Illinois Press, 1979.

Bergeron, Paul H. *The Presidency of James K. Polk.* Lawrence: University Press of Kansas, 1987.

Berlin, Ira. *Many Thousands Gone: The First Two Centuries of Slavery in North America.* Cambridge, Mass.: Harvard University Press, 1998.

Billington, Ray Allen. *The Far Western Frontier, 1830–1860.* New York: Harper, 1956.

Brodie, Fawn. *No Man Knows My History: The Life of Joseph Smith.* New York: Knopf, 1945.

Davis, David Brion. *Antebellum American Culture: An Interpretative Anthology.* Lexington, Mass: Heath, 1979.

Degler, Carl. *At Odds: Women and the Family in America from the Revolution to the Present.* New York: Oxford University Press, 1980.

Douglass, Frederick. *The Life and Times of Frederick Douglass, An American Slave, Written by Himself.* 1845. Reprint, Boston: Bedford Books, 1993.

Dubois, Ellen Carol. *Feminism and Suffrage: The Emergence of the Independent Women's Movement in America, 1848–1869.* Ithaca, N.Y.: Cornell University Press, 1978.

Durham, Michael S. *Desert Between the Mountains: Mormons, Miners, Padres, Mountain Men, and the Opening of the Great Basin, 1772–1869.* New York: Henry Holt and Company, 1997.

Eisenhower, John S. D. *So Far from God: The U. S. War with Mexico, 1846–1848.* New York: Random House, 1989.

Faragher, John Mack. *Daniel Boone: The Life and Legend of an American Pioneer.* New York: Henry Holt & Company, 1992.

———. *Women and Men on the Overland Trail.* New Haven, Conn.: Yale University Press, 1979.

Fehrenbacher, Don E. *Sectional Crisis and Southern Constitutionalism.* Baton Rouge: Louisiana State University Press, 1995.

Flanders, Robert B. *Nauvoo: Kingdom on the Misssissippi.* Urbana: University of Illinois Press, 1965.

Foner, Eric. *Free Soil, Free Labor, Free Men: The Ideology of the Republican Party before the Civil War.* New York: Oxford University Press, 1970.

Freeling, William H. *Prelude to Civil War: The Nullification Controversy in South Carolina.* New York: Oxford University Press, 1992.

Grossberg, Michael. *Governing the Hearth: Law and Family in Nineteenth Century America.* Chapel Hill: University of North Carolina Press, 1985.

Gutman, Herbert. *Who Built America: Working People and the Nation 's Economy, Politics, Culture, and Society,* Vol. 1. New York: Pantheon Books, 1989.

Hickey, Donald R. *The War of 1812: A Forgotten Conflict.* Urbana: University of Illinois Press, 1989.

Hirsch, Adam Jay. *The Rise of the Penitentiary: Prisons and Punishment in Early America.* New Haven, Conn.: Yale University Press, 1992.

Hurt, R. Douglas. *American Agriculture: A Brief History.* Ames: Iowa State University Press, 1994.

Irons, Peter. *A People's History of the Supreme Court: The Men and Woman Whose Cases and Decisions Have Shaped Our Constitution.* New York: Viking, 1999.

Jeffrey, Julie Roy. *Converting the West: A Biography of Narcissa Whitman.* Norman: University of Oklahoma Press, 1991.

———. *The Great Silent Army of Abolitionism: Ordinary Women and the Antislavery Movement.* Chapel Hill: University of North Carolina Press, 1998.

Johannsen, Robert W. *Stephen A. Douglas.* New York: Oxford University Press, 1973.

———. *To the Halls of Montezuma: The Mexican War in the American Imagination.* New York: Oxford University Press, 1985.

Larkin, John. *The Reshaping of Everyday Life, 1790–1840.* New York: Harper & Row, 1988.

Levine, Bruce. *Half Slave, Half Free: The Roots of the Civil War.* New York: Hill & Wang, 1992.

Litwack, Leon F. *North of Slavery: The Negro in the Free States, 1790–1860.* Chicago: University of Chicago Press, 1960.

Merk, Frederick. *The Monroe Doctrine and American Expansion.* New York: Knopf, 1966.

Mintz, Steven. *Moralists and Modernizers: America's Pre-Civil War Reformers.* Baltimore: Johns Hopkins University Press, 1995.

Morrison, Michael A. *Slavery and the American West: The Eclipse of Manifest Destiny and the Coming of the Civil War.* Chapel Hill: University of North Carolina Press, 1997.

Owsley, Frank L. *Filibusters and Expansionists: Jeffersonian Manifest Destiny, 1800–1821.* Tuscaloosa: University of Alabama Press, 1997.

Perdue, Theda and Michael D. Green, eds. *The Cherokee Removal: A Brief History with Documents.* Boston: Bedford Books, 1995.

Perry. Lewis. *Radical Abolitionism: Anarchy and the Government of God in Antislavery Thought.* Ithaca, N.Y.: Cornell University Press, 1973.

Peterson, Merrill. *The Great Triumvirate: Webster, Clay, and Calhoun.* New York: Oxford University Press, 1987.

Pletcher, David. *The Diplomacy of Annexation: Texas, Oregon, and the Mexican War.* Columbia: University of Missouri Press, 1973.

Prucha, Francis Paul. *The Great Father: The United States Government and the American Indians.* 2 vols. Lincoln: University of Nebraska Press, 1984.

Remini, Robert V. *Henry Clay: Statesman for the Union.* New York: W. W. Norton, 1991.

———. *The Life of Andrew Jackson.* New York: Harper & Row, 1988.

Rohrbough, Malcolm J. *Days of Gold: The California Gold Rush and the American Nation.* Berkeley: University of California Press, 1997.

———. *The Trans-Appalachian Frontier: People, Societies, and Institutions, 1775–1850.* New York: Oxford University Press, 1978.

Romero, Lora. *Home Fronts: Domesticity and Its Critics in the Antebellum United States.* Durham, N.C.: Duke University Press, 1997.

Rorabaugh, William J. *The Alcoholic Republic: An American Tradition.* New York: Oxford University Press, 1979.

Rosenberg, Charles E. *The Cholera Years: The United States in 1832, 1849, and 1866.* Chicago: University of Chicago Press, 1962.

Sellers, Charles Grier. *The Market Revolution: Jacksonian America, 1815–1848.* New York: Oxford University Press, 1991.

Sewall, Richard H. *Ballots for Freedom: Antislavery Politics in the United States, 1837–1860.* New York: Oxford University Press, 1976.

Stegmaier, Mark J. *Texas, New Mexico, and the Compromise of 1850: Boundary Dispute and Section Crisis.* Kent, Ohio: Kent State University Press, 1996.

Stevens, Kenneth R. *William Henry Harrison: A Biography.* Westport, Conn.: Greenwood Press, 1996.

Stewart, James B. *Wendell Phillips, Liberty's Hero.* Baton Rouge: Louisiana State University Press, 1998.

Stover, John F. *Iron Road to the West: American Railroads in the 1850s.* New York: Columbia University Press, 1978.

Takaki, Ronald. *Iron Cages: Race and Culture in 19th Century America.* New York: Oxford University Press, 1979.

Tompkins, Jane. *Sensational Designs: The Cultural Work of American Fiction, 1790–1860.* New York: Oxford University Press, 1985.

Unruh, John D. *The Plains Across: The Overland Emigrants and the Trans-Mississippi West, 1840–1860.* Urbana: University of Illinois Press, 1979.

Wacker, Grant. *Religion in Nineteenth Century America.* New York: Oxford University Press, 2000.

Walter, Ronald G. *American Reformers, 1815–1860.* New York: Hill & Wang: 1978.

Weber, David J. *The American Frontier, 1821–1846: The American Southwest Under Mexico.* Albuquerque: University of New Mexico Press, 1982.

Weeks, Philip. *Farewell My Nation. The American Indian and the United States, 1820–1890.* Arlington Heights, Ill.: H. Davidson, 1990.

Wolff, Gerald W. *The Kansas-Nebraska Bill: Party, Section, and the Coming of the Civil War.* Brooklyn, N.Y.: The Revisionist Press, 1977.

Yellin, Jean Fagan. *Women & Sisters: The Antislavery Feminists in American Culture.* New Haven, Conn.: Yale

Index

Boldface page numbers denote extensive treatment of a topic. *Italic* page numbers refer to illustrations; *c* refers to the Chronology; and *m* indicates a map.

C

G

Q

R

U

V

X

Y

Z